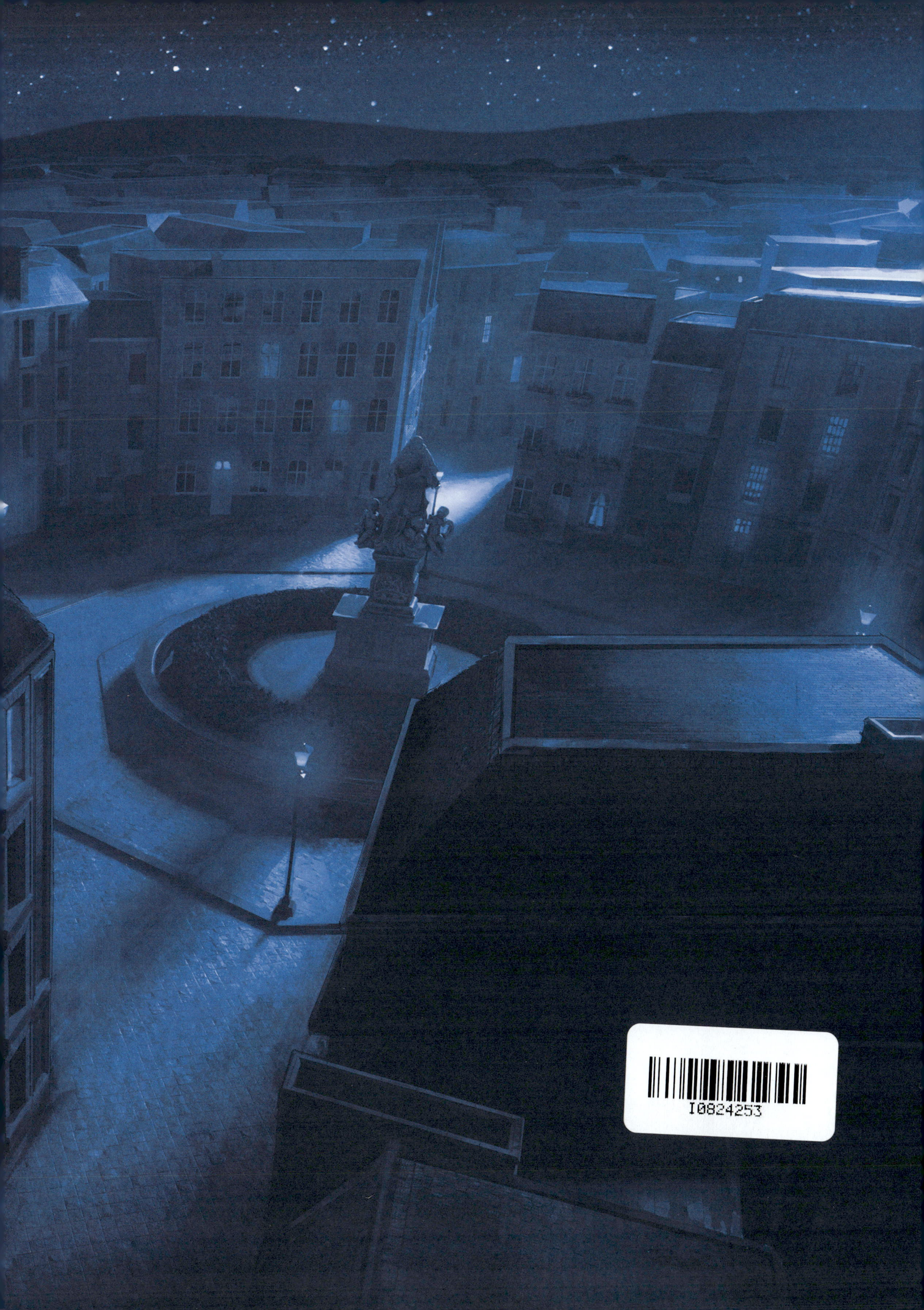

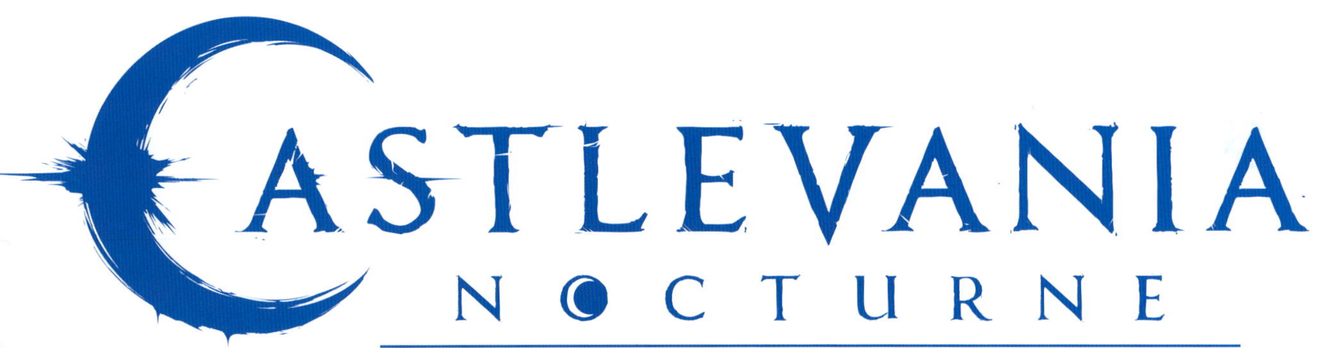
CASTLEVANIA
NOCTURNE
THE ART OF THE ANIMATED SERIES

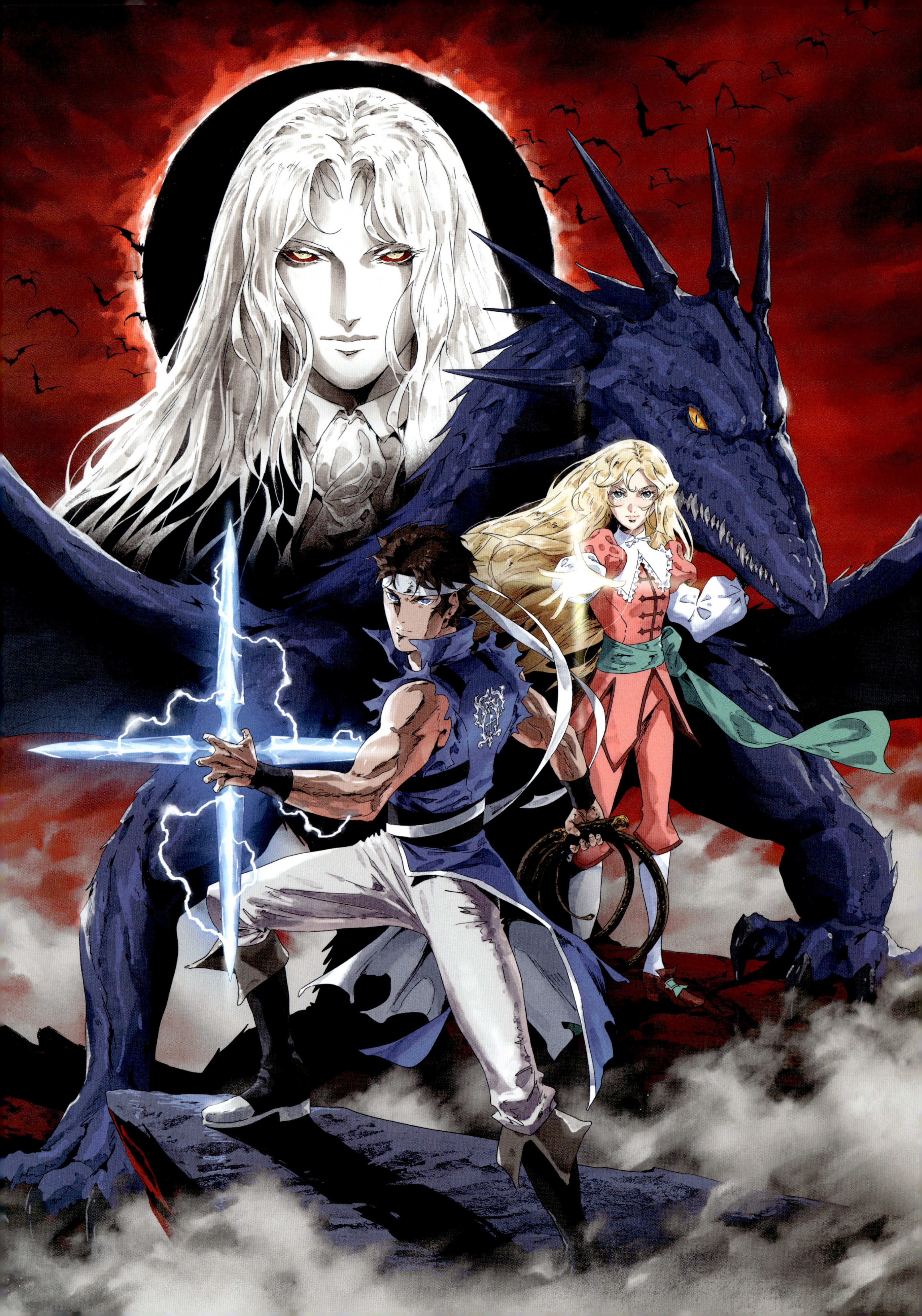

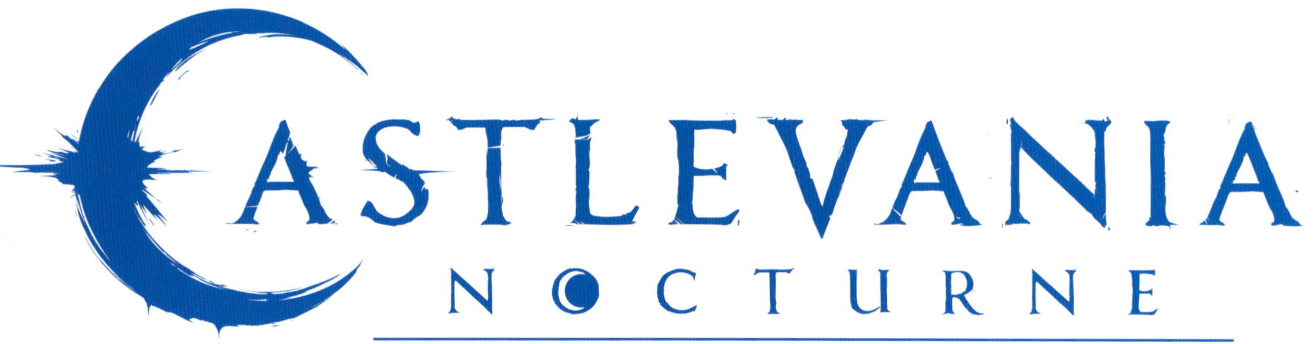

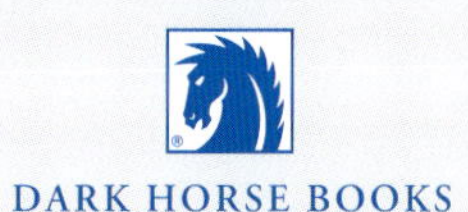

DARK HORSE BOOKS

President and Publisher
Mike Richardson

Editor
Ian Tucker

Assistant Editor
Jennifer Wurtele

Designer
Stephen Reichert

Digital Art Technician
Betsy Howitt

Prepress
Maureen Heaster

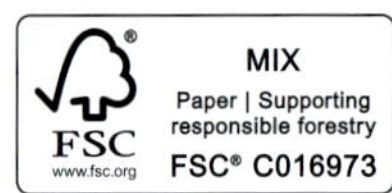

Published by Dark Horse Books
A division of Dark Horse Comics LLC
10956 SE Main Street
Milwaukie, OR 97222

Represented in the EU by Authorised Rep Compliance Ltd.
Ground Floor, 71 Lower Baggot Street
Dublin, D02 P593, Ireland
ARCCompliance.com

DarkHorse.com

Library of Congress Cataloging-in-Publication Data

Names: Ratcliffe, Amy, author.
Title: Castlevania nocturne : the art of the animated series / written by Amy Ratcliffe.
Description: First edition. | Milwaukie, OR : Dark Horse Books, 2026.
Identifiers: LCCN 2025011350 (print) | LCCN 2025011351 (ebook) | ISBN 9781506750842 hardcover | ISBN 9781506753348 ebook
Subjects: LCSH: Castlevania nocturne
Classification: LCC NC1766.U53 C394 2026 (print) | LCC NC1766.U53 (ebook) | DDC 791.45/75--dc23/eng/20250619
LC record available at https://lccn.loc.gov/2025011350
LC ebook record available at https://lccn.loc.gov/2025011351

First edition: March 2026
Ebook ISBN 978-1-50675-334-8
Hardcover ISBN 978-1-50675-084-2

1 3 5 7 9 10 8 6 4 2
Printed in China

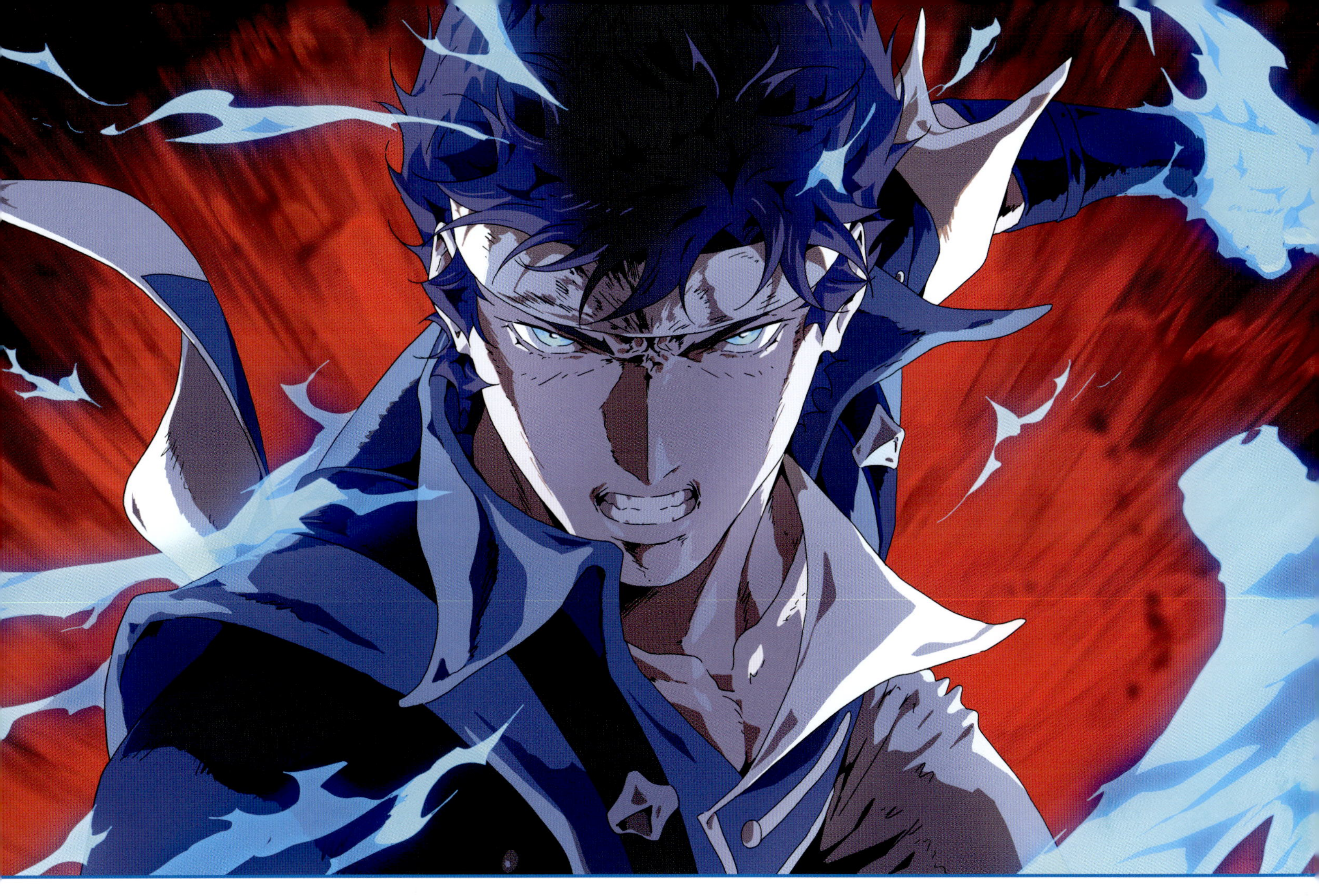

Table of Contents

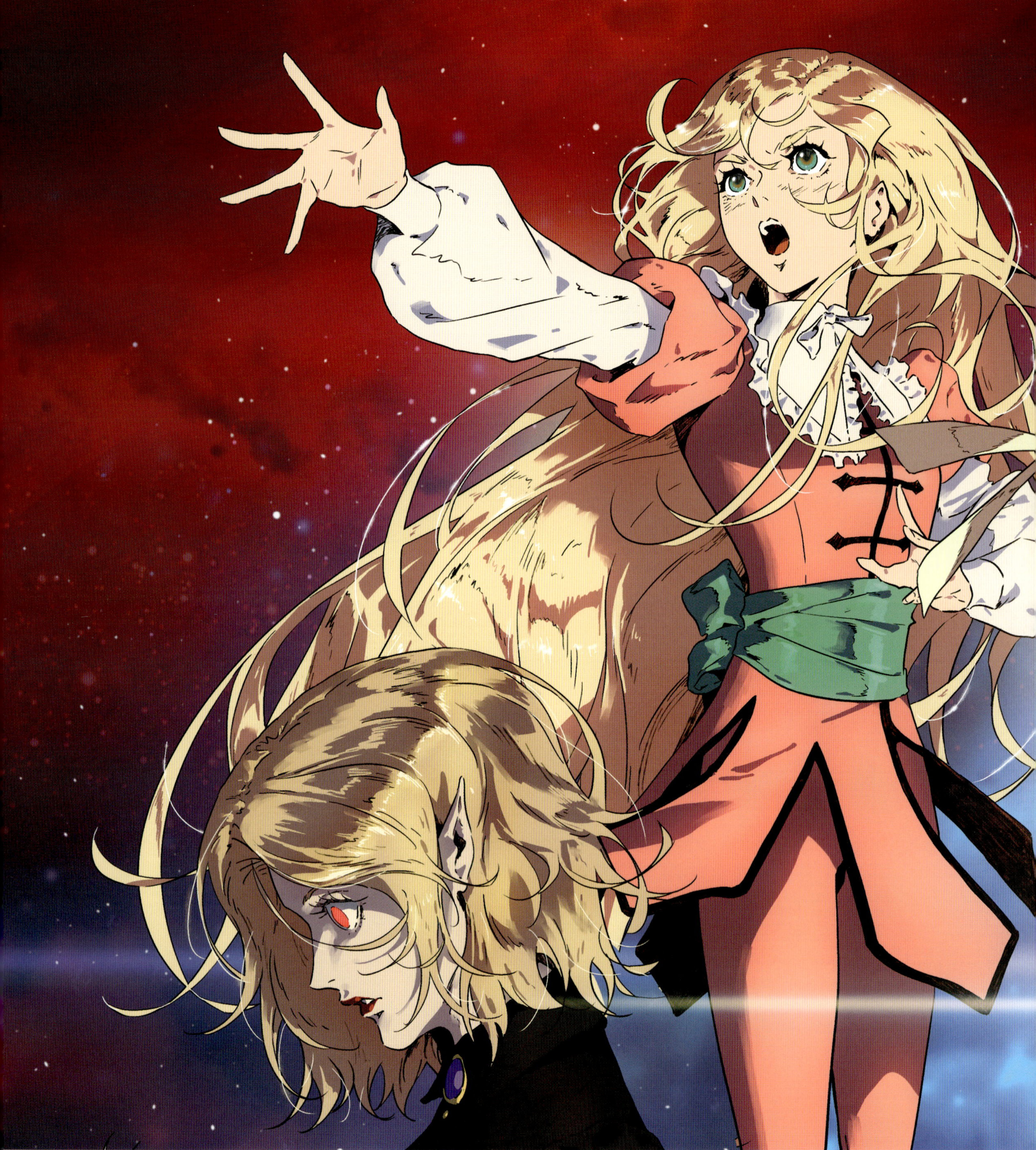

Art by Samuel Deats.

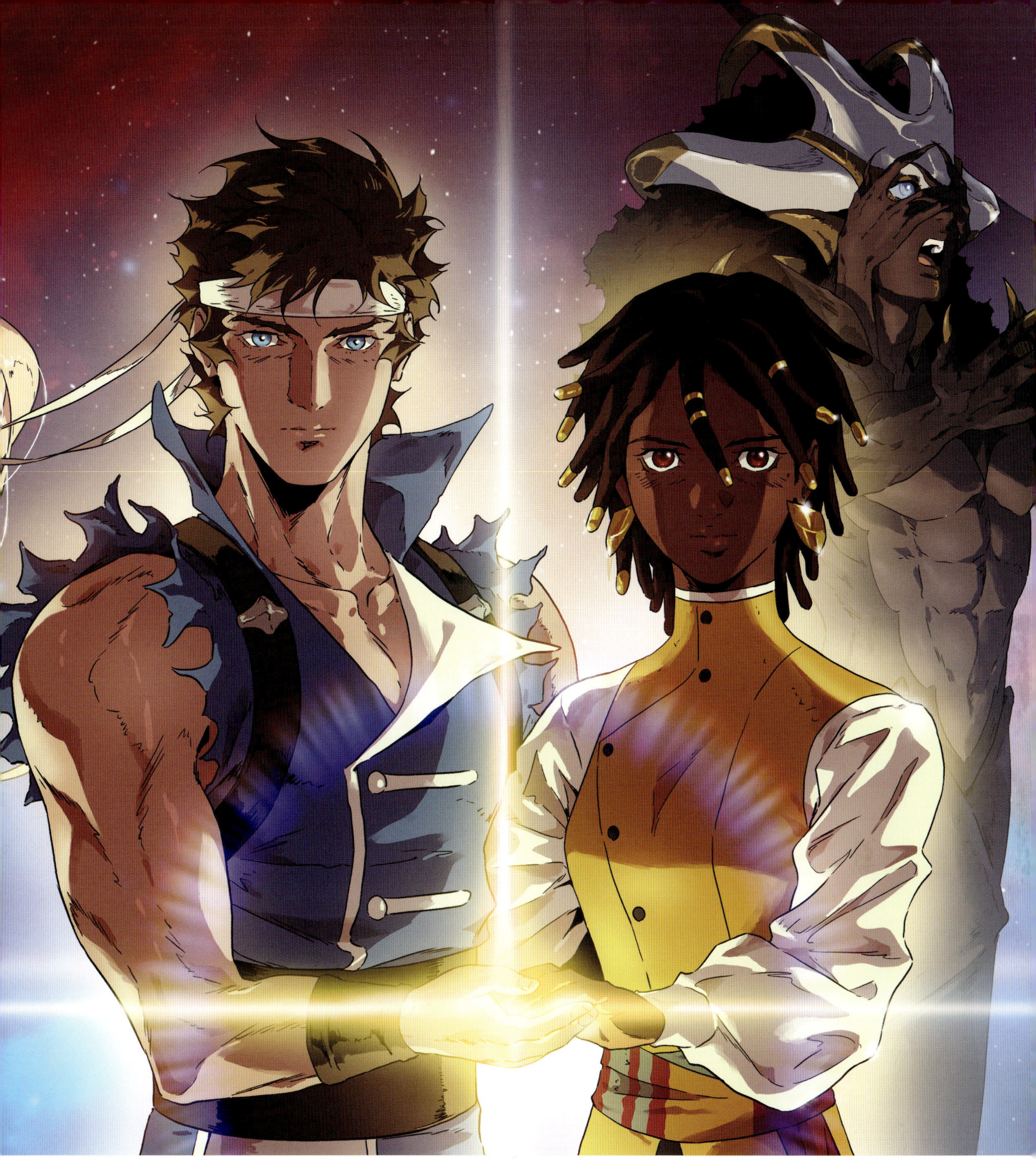

CHAPTER I

Saviors and the Innocent

Richter Belmont

Richter Belmont comes from a long line of vampire hunters. With a rich history in the world of *Castlevania*, having appeared in multiple games with various looks, he was a difficult character to capture in the animated series. When *Castlevania: Nocturne* begins, he isn't using his powers—not yet. Richter carries the trauma of witnessing his mother's murder and has to find his way.

Executive producer Sam Deats shared that finding the right, balanced design to represent all the different versions of Richter was exceptionally tricky. He worked on a variety of looks, as did character design supervisor Kathryn (Katie) Silva, who teased that Richter was Sam's favorite character and therefore the most challenging to get right.

Art by Samuel Deats.

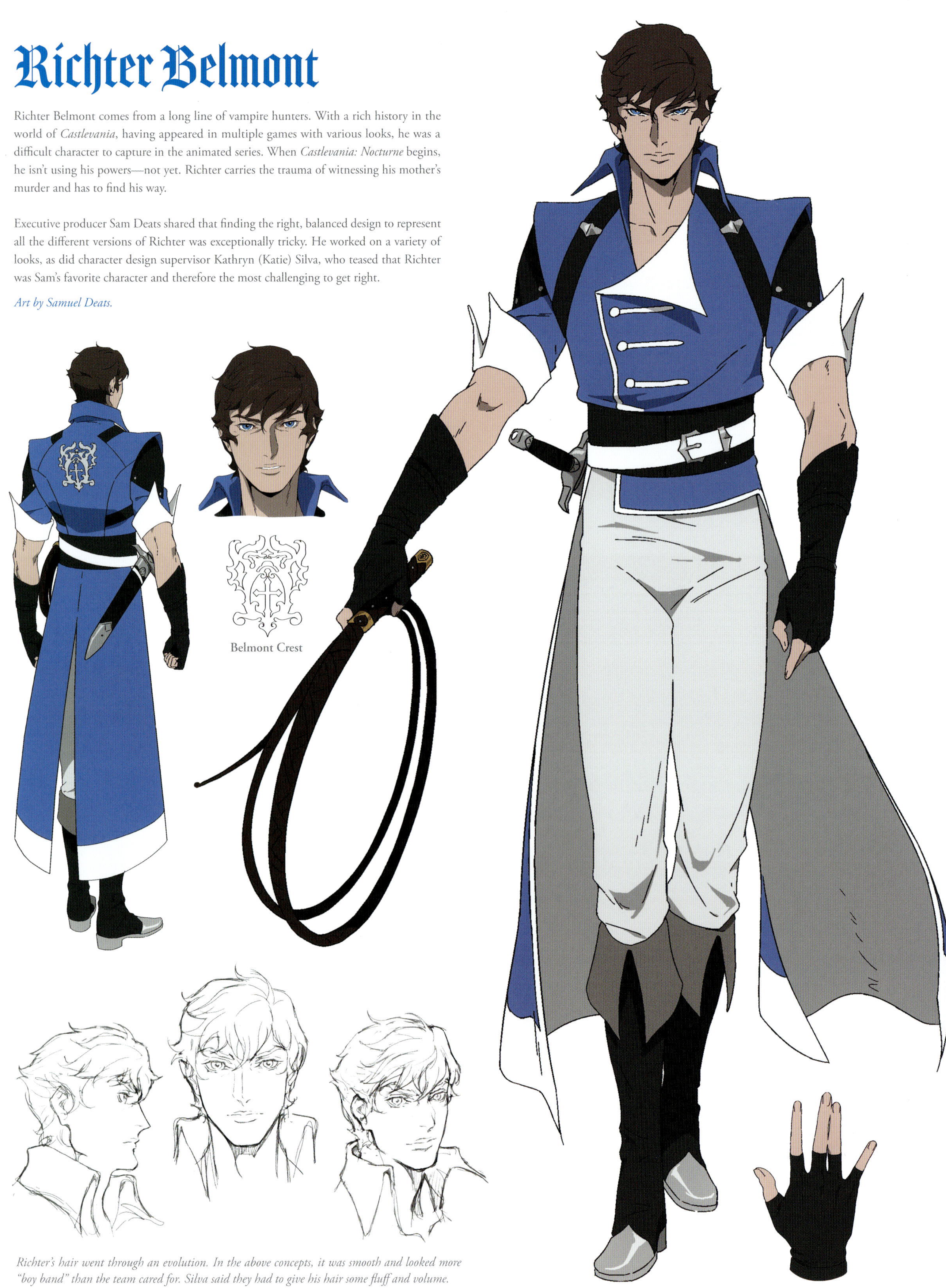

Richter's hair went through an evolution. In the above concepts, it was smooth and looked more "boy band" than the team cared for. Silva said they had to give his hair some fluff and volume.

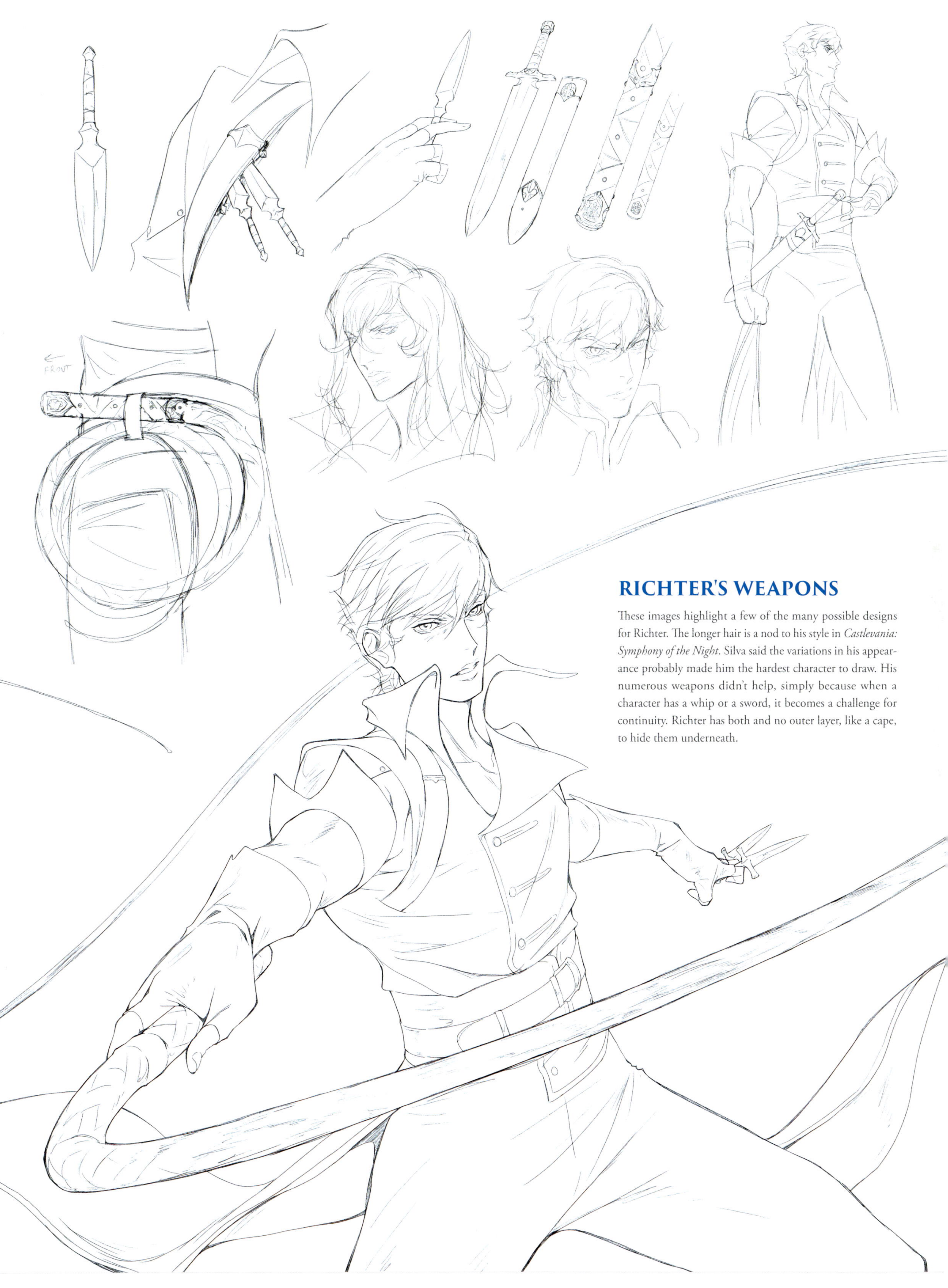

RICHTER'S WEAPONS

These images highlight a few of the many possible designs for Richter. The longer hair is a nod to his style in *Castlevania: Symphony of the Night*. Silva said the variations in his appearance probably made him the hardest character to draw. His numerous weapons didn't help, simply because when a character has a whip or a sword, it becomes a challenge for continuity. Richter has both and no outer layer, like a cape, to hide them underneath.

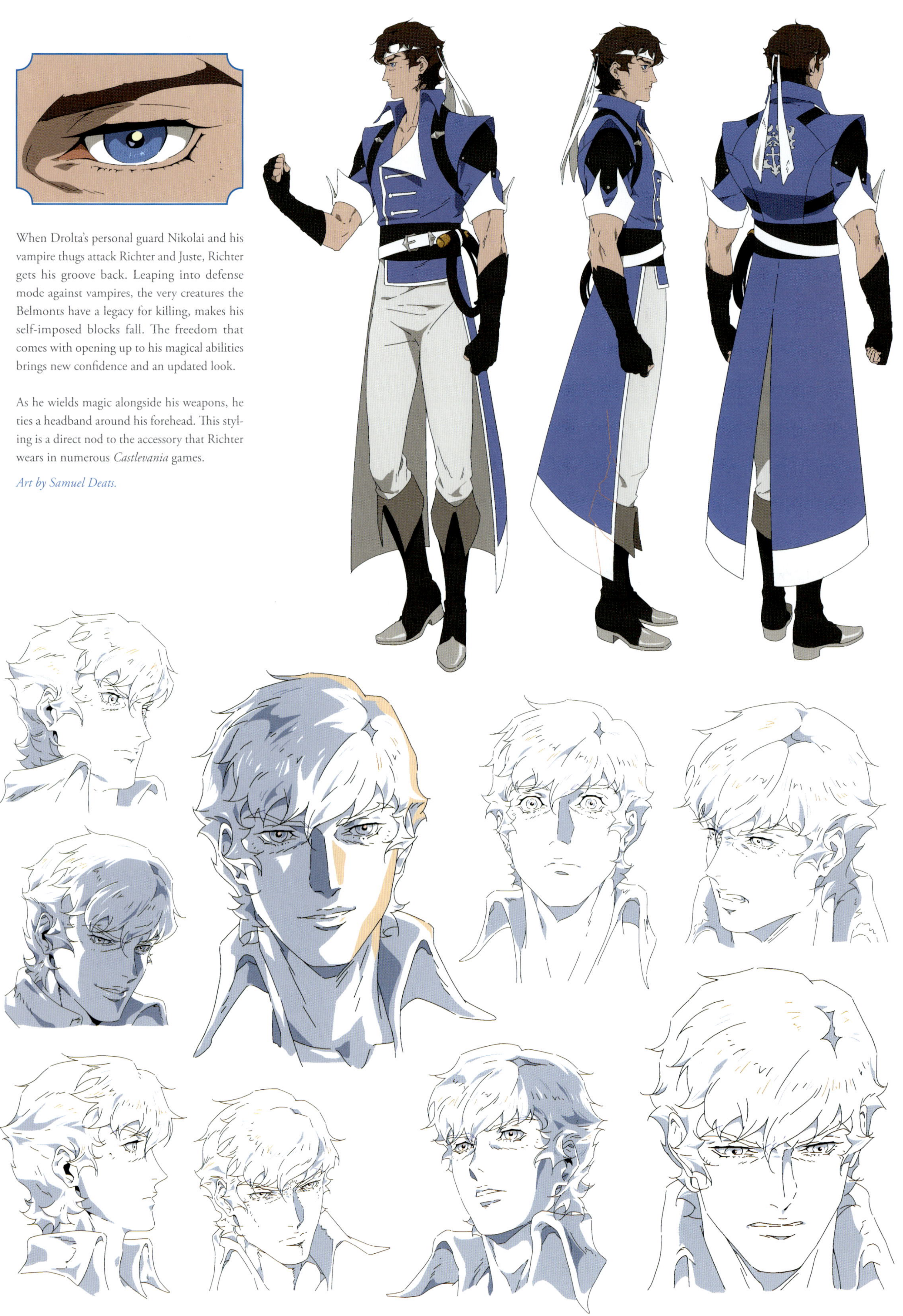

When Drolta's personal guard Nikolai and his vampire thugs attack Richter and Juste, Richter gets his groove back. Leaping into defense mode against vampires, the very creatures the Belmonts have a legacy for killing, makes his self-imposed blocks fall. The freedom that comes with opening up to his magical abilities brings new confidence and an updated look.

As he wields magic alongside his weapons, he ties a headband around his forehead. This styling is a direct nod to the accessory that Richter wears in numerous *Castlevania* games.

Art by Samuel Deats.

Art by Samuel Deats, layouts by Kathryn Layno.

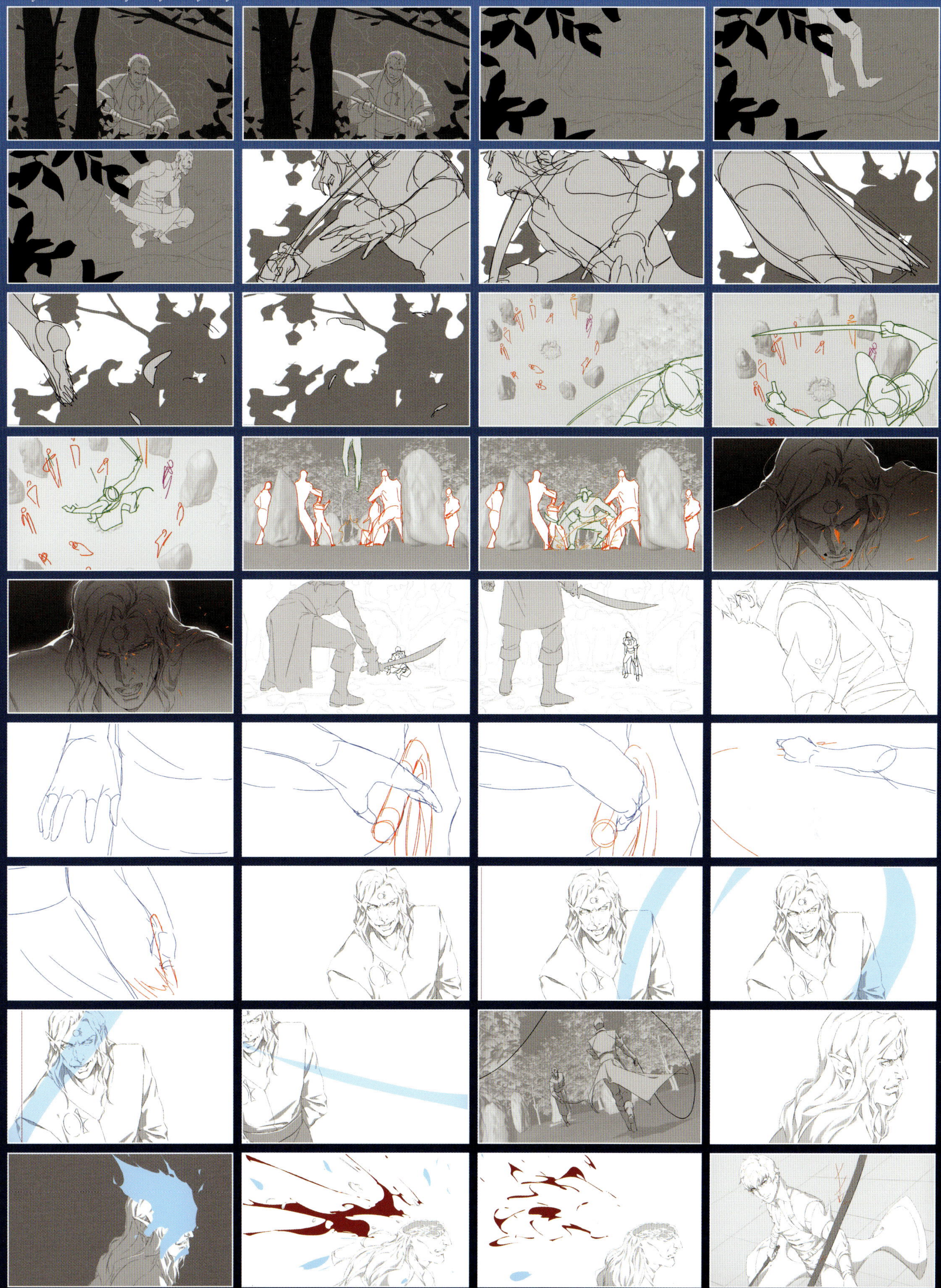

"Here, we're introducing Richter and Maria for the first time. I wanted to give Richter a little bit of that mystique where we're not showing his face at first, then a quick draw effect on the whip snap and then that nice delay before the head pops off." —Sam Deats

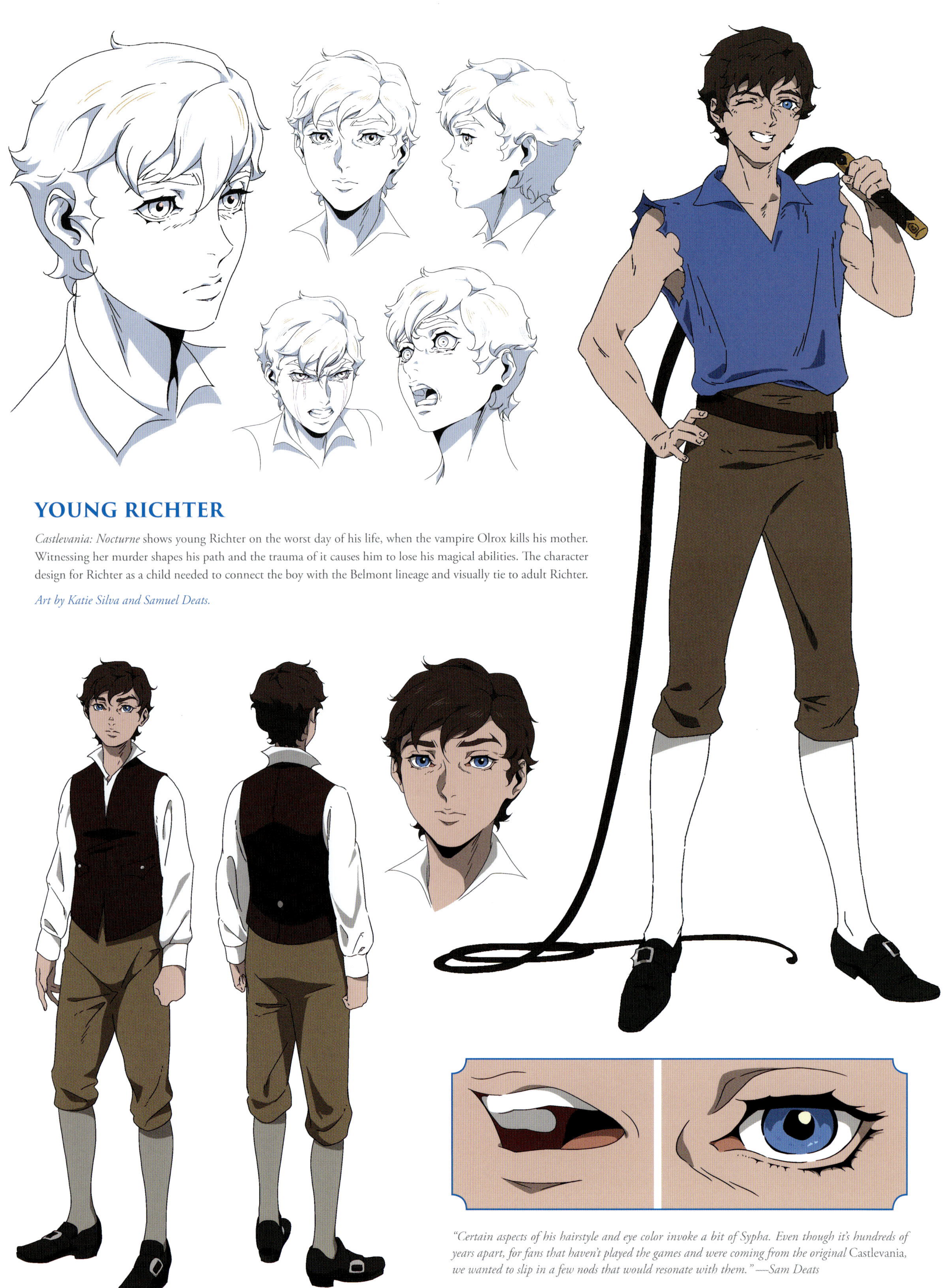

YOUNG RICHTER

Castlevania: Nocturne shows young Richter on the worst day of his life, when the vampire Olrox kills his mother. Witnessing her murder shapes his path and the trauma of it causes him to lose his magical abilities. The character design for Richter as a child needed to connect the boy with the Belmont lineage and visually tie to adult Richter.

Art by Katie Silva and Samuel Deats.

"Certain aspects of his hairstyle and eye color invoke a bit of Sypha. Even though it's hundreds of years apart, for fans that haven't played the games and were coming from the original Castlevania*, we wanted to slip in a few nods that would resonate with them." —Sam Deats*

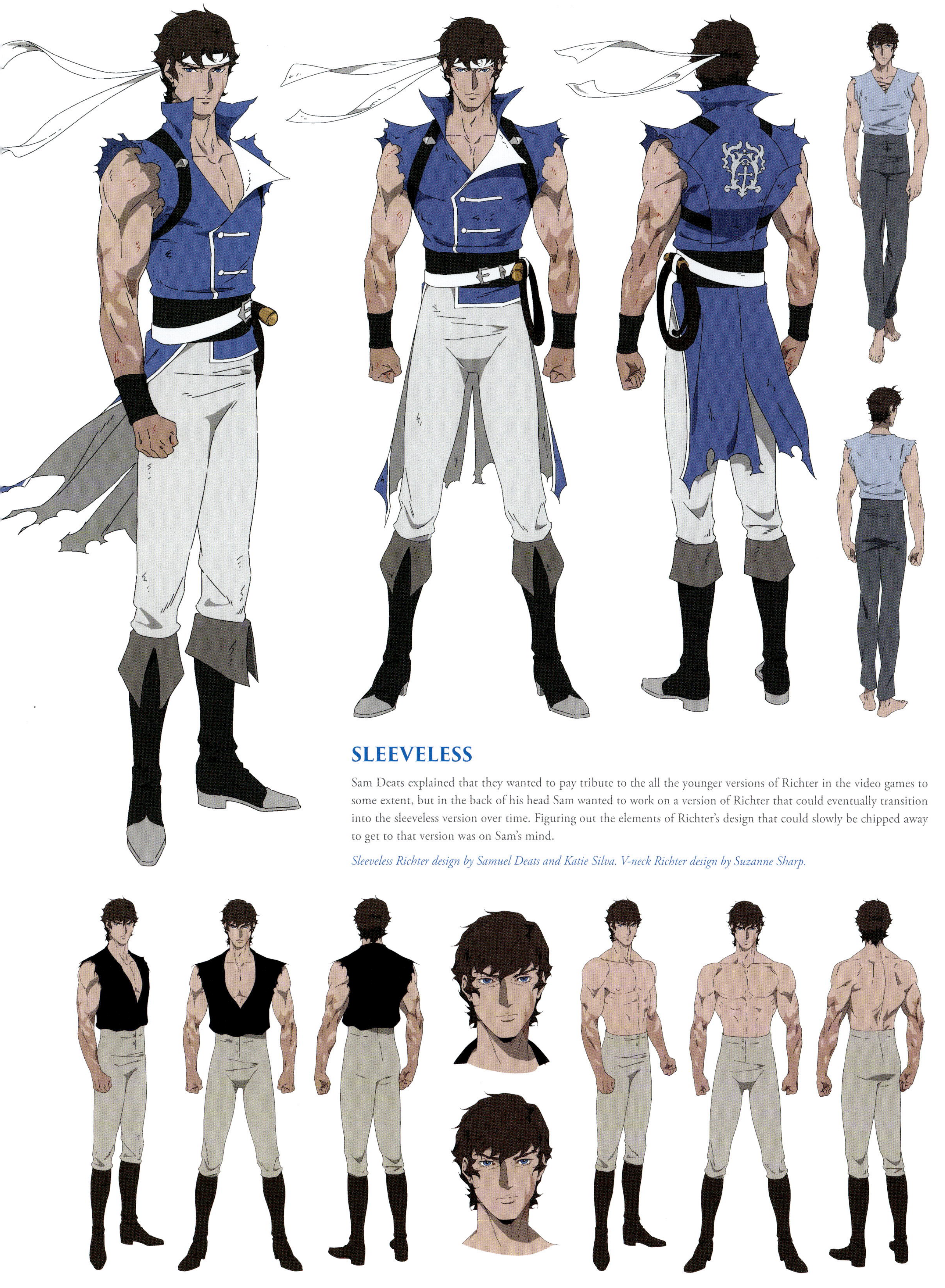

SLEEVELESS

Sam Deats explained that they wanted to pay tribute to the all the younger versions of Richter in the video games to some extent, but in the back of his head Sam wanted to work on a version of Richter that could eventually transition into the sleeveless version over time. Figuring out the elements of Richter's design that could slowly be chipped away to get to that version was on Sam's mind.

Sleeveless Richter design by Samuel Deats and Katie Silva. V-neck Richter design by Suzanne Sharp.

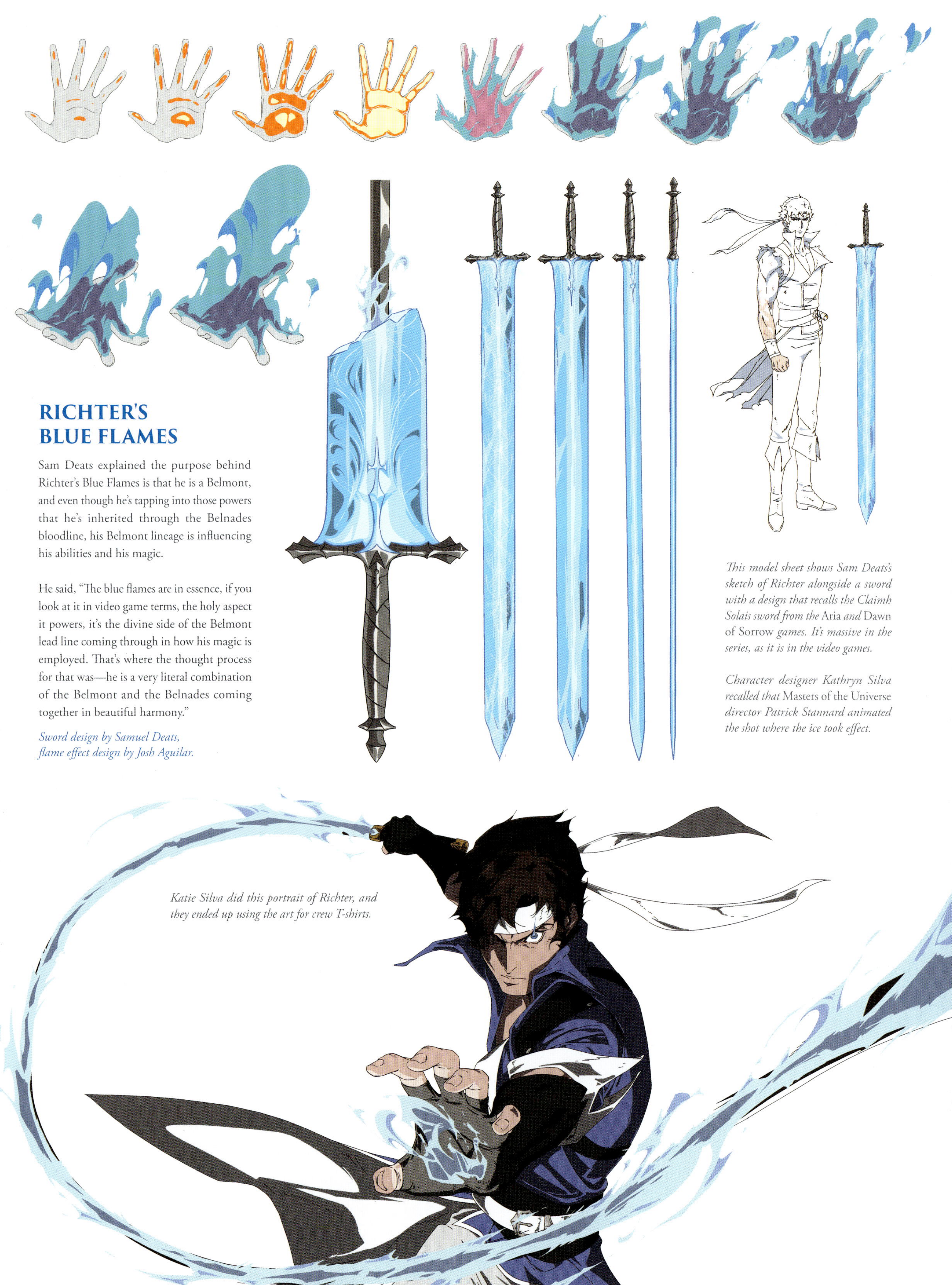

RICHTER'S BLUE FLAMES

Sam Deats explained the purpose behind Richter's Blue Flames is that he is a Belmont, and even though he's tapping into those powers that he's inherited through the Belnades bloodline, his Belmont lineage is influencing his abilities and his magic.

He said, "The blue flames are in essence, if you look at it in video game terms, the holy aspect it powers, it's the divine side of the Belmont lead line coming through in how his magic is employed. That's where the thought process for that was—he is a very literal combination of the Belmont and the Belnades coming together in beautiful harmony."

Sword design by Samuel Deats, flame effect design by Josh Aguilar.

This model sheet shows Sam Deats's sketch of Richter alongside a sword with a design that recalls the Claimh Solais sword from the Aria *and* Dawn of Sorrow *games. It's massive in the series, as it is in the video games.*

Character designer Kathryn Silva recalled that Masters of the Universe *director Patrick Stannard animated the shot where the ice took effect.*

Katie Silva did this portrait of Richter, and they ended up using the art for crew T-shirts.

Storyboards by Samuel Deats.

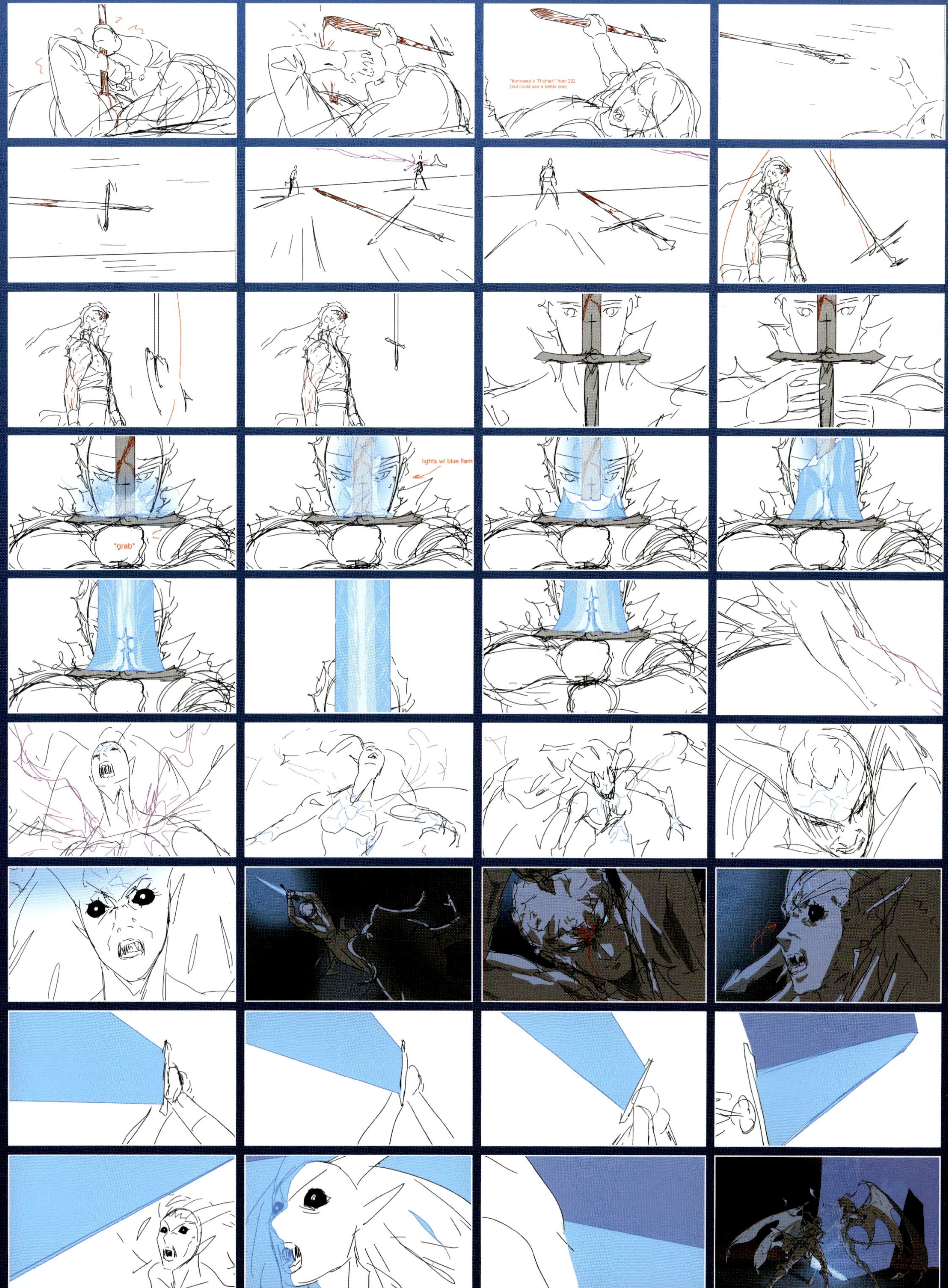

Sam Deats wanted this sequence to illustrate the moment of Richter becoming a true Belmont. He started on the Belmont crest, zoomed around and flashed into impact frame effects that they used for the opening of the original series and then throughout the show for important moments and big attacks.

Juste Belmont

Juste appears in his sixties in *Nocturne*, so as Sam Deats noted, he doesn't have the same outfit anymore but he still rocks. He explained, "I wanted to incorporate elements of the shape language from the speaker magicians of the original series. So you're seeing some of the same touches. There's this diamond shape at the edges of the speaker robes that I'm incorporating into a very Belmont-looking cloak as well as the bird-shaped pins that Sypha had on her outfit. It's also in the robe as well as the buttons facing inward." He adds that the armor is a direct nod to the type of armor Juste wears in the game.

Art by Samuel Deats with Mari Arakaki.

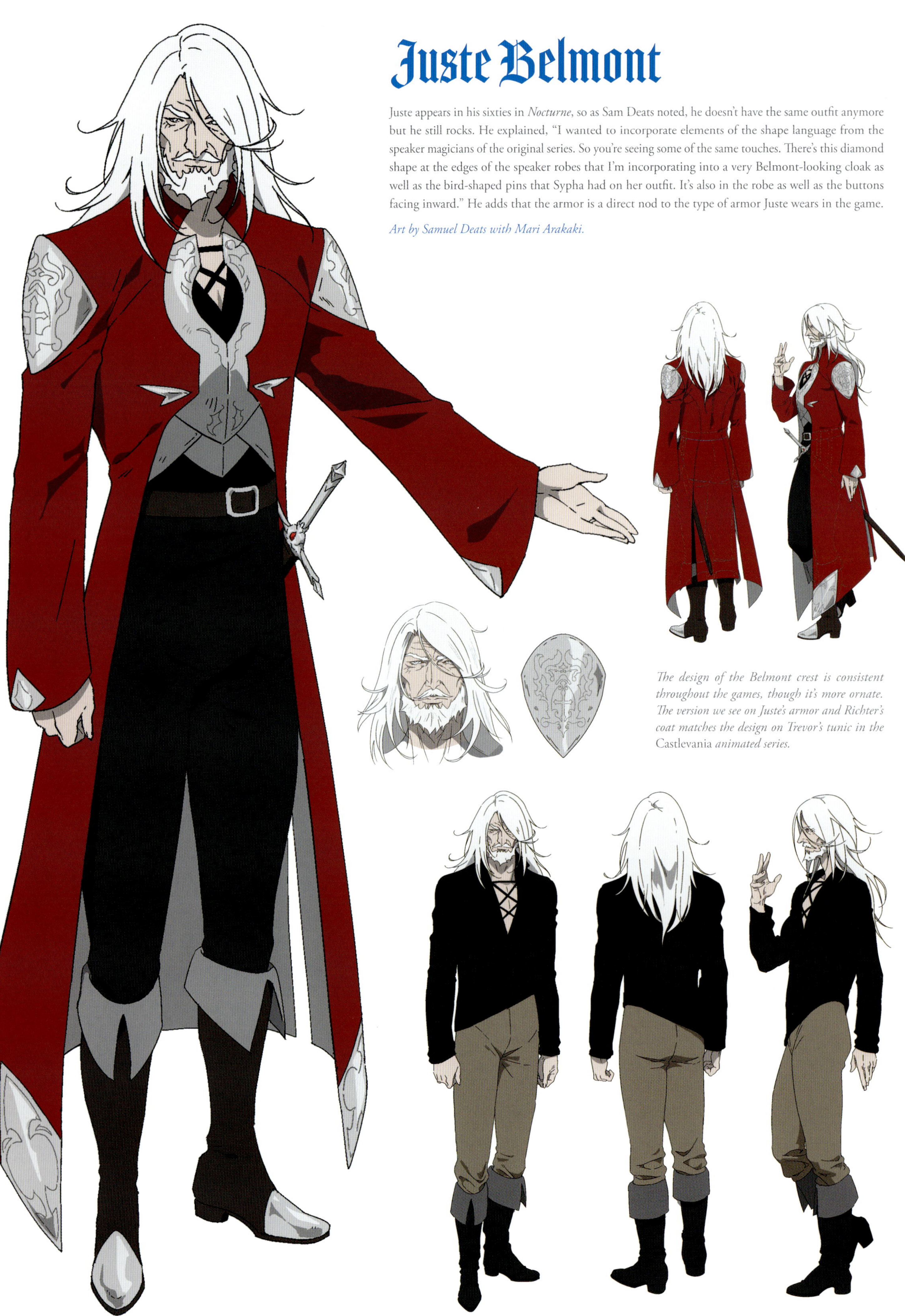

The design of the Belmont crest is consistent throughout the games, though it's more ornate. The version we see on Juste's armor and Richter's coat matches the design on Trevor's tunic in the Castlevania *animated series.*

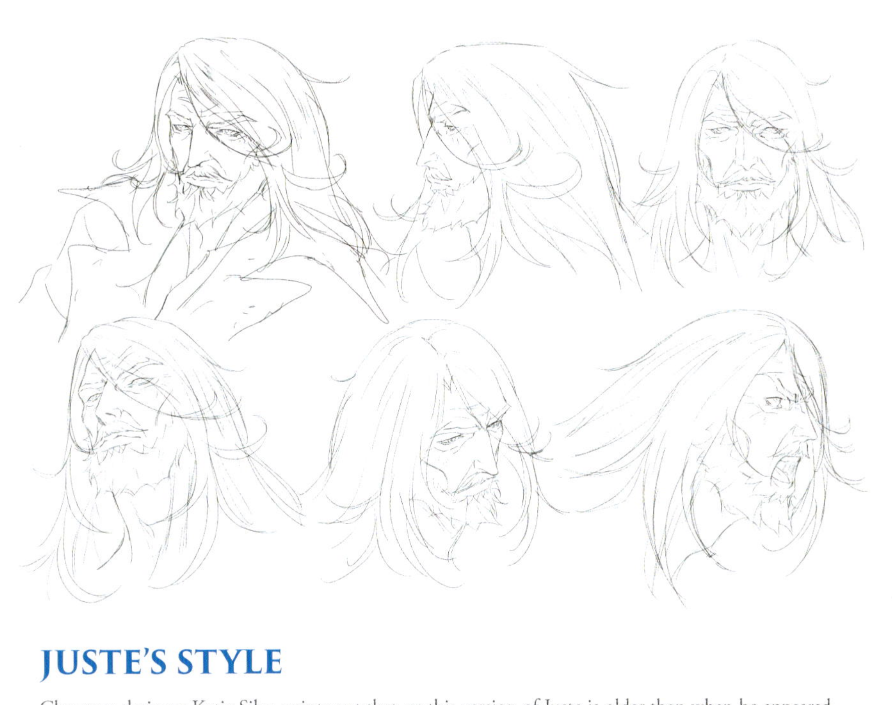

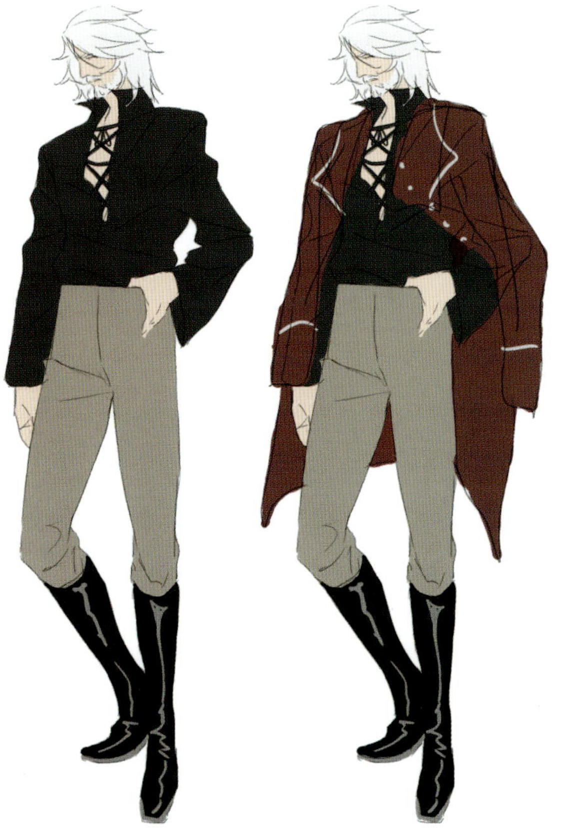

JUSTE'S STYLE

Character designer Katie Silva points out that, as this version of Juste is older than when he appeared in *Castlevania: Harmony of Dissonance*, they leaned into a little of a silver fox look. She said Sam did most of the initial sketches and design for Juste, noting the loose strand of hair that falls across his face was a challenge for animation.

Art by Samuel Deats.

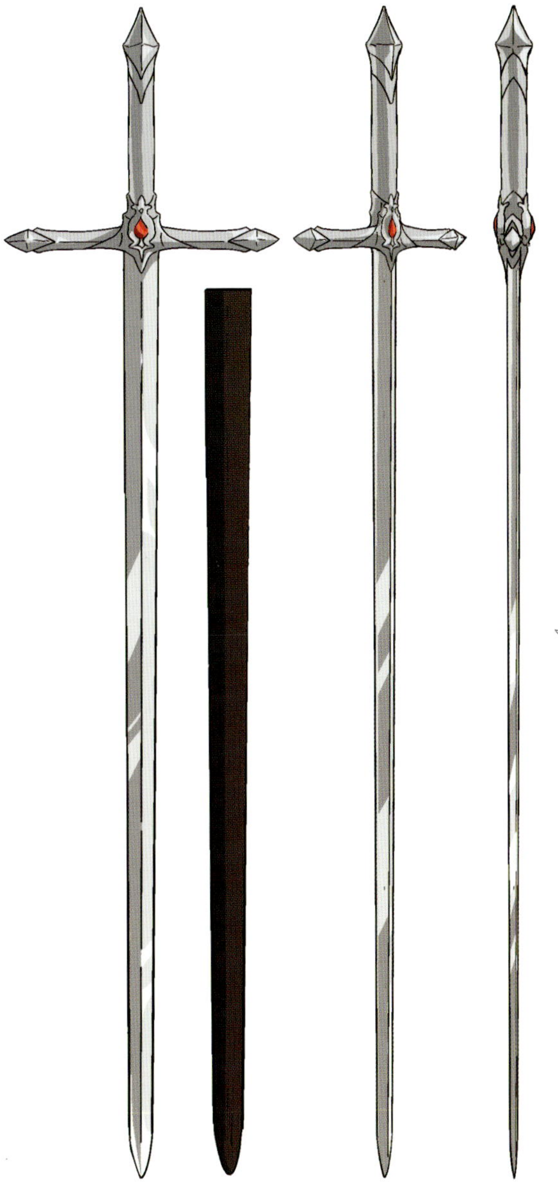

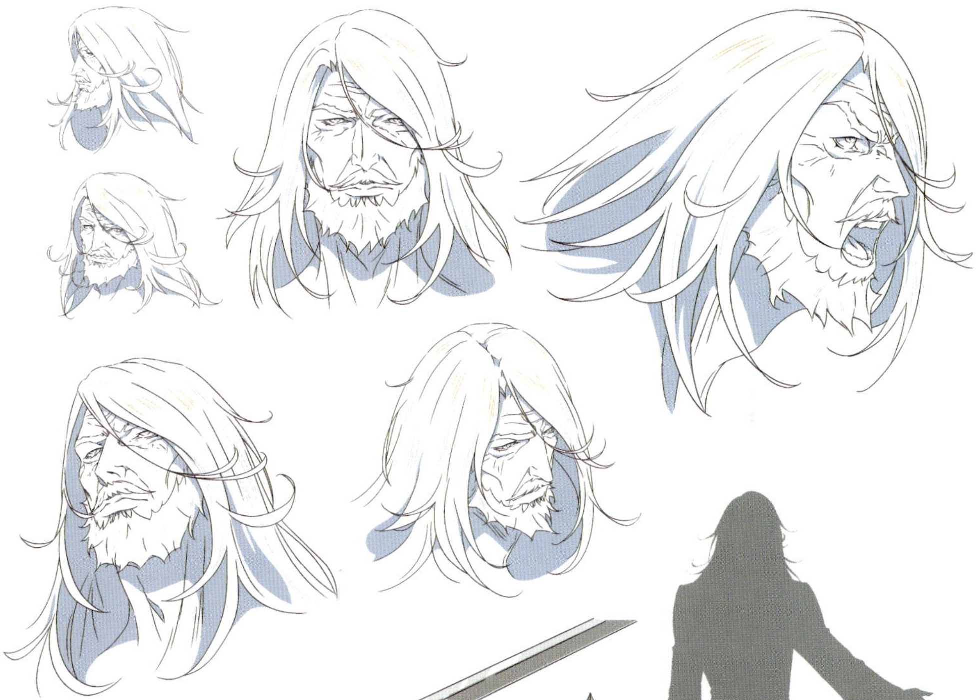

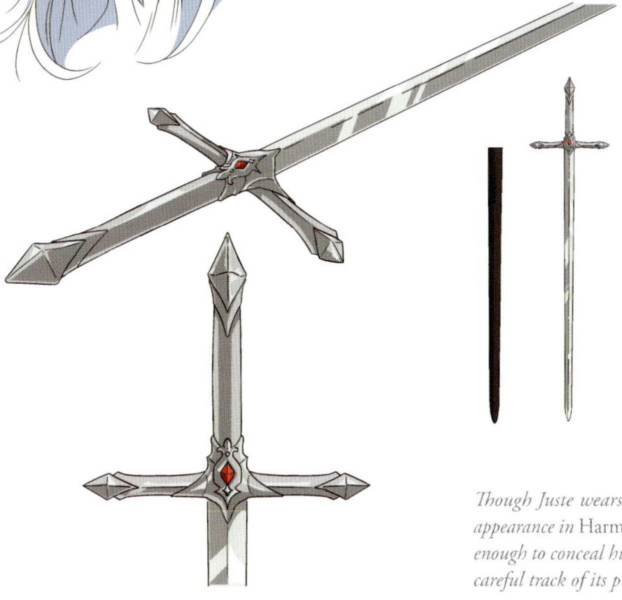

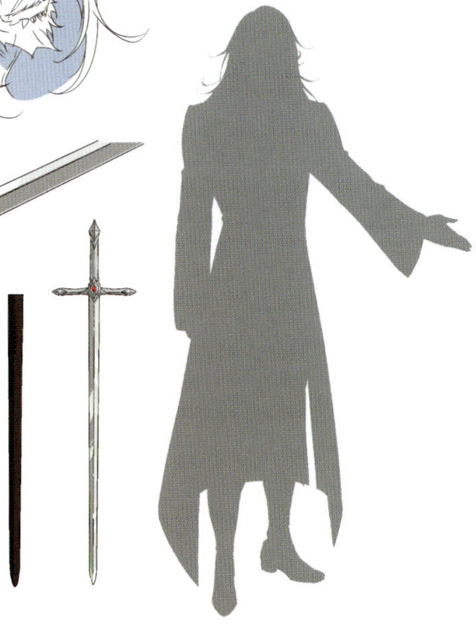

Though Juste wears a long red jacket—a reference to his appearance in Harmony of Dissonance*—it's not quite long enough to conceal his sword, which meant they had to keep careful track of its placement and angle when animating.*

Julia Belmont

The descendant of Trevor Belmont and Sypha Belnades, Julia Belmont is not to be trifled with. As the wielder of the Vampire Killer whip, she's a formidable hunter. Her strategic fighting style is on display in *Nocturne*, when we see her fight—and ultimately lose—against Olrox, who is seeking revenge for Julia killing his vampire lover.

Katie Silva noted that there are few female Belmonts who are vampire killers in *Castlevania*, so Sam Deats got to design an original character. Visual cues in her costume connect her to her son Richter and her father Juste. She has the same coat silhouette as Juste, though her lapels look a little more 18th century.

Art by Samuel Deats with Katie Silva.

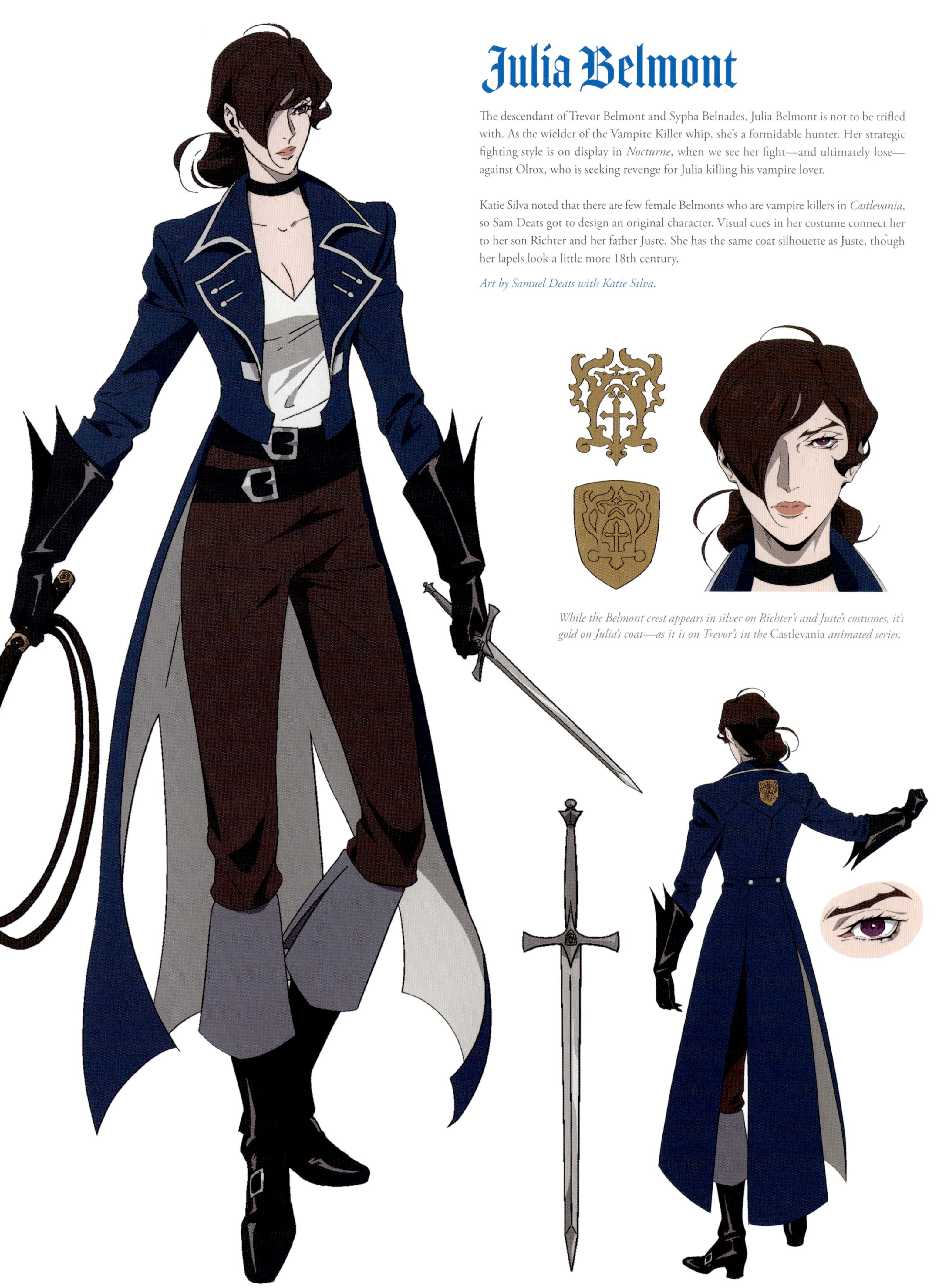

While the Belmont crest appears in silver on Richter's and Juste's costumes, it's gold on Julia's coat—as it is on Trevor's in the Castlevania *animated series.*

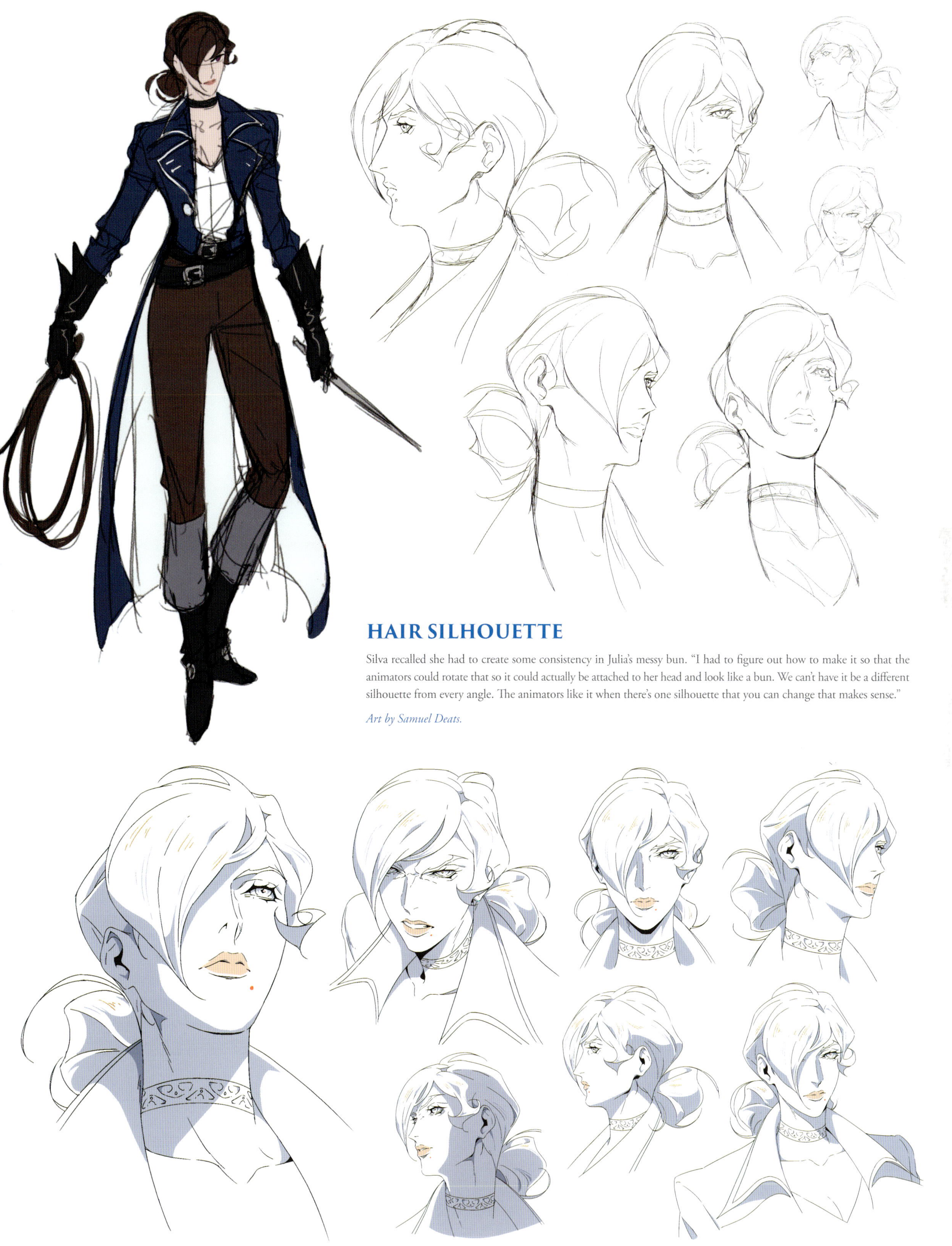

HAIR SILHOUETTE

Silva recalled she had to create some consistency in Julia's messy bun. "I had to figure out how to make it so that the animators could rotate that so it could actually be attached to her head and look like a bun. We can't have it be a different silhouette from every angle. The animators like it when there's one silhouette that you can change that makes sense."

Art by Samuel Deats.

Storyboards by Samuel Deats.

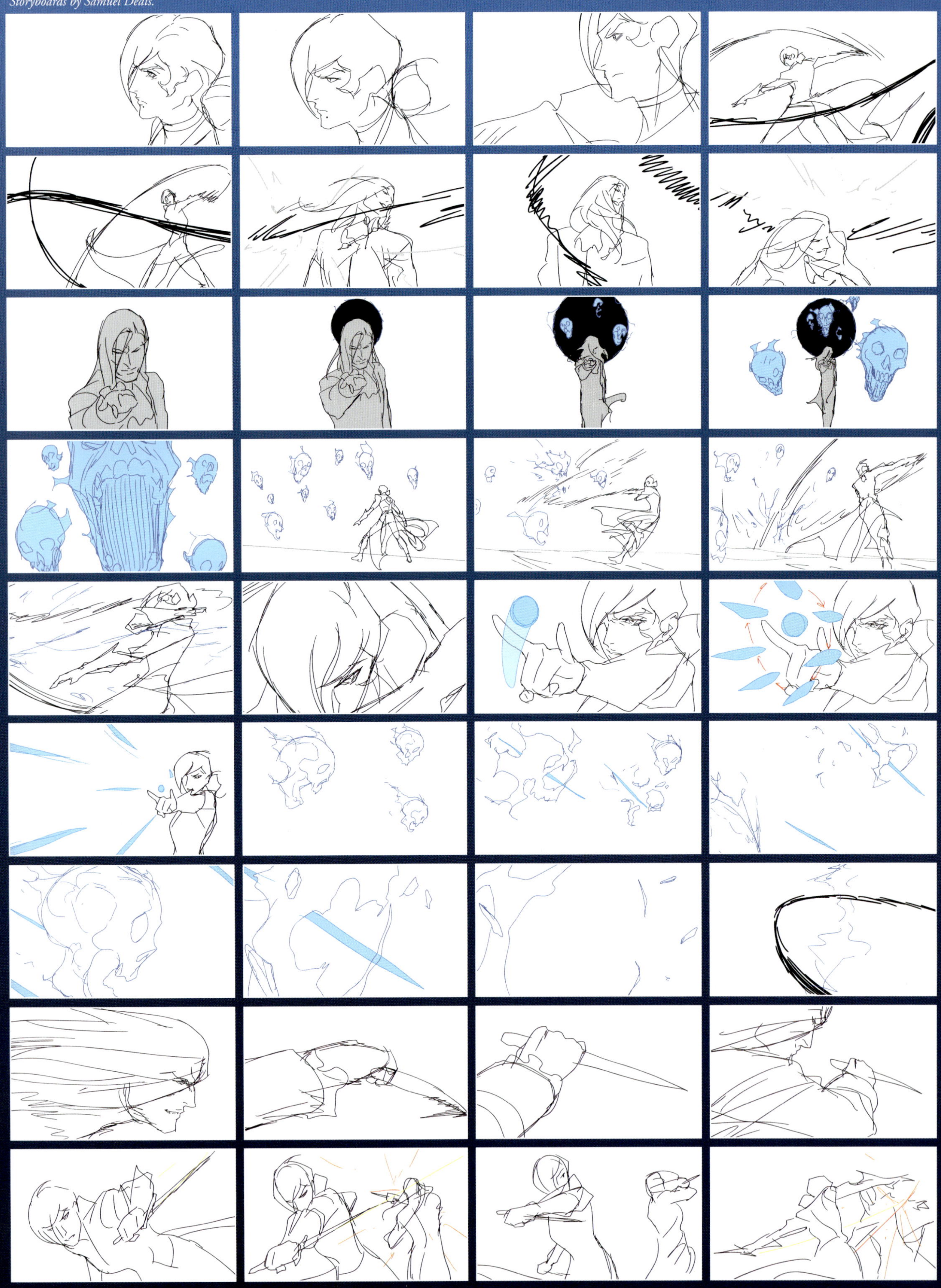

The storyboards for this sequence with Julia Belmont were the first completed for the show. Sam said, "The obvious goal was we have to make sure that people fall in love with this character as early as possible. I wanted to showcase her unique fighting style and how she's dealing with the combination of her magic and whip skills."

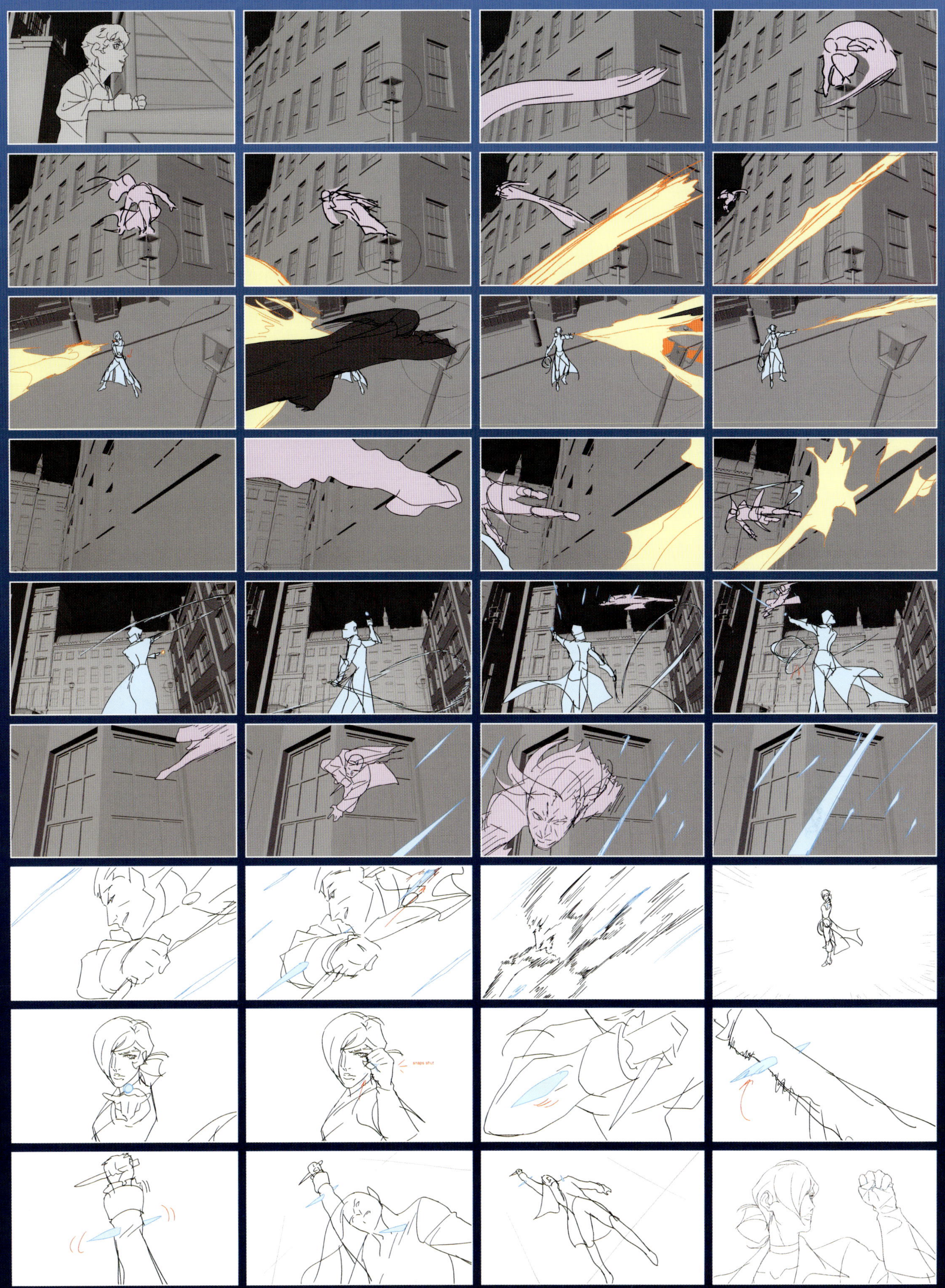

"One of the things that is important to me as a storyboard artist when I'm storyboarding an action sequence is showing the character's thinking, not just showing them flailing about," Sam explained. That's what he tried to show here with Julia shooting ice needles into Olrox, because she can control the needles and then lock him into place.

Tera Renard

Tera appears in the *Castlevania* games, but the Tera Renard depicted in *Castlevania: Nocturne* is a quite different character. A talented Speaker who fled her home and ended up in Machecoul, Tera is both fierce and kind. She's a literal mother to Maria and an adoptive mother to Richter, pushing them both to realize their full potential. She herself goes through a transformation when she's turned into a vampire.

Sam Deats did a lot of designs for Tera, though Katie Silva worked on Tera as well. The blue in Tera's costume is a reference to Speaker magic—Sypha Belnades and Julia Belmont both wear blue—and the shirt is more of a Victorian style.

Base design by Samuel Deats with expression sheet by Katie Silva.

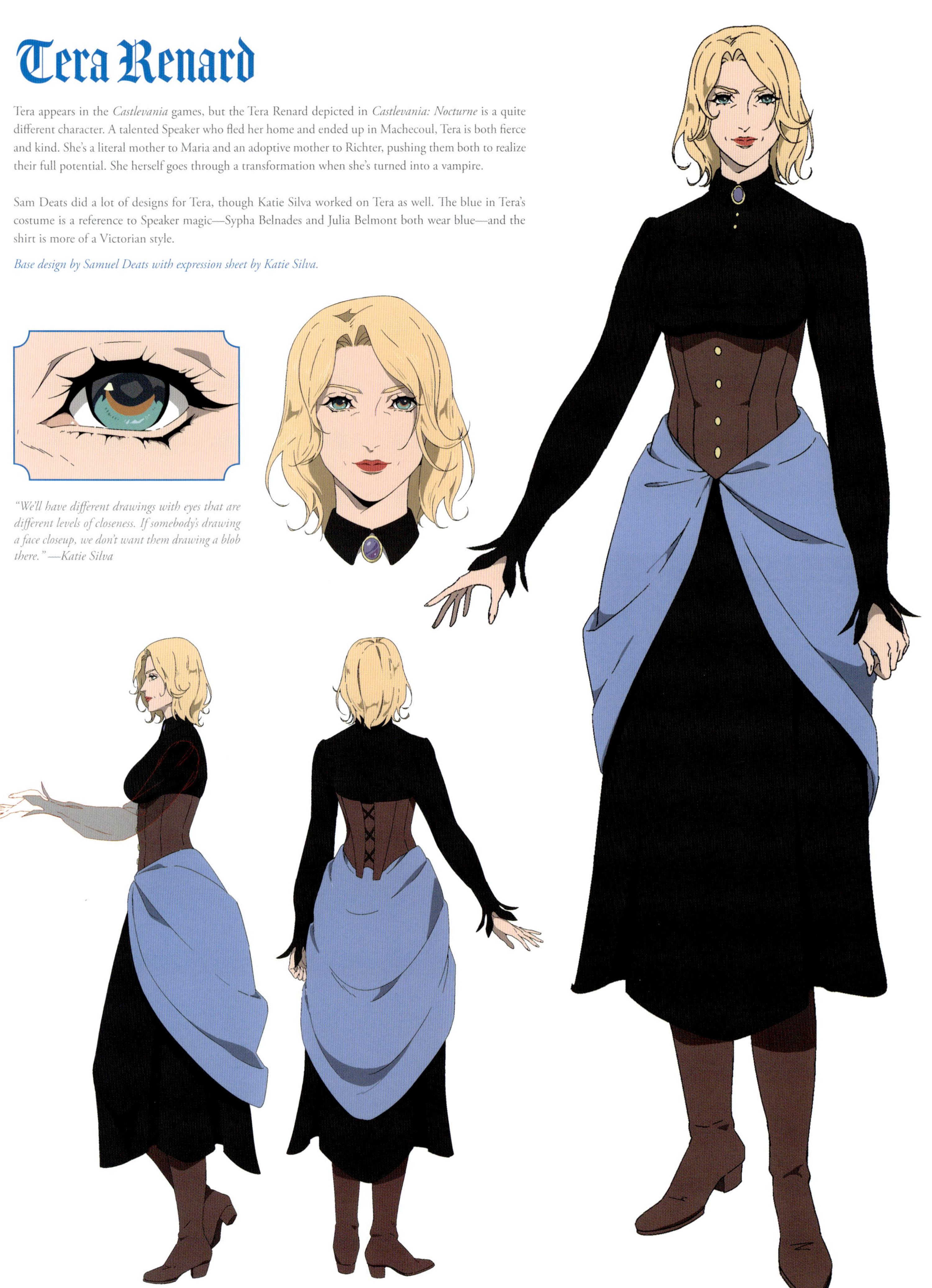

"We'll have different drawings with eyes that are different levels of closeness. If somebody's drawing a face closeup, we don't want them drawing a blob there." —Katie Silva

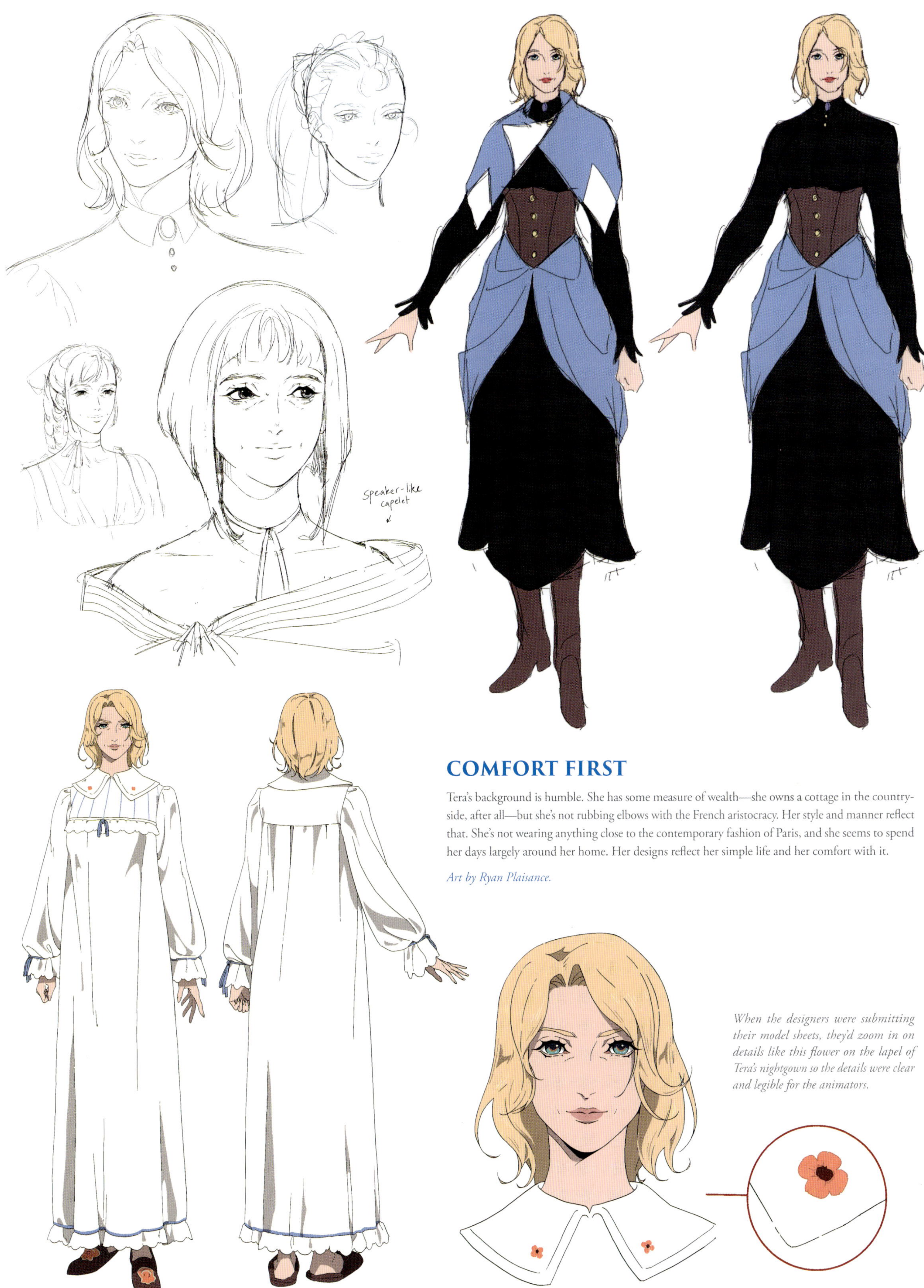

COMFORT FIRST

Tera's background is humble. She has some measure of wealth—she owns a cottage in the countryside, after all—but she's not rubbing elbows with the French aristocracy. Her style and manner reflect that. She's not wearing anything close to the contemporary fashion of Paris, and she seems to spend her days largely around her home. Her designs reflect her simple life and her comfort with it.

Art by Ryan Plaisance.

When the designers were submitting their model sheets, they'd zoom in on details like this flower on the lapel of Tera's nightgown so the details were clear and legible for the animators.

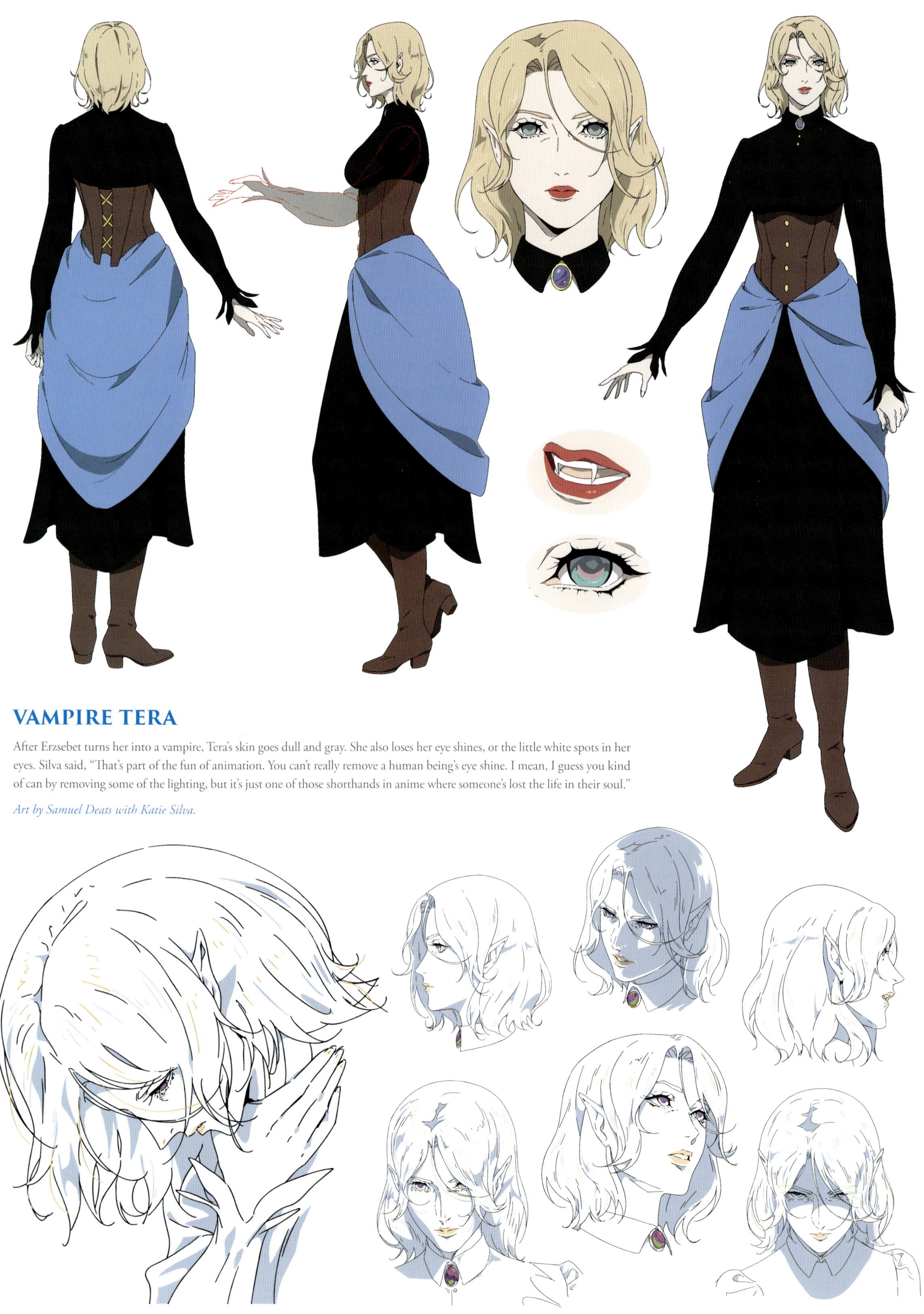

VAMPIRE TERA

After Erzsebet turns her into a vampire, Tera's skin goes dull and gray. She also loses her eye shines, or the little white spots in her eyes. Silva said, "That's part of the fun of animation. You can't really remove a human being's eye shine. I mean, I guess you kind of can by removing some of the lighting, but it's just one of those shorthands in anime where someone's lost the life in their soul."

Art by Samuel Deats with Katie Silva.

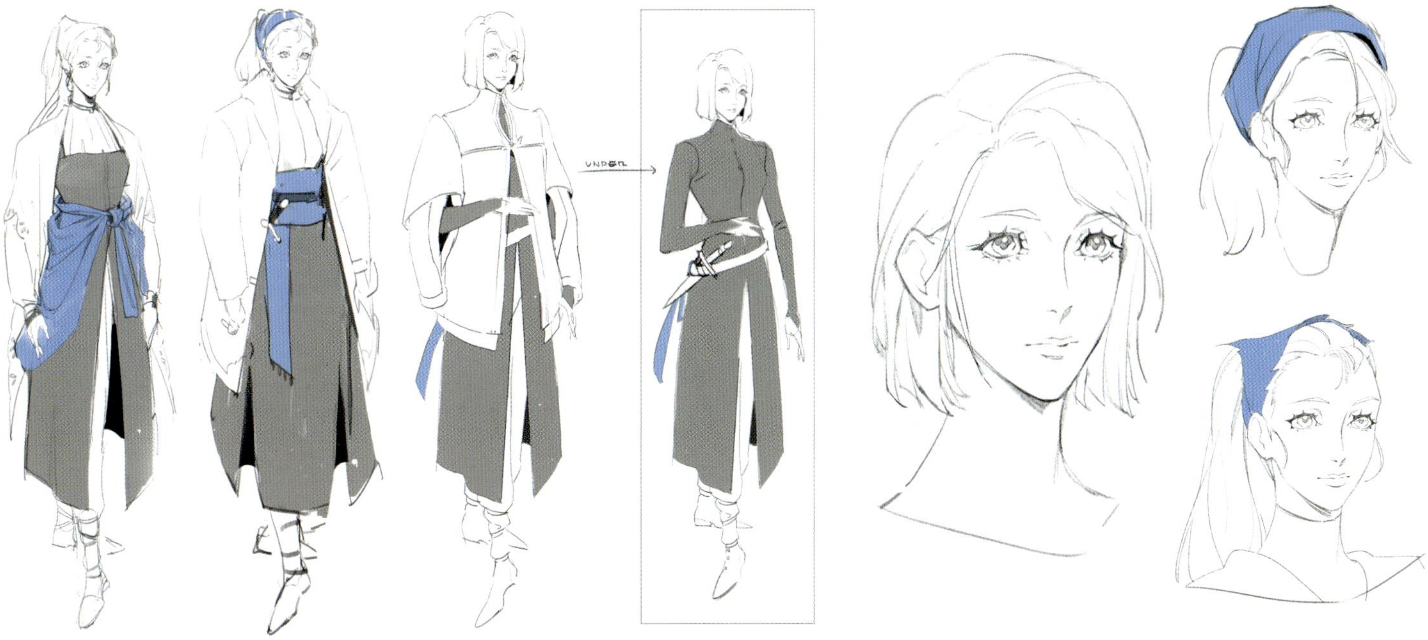

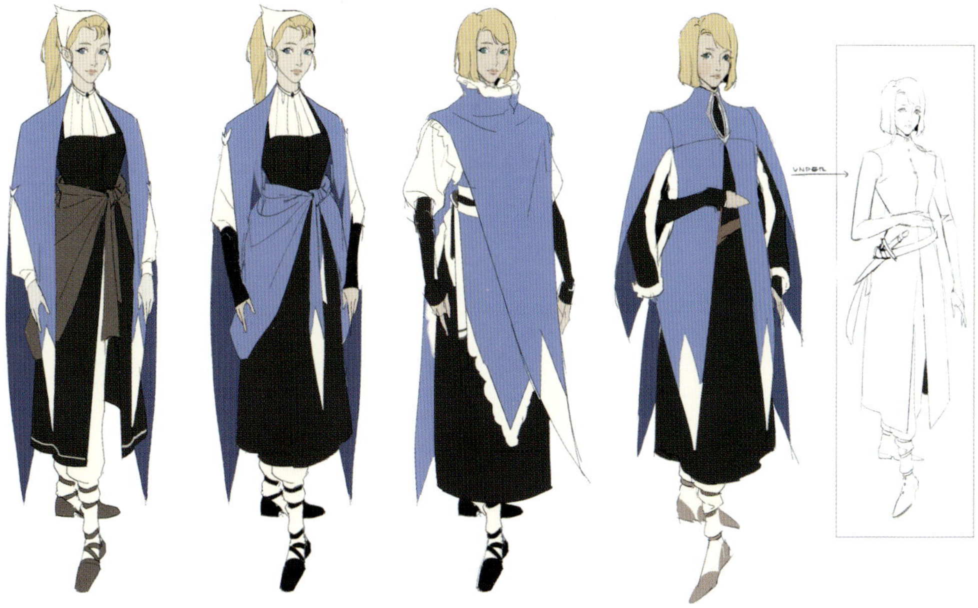

YOUNG TERA

Though the Tera who appears in *Castlevania: Rondo of Blood* is not the same—she's a nun who gets held hostage in Demon Castle—the hairstyles of Young Tera are throwbacks to the character in the video game. In the 1993 game, her long green hair is tied in a ponytail with a bow. The design with the headband emulates that.

The Speaker blue remains present throughout iterations for Tera's costume. At this point in her story, Tera is in a Russian village with her family (hence the attire fitting for colder weather) and other Speakers. Erzsebet hunts them, kills most of Tera's family, and captures Tera's younger sister.

Art by Mari Arakaki.

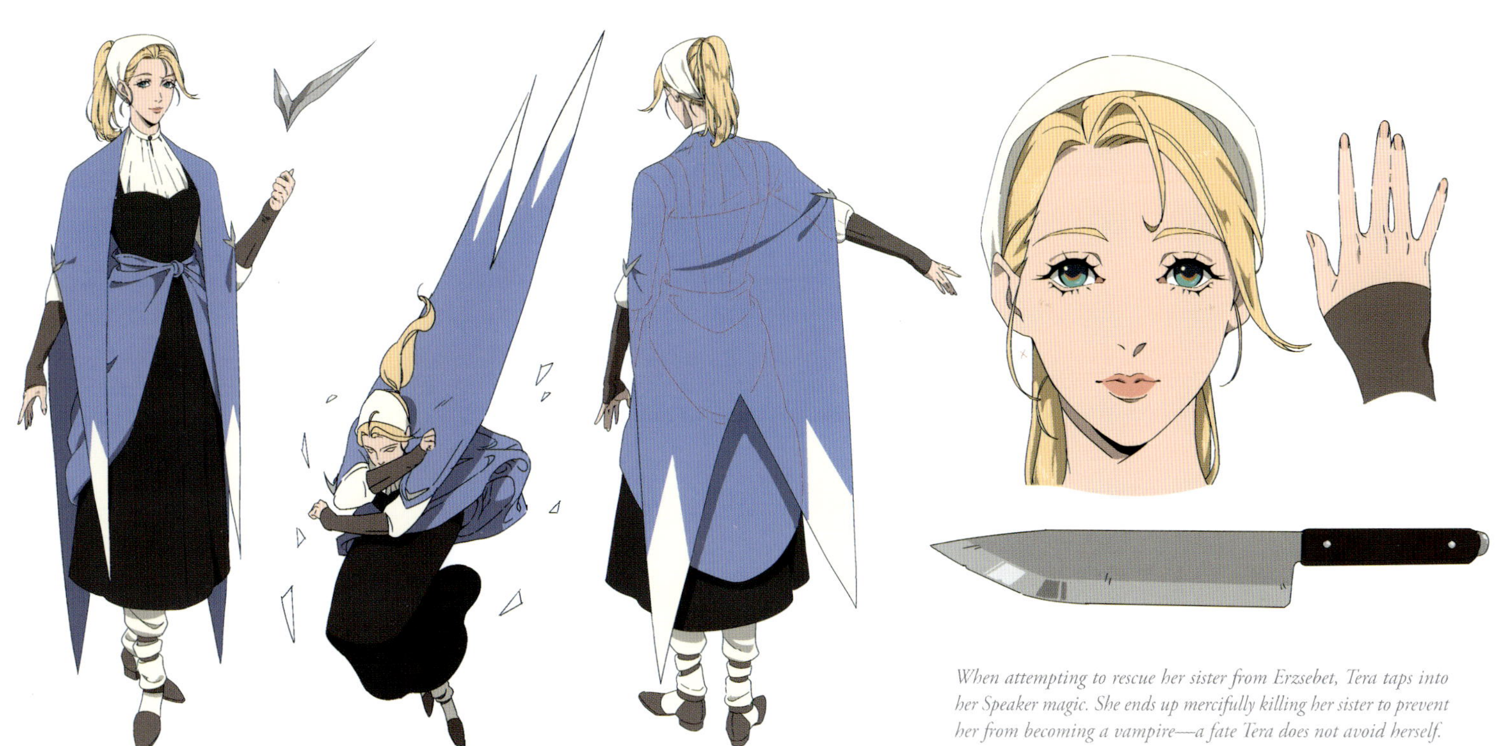

When attempting to rescue her sister from Erzsebet, Tera taps into her Speaker magic. She ends up mercifully killing her sister to prevent her from becoming a vampire—a fate Tera does not avoid herself.

Maria Renard

Like other recurring characters in the *Castlevania* video games, Maria Renard takes on a new life in *Nocturne*. Her powerful summoning magic from the game series assists her in her role as a leader of the revolutionaries in Machecoul (though at one point, Maria was only going to have Speaker magic). Her appearance in the series, particularly her outfit, looks like her redesign in *Castlevania: The Dracula X Chronicles*.

Character designer Katie Silva said, "This is one of the designs where I feel like you can really see the difference between the original *Castlevania* series style and then *Nocturne*. If you look at her hair, we were just doing all of these Rococo curls and way fewer sharp lines and angles."

Art by Katie Silva.

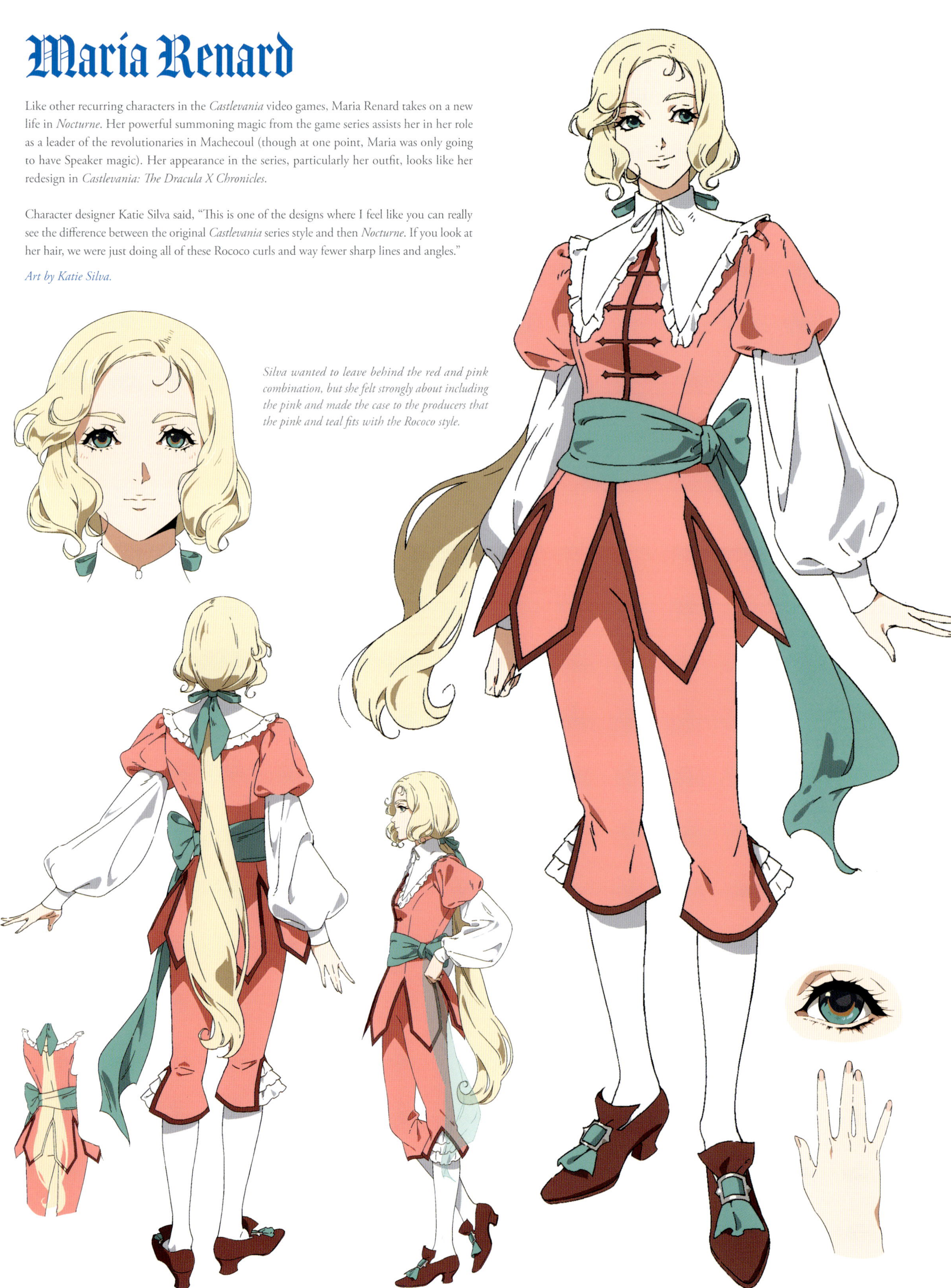

Silva wanted to leave behind the red and pink combination, but she felt strongly about including the pink and made the case to the producers that the pink and teal fits with the Rococo style.

MARIA'S EYES

Maria's eye color closely matches Tera's. Silva said, "We added multiple eye colors because in the previous *Castlevania*, every character just had one eye color. But in the Ayami Kojima art of Maria specifically, she has all these different colors in her eyes. It ended up being a little bit more difficult because you have to draw all these colors individually and then blur them together at different distances to the camera."

Art by Katie Silva with colors by Samuel Deats.

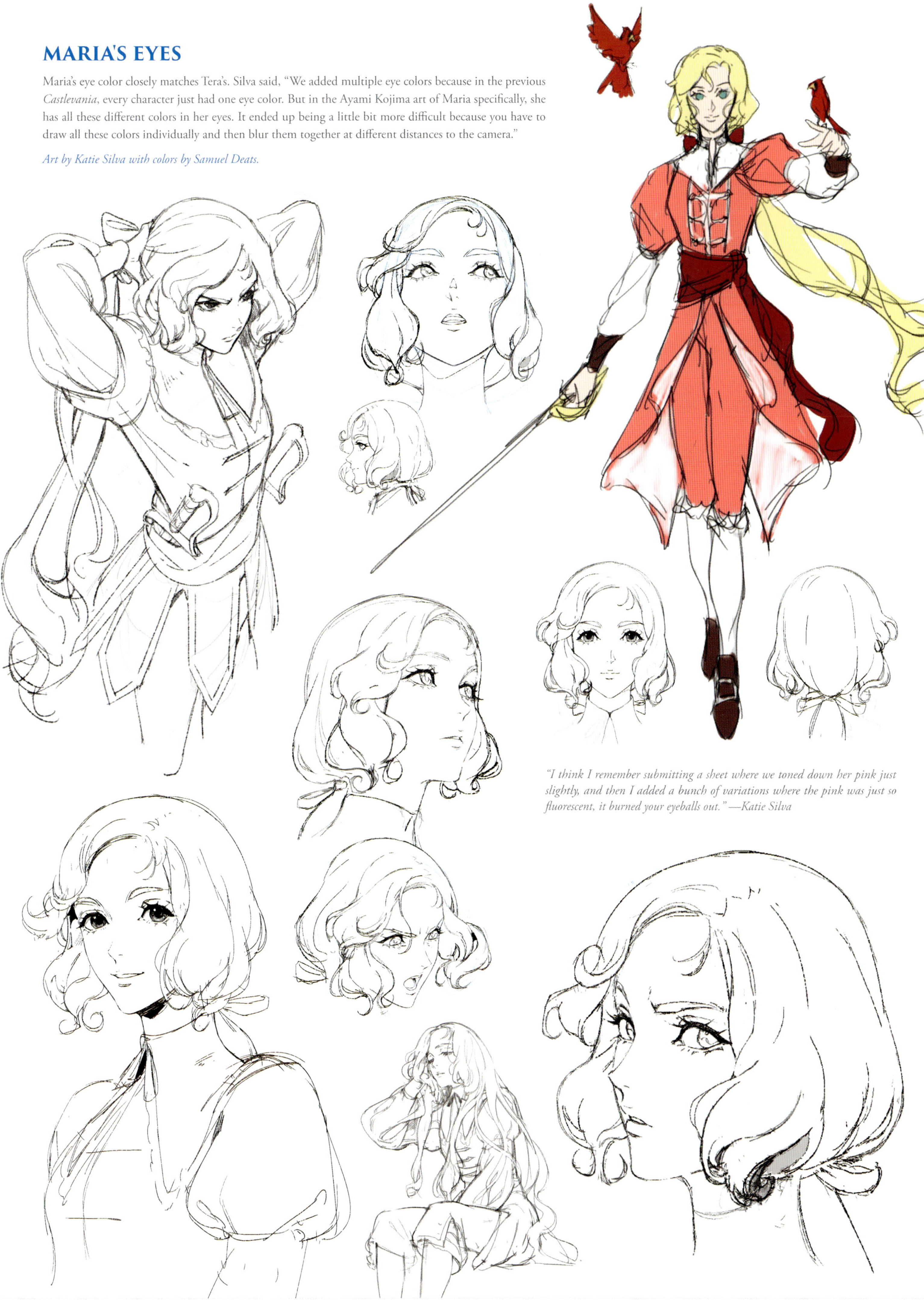

"I think I remember submitting a sheet where we toned down her pink just slightly, and then I added a bunch of variations where the pink was just so fluorescent, it burned your eyeballs out." —Katie Silva

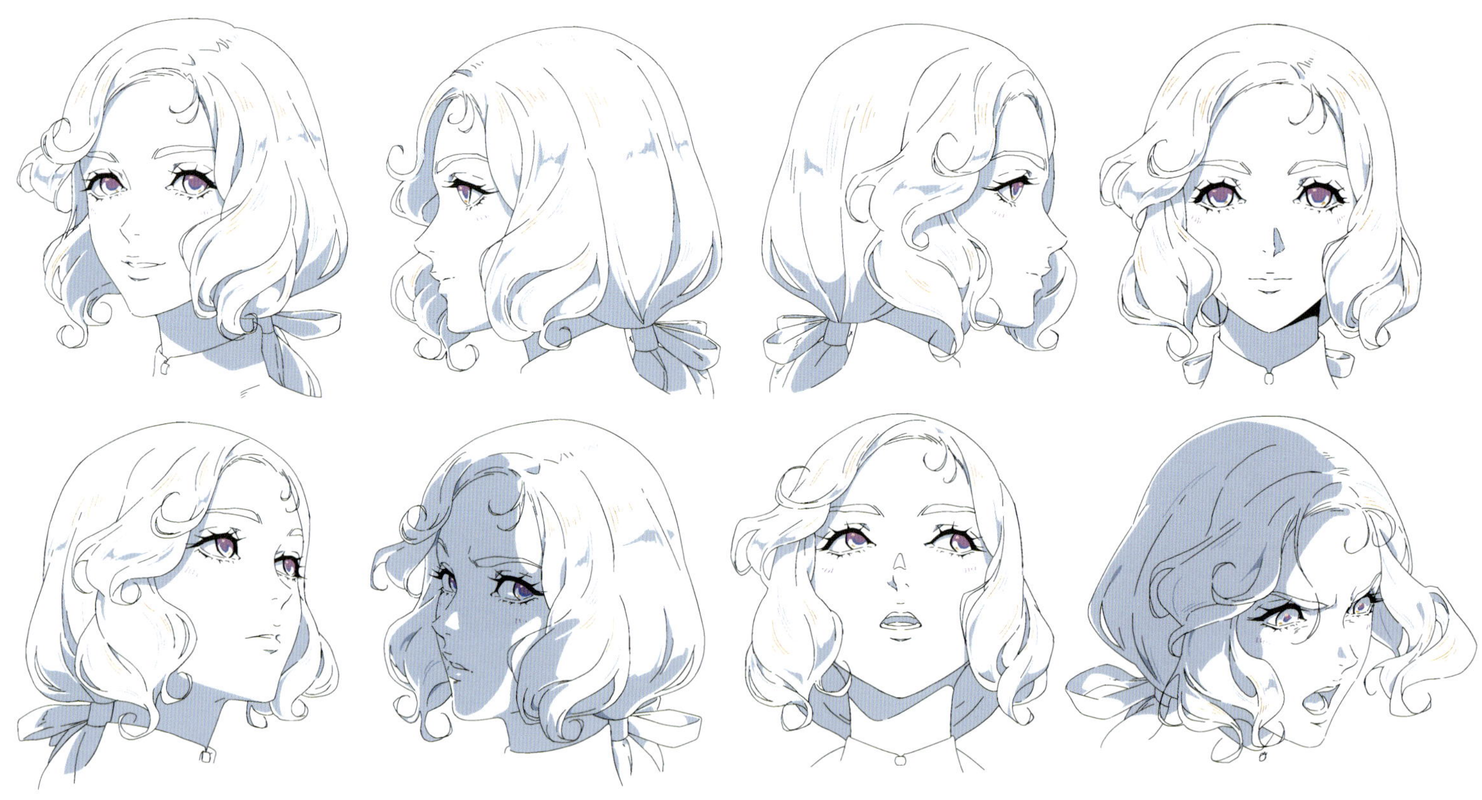

Silva said she's happy with the design they ended up with because it's close to the original game. Maria has a very "lady knight" look and her hair story follows her character arc too—it's down when she's more serious.

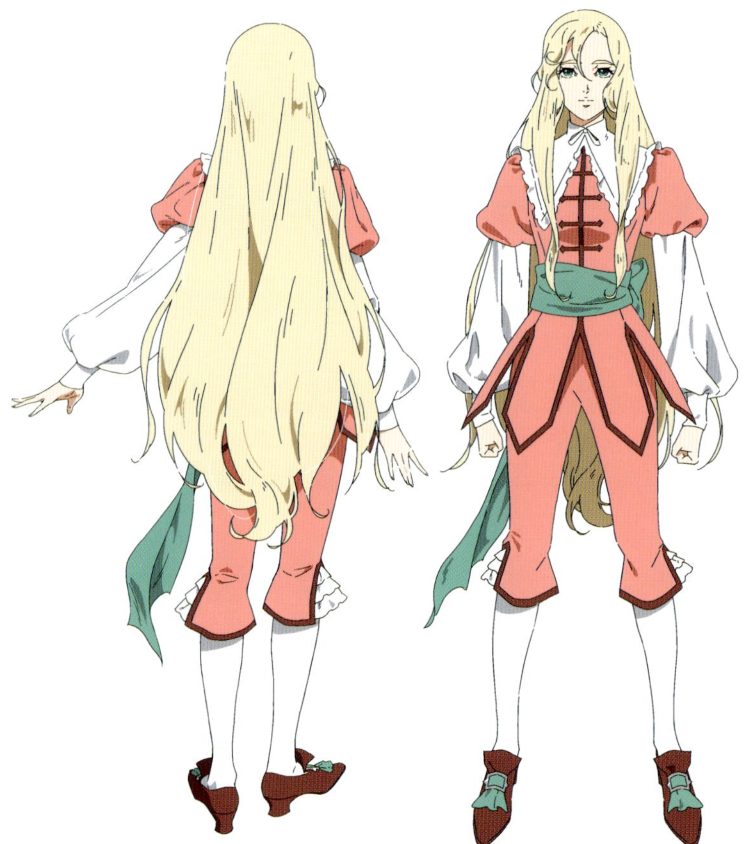

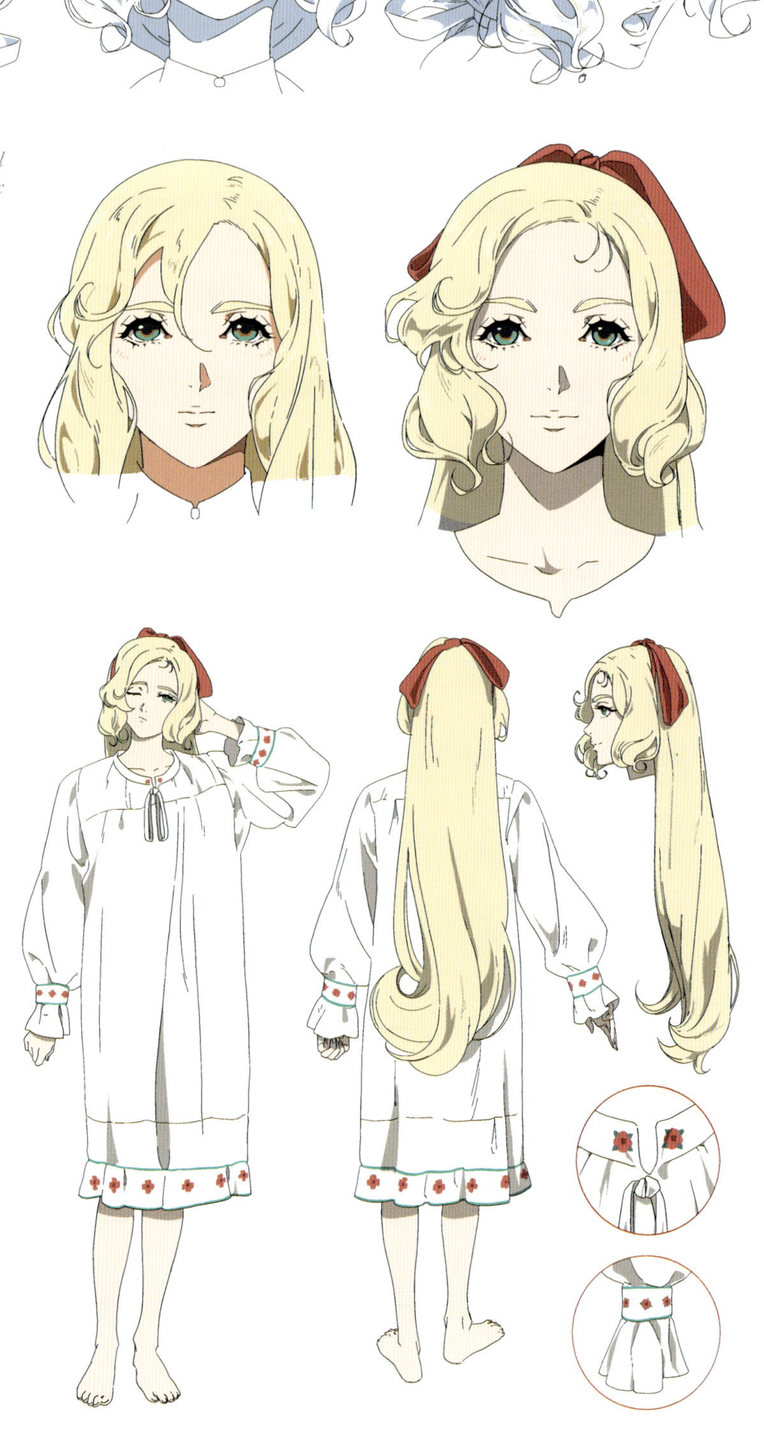

BRIGHTNESS IN THE DARK

As *Castlevania: Nocturne* progresses, the story gets darker in tone and the overall environment shifts to match, particularly after the eclipse at the end of season one. Maria's bright pink costume proved to be a challenge in that regard. Silva recalled, "The compositors had a lot of fun trying to make her look like she existed in the same scene as the other people."

Nightgown design by Ryan Plaisance. Hair and expressions by Katie Silva.

MARIA'S MAGIC

With her special abilities, Maria can Summon Four Holy Beasts; they're also known as the Four Symbols. The magic and creatures appear in *Symphony of the Night* and *Grimoire of Souls*, though they look quite different in the games. For *Nocturne*, the designers had the opportunity to flesh them out and have their aesthetic match the brightness of Maria. The beasts—Byakko, Seiryuu, Genbu, and Suzaku—assist her and her allies in battle. Each represents the four points on a compass. Maria can direct their actions in battle, and as her powers grow, her connection to the beasts deepens.

Initial concept design by Samuel Deats with art by Dooz Leslie and Suzanne Sharp.

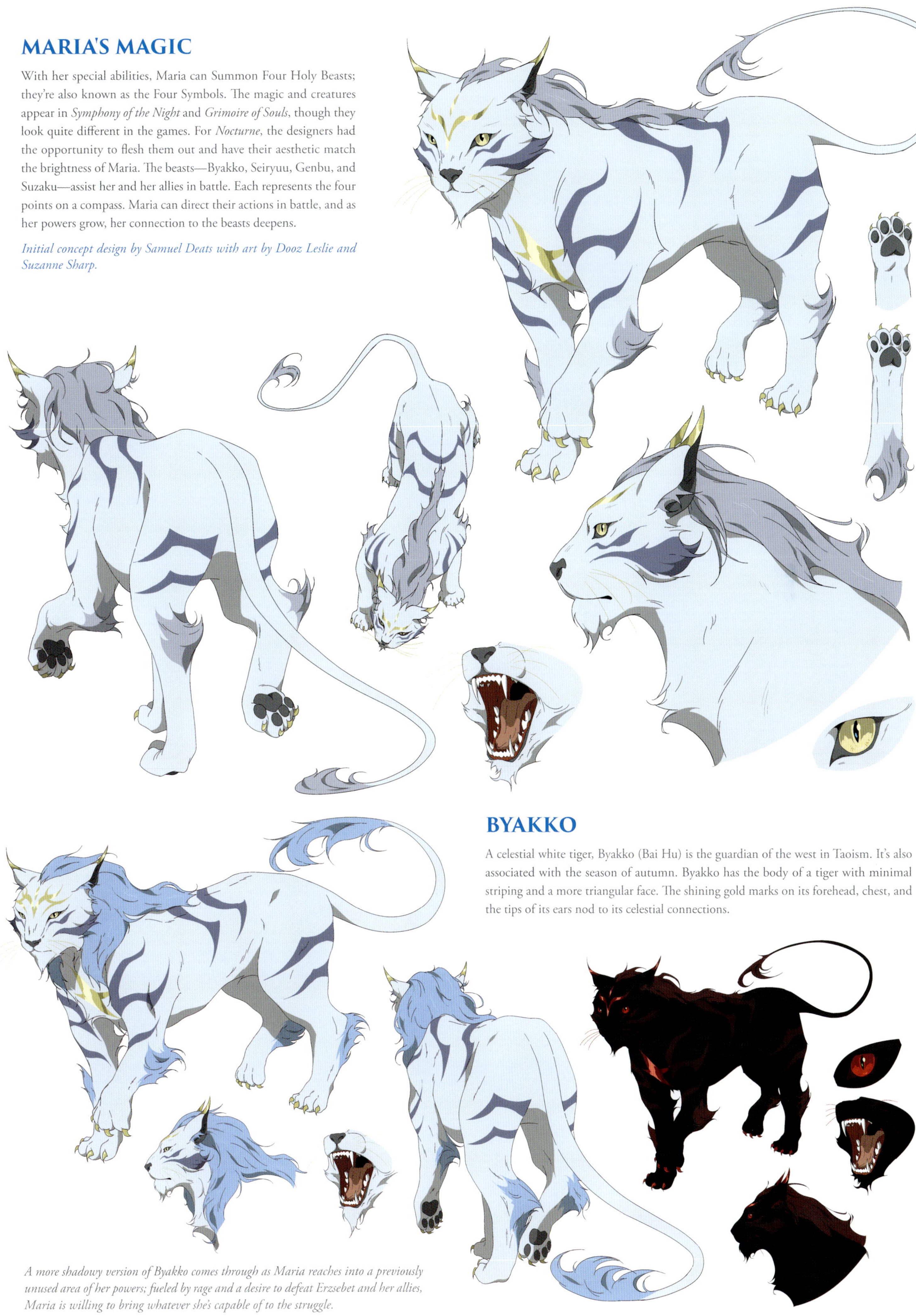

BYAKKO

A celestial white tiger, Byakko (Bai Hu) is the guardian of the west in Taoism. It's also associated with the season of autumn. Byakko has the body of a tiger with minimal striping and a more triangular face. The shining gold marks on its forehead, chest, and the tips of its ears nod to its celestial connections.

A more shadowy version of Byakko comes through as Maria reaches into a previously unused area of her powers; fueled by rage and a desire to defeat Erzsebet and her allies, Maria is willing to bring whatever she's capable of to the struggle.

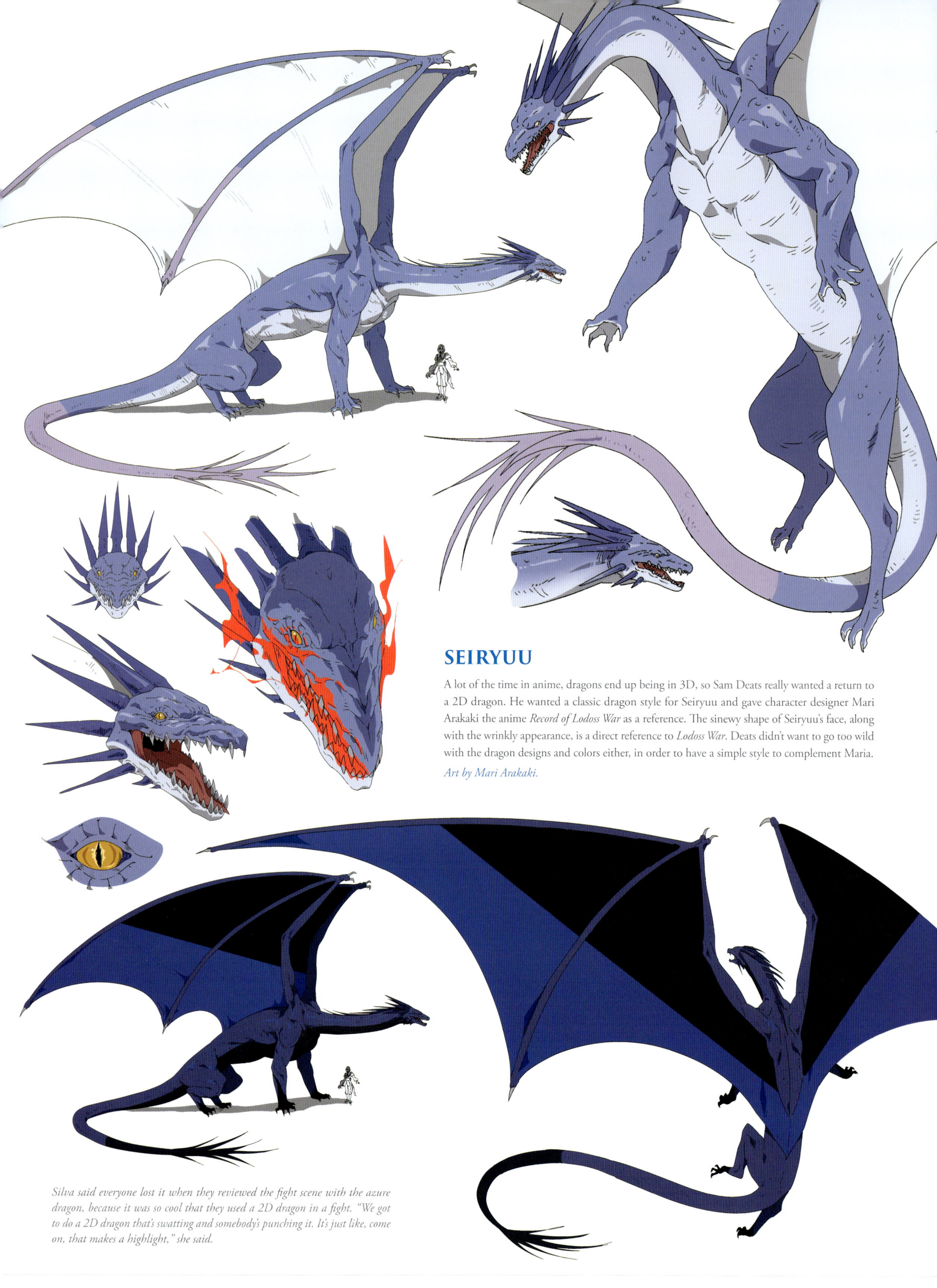

SEIRYUU

A lot of the time in anime, dragons end up being in 3D, so Sam Deats really wanted a return to a 2D dragon. He wanted a classic dragon style for Seiryuu and gave character designer Mari Arakaki the anime *Record of Lodoss War* as a reference. The sinewy shape of Seiryuu's face, along with the wrinkly appearance, is a direct reference to *Lodoss War*. Deats didn't want to go too wild with the dragon designs and colors either, in order to have a simple style to complement Maria.

Art by Mari Arakaki.

Silva said everyone lost it when they reviewed the fight scene with the azure dragon, because it was so cool that they used a 2D dragon in a fight. "We got to do a 2D dragon that's swatting and somebody's punching it. It's just like, come on, that makes a highlight," she said.

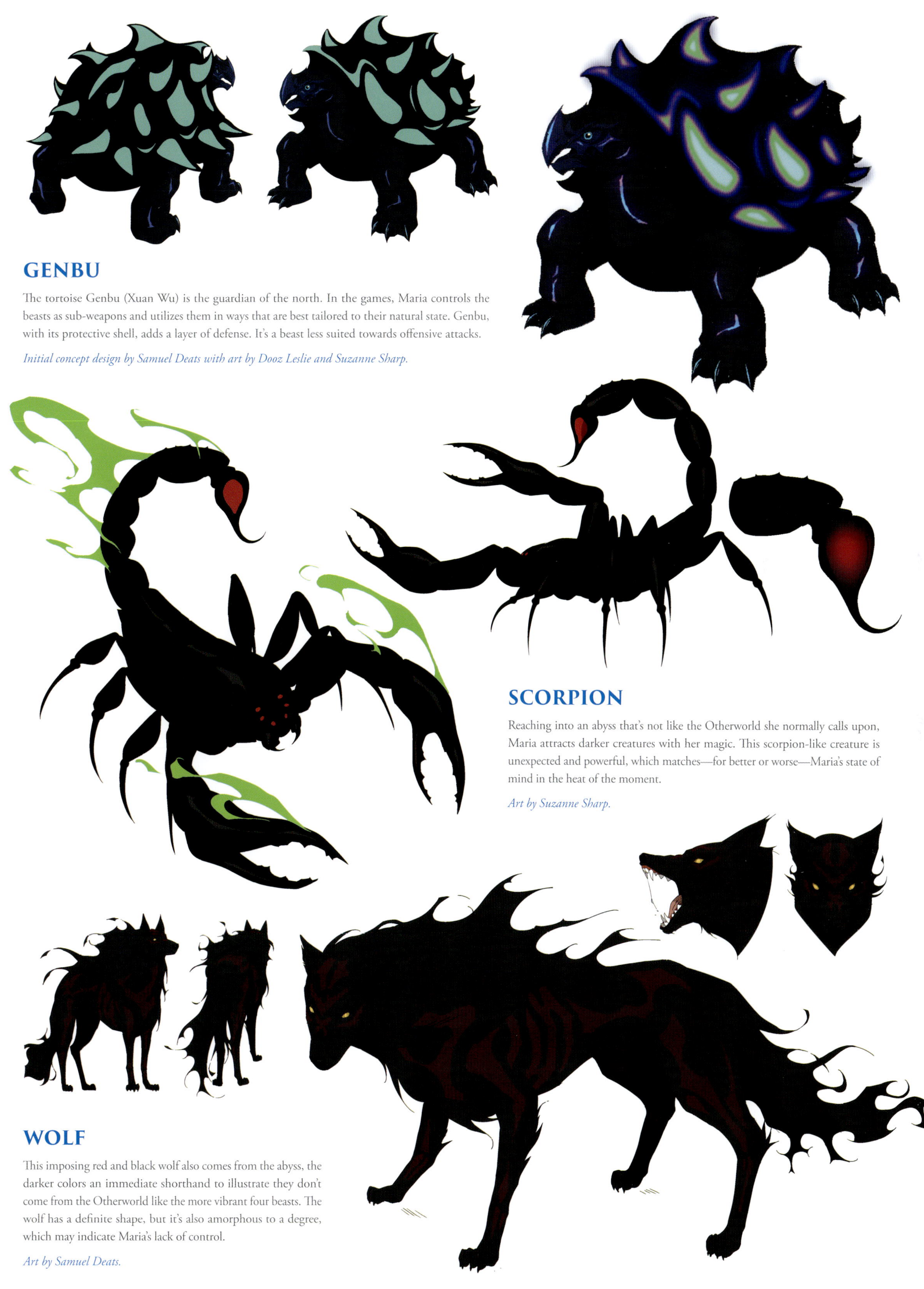

GENBU

The tortoise Genbu (Xuan Wu) is the guardian of the north. In the games, Maria controls the beasts as sub-weapons and utilizes them in ways that are best tailored to their natural state. Genbu, with its protective shell, adds a layer of defense. It's a beast less suited towards offensive attacks.

Initial concept design by Samuel Deats with art by Dooz Leslie and Suzanne Sharp.

SCORPION

Reaching into an abyss that's not like the Otherworld she normally calls upon, Maria attracts darker creatures with her magic. This scorpion-like creature is unexpected and powerful, which matches—for better or worse—Maria's state of mind in the heat of the moment.

Art by Suzanne Sharp.

WOLF

This imposing red and black wolf also comes from the abyss, the darker colors an immediate shorthand to illustrate they don't come from the Otherworld like the more vibrant four beasts. The wolf has a definite shape, but it's also amorphous to a degree, which may indicate Maria's lack of control.

Art by Samuel Deats.

SHADOW MONSTER

As Sam noted, in the games, Maria summons more than only the four sacred beasts. They expanded that to the idea that there's more she can tap into from this place—and not just friendly creatures. He explained, "We started getting into some of these darker creatures. We start to play with the idea that they're her own. She influences the things that she's pulling through and in turn, as she starts to connect with them more closely, they influence her as well."

Art by Chance Kubesh.

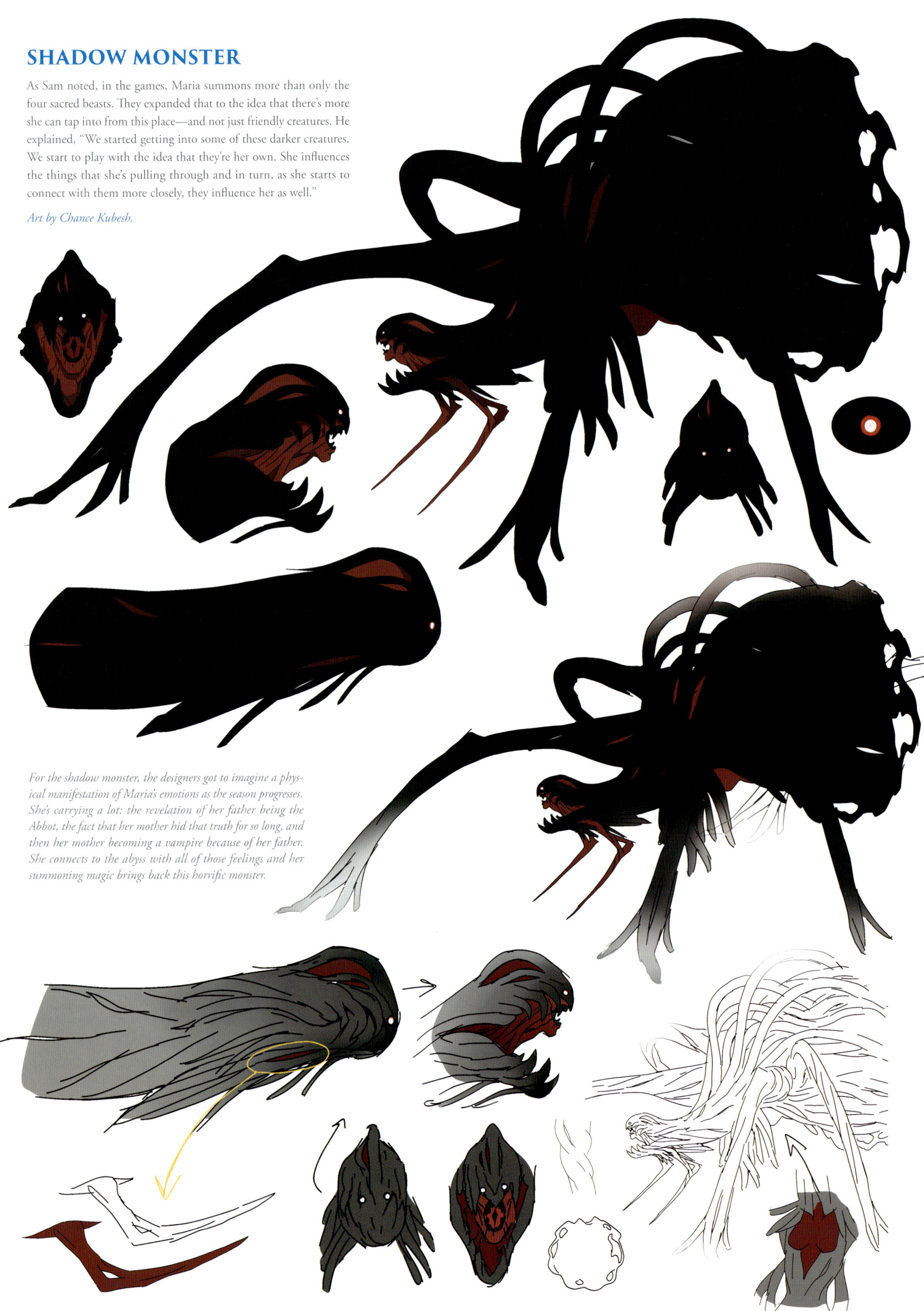

For the shadow monster, the designers got to imagine a physical manifestation of Maria's emotions as the season progresses. She's carrying a lot: the revelation of her father being the Abbot, the fact that her mother hid that truth for so long, and then her mother becoming a vampire because of her father. She connects to the abyss with all of those feelings and her summoning magic brings back this horrific monster.

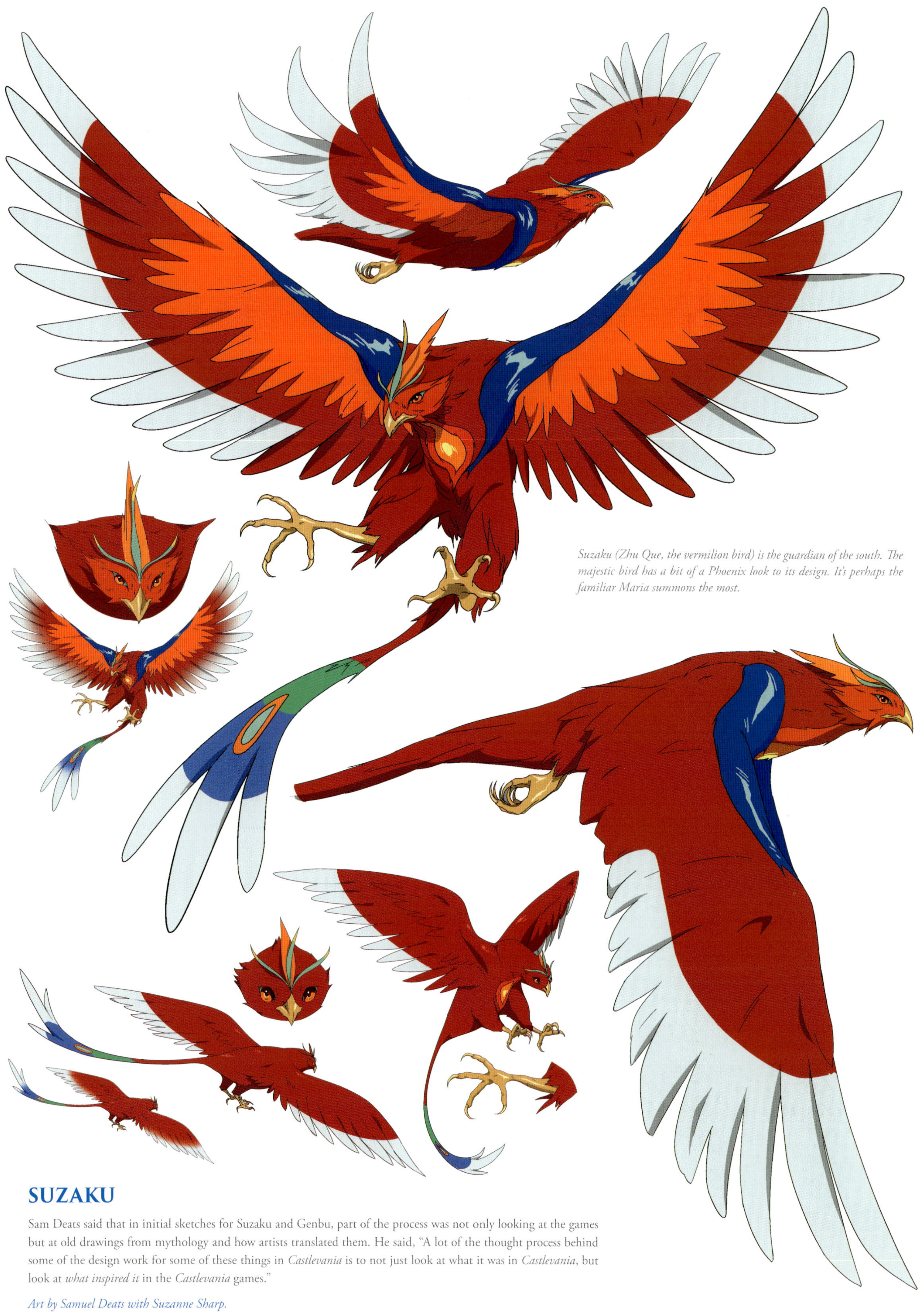

Suzaku (Zhu Que, the vermilion bird) is the guardian of the south. The majestic bird has a bit of a Phoenix look to its design. It's perhaps the familiar Maria summons the most.

SUZAKU

Sam Deats said that in initial sketches for Suzaku and Genbu, part of the process was not only looking at the games but at old drawings from mythology and how artists translated them. He said, "A lot of the thought process behind some of the design work for some of these things in *Castlevania* is to not just look at what it was in *Castlevania*, but look at *what inspired it* in the *Castlevania* games."

Art by Samuel Deats with Suzanne Sharp.

Storyboards by Samuel Deats.

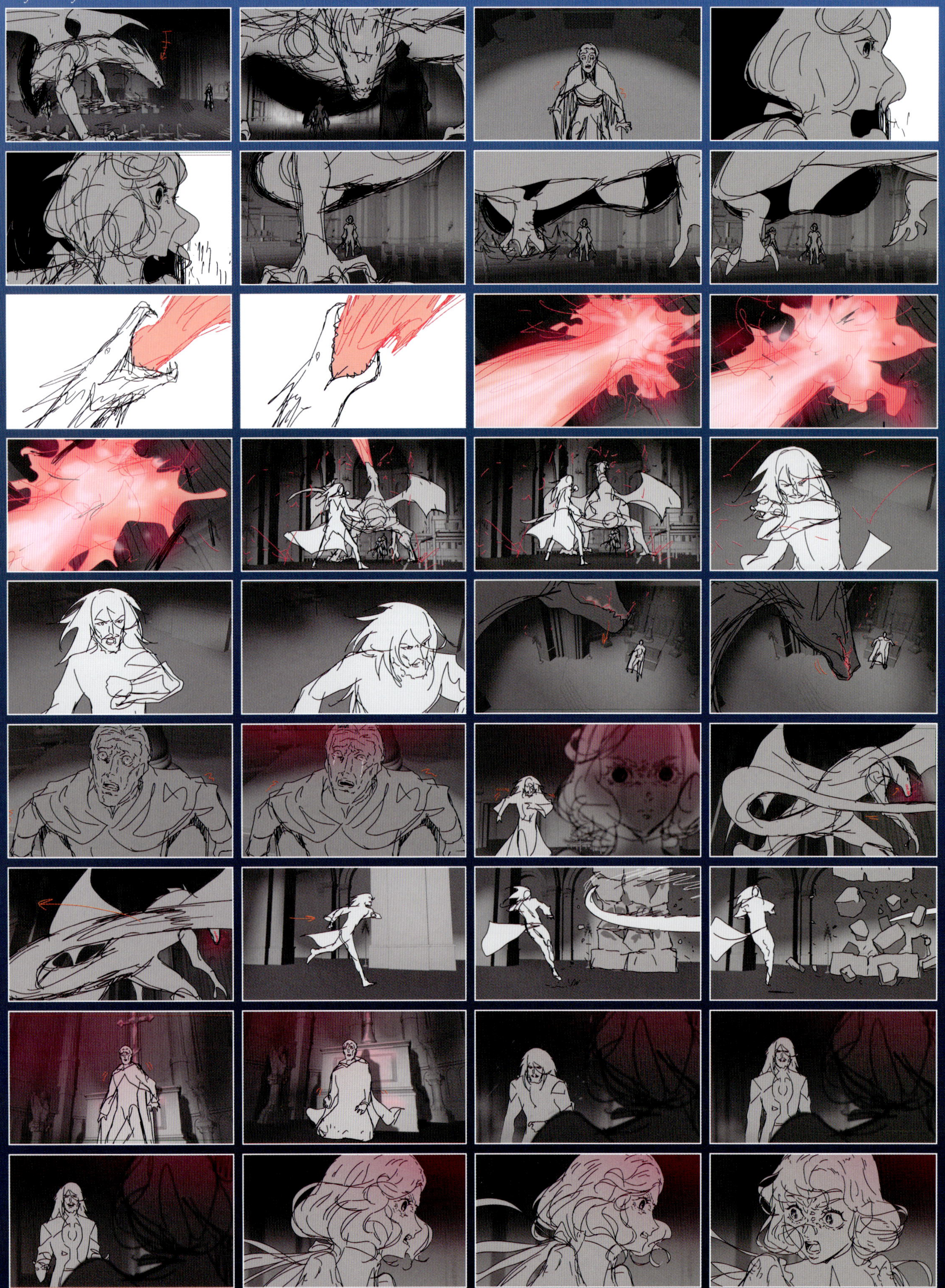

Sam recalled, "This was a turning point for Maria, symbolically, she didn't know it yet, but a wakeup call. So it was very important that we nailed it as perfectly as we could manage." Adam Deats adds that was especially true because it was one of the moodier things they got to do in an otherwise action-heavy season.

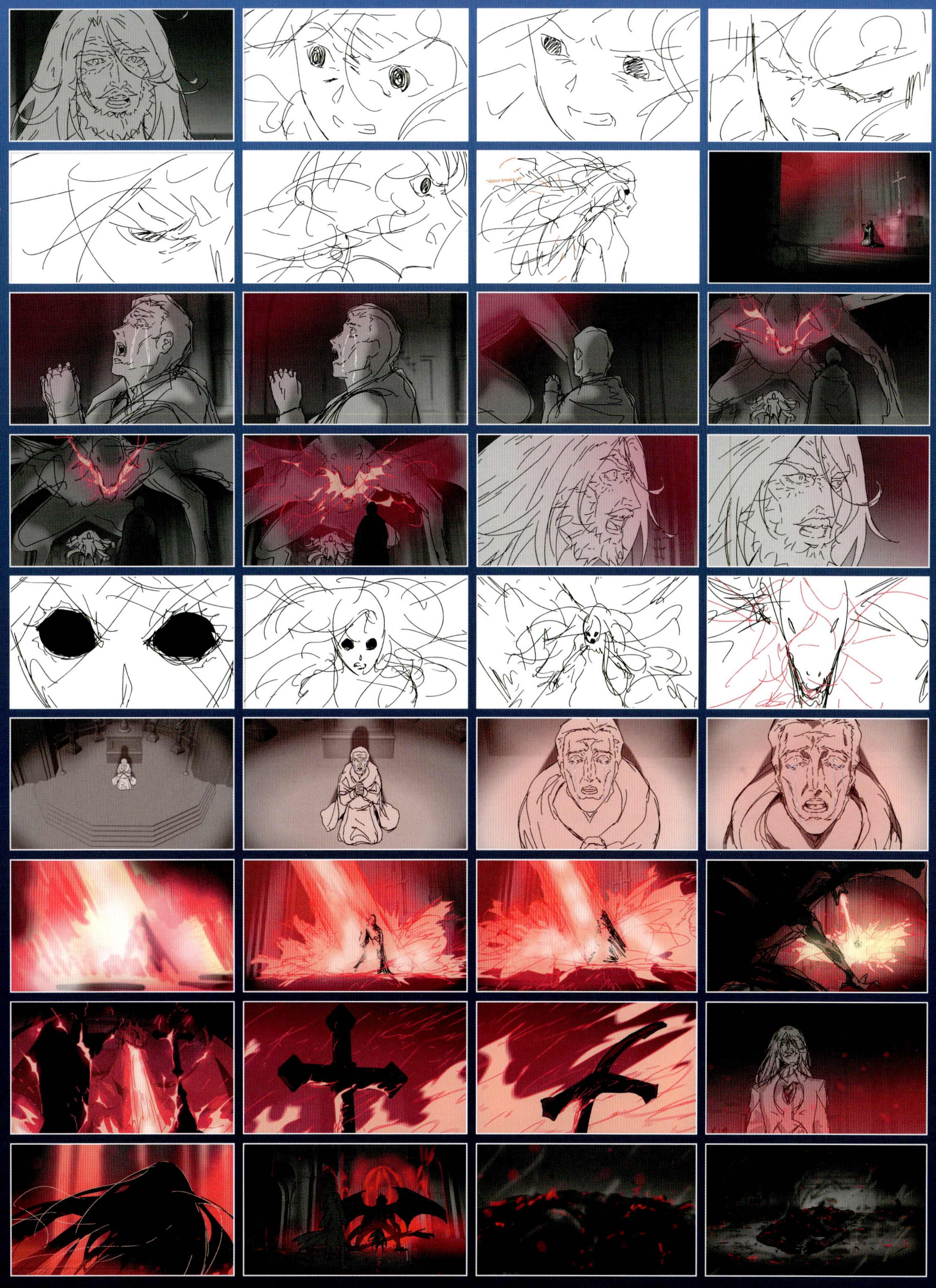

"I remember being particular about the timing of the Abbott's last shocked moments," Sam noted. "It was this really difficult line to walk because that that could end up feeling comedic and I was worried about that. You want to be a little bit satisfied that this absolute bastard is getting his due, but you don't want to be pulled out of the drama of the moment."

Annette

Born a slave on Saint-Domingue, Annette is a descendant of the orisha Ogun and can access his power to wield magic pulled from the Earth. She is also a skilled fighter. With her friend Edouard, she escapes her slaver and joins the revolution against slavery in Saint-Domingue before traveling to find a Belmont to help stop the dangerous Vampire Messiah. That Belmont ends up being Richter.

Silva said Annette's design carries a little of the Lady Belmont vibe we see with Julia earlier as far as the styling of her clothing. The pieces are more snug and therefore more suited for the motion a fighter needs, and she has a sash to secure her weapons.

Art by Katie Silva.

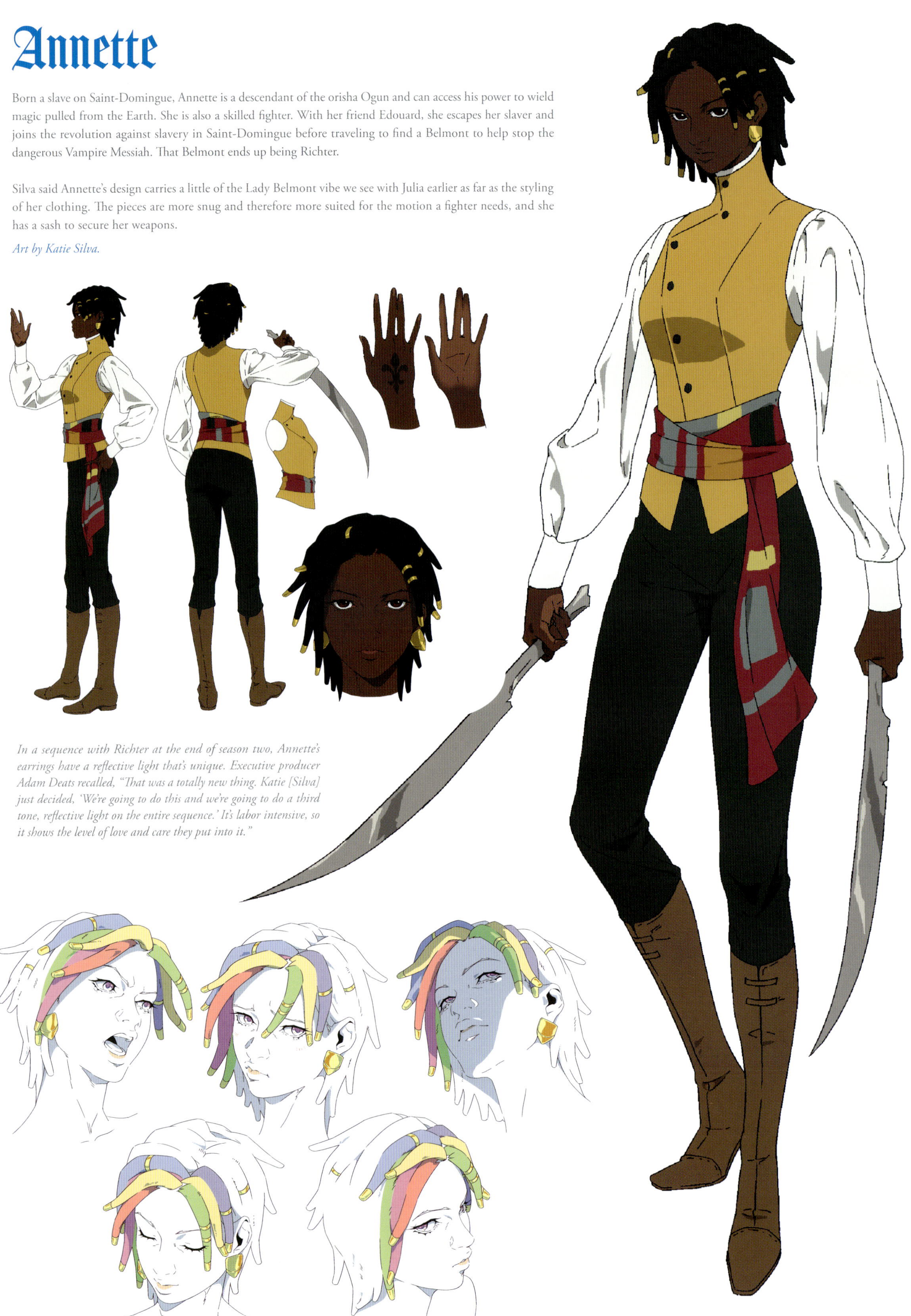

In a sequence with Richter at the end of season two, Annette's earrings have a reflective light that's unique. Executive producer Adam Deats recalled, "That was a totally new thing. Katie [Silva] just decided, 'We're going to do this and we're going to do a third tone, reflective light on the entire sequence.' It's labor intensive, so it shows the level of love and care they put into it."

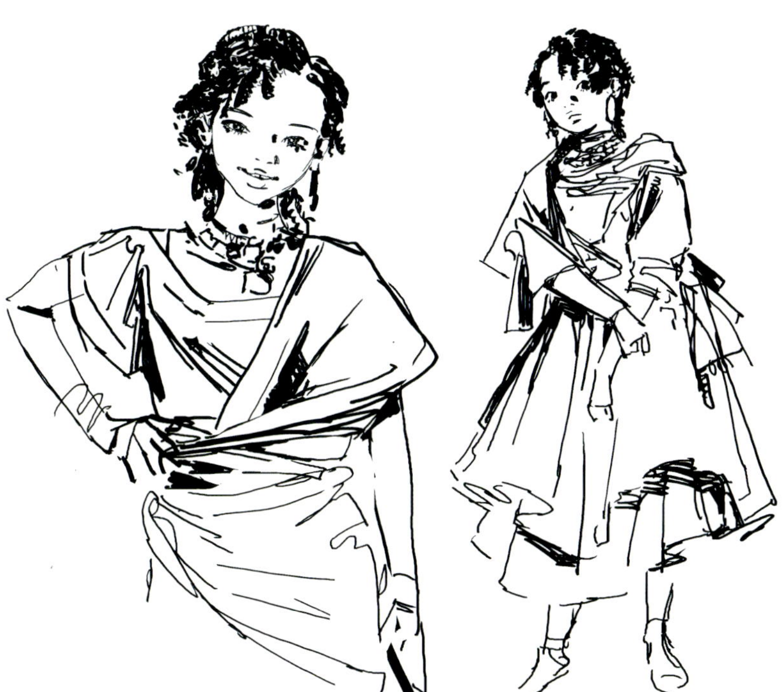

FINDING ANNETTE'S LOOK

Character designer Saskia Gutekunst helped refine Annette's design. Silva said they brought Gutekunst on board to bring more variety to the character design and have an anime character with a wider nose and Black features. Saskia's designs are on the right and many features are visible in Annette's final look.

Art by Saskia Gutekunst.

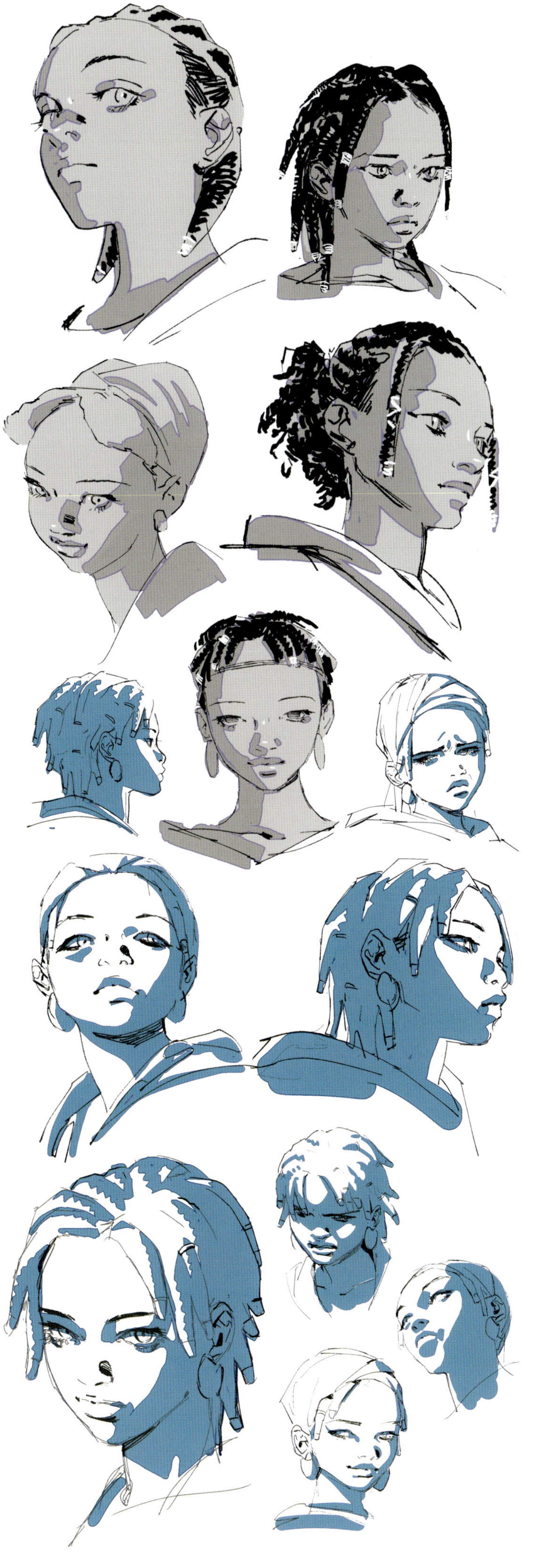

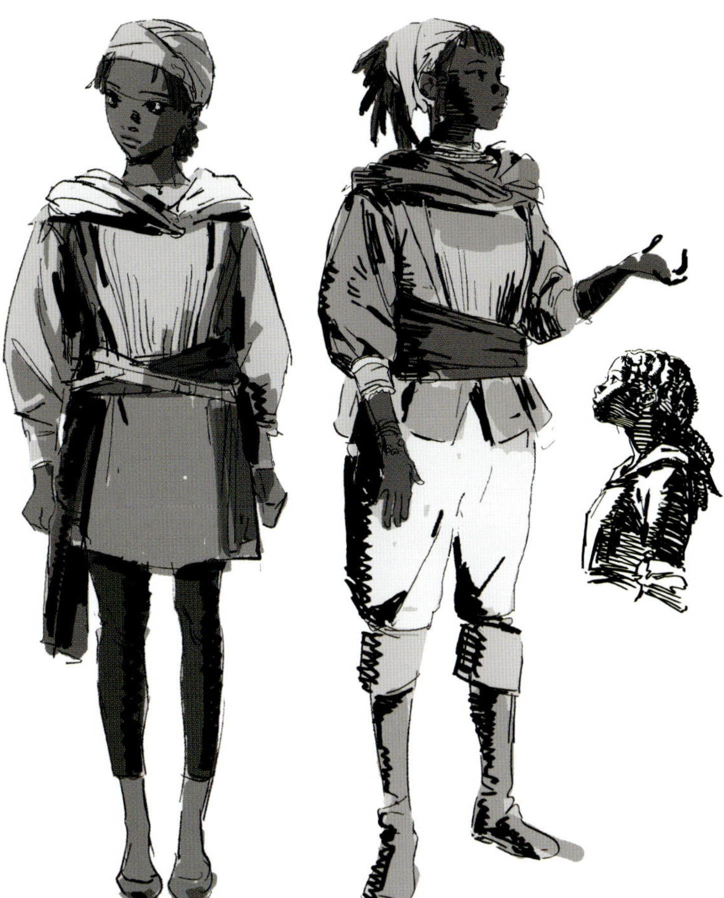

The left image helps animators identify particular pieces of hair so they can keep track of their movement in different shots. The artists use this kind of color coding for pieces of hair—also in storyboards—and the various hues make pieces that need to be animated separately stand apart at a quick glance. Here, the colors show which of Annette's locs are framing her face.

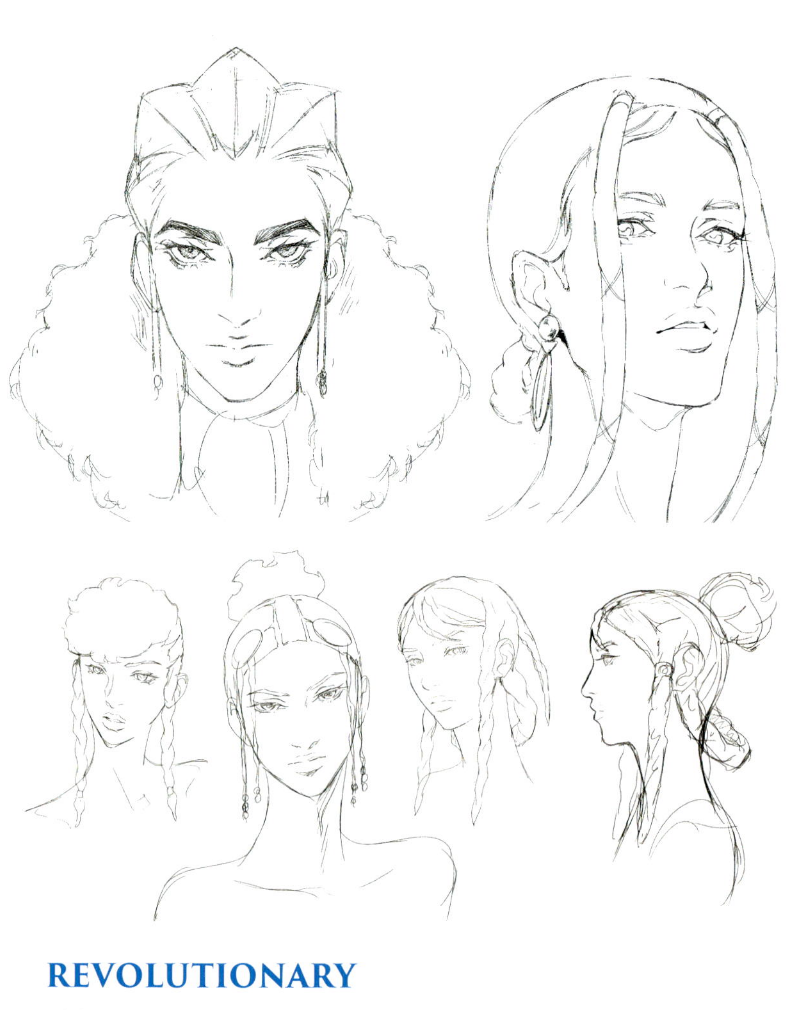

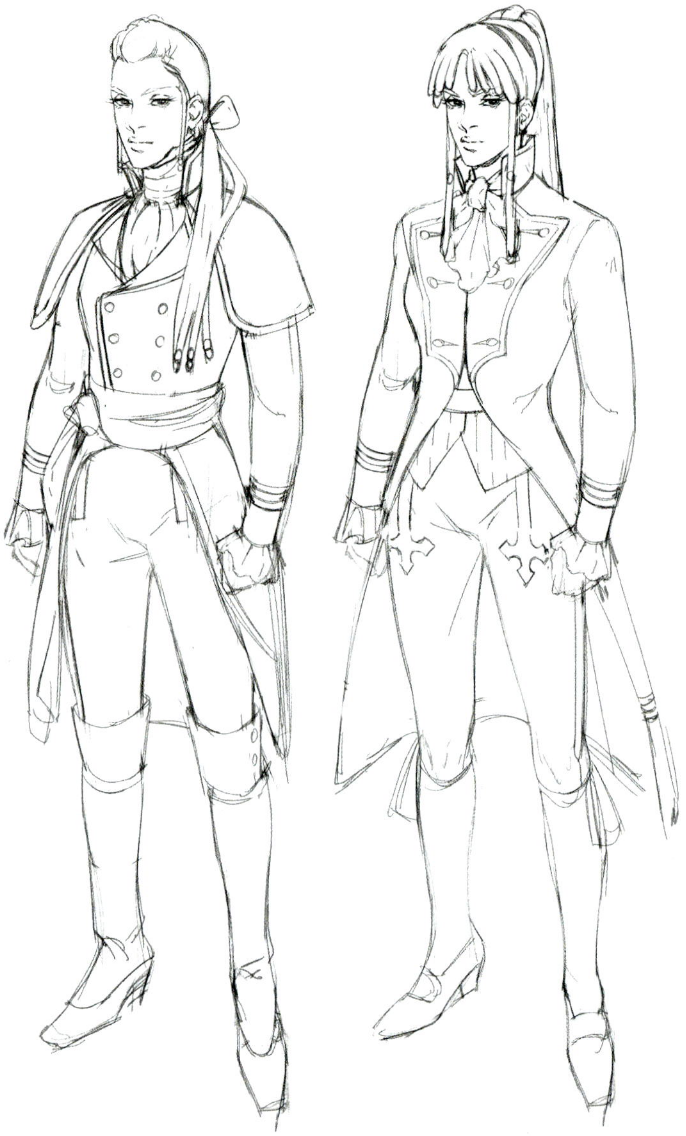

REVOLUTIONARY

While Annette did have a role to play in the fight against slavery, she ended up taking a more swashbuckling adventurer turn and sailed across the sea to find Richter Belmont. However, she was envisioned as a military leader at one point. They looked to a real-life general from the Haitian revolution, Toussaint Louverture, for inspiration for Annette. The above right designs show her in a possible buttoned-up, militaristic ensemble.

Explorations by Samuel Deats and Katie Silva.

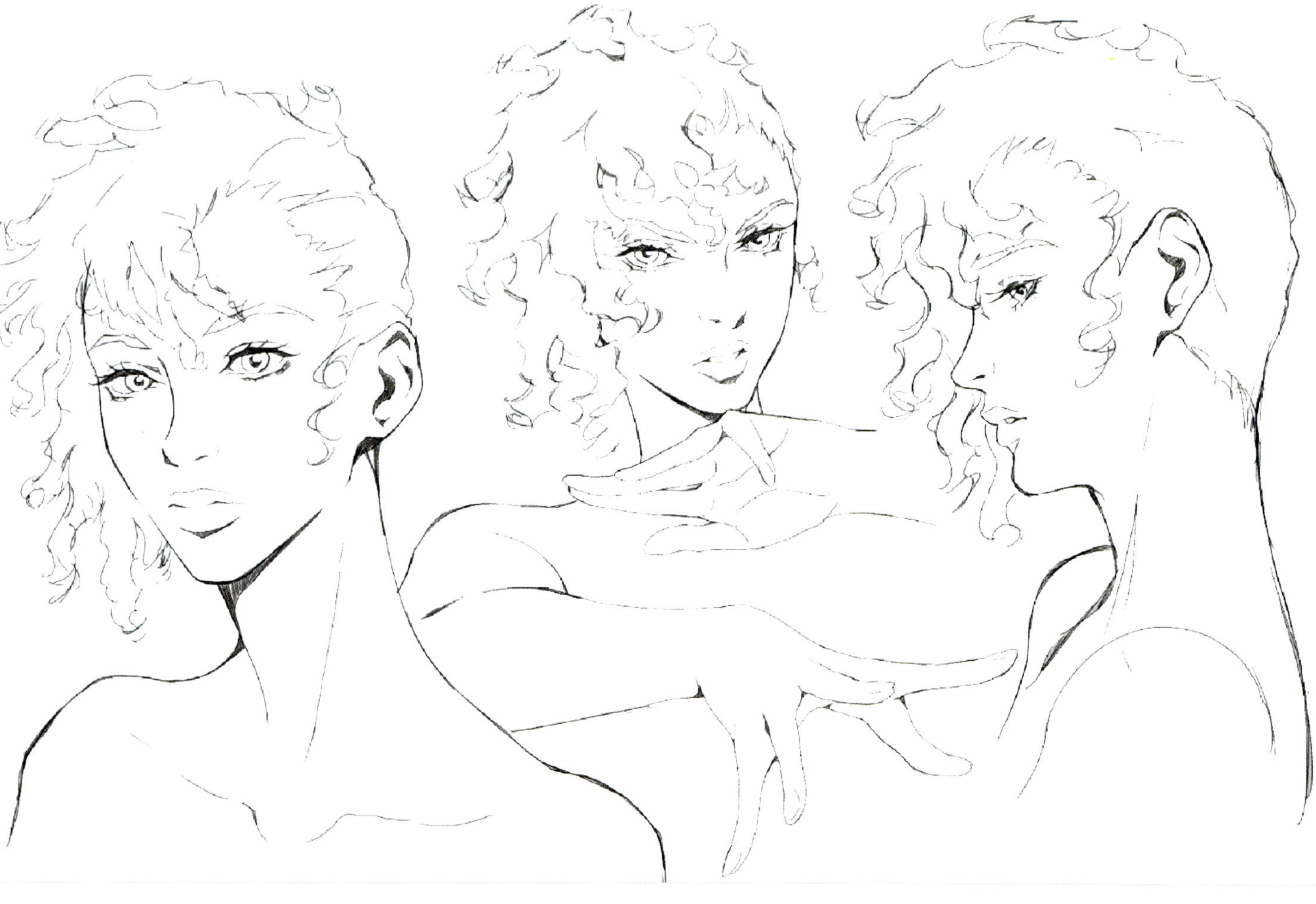

Storyboards by Kamille Areopagita.

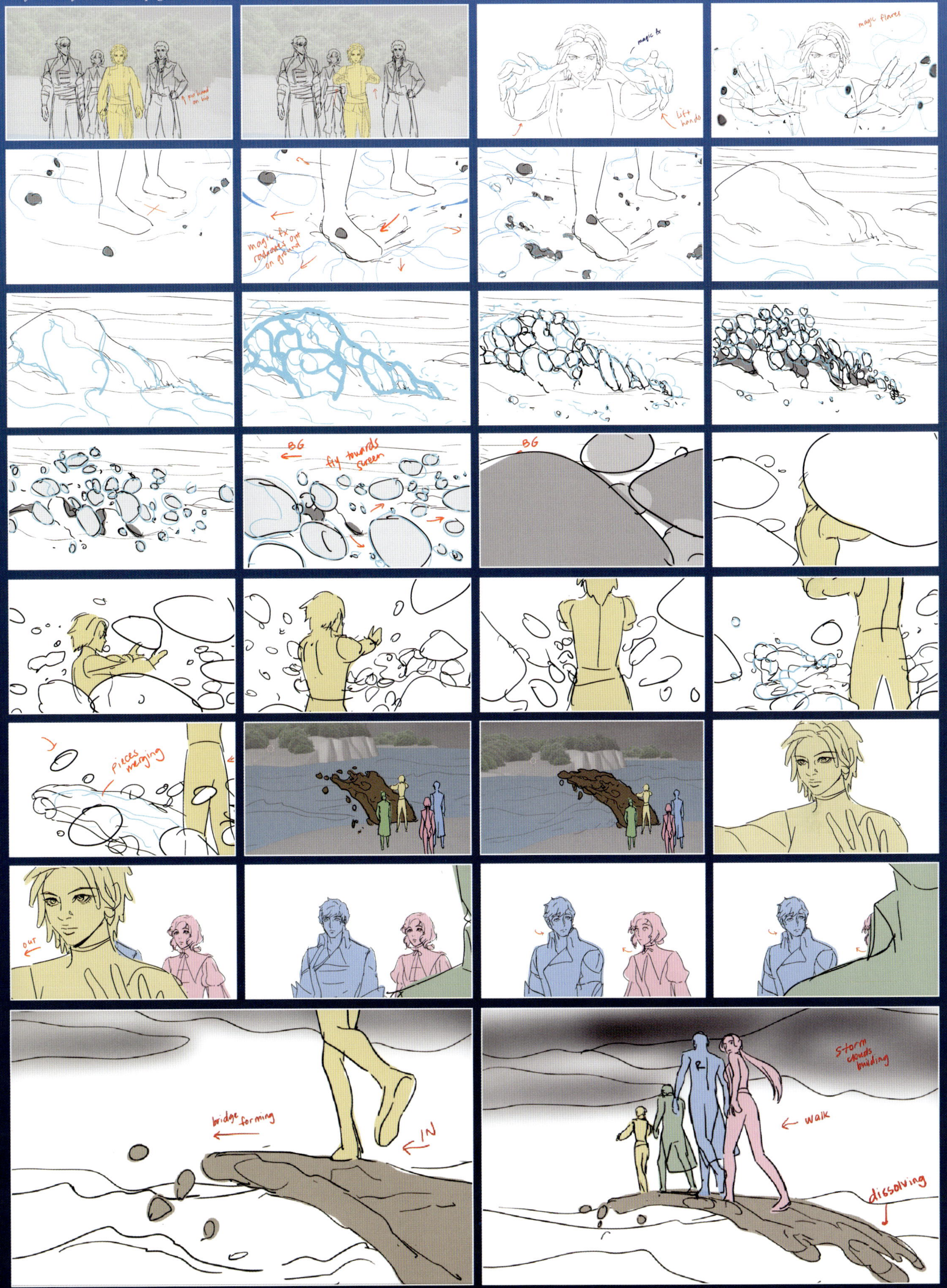

Artist Kamille Areopagita illustrated these storyboards showing Annette using her orisha magic. They wanted to depict Annette's abilities differently than other magic in the show. Specifically, they wanted to consider the importance of her environment to her magic by showing how she reacts and uses what's around her to her advantage in a fight.

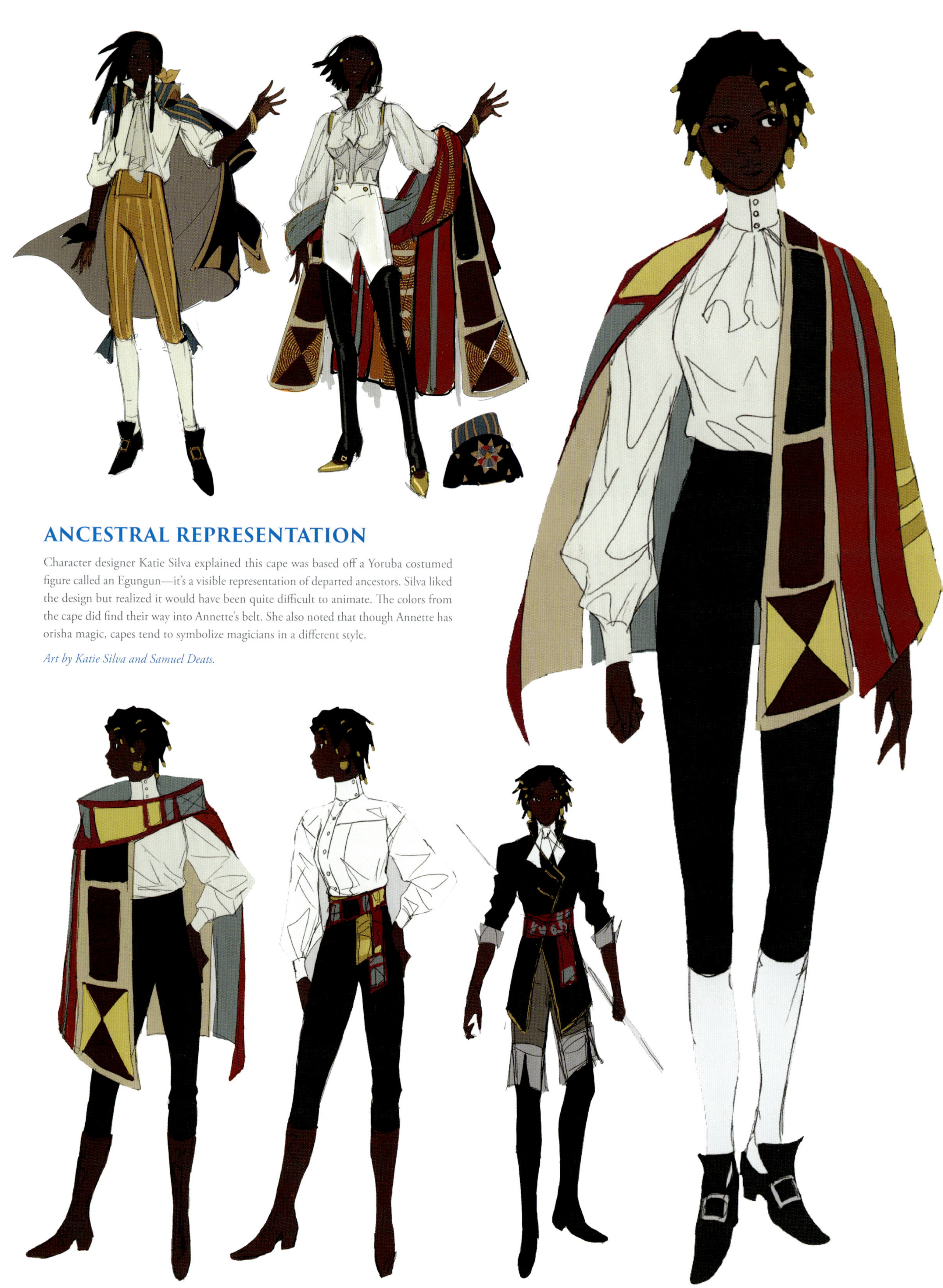

ANCESTRAL REPRESENTATION

Character designer Katie Silva explained this cape was based off a Yoruba costumed figure called an Egungun—it's a visible representation of departed ancestors. Silva liked the design but realized it would have been quite difficult to animate. The colors from the cape did find their way into Annette's belt. She also noted that though Annette has orisha magic, capes tend to symbolize magicians in a different style.

Art by Katie Silva and Samuel Deats.

SOFTER STYLE

When Annette finally gets to rest at the end of season two, her clothing reflects it. Silva said, "This is a Haitian traditional outfit. Sam [Deats] requested that she have a different outfit, and I was really pushing for her to look more soft and romantic. And also I thought that she should have a Karabela dress because it looks soft and romantic."

Art by Katie Silva.

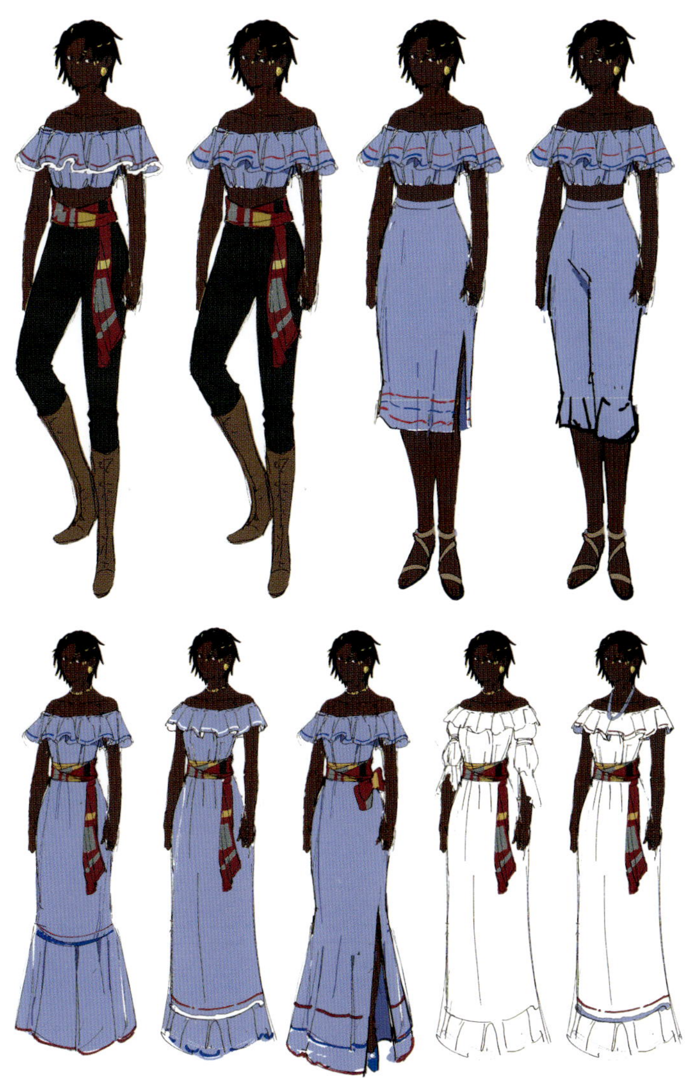

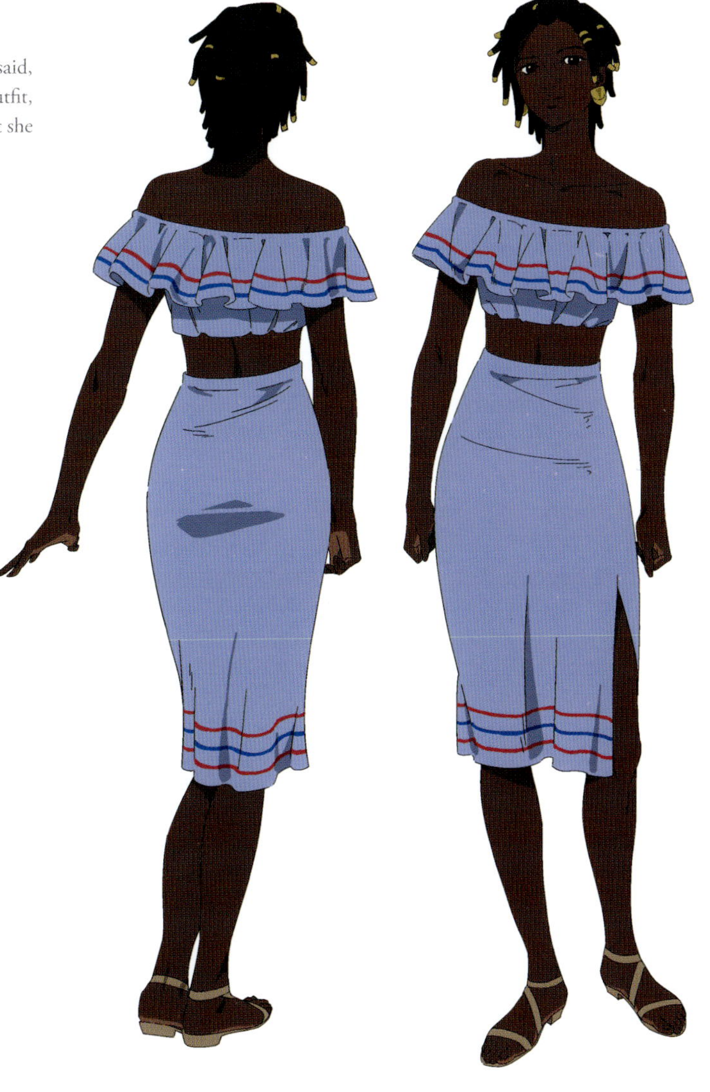

Because the series shows Annette fighting so much and being practical, the idea of her mixing and matching the top of a Karabela dress with her pants and belt was a possibility. Ultimately, the outfit worked best with Annette figuratively letting her hair down and relaxing.

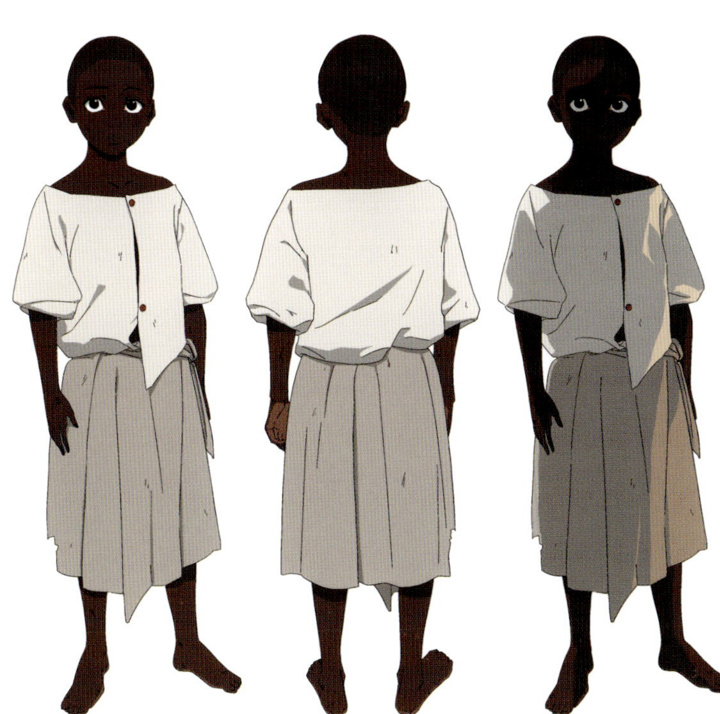

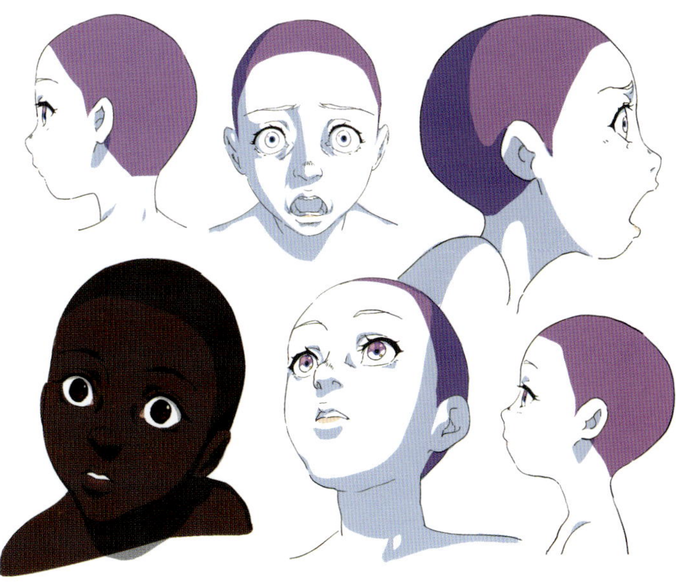

YOUNG ANNETTE

Silva said they referenced historical paintings for young Annette's look. "We wanted her to have a bit of a hair journey," she said. "You're not really allowed to have hair as a slave, so we gave her a loc growth journey. We made different model sheets for her hair growth at different lengths."

Art by Mari Arakaki.

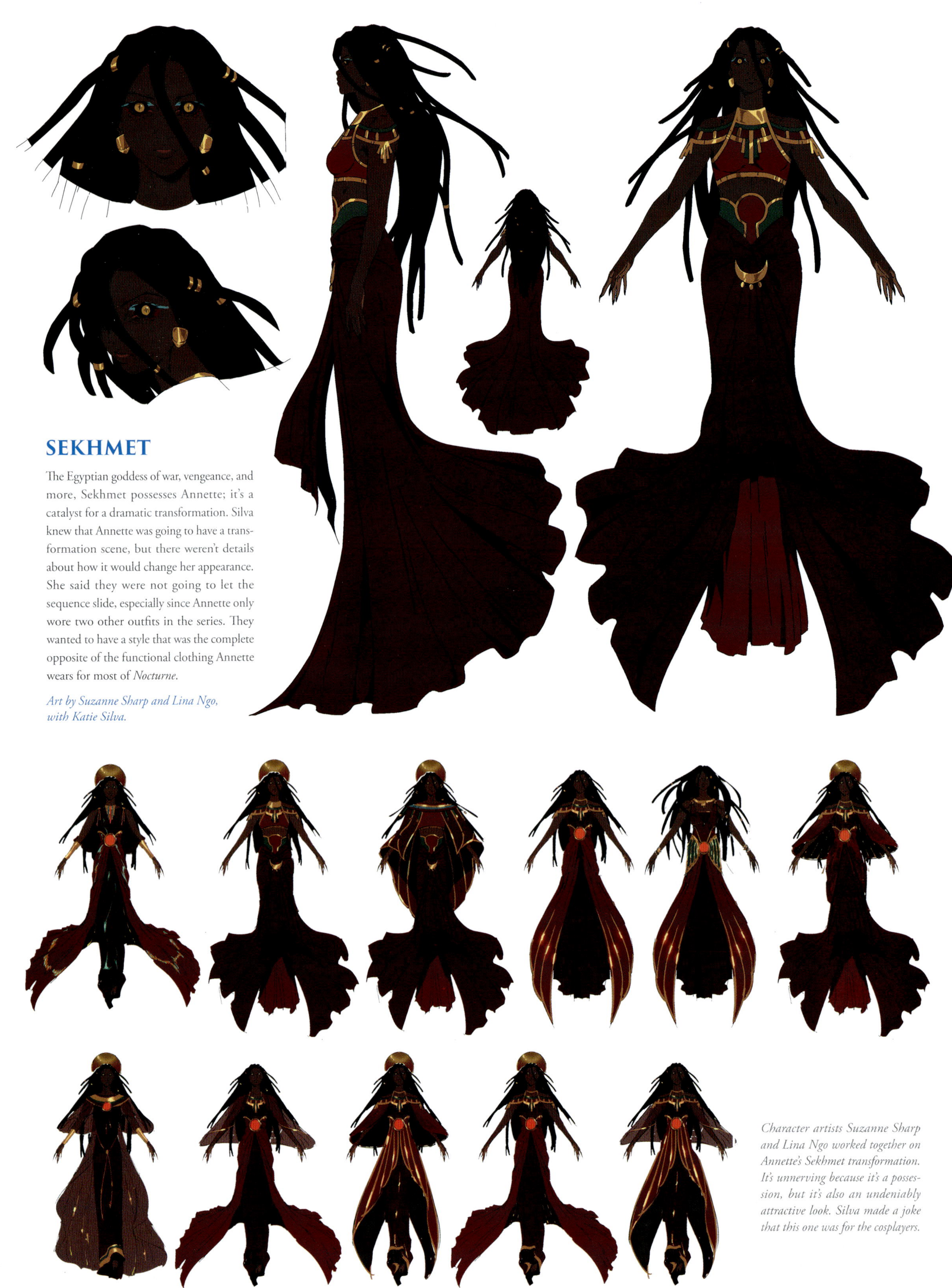

SEKHMET

The Egyptian goddess of war, vengeance, and more, Sekhmet possesses Annette; it's a catalyst for a dramatic transformation. Silva knew that Annette was going to have a transformation scene, but there weren't details about how it would change her appearance. She said they were not going to let the sequence slide, especially since Annette only wore two other outfits in the series. They wanted to have a style that was the complete opposite of the functional clothing Annette wears for most of *Nocturne*.

Art by Suzanne Sharp and Lina Ngo, with Katie Silva.

Character artists Suzanne Sharp and Lina Ngo worked together on Annette's Sekhmet transformation. It's unnerving because it's a possession, but it's also an undeniably attractive look. Silva made a joke that this one was for the cosplayers.

Storyboards by Chance Kubesh and Chansard Vincent.

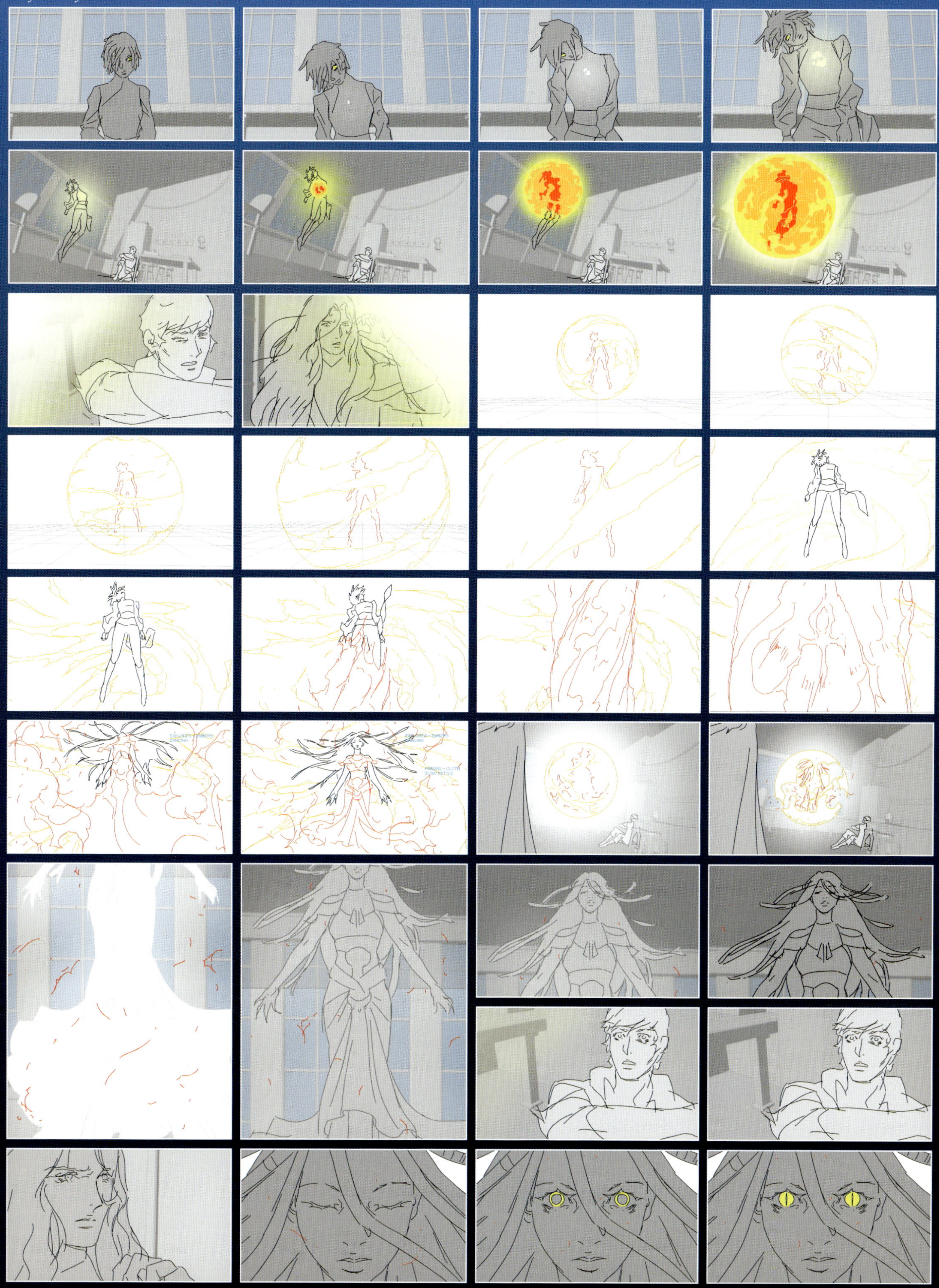

While this sequence was a bit of a magical-girl transformation for Annette, it's also unsettling because we don't know what the possession means. "It's a combination of wanting to make it cool but also unnerving. We want to make sure that there's some tension for the characters going into the next episode," Sam Deats said.

Esther

Esther was a gentle, strong woman enslaved by Vaublanc, a secret vampire and owner of a plantation on Saint-Domingue. She loved her daughter Annette and used what she knew of Vodou magic to protect her. Esther's use of Vodou provoked Vaublanc, however, and he murdered her in front of Annette—in doing so, he set Annette's path and provoked her desire to fight against slavery.

Art by Mari Arakaki.

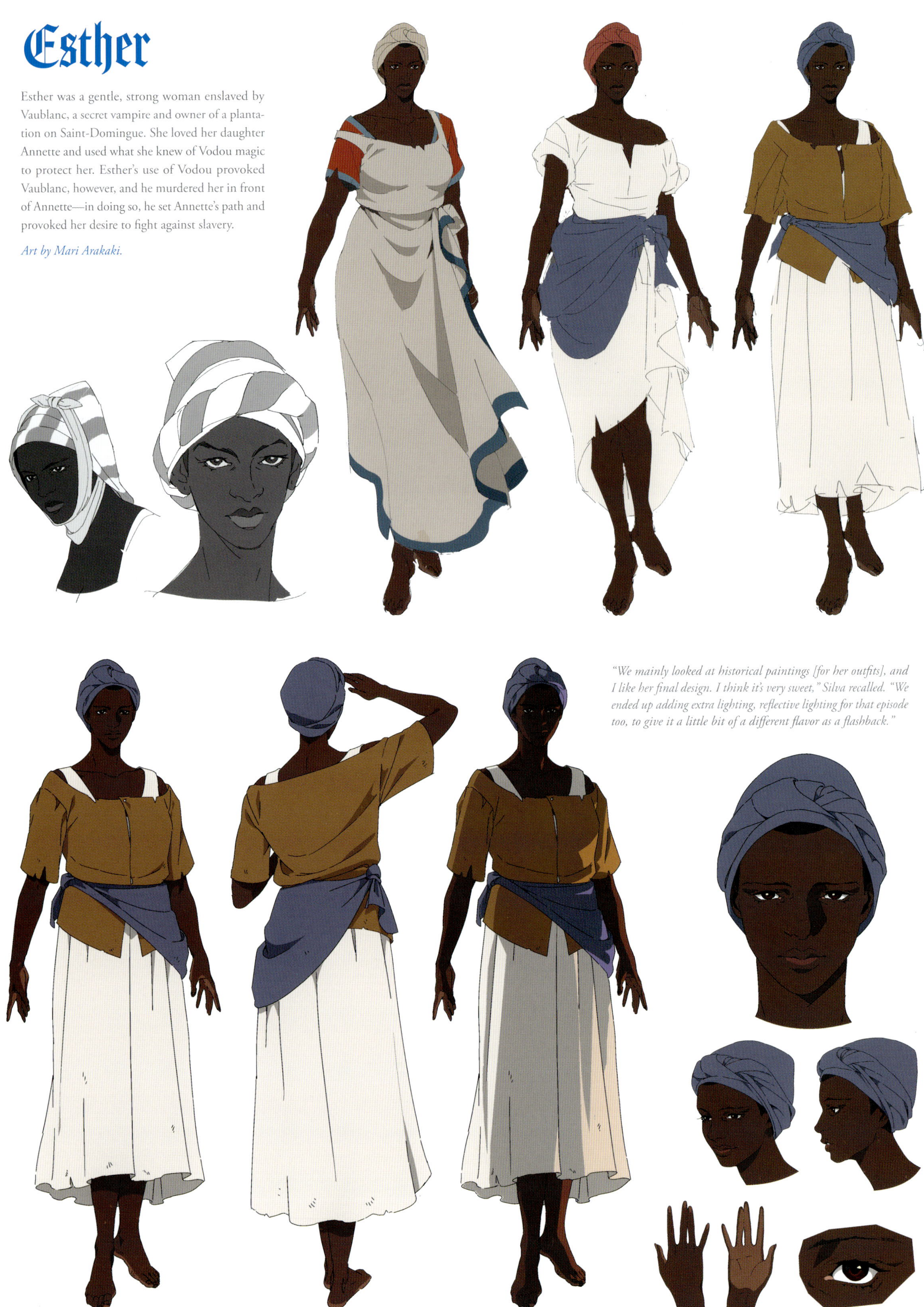

"We mainly looked at historical paintings [for her outfits], and I like her final design. I think it's very sweet," Silva recalled. "We ended up adding extra lighting, reflective lighting for that episode too, to give it a little bit of a different flavor as a flashback."

Papa Legba

In Haitian Vodou, Papa Legba is an Iwa. He appears to Annette as the guardian of the Spirit World in *Nocturne*. The design team worked with a historical consultant (Haitian American scholar Cécile Accilien) who provided them with information and guides for characters such as Papa Legba, as well as for characters and locations key to the Haitian revolution. *Castlevania: Nocturne* may be a show about vampires, but Silva said they all wanted to do their due diligence.

Art by Mari Arakaki.

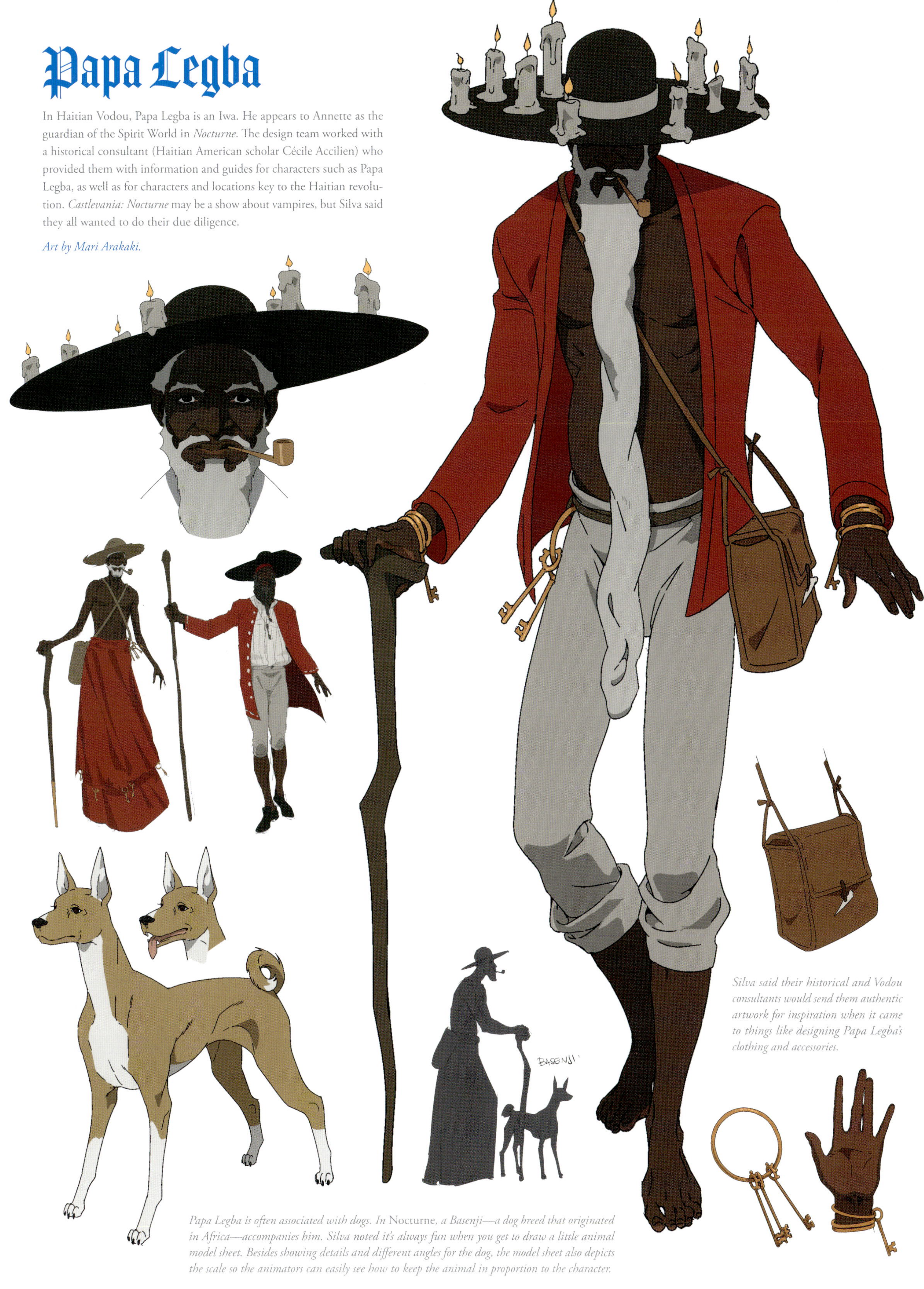

Silva said their historical and Vodou consultants would send them authentic artwork for inspiration when it came to things like designing Papa Legba's clothing and accessories.

Papa Legba is often associated with dogs. In Nocturne*, a Basenji—a dog breed that originated in Africa—accompanies him. Silva noted it's always fun when you get to draw a little animal model sheet. Besides showing details and different angles for the dog, the model sheet also depicts the scale so the animators can easily see how to keep the animal in proportion to the character.*

Cécile Fatiman

A leader in the Haitian Revolution and a Vodou practitioner, Cécile Fatiman is an inimitable historical figure. In both *Nocturne* and history, Cécile was born in Saint-Domingue. *Castlevania's* world sees her become a mentor to Annette, teaching her about her ancestry and how to tap into her magical potential—all while leading the slave rebellion. Cécile is the one who sends Annette on the quest to find Richter Belmont because she senses the threat of the Vampire Messiah.

Art by Mari Arakaki.

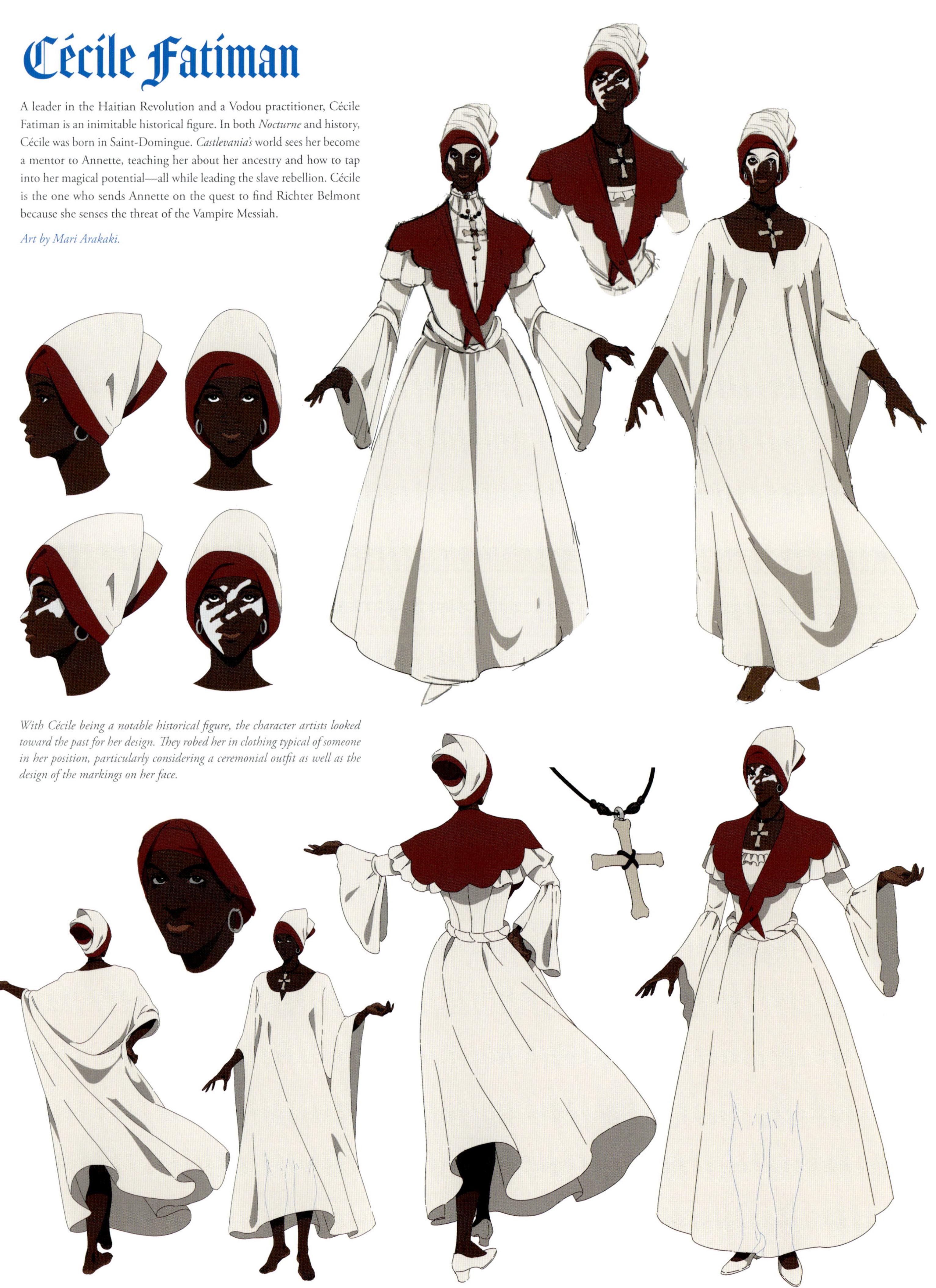

With Cécile being a notable historical figure, the character artists looked toward the past for her design. They robed her in clothing typical of someone in her position, particularly considering a ceremonial outfit as well as the design of the markings on her face.

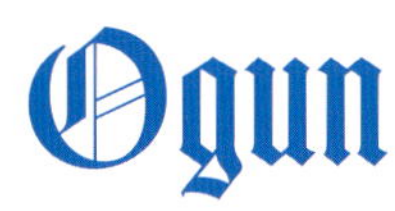
Ogun

Annette meets with Ogun, the orisha god of iron and war, in the Spirit World. She's his descendant. Artist Mari Arakaki did the design for Ogun, bringing his abilities and formidable nature into his appearance. She also included his vèvè, a religious symbol used in Haitian Vodou; it appears on his head and then moves to his shield as protection.

Art by Mari Arakaki.

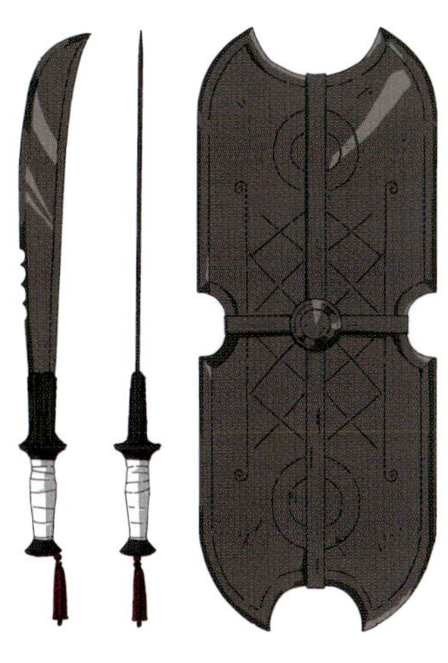

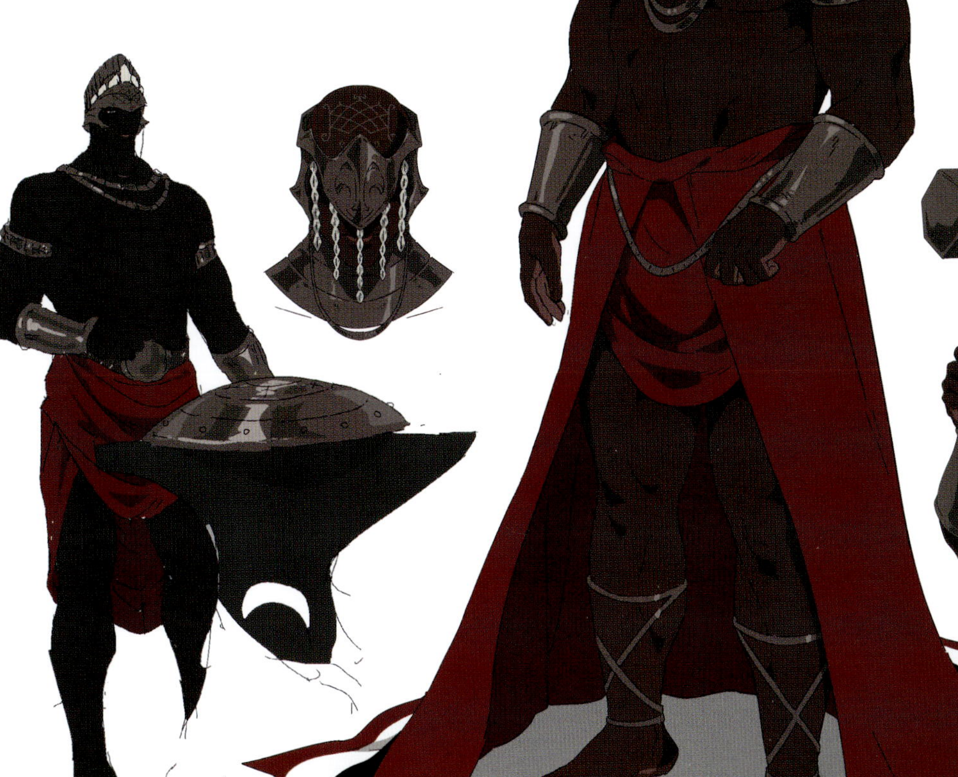

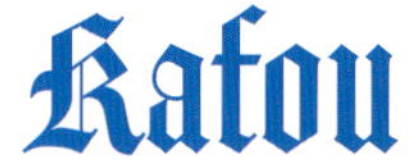
Kafou

Before they meet in the Spirit World, Papa Legba seems to appear to Annette as this mysterious three-faced deity. Kafou has more of a trickster type of vibe. This design ended up being a challenge to animate because it wasn't only silhouettes but three different faces with four horns on a single head and two horns on each of the other heads. Silva joked that it was definitely an instance of them having to stew in a soup of their own making.

Art by Suzanne Sharp.

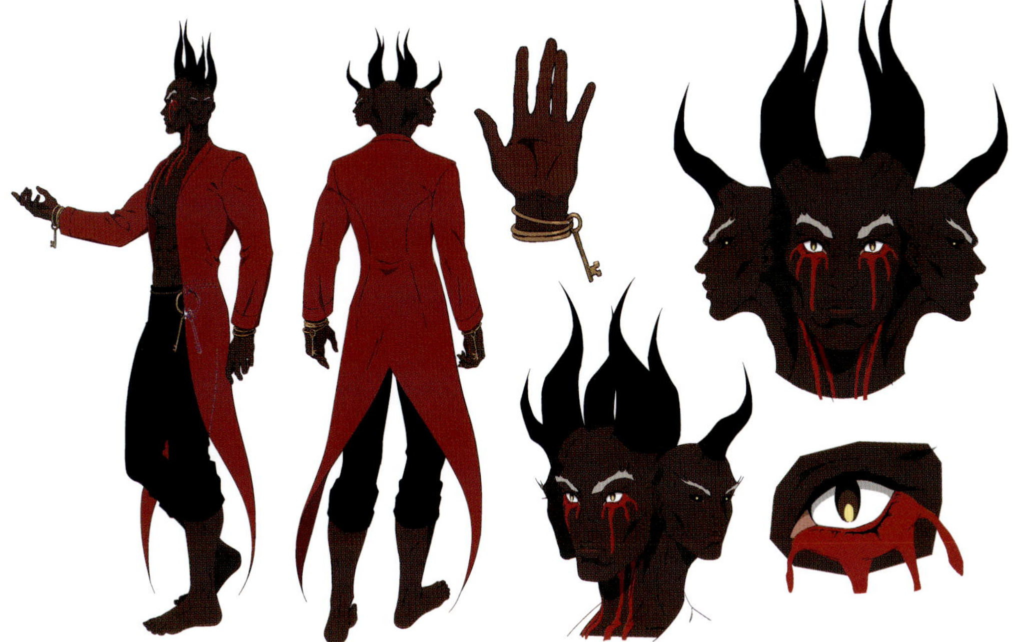

Edouard

An opera singer turned revolutionary turned Night Creature, Edouard goes on a transformative journey—symbolically and otherwise. Throughout it all, he retains his humanity and his voice. He becomes fast friends with Annette after she escapes from Vaublanc's plantation and accompanies her across the ocean to France on her quest to find the Belmont who can stop the Vampire Messiah. But in France, that quest leads him to darkness.

Character designer Katie Silva noted that his design has more of a historical silhouette than others in the show. And while this look is put together, Silva joked that this is his "slumming it in France outfit." He would dress up more nicely in Saint-Domingue, but his outfit for boarding a ship is still slick.

Art by Katie Silva.

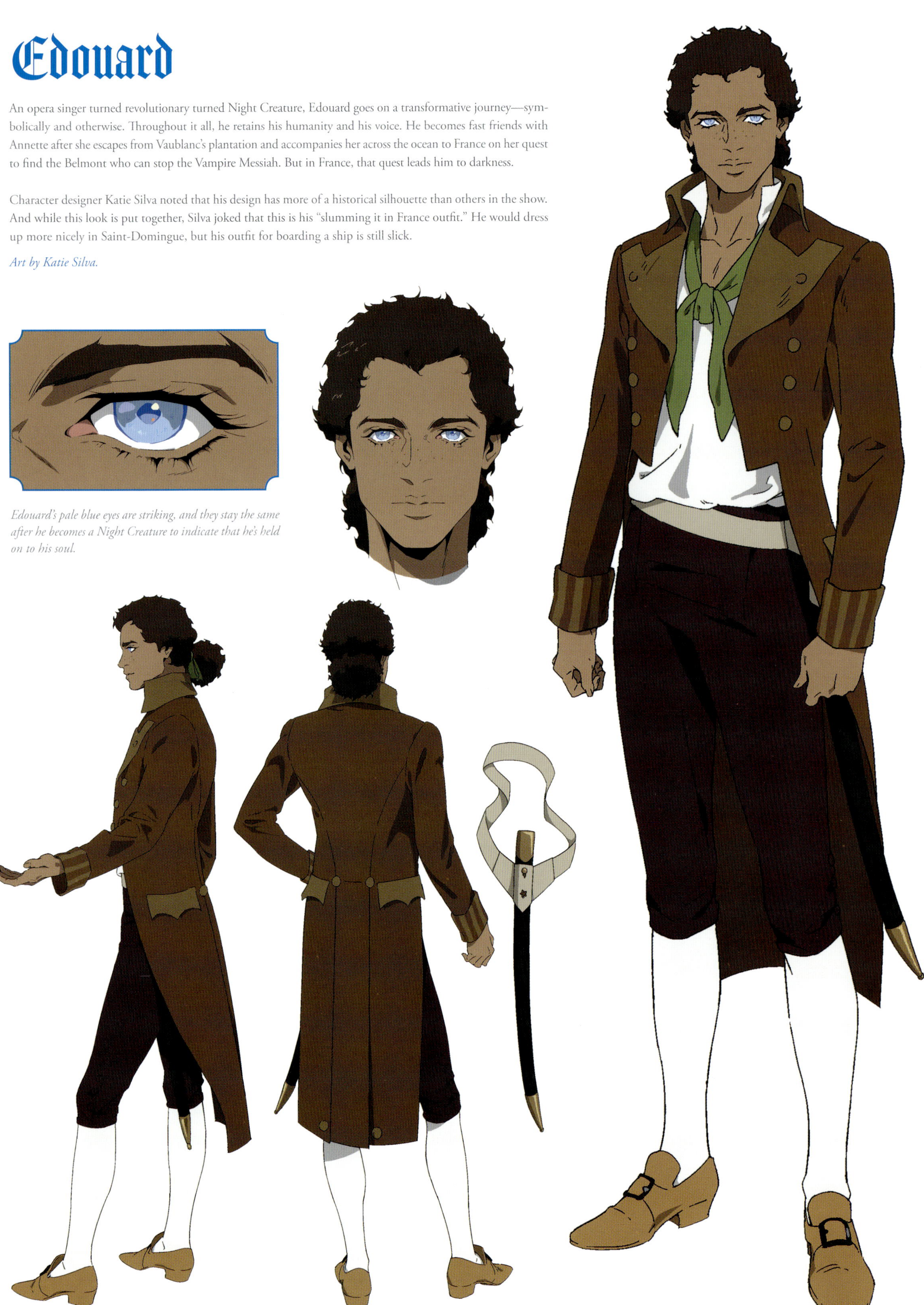

Edouard's pale blue eyes are striking, and they stay the same after he becomes a Night Creature to indicate that he's held on to his soul.

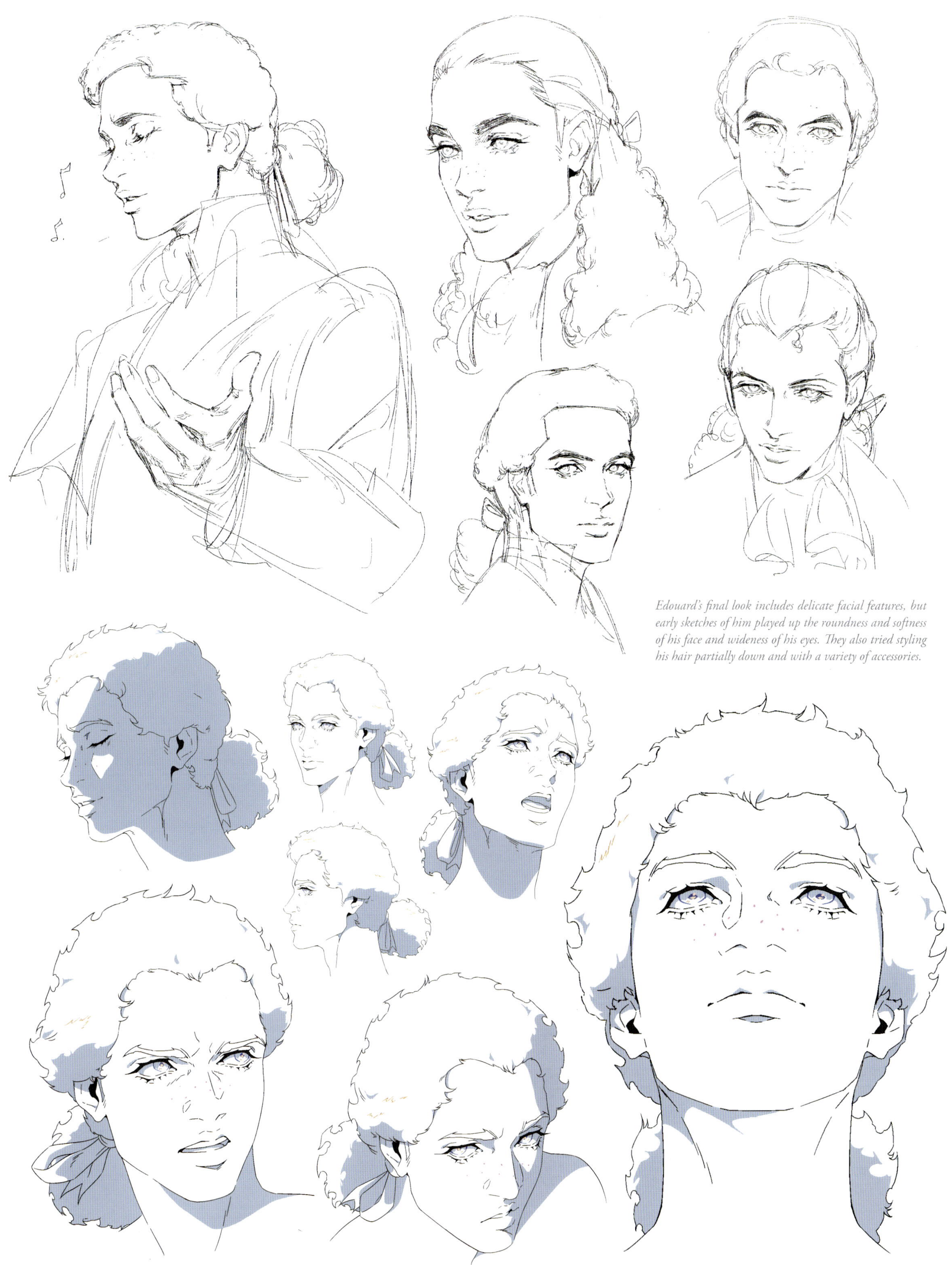

Edouard's final look includes delicate facial features, but early sketches of him played up the roundness and softness of his face and wideness of his eyes. They also tried styling his hair partially down and with a variety of accessories.

In early explorations for Edouard, the character artist team experimented with different textures for his hair. Silva said it's on the curlier side and closer to 3C hair than 4C hair. Since he's a performer, they also got to explore his expressiveness with a wider range of emotions than other characters.

GOING GOLD

Edouard's opera performance outfit does not hold back. When he performs on the stage at the Comédie du Cap in Saint-Domingue, he's in his element. The grand setting demands a grand ensemble with all the frills. Katie Silva said she insisted on taking the opera outfit for herself and doing all the model sheets for it. She drew a closeup shot of his shoes and joked that she put ten different gold tones in them, much to the chagrin of the compositors.

Art by Katie Silva.

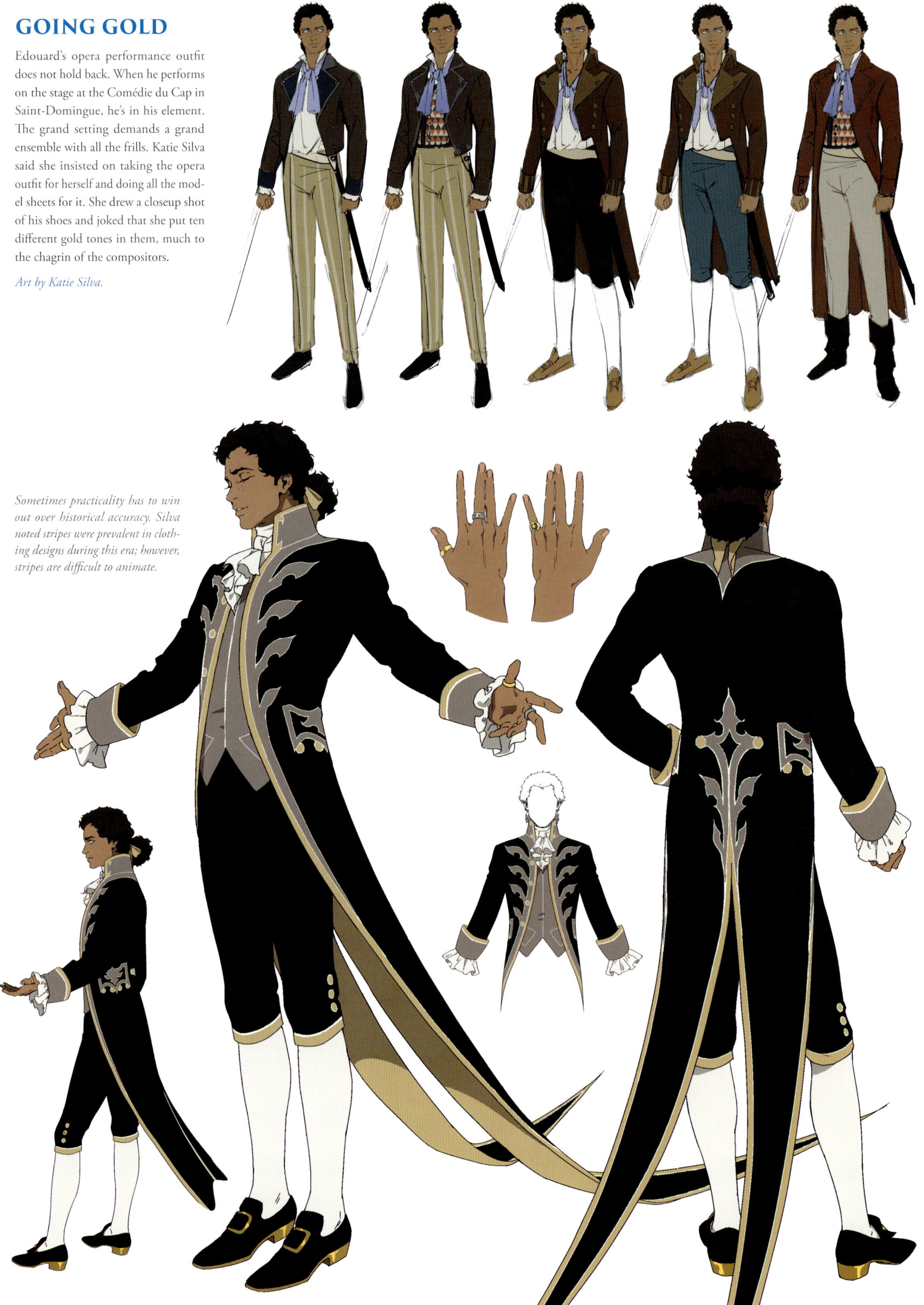

Sometimes practicality has to win out over historical accuracy. Silva noted stripes were prevalent in clothing designs during this era; however, stripes are difficult to animate.

NIGHT CREATURE EDOUARD

When Annette first met Edouard in Saint-Domingue, he was somebody who represented a certain level of freedom and positivity to her, executive producer Adam Deats said. But then Edouard loses himself and Annette has to face that and what it means for them both. His struggle as a lost soul is a striking part of his story, as is the way he finds himself again in this form—a Night Creature distorted by Abbot Emmanuel's imperfect Forgemaster abilities. Edouard's attempts to hold onto shreds of his human self come through in the way his transformation manifests.

Art by Katie Silva.

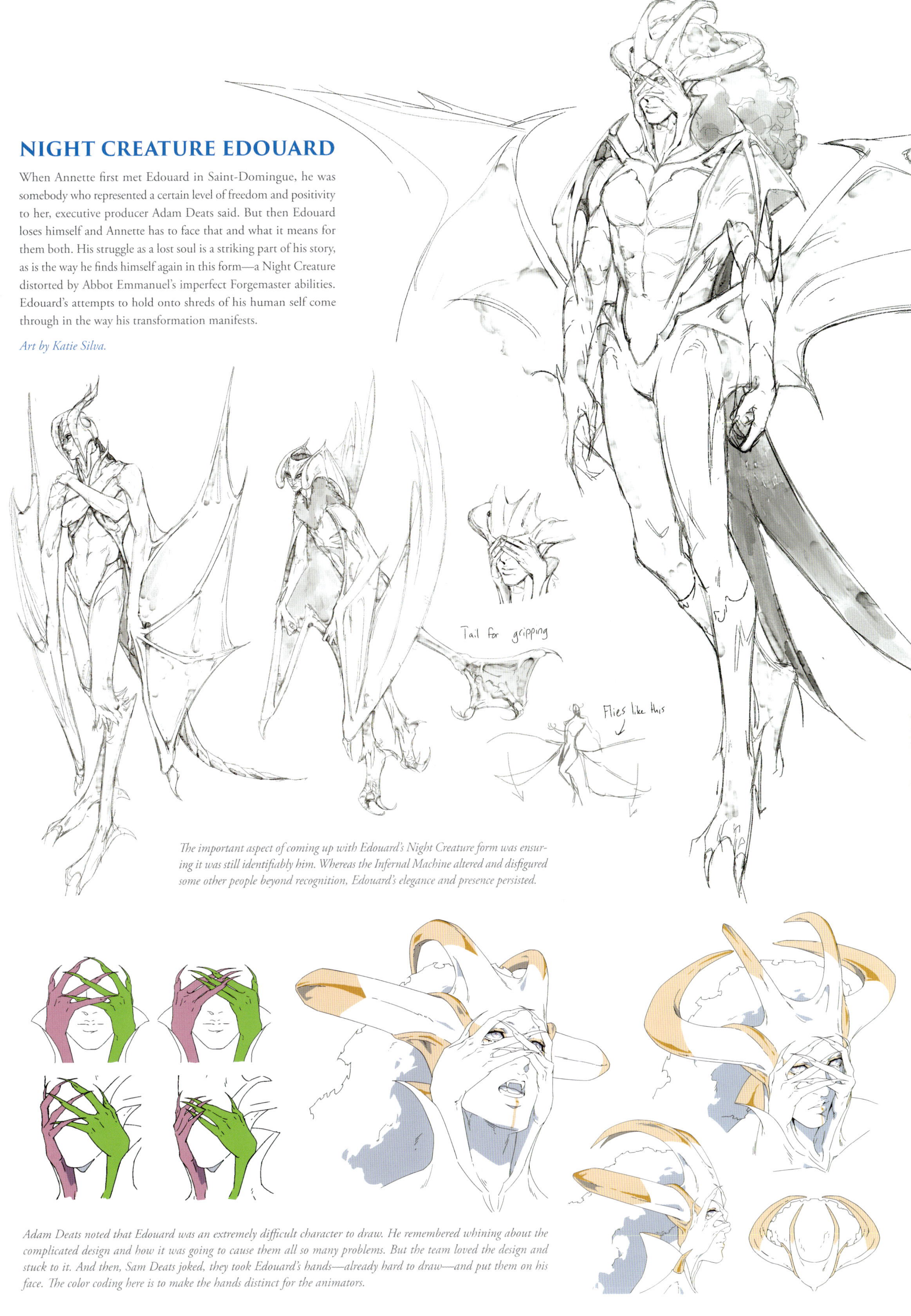

The important aspect of coming up with Edouard's Night Creature form was ensuring it was still identifiably him. Whereas the Infernal Machine altered and disfigured some other people beyond recognition, Edouard's elegance and presence persisted.

Adam Deats noted that Edouard was an extremely difficult character to draw. He remembered whining about the complicated design and how it was going to cause them all so many problems. But the team loved the design and stuck to it. And then, Sam Deats joked, they took Edouard's hands—already hard to draw—and put them on his face. The color coding here is to make the hands distinct for the animators.

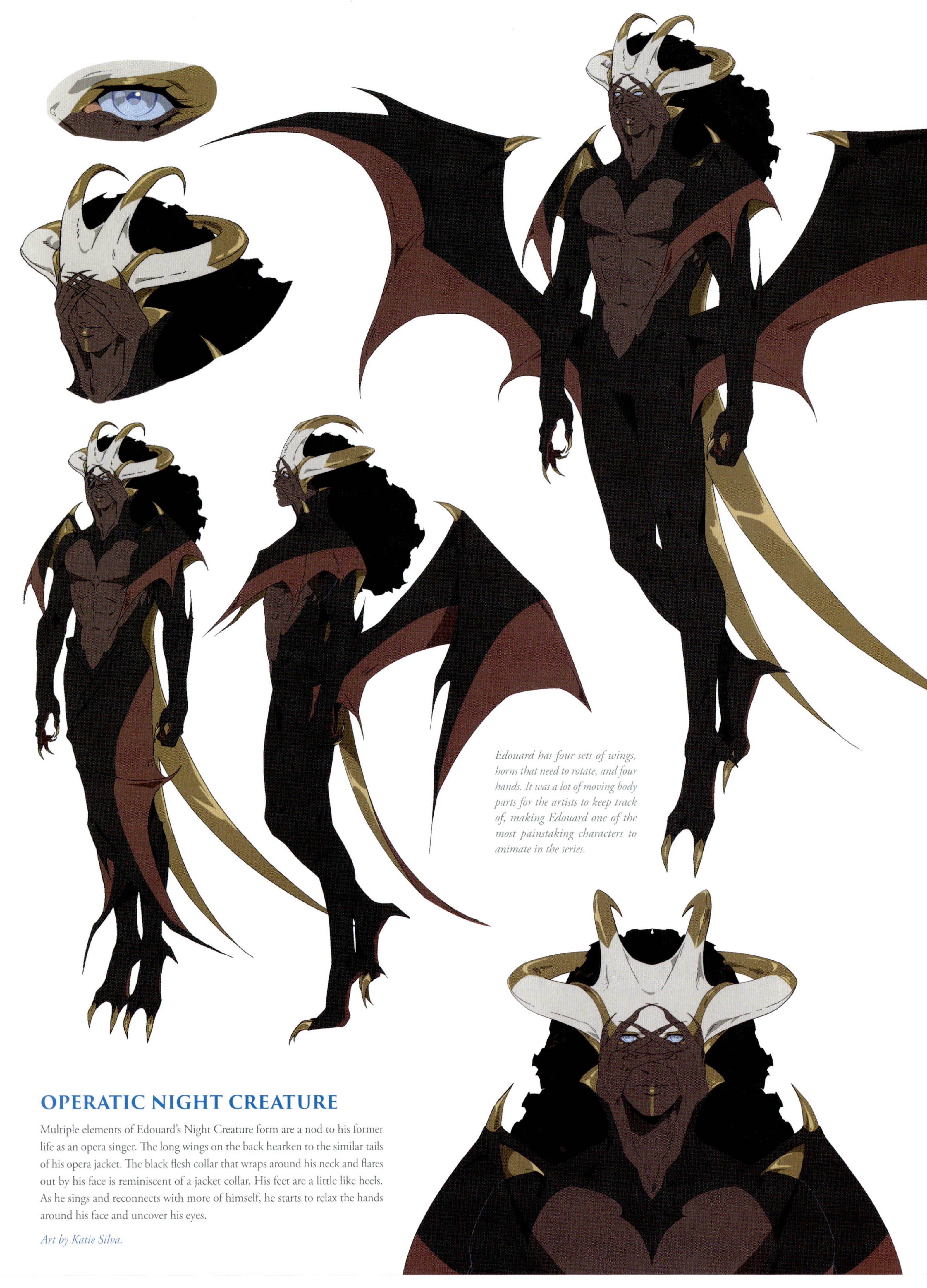

Edouard has four sets of wings, horns that need to rotate, and four hands. It was a lot of moving body parts for the artists to keep track of, making Edouard one of the most painstaking characters to animate in the series.

OPERATIC NIGHT CREATURE

Multiple elements of Edouard's Night Creature form are a nod to his former life as an opera singer. The long wings on the back hearken to the similar tails of his opera jacket. The black flesh collar that wraps around his neck and flares out by his face is reminiscent of a jacket collar. His feet are a little like heels. As he sings and reconnects with more of himself, he starts to relax the hands around his face and uncover his eyes.

Art by Katie Silva.

Storyboards by Sara Syed, layouts by Abroo Khan.

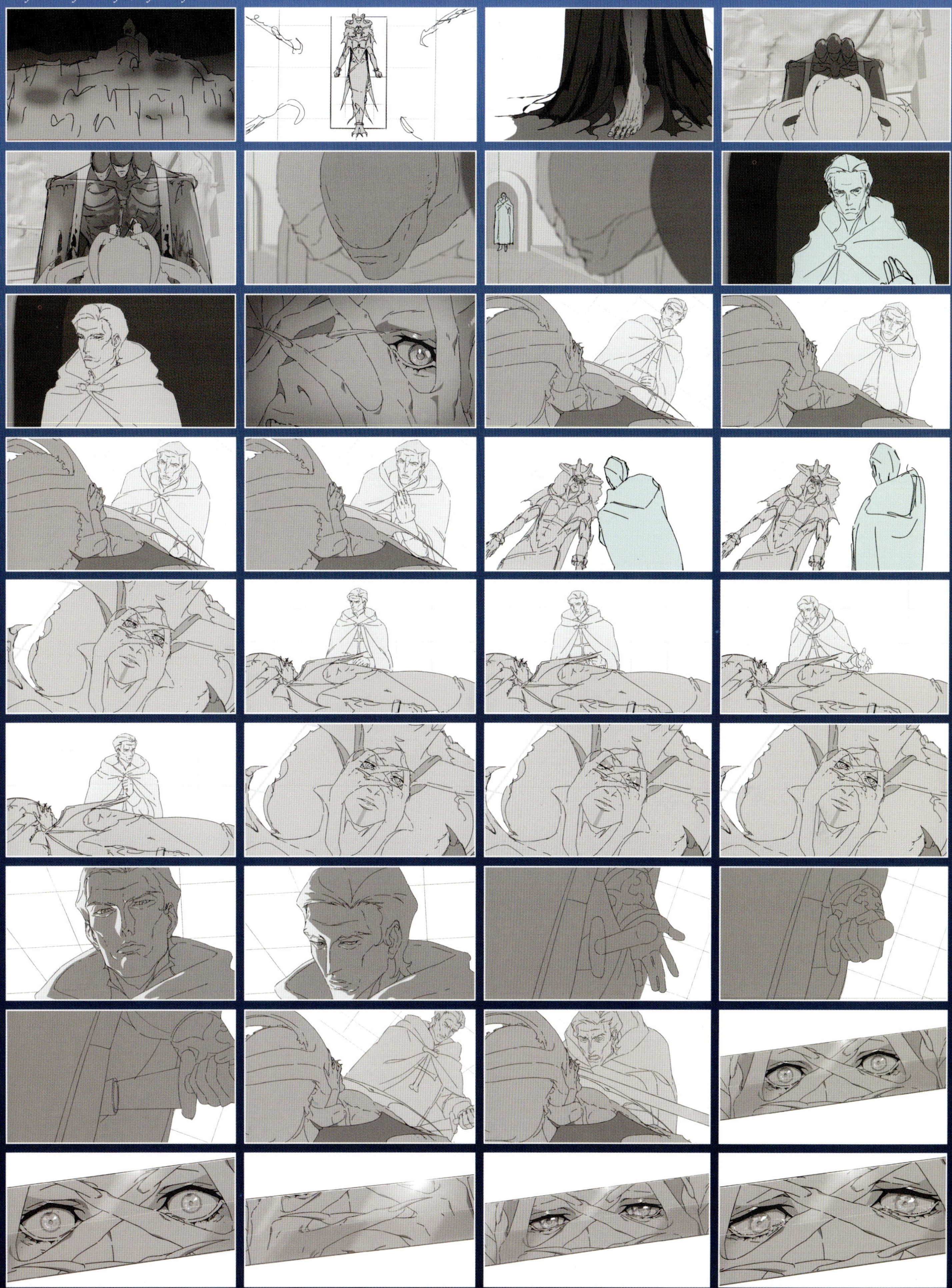

Because the Abbot is not the kind of Forgemaster Hector and Isaac were, the process of creating Night Creatures is less controlled. Through Edouard's transformation, this sequence reveals how a Night Creature can sometimes still retain their soul and what it means to remember themselves and who they were and are. On the other side, we see the Abbot realizing his process is imperfect and trying to understand how the machine left traces of Edouard's humanity intact.

Jacques

Jacques is part of Maria Renard's secret group of revolutionaries. Vampires capture him and give him to Abbot Emmanuel for the Infernal Machine. Like other Night Creatures, Jacques doesn't remember his human life—not at first. Edouard is able to reach him and remind Jacques of who he was, which leads Jacques to fight back against his captors. His transformation is more extreme, but despite that, Jacques's human face remains.

Human Jacques design by Suzanne Sharp.
Night Creature Jacques design by Mari Arakaki.

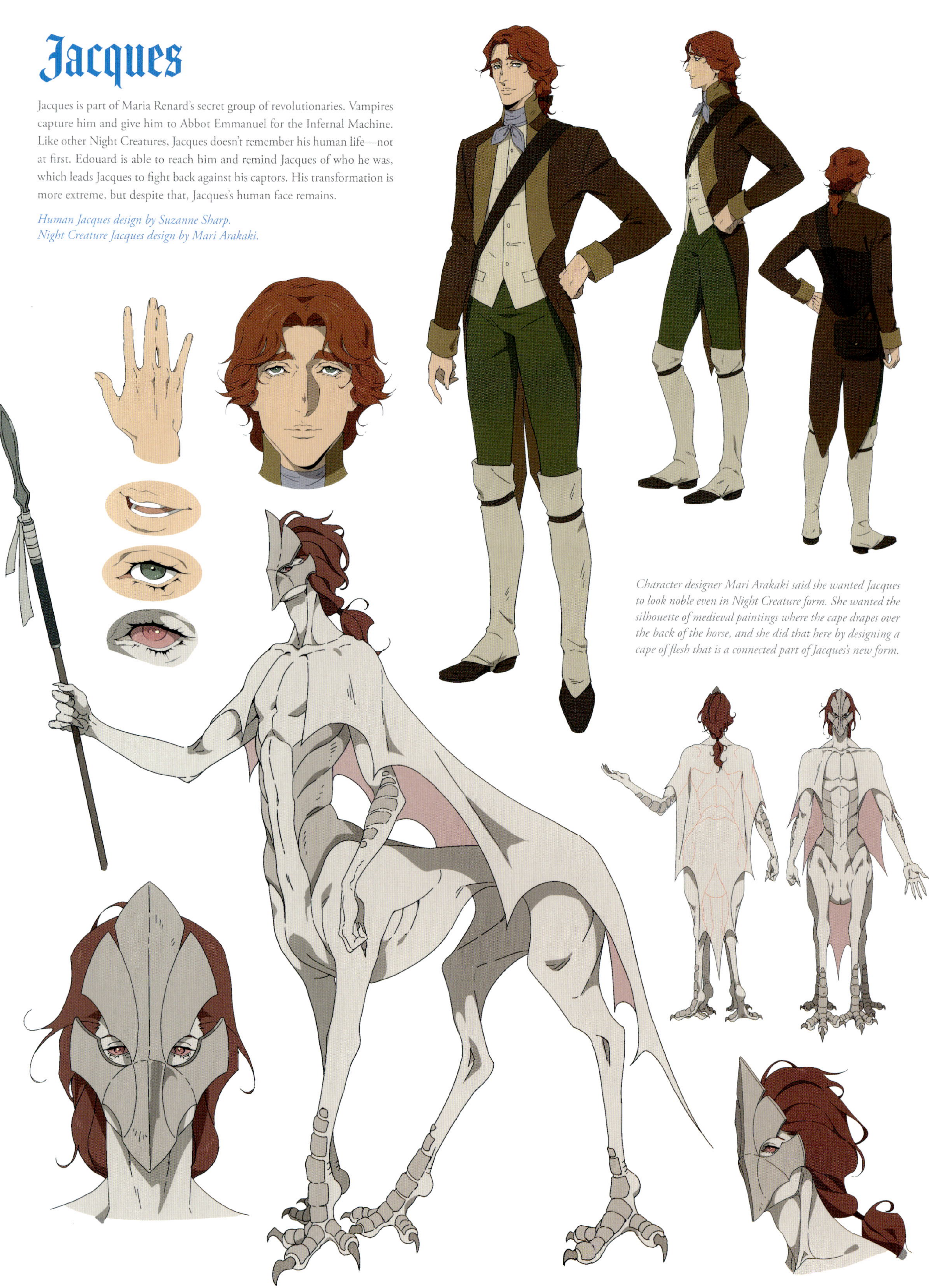

Character designer Mari Arakaki said she wanted Jacques to look noble even in Night Creature form. She wanted the silhouette of medieval paintings where the cape drapes over the back of the horse, and she did that here by designing a cape of flesh that is a connected part of Jacques's new form.

The Captain

The Captain leads the National Guard until she and her squadron cross Drolta's path. They become further fuel for the Night Creature–crafting machine. Remembering some part of who she was, she goes on to lead the other Night Creatures in a rebellion against the vampires. She does so even while mourning her transformed state. Silva noted her Night Creature form is from the games: the Frozen Shade. The character was an enemy in multiple games and here, the crystalline blue figure gets to be one of the heroes.

Art by Mari Arakaki.

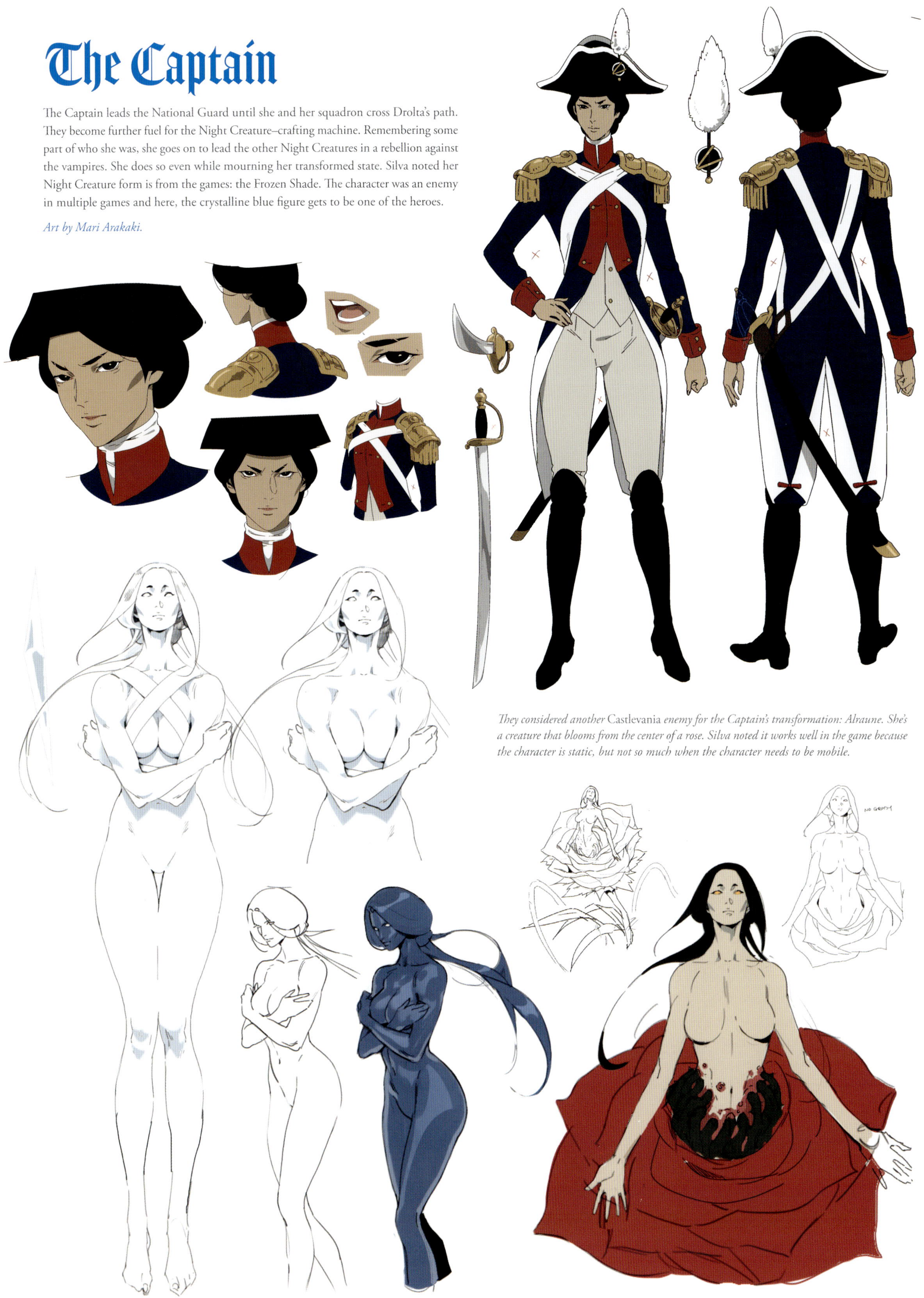

They considered another Castlevania *enemy for the Captain's transformation: Alraune. She's a creature that blooms from the center of a rose. Silva noted it works well in the game because the character is static, but not so much when the character needs to be mobile.*

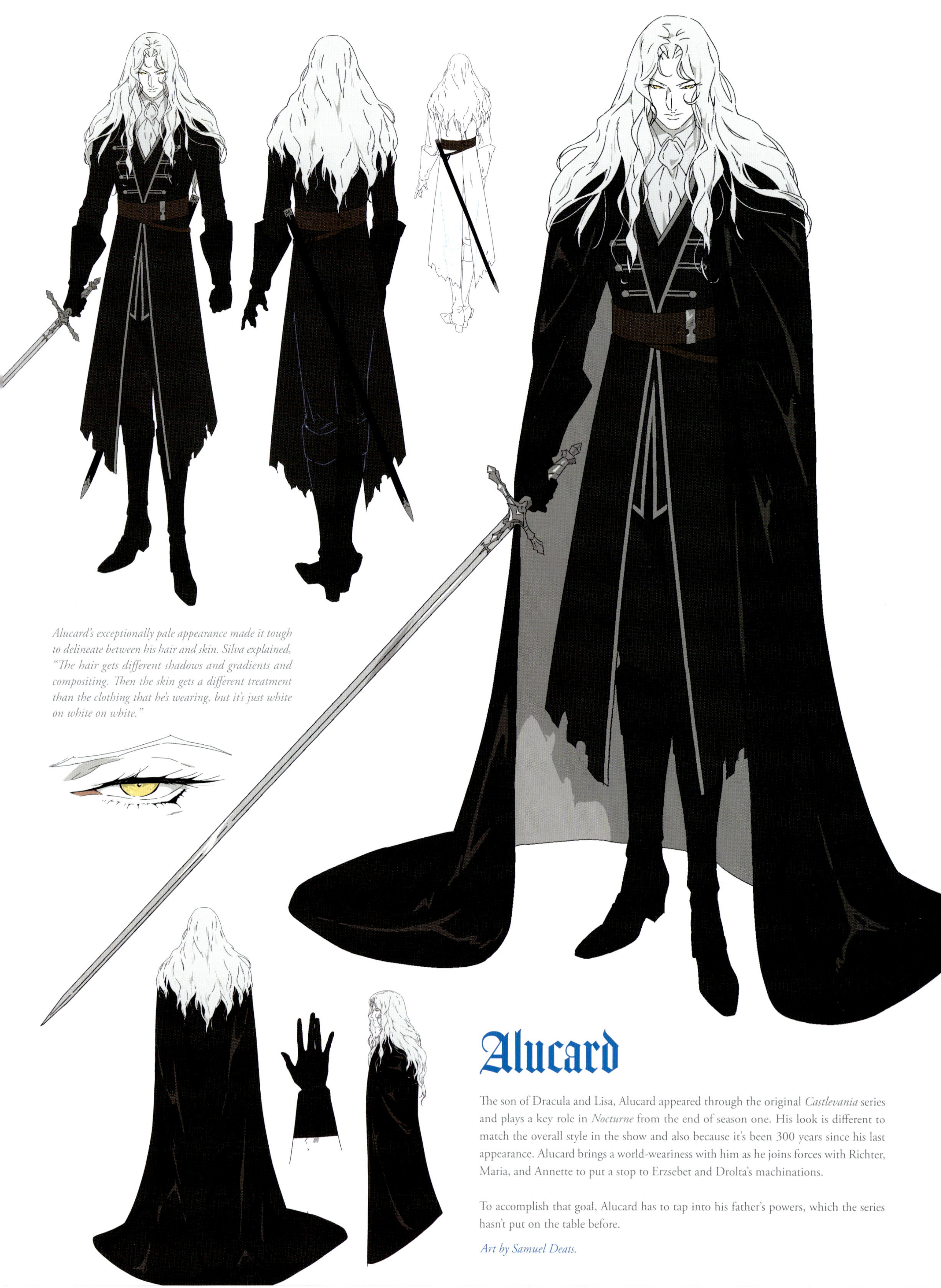

Alucard's exceptionally pale appearance made it tough to delineate between his hair and skin. Silva explained, "The hair gets different shadows and gradients and compositing. Then the skin gets a different treatment than the clothing that he's wearing, but it's just white on white on white."

Alucard

The son of Dracula and Lisa, Alucard appeared through the original *Castlevania* series and plays a key role in *Nocturne* from the end of season one. His look is different to match the overall style in the show and also because it's been 300 years since his last appearance. Alucard brings a world-weariness with him as he joins forces with Richter, Maria, and Annette to put a stop to Erzsebet and Drolta's machinations.

To accomplish that goal, Alucard has to tap into his father's powers, which the series hasn't put on the table before.

Art by Samuel Deats.

NOD TO THE PAST

Katie did the model sheets based on Sam Deats's design, and this look reminded her of a forest creature from Mamoru Oshii's *Angel's Egg*. That movie has an ethereal, ghostly look that is present in this desaturated otherworldly look for Alucard. The designs at the bottom of the page are a far more colorful look for the character. Silva said, "The clothing and the hood are very much a reference to Lisa's outfit when she walks into Dracula's Castle for the first time."

Art by Samuel Deats.

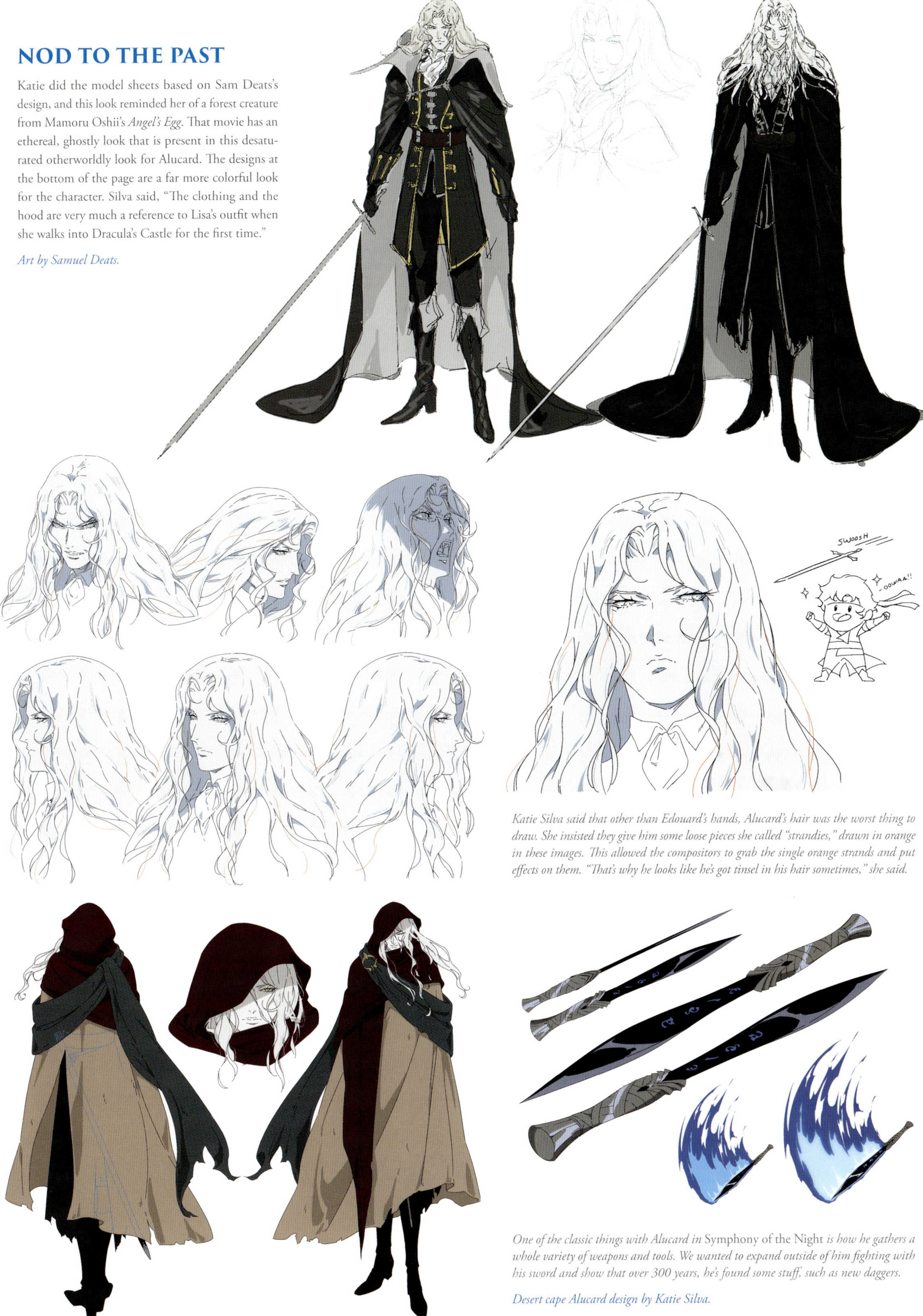

Katie Silva said that other than Edouard's hands, Alucard's hair was the worst thing to draw. She insisted they give him some loose pieces she called "strandies," drawn in orange in these images. This allowed the compositors to grab the single orange strands and put effects on them. "That's why he looks like he's got tinsel in his hair sometimes," she said.

One of the classic things with Alucard in Symphony of the Night *is how he gathers a whole variety of weapons and tools. We wanted to expand outside of him fighting with his sword and show that over 300 years, he's found some stuff, such as new daggers.*

Desert cape Alucard design by Katie Silva.

Storyboards by Samuel Deats.

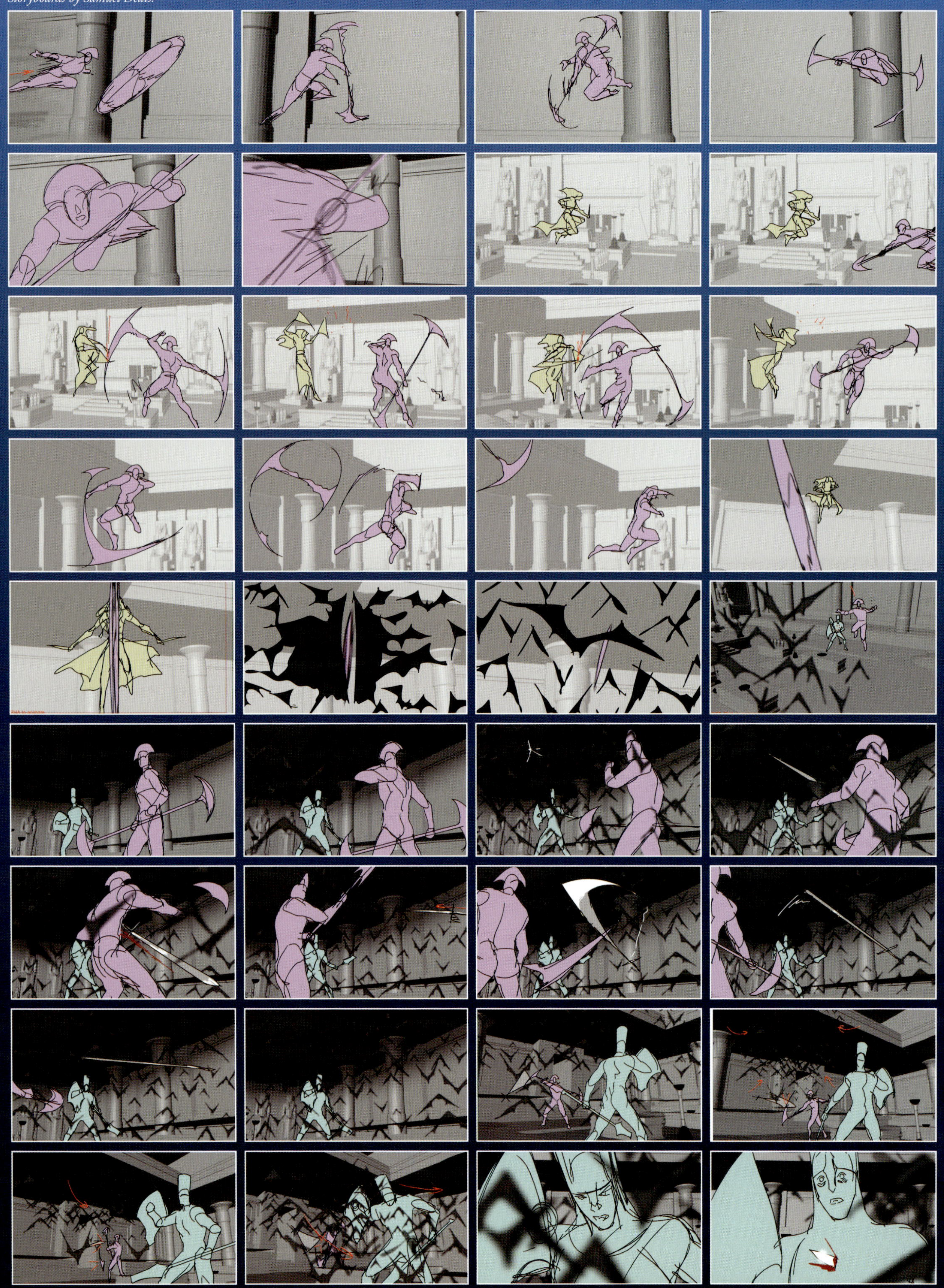

This sequence with Alucard was not in the original outline—season two was going to start with a Drolta flashback—but they decided to go with this scene to celebrate Alucard's return and have fun with it. Sam said he got to scratch an *Indiana Jones* itch with the classic adventure elements at the beginning of the scene.

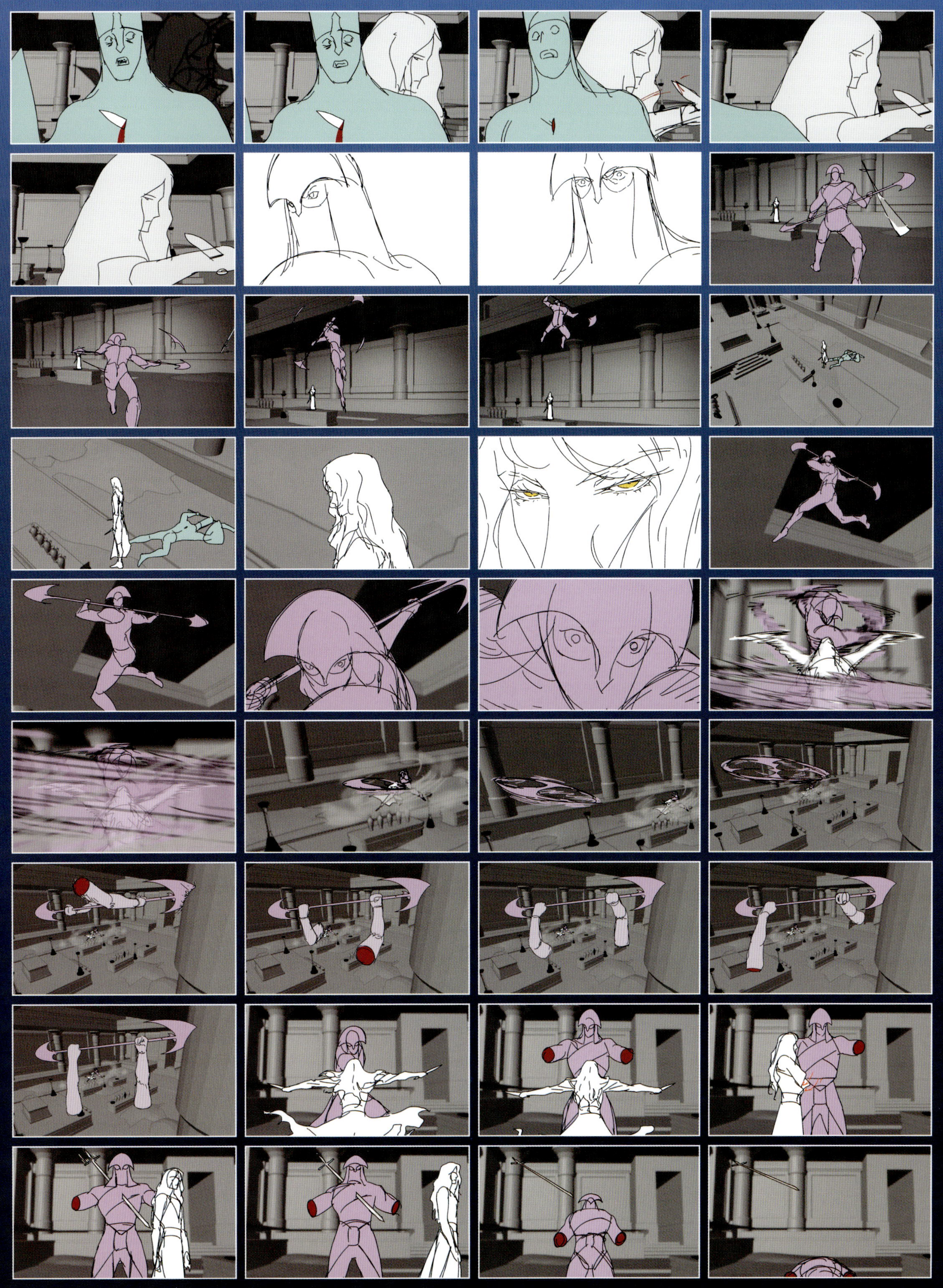

In this Alucard scene, they wanted to have pulpy fun. "This is showing the playful side of doing an action sequence, which is we're showing off a character's moves and ability set, new stuff they can do, and then, not just doing a cool finisher, but making someone smile in a devious sort of way," Sam said.

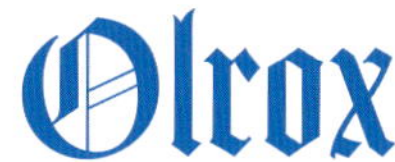

Olrox

The Olrox of *Castlevania: Nocturne* is an ancient vampire from the Aztec Empire with only some personality traits in common with his game character. He follows a nebulous code of his own that sees his alignment change depending on his needs and desires. For example, he murders Julia Belmont in an act of vengeance (Julia killed his lover, also a vampire) but spares her young son because he is, to Olrox's mind, separate from the transaction.

Character designer Katie Silva, who illustrated the portrait on the right, said a lot of people think they designed Olrox to look like his voice actor, Zahn McClarnon, but she mentioned the character looks are usually done before casting.

Art by Katie Silva.

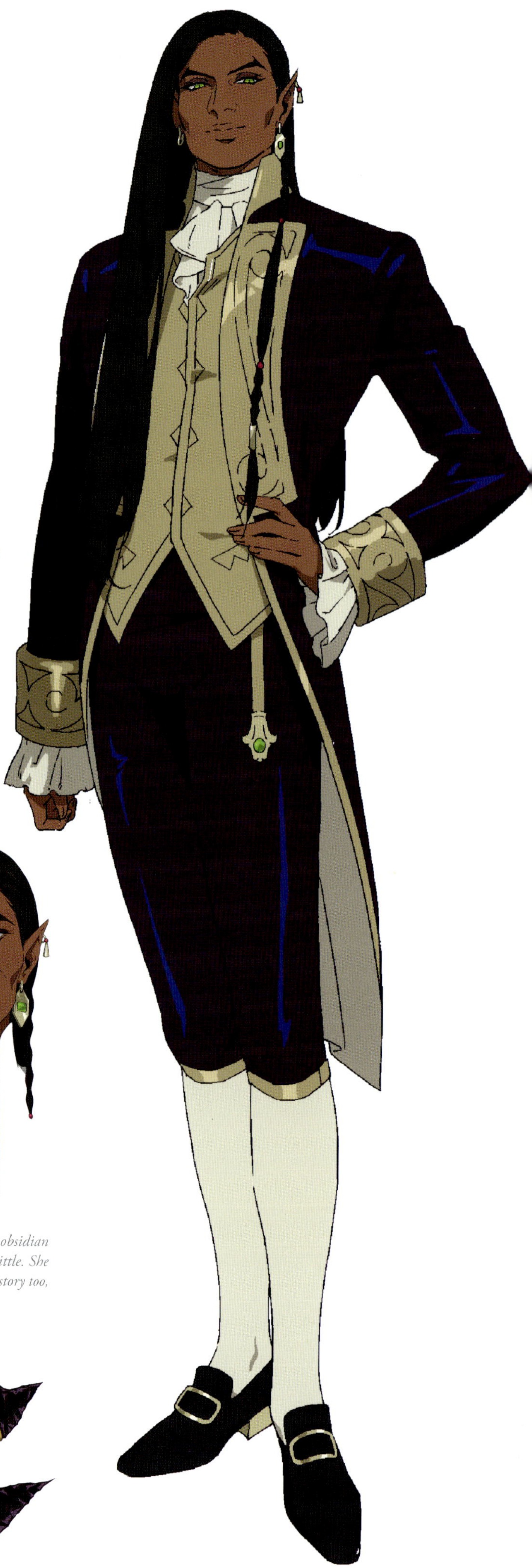

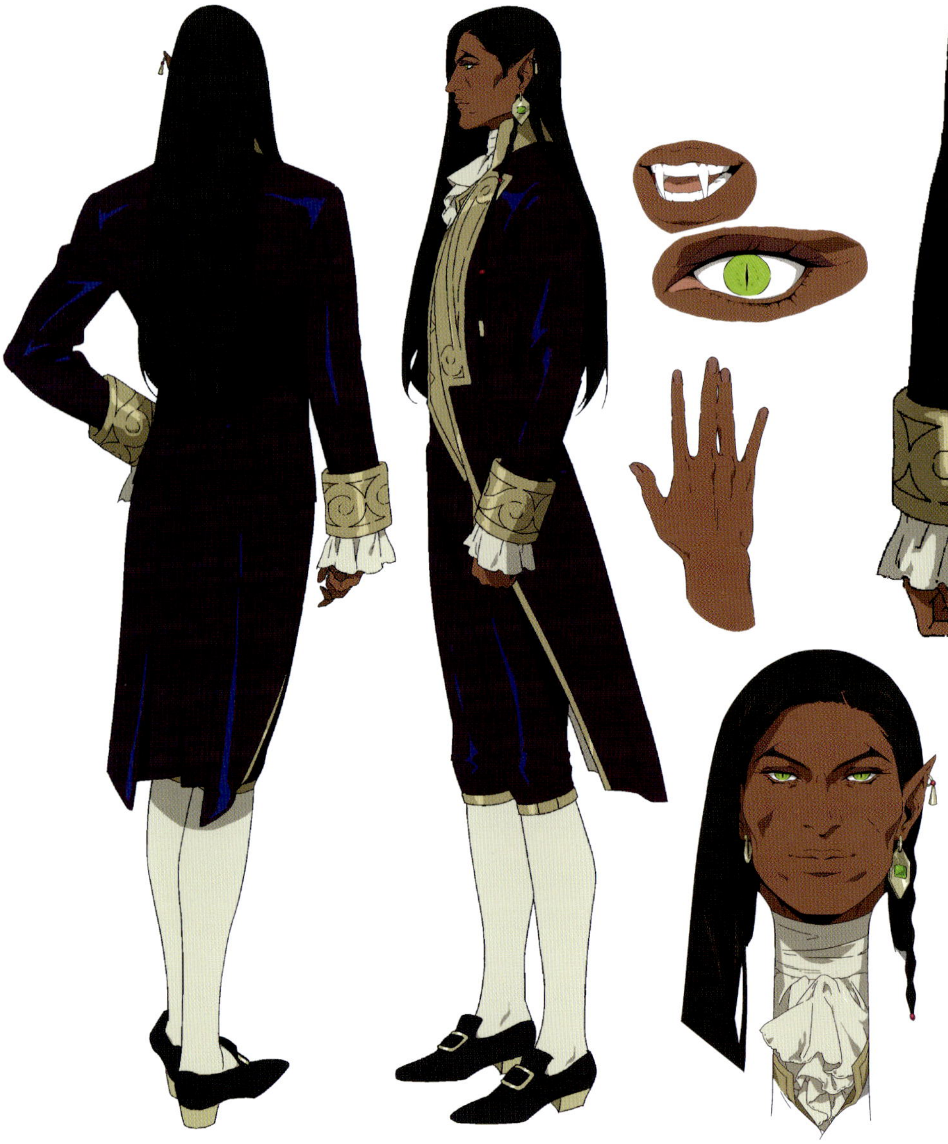

Every aspect of Olrox is stylish, including his weaponry. The vampire carries a richly decorated dagger with an obsidian blade. As Katie pointed out, the obsidian would be completely useless in real life because the material is so brittle. She kidded that a nameless vampire technology makes it lethal, and we see that in the series. It connects with his history too, as the Aztecs valued the volcanic glass.

Knife design by Stephanie McCrea Rainosek.

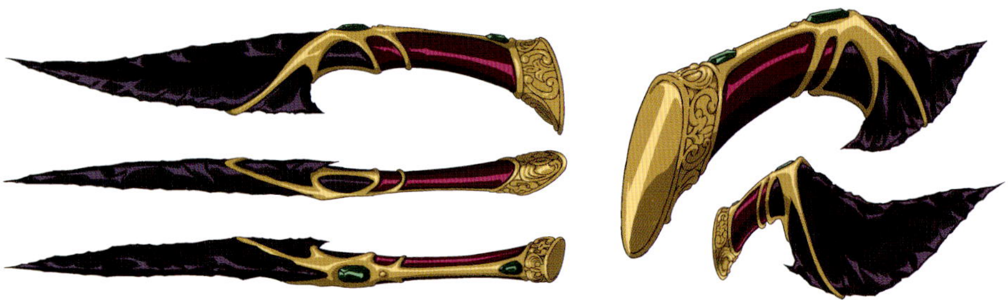

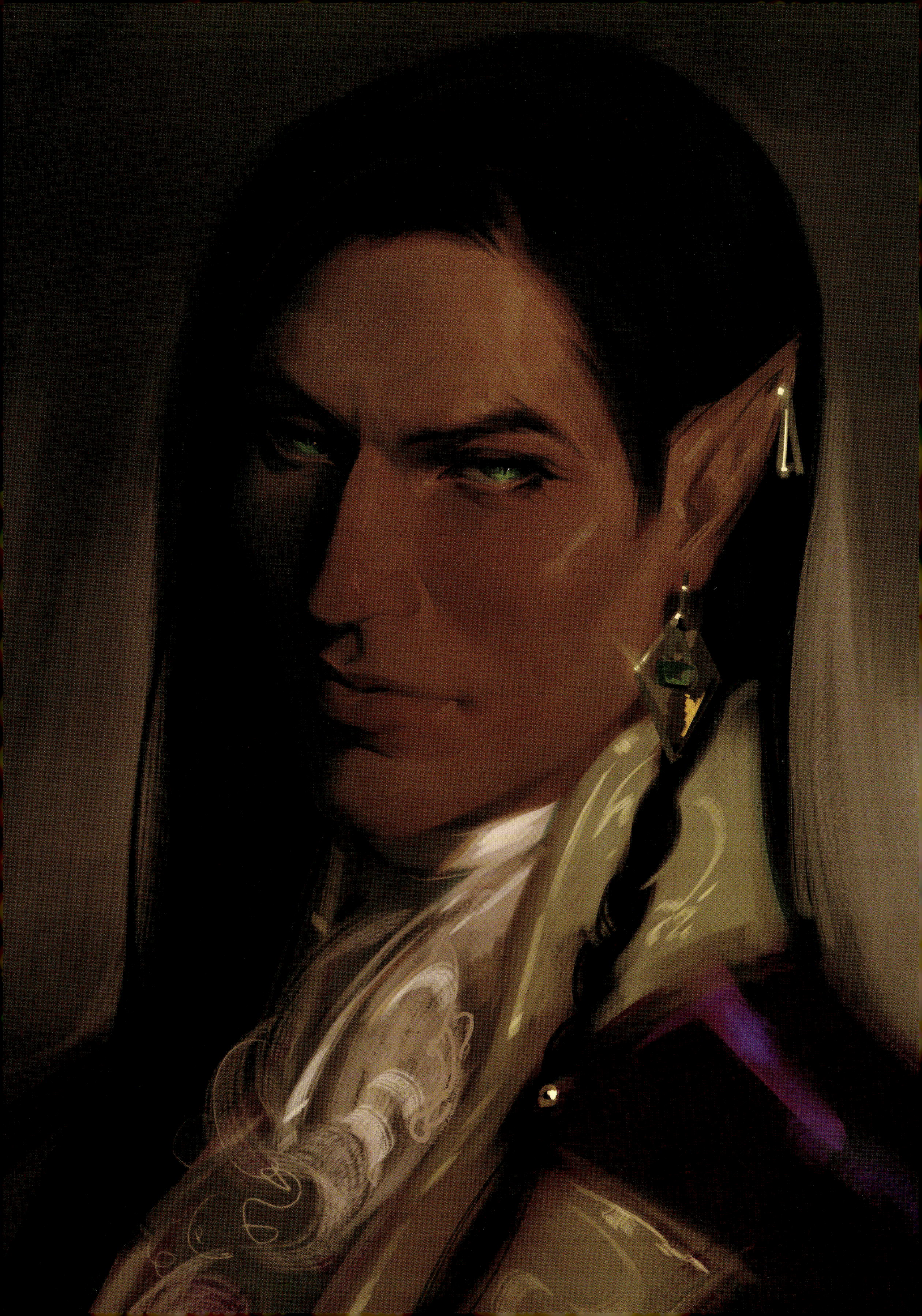

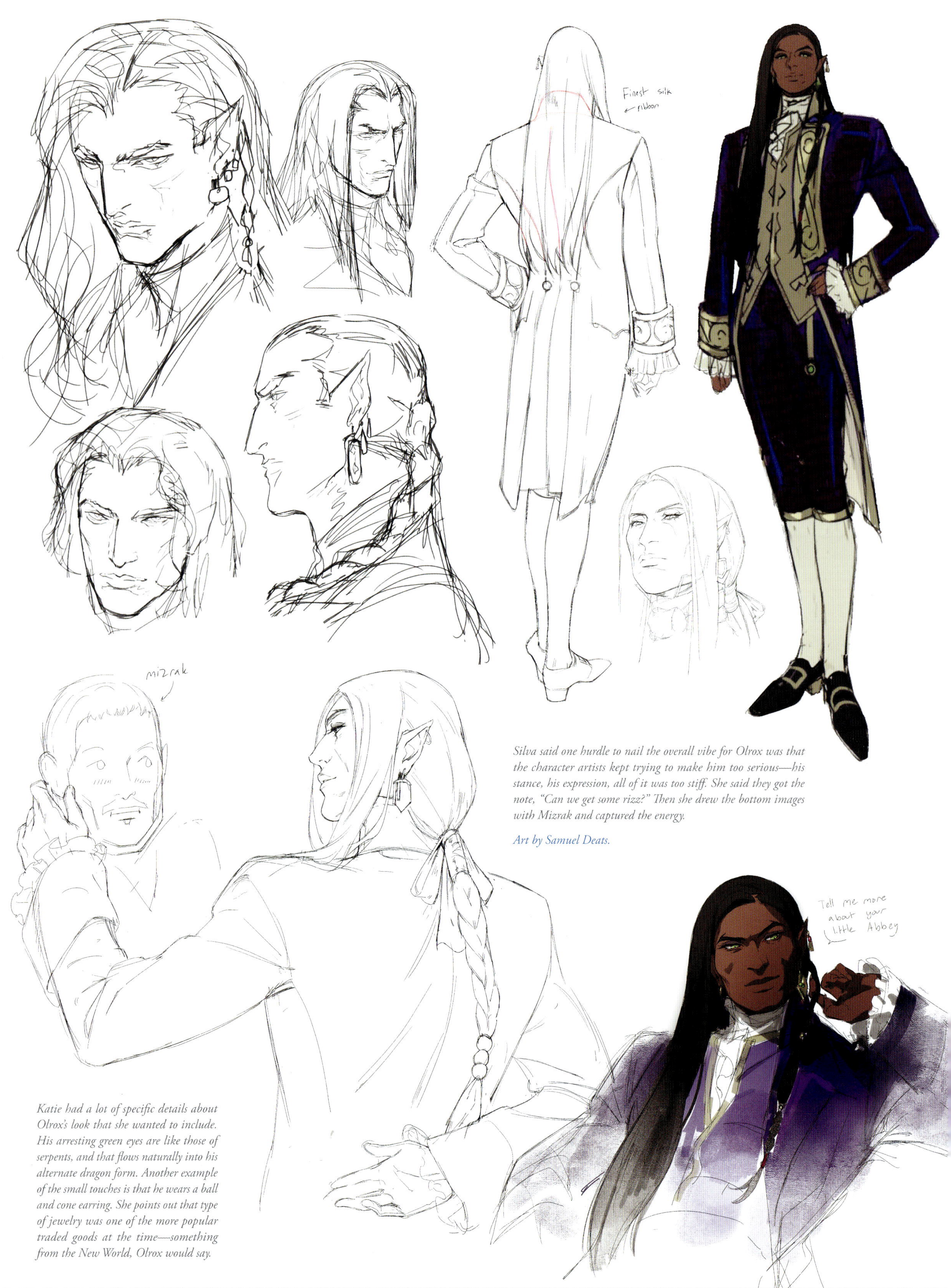

Silva said one hurdle to nail the overall vibe for Olrox was that the character artists kept trying to make him too serious—his stance, his expression, all of it was too stiff. She said they got the note, "Can we get some rizz?" Then she drew the bottom images with Mizrak and captured the energy.

Art by Samuel Deats.

Katie had a lot of specific details about Olrox's look that she wanted to include. His arresting green eyes are like those of serpents, and that flows naturally into his alternate dragon form. Another example of the small touches is that he wears a ball and cone earring. She points out that type of jewelry was one of the more popular traded goods at the time—something from the New World, Olrox would say.

ELEGANT LINES

Olrox's face is unique in anime, Katie said. "Anime masculinity tends to be the pointiest of chins, but specifically, elegant masculinity tends to be really pointy chins. But we wanted him to have that elegant, almost feminine look, including his cheekbones. So, I was really specific about him and his model sheet."

Art by Katie Silva.

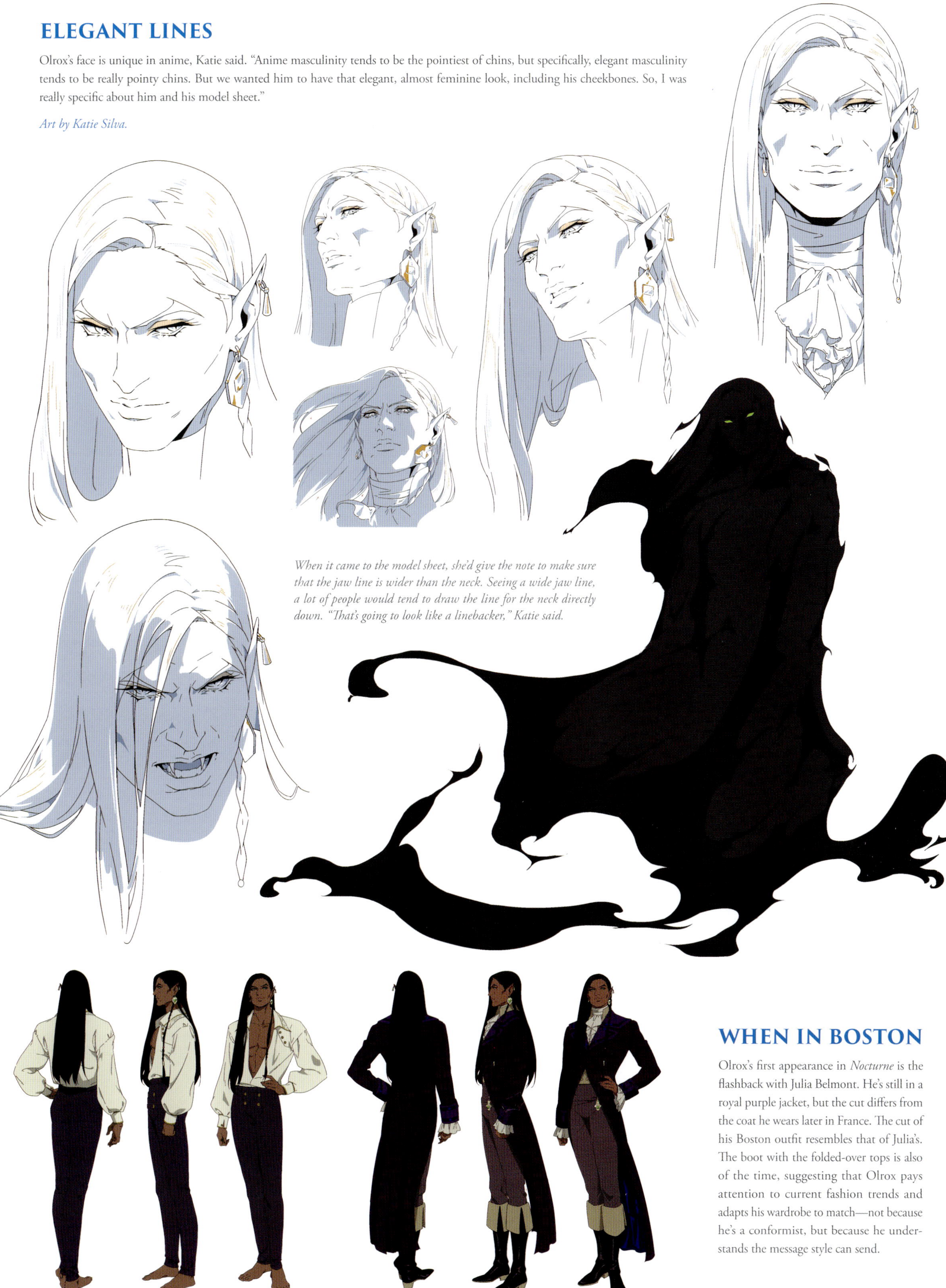

When it came to the model sheet, she'd give the note to make sure that the jaw line is wider than the neck. Seeing a wide jaw line, a lot of people would tend to draw the line for the neck directly down. "That's going to look like a linebacker," Katie said.

WHEN IN BOSTON

Olrox's first appearance in *Nocturne* is the flashback with Julia Belmont. He's still in a royal purple jacket, but the cut differs from the coat he wears later in France. The cut of his Boston outfit resembles that of Julia's. The boot with the folded-over tops is also of the time, suggesting that Olrox pays attention to current fashion trends and adapts his wardrobe to match—not because he's a conformist, but because he understands the message style can send.

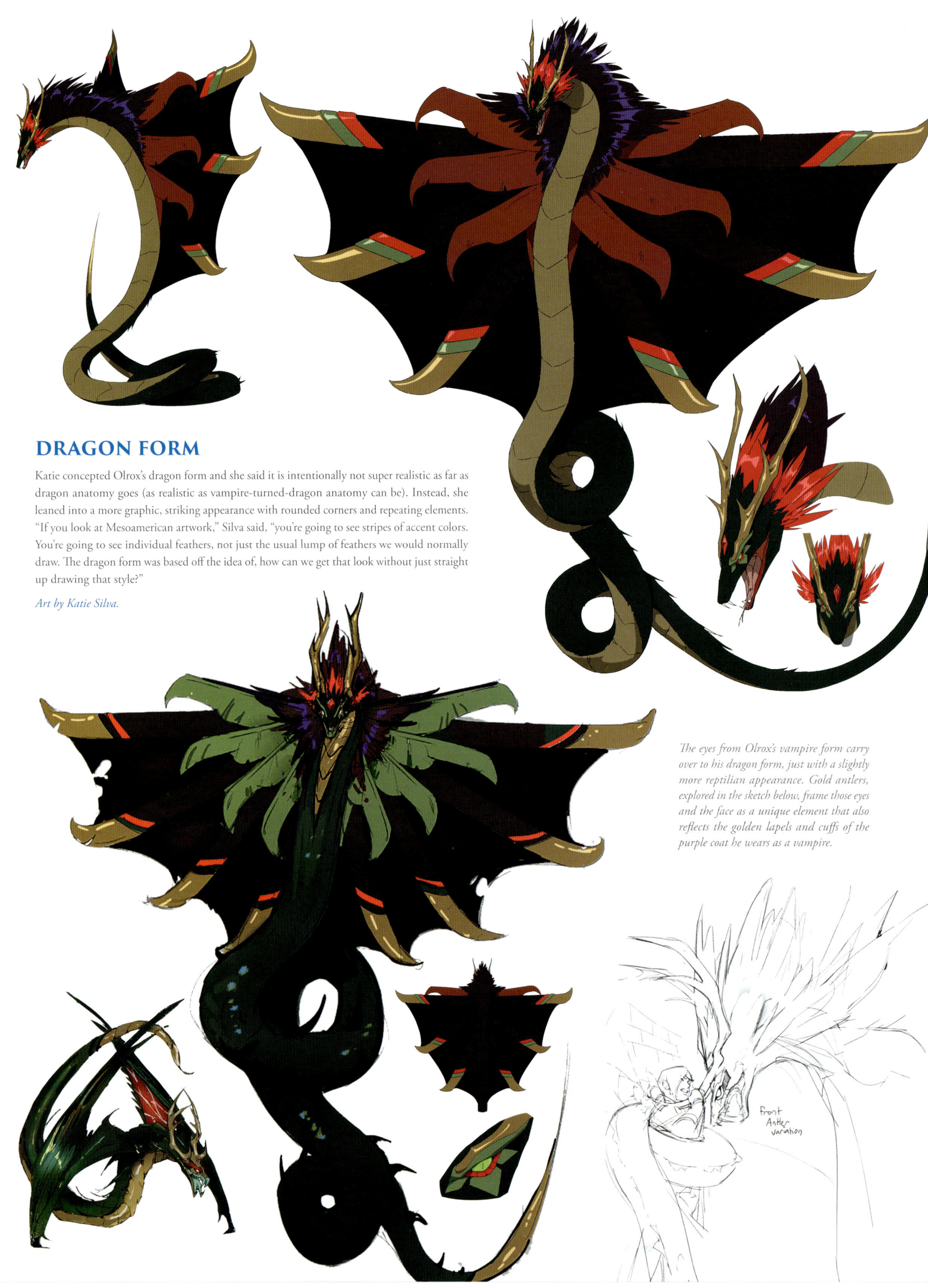

DRAGON FORM

Katie concepted Olrox's dragon form and she said it is intentionally not super realistic as far as dragon anatomy goes (as realistic as vampire-turned-dragon anatomy can be). Instead, she leaned into a more graphic, striking appearance with rounded corners and repeating elements. "If you look at Mesoamerican artwork," Silva said, "you're going to see stripes of accent colors. You're going to see individual feathers, not just the usual lump of feathers we would normally draw. The dragon form was based off the idea of, how can we get that look without just straight up drawing that style?"

Art by Katie Silva.

The eyes from Olrox's vampire form carry over to his dragon form, just with a slightly more reptilian appearance. Gold antlers, explored in the sketch below, frame those eyes and the face as a unique element that also reflects the golden lapels and cuffs of the purple coat he wears as a vampire.

Storyboards by Armando Atencio.

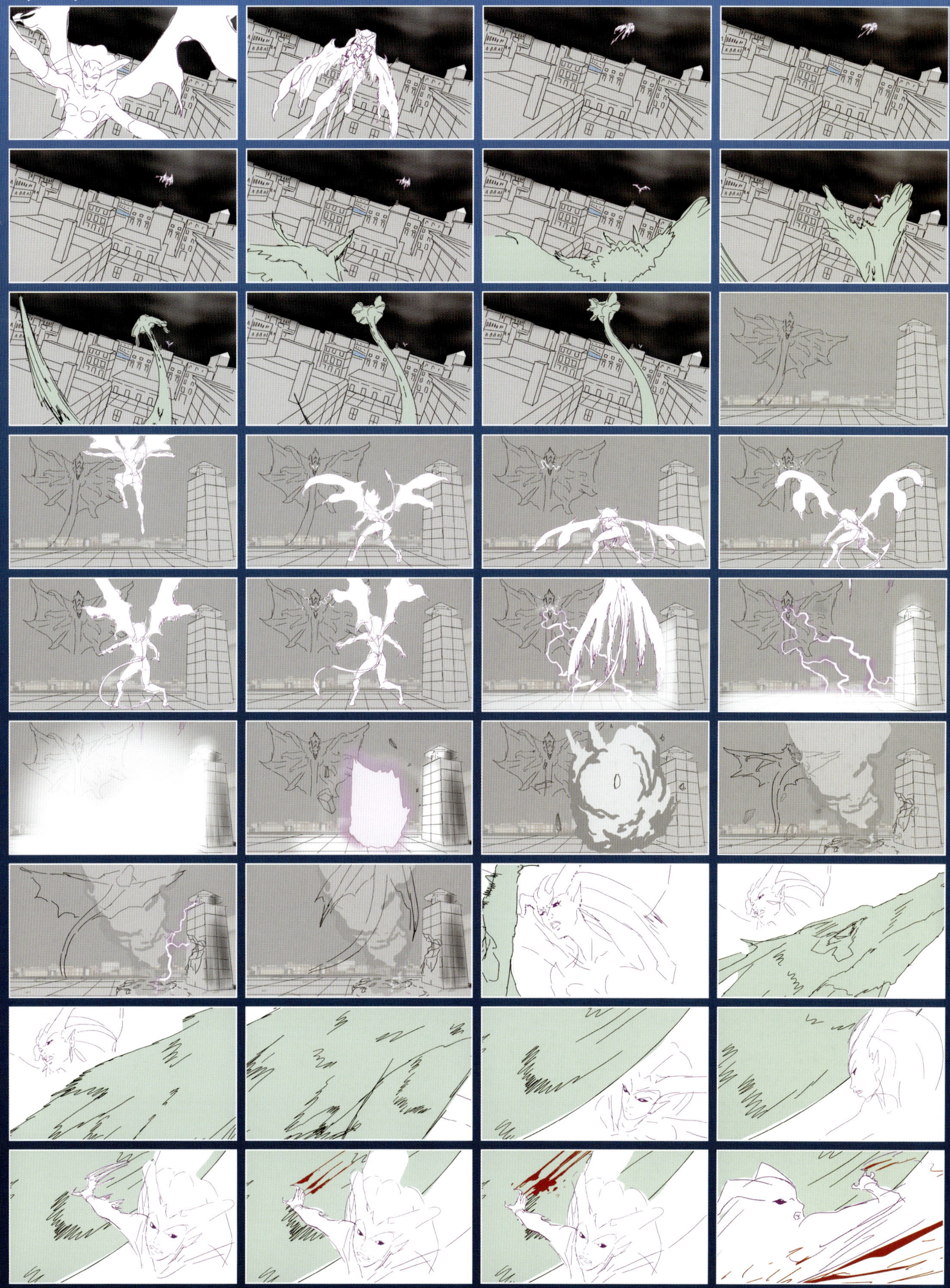

Olrox and Drolta, at this particular moment, are pretty evenly matched. The episode with this sequence features a lot of crowds, and with Olrox's dragon form and Drolta's wings, they wanted to get away from the ground level. Sam remembered, "I wanted some of these things to break away from the crowds for production reasons, but also so that we can be more focused on the characters, their own struggles, and not so much what's going on elsewhere."

Mizrak

A warrior monk devoted to his faith, Mizrak is a member of the Knights of Saint John. His stoic nature is visible in his countenance, his angular face often making it look as if his jaw is clenched. He moves with the weight of the religion he carries—particularly when those he follows make questionable decisions that do not align with holiness.

Because of his religious nature, Silva said she tried to give him a scapular underneath his clothing. The garment tends to be suspended over the shoulders. It didn't make it to the final design by character artist Suzanne Sharp, because the ensemble is more focused on Mizrak's warrior build.

Art by Katie Silva and Suzanne Sharp, with Mari Arakaki.

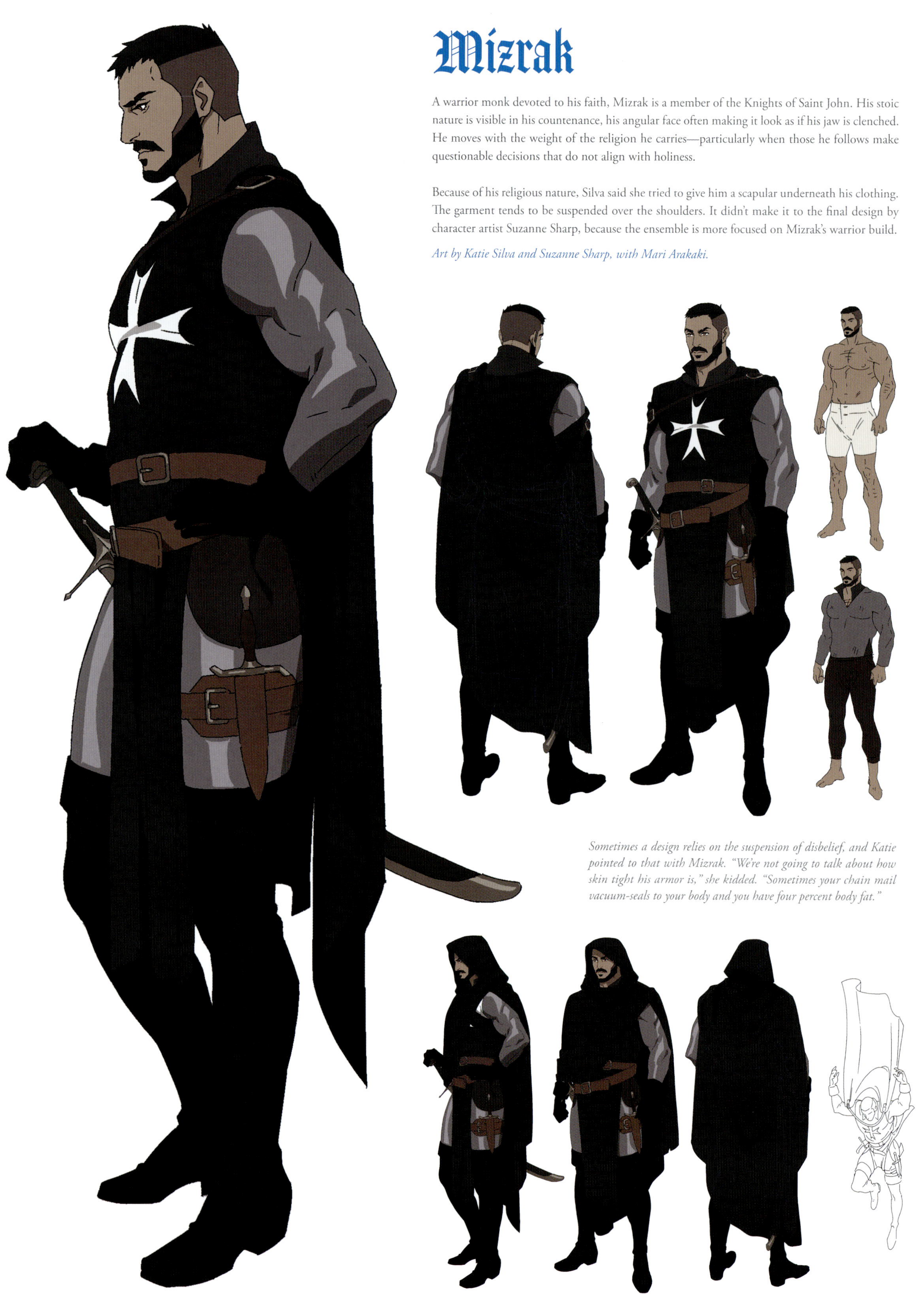

Sometimes a design relies on the suspension of disbelief, and Katie pointed to that with Mizrak. "We're not going to talk about how skin tight his armor is," she kidded. "Sometimes your chain mail vacuum-seals to your body and you have four percent body fat."

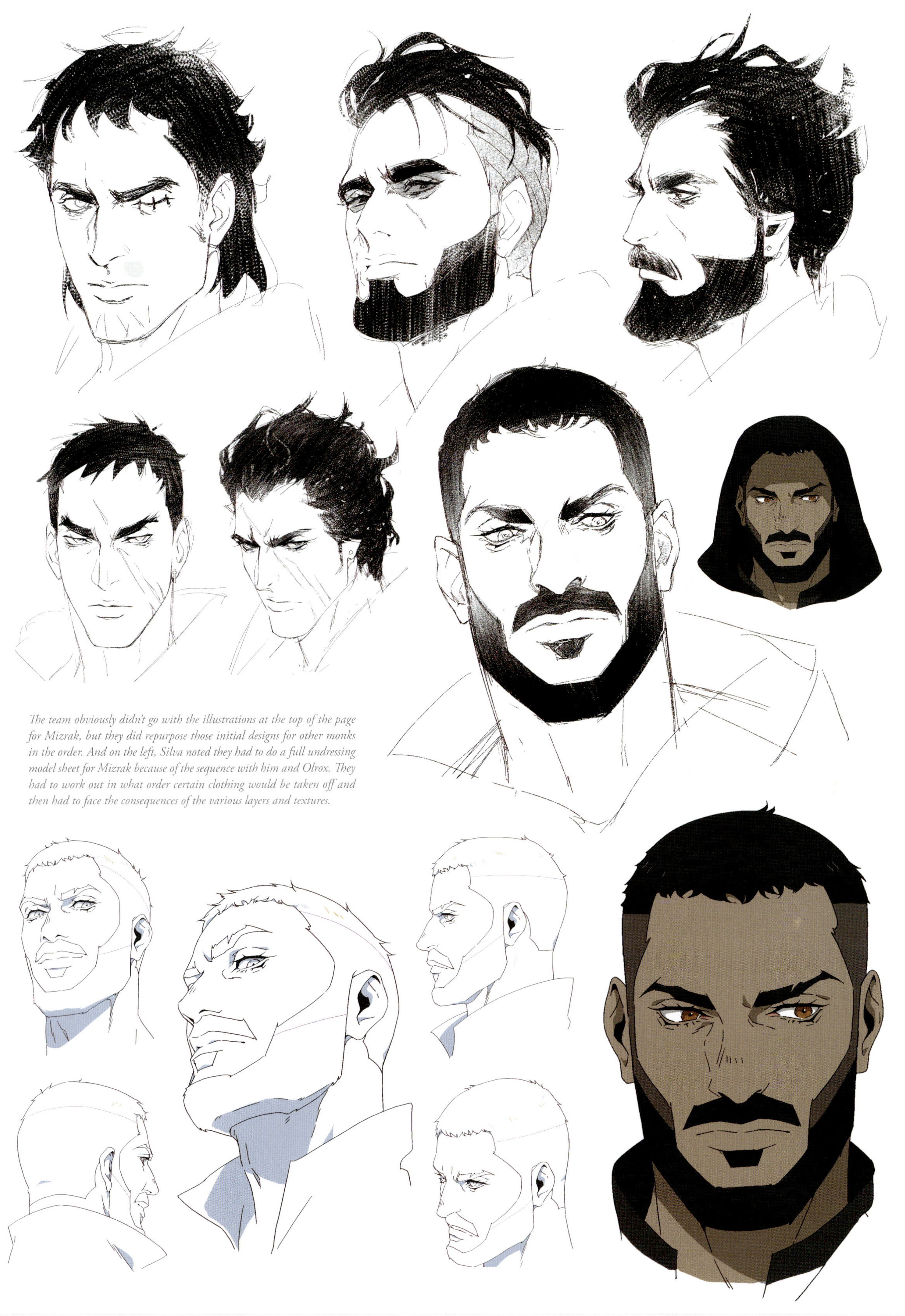

The team obviously didn't go with the illustrations at the top of the page for Mizrak, but they did repurpose those initial designs for other monks in the order. And on the left, Silva noted they had to do a full undressing model sheet for Mizrak because of the sequence with him and Olrox. They had to work out in what order certain clothing would be taken off and then had to face the consequences of the various layers and textures.

Storyboards by Chance Kubesh.

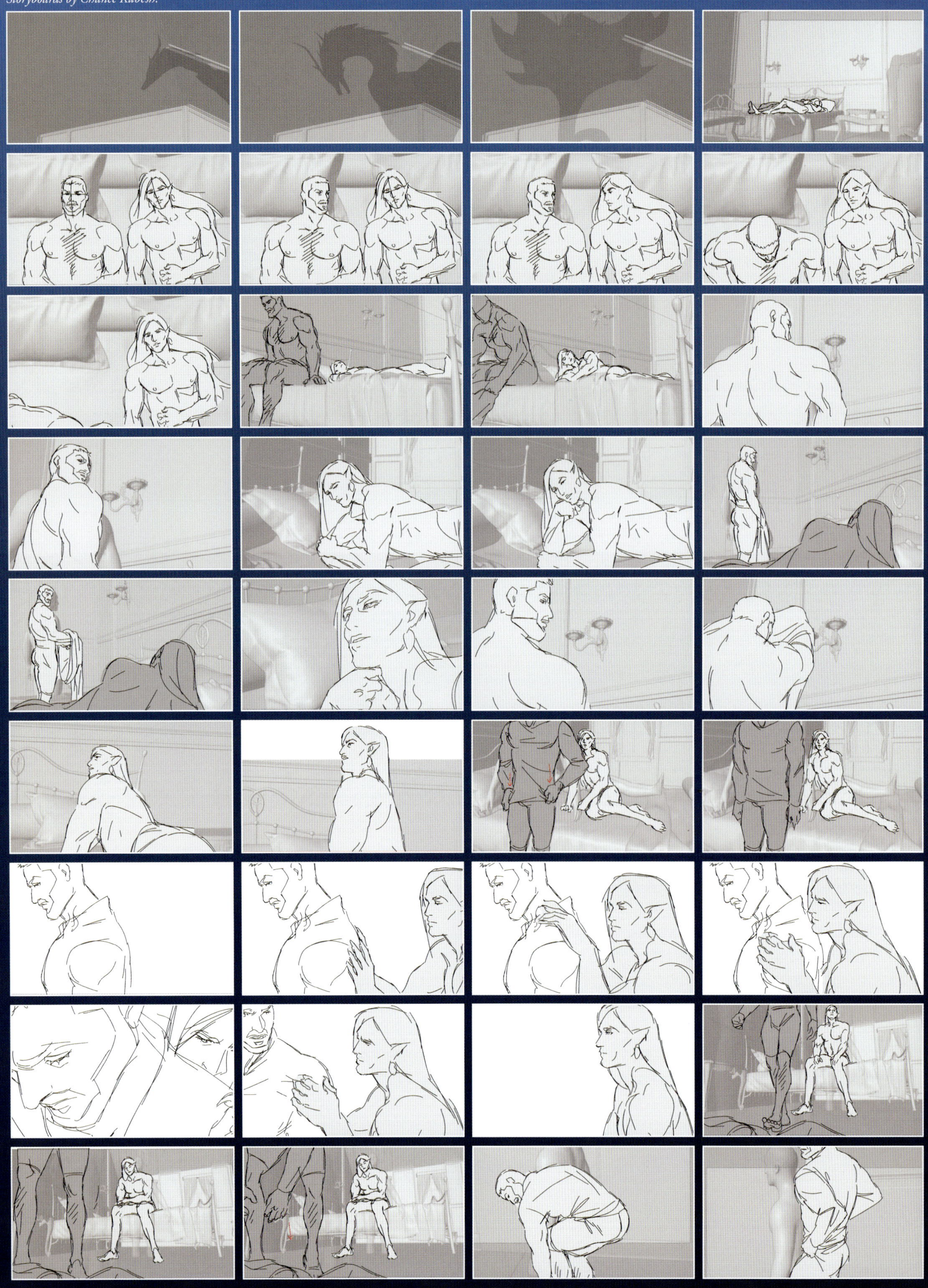

Storyboard artist Chance Kubesh brought tenderness and uncertainty to Mizrak's and Olrox's body language in these scenes. Like Sam Deats pointed out, Olrox's feelings aren't there yet and you can't tell if there's manipulation here or if something is starting to brew between them.

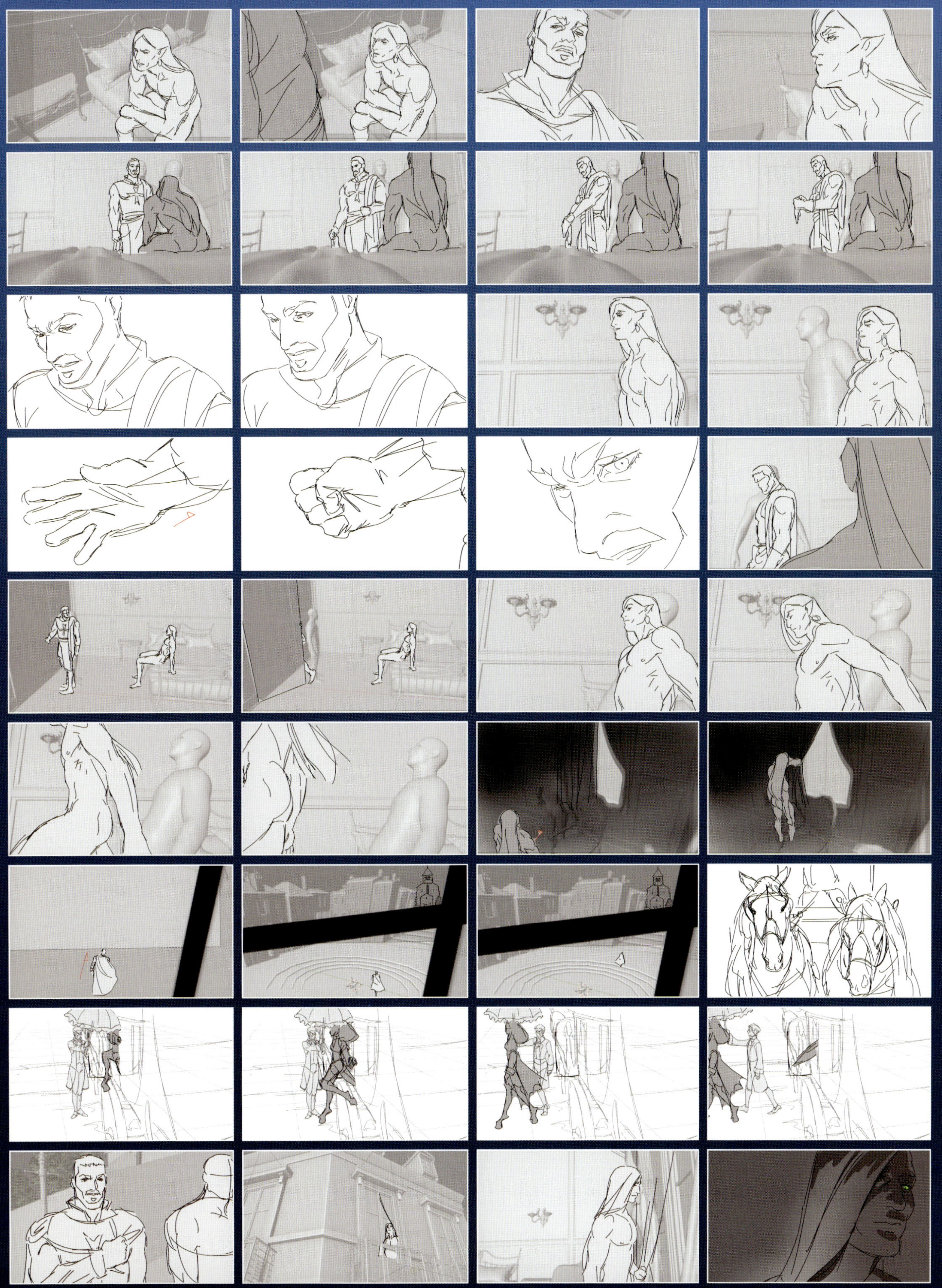

Sam said of Mizrak, "He's much more inhibited. I mean, he is the soldier. He doesn't know. He feels more shame over this than Olrox, who is very comfortable in his own skin. Chance did a great job of showing the character's personalities and their feelings in that body language."

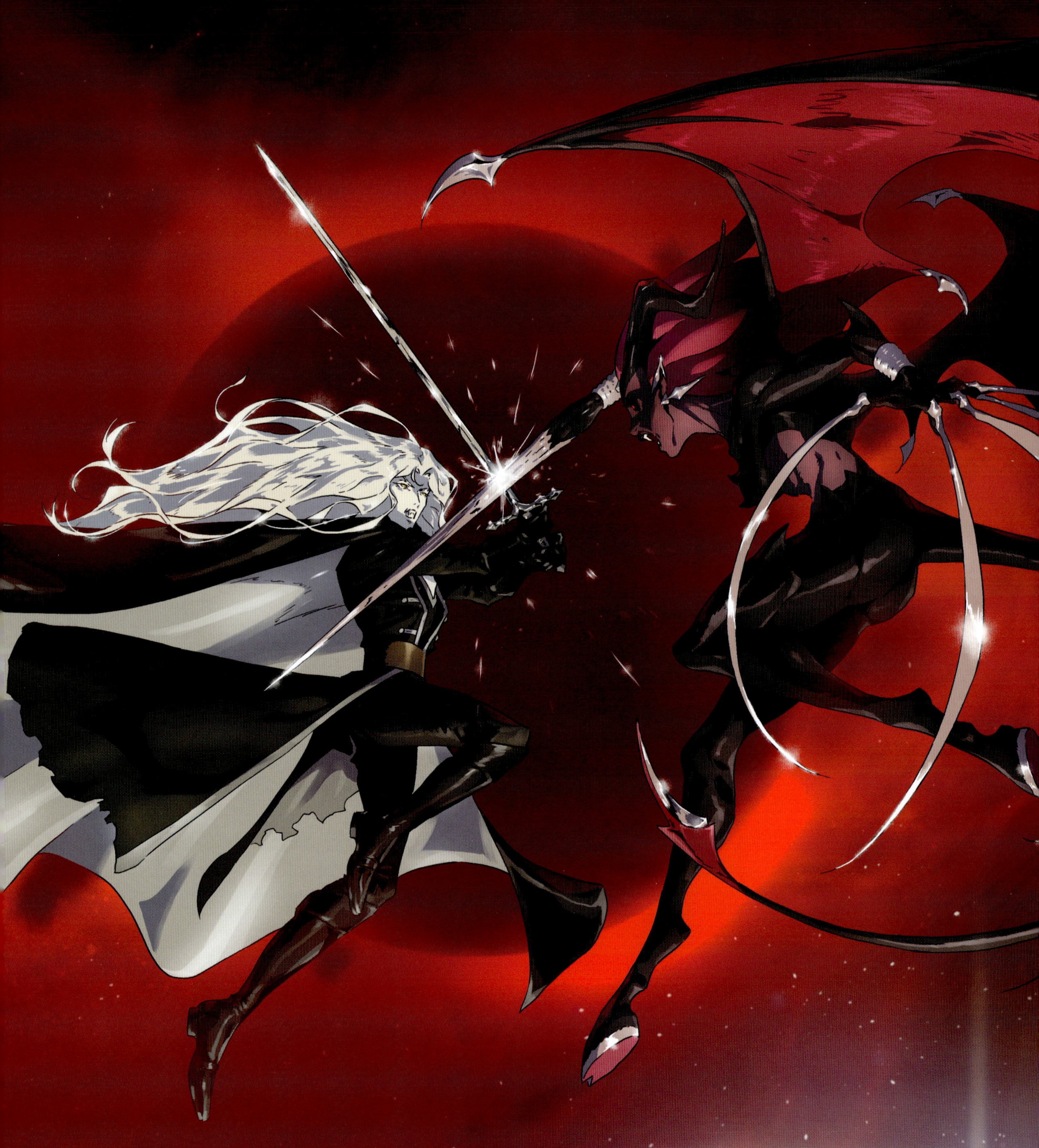

Art by Samuel Deats.

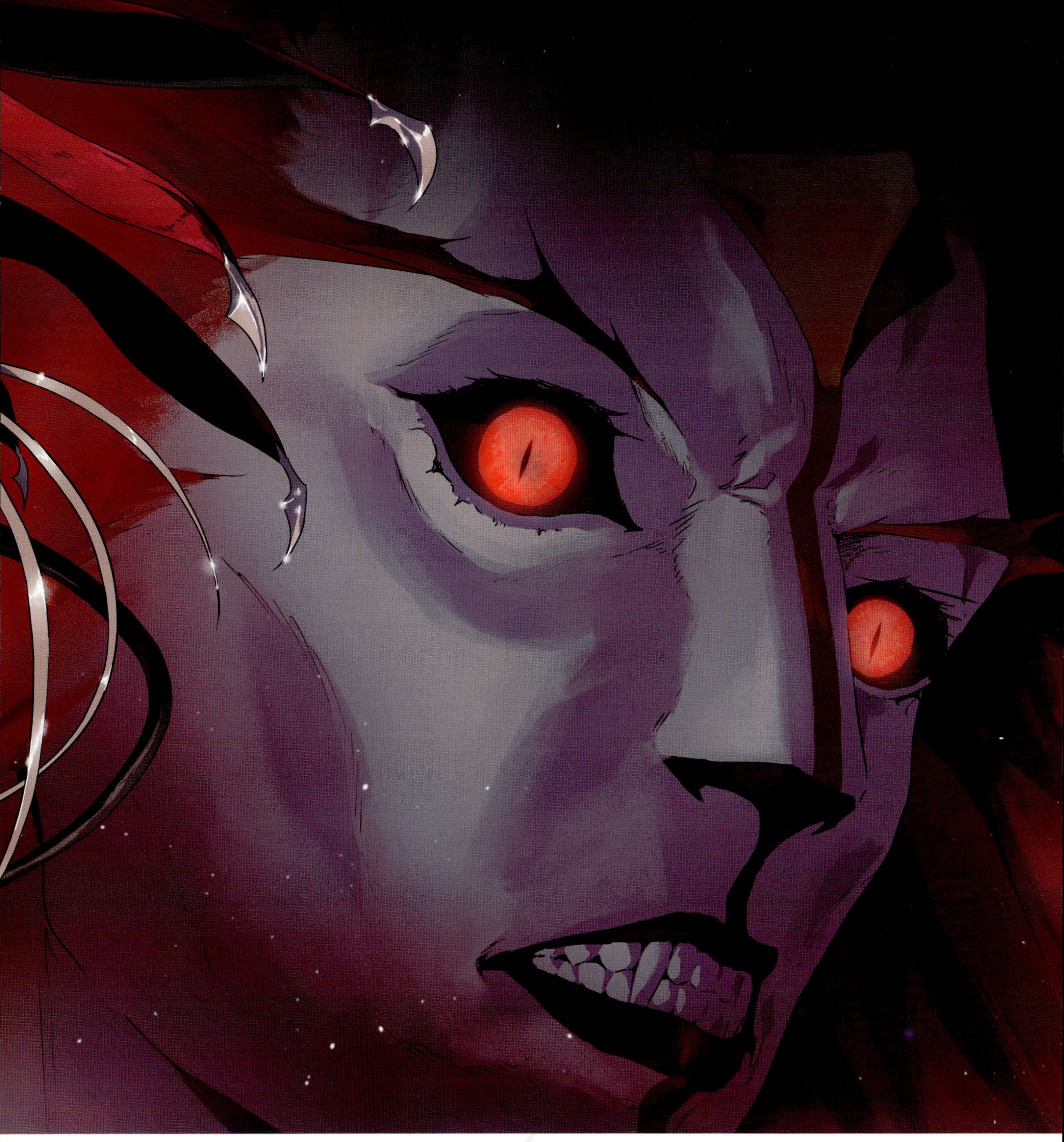

CHAPTER II

Demons and the Damned

Erzsebet Báthory

Countess Erzsebet Báthory was once human—a human responsible for the death of hundreds of women and children. She left that form behind to become a vampire and goddess at the tips of Drolta's fangs. Believing herself to be the only possible vessel for Sekhmet, Erzsebet followed a path to power through slowly drinking Sekhmet's blood over time. She pursued what she believed to be her righteous destiny: to be the queen of all vampires, the Vampire Messiah.

With each step she takes to enact her plan to spite Ra and bring perpetual darkness for the vampires to roam freely, she becomes more narrow minded and sees only her victory. Her statuesque form matches her defiant personality.

Art by Suzanne Sharp. Horses by Stephanie McCrea Rainosek.

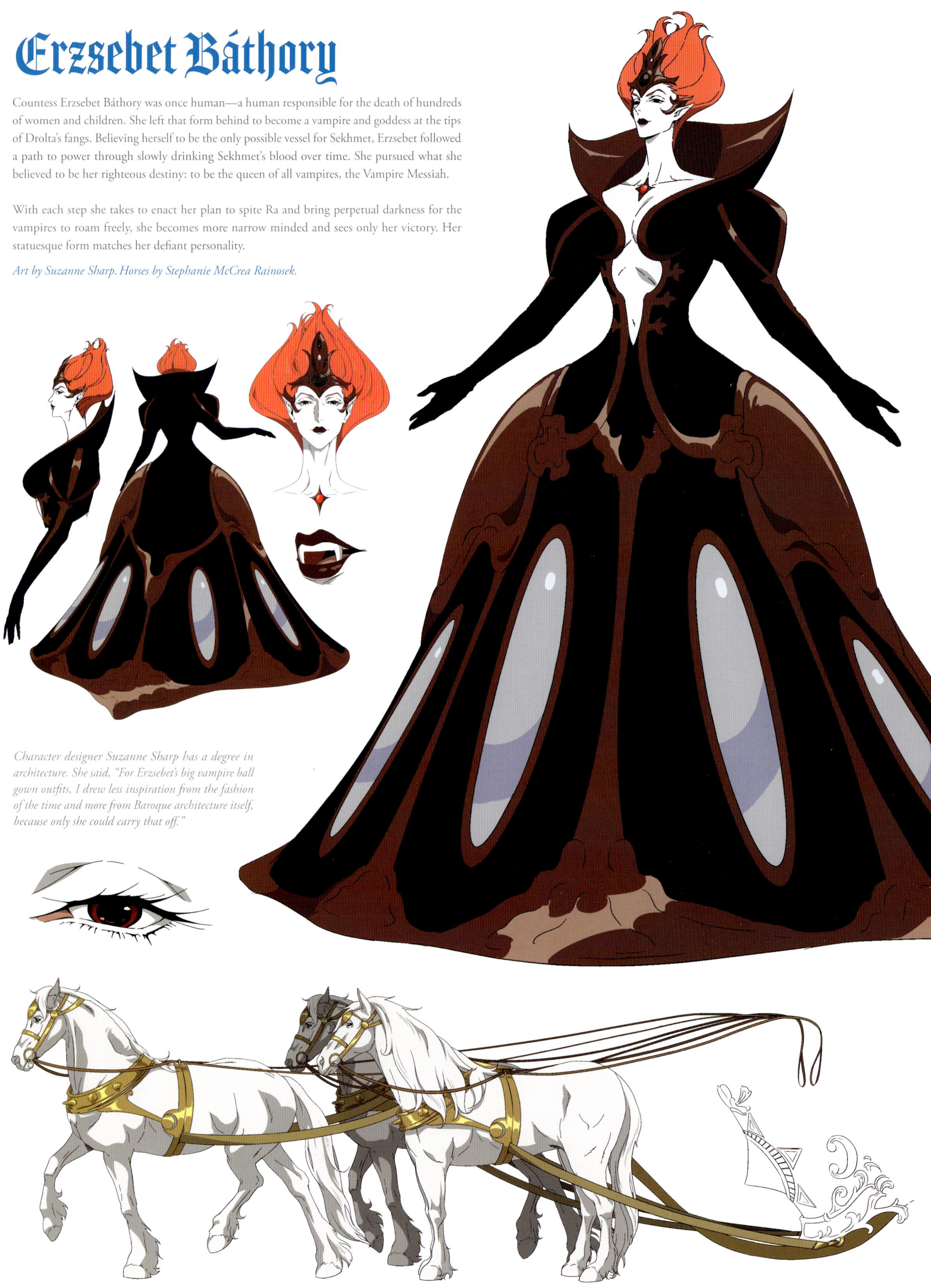

Character designer Suzanne Sharp has a degree in architecture. She said, "For Erzsebet's big vampire ball gown outfits, I drew less inspiration from the fashion of the time and more from Baroque architecture itself, because only she could carry that off."

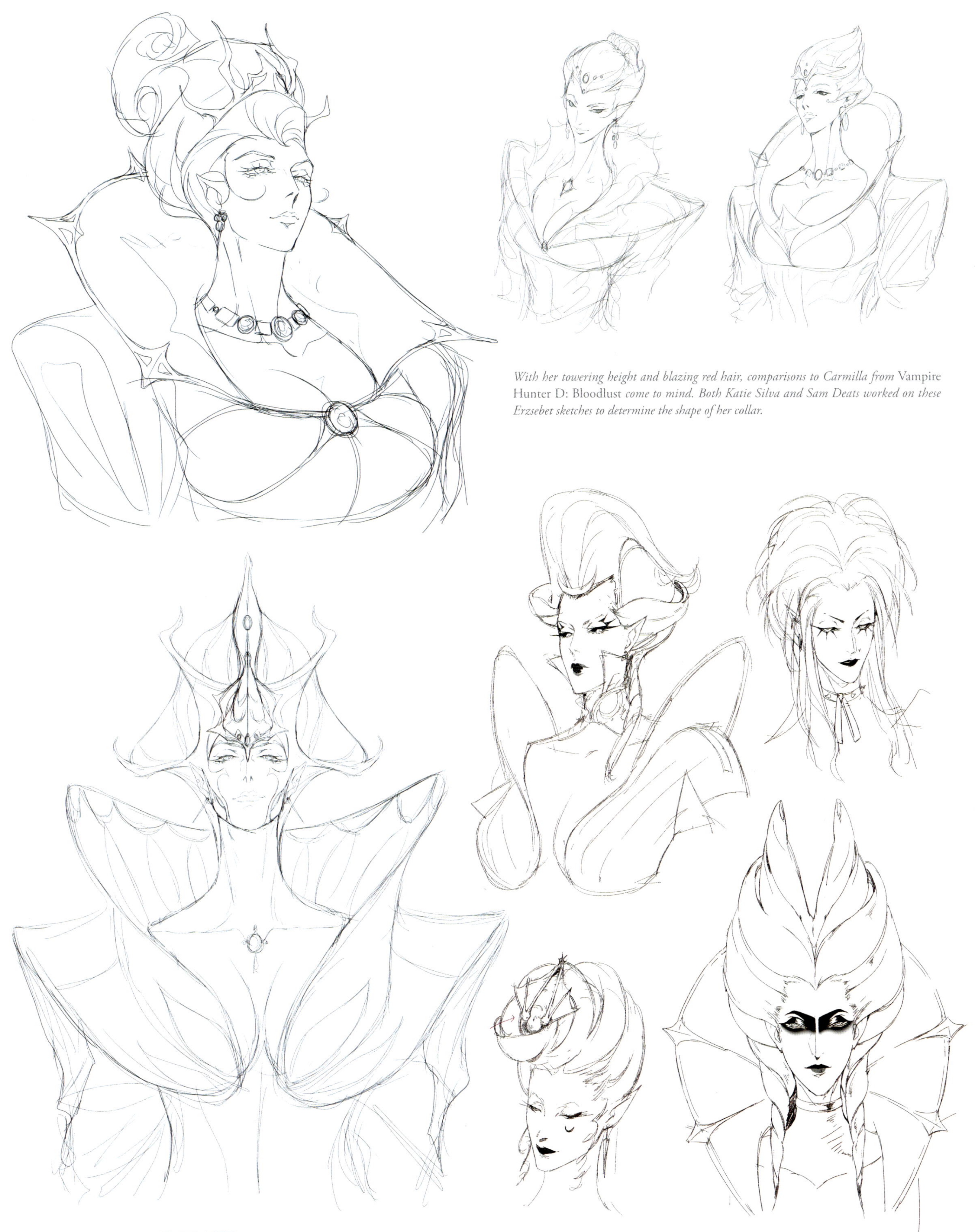

With her towering height and blazing red hair, comparisons to Carmilla from Vampire Hunter D: Bloodlust *come to mind. Both Katie Silva and Sam Deats worked on these Erzsebet sketches to determine the shape of her collar.*

TOWERING HAIR

Nothing about Erzsebet is conventional, which means her hairstyle had to complement her equally imposing and distinct couture. As a human, Erzsebet's long hair flowed down her back, but as a vampire, it adds to her height. It's another carefully sculpted and presented element of her outward appearance. The designers explored various silhouettes with circlets, tiaras, and other hair accessories for her before landing on the final look. The looser hairstyle on the top right was modeled on Mana from the Japanese Visual Kei gothic metal band Moi dix Mois.

Art by Katie Silva and Samuel Deats.

VAMPIRE QUEEN

Erzsebet ended up with more of a historical hair shape than other styles in the series as far as her locks being piled on top of her head. The bulbous shape came to a point on the top, which some fans compared to an onion. However, it was another powerful shape that set her apart from everyone else, human or vampire. Erzsebet is here to make a statement in every possible way.

Art by Suzanne Sharp, Katie Silva, and Samuel Deats.

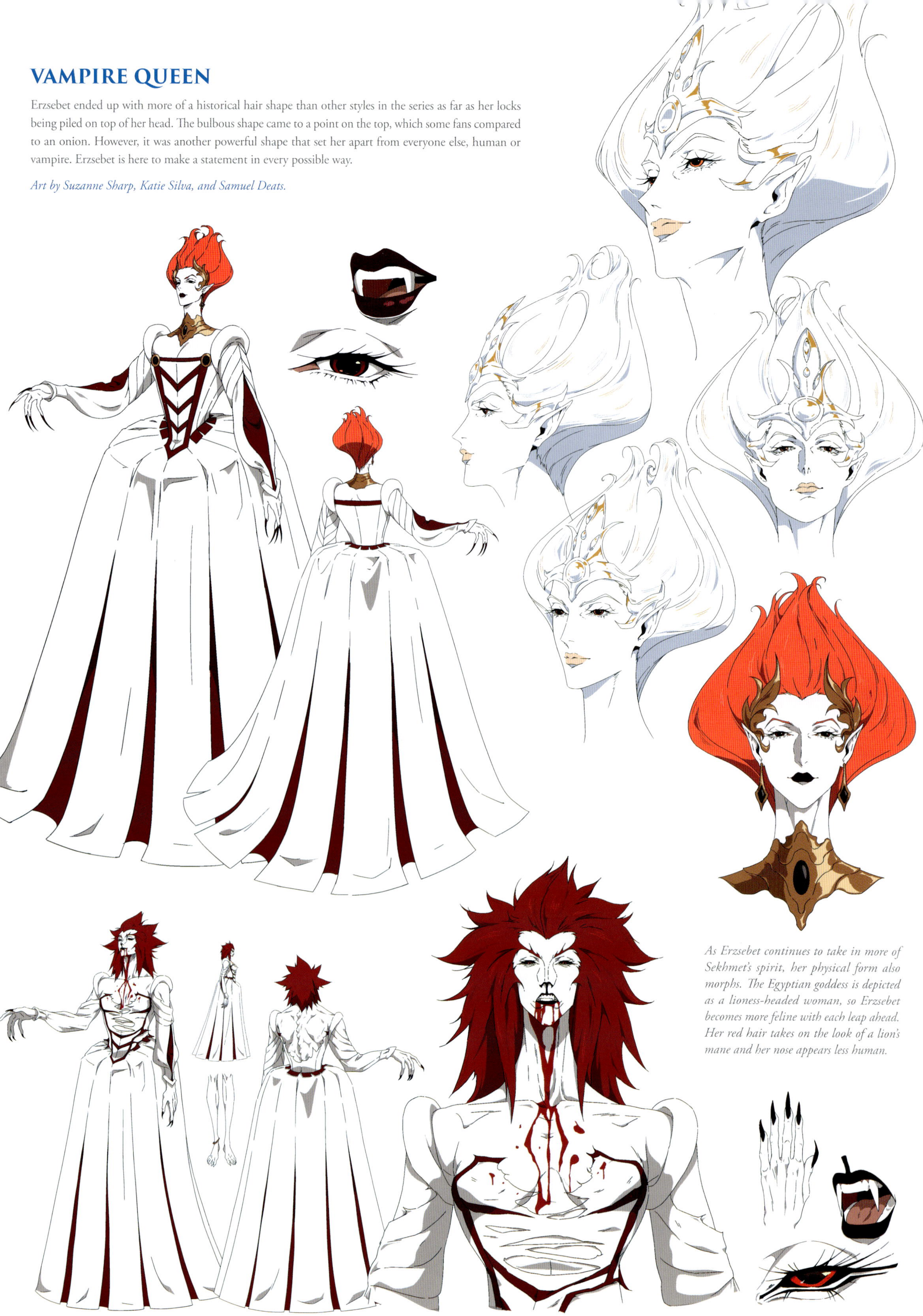

As Erzsebet continues to take in more of Sekhmet's spirit, her physical form also morphs. The Egyptian goddess is depicted as a lioness-headed woman, so Erzsebet becomes more feline with each leap ahead. Her red hair takes on the look of a lion's mane and her nose appears less human.

BECOMING A GODDESS

Before Drolta found Erzsebet, previous vessels didn't survive the absorption of Sekhmet's power. The vampire queen is able to withstand hosting one of Sekhmet's three souls, and the additional changes in physiology and powers happen as she consumes the remaining souls. The golden disk behind her head also comes from how Sekhmet is depicted. The goddess has a solar disk that sits on the top of her head, while Erzsebet's seems to extend from the back of her dress.

Art by Mari Arakaki and Katie Silva.

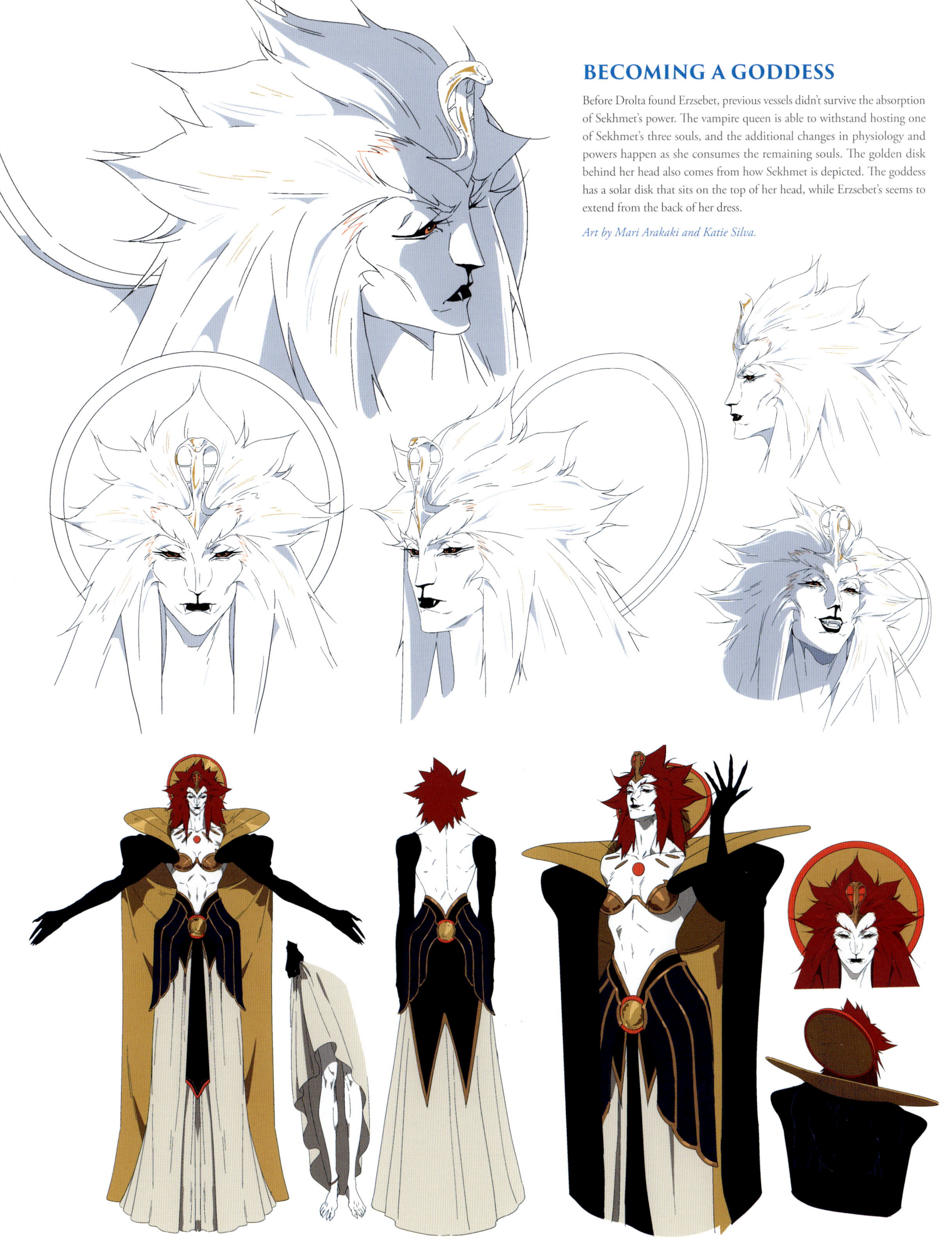

Mari Arakaki and Suzanne Sharp put together these designs, again bringing architectural and graphic aspects to Erzsebet's dress beyond the fashion of the time. The cut of this particular dress shows how her body is taking on more leonine musculature and starting to become even more intimidating.

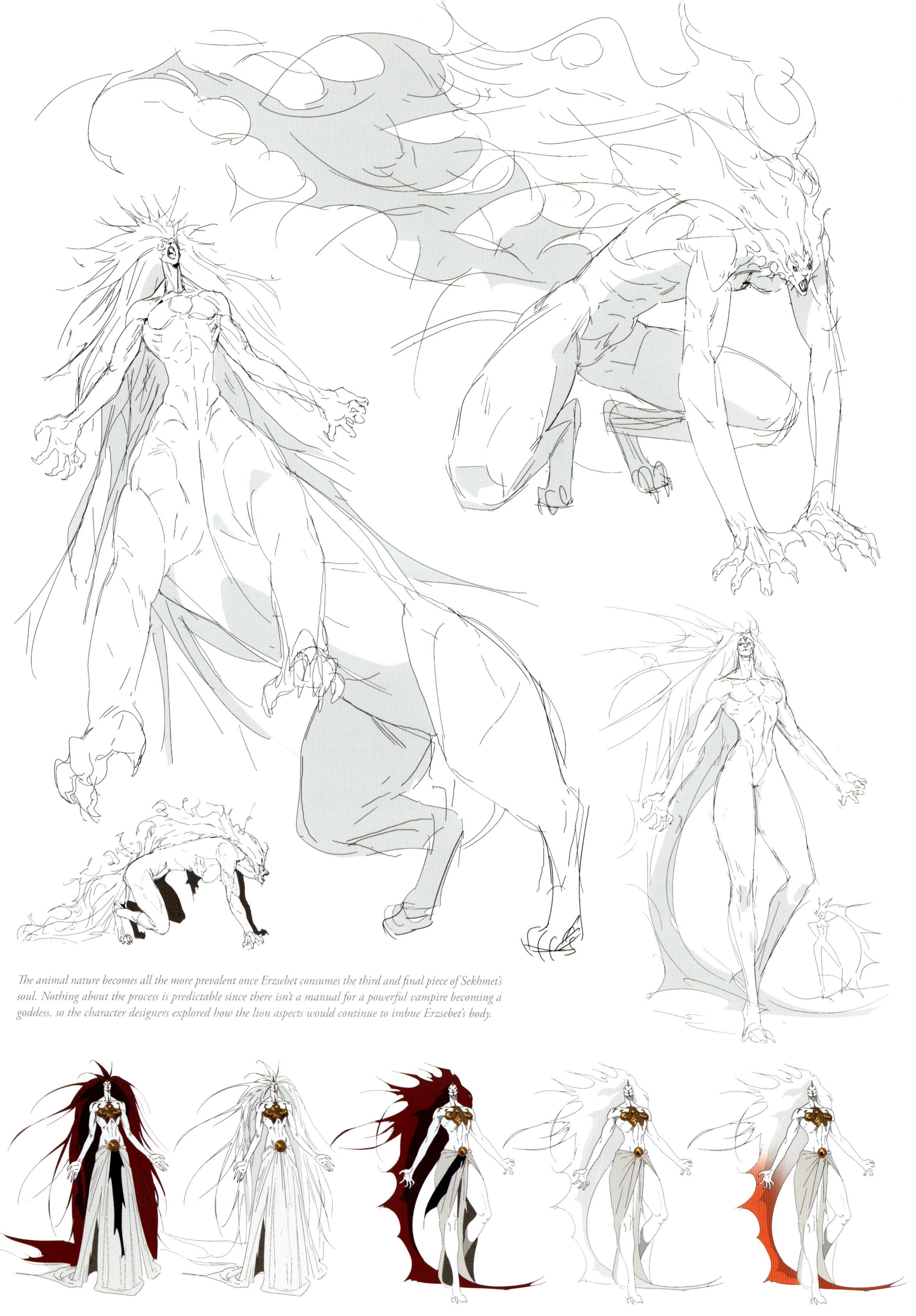

The animal nature becomes all the more prevalent once Erzsebet consumes the third and final piece of Sekhmet's soul. Nothing about the process is predictable since there isn't a manual for a powerful vampire becoming a goddess, so the character designers explored how the lion aspects would continue to imbue Erzsebet's body.

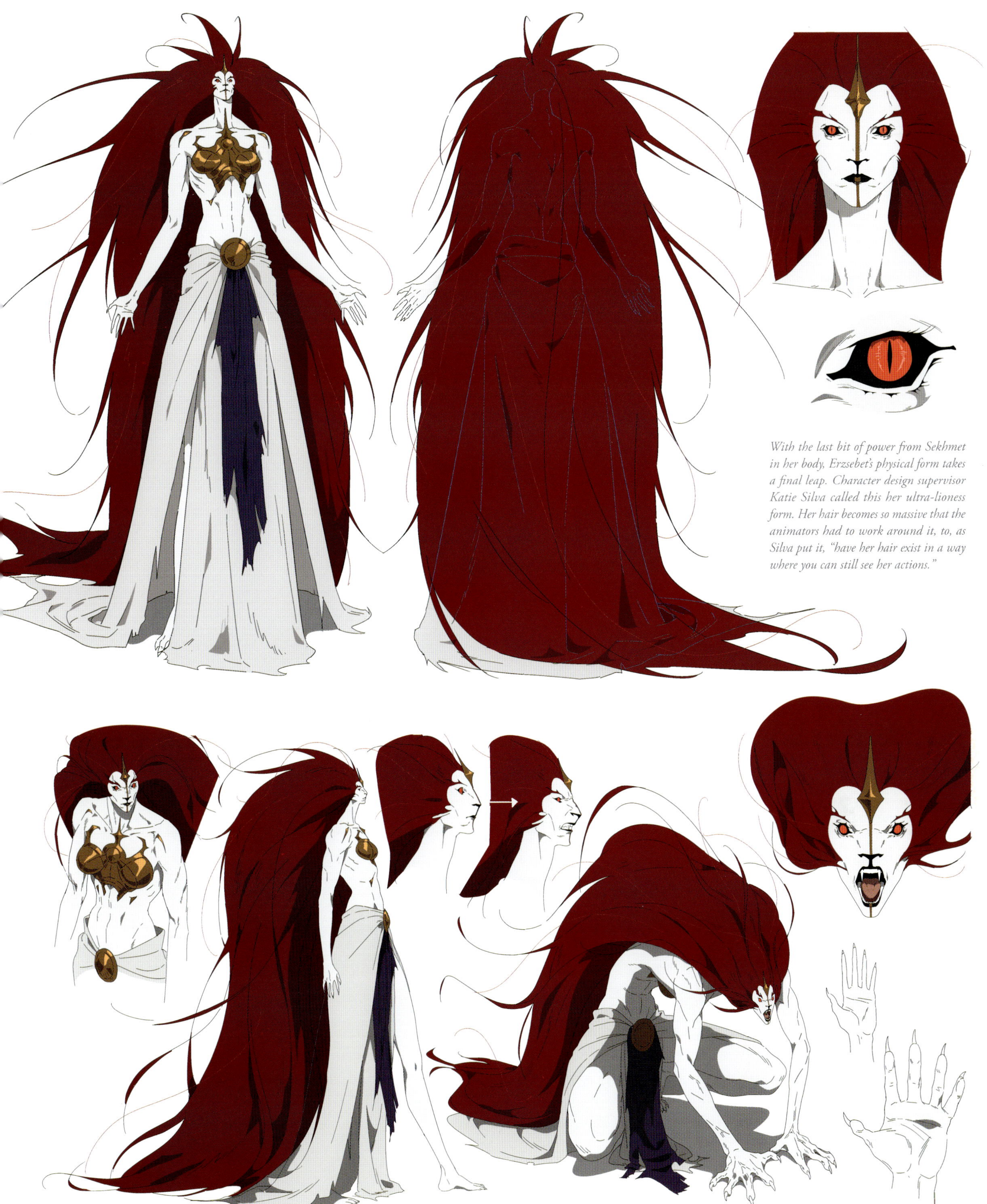

With the last bit of power from Sekhmet in her body, Erzsebet's physical form takes a final leap. Character design supervisor Katie Silva called this her ultra-lioness form. Her hair becomes so massive that the animators had to work around it, to, as Silva put it, "have her hair exist in a way where you can still see her actions."

FINAL TRANSFORMATION

Considering the sizable real estate of Erzsebet's hair and how challenging it made her to draw and animate, the character artists opted to keep the rest of her look somewhat simple. She has three pieces of fabric on her lower half, all the same color so the animators could merge them into one if necessary. As they honed how feral her face would become, they leaned into a strong feline profile. Erzsebet looks increasingly out of control as she gets to this final form because she can barely grasp Sekhmet's power.

Art by Mari Arakaki.

HUMAN ERZSEBET

Whereas the vampire form of Erzsebet is dressed in gowns styled after building design, the human form puts on more of a historical silhouette. She's still imposing (after all she's a murderer) but she isn't untouchable. Though she doesn't have status at this point, Erzsebet still carries herself like nobility and treats others, including Drolta, as if they should be grateful to be in her presence. That haughty personality comes through in these illustrations.

Art by Suzanne Sharp.

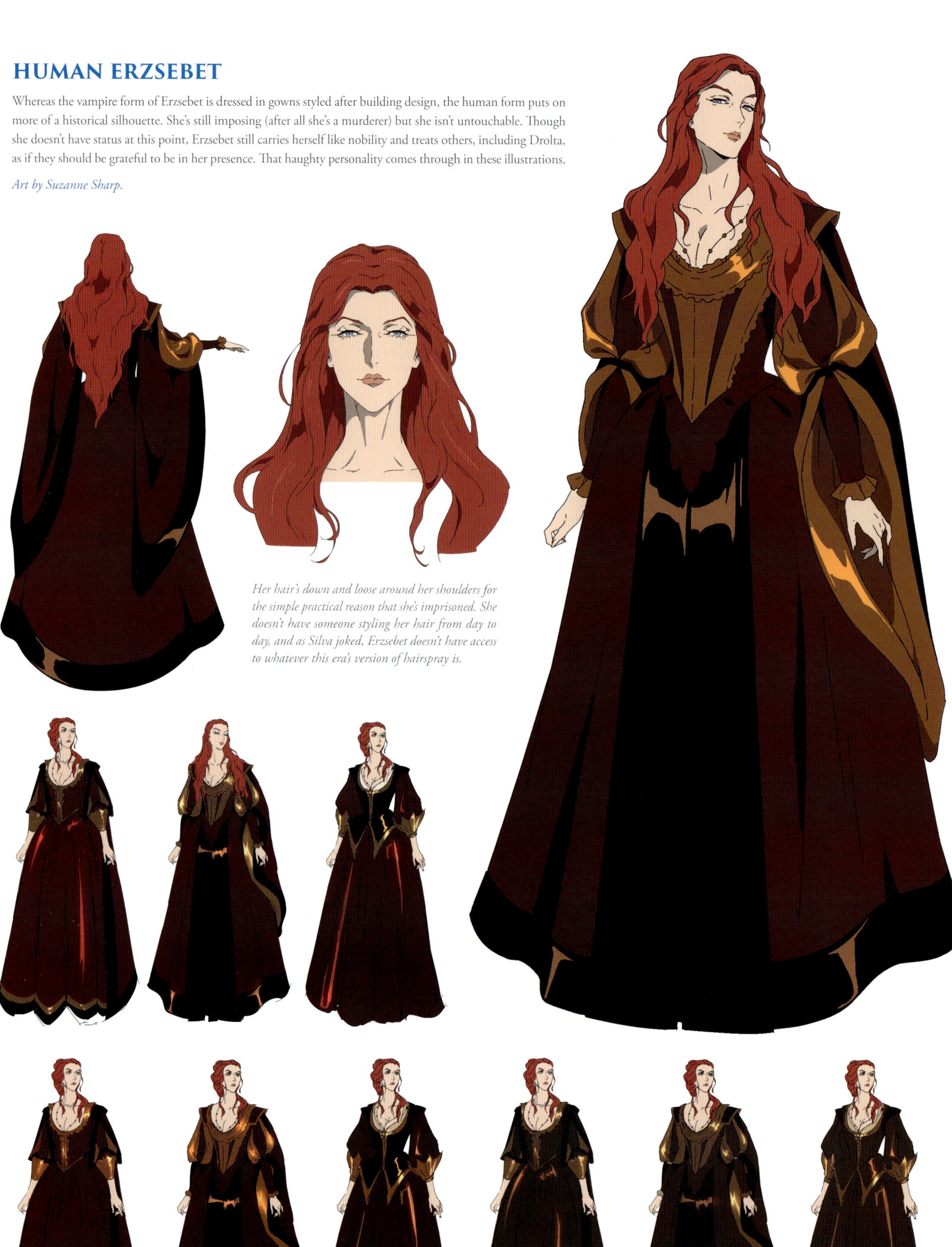

Her hair's down and loose around her shoulders for the simple practical reason that she's imprisoned. She doesn't have someone styling her hair from day to day, and as Silva joked, Erzsebet doesn't have access to whatever this era's version of hairspray is.

Storyboards by Armando Atencio.

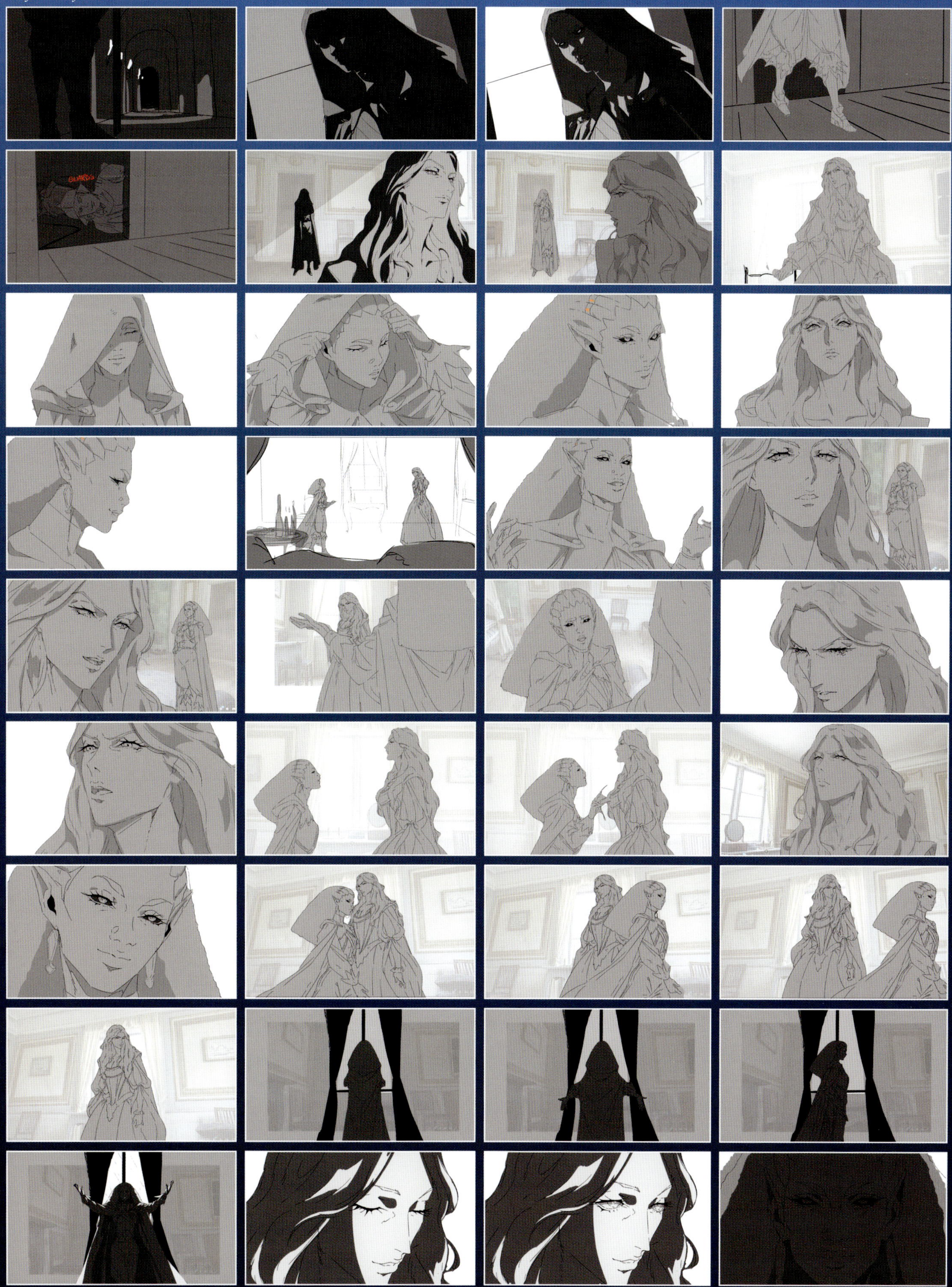

Erzsebet Báthory was a sociopathic human long before she became a vampire goddess. Adam Deats noted the importance of these flashbacks: "These are the only backstory that you get about Drolta, and they're short-winded. We had to make sure they were as clean and readable as possible. We revised a few things in the boarding stage of this one because the staging of her walking up the soldier, the flash of lightning that revealed her, it was difficult."

Nikolai

As Drolta's personal guard, Nikolai has to exude toughness. One only has to be around Drolta a short while to see she's perfectly capable of handling herself. Nikolai, however, does bring muscle to the table. He's there to do the job—as long as the job involves violence—and to do it well.

Since he protects Drolta, Nikolai follows Erzsebet by default and sports a brand of the solar eclipse she plans to set into motion. It's her symbol. In one of Katie Silva's sketches, she illustrated him taking a poker to his own face to prove his loyalty to the vampire queen because he seems like the type who would go that far.

Art by Katie Silva.

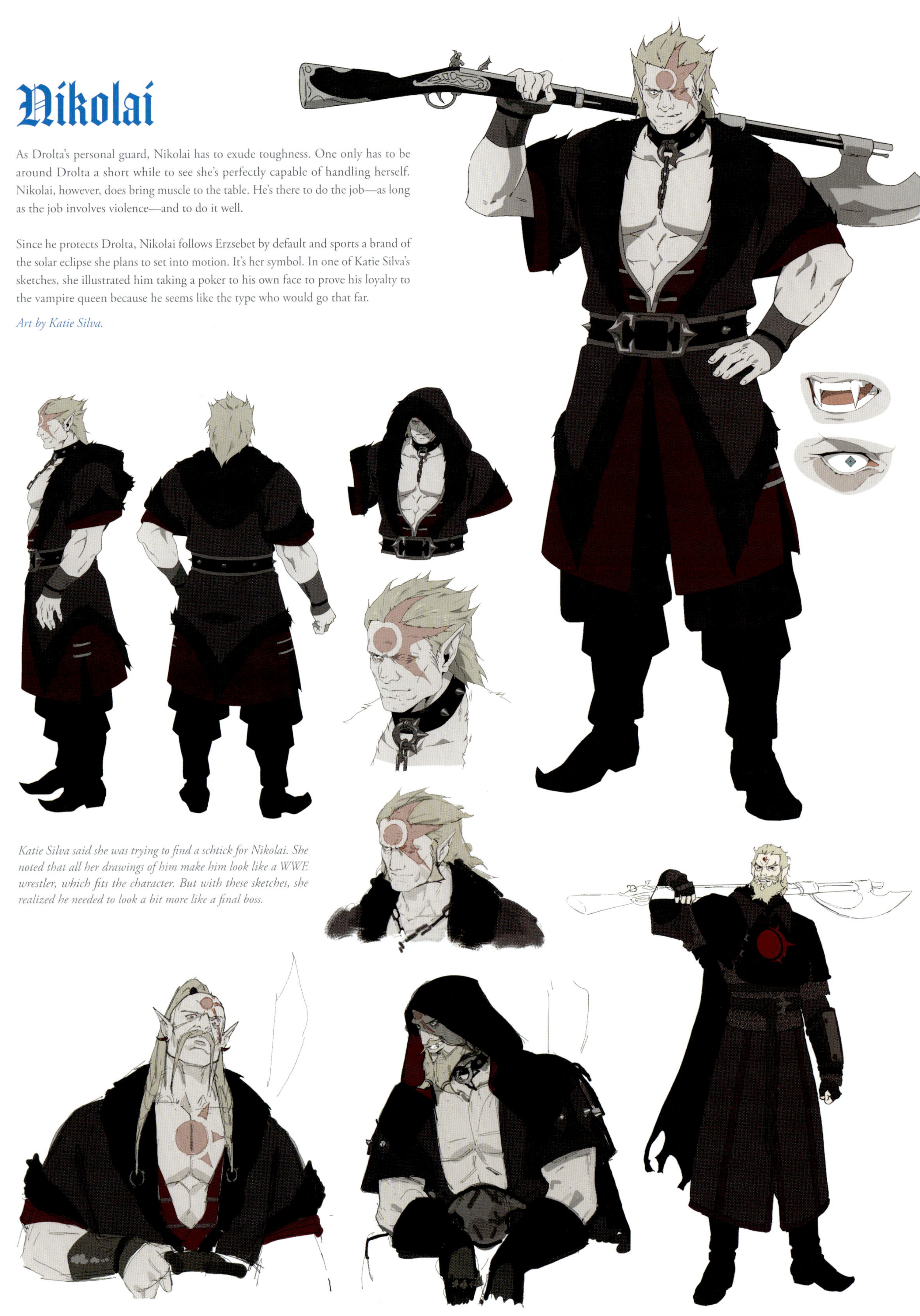

Katie Silva said she was trying to find a schtick for Nikolai. She noted that all her drawings of him make him look like a WWE wrestler, which fits the character. But with these sketches, she realized he needed to look a bit more like a final boss.

Vampire Allies

The vampire allies are really more vampire thugs. They're extra muscle, brute force that more cunning vampires can throw at heavy hitters—not unlike vampire infantry. They each get discrete weaponry and costumes. However, in the case of this top vampire, his visage is one of the discarded designs for Nikolai. The designers efficiently repurposed the sketch, changing Nikolai's blond hair to red.

Art by Mari Arakaki.

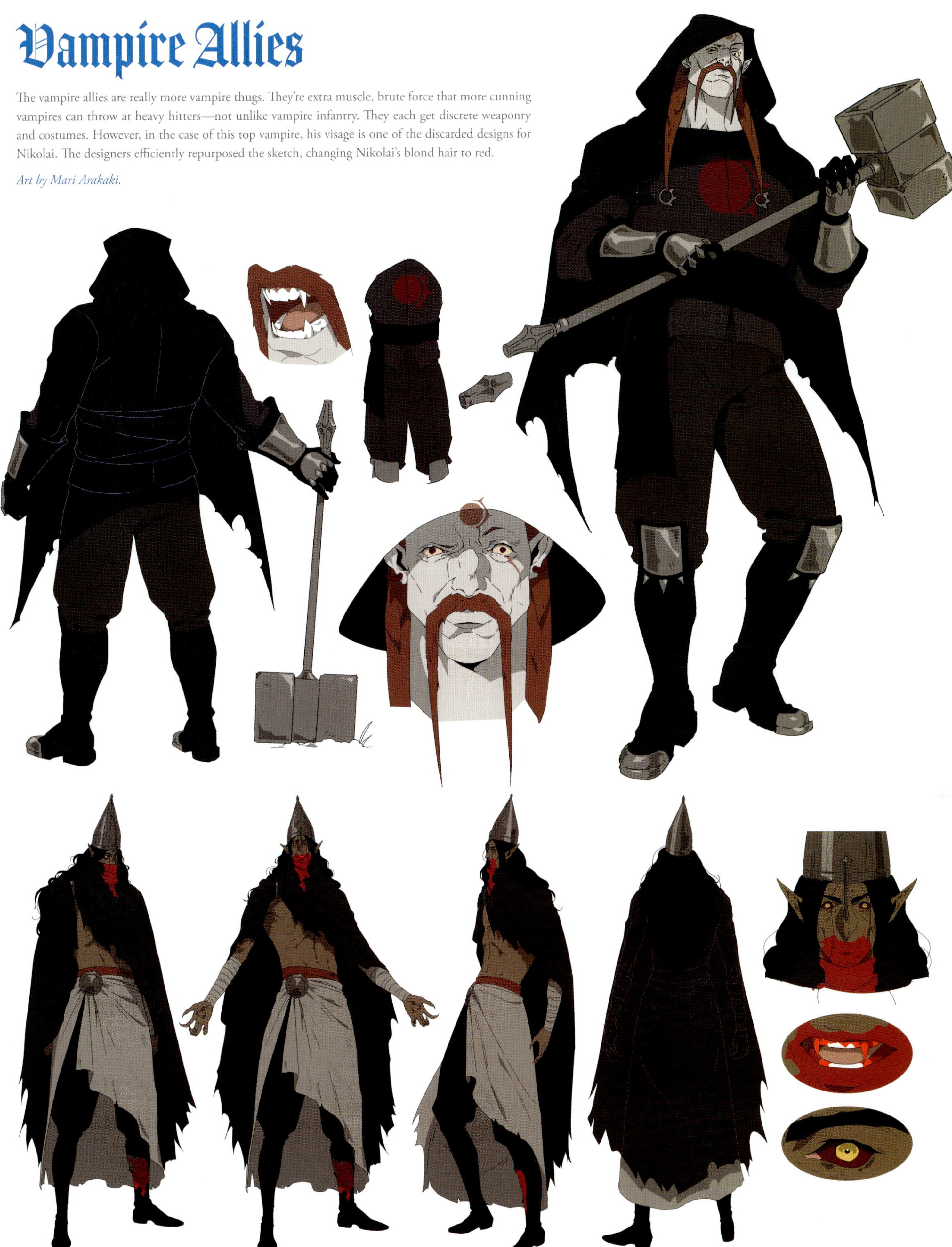

The human version of Drolta encounters this vampire in Sekhmet's Temple; she believes the goddess herself sent the vampire in answer to her prayers to become stronger. Silva said that internally they referred to this character as Cone Head. The vampire makes the mistake of insulting Drolta and her goddess, which results in his demise as Drolta slays him and drinks his fresh blood to turn herself into a vampire.

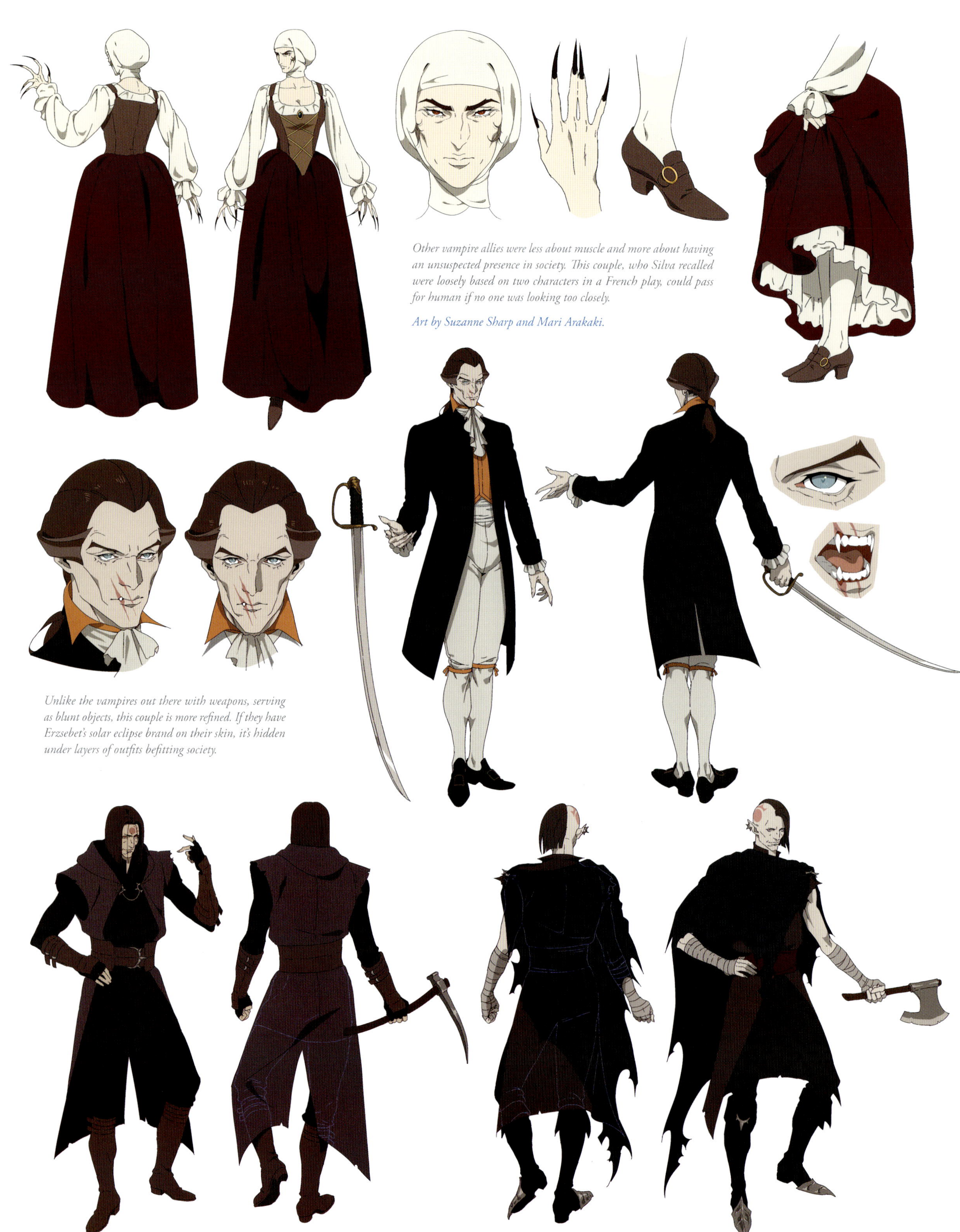

Other vampire allies were less about muscle and more about having an unsuspected presence in society. This couple, who Silva recalled were loosely based on two characters in a French play, could pass for human if no one was looking too closely.

Art by Suzanne Sharp and Mari Arakaki.

Unlike the vampires out there with weapons, serving as blunt objects, this couple is more refined. If they have Erzsebet's solar eclipse brand on their skin, it's hidden under layers of outfits befitting society.

Proper petticoats and fancy swords are not the province of the vampires who've been branded in service of the vampire queen. Their designs have varying silhouettes thanks to mix-and-match style costume pieces, but both of these characters are dressed to blend into the shadows.

The Prussian

The Prussian is Katie Silva's design. "He's one of my favorite designs in the world. And we were really hoping we could get Danny DeVito to voice perform him," she said. "Sometimes you just get really attached to a little side character. And that's this guy for me." Anytime Sam Deats would do boards with the character, he'd send them to Katie because of her affection for him. It didn't matter to her that he didn't have a single speaking line in the series.

Art by Katie Silva.

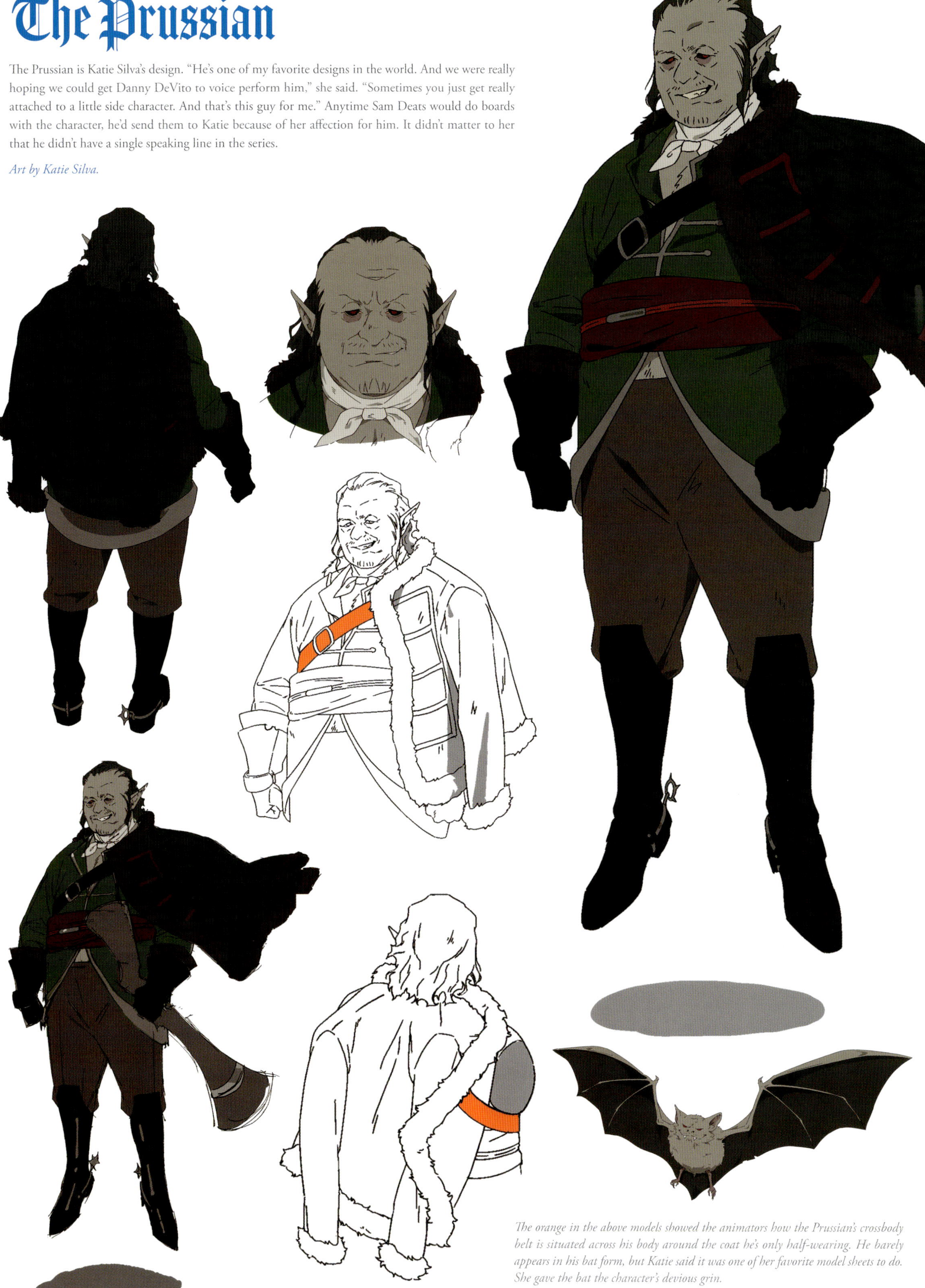

The orange in the above models showed the animators how the Prussian's crossbody belt is situated across his body around the coat he's only half-wearing. He barely appears in his bat form, but Katie said it was one of her favorite model sheets to do. She gave the bat the character's devious grin.

Vampire Priests

The vampire priests who believe in Erzsebet's plan to lift them up by creating a solar eclipse wear the Vampire Messiah's symbol on their forehead. Katie recalled that these particular characters were some of the first vampire designs Sam Deats did for the series because they fought in the first episode. Necessity demanded that Sam had to jump on the task and design the vampires quickly. She joked that they referred to two of the priests as Tall and Bulky.

They're meant to look serious, focused, and loyal. These are utility players that Erzsebet can employ as needed.

Art by Samuel Deats, Suzanne Sharp, Dominique Ferro, and Stephanie McCrea Rainosek.

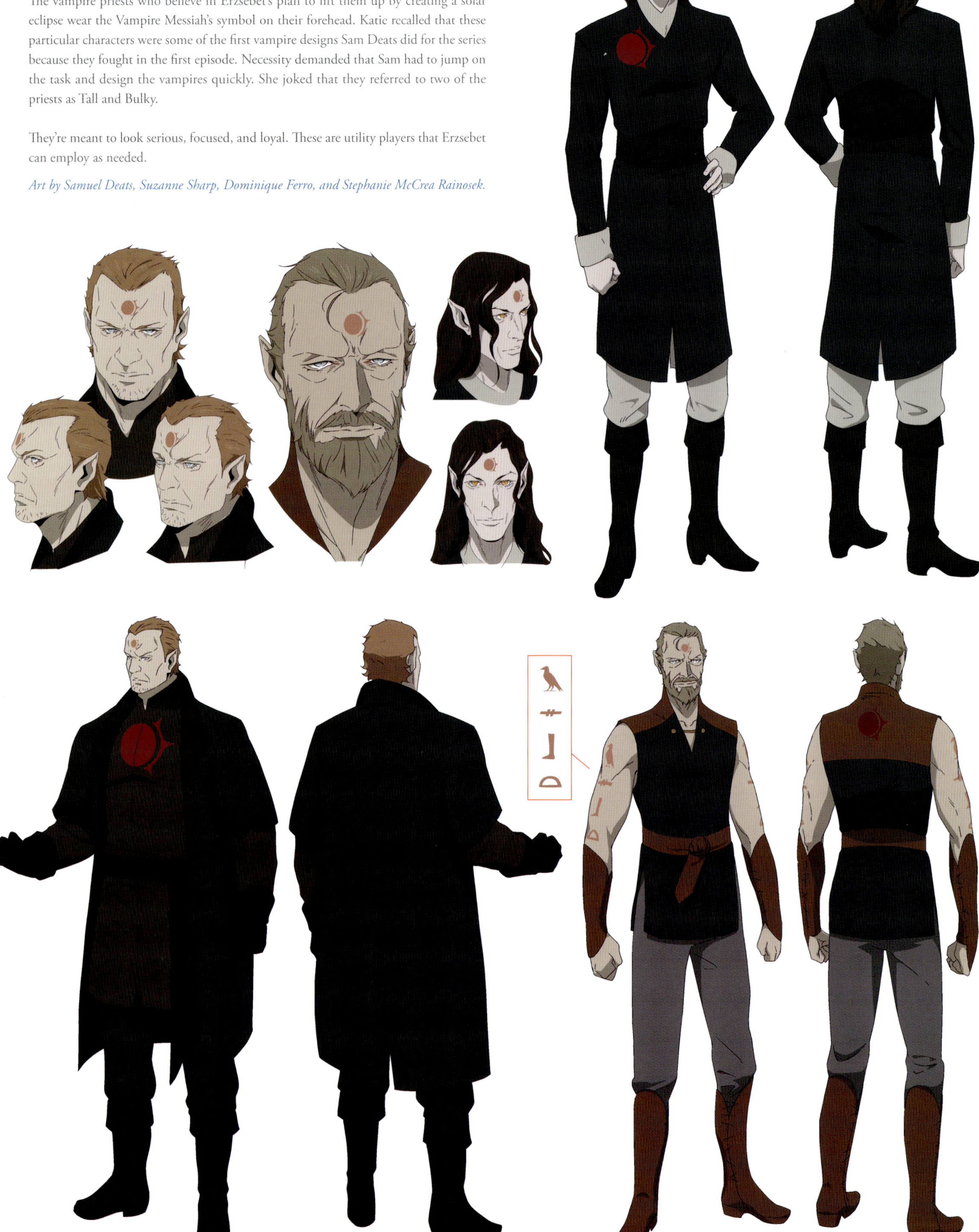

Erzsebet's mark is a common feature on her followers' attire and skin, but this design plays around with using Egyptian hieroglyphs that spell out the goddess Sekhmet's name.

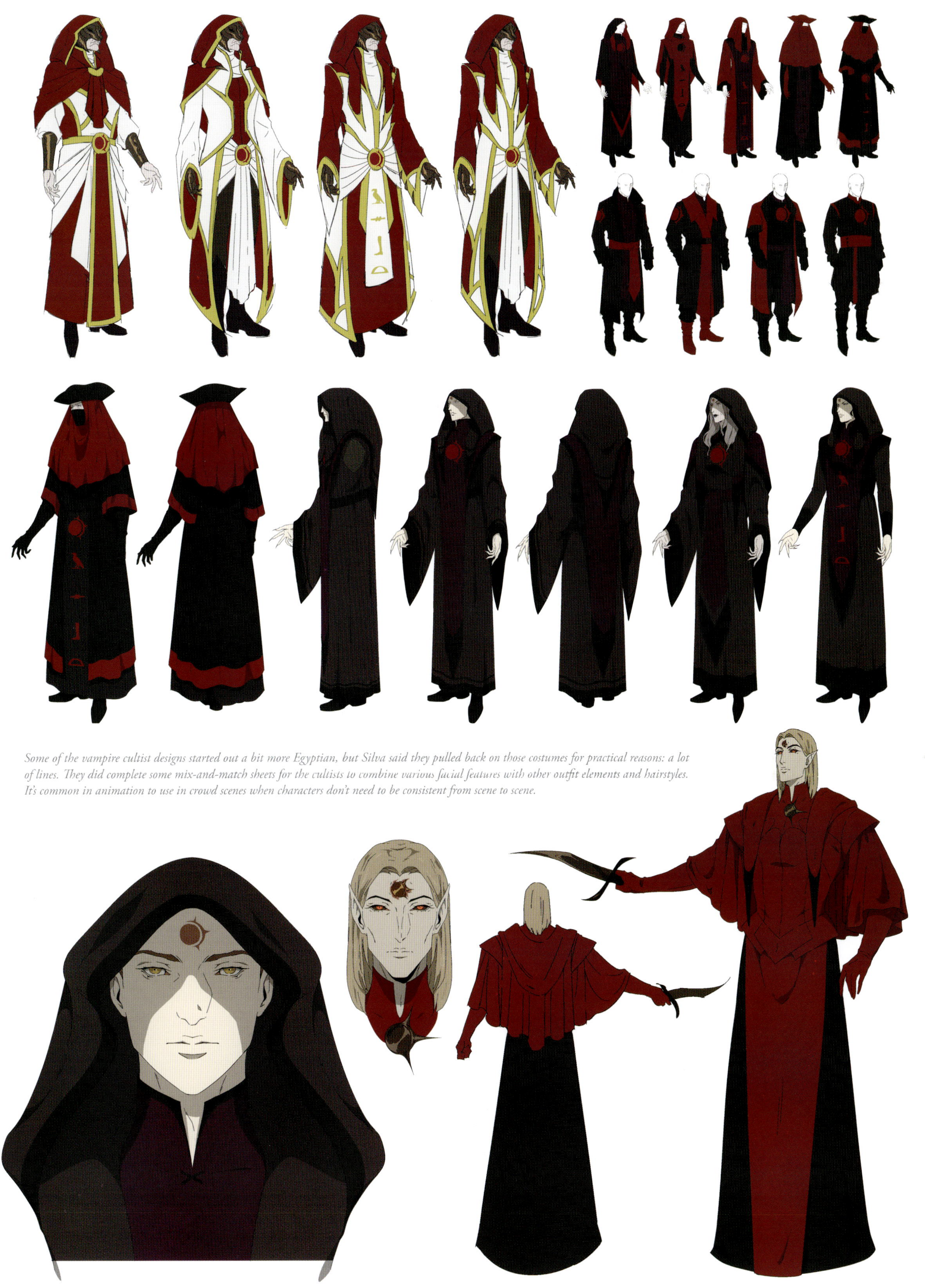

Some of the vampire cultist designs started out a bit more Egyptian, but Silva said they pulled back on those costumes for practical reasons: a lot of lines. They did complete some mix-and-match sheets for the cultists to combine various facial features with other outfit elements and hairstyles. It's common in animation to use in crowd scenes when characters don't need to be consistent from scene to scene.

Drolta Tzuentes

Drolta's story begins with her trying to elevate others to the position of her goddess, Sekhmet. She was the High Priestess in a temple before she turned herself into a vampire. Drolta deemed Erzsebet Báthory worthy and served her over the years as she rose in power. But after a resurrection as a Night Creature and vampire hybrid, Drolta eventually betrays Erzsebet and claims Sekhmet's power as her own.

Her constantly shifting plans and motivations lead Drolta through metamorphosis again and again. The antagonist's appearance changes each time in big, bombastic ways. Both Sam and Adam Deats tease that Drolta was one character where they had to give notes to dial it back. But nothing was off the table in initial ideas for her looks.

Art by Katie Silva.

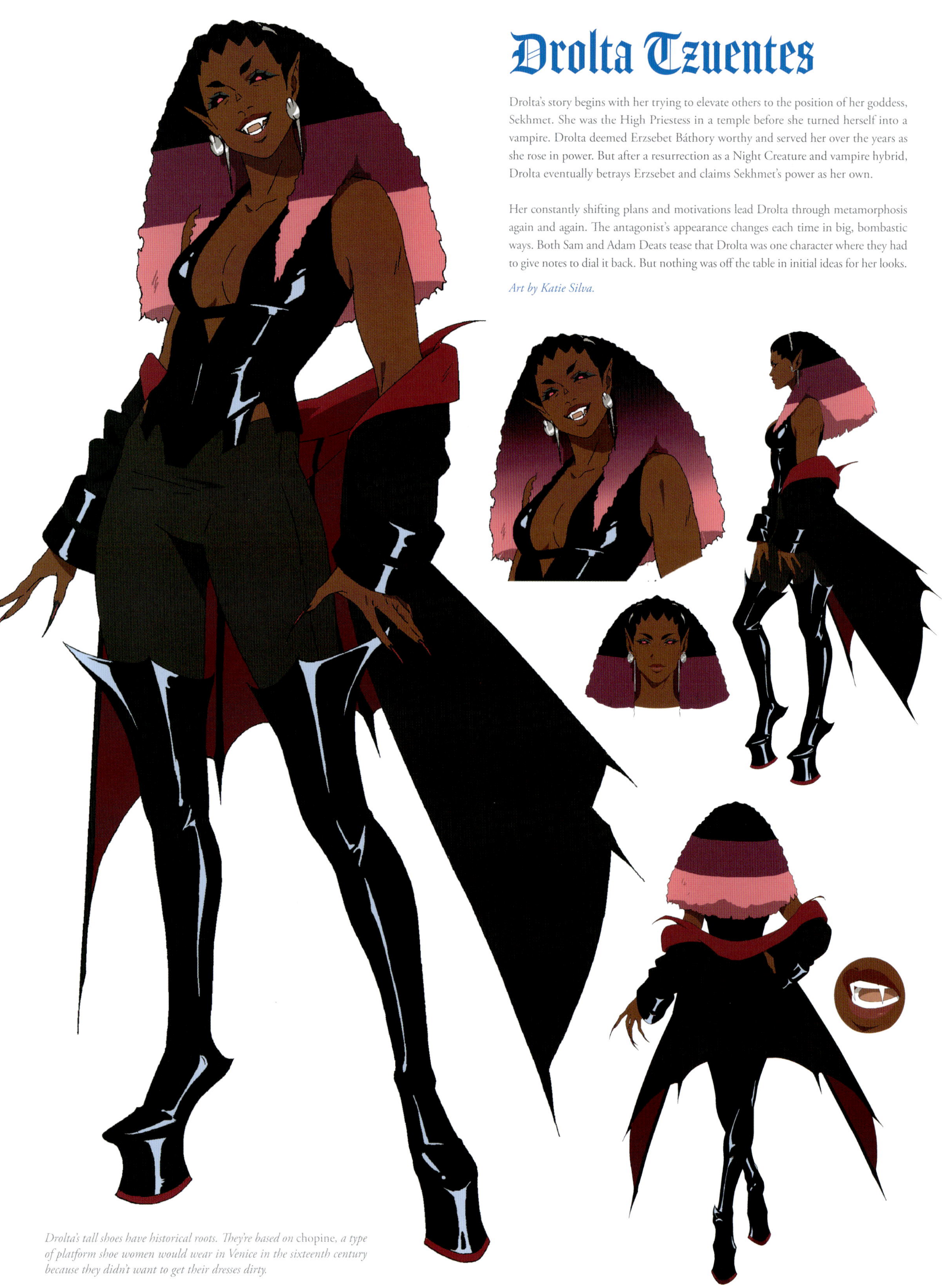

Drolta's tall shoes have historical roots. They're based on chopine, *a type of platform shoe women would wear in Venice in the sixteenth century because they didn't want to get their dresses dirty.*

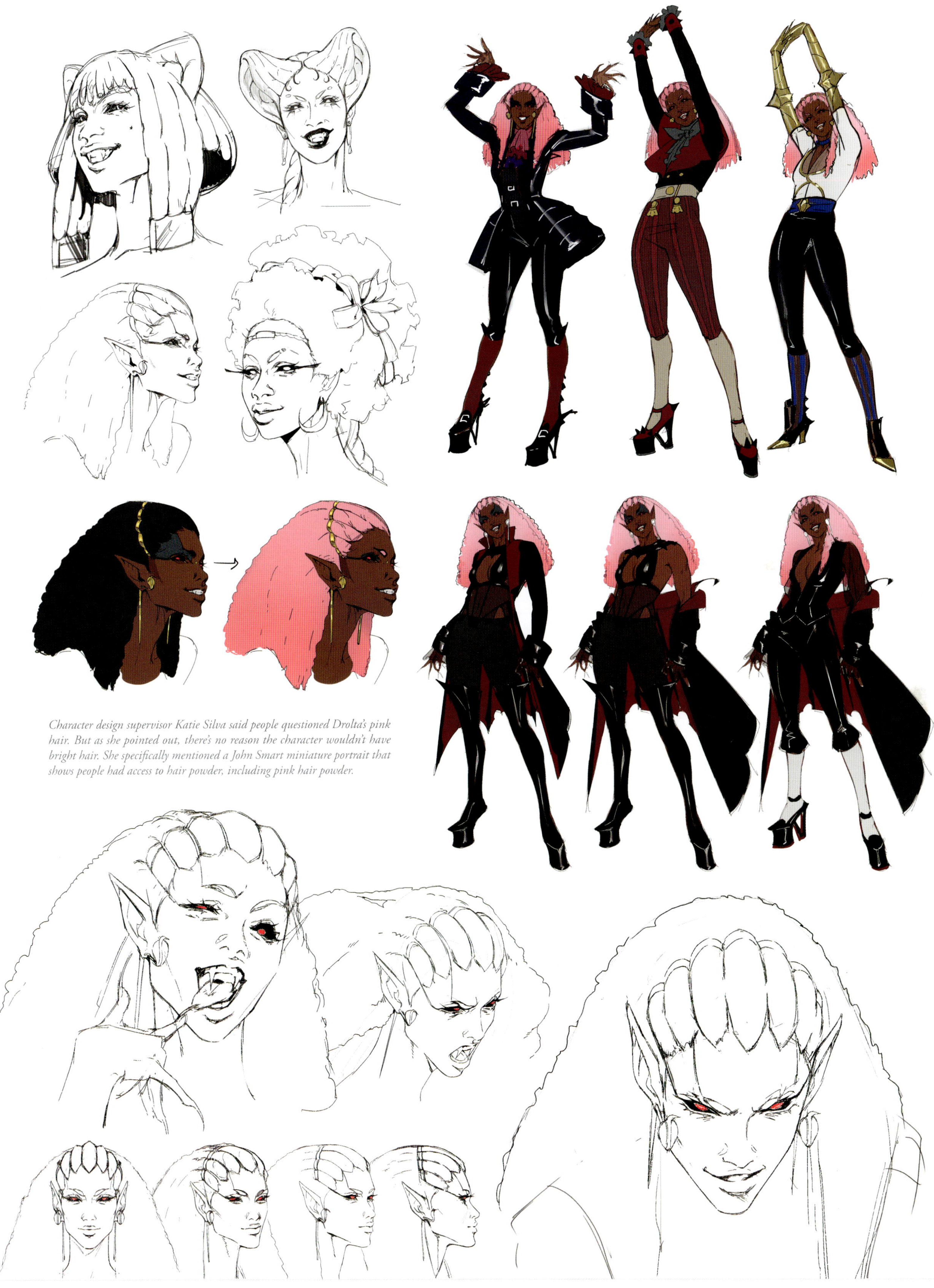

Character design supervisor Katie Silva said people questioned Drolta's pink hair. But as she pointed out, there's no reason the character wouldn't have bright hair. She specifically mentioned a John Smart miniature portrait that shows people had access to hair powder, including pink hair powder.

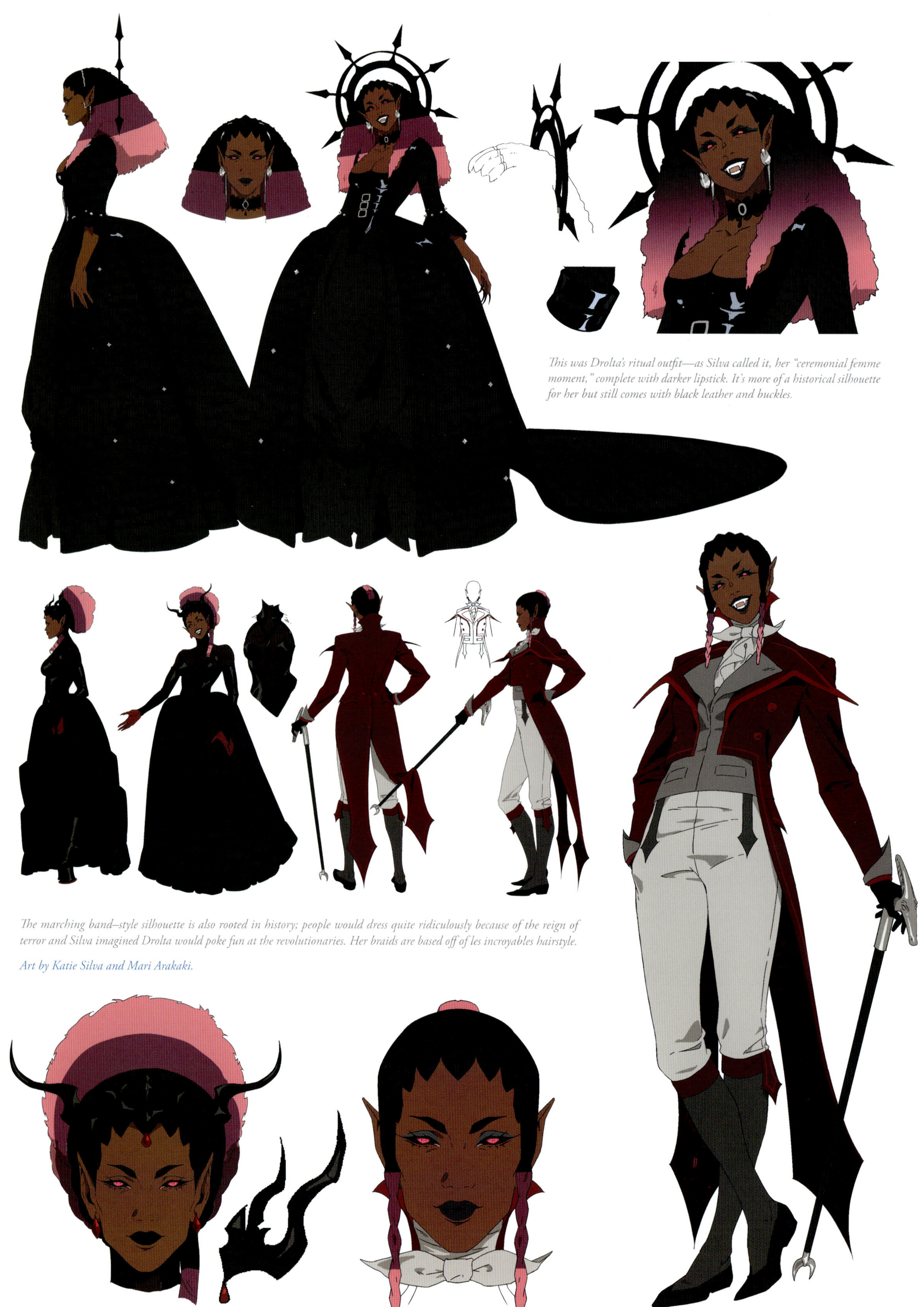

This was Drolta's ritual outfit—as Silva called it, her "ceremonial femme moment," complete with darker lipstick. It's more of a historical silhouette for her but still comes with black leather and buckles.

The marching band–style silhouette is also rooted in history; people would dress quite ridiculously because of the reign of terror and Silva imagined Drolta would poke fun at the revolutionaries. Her braids are based off of les incroyables hairstyle.

Art by Katie Silva and Mari Arakaki.

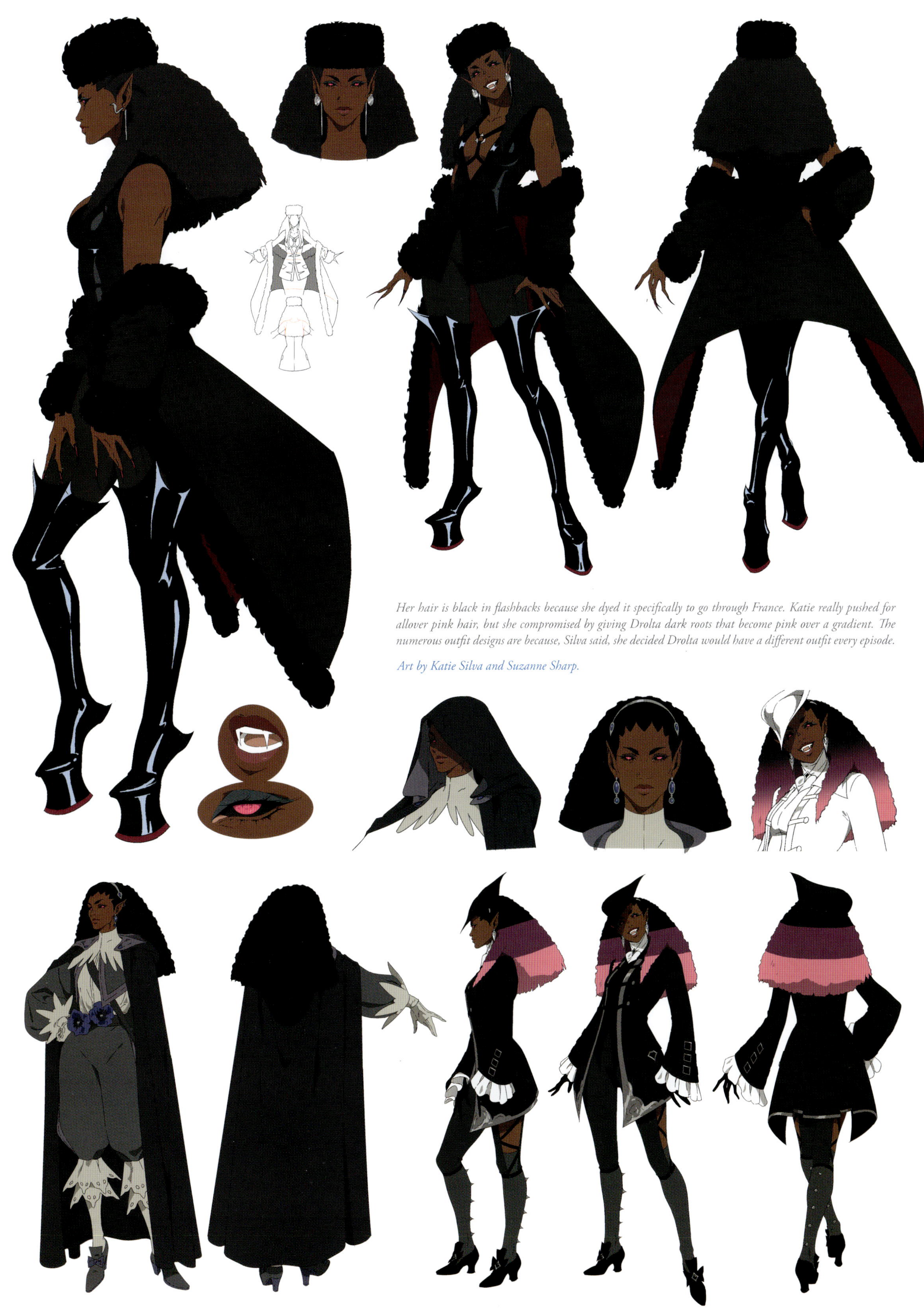

Her hair is black in flashbacks because she dyed it specifically to go through France. Katie really pushed for allover pink hair, but she compromised by giving Drolta dark roots that become pink over a gradient. The numerous outfit designs are because, Silva said, she decided Drolta would have a different outfit every episode.

Art by Katie Silva and Suzanne Sharp.

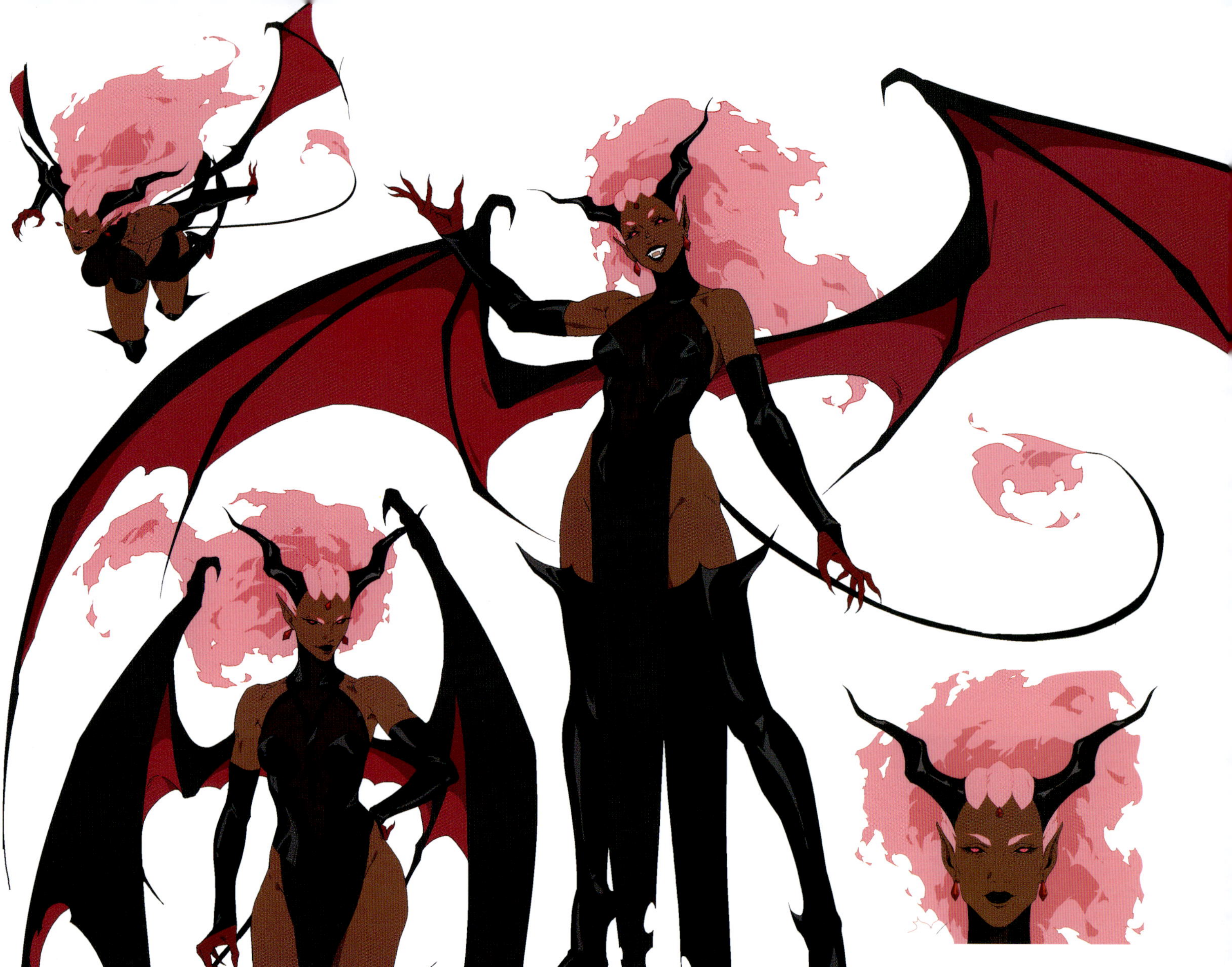

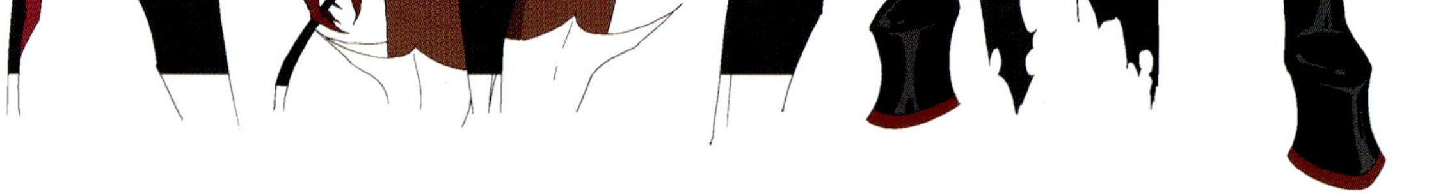

Drolta's hair got to go full pink in her succubus form. It has a less-defined shape aside from the pieces that cover her forehead.

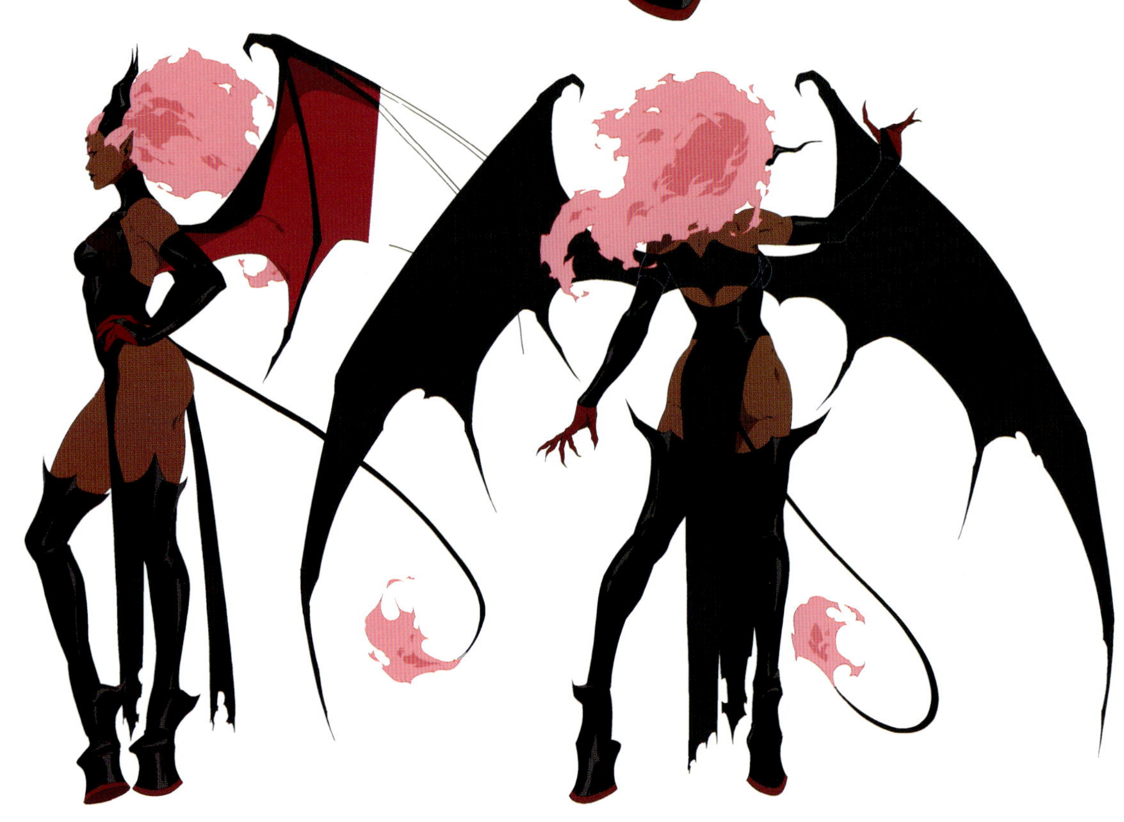

SUCCUBUS FORM

Katie said Drolta started out with a different role in the story and then became a succubus-type character. That meant she was leaning into more sexy, powerful looks from early design stages. For this specific version of Drolta, they did a bunch of different designs and then realized they should have her rip off the sides of her skirt from her ballroom outfit.

With this look, they played it up in the model sheets. They included a lot of different angles to show Drolta flying towards the screen and added extra poses to show what the outfit looks like from other perspectives. Silva said they could have just drawn her as a symmetrical mannequin, but she wanted the sheets to look fun.

Art by Katie Silva.

Storyboards by Chance Kubesh and Chansard Vincent.

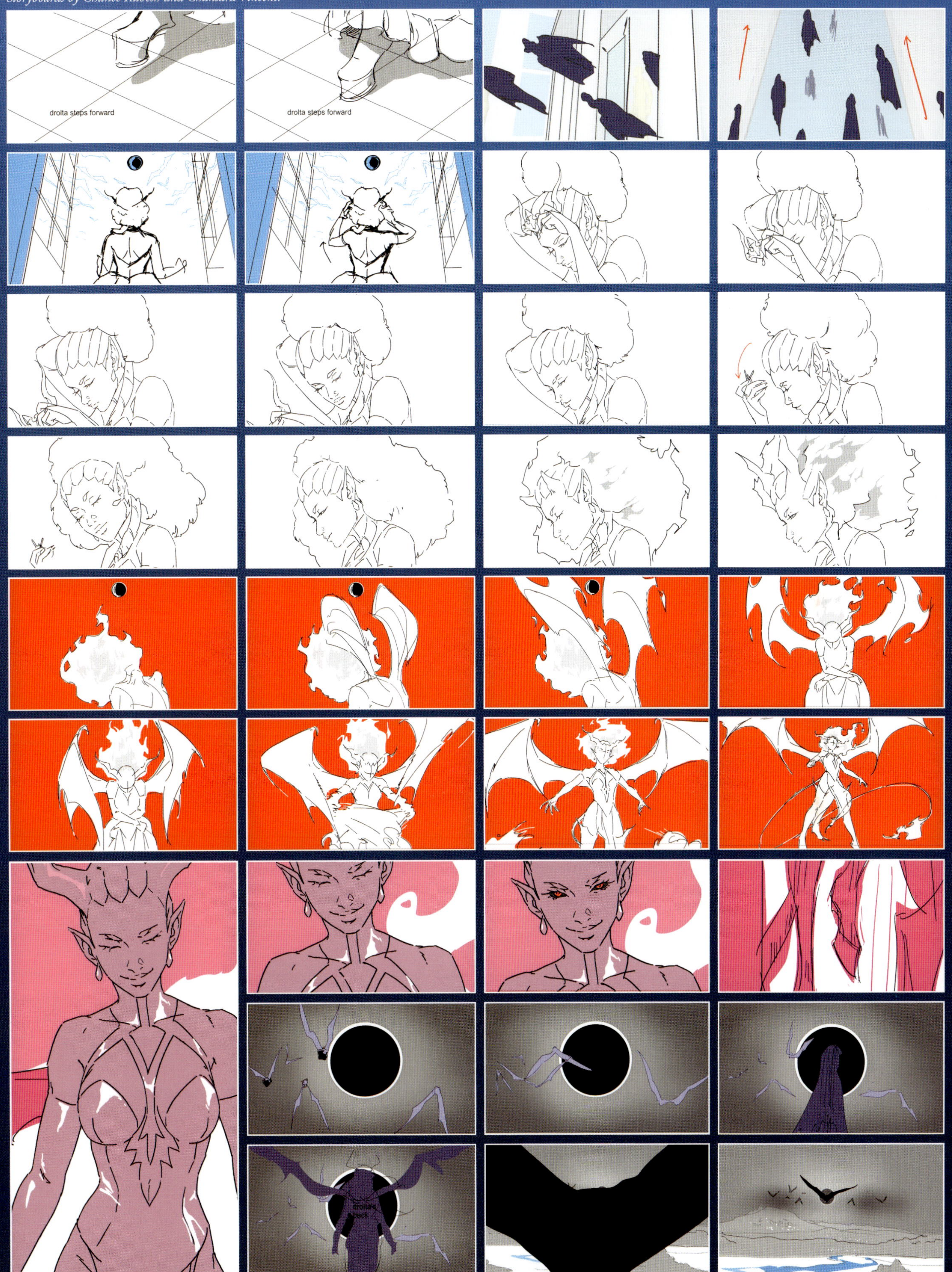

Drolta continues to transform throughout the series, and this scene illustrates an important part of her journey. Adam remembered they tweaked things in post to better serve the moment. He took what was there, sped some of it up, and then cut out parts of layers and turned them into objects that moved and flew by the camera really quickly. Sam recalled debating whether they would show the vampires flying away in human form or as bats: "I kept harping on how this is a vampire show—where're all the bats?"

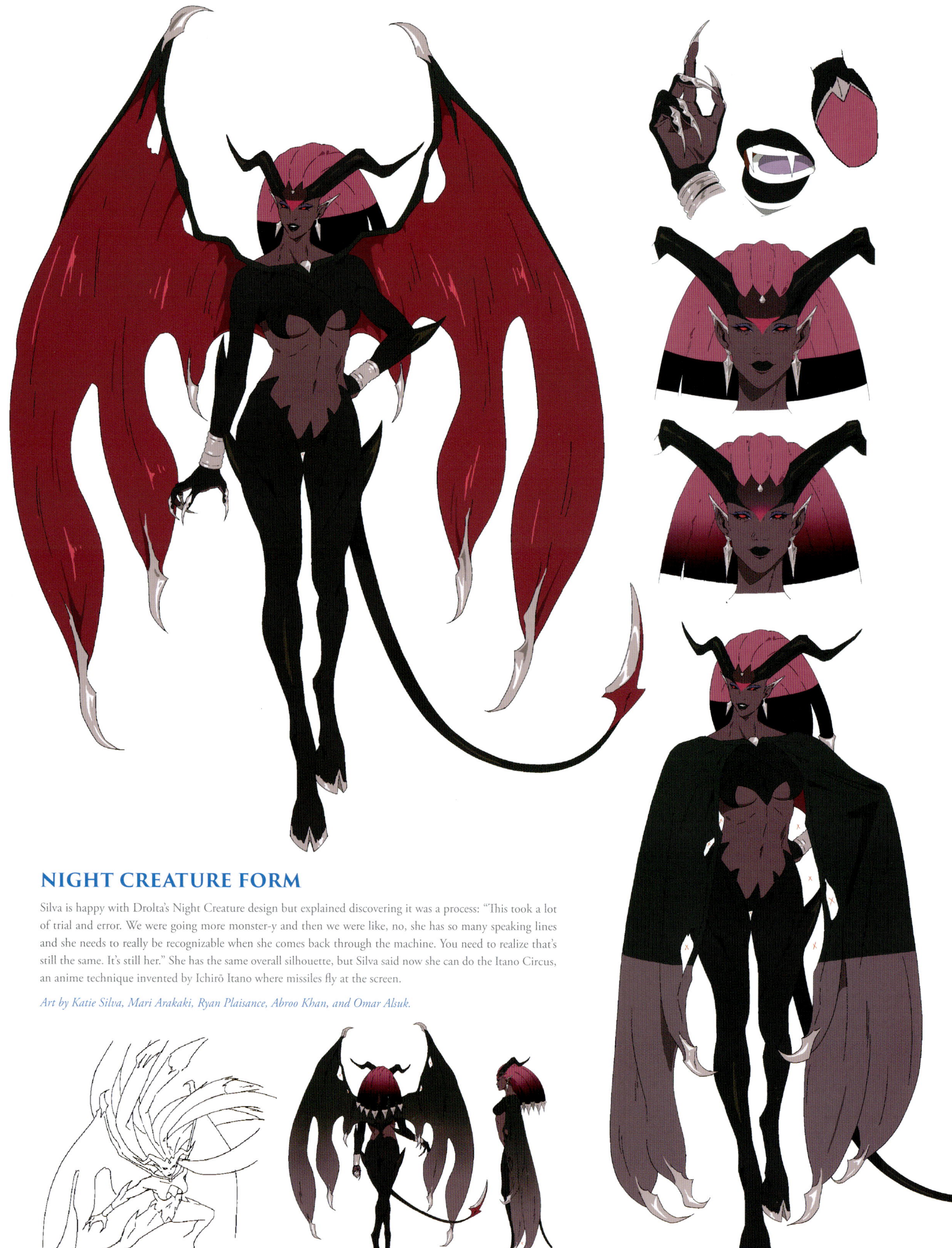

NIGHT CREATURE FORM

Silva is happy with Drolta's Night Creature design but explained discovering it was a process: "This took a lot of trial and error. We were going more monster-y and then we were like, no, she has so many speaking lines and she needs to really be recognizable when she comes back through the machine. You need to realize that's still the same. It's still her." She has the same overall silhouette, but Silva said now she can do the Itano Circus, an anime technique invented by Ichirō Itano where missiles fly at the screen.

Art by Katie Silva, Mari Arakaki, Ryan Plaisance, Abroo Khan, and Omar Alsuk.

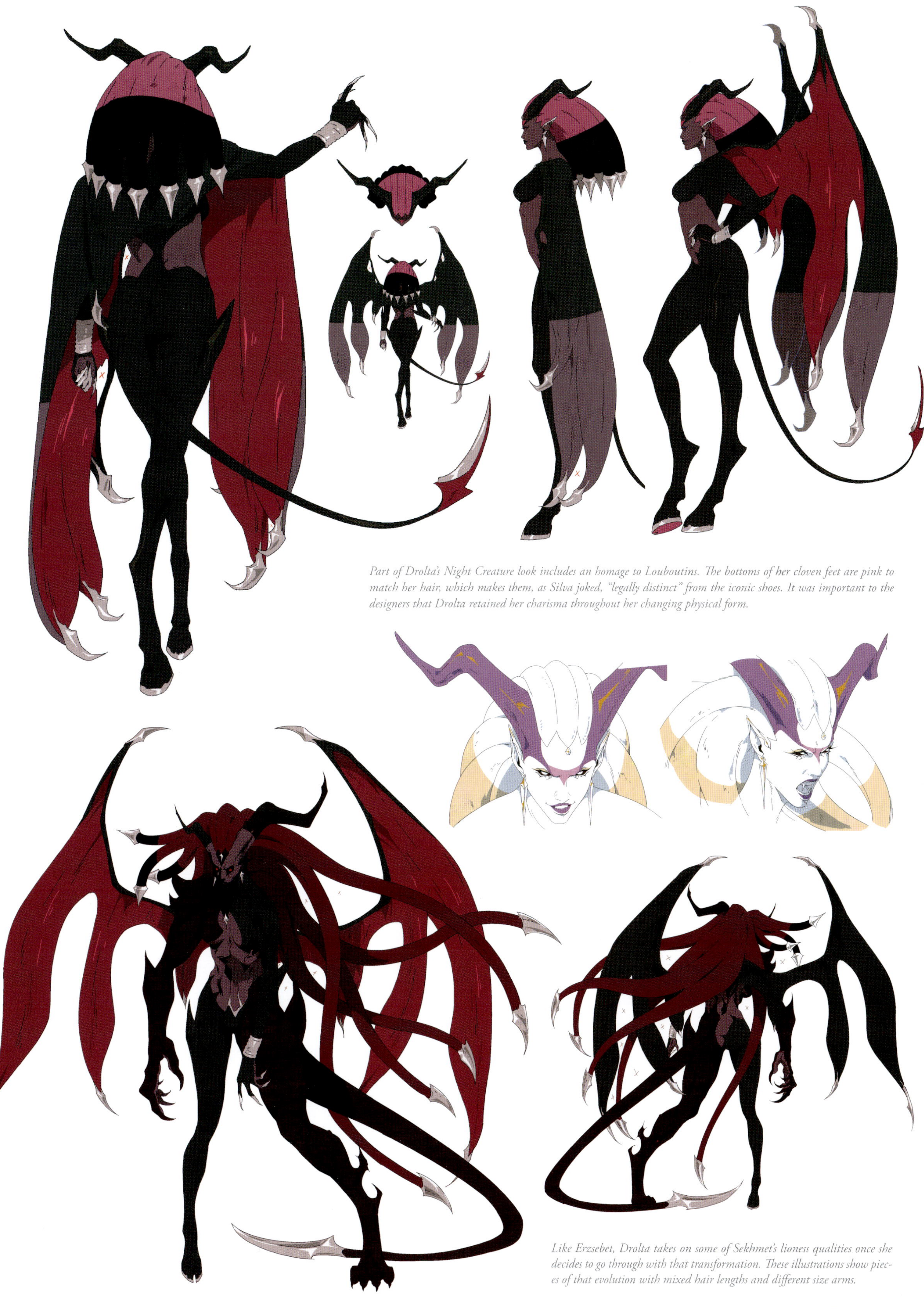

Part of Drolta's Night Creature look includes an homage to Louboutins. The bottoms of her cloven feet are pink to match her hair, which makes them, as Silva joked, "legally distinct" from the iconic shoes. It was important to the designers that Drolta retained her charisma throughout her changing physical form.

Like Erzsebet, Drolta takes on some of Sekhmet's lioness qualities once she decides to go through with that transformation. These illustrations show pieces of that evolution with mixed hair lengths and different size arms.

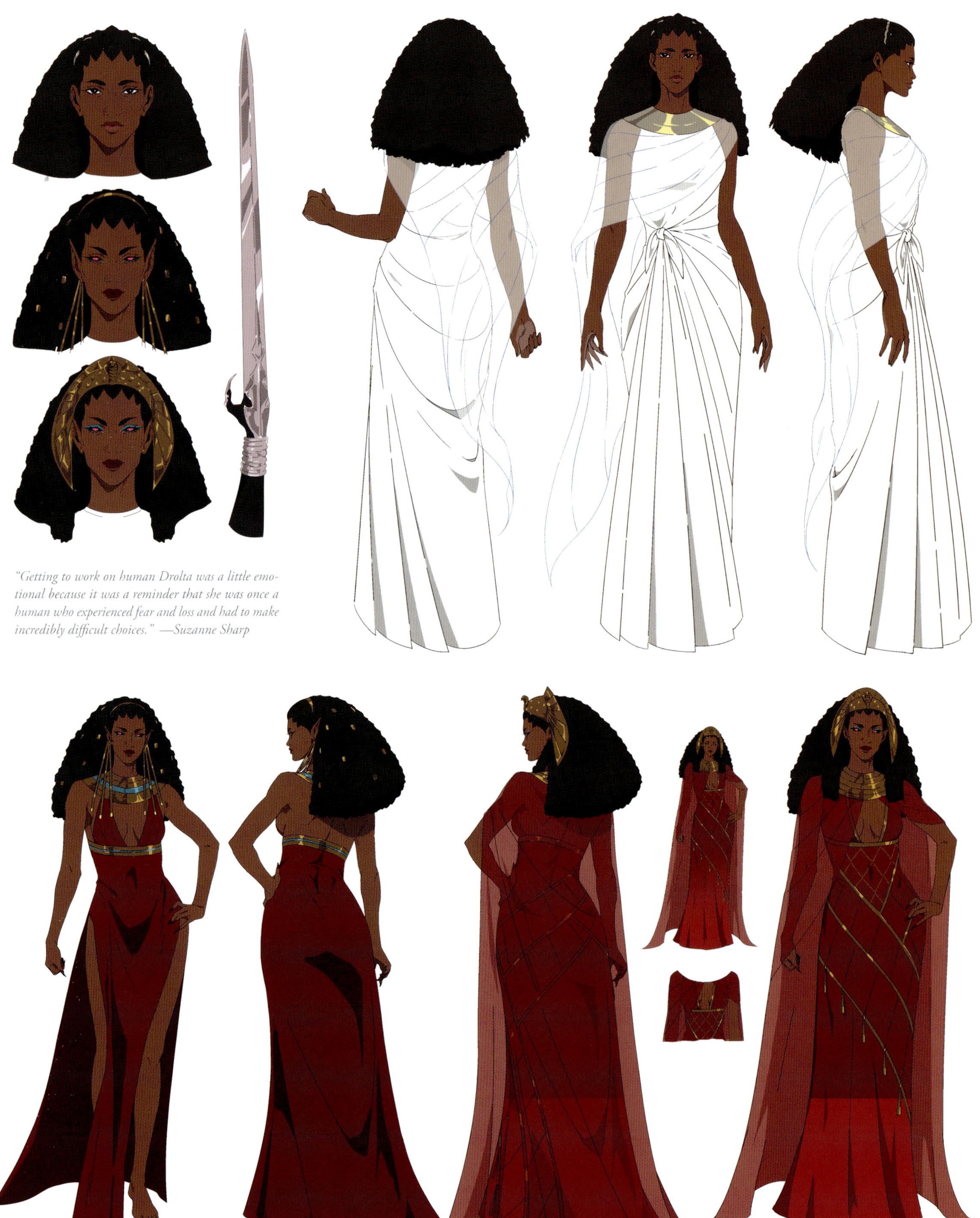

"Getting to work on human Drolta was a little emotional because it was a reminder that she was once a human who experienced fear and loss and had to make incredibly difficult choices." —Suzanne Sharp

HIGH PRIESTESS

Drolta was once a humble High Priestess trying her best to serve her chosen goddess, Sekhmet. Her temple was struck by tragedy when raiders invaded and killed her fellow worshipers. Feeling helpless in the wake of such an attack prompted Drolta to look at other opportunities for survival. The white robes were common for more everyday priestess duties, while the red look is ceremonial garb.

Art by Katie Silva, Lina Ngo, and Suzanne Sharp.

Sekhmet

The goddess Sekhmet is a continuous thread throughout the series, a driving factor in both Erzsebet's and Drolta's desire for power. Each of the women believe they are carrying out the goddess's utmost desire: to be resurrected in another vessel with all three pieces of her soul and reign from a position of power. When she finally appears as herself, it's not in a lioness form, but touches of a hunting carnivore are evident in her cat-like facial features. That lion connection is why she has pointed teeth on the top *and* bottom.

Art by Lina Ngo.

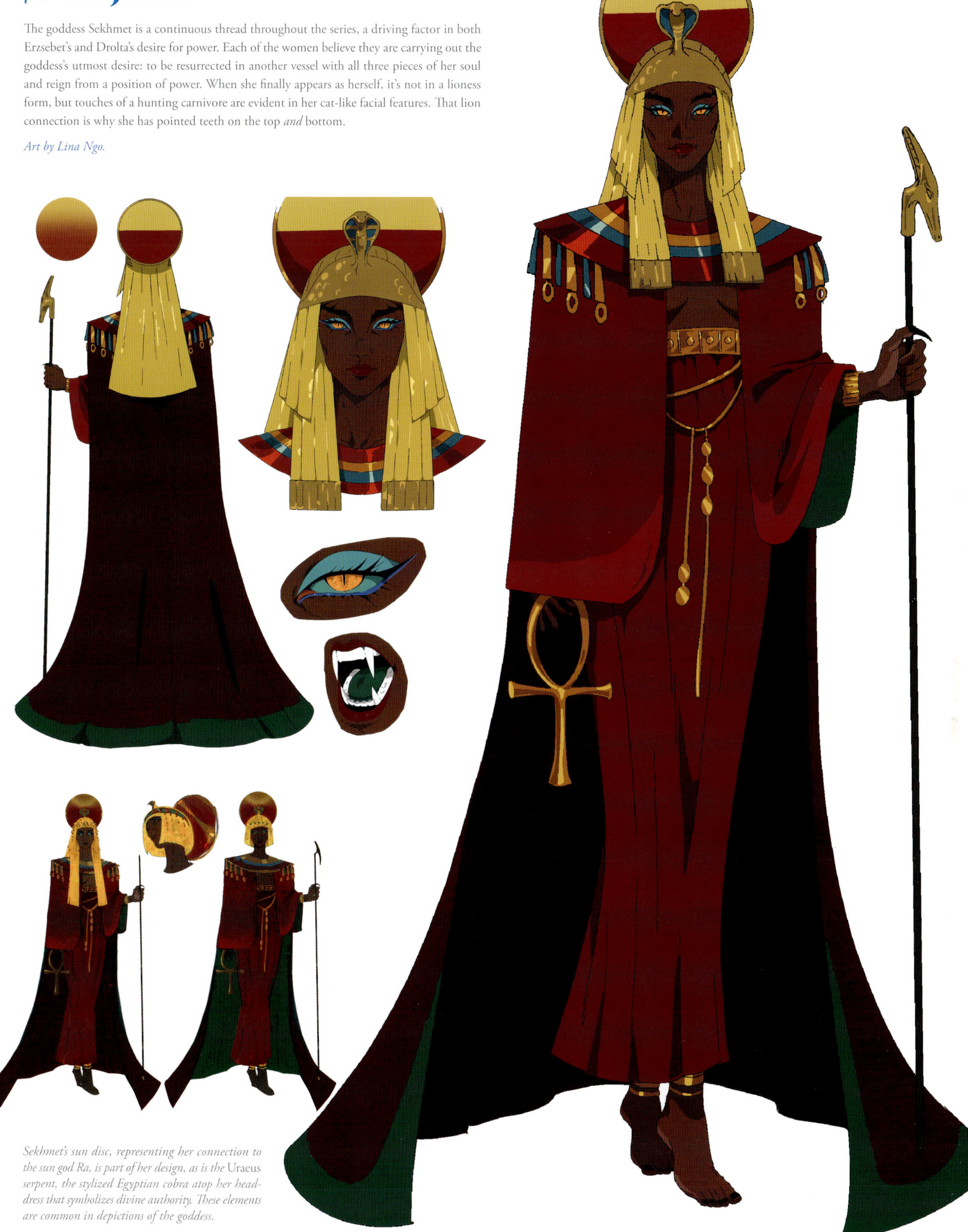

Sekhmet's sun disc, representing her connection to the sun god Ra, is part of her design, as is the Uraeus *serpent, the stylized Egyptian cobra atop her headdress that symbolizes divine authority. These elements are common in depictions of the goddess.*

Temple Vampires

After seeing the other followers of Sekhmet murdered, Drolta uses her new vampiric abilities to create an immortal cult. She transforms humans into temple guards and priestesses, ensuring that they can protect both the temple *and* themselves from any attempts at human-inflicted harm.

The deep maroon visible in this design ties visually to Sekhmet herself and her followers; we see the hue in Drolta's vampire high priestess dress as well as when the goddess possesses Annette.

Art by Mari Arakaki.

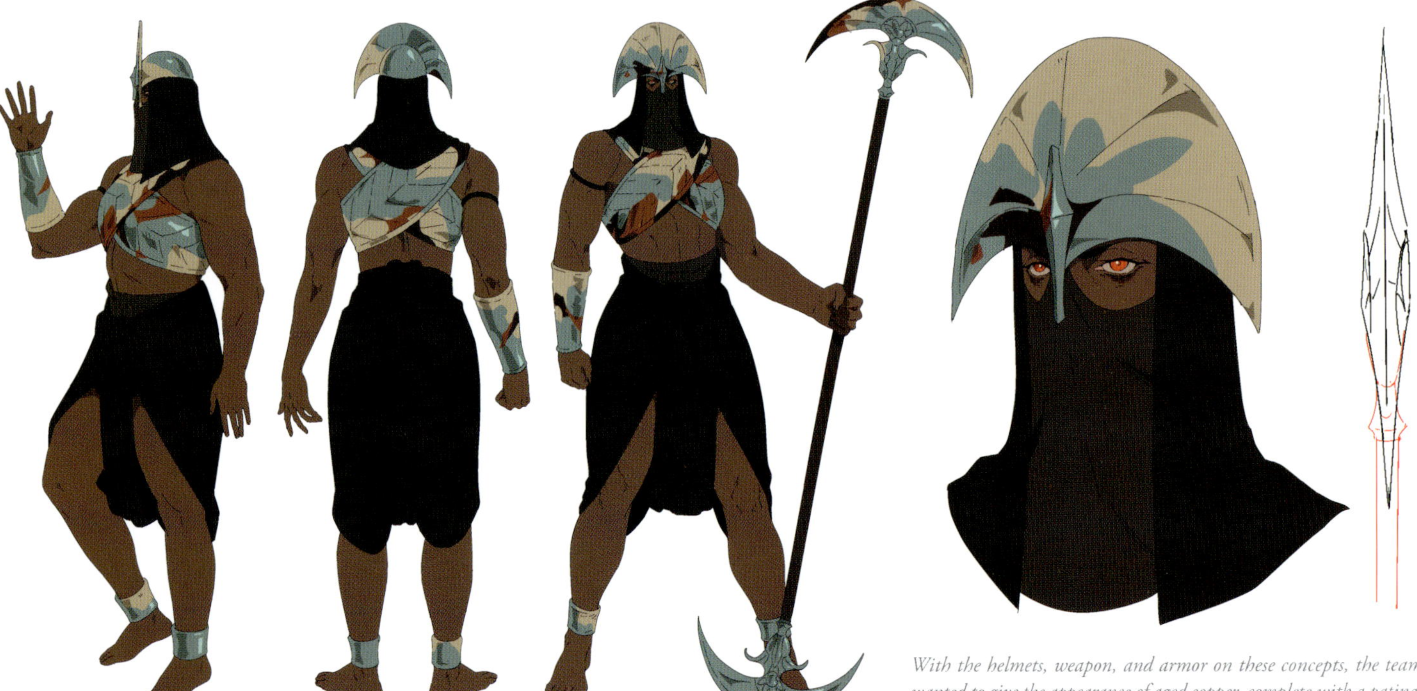

With the helmets, weapon, and armor on these concepts, the team wanted to give the appearance of aged copper, complete with a patina.

Vampire Priestesses

With a new lease on life, Drolta puts aside her simple white priestess robes and seems to relish her position more. She dons red as the high vampire priestess of Sekhmet's temple, so the priestesses that follow her should have a similar style. They, like Drolta, wear deep red robes—red, perhaps to emphasize the less innocent purpose of their temple. The character artists also experimented with giving the priestesses Erzsebet's brand.

Art by Katie Silva, Ryan Plaisance, and Omar Alsuk.

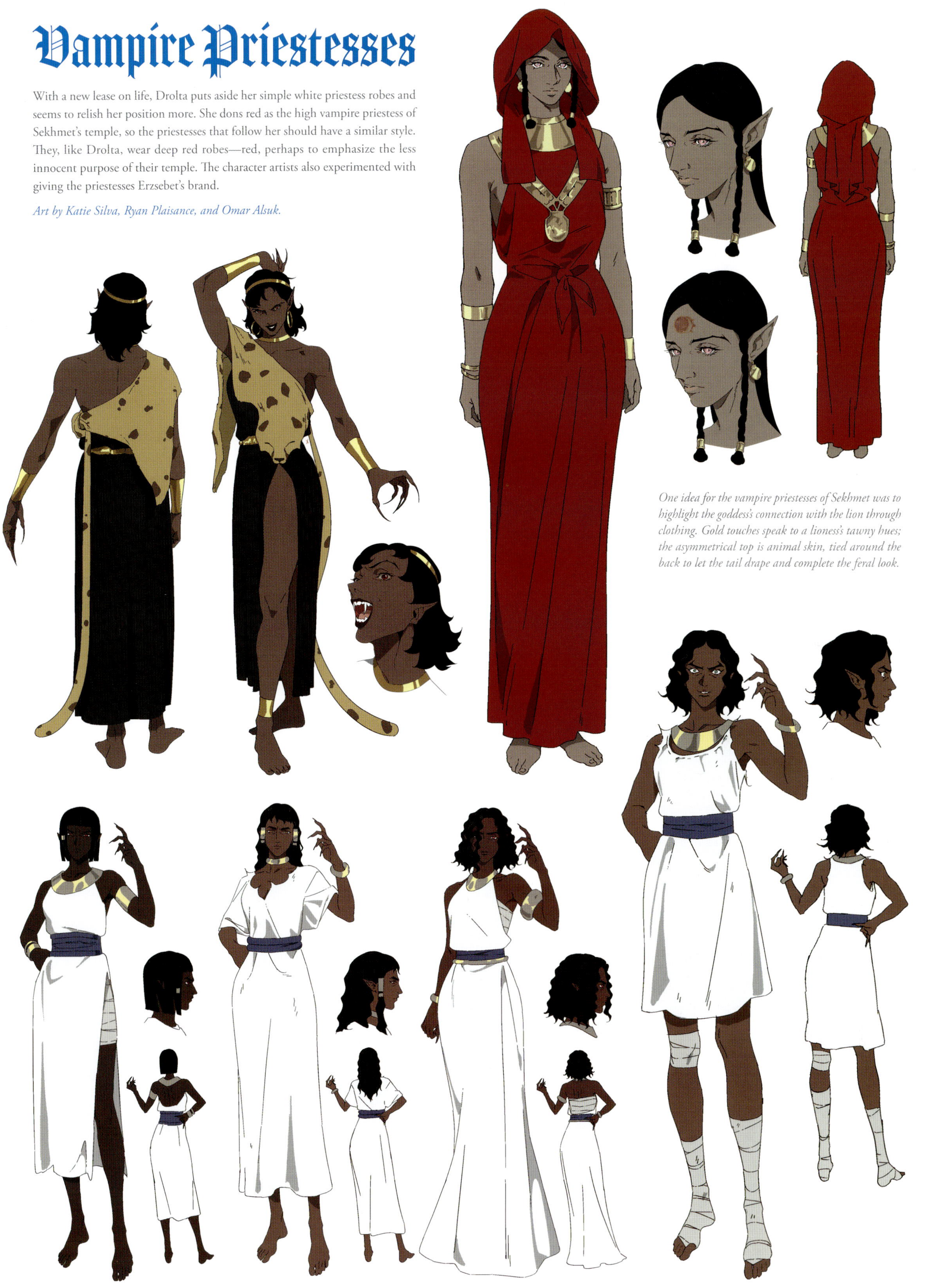

One idea for the vampire priestesses of Sekhmet was to highlight the goddess's connection with the lion through clothing. Gold touches speak to a lioness's tawny hues; the asymmetrical top is animal skin, tied around the back to let the tail drape and complete the feral look.

Abbot Emmanuel

Not all enemies reveal their nature with fangs and ostentatious clothing; some hide among the everyday, present and insidious. Emmanuel believes that the revolution endangers the institutions that he holds sacred, and his questionable decisions are all made in service of preserving the church's power. To him, the ends justify the means, which include trading the souls of himself and his knights to Mephistopheles for the dark power to create an army of Night Creatures, or bargaining with Erzsebet and the vampires. Emmanuel plans to betray Erzsebet, but the vampire queen is ultimately far too powerful.

His face is austere and gaunt, his clothing simple but with more ornate touches than warrior monks such as Mizrak. The Abbot's story is one of contradictions, as he claims a holy path but sacrifices his former lover Tera to Erzsebet and in doing so, betrays his daughter Maria.

Art by Samuel Deats and Katie Silva, with Stephanie McCrea Rainosek.
Book design by Suzanne Sharp.

Art by Suzanne Sharp, Mari Arakaki, and Katie Silva.

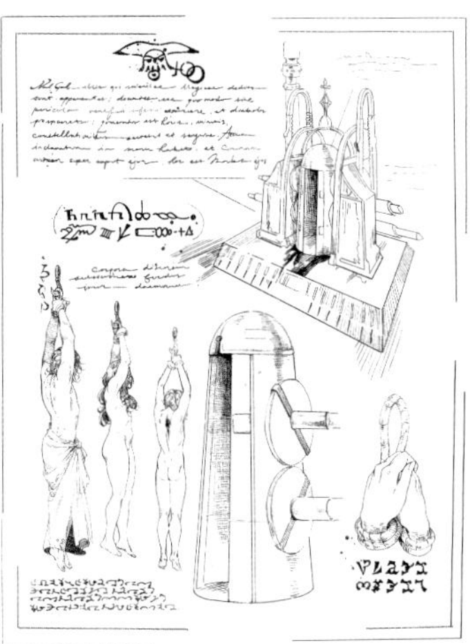

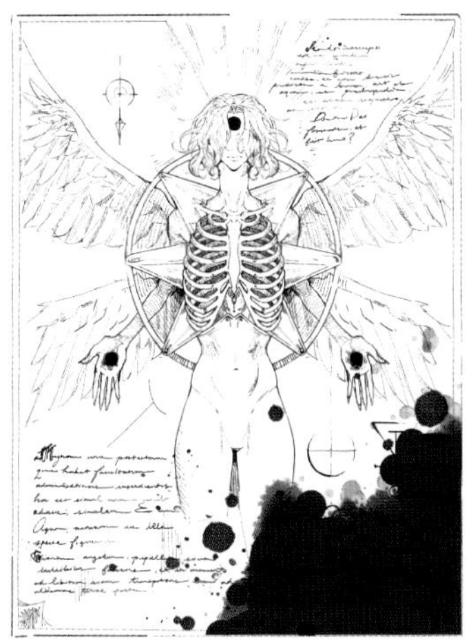

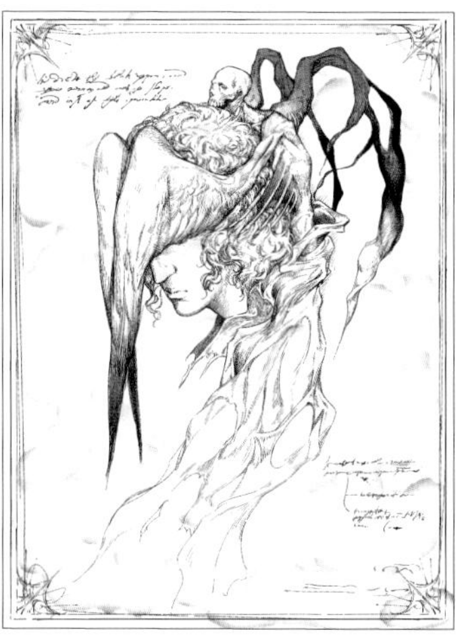

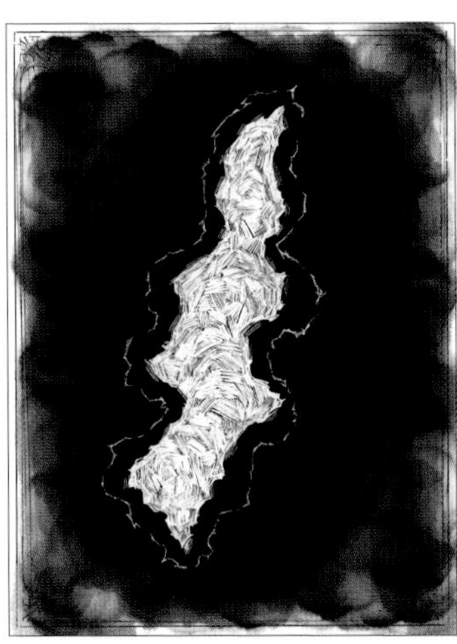

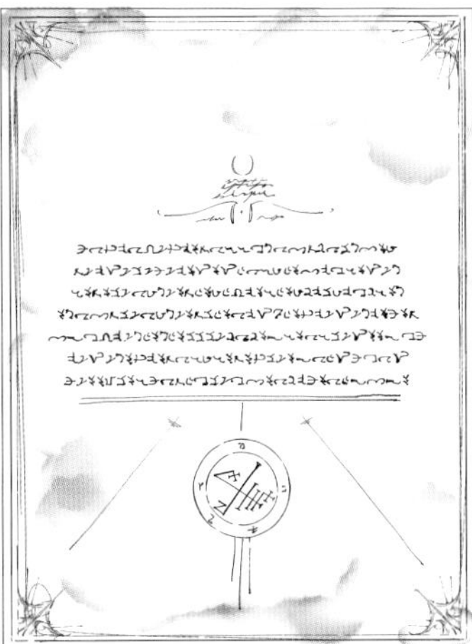

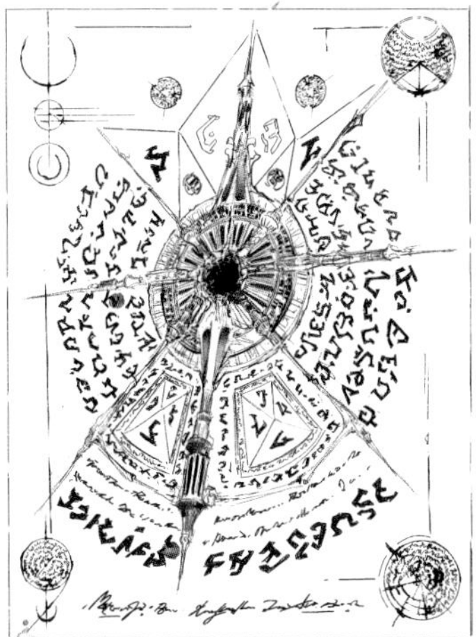

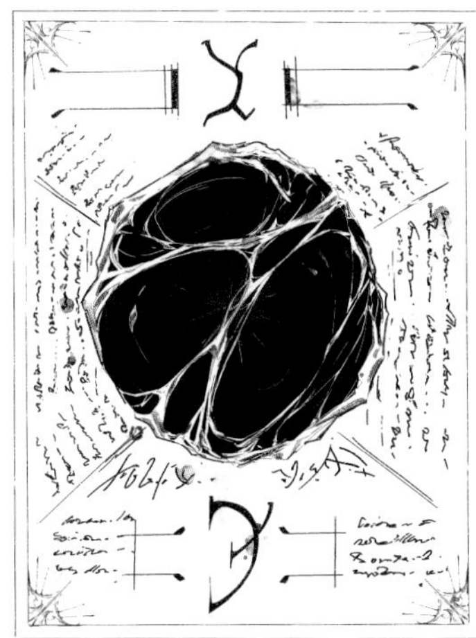

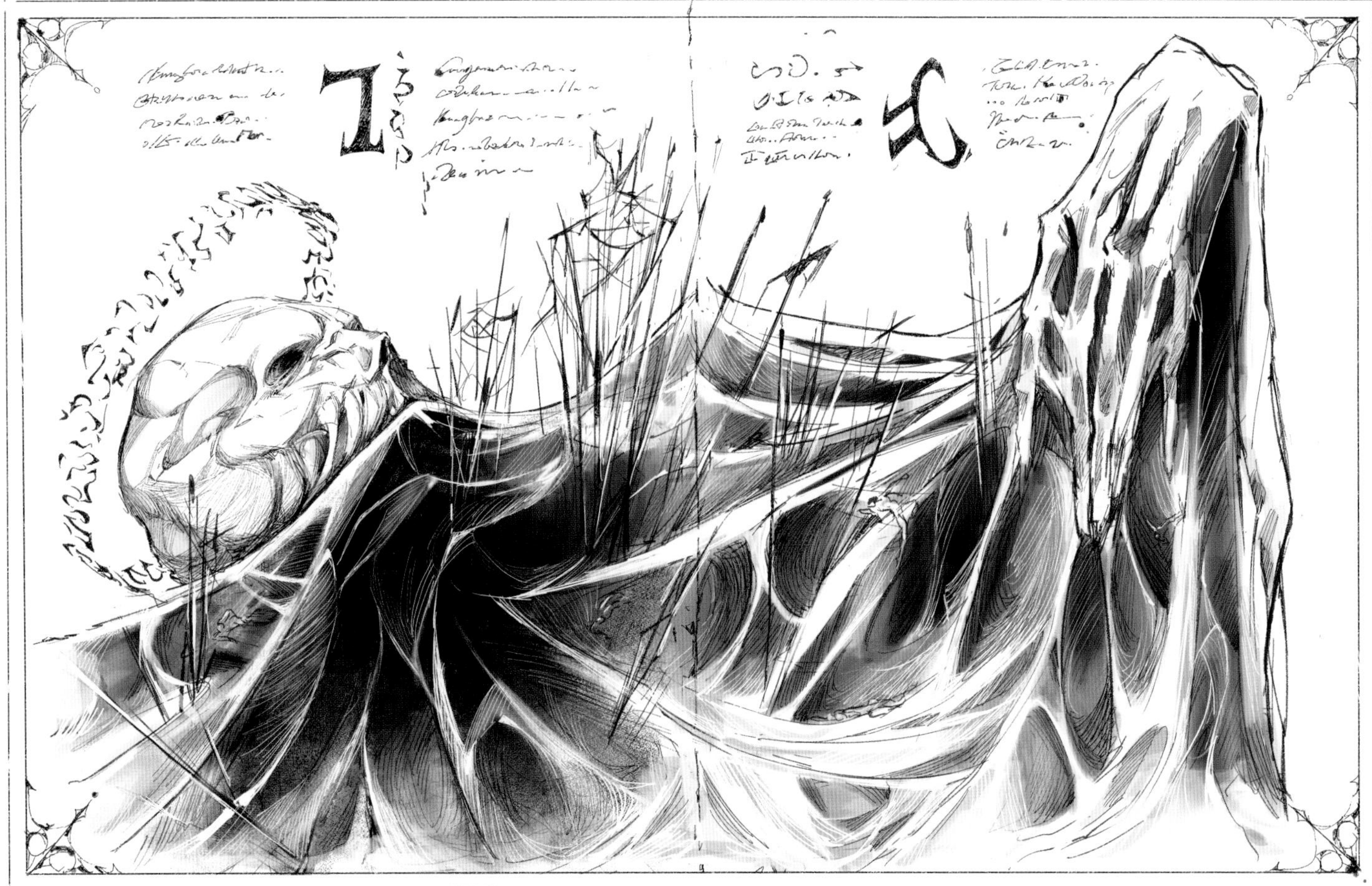

Abbot Emmanuel references an Enochian spell book to become the Forgemaster, using the Infernal Machine to create Night Creatures. The interior features crude instructions and mysterious notes. It shows plans for the machine, of which there were numerous iterations, and hints at the process. But mostly, Adam noted, they didn't give specifics for what the book should include but vibes. They wanted it to be cryptic and creepy and to give the artists creative freedom to play around and keep things vague so the contents of the book wouldn't "break" anything or have details the story would later be beholden to.

Night Creatures

The way the Night Creatures are made in *Castlevania: Nocturne* is different than in the original *Castlevania* animated series. Each Forgemaster has their own style, and Abbot Emmanuel is learning the process from a book. Katie Silva explained that for this series, they wanted the designs to be less scary-and-gross and more scary-but-elegant—and most importantly, human. Keeping sight of that aspect was important for the designs.

"As you're learning, they're not randomized souls that get placed into this machine. This machine seems to call back the individual person," Silva said. "If it's a character that gets transformed into a Night Creature in the story, they retain a bit more of their humanity."

Art by Mari Arakaki.

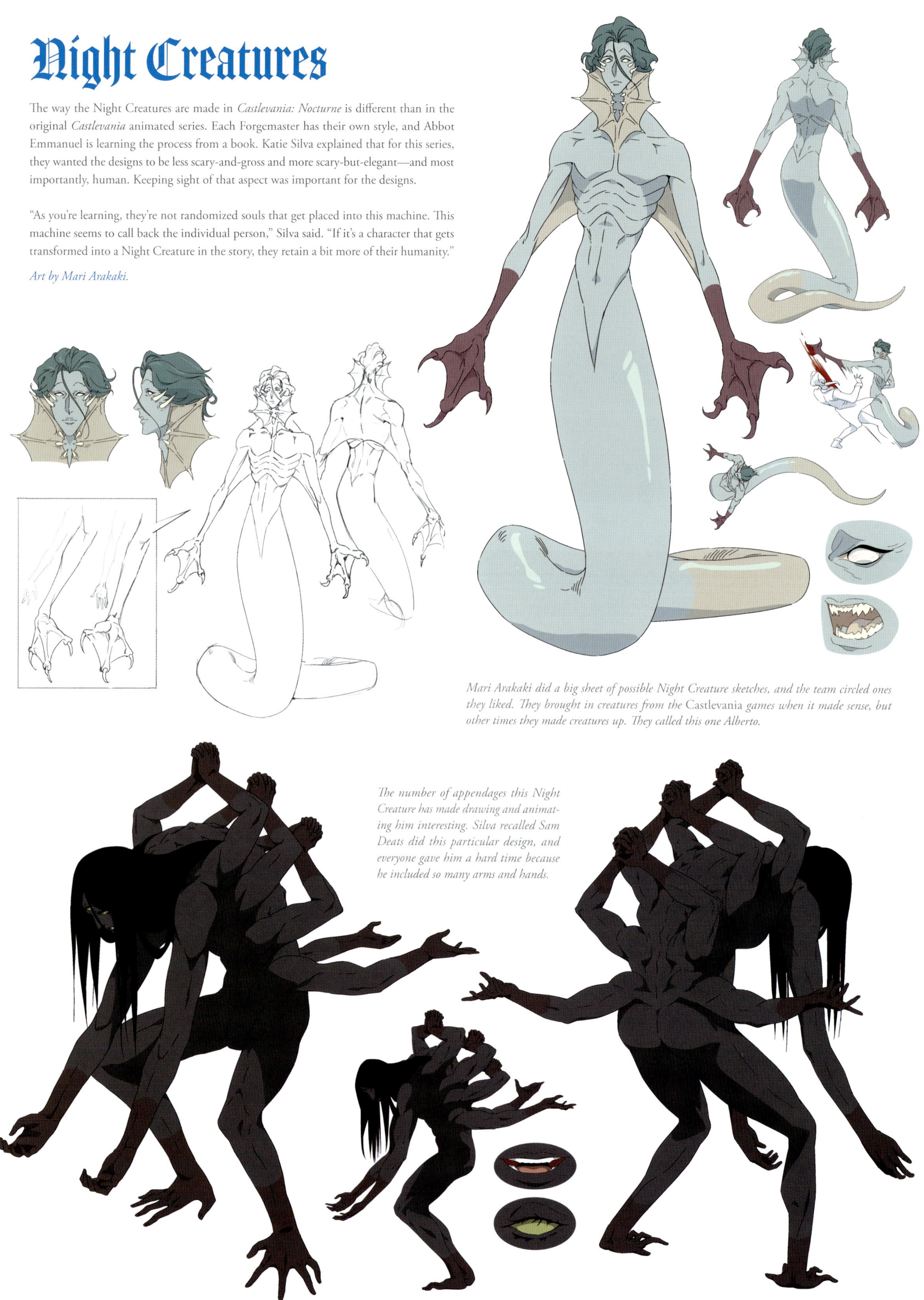

Mari Arakaki did a big sheet of possible Night Creature sketches, and the team circled ones they liked. They brought in creatures from the Castlevania *games when it made sense, but other times they made creatures up. They called this one Alberto.*

The number of appendages this Night Creature has made drawing and animating him interesting. Silva recalled Sam Deats did this particular design, and everyone gave him a hard time because he included so many arms and hands.

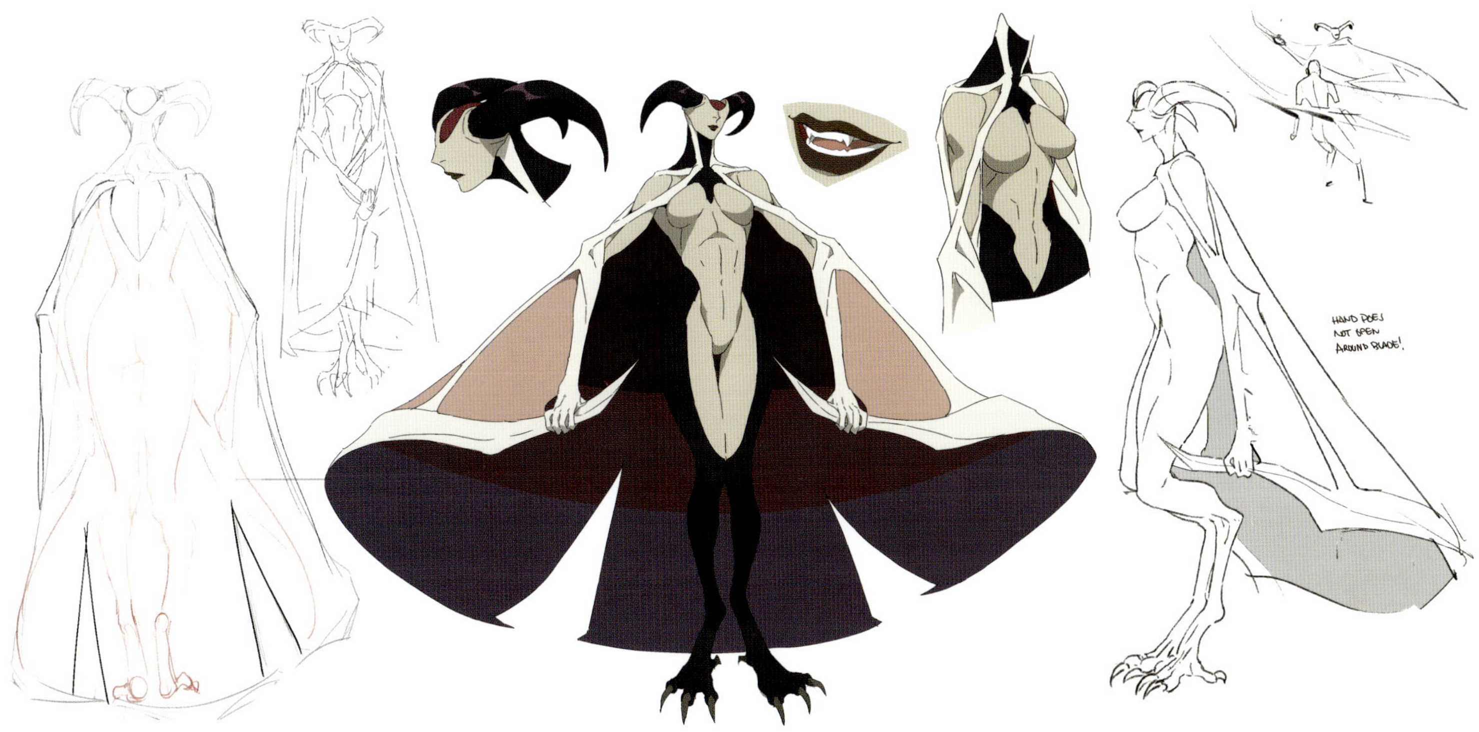

While the artists made sure to stay homed in on the human aspects of each Night Creature, they also kept one foot firmly in the realm of creepy. Silva noted sometimes it could be as easy as covering someone's eyes or mouth, taking away the mouth, or putting a head or a hand in a place those body parts don't traditionally appear.

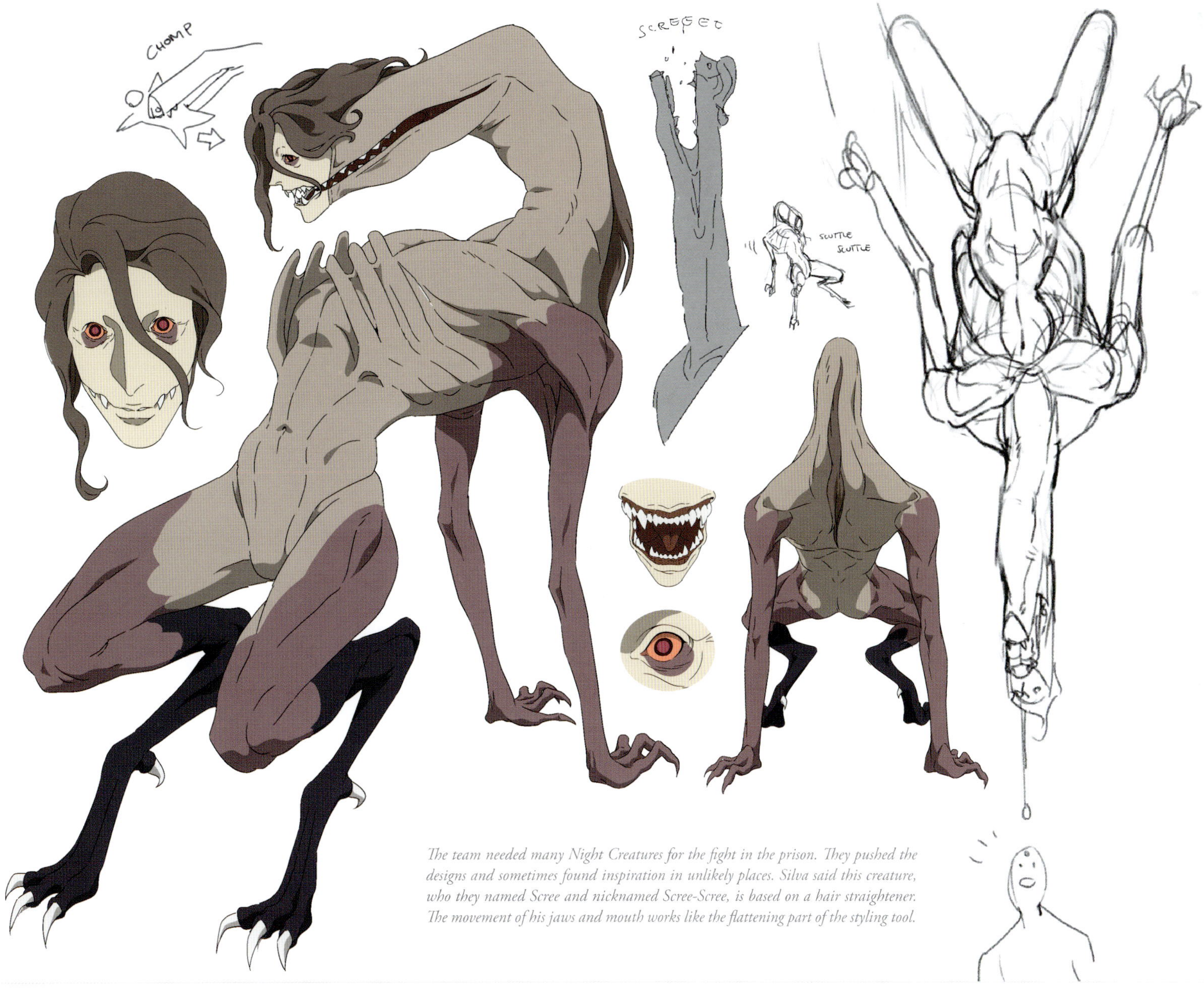

The team needed many Night Creatures for the fight in the prison. They pushed the designs and sometimes found inspiration in unlikely places. Silva said this creature, who they named Scree and nicknamed Scree-Scree, is based on a hair straightener. The movement of his jaws and mouth works like the flattening part of the styling tool.

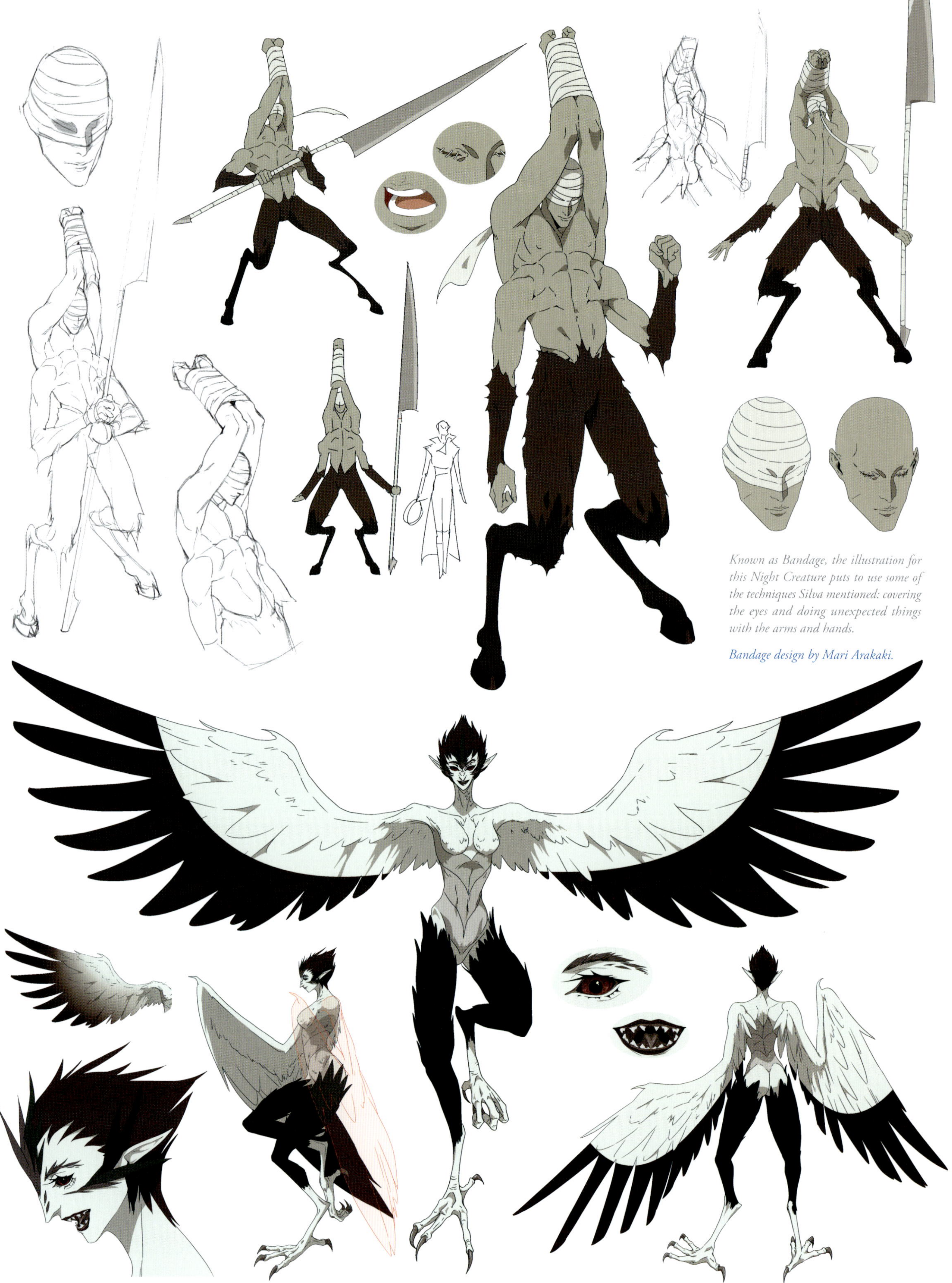

Known as Bandage, the illustration for this Night Creature puts to use some of the techniques Silva mentioned: covering the eyes and doing unexpected things with the arms and hands.

Bandage design by Mari Arakaki.

Incorporating elements from animals gave the artists another way to add diversity to their Night Creature sketches. This design brings in the traits of a bird, from the feathered haunches to feet with talons. Putting the bird-like features onto a human face added an unexpected kind of beauty to this Night Creature.

Harpy design by Samuel Deats with Stephanie McCrea Rainosek.

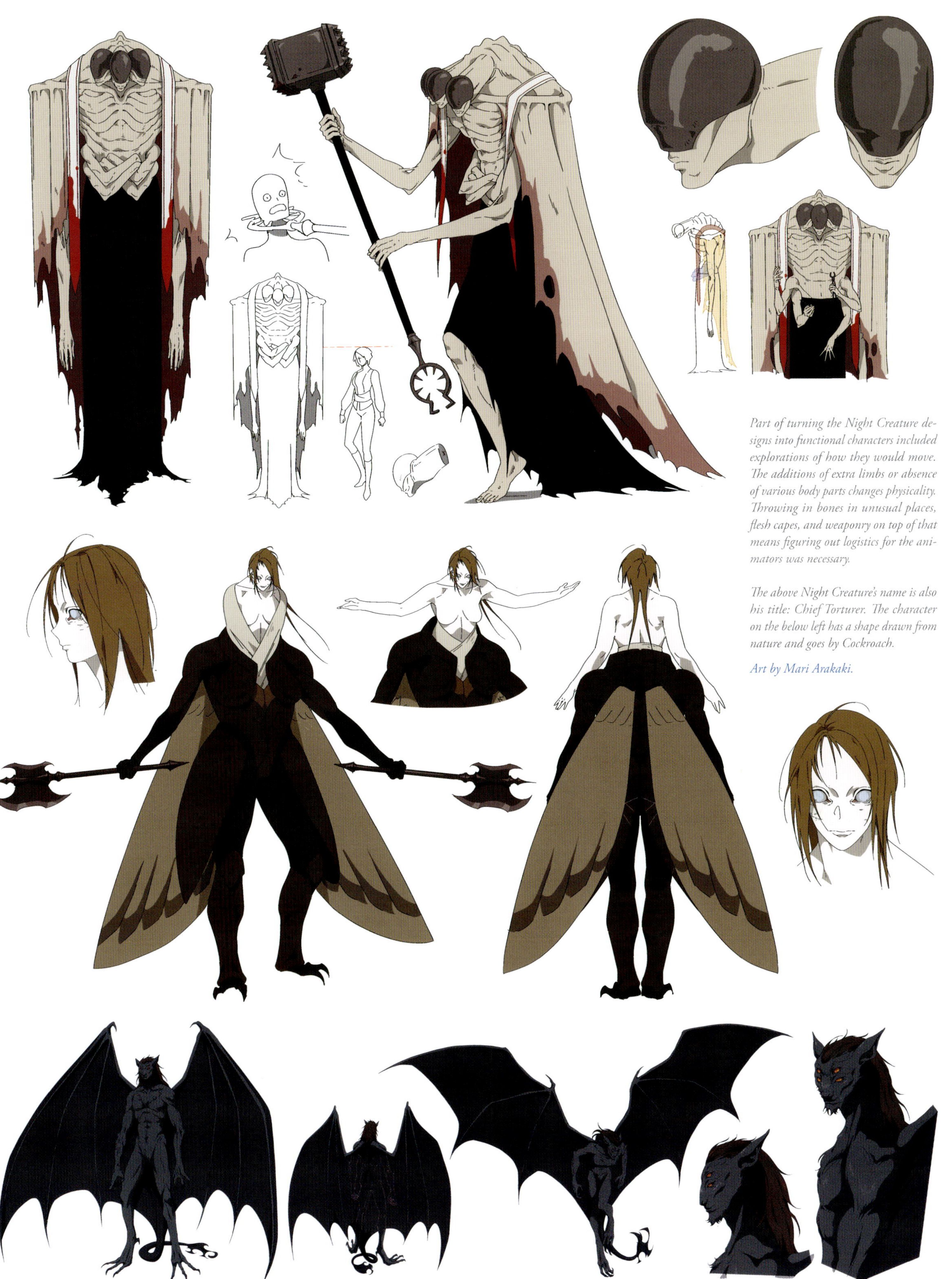

Part of turning the Night Creature designs into functional characters included explorations of how they would move. The additions of extra limbs or absence of various body parts changes physicality. Throwing in bones in unusual places, flesh capes, and weaponry on top of that means figuring out logistics for the animators was necessary.

The above Night Creature's name is also his title: Chief Torturer. The character on the below left has a shape drawn from nature and goes by Cockroach.

Art by Mari Arakaki.

Bats are sprinkled through Nocturne, *but usually as an alternate form for the vampires. This Night Creature's look brings angular bat wings and ears to a face with eyes almost like a fly's.*

Two other approaches for making a creature instantly creepy: extra teeth and long fingers ending in claws. Both additions work to great effect for this Night Creature. It also has an unusual profile and a hole in the side of its mouth; the green blocks behind the face on the model sheet show the animators where to leave gaps.

Art by Chance Kubesh.

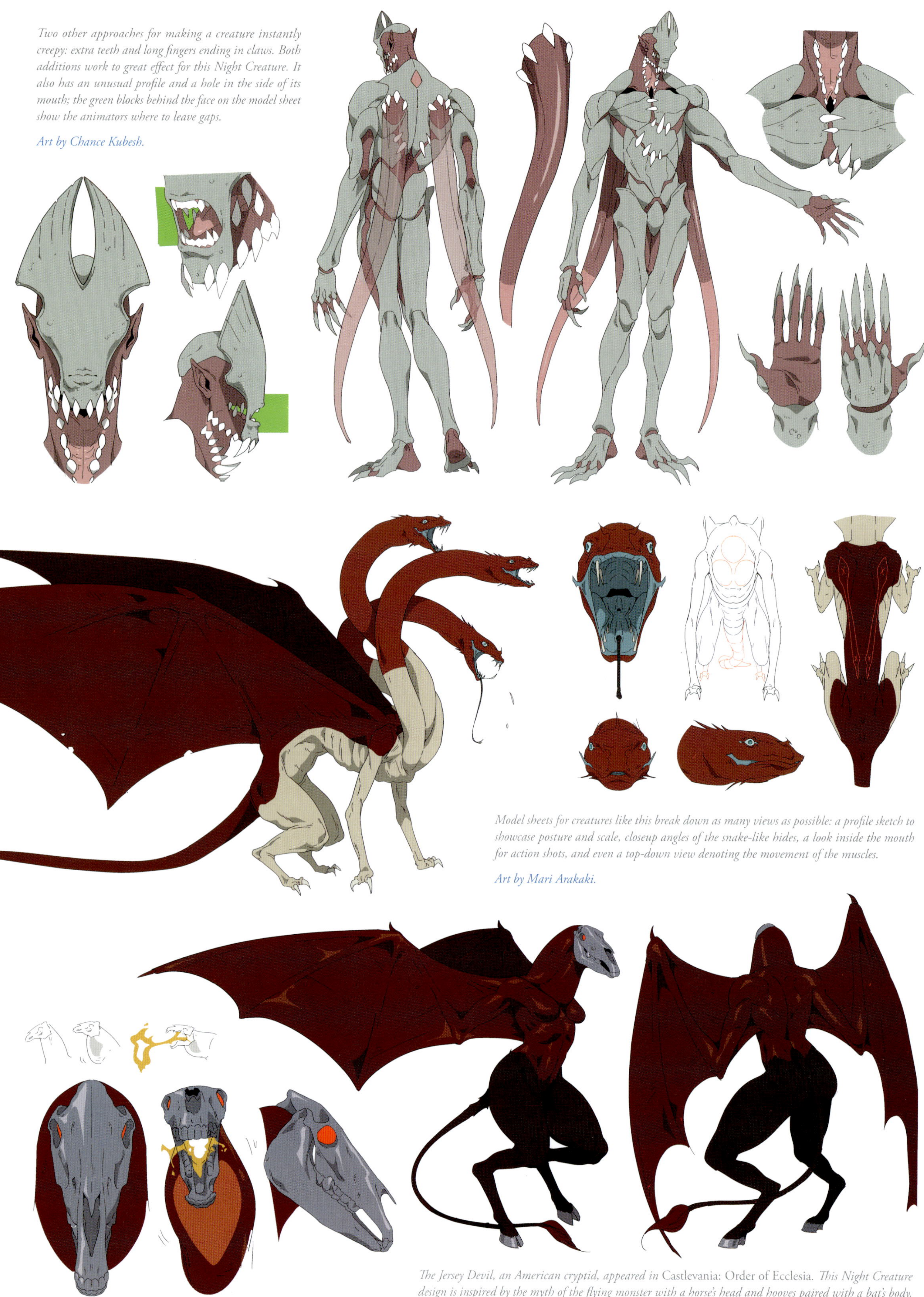

Model sheets for creatures like this break down as many views as possible: a profile sketch to showcase posture and scale, closeup angles of the snake-like hides, a look inside the mouth for action shots, and even a top-down view denoting the movement of the muscles.

Art by Mari Arakaki.

The Jersey Devil, an American cryptid, appeared in *Castlevania: Order of Ecclesia*. This Night Creature design is inspired by the myth of the flying monster with a horse's head and hooves paired with a bat's body.

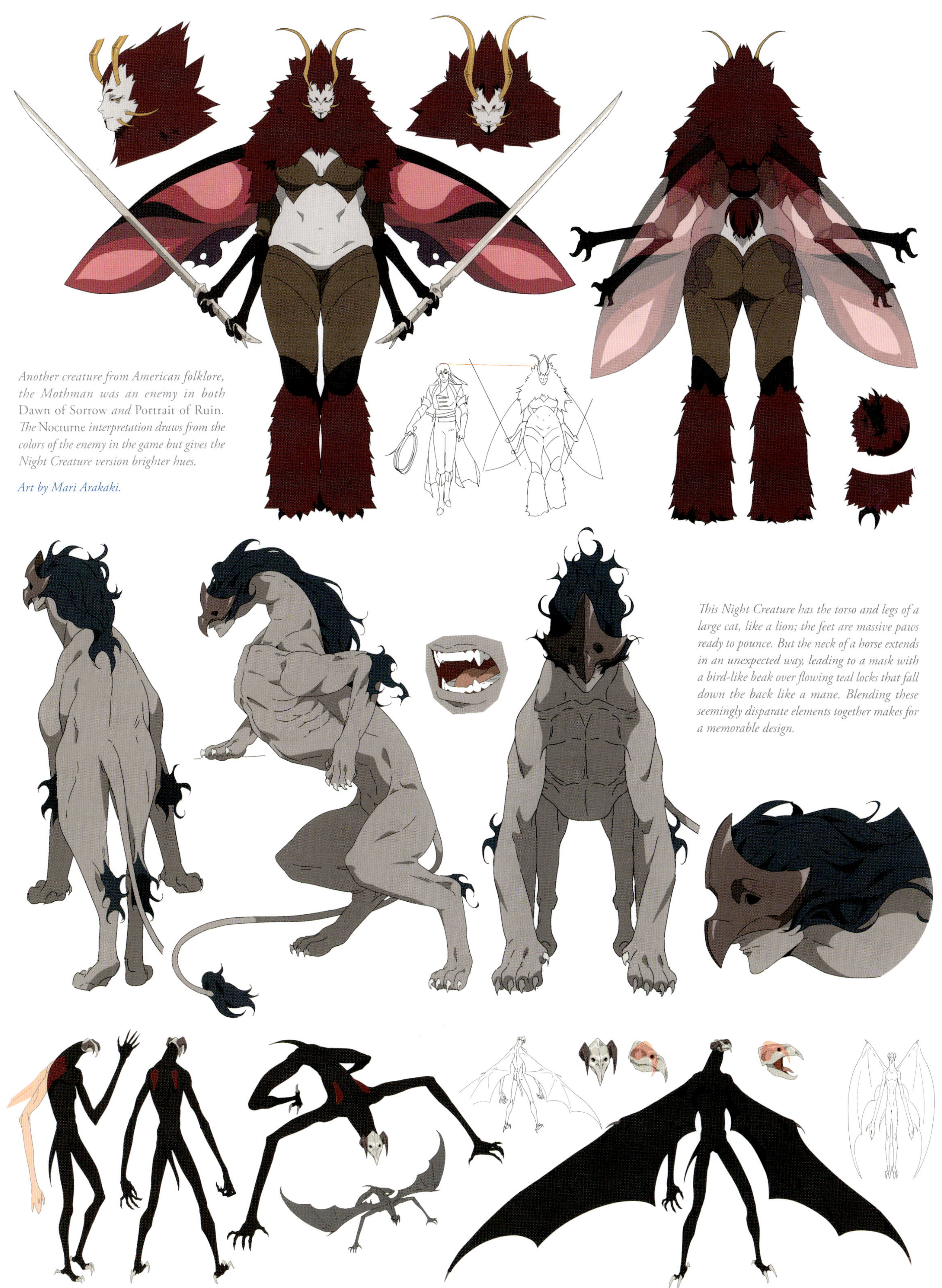

Another creature from American folklore, the Mothman was an enemy in both Dawn of Sorrow *and* Portrait of Ruin. *The* Nocturne *interpretation draws from the colors of the enemy in the game but gives the Night Creature version brighter hues.*

Art by Mari Arakaki.

This Night Creature has the torso and legs of a large cat, like a lion; the feet are massive paws ready to pounce. But the neck of a horse extends in an unexpected way, leading to a mask with a bird-like beak over flowing teal locks that fall down the back like a mane. Blending these seemingly disparate elements together makes for a memorable design.

Because of the quantity of Night Creatures required for the uprising, Silva noted they made mix-and-match sheets to maximize the designs for various elements: unusual wings, skulls, and heads. These sketches are examples of how they used similar, smaller pieces to build unique Creatures.

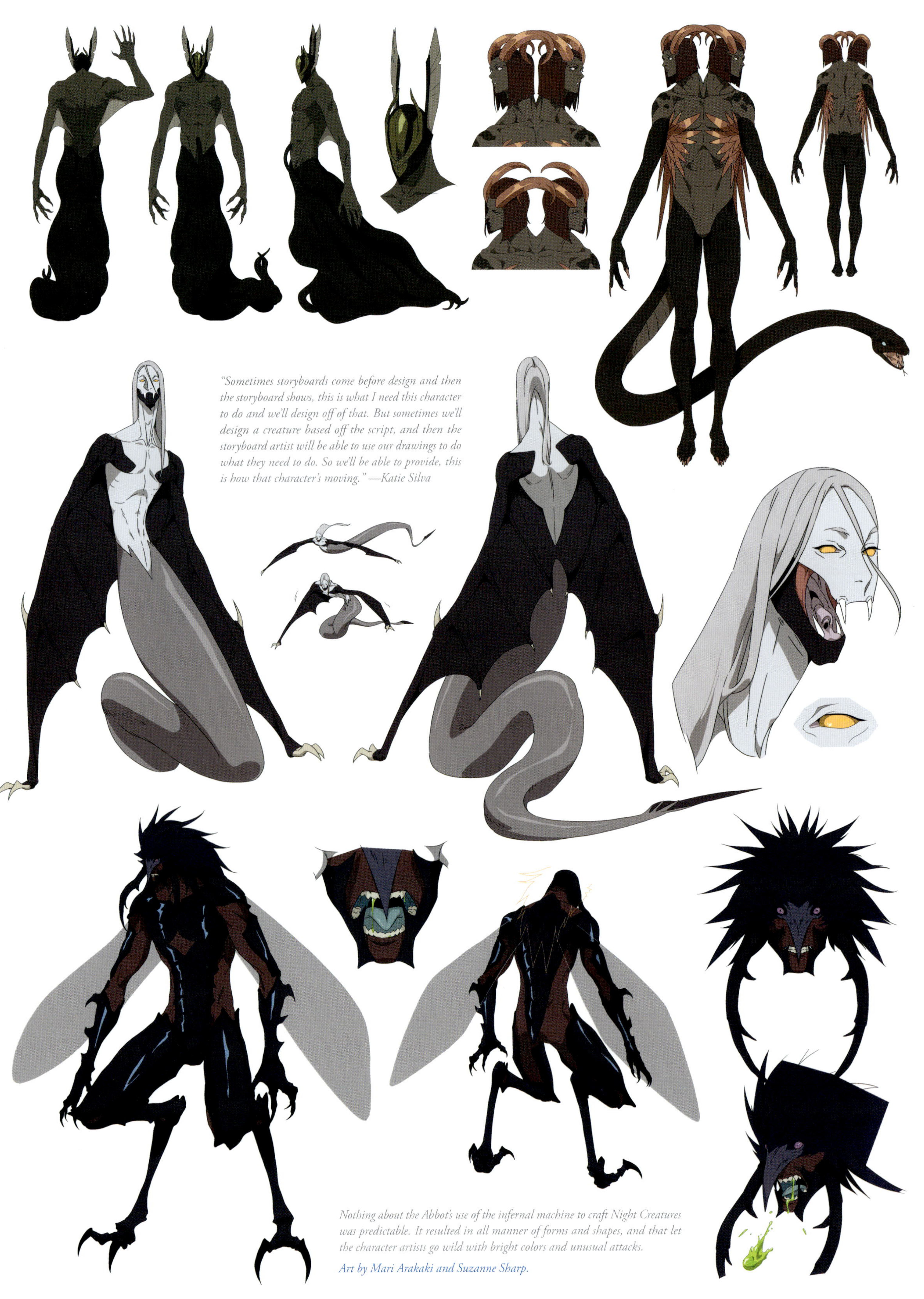

"Sometimes storyboards come before design and then the storyboard shows, this is what I need this character to do and we'll design off of that. But sometimes we'll design a creature based off the script, and then the storyboard artist will be able to use our drawings to do what they need to do. So we'll be able to provide, this is how that character's moving." —Katie Silva

Nothing about the Abbot's use of the infernal machine to craft Night Creatures was predictable. It resulted in all manner of forms and shapes, and that let the character artists go wild with bright colors and unusual attacks.

Art by Mari Arakaki and Suzanne Sharp.

Storyboards by Armando Atencio.

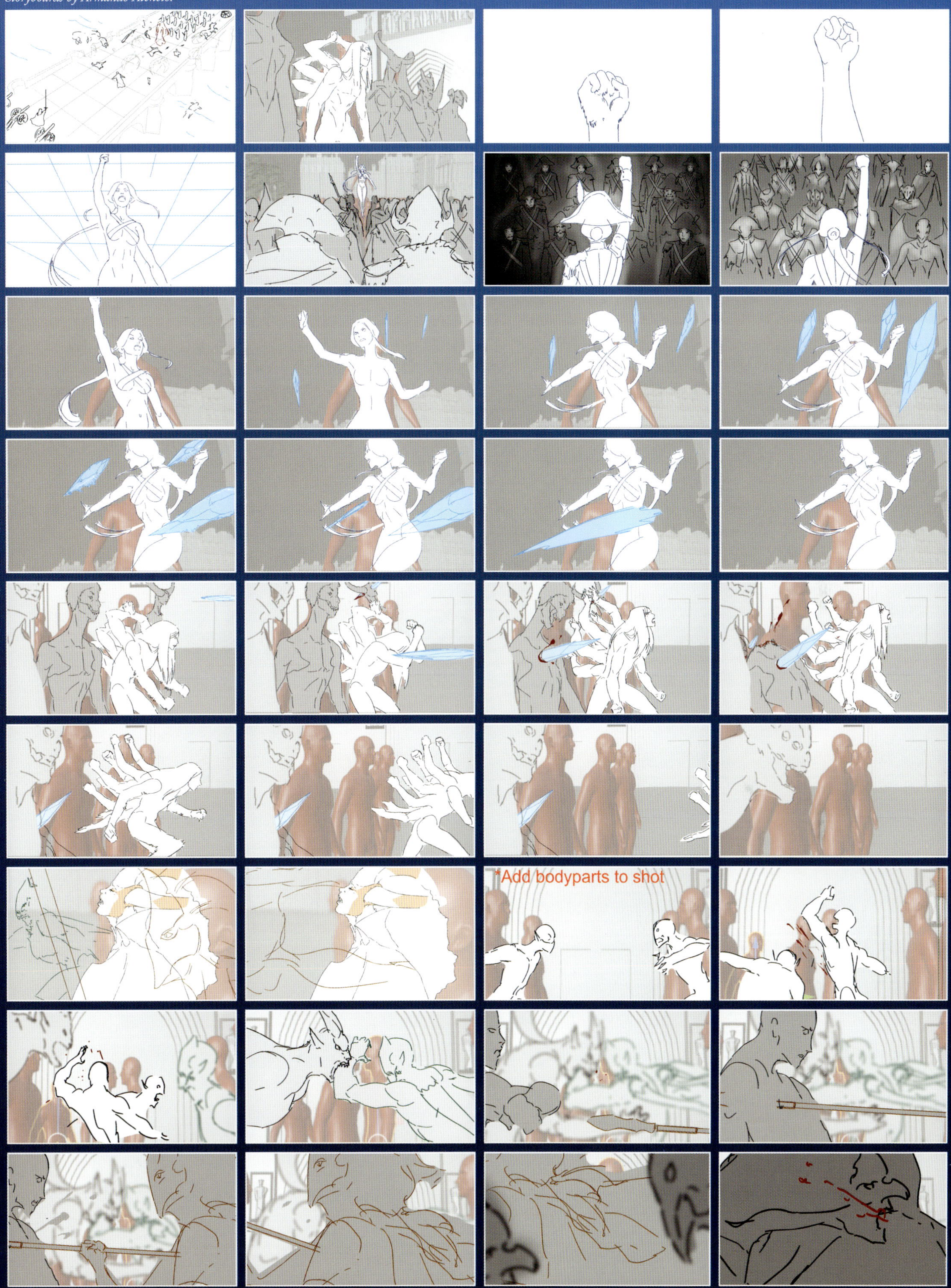

"I really like the transition from the captain and her soldiers as they originally were into the Night Creatures shot," Sam said. "That really got into the heart of what's happening here. They managed to find their way back to themselves and are fighting the good fight in a similar manner that they were before but against a very different kind of foe." As for the "add body parts to the shot" note, that was a common way for Sam to share simple notes on the storyboard file.

Spirit Creatures

The Spirit World contains a number of surprises for Annette. The supernatural plane seems to be connected to varying mythologies and realms—she meets Ogun there, but can also visit her mother and Sekhmet's temple. Navigating the intricacies of the Spirit World is something Annette is called to do through her magical abilities, rooted in orisha and Vodou traditions.

Because she believes it will provide a path towards stopping Erzsebet, Annette bravely enters the realm, on guard but unaware of what to expect once there. The otherworldly dimension tests her resolve, mentally and physically. She must face not only her ancestors, but dangerous spirit creatures.

Art by Mari Arakaki.

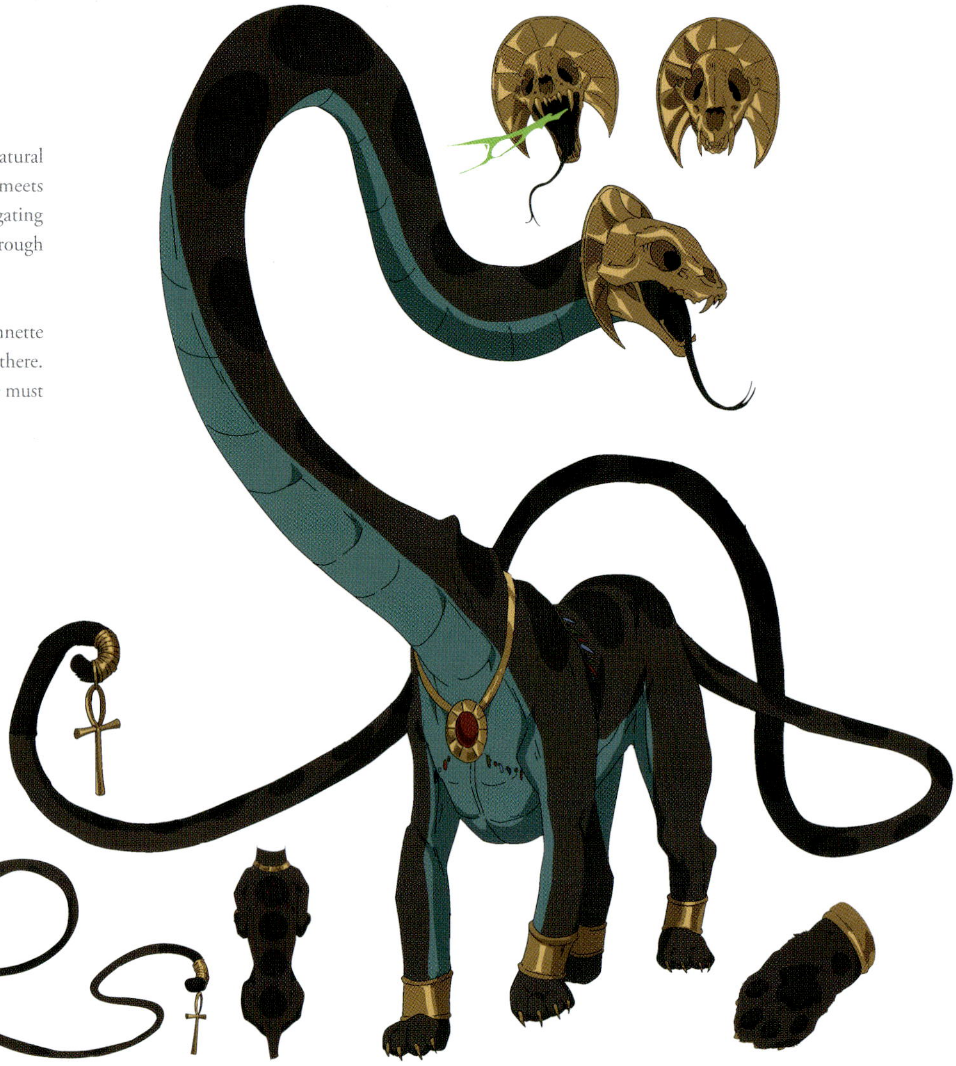

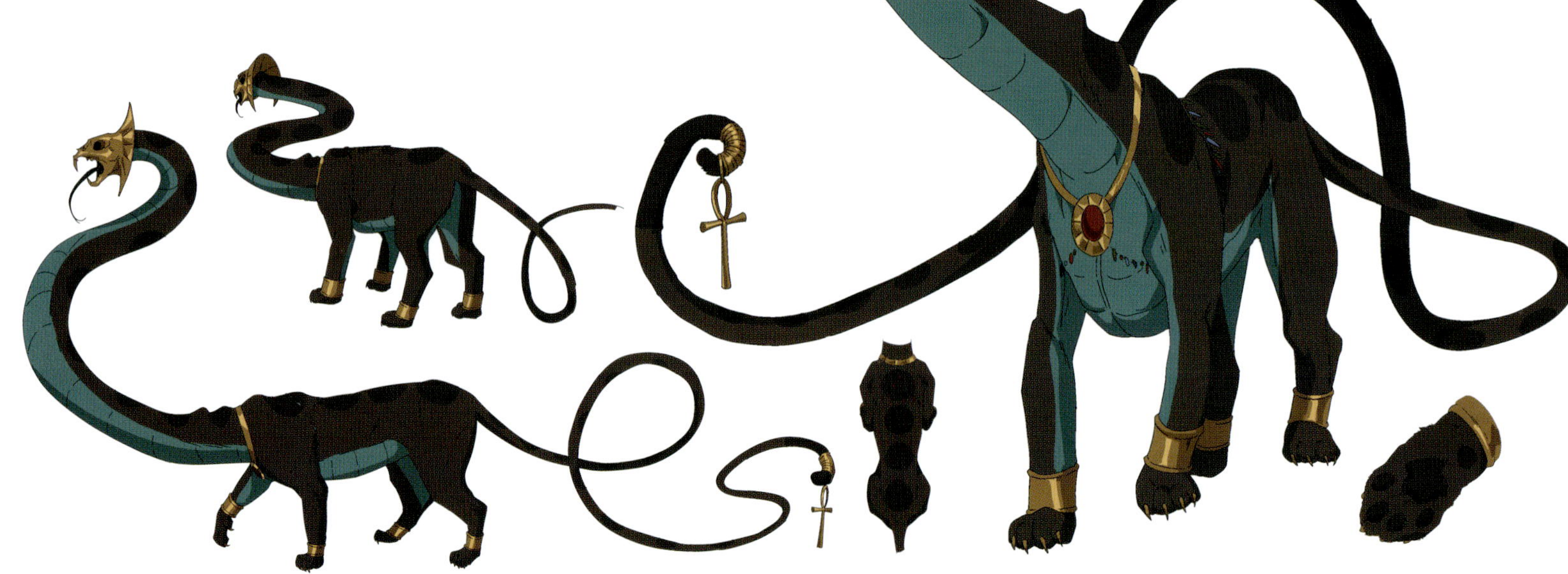

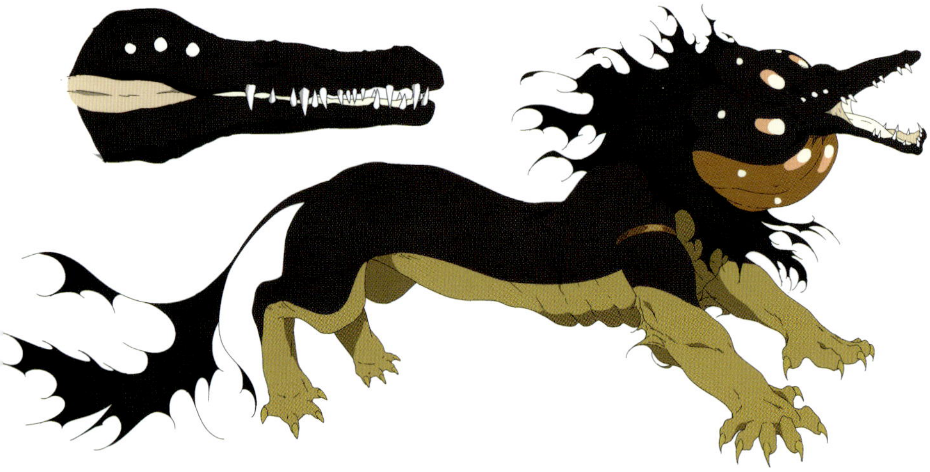

Annette's encounter with this hulking underwater creature nearly costs her life. Without Ogun's shield, she may not have survived. The way the creature moves calls sea serpents such as the Loch Ness Monster to mind. Katie Silva noted she added the golden skull plate to this character simply because it looks fun.

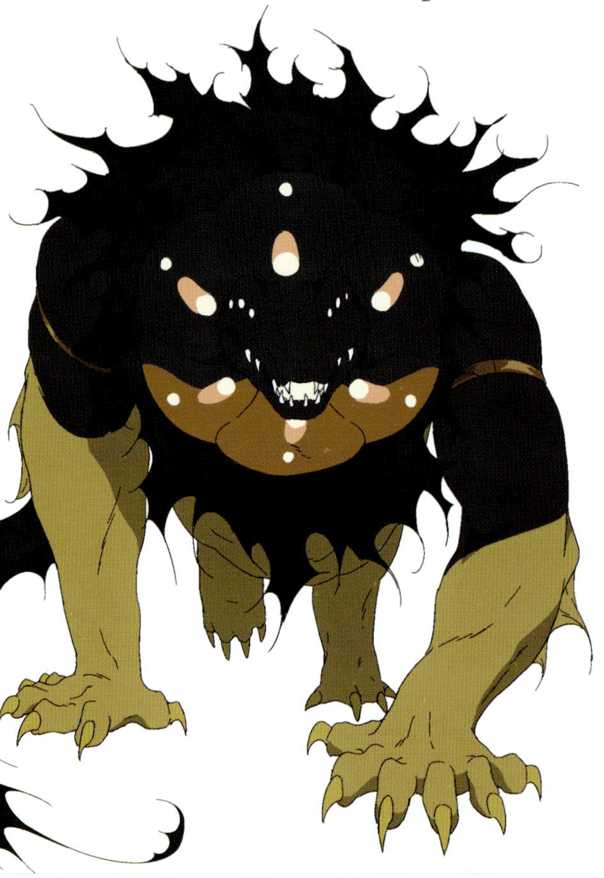

This nightmare-fuel creature combines the musculature and snout of a crocodile with almost feline movements. The strong legs cover more ground than a crocodile's would—that combined with its numerous teeth make for an unsettling and frightening creature.

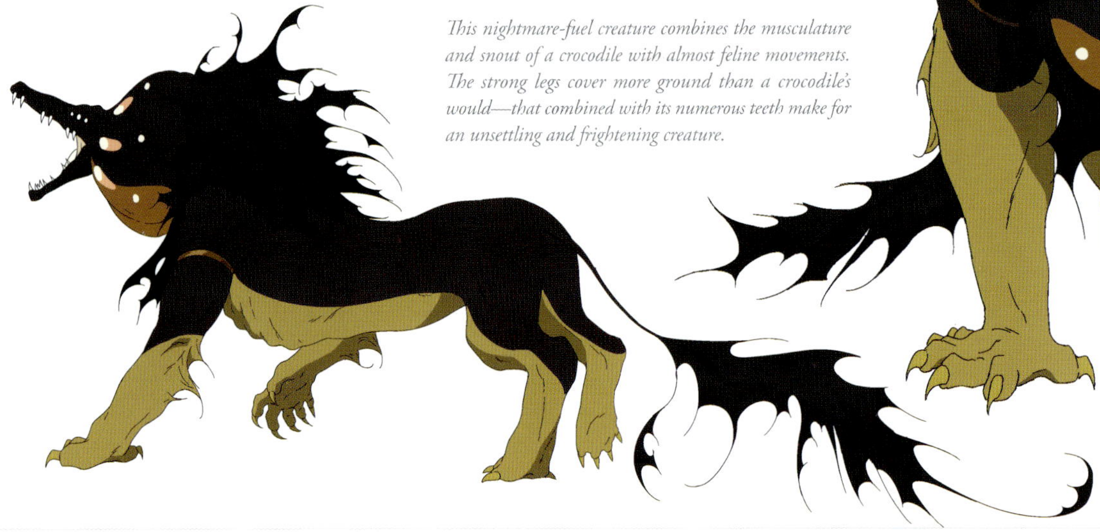

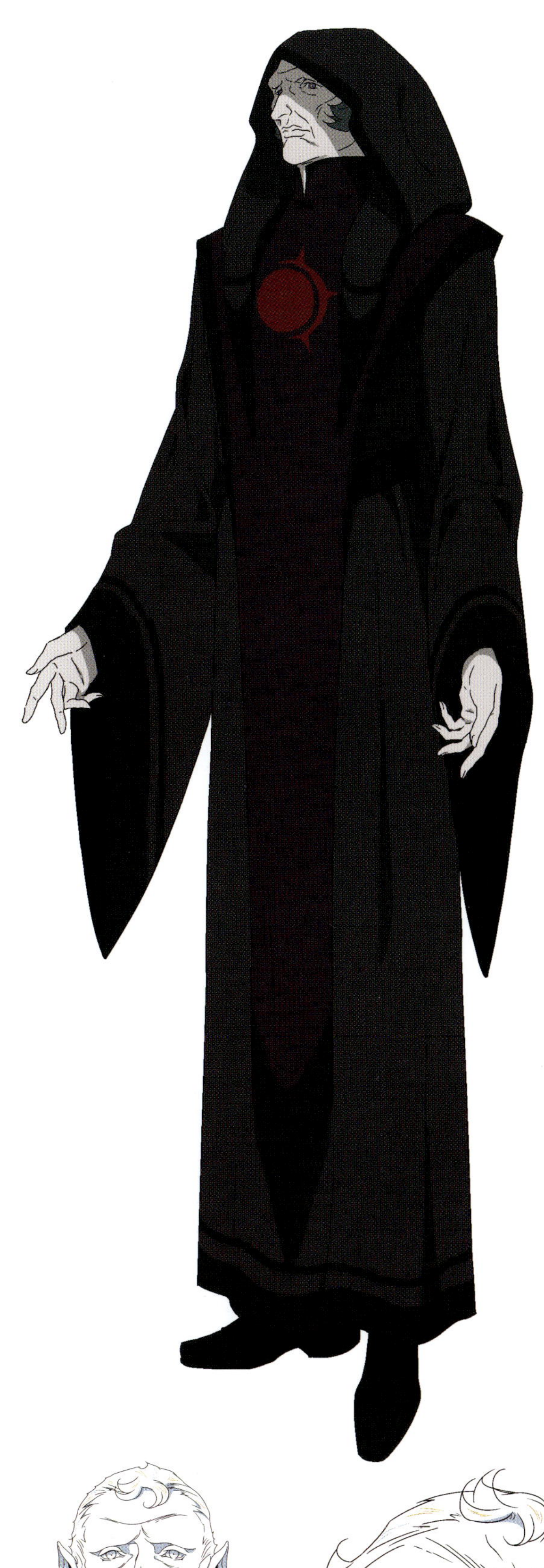

Comte de Vaublanc

The owner of a sugar plantation in Saint-Domingue, Vaublanc perpetuates slavery, murder (he killed Annette's mother, Esther), and other atrocities. It's in his best interest to answer Drolta's command for assistance, but Vaublanc also sees it as a way to amass more power for himself. Since he serves Drolta and Erzsebet, Silva said Sam Deats explored the idea of leaning into more of an Egypt-inspired look for Vaublanc. Ultimately, however, he ended up with a white Southern-style plantation suit.

Branded Vaublanc design by Suzanne Sharp. White suit design by Samuel Deats. Bat design by Evgeny Kubaev.

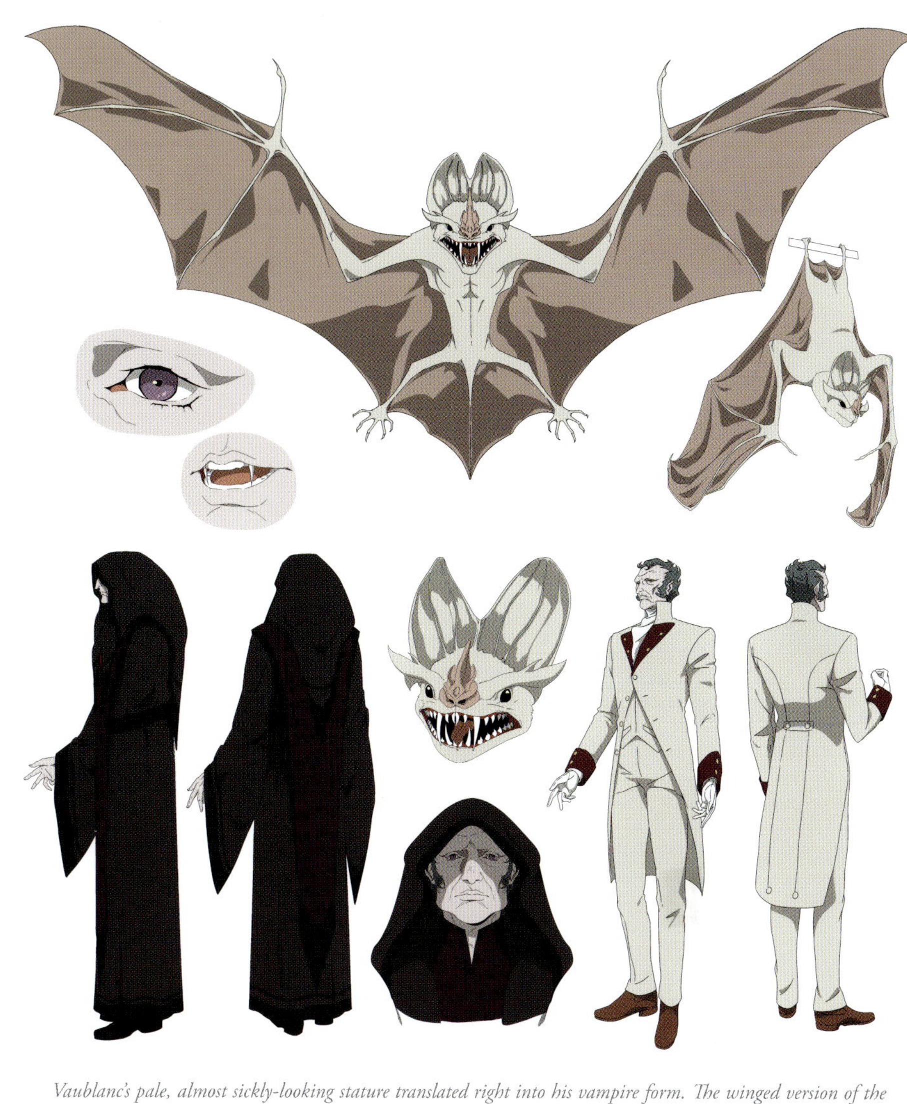

Vaublanc's pale, almost sickly-looking stature translated right into his vampire form. The winged version of the slave owner appears similarly gaunt, like skin stretched over not enough bones, with an oily and malevolent grin.

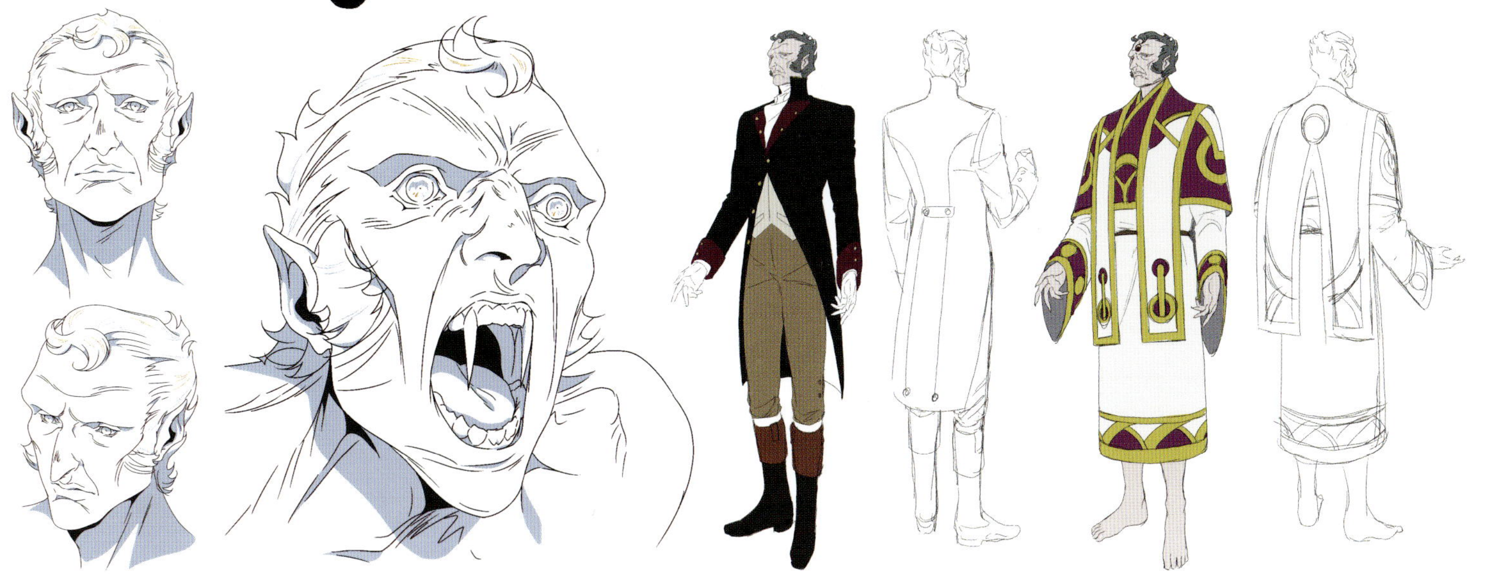

Marquis & Marchioness

Members of the French vampire aristocracy, the Marquis and Marchioness relish in their wealth and power. The Marquis owns a sprawling chateau, the Vendée, modeled on the Palace of Versailles. They embrace every facet of their nobility while acting abominably. Their way of life underscores a recurring theme in *Castlevania: Nocturne*: those who grasp at status and money tend to leech on those in the lower classes—or anyone not deemed "worthy" by their standards. Their ensembles are all about the fashion of the time turned up to eleven, because they both believe more is better. They are so confident in themselves and their place that they choose gaudiness, believing it to be impressive.

Marquis design by Samuel Deats and Dominique Ferro. Marchioness design by Suzanne Sharp.

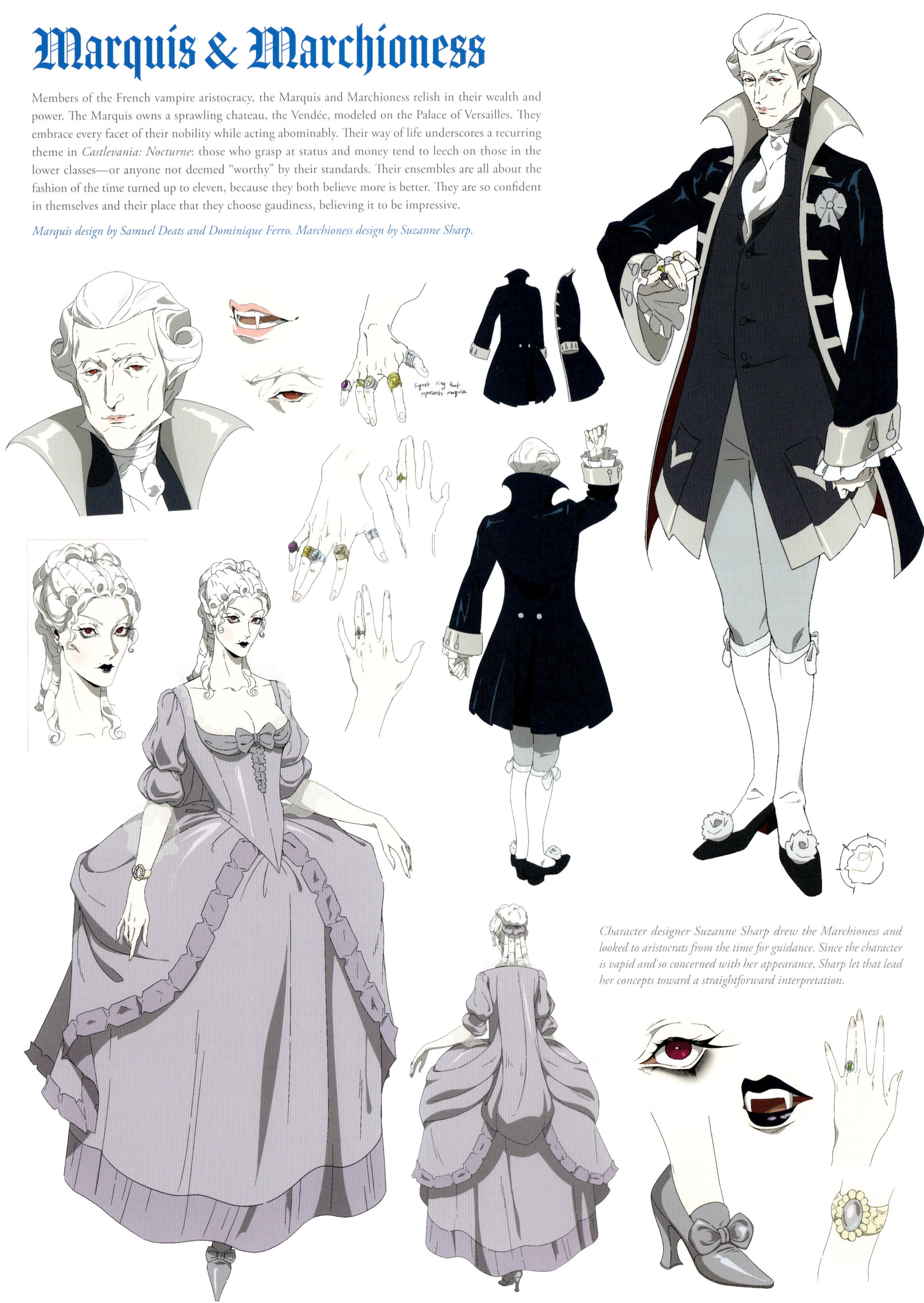

Character designer Suzanne Sharp drew the Marchioness and looked to aristocrats from the time for guidance. Since the character is vapid and so concerned with her appearance, Sharp let that lead her concepts toward a straightforward interpretation.

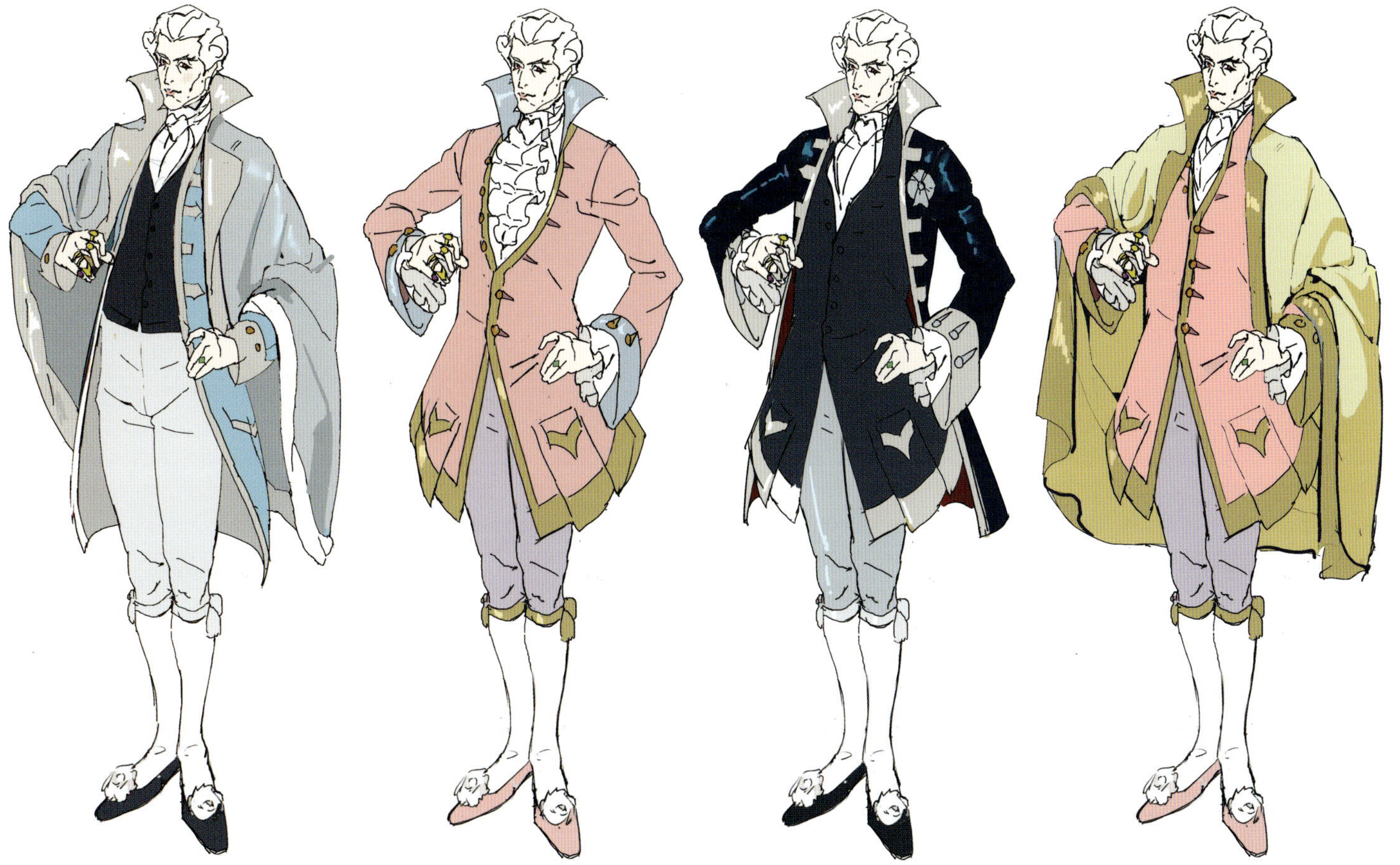

Silva recalled that Sam Deats worked on the Marquis's face and that he referenced old paintings where the artists drew the most delicate, tiny features. The lips would be "these ultra-European tiniest lips." Sam translated those old portraits into functional character design.

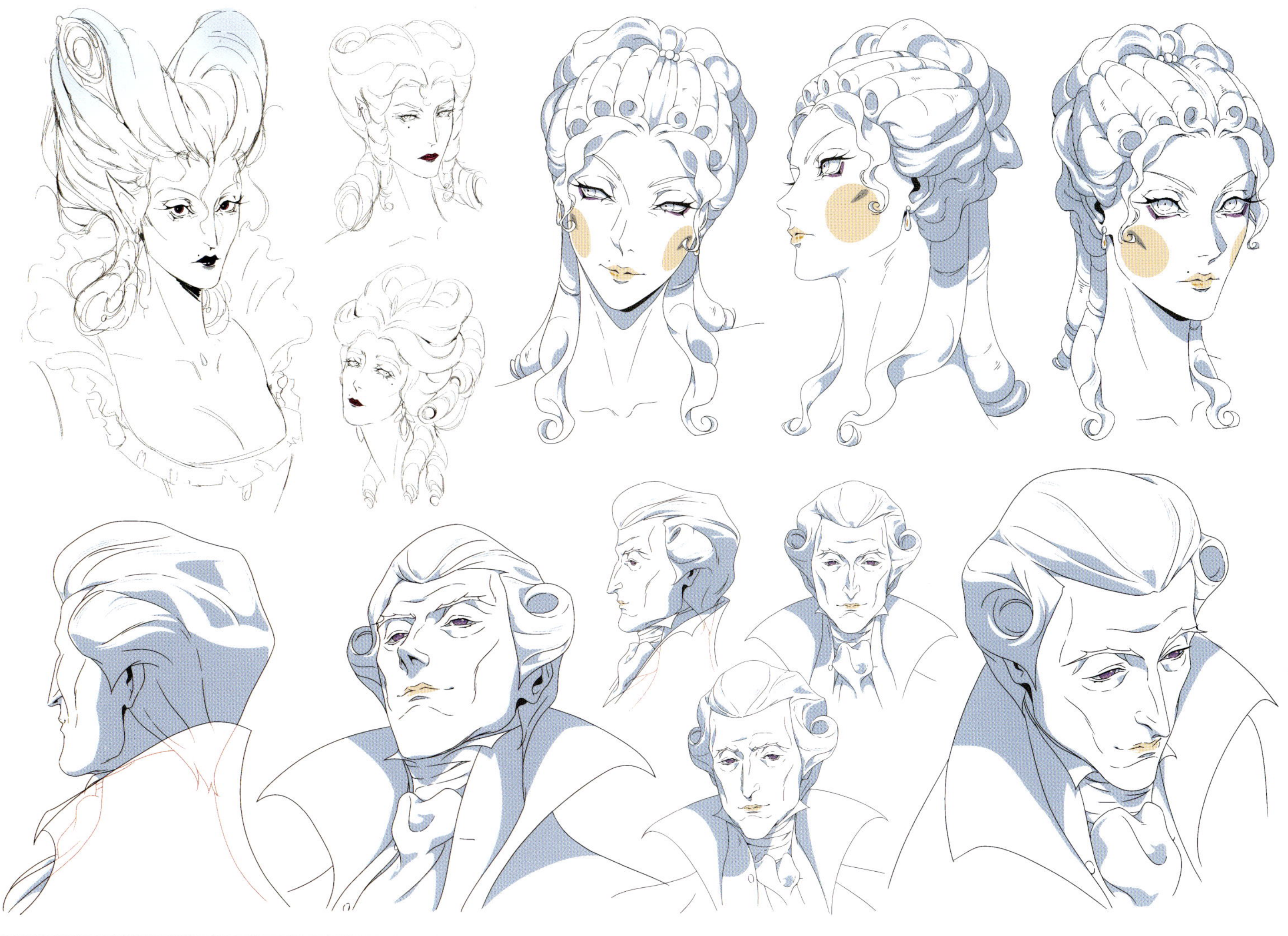

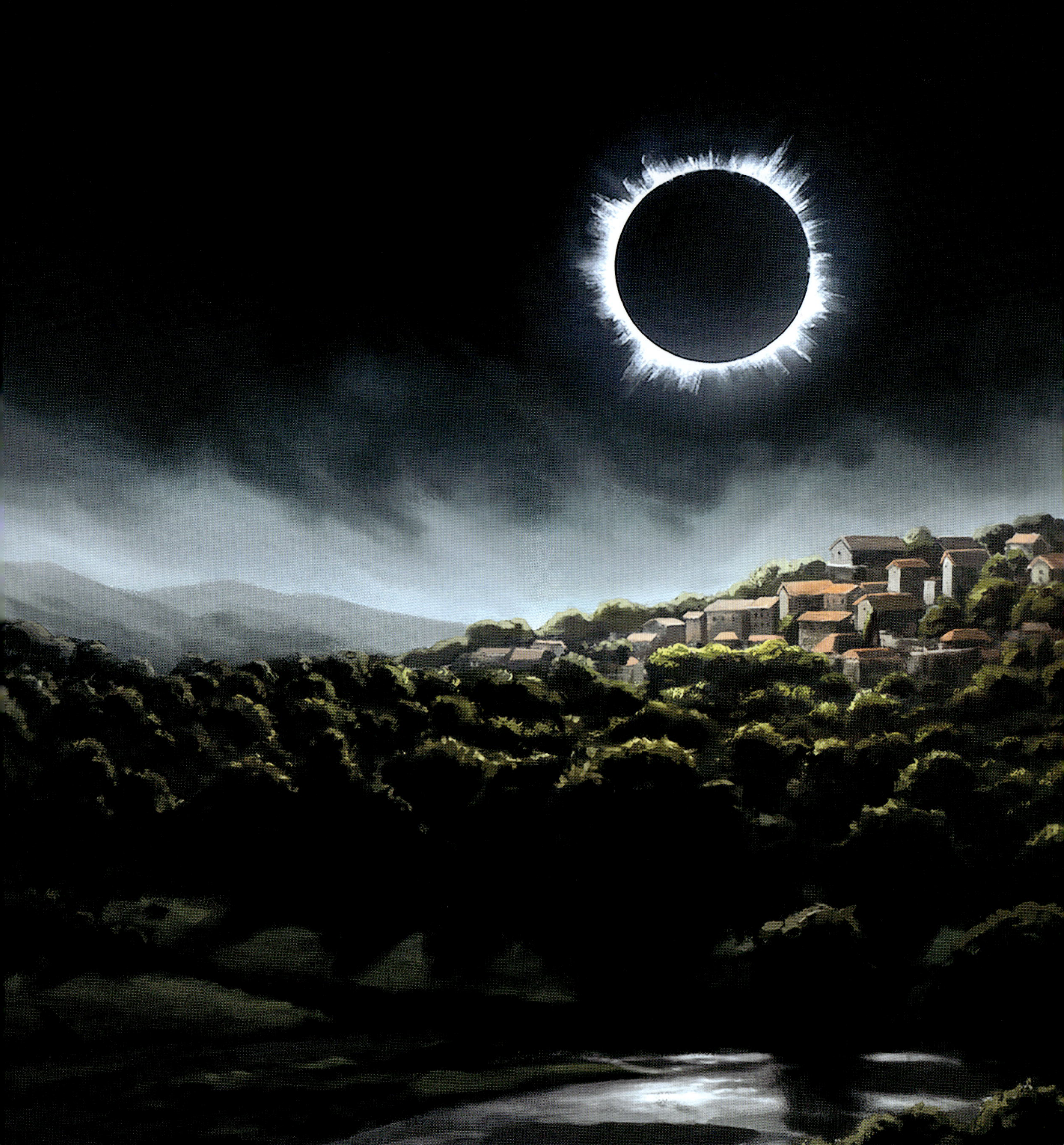

Art by Sam Kesier.

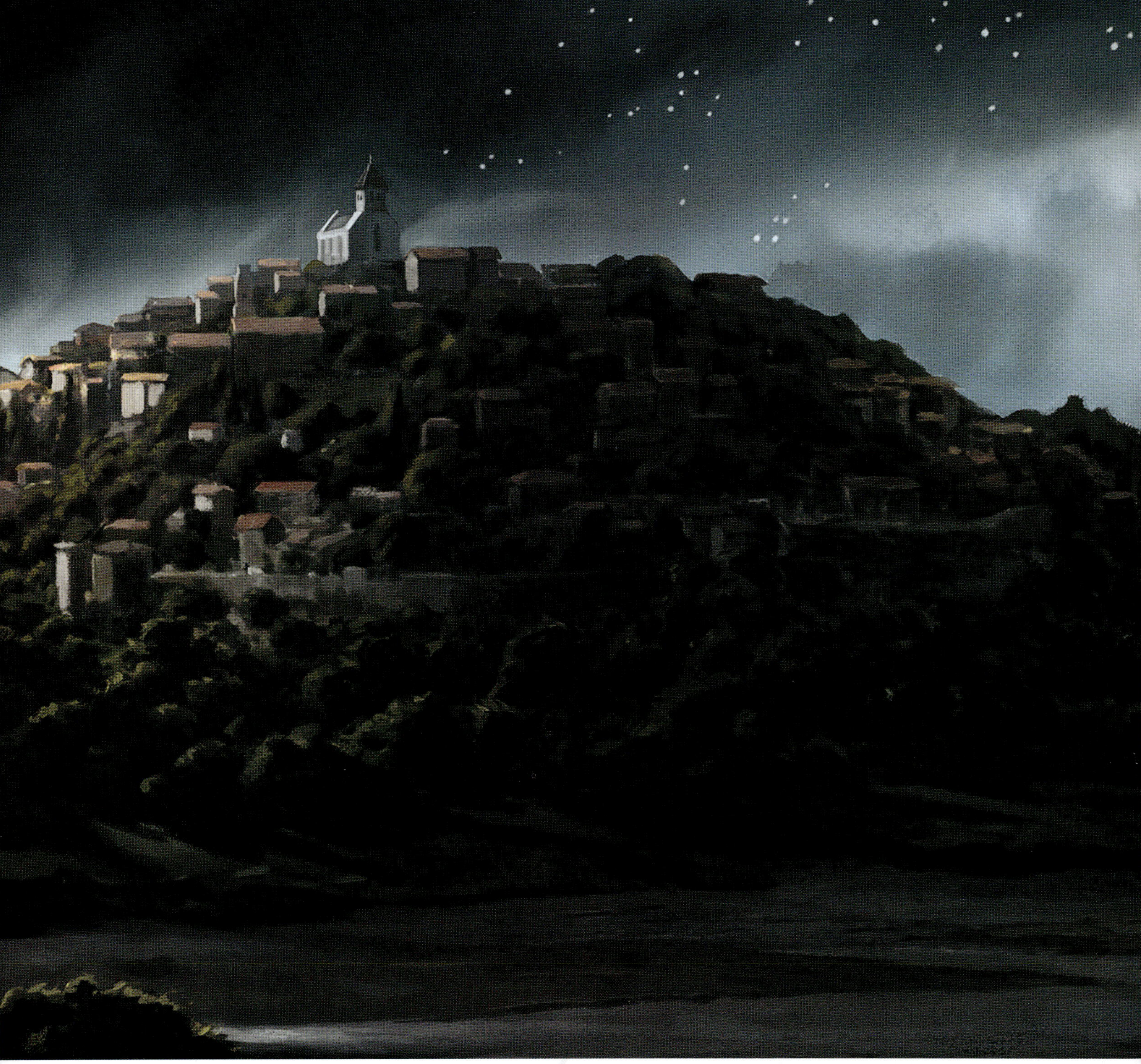

CHAPTER III

Machecoul and the Lands Beyond

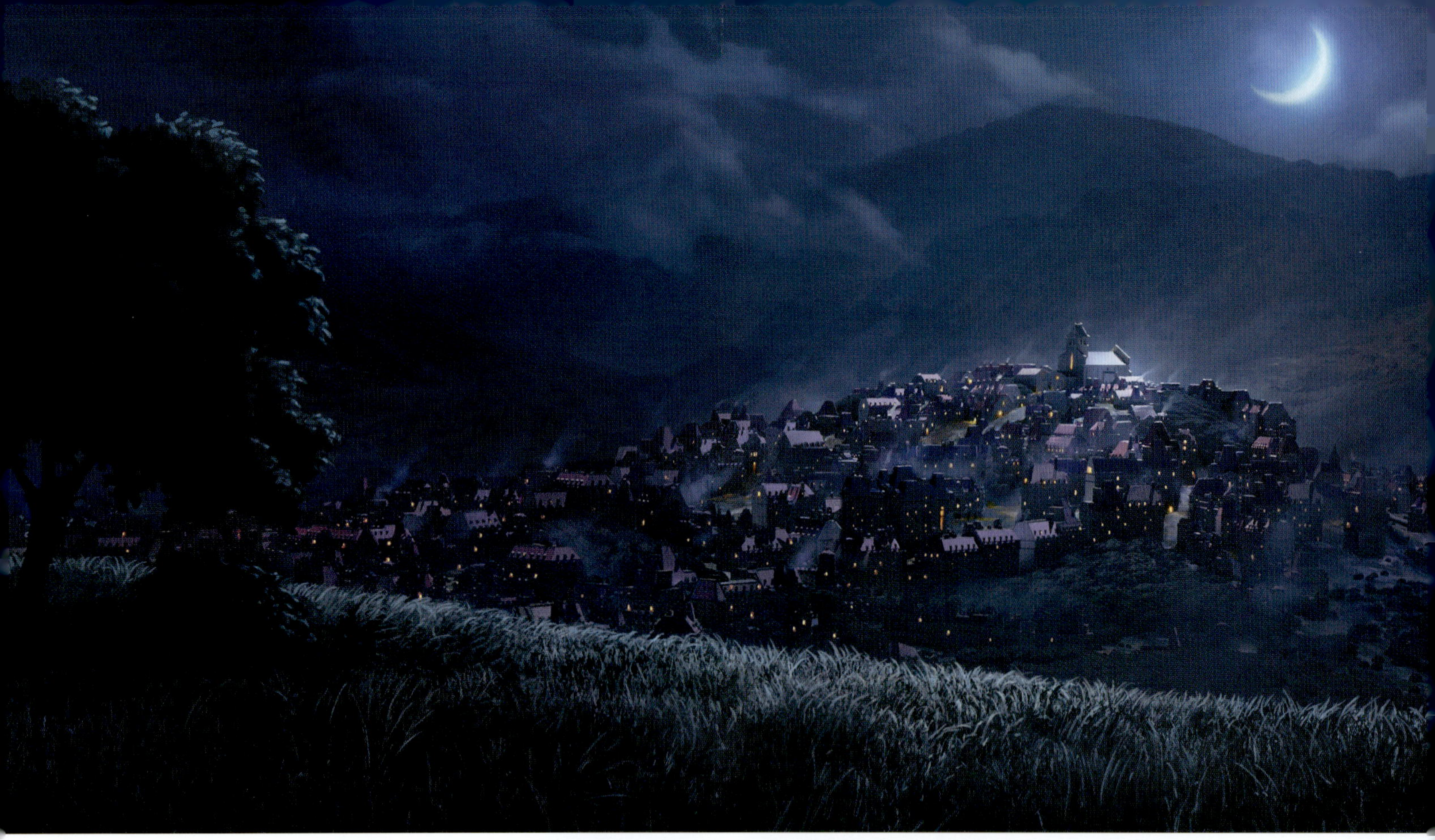

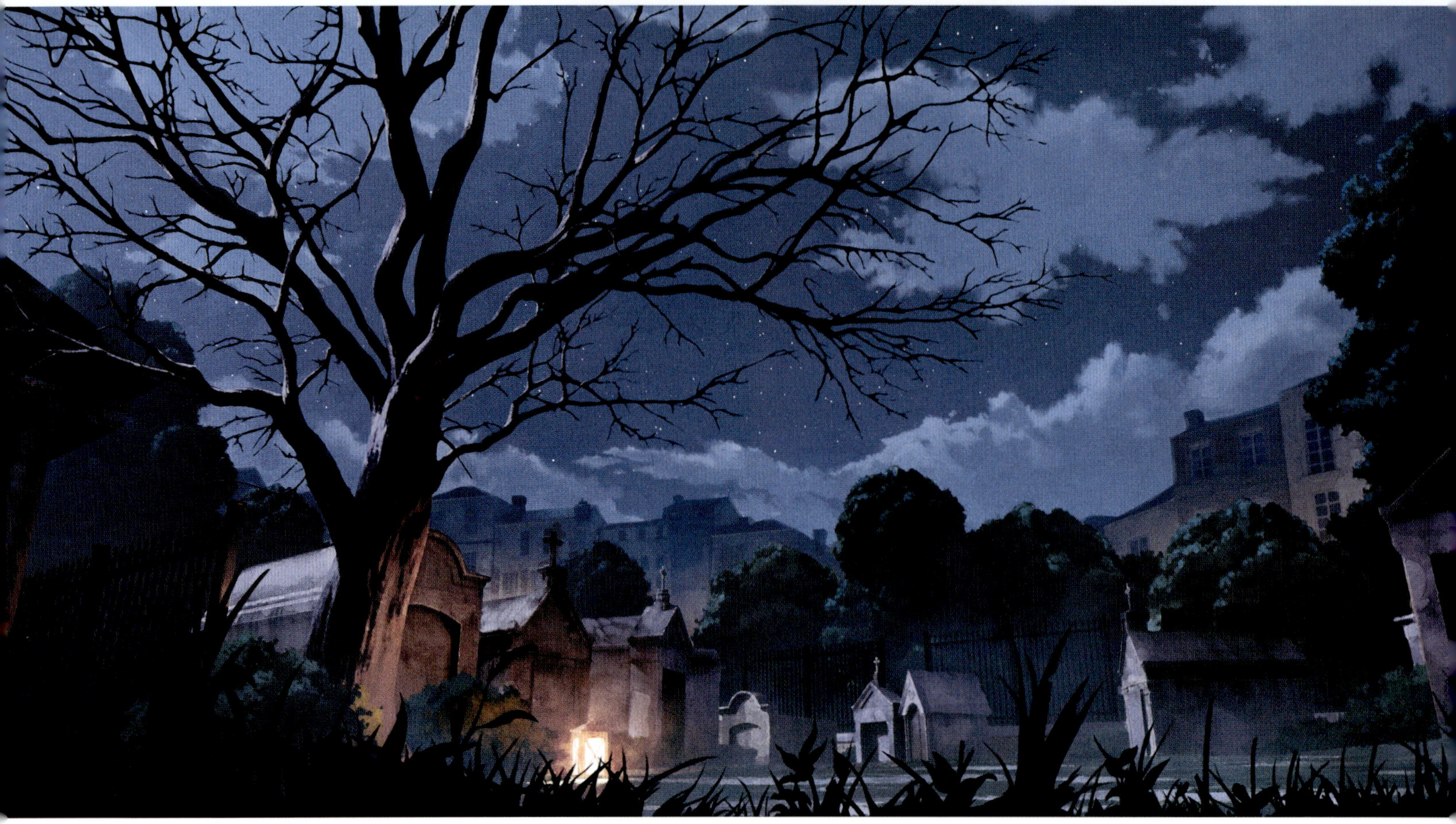

Machecoul

Erzsebet's battle for control and power unfolds against the backdrop of Machecoul, a French town. Supervising background designer Stephen Stark looked at other cities in France to inform the appearance of Machecoul. He ended up using the older parts of Lyon for reference. Then they went back and forth with series creator and writer Clive Bradley on the size of the city. One aspect that helped determine the scale is that Bradley wanted the abbey to sit above the town, to basically be visible regardless of where someone is located in the city. For the exterior of the building, the design team looked to the abbey on the island of Mont Saint-Michel and the way it stretches above the ocean. They refined the look of the abbey to be more of an unassuming church rather than being super ornate.

Opposite top: Sam Keiser, Opposite bottom: Stephen Stark. This page: Stephen Stark, Bottom right: Sam Keiser.

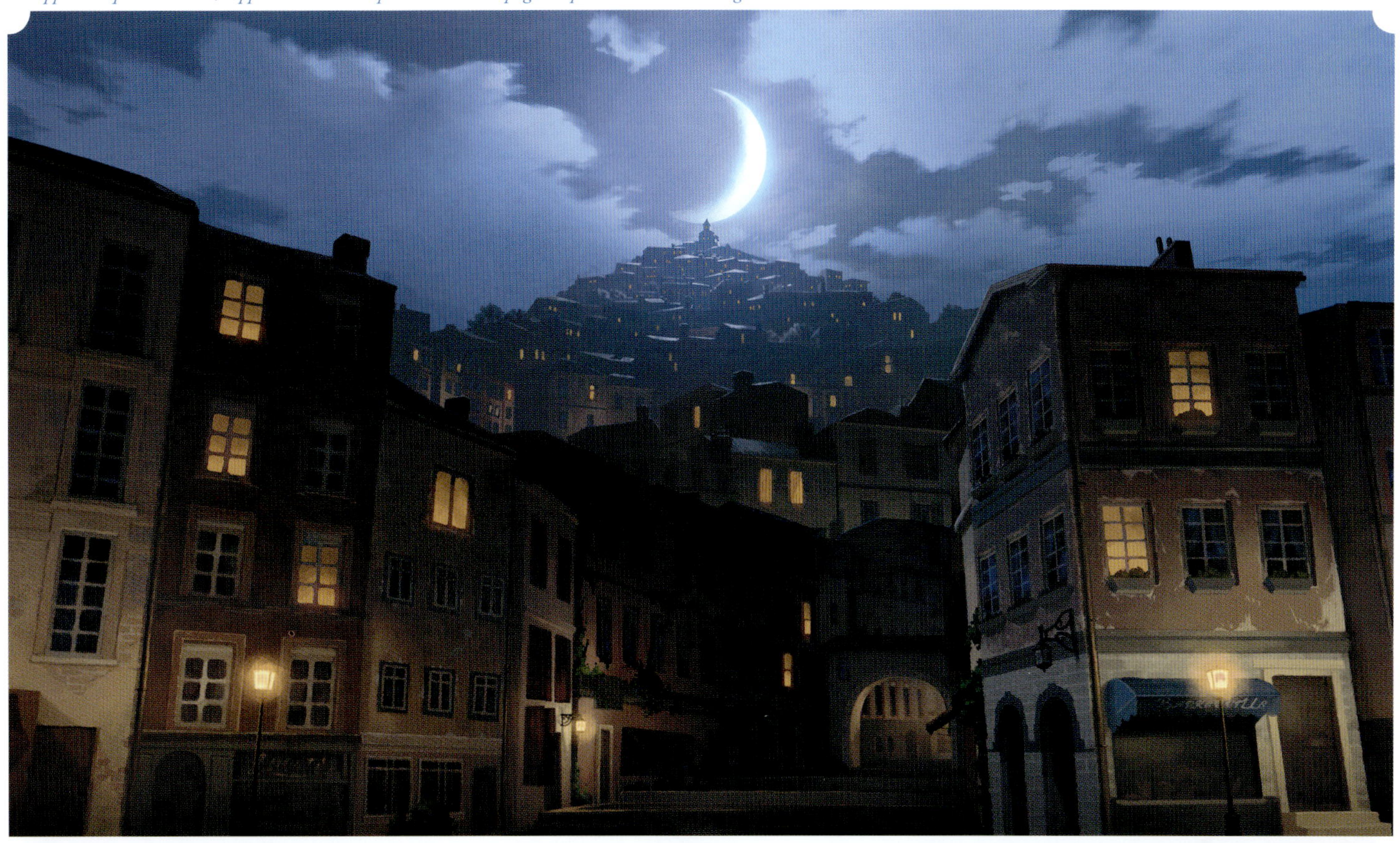

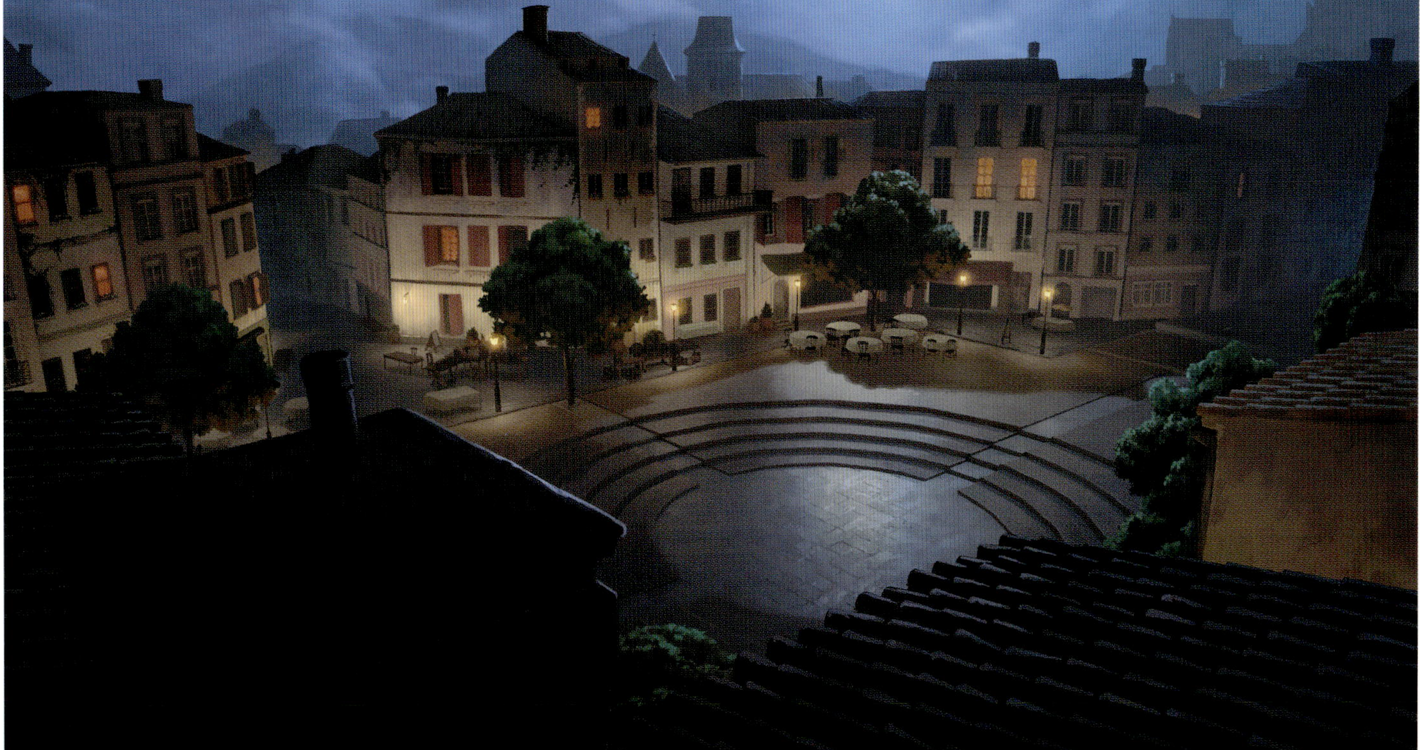

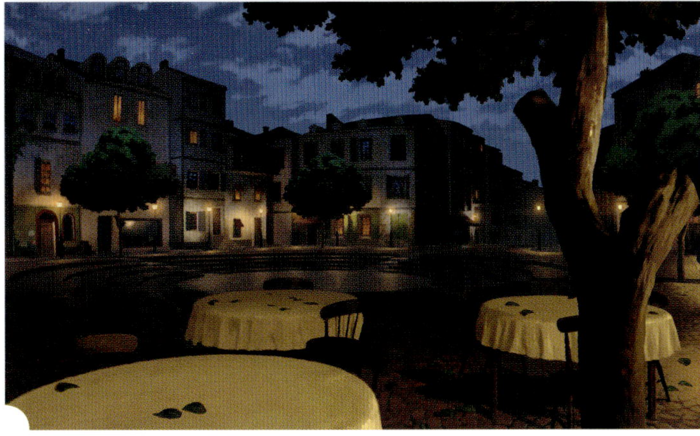

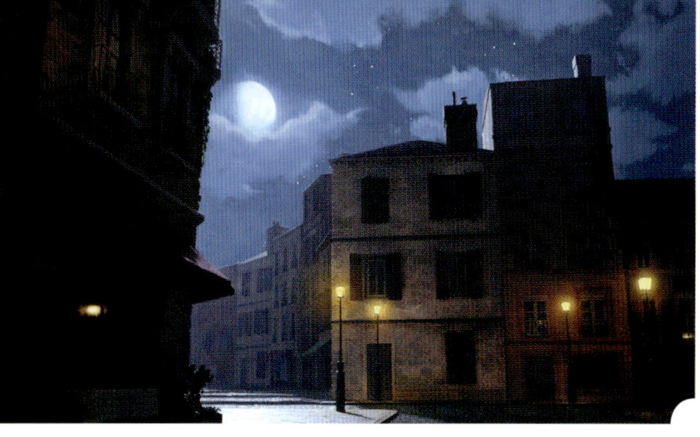

Top: Bo Li, Middle row and bottom right: Sean Randolph, Bottom left: Bo Li. Opposite top: Cullen Cole, Opposite bottom: Sabina Lewis.

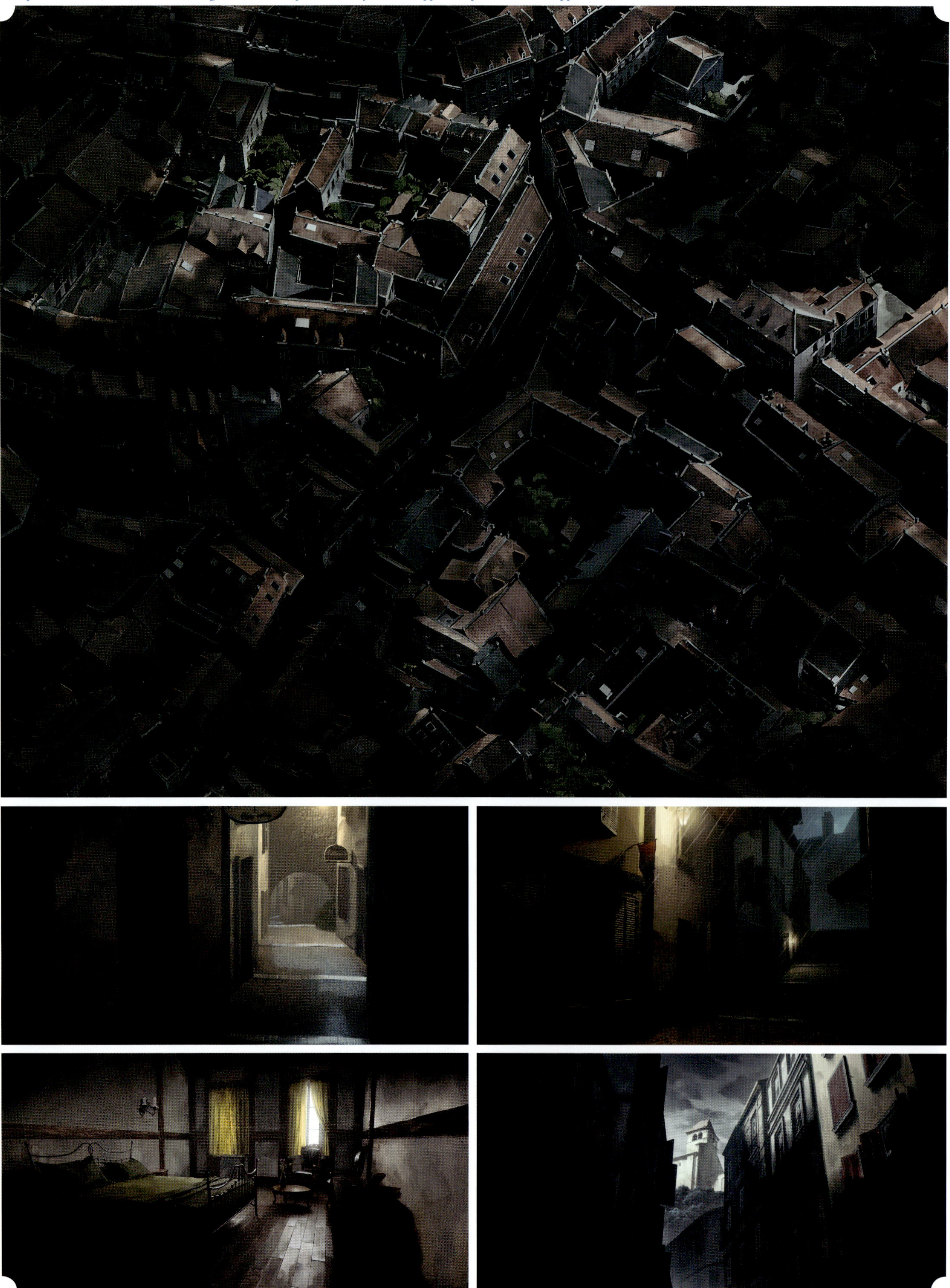

Early on in the series Stark spoke with production designer Sam Deats about the background style of *Nocturne*. To differentiate it from the original *Castlevania*, Stark wanted to do a juxtaposition with the backgrounds and the tone of the series. They wanted Machecoul and everywhere else to have an idyllic, Studio Ghibli–influenced look. But then as the story darkens towards the end of season one, the backgrounds gravitate more towards the photorealistic style of *Castlevania* because the fantasy tale Richter and Maria have been living in is no longer true.

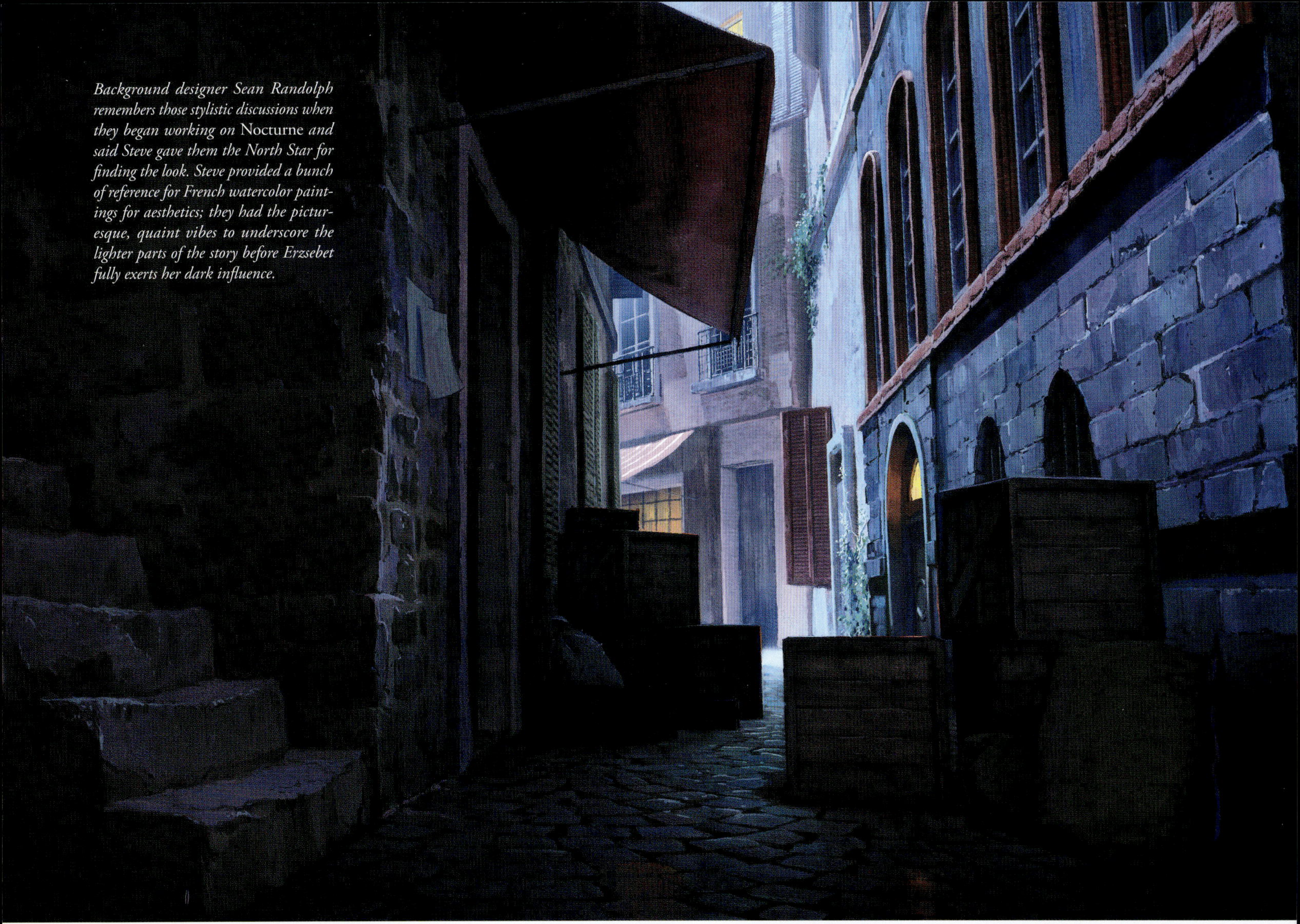

Background designer Sean Randolph remembers those stylistic discussions when they began working on Nocturne *and said Steve gave them the North Star for finding the look. Steve provided a bunch of reference for French watercolor paintings for aesthetics; they had the picturesque, quaint vibes to underscore the lighter parts of the story before Erzsebet fully exerts her dark influence.*

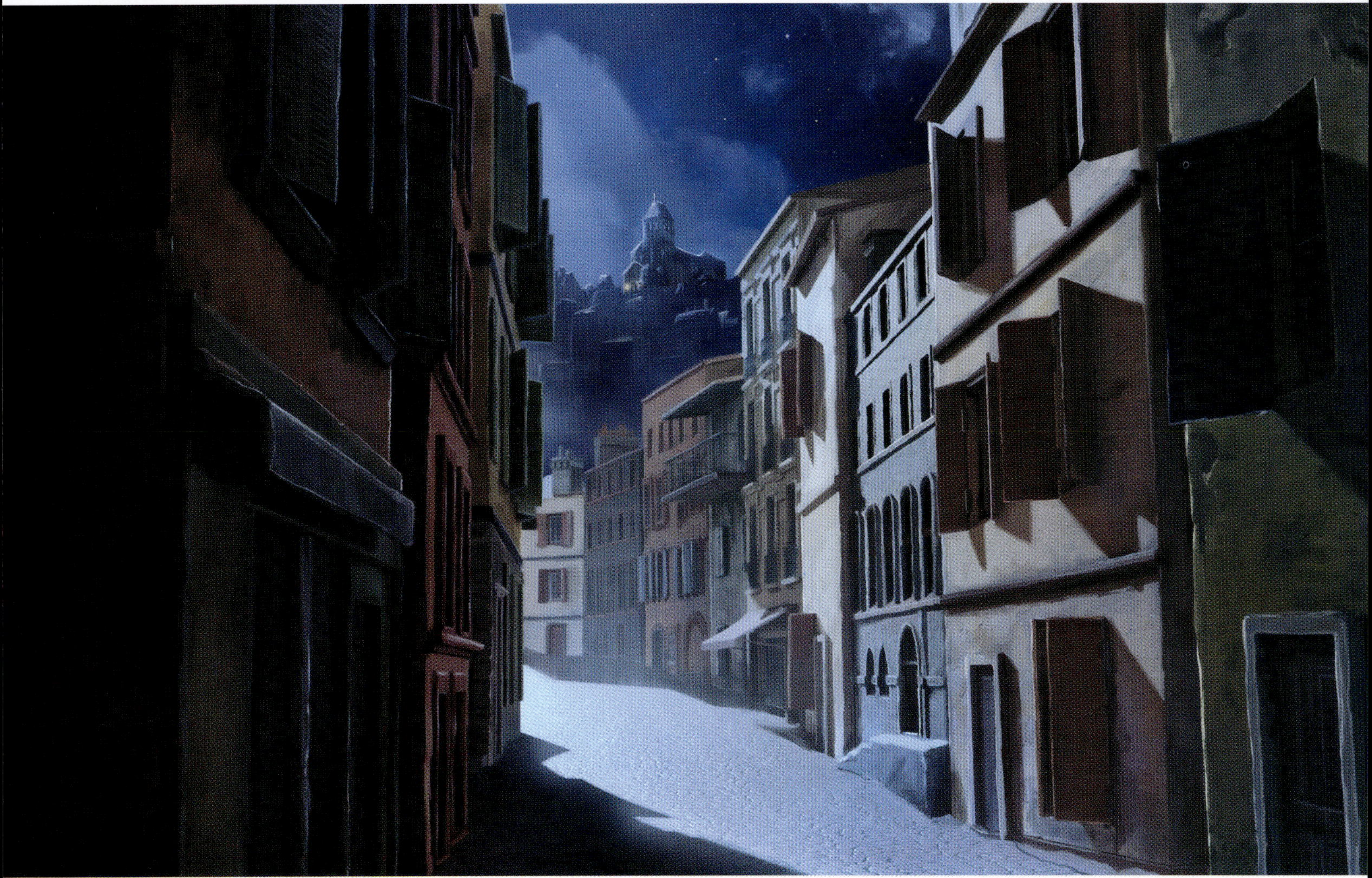

Top: Sabina Lewis, Middle: Blaise Rhein, Bottom: Sam Keiser. Opposite page: Stephen Stark.

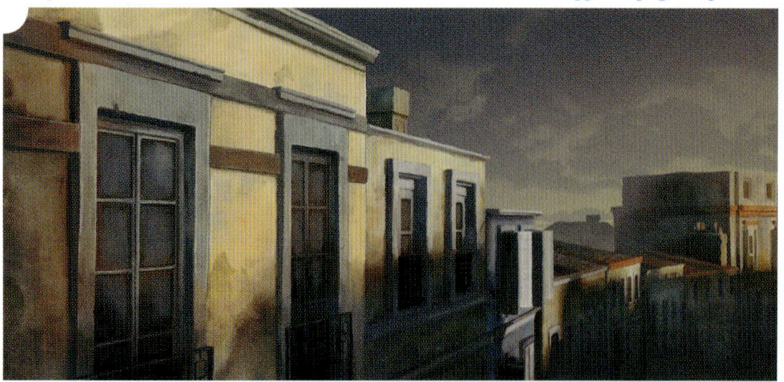

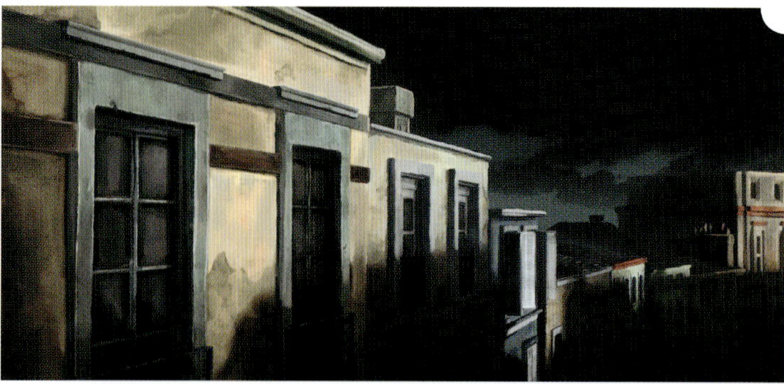

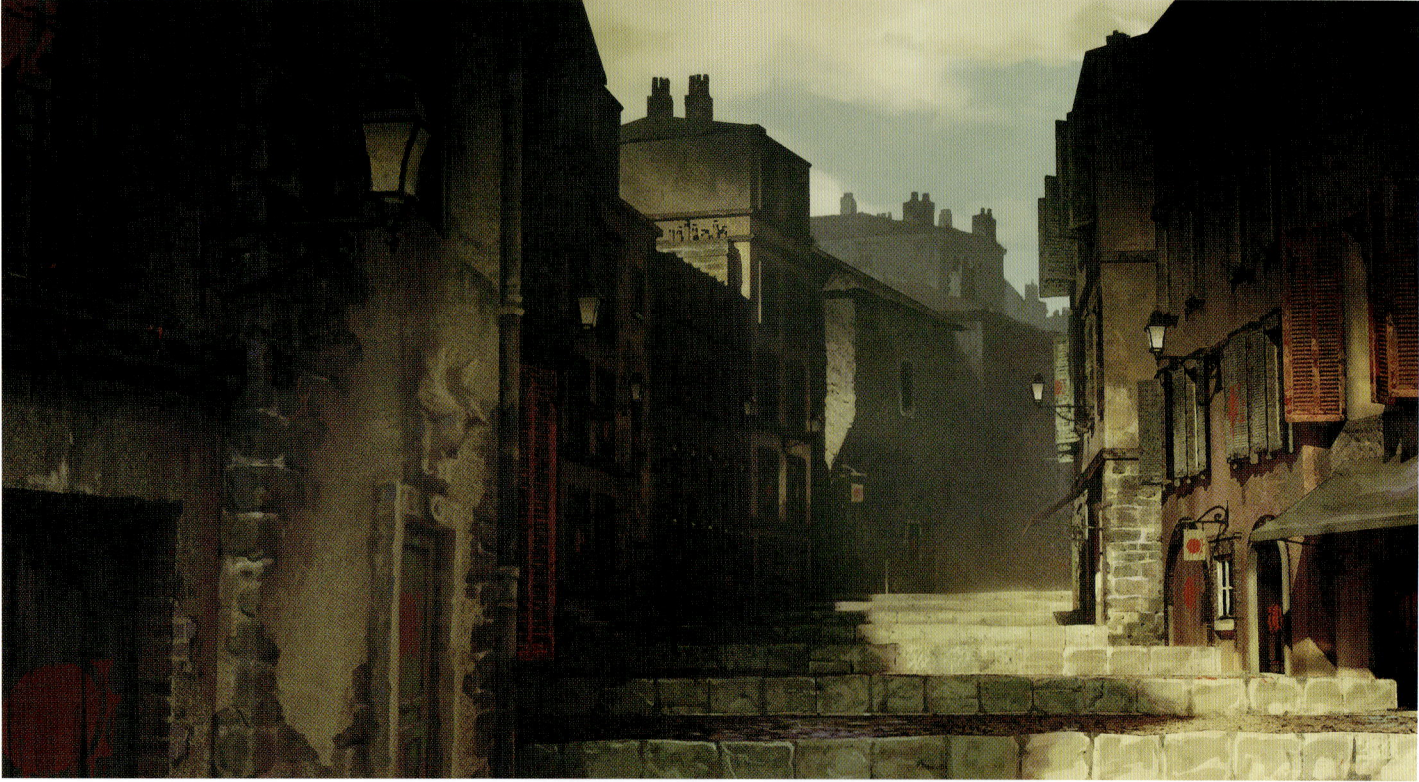

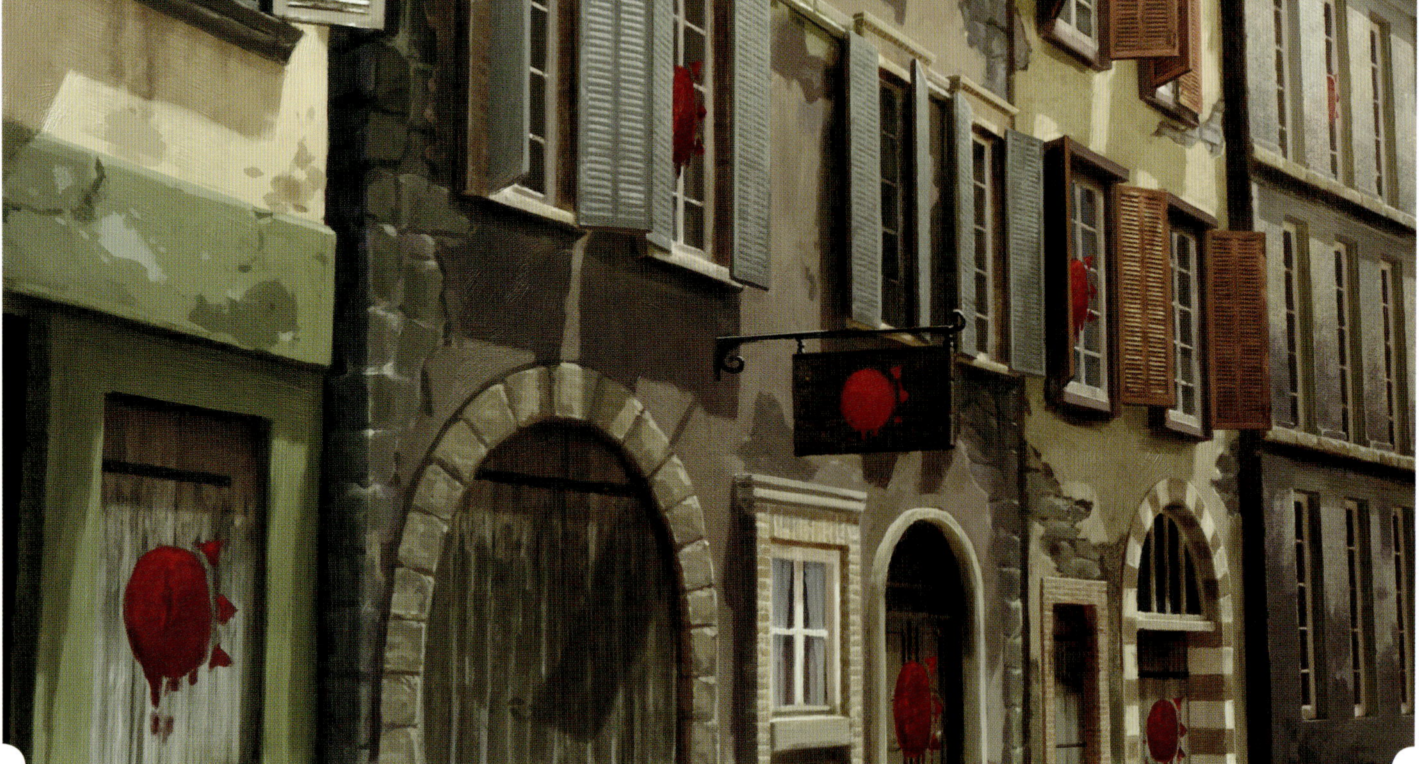

"This is, I think, a fun contrast and a perfect example of what Steve was talking about in terms of going towards 'grittified' in season two versus the idyllic side in season one. The image on the right is when we really found our stride for season one and started to nail that colorful, cheerier vibe. But the images on the left are much grittier, much darker," background designer Sam Keiser said. He noted the artist who did the middle images included some nods to the game *Bloodborne*.

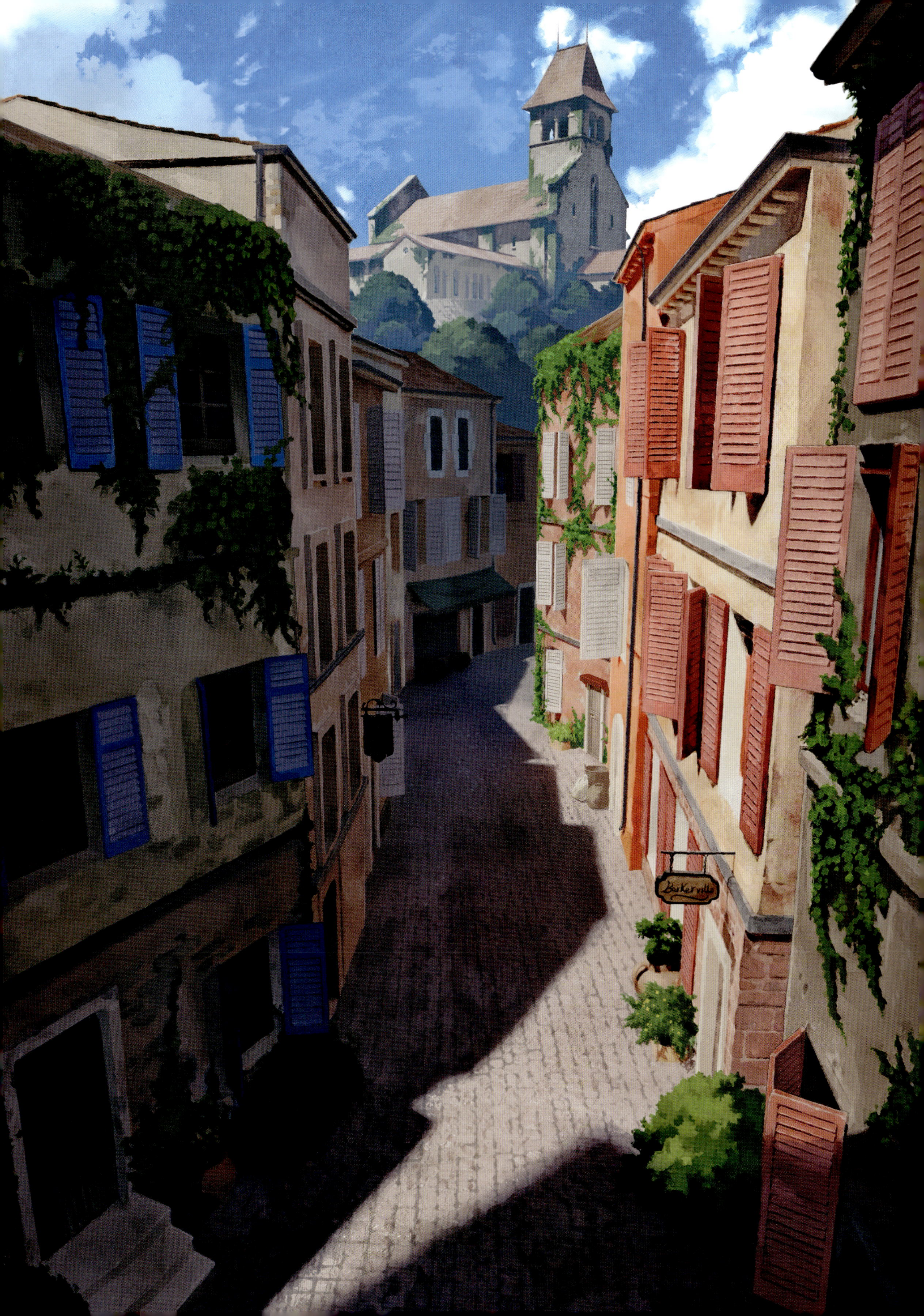

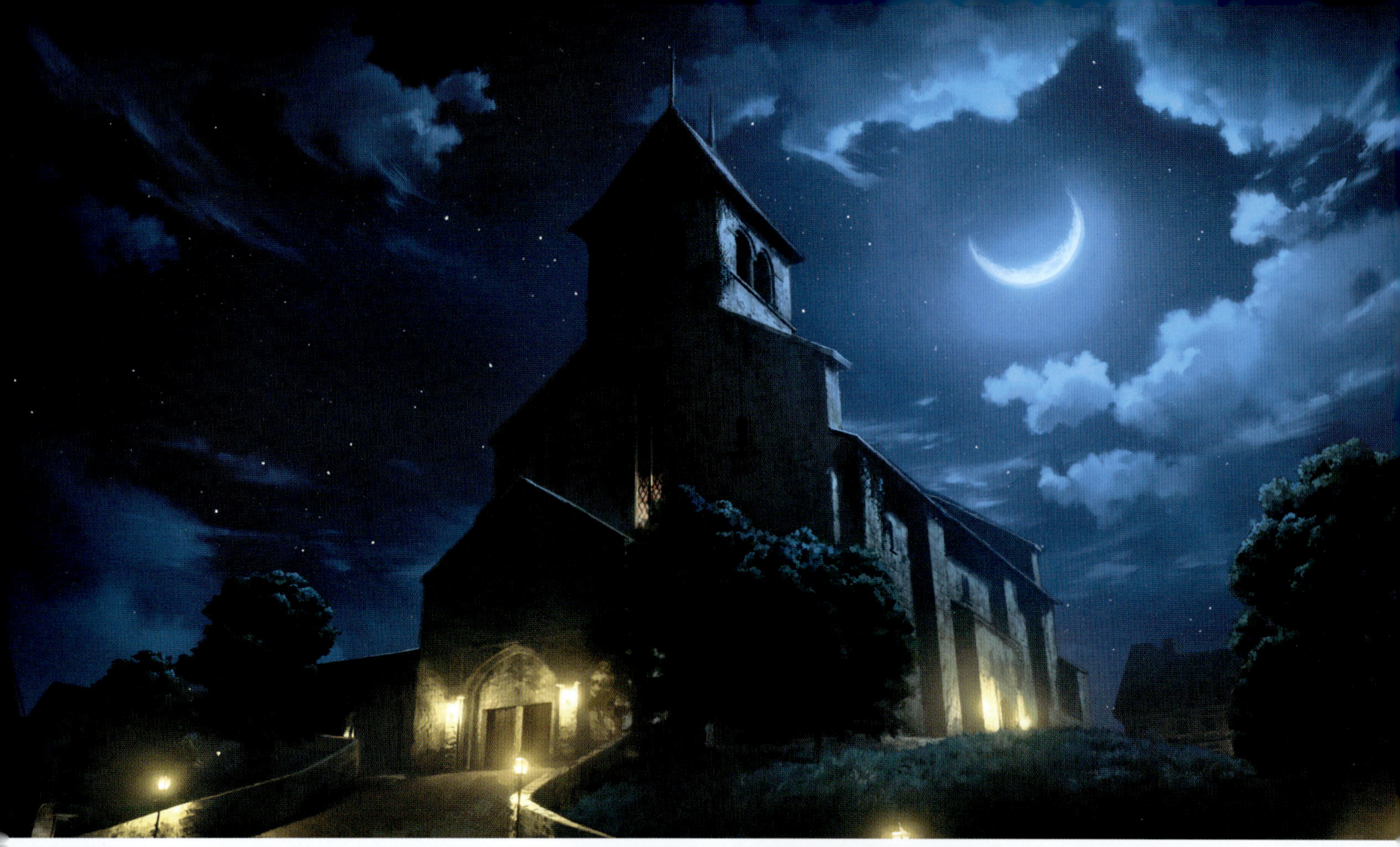

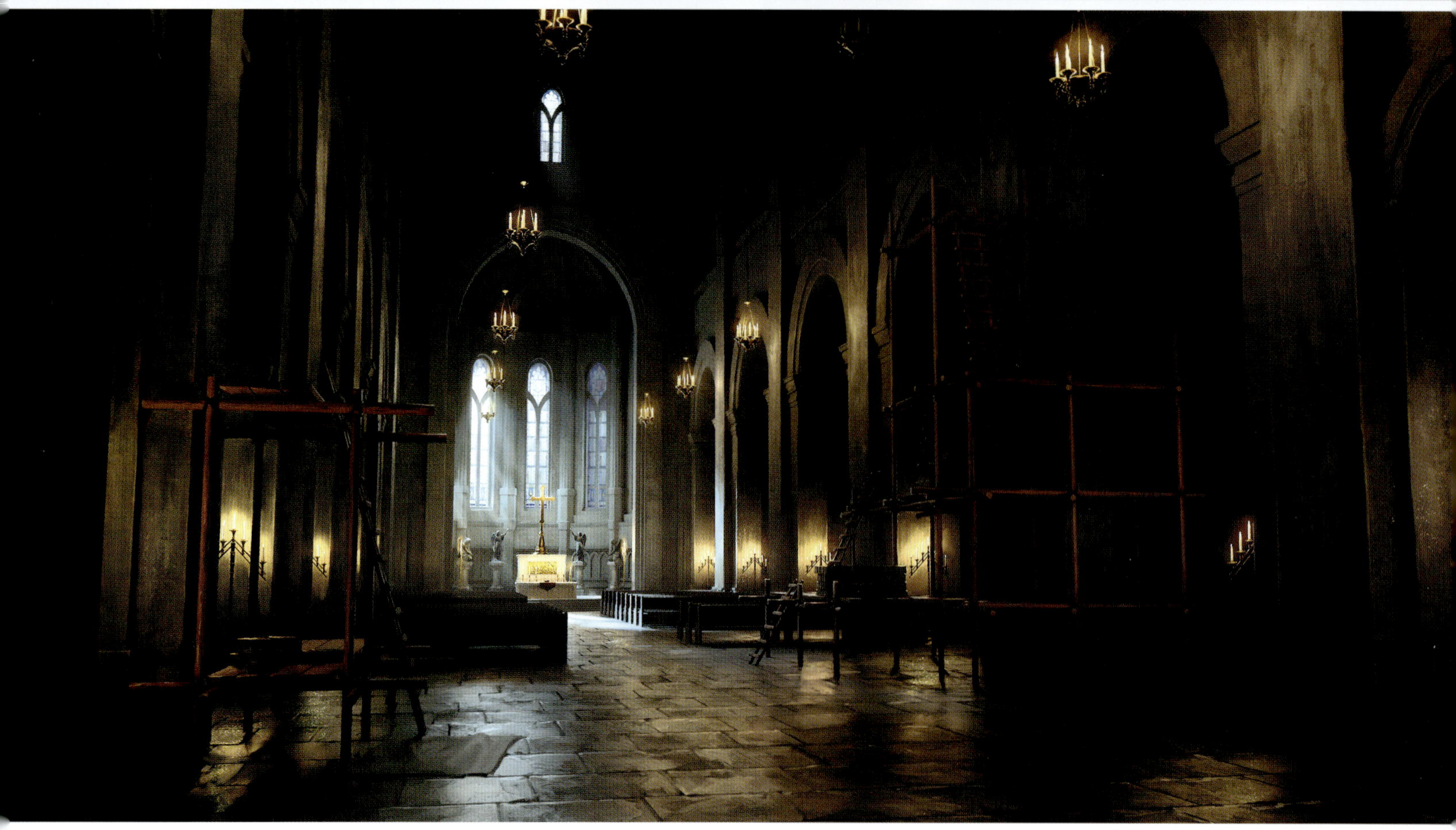

The Abbey

Both a place of divine worship and nefarious secrets, the team wanted the Abbey's design to reflect the dichotomy of its interior and purpose. Randolph said for the tone of the building he wanted to hit a middle note. In the first full exterior shot of the Abbey in the series, as seen above, he wanted the mood to look like it could be a normal night in a church or be a place with a bit more of an ominous edge. He wanted to reflect, that, though Abbot Emmanuel is a villain, the audience is not aware of his full involvement at this point. When he finalized the exterior, he passed that shape off to Keiser to take charge of the abbey's interior architecture.

Opposite top: Sean Randolph, Opposite bottom: Sam Keiser. Top left: Sean Randolph, Top right: Sam Keiser, Middle: Ian Jun Wei Chiew, Middle row: Sean Randolph, Bottom: Sam Keiser.

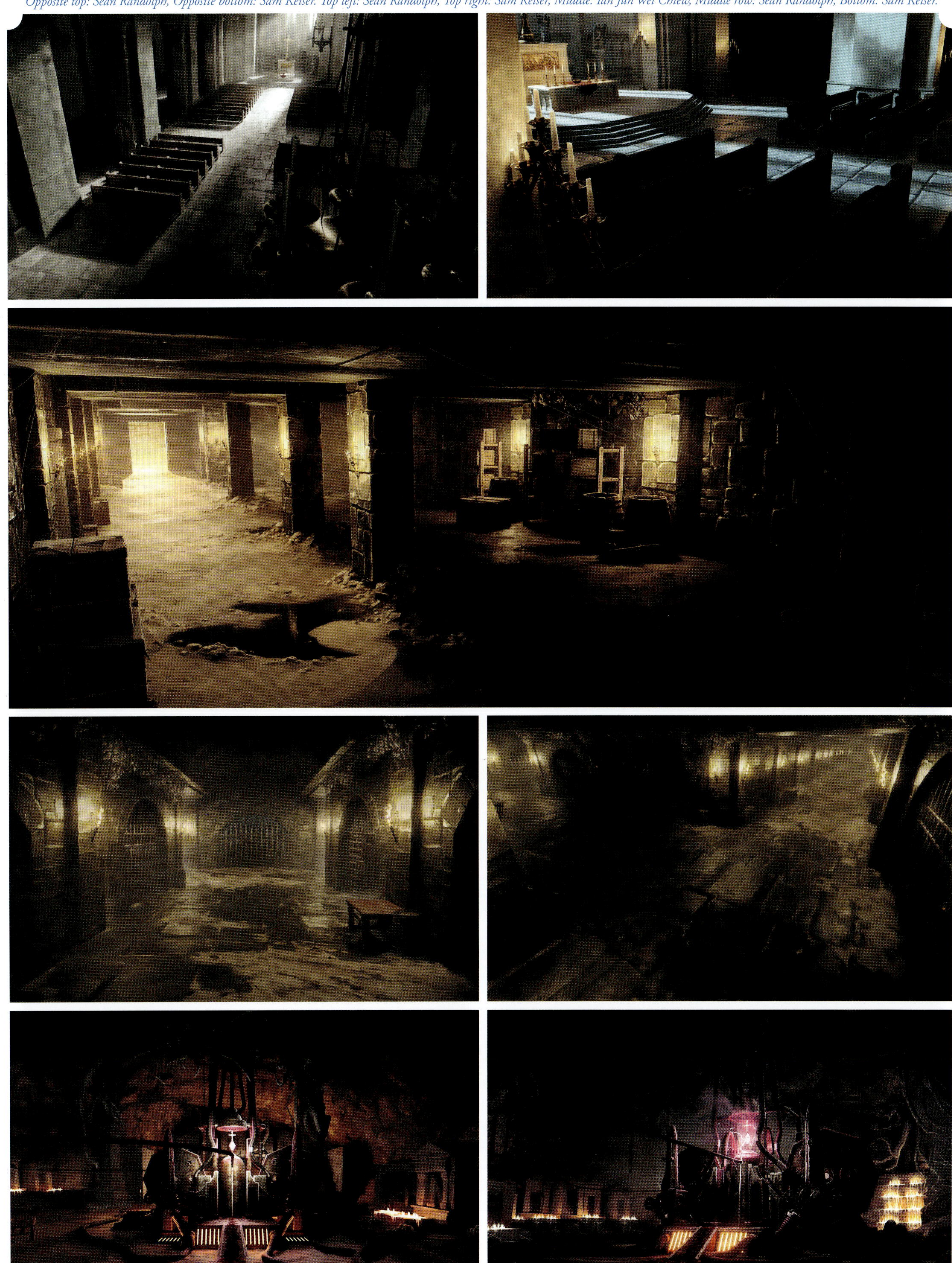

Keiser said one of the art direction notes he got and really held onto was that the inside of the Abbey should show someplace that's past its prime, but still demonstrate that it did once have its glory days. He noted, "That's the reason why I started putting things like the scaffolding in there. There's a lot more wear and tear on the sides. At first, I had the sides filled with alcoves like in Notre Dame, but I realized it was too grand."

Storyboards by Samuel Deats.

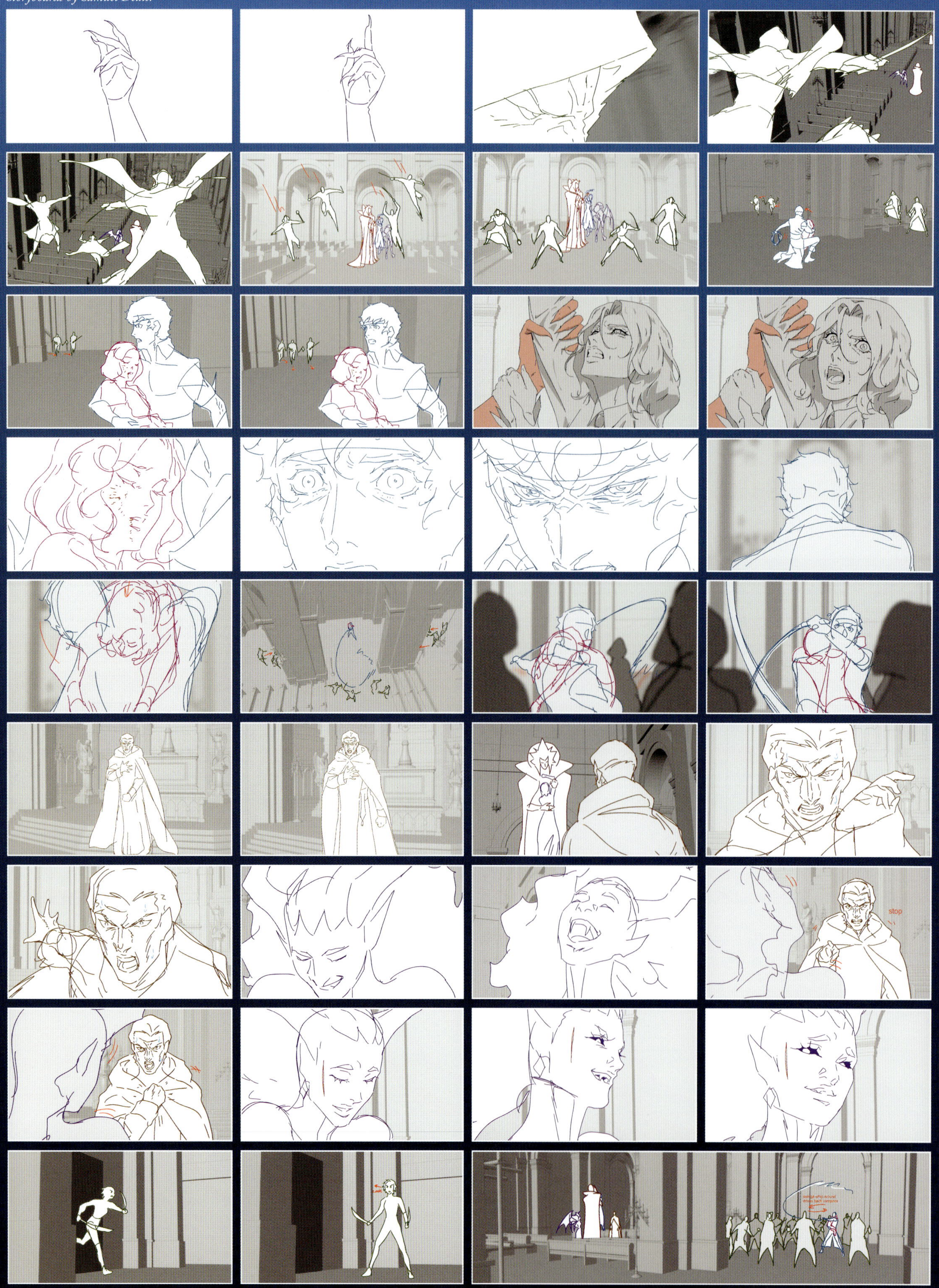

This episode, as Sam recalled, was very chaotic. He said, "There were a lot of balancing acts between what's going on upstairs versus what's happening downstairs with the portal opening and what Annette is doing. You're having to constantly have a mental chess board going on to be like, okay, this character's here, this character's over here."

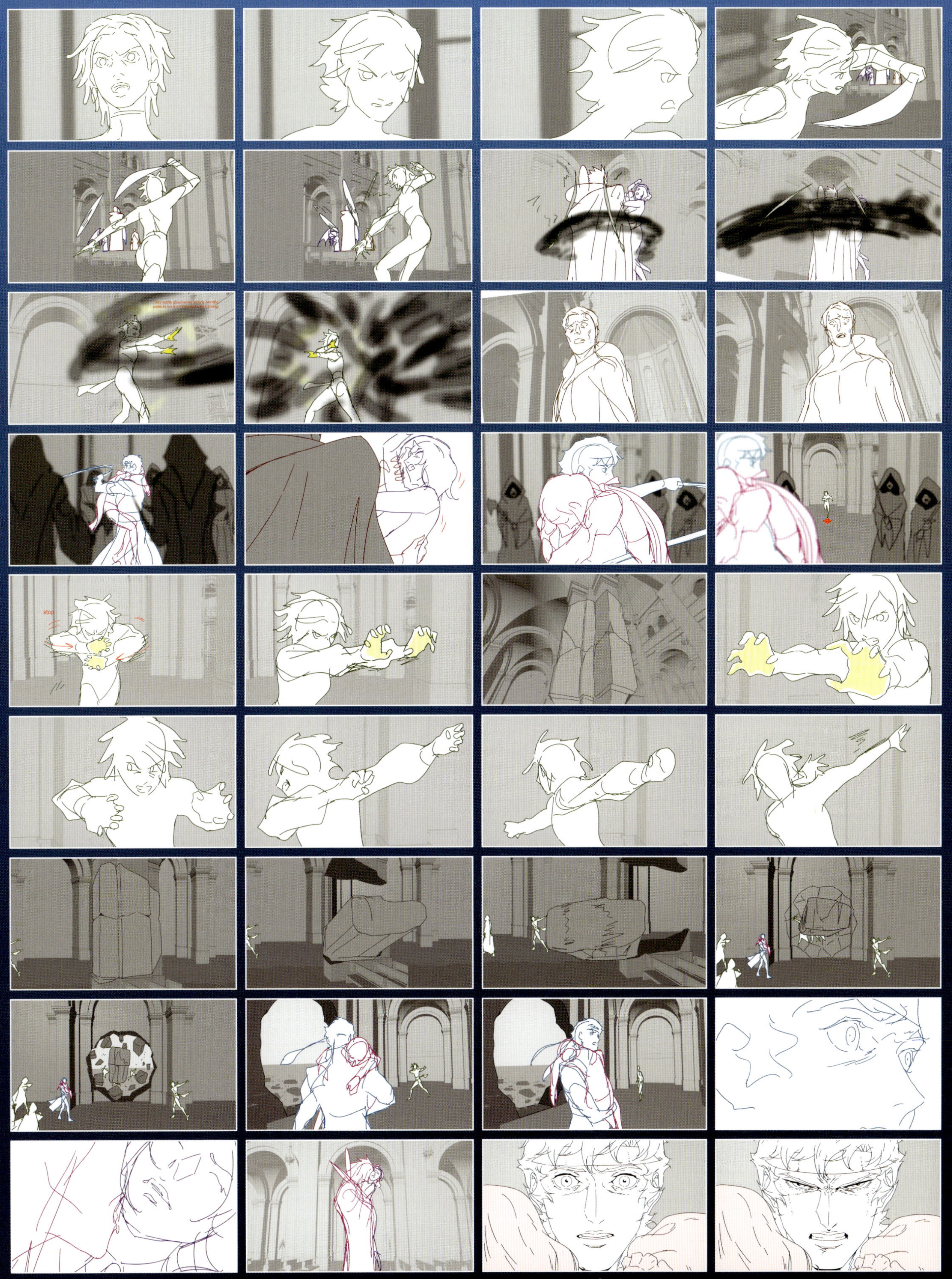

Sam handled the action happening upstairs and handed off the downstairs shots. The fight destroyed many elements of the interior. "It was very tricky, constantly having to work out what's getting broken in the environment where the characters are progressively moving—a fun challenge, but a difficult one," Sam said. These rough layouts plot the complex action that took place across the various abbey locations.

Storyboards by Samuel Deats.

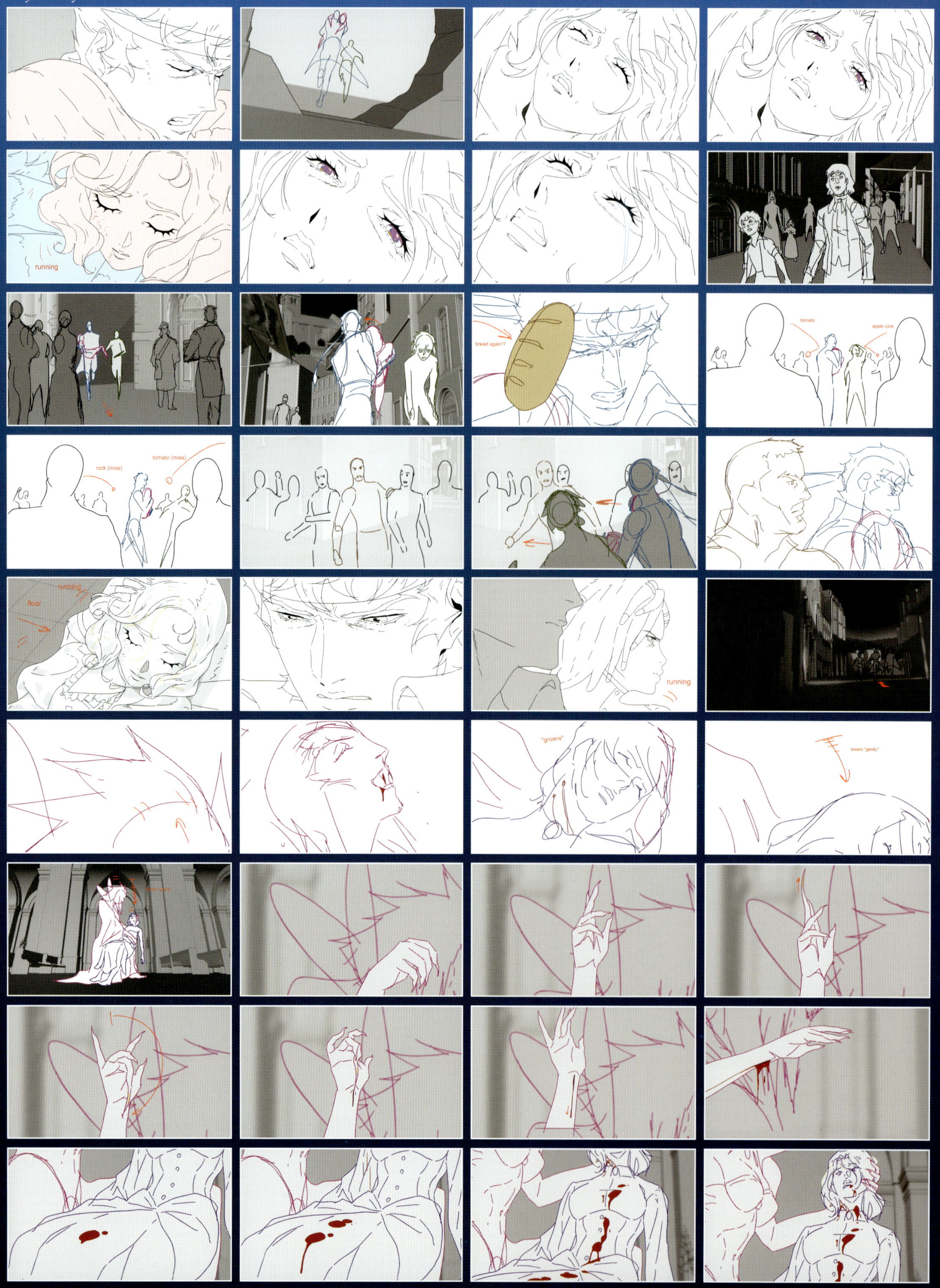

"The sequence of Tera turning was a really important one for me," Sam said. "I was wanting to get across just how unsettling and horrible it is to see someone who's effectively been a mother to Richter—is literally Maria's mother's—who is literally infected by something and it's possessing her,"

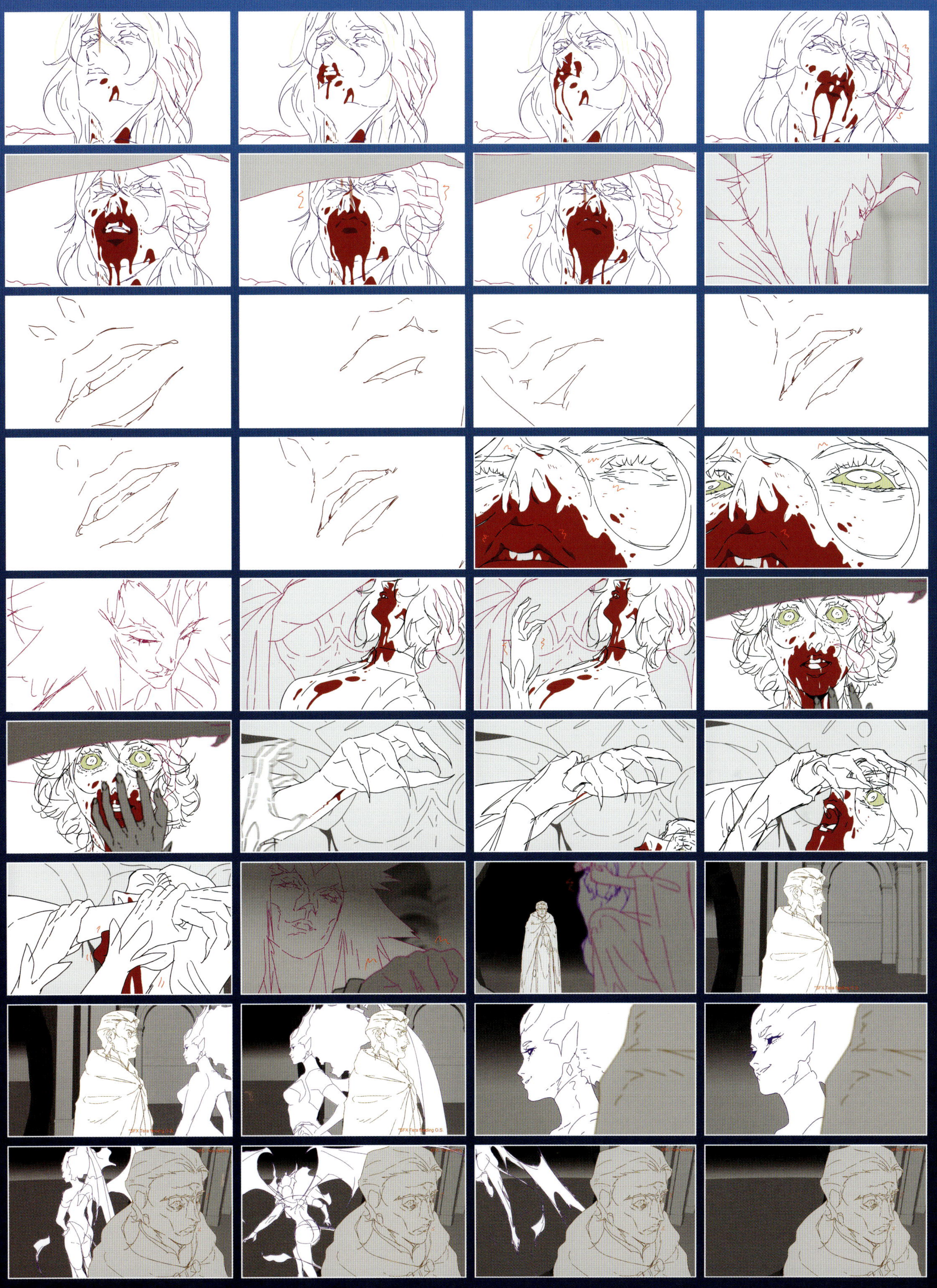

They put special effort into this sequence to make it gruesome and messy, to make the audience's skin crawl. They gave the Abbot a character beat here as well. Sam said, "He could have turned away and not looked, but he doesn't. He owes it to Tera to watch this happen."

Top left: Sam Keiser, Top right: Sean Randolph, Middle: Sean Randolph, Bottom: Sean Randolph.

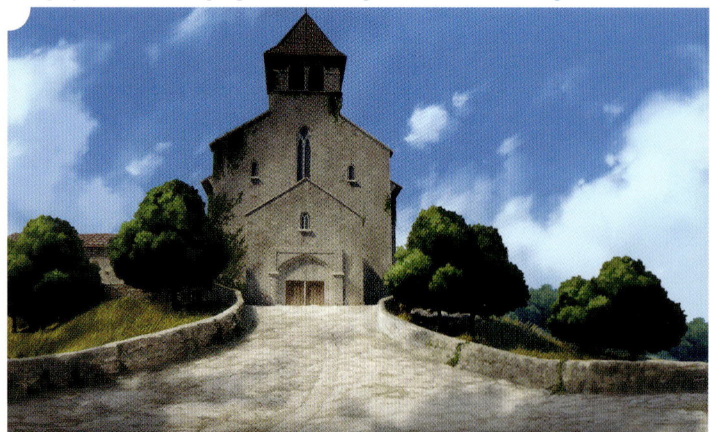

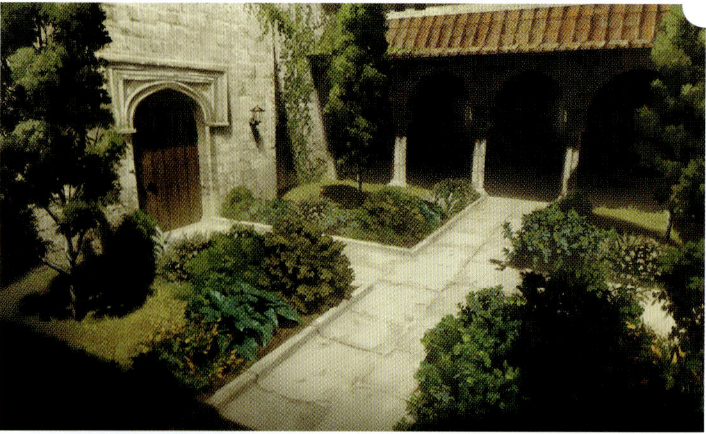

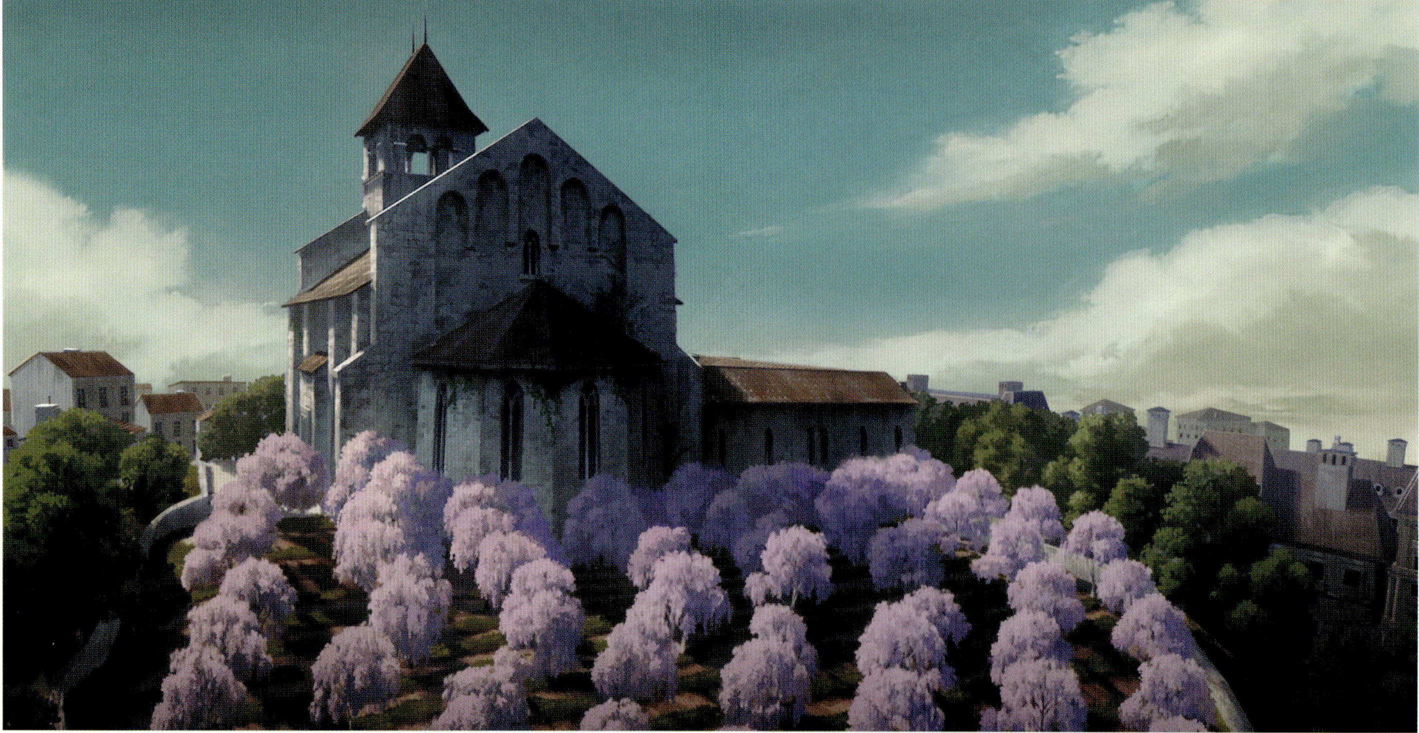

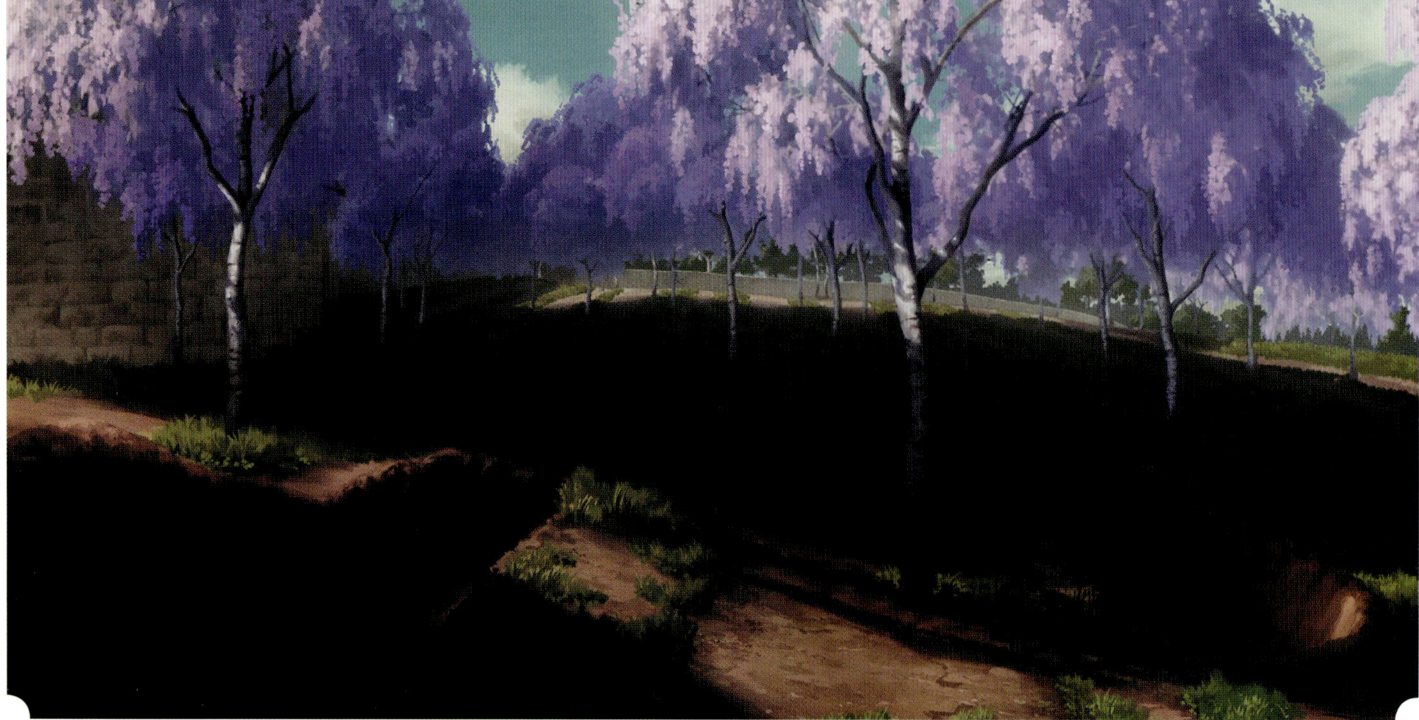

"For the Abbey design," Randolph said, "I added the little side garden area. Specifically, I had the scene in mind where Mizrak and Olrox are having their very gay talk. I had the idea of having this square area because I knew that if the sun hit it in a certain way, half of the area would be covered in shadow. I thought it would be a fun backdrop for a certain time of day. I also designed these trees in the background, but we never really had an opportunity to see the back of the Abbey."

Top: Stephen Stark, Bottom: Sean Randolph.

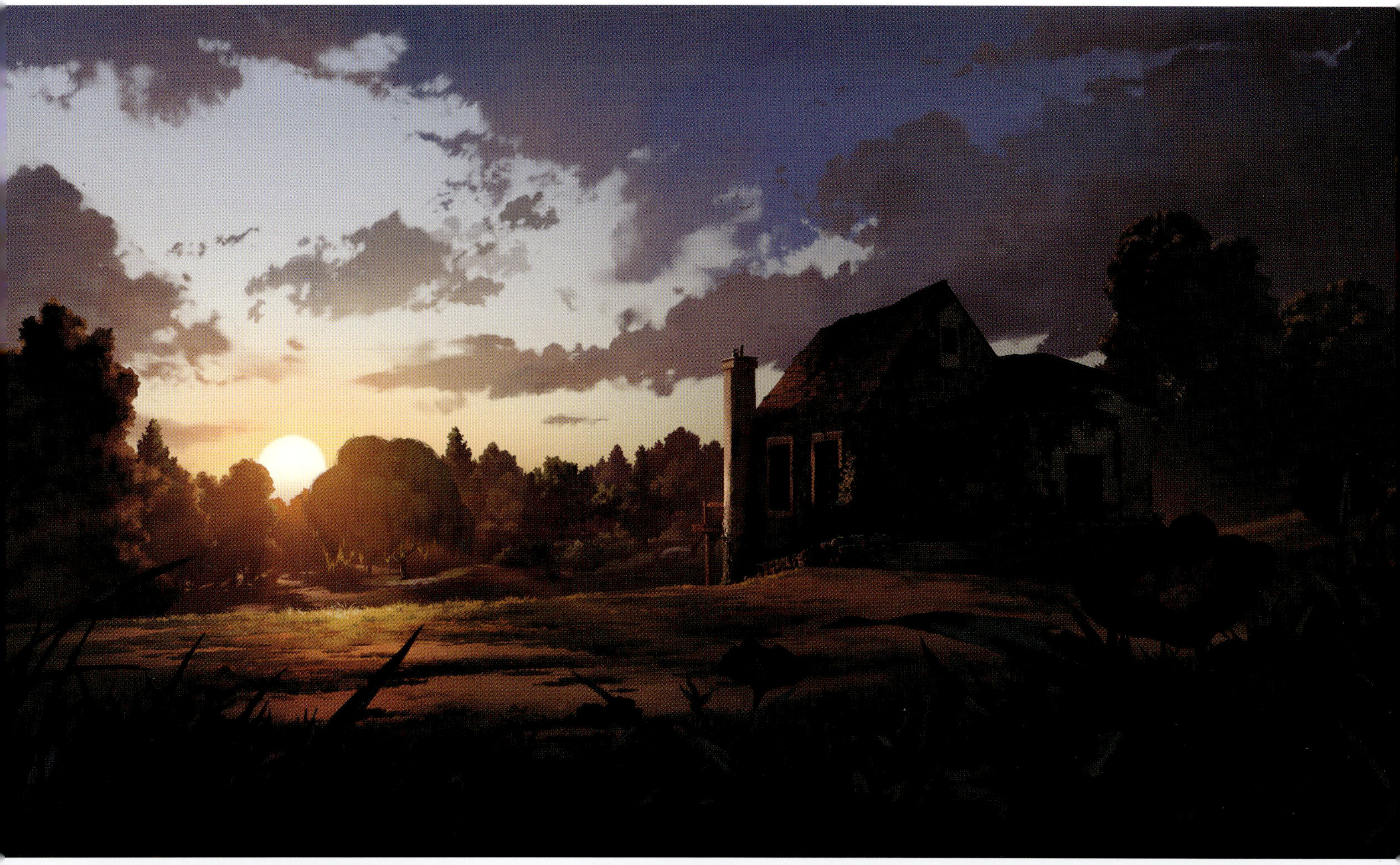

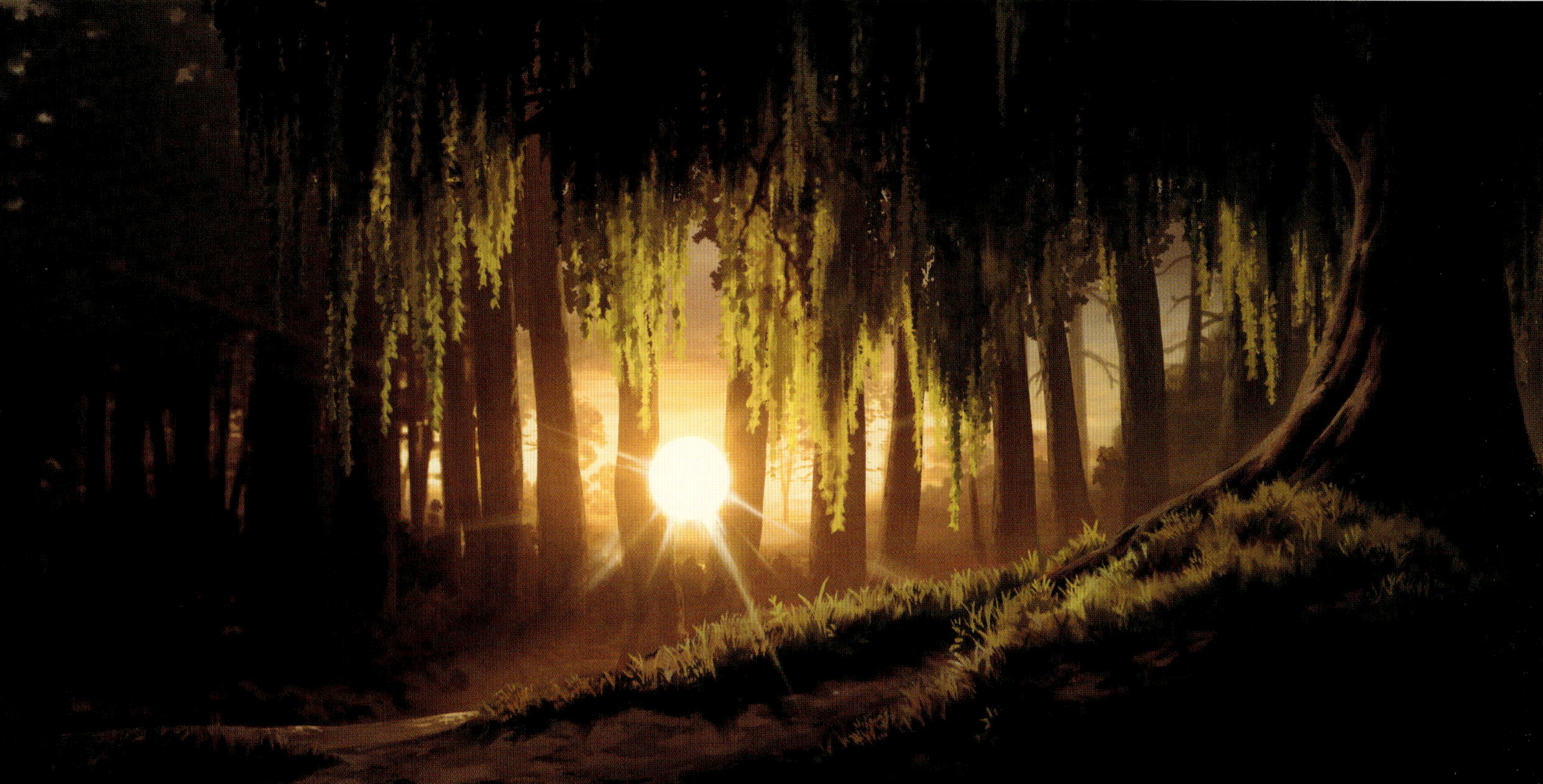

Tera's House

Tera's house is in the countryside in a storybook setting. The willow tree seen above was in the script for outside of her home and it arches gracefully with a mournful design for a specific scene. But overall, Stark remembered he wanted to give the home a cottage core vibe. In his personal canon, Tera had some amount of disposable income and was thus able to live slightly away from Machecoul, decorating the home she's made for her and her daughter in comfort, if not in opulence.

Top: Bo Li, Middle and bottom: Stephen Stark.

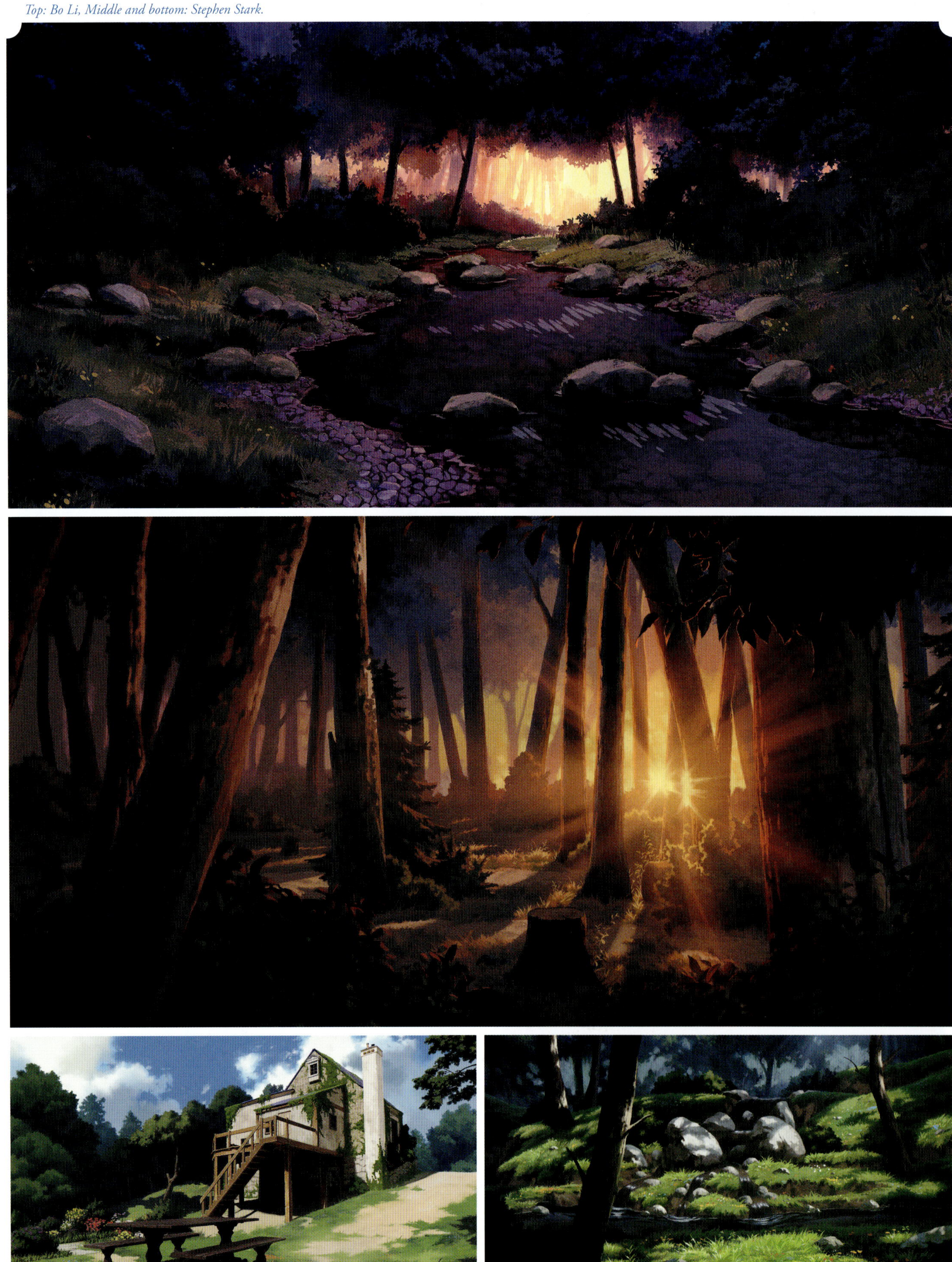

Stark specifically recalled the picnic table design for Tera's house; he said he was in a meeting with the writer and the producer and they made fun of the table for looking like it was right out of an American National Park. He went back to the drawing board to create something more in line with rural France. The image also shows some of Tera's garden, which Stark modeled on the garden from his childhood home.

Top: Stephen Stark, Insert: Sean Randolph, Middle: Sam Keiser, Bottom: Sam Keiser.

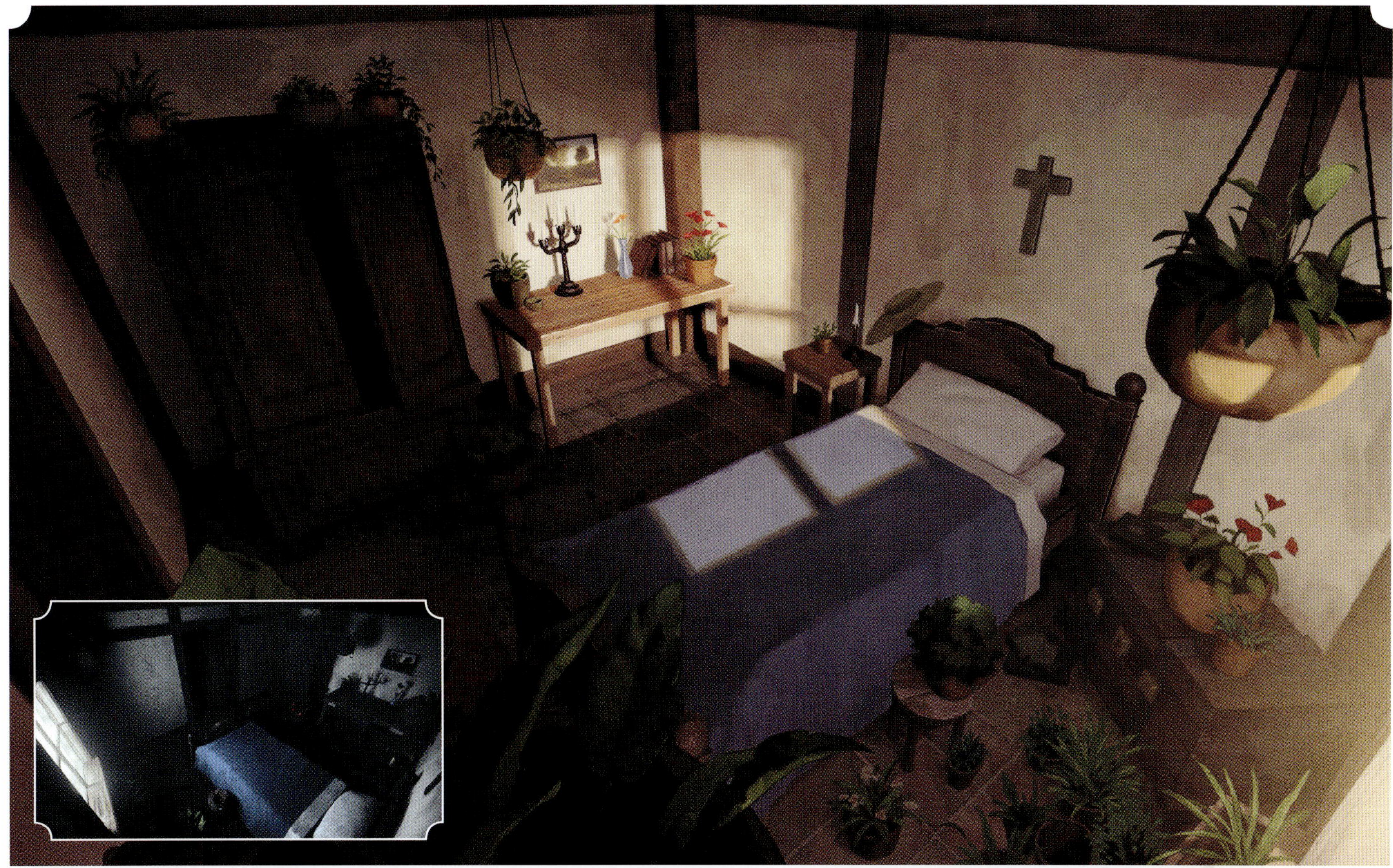

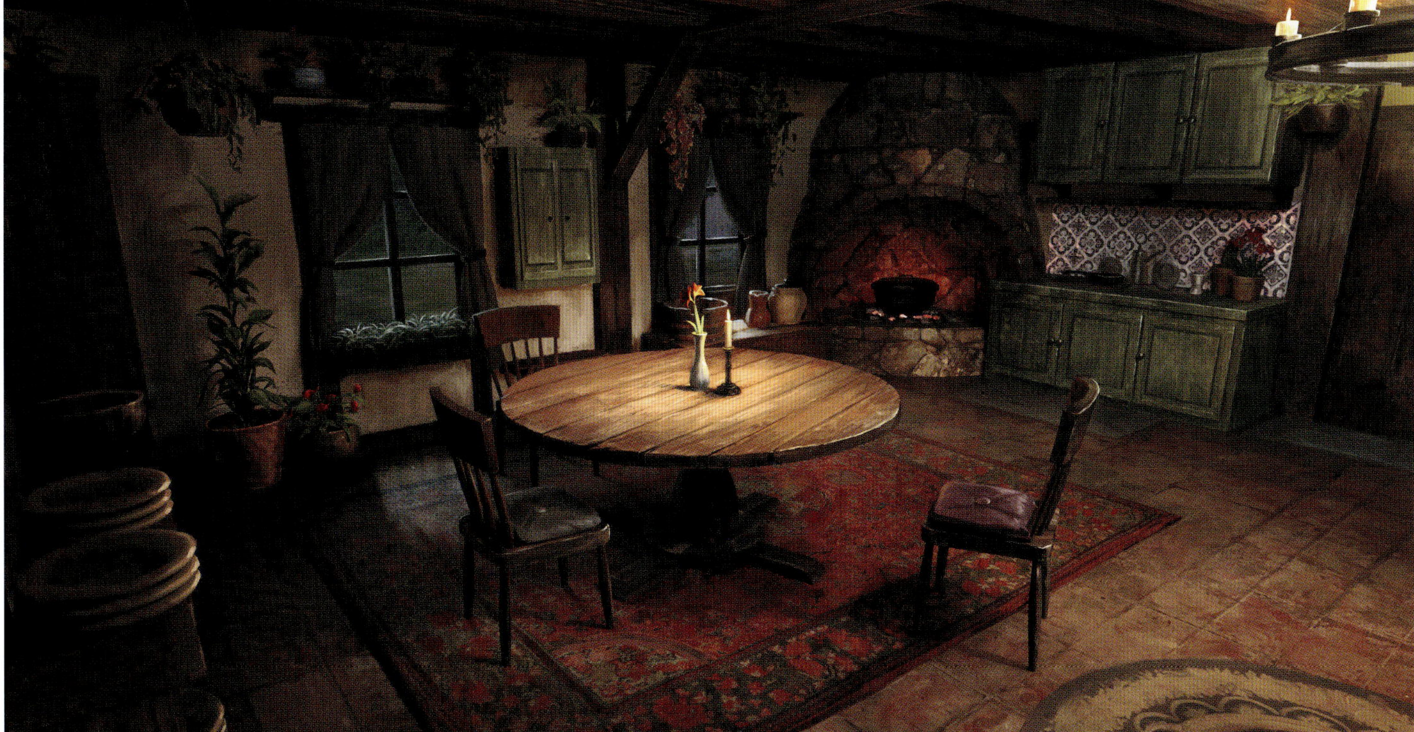

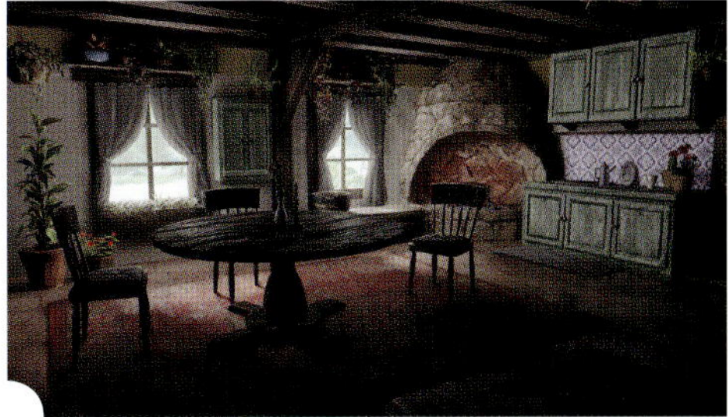

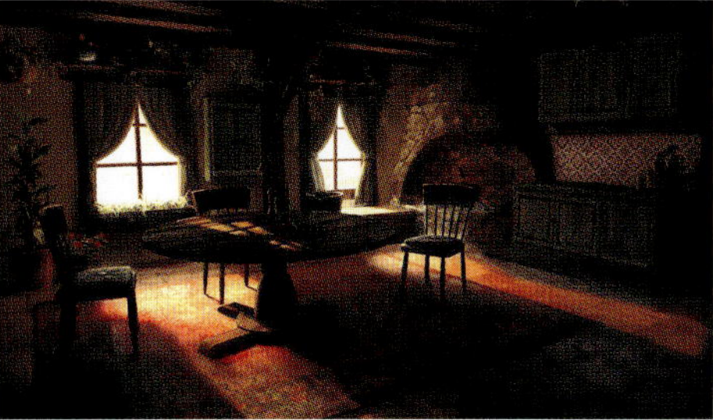

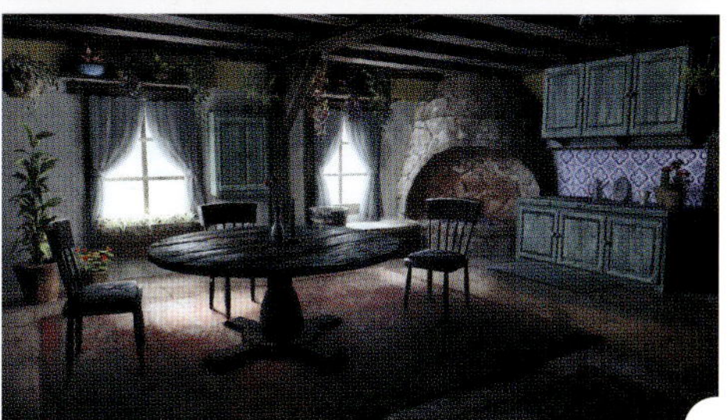

Keiser followed the cottage-core theming for the interiors in Tera's house. Plaster and wallpaper were just starting to become a thing around that time period, so they thought Tera would bring some of that into her home. He said, "In one of the concepts for some reason I did something where there was just a bunch of plants everywhere, and we dialed that back for the final concepts. She just really loves trying to nurture things and trying to bring them to life in some way."

Top: Stephen Stark, Insert: Stephen Stark, Bottom: Bo Li.

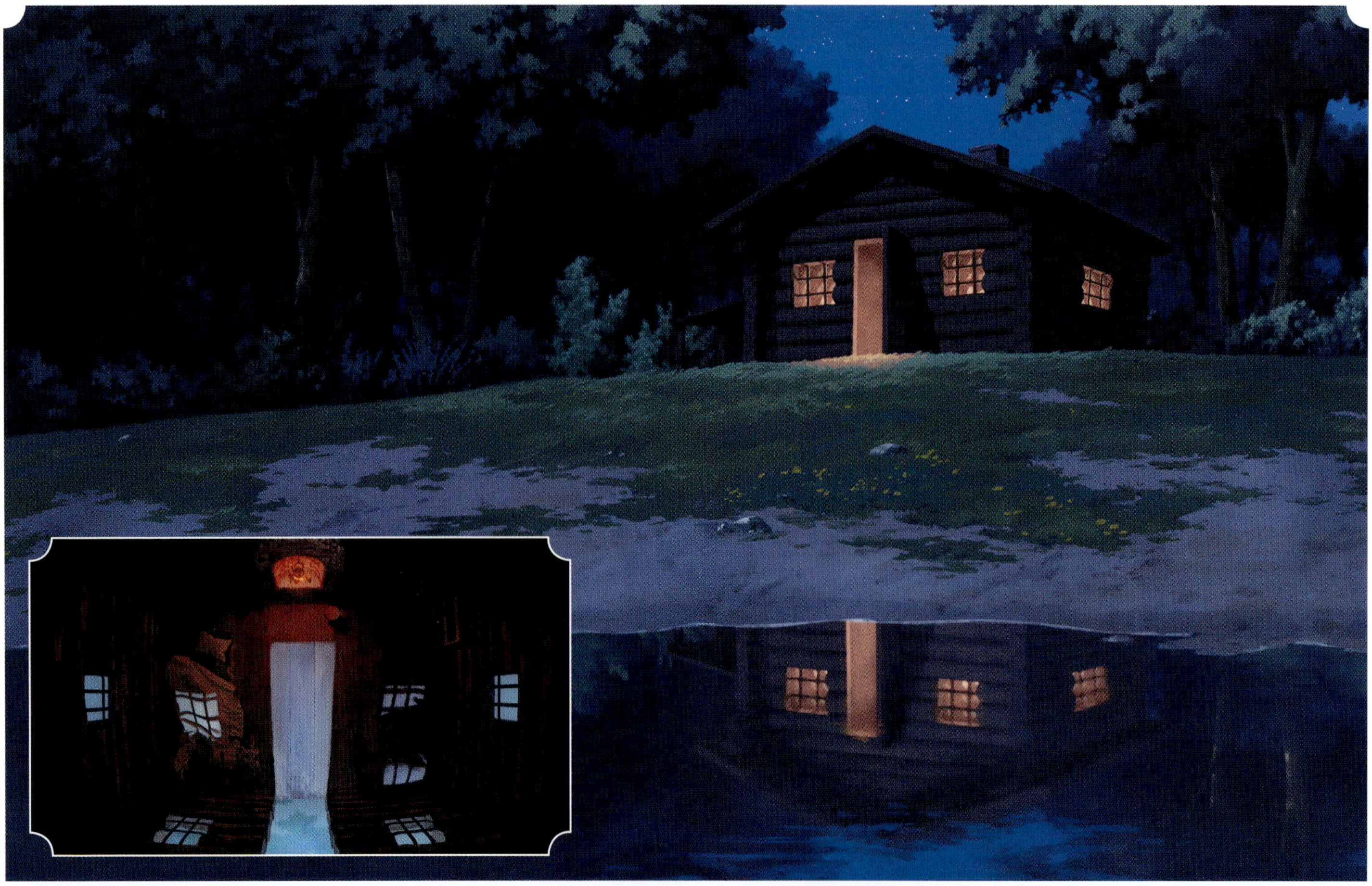

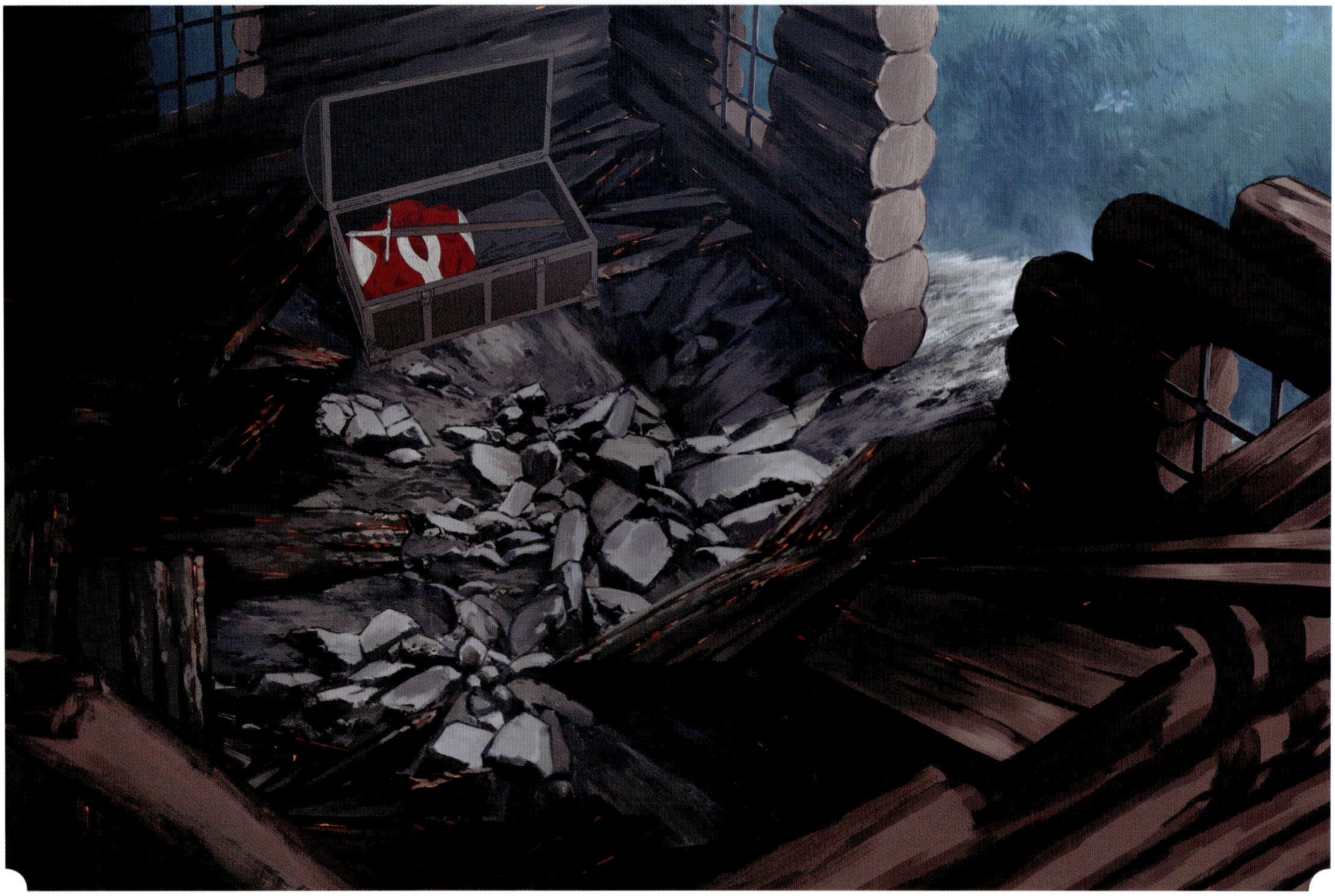

JUSTE'S HOUSE

Juste Belmont has made a simple life for himself, hiding away from the world. His cabin reflects that, with the idea being that he built the home in a short amount of time for function and shelter and moved on. It's without frills. He does, however, have a chest with a treasure. Randolph explained it continues the tradition from the first series of having some important piece of loot—Juste's sword, in this case—come out of a cool video game chest.

Storyboards by Samuel Deats.

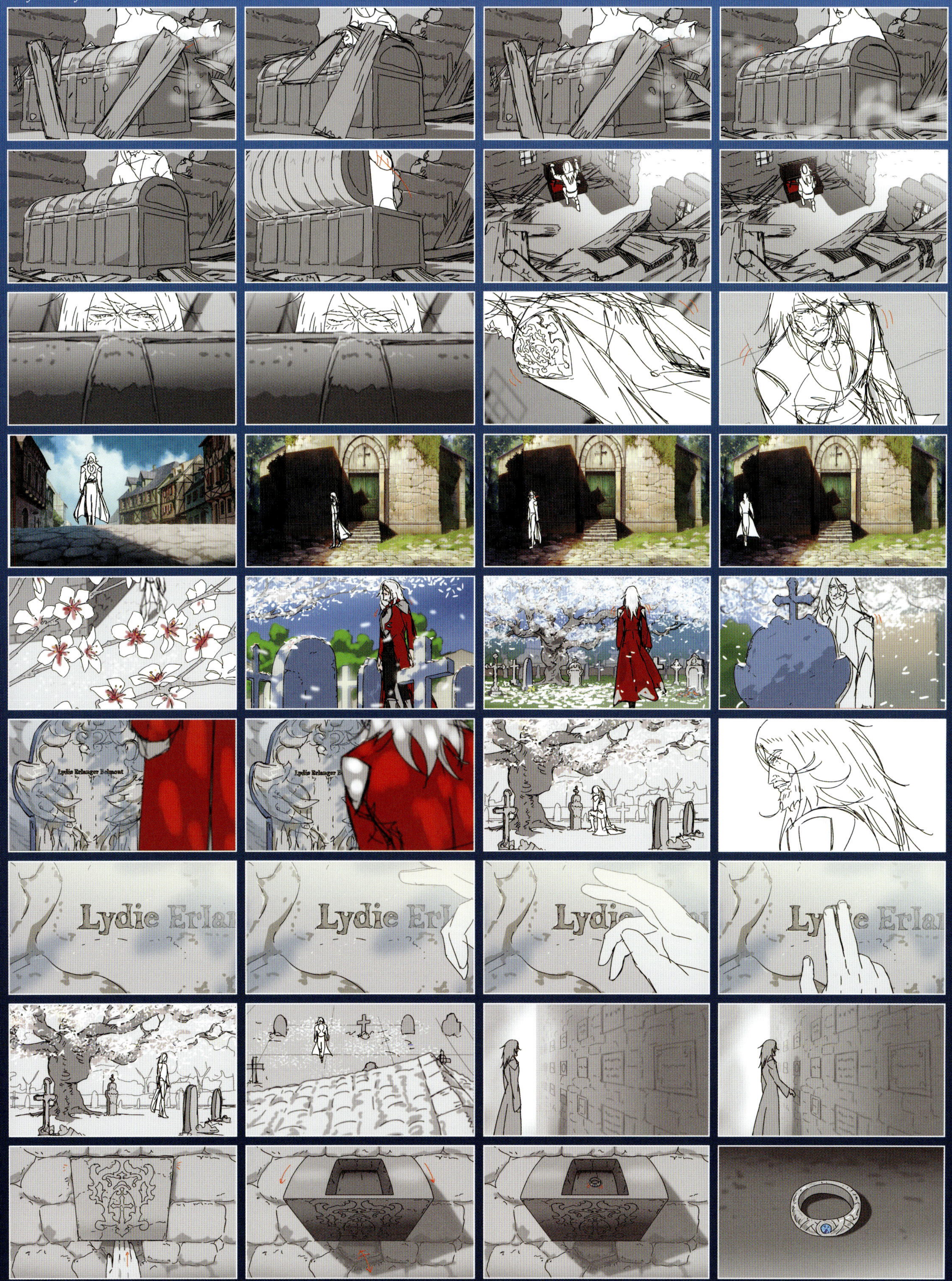

Here, Juste has decided to re-enter the fight as an active participant, no longer hiding away in his cabin. He pays his respects to Lydie, his departed wife, before embracing who he is. The almond tree by Lydie's grave has special significance. "I was playing to the combination of colors from Juste's red and Lydie colors with the bits of yellow that are in the bloom of the almond tree flower, and then white," Sam said. These rough layouts showcase the location of Juste's cabin.

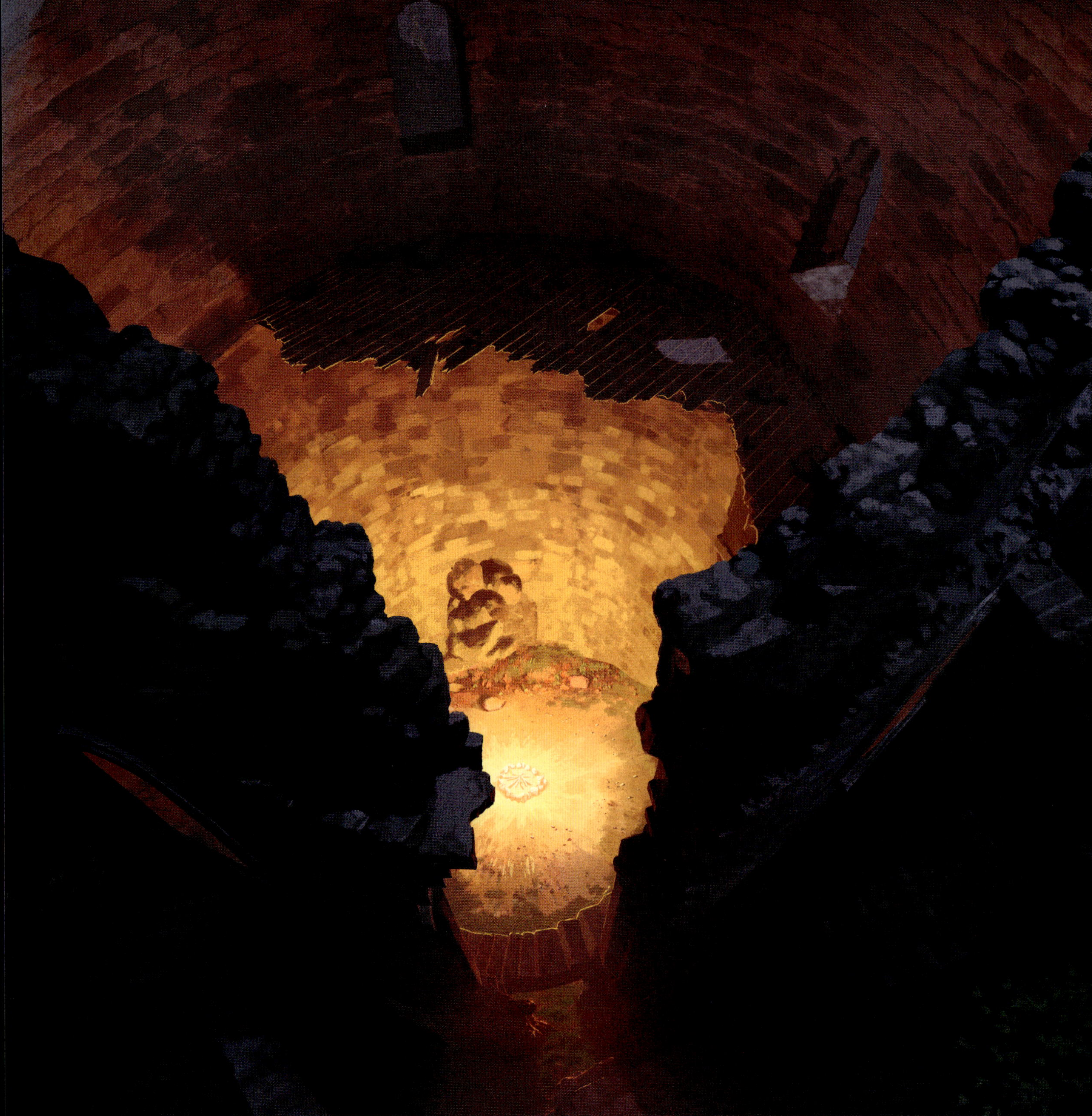

Castle Ruins

Castlevania: Nocturne notably does not include Dracula's castle, a cornerstone of the video games and the previous animated series, but it's not without castles altogether. The backdrop of France means a Western European sort of castle, quite separate in design from Dracula's manse. To illustrate the ruins, the background team researched both intact and crumbling castles of the era, considering the type of masonry and stone used and what it would look like it as it aged and fell into ruin.

Opposite: Stephen Stark. Top: Sean Randolph, Middle: Stephen Stark, Bottom left: Stephen Stark, Bottom right: Sean Randolph.

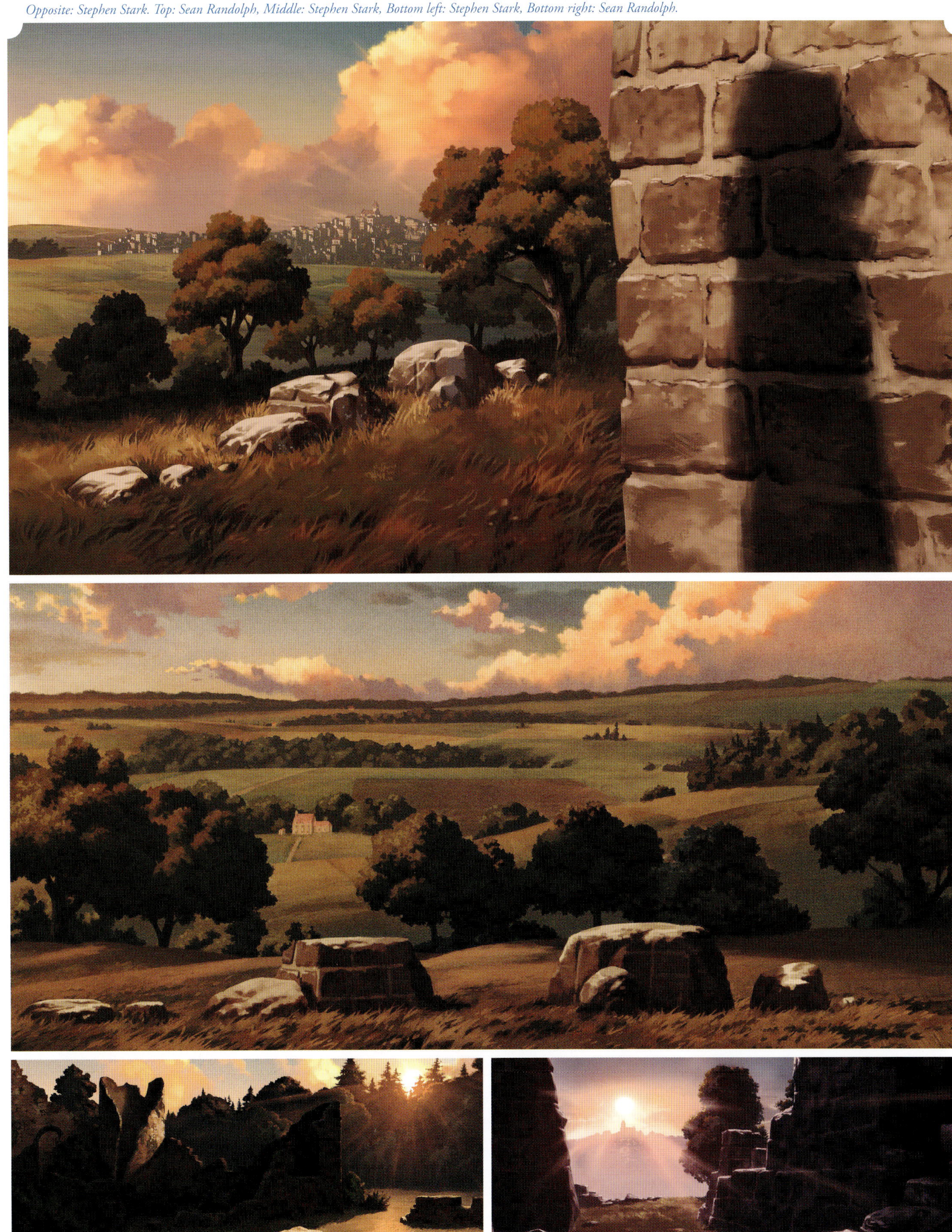

"The middle image is a direct reference, I believe, to *Kiki's Delivery Service*. I saw it while looking through images one day and loved the sweeping hills," Stark recalled. "I referenced that painting pretty directly, especially that little house in the middle. The foreground stuff, the line of trees, and the ruined seats from the castle are ours."

Art by Stephen Stark.

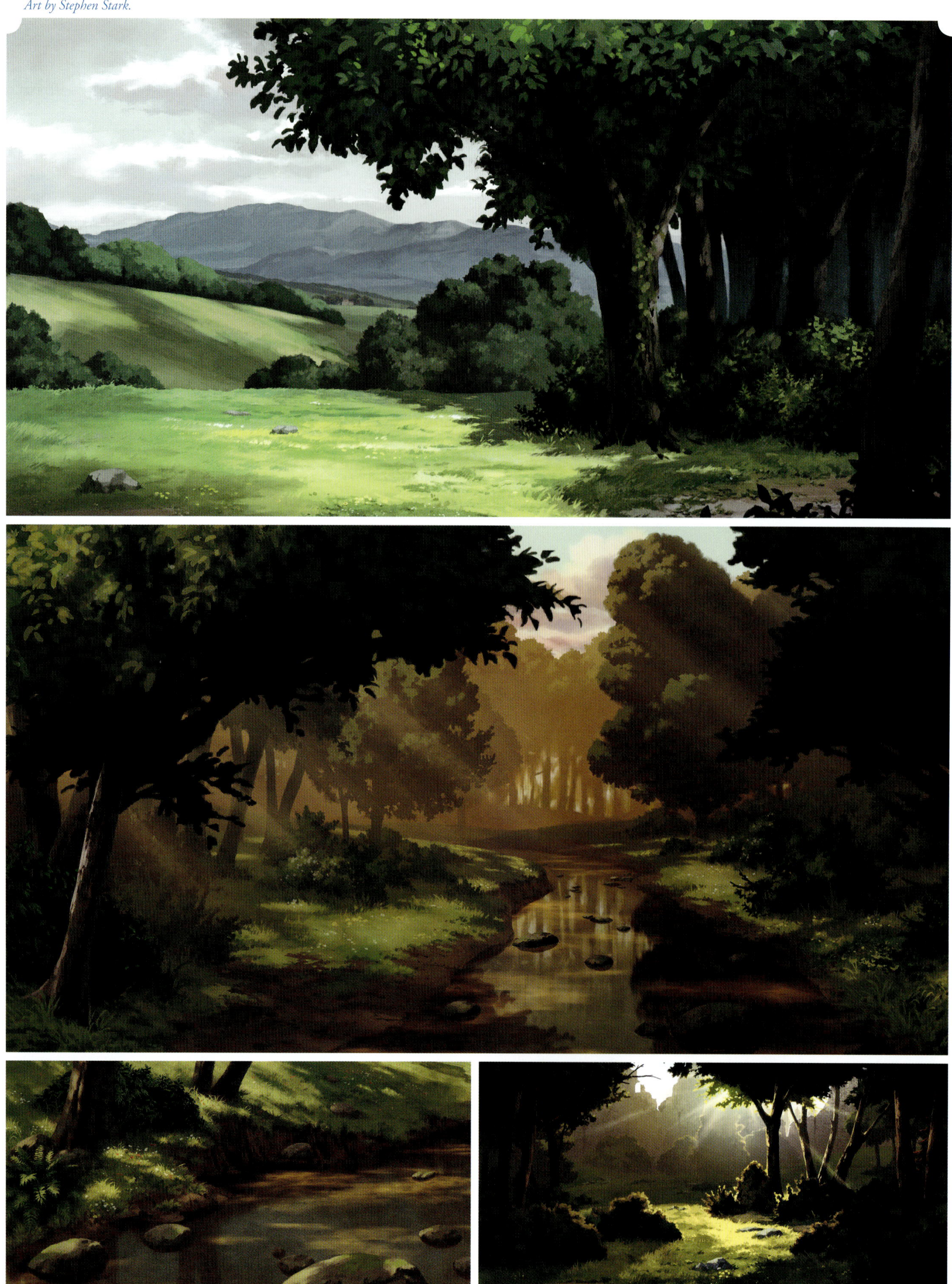

Studio Ghibli influenced, in part, the dreamy forests in *Nocturne*. Stark was hands-on with illustrating the forests, and he also experimented with doing some of the river animation himself by drawing three sets of the environment in slightly different spaces relative to one another. His cohorts credit him with being the first on the show's background team to animate the camera.

Storyboards by Samuel Deats, layouts by Jett Vaultz.

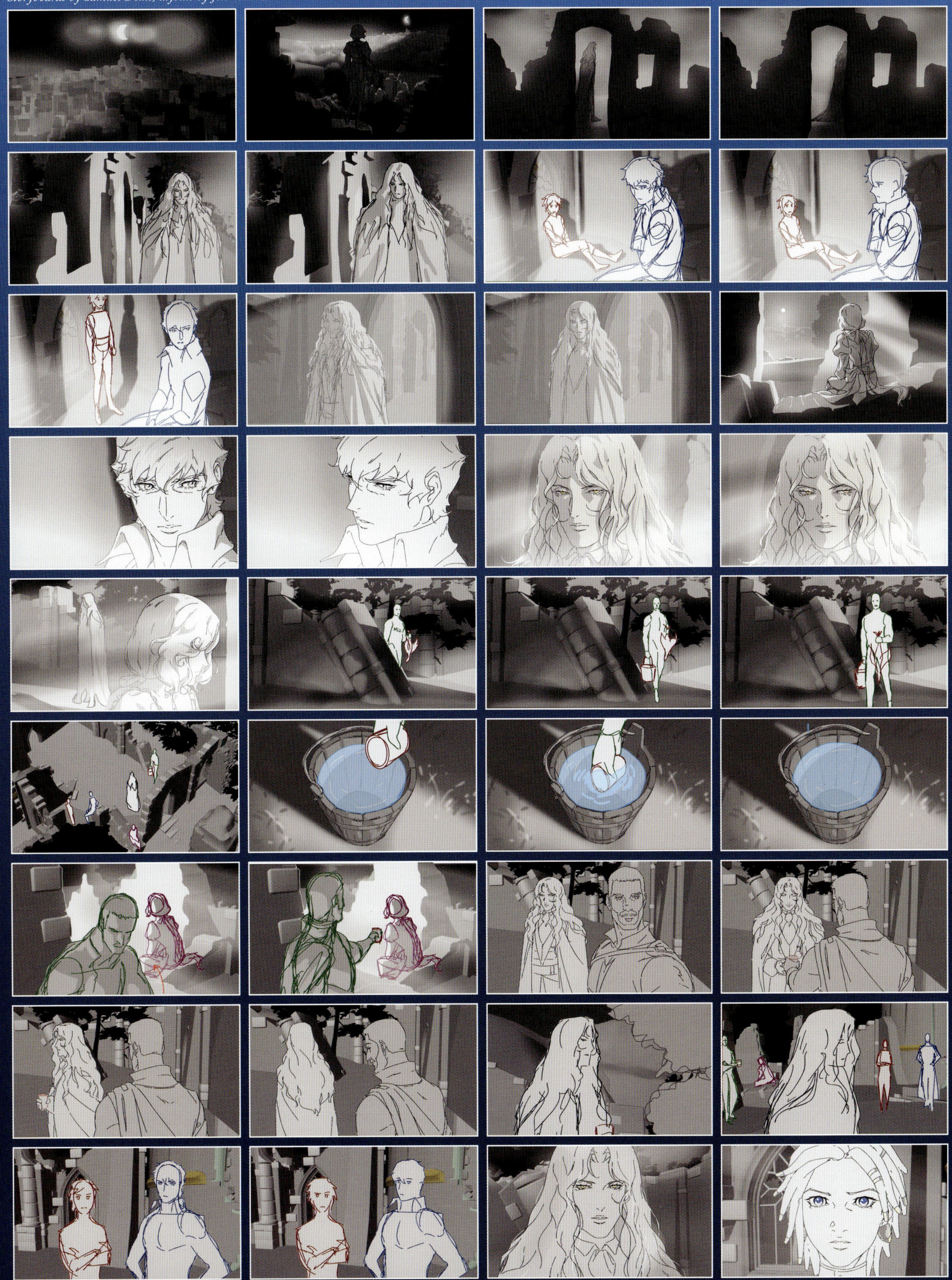

"This was a nice moment where we're getting to see Daddy Mizrak taking care of everyone," Sam said. "We're getting a little nod to his character and how he's chosen to now look out for these people and take care of them. We're also getting a moment of calm where the characters are getting to interact with Alucard. I wanted to get across a little bit of that mystique through their eyes when they're looking at him." These rough layouts plot this memorable moment that occurred near the castle ruins.

Top: Sean Randolph, Middle left: Sabina Lewis, Middle right: Sam Keiser, Bottom: Sabina Lewis.

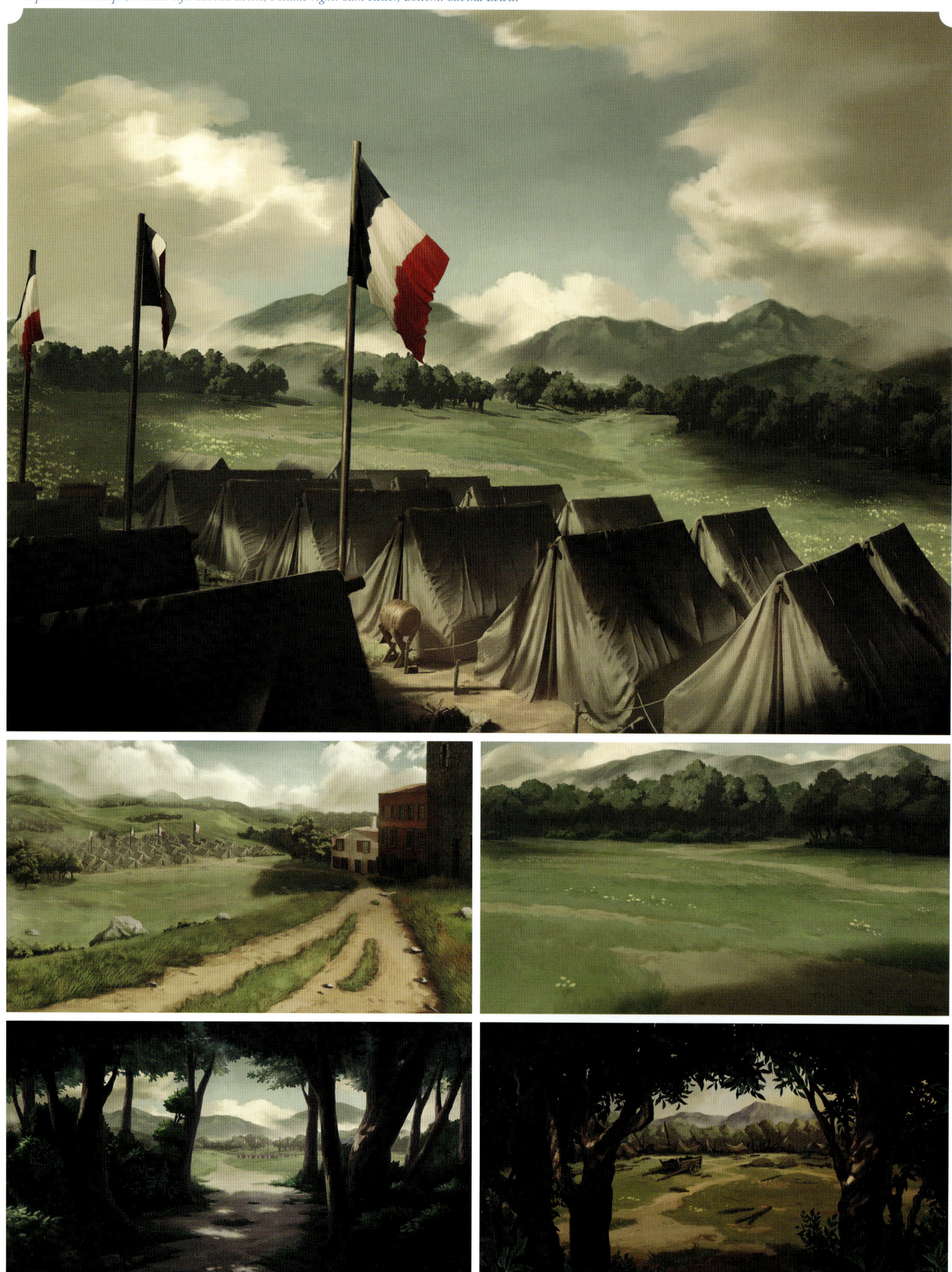

While the vampires are leveraging the egos of the aristocracy to enable their plans, the French Revolution plays out in the background—the struggle for power mirroring the battle of humans against Erzsebet and Drolta. The tidy layout of the military camp reflects the utilitarian and functional design one would expect. This is one of those environments that gets realized only for a character to destroy it.

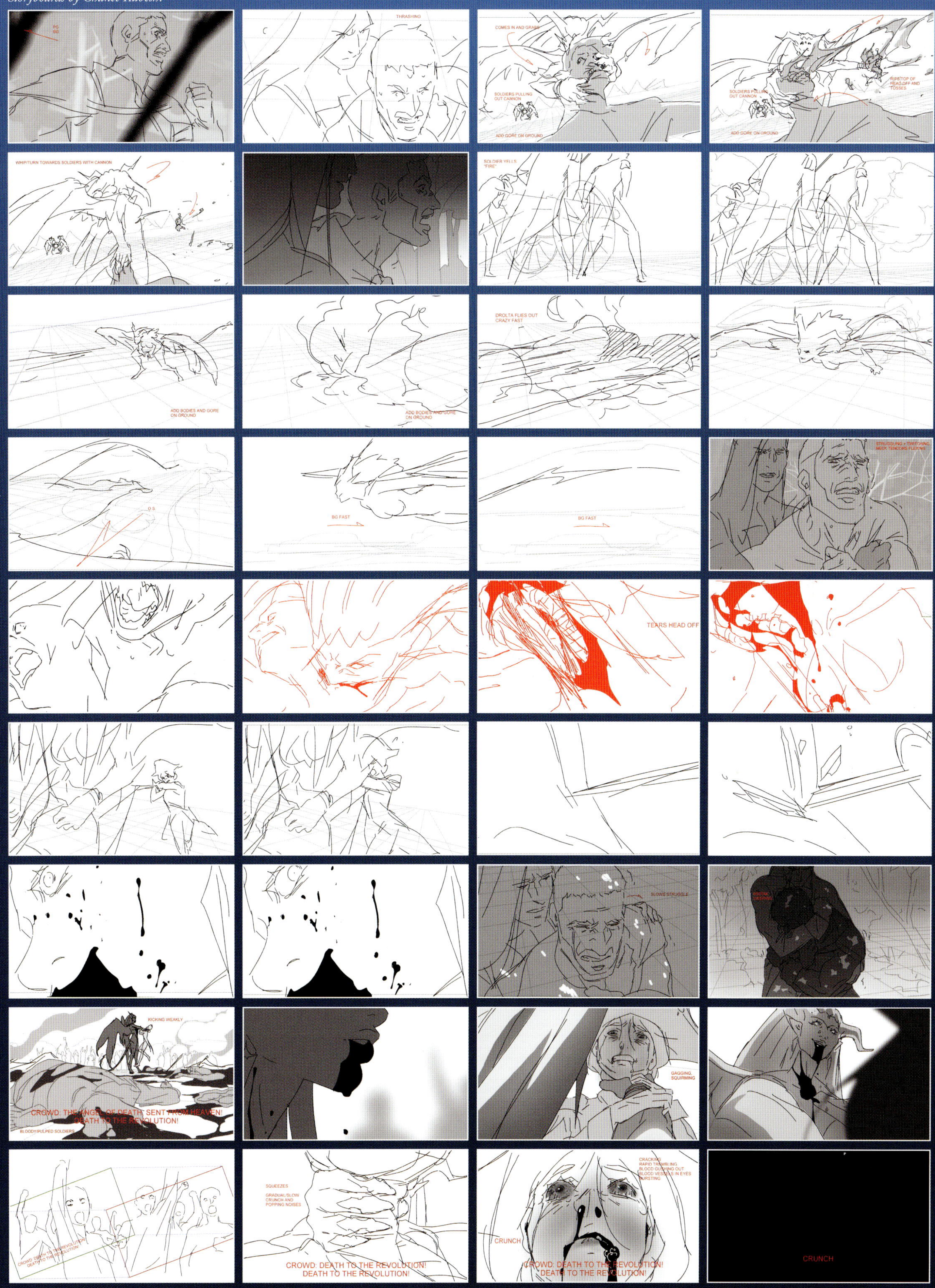

Storyboards by Chance Kubesh.

The line between layouts and raw storyboards can be blurry in this digital age, but executive producer Adam Deats clarified that the storyboard is the foundation, the rough drawing. Then, depending on the production, some folks might take that to a clean board, which is a tighter drawing more on model, or a layout, which is an even tighter version.

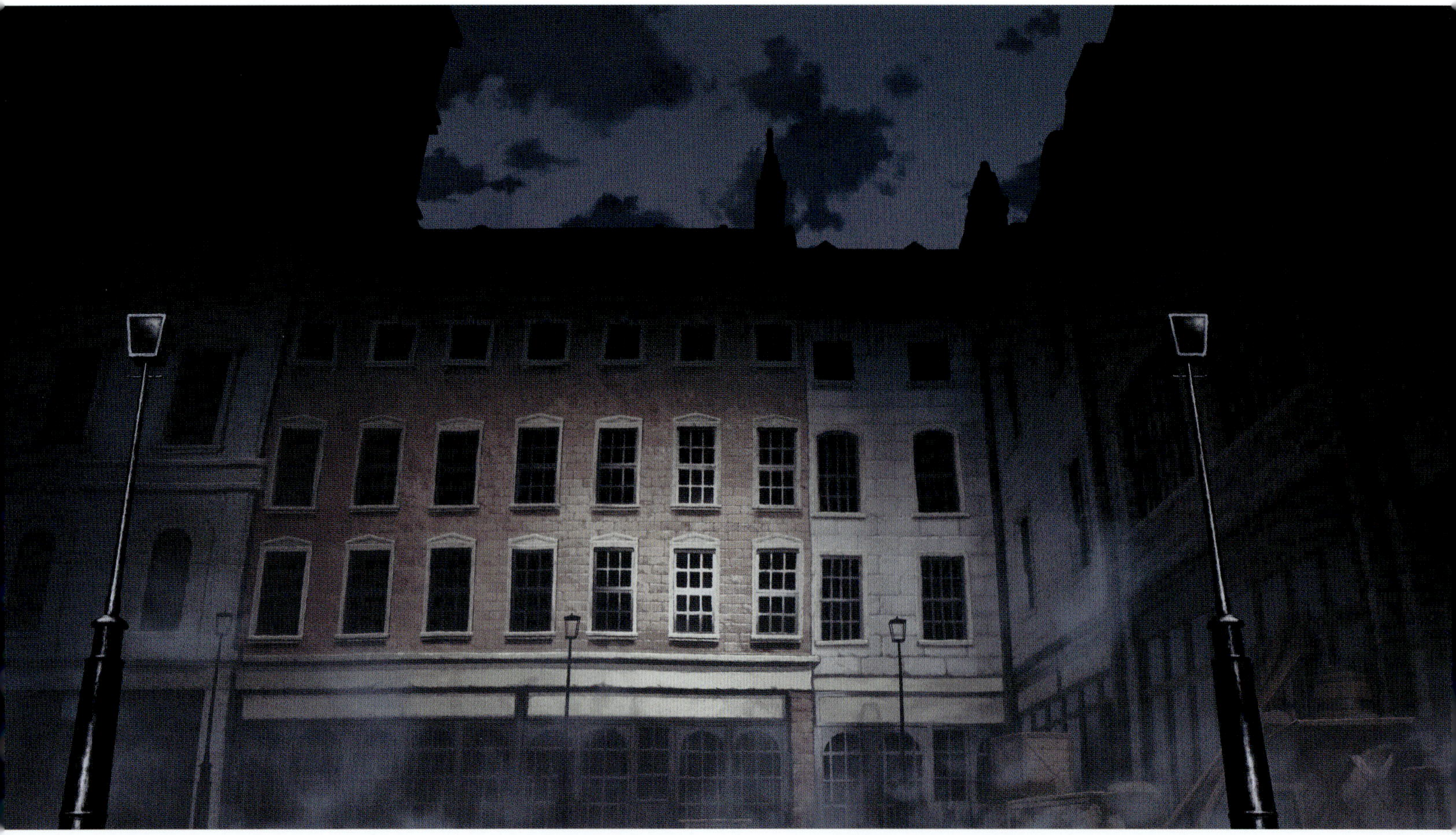

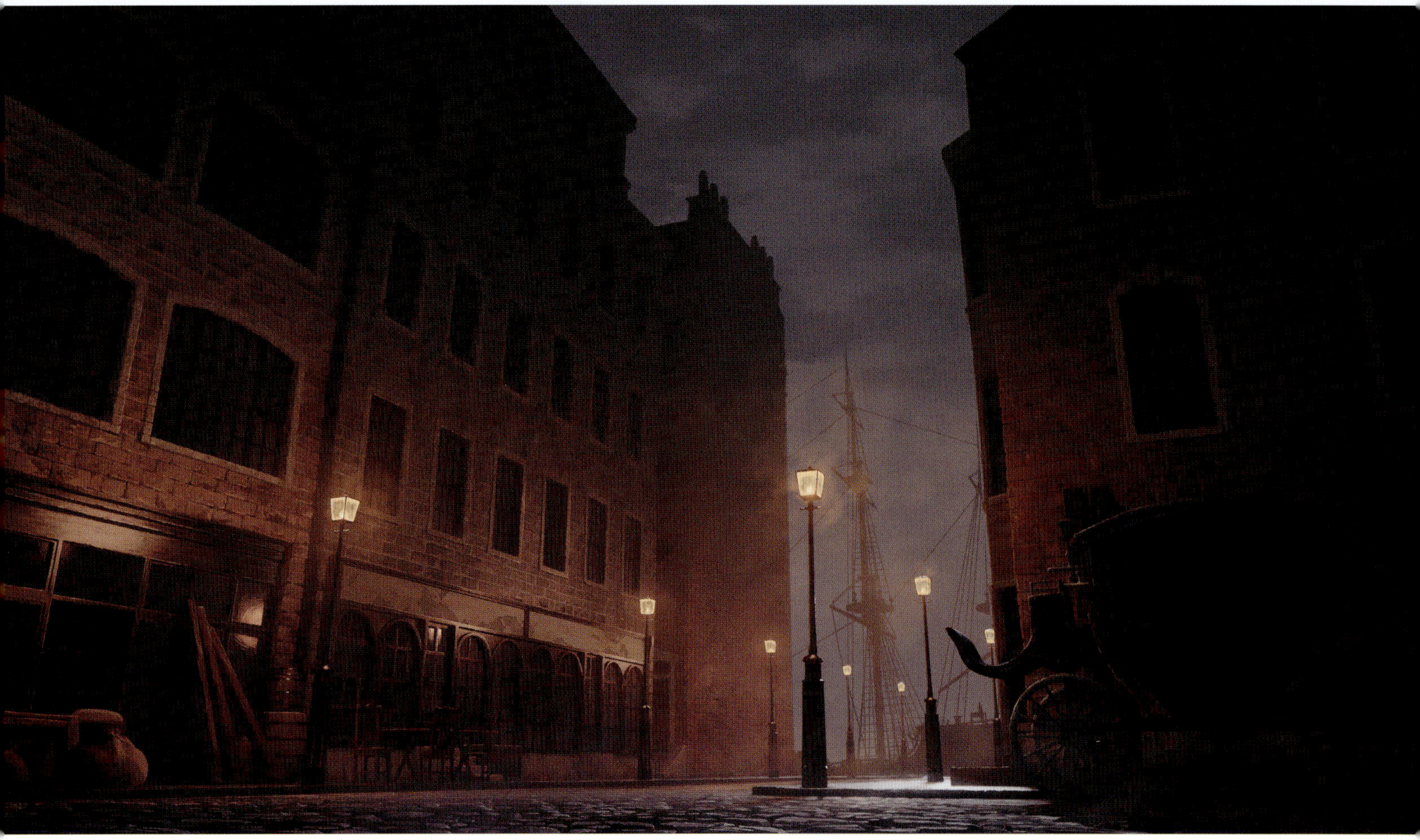

Boston

A young Richter Belmont witnessed the death of his mother on the streets of Boston in 1783. Stephen Stark imbued the backgrounds of that flashback with a variety of moods to accompany the story. The bottom left is the beginning of the scene; it's well-lit and appears more inviting (Stark also joked that he added a Dunkin' Donuts logo to make it feel more like home). Whereas on the top left, he wanted the environment where Julia was fighting Olrox to look more oppressive. He said, "I saw some anime

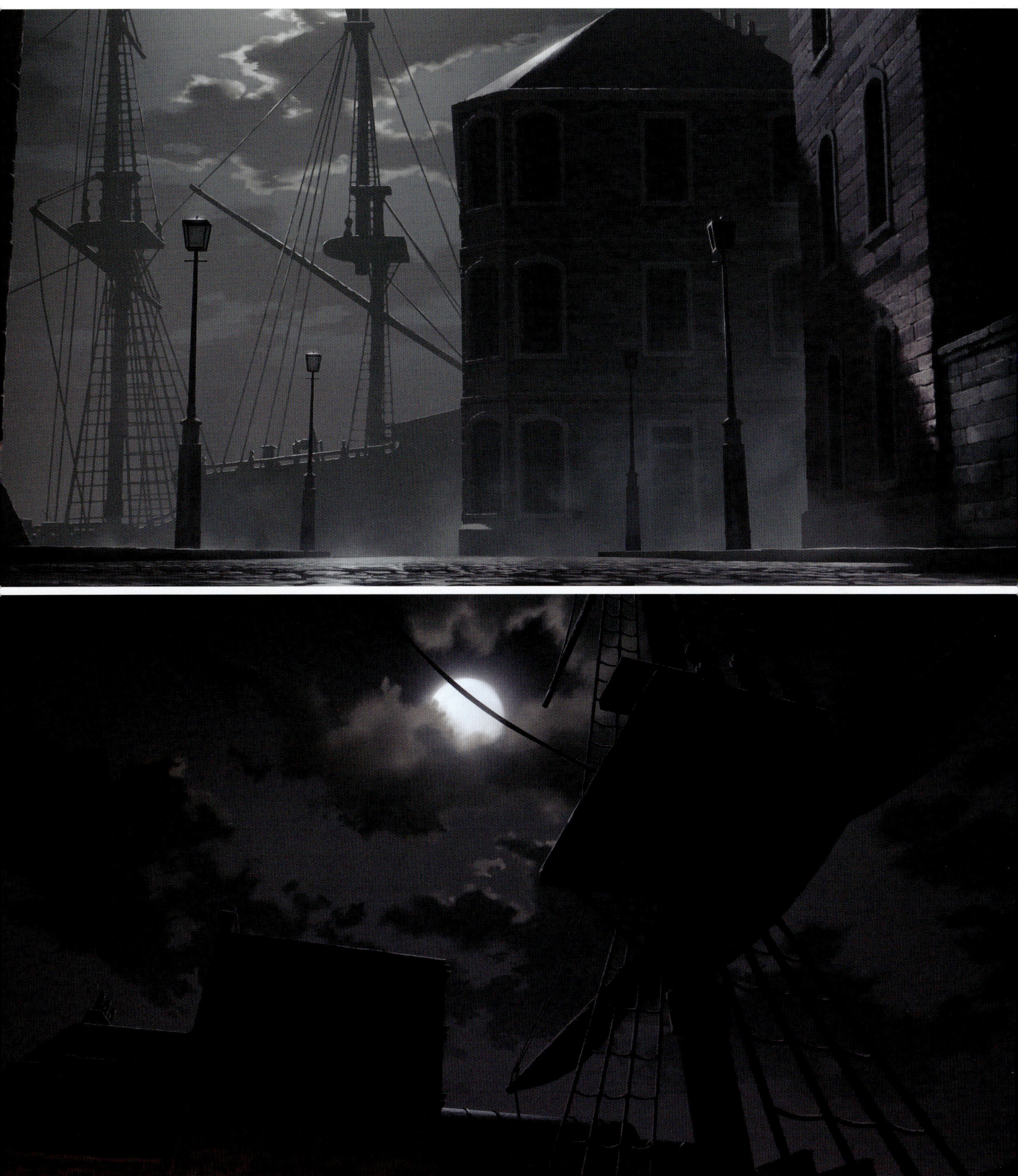

Art by Stephen Stark.

background where they had some crazy oppressive black shadow at the top, and I'm like, I want to do that." In the top right image, Olrox is talking to "Little Boy Belmont," as he calls him. Stark wanted that to feel disgusting and uncomfortable. He noted, "Richter is just internally just wanting to throw up just from everything that's happening, so I went with a very sickly vibe."

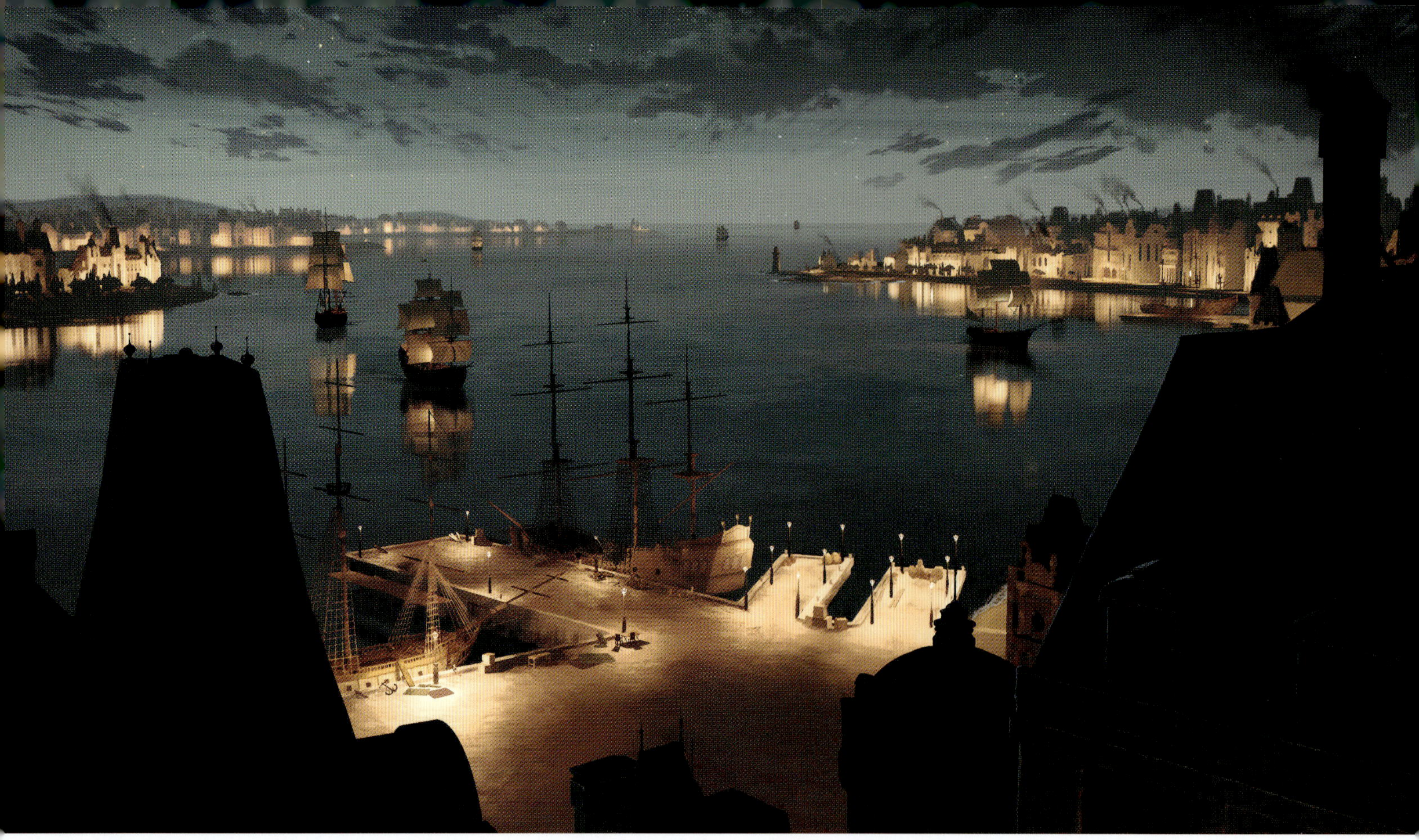

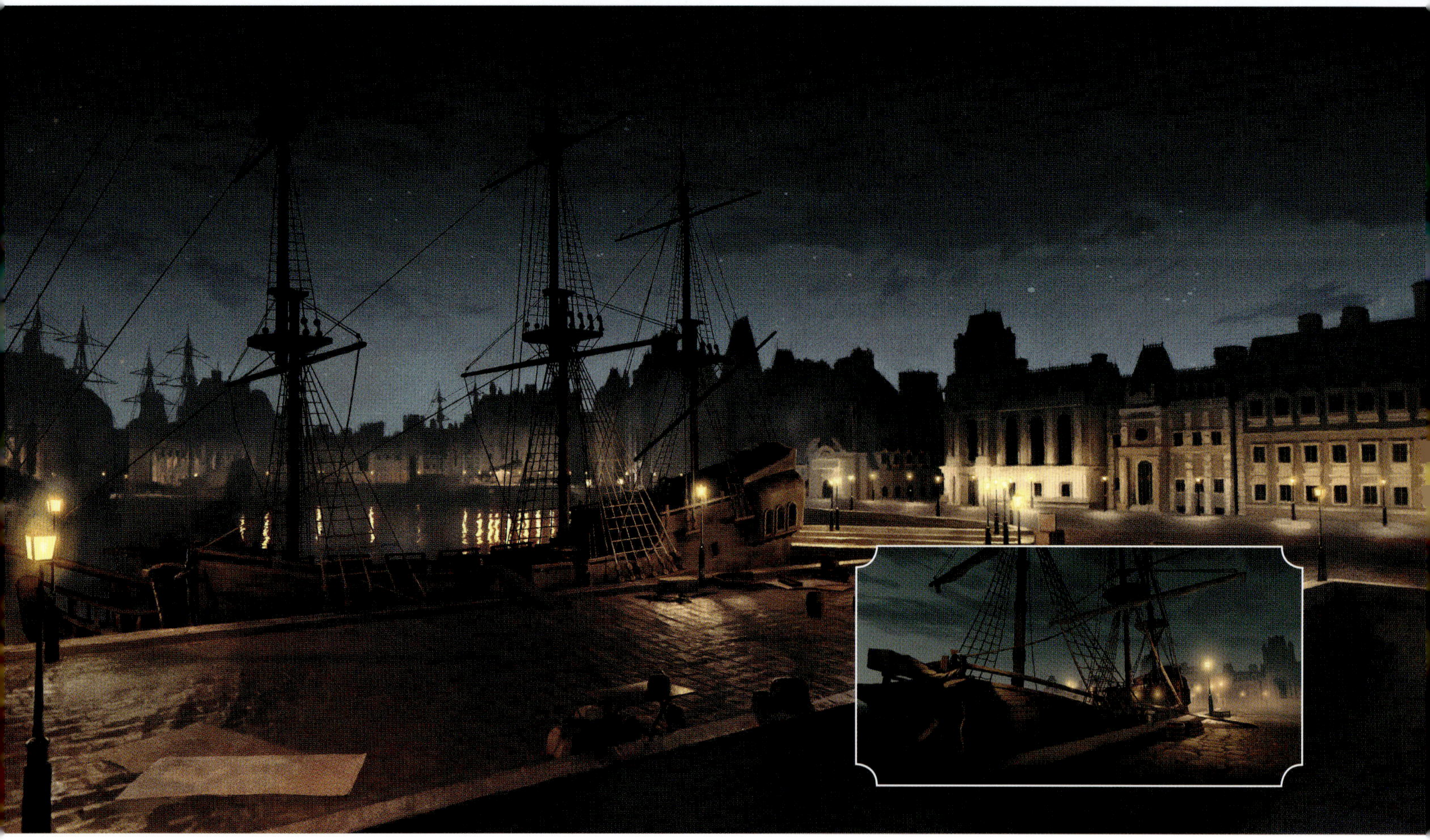

Nantes

For the harbor in Nantes, the name of the game was making it feel more lived in and usable. Keiser called out "greasy" as an overall vibe. In the top right image, he illustrated this with putting visible mud and horse leavings on the cobblestone.

But Stark also wanted Nantes to represent an unknown future for the characters, too. He said, "The sky is so open compared to anywhere else in the show. I went with a very wide lens to get that look for the sky and to show that, beyond this port, anything is possible."

Opposite top: Stephen Stark, Opposite bottom: Sam Keiser, Opposite insert: Stephen Stark. Top: Sam Keiser, Bottom: Sam Keiser.

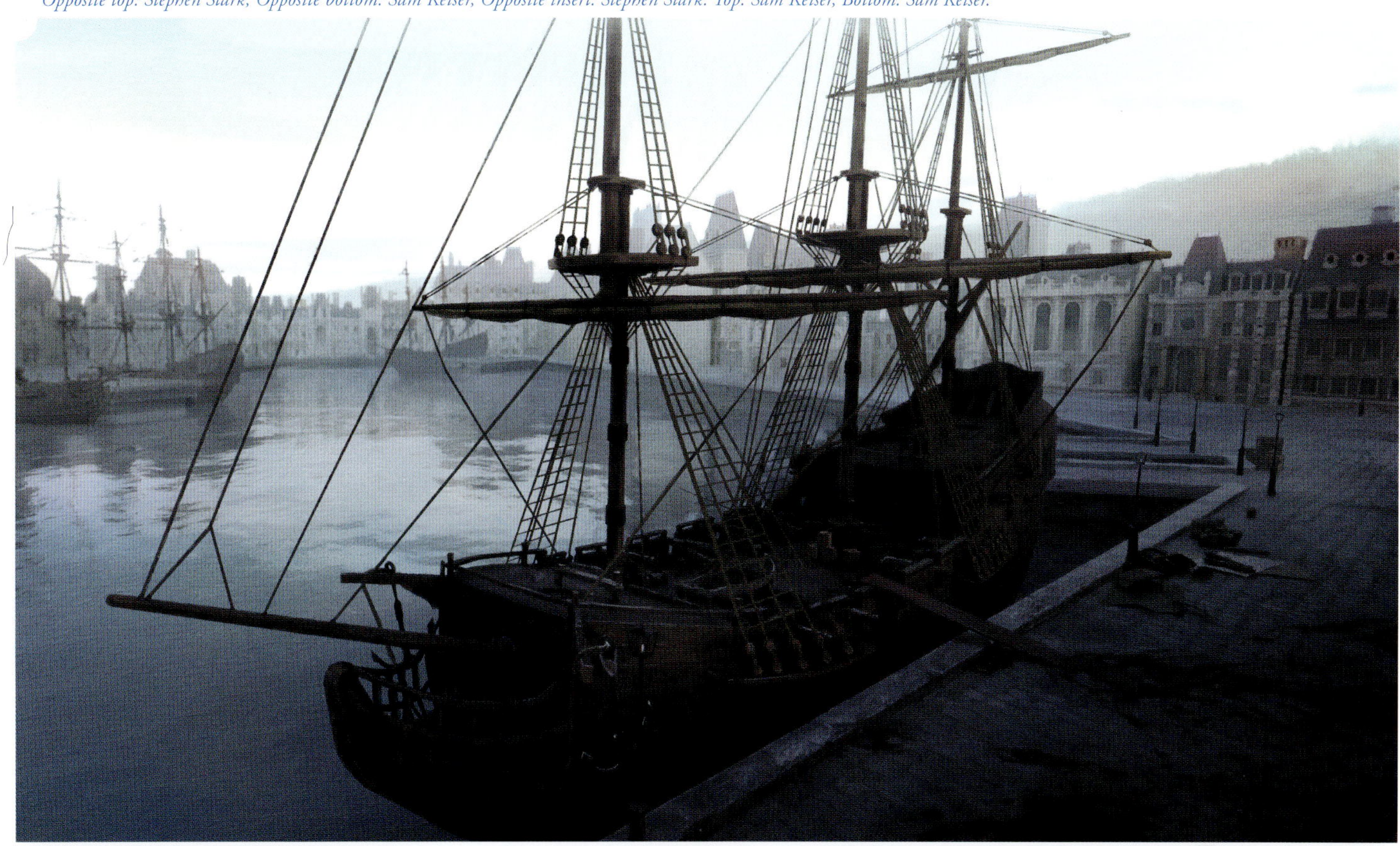

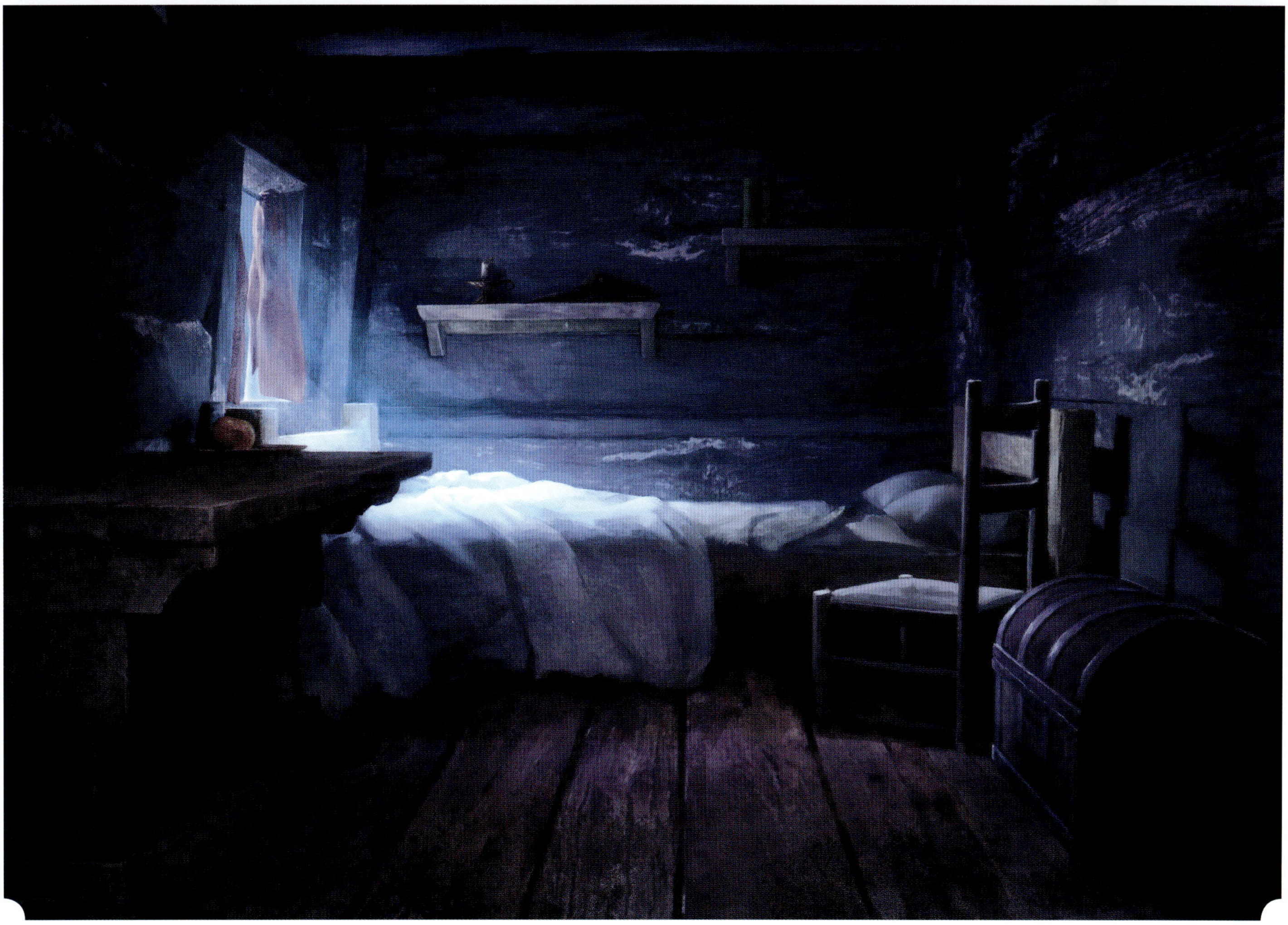

HARBOR SHIPS

Here, Richter and Annette finally have a moment of quiet from battling forces of evil, so this ship cabin needed to have a romantic feel. "I did want to do something cozy," Keiser recalled. "I knew the light would actually play a very strong role because opposite the two sequences where this has happened, there's actually a lot of moonlight and then the sunlight coming in. It's just about making a spot have an appropriate place for that spotlight to come in."

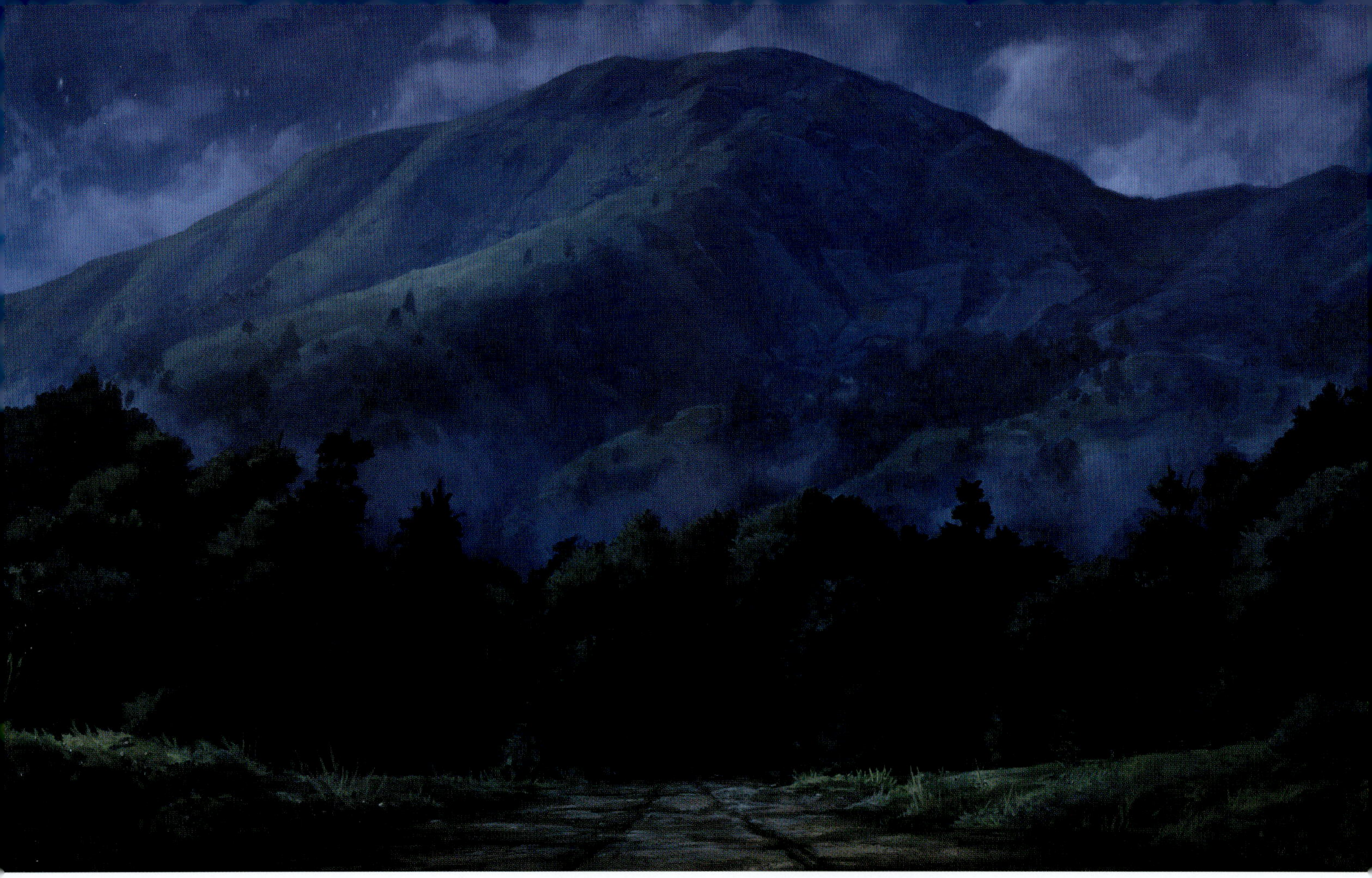

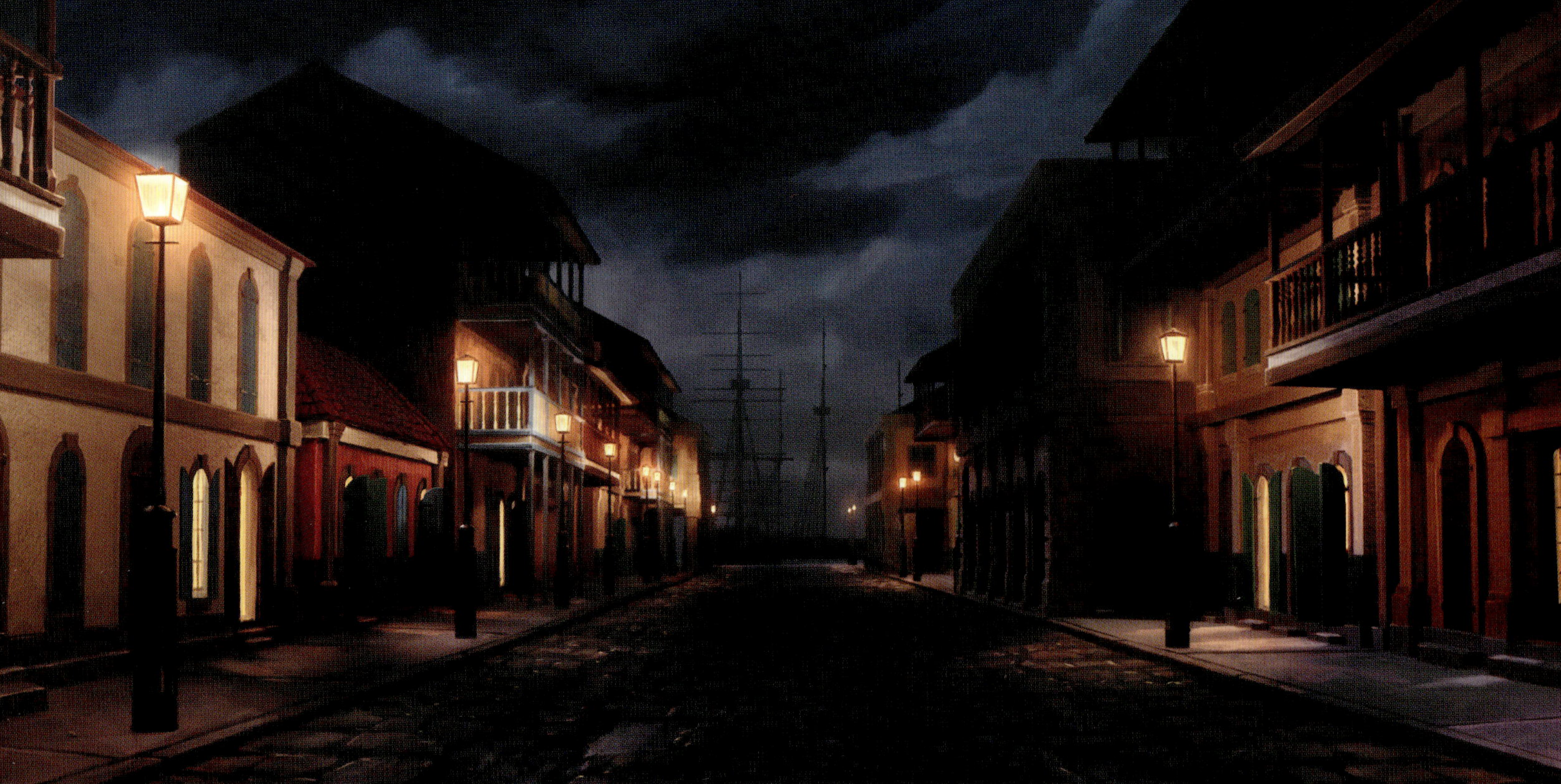

Saint-Domingue

Annette and Edouard come from the French colony of Saint-Domingue, which is in the area of contemporary Haiti. It's where they both engage in the revolution and eventually fight the vampire Vaublanc. For about two and a half weeks, Keiser said he lived and breathed everything Saint-Domingue to get the backgrounds right. He went deep into research until he found references for actual buildings that existed during the time of *Nocturne*. He modeled those buildings out—seen in the art immediately above—including the exterior of the Comédie du Cap Opera House, though not all the exteriors ended up in the series.

Opposite page: Sam Keiser. Top: Sean Randolph, Middle row: Sean Vo, Bottom row: Bo Li.

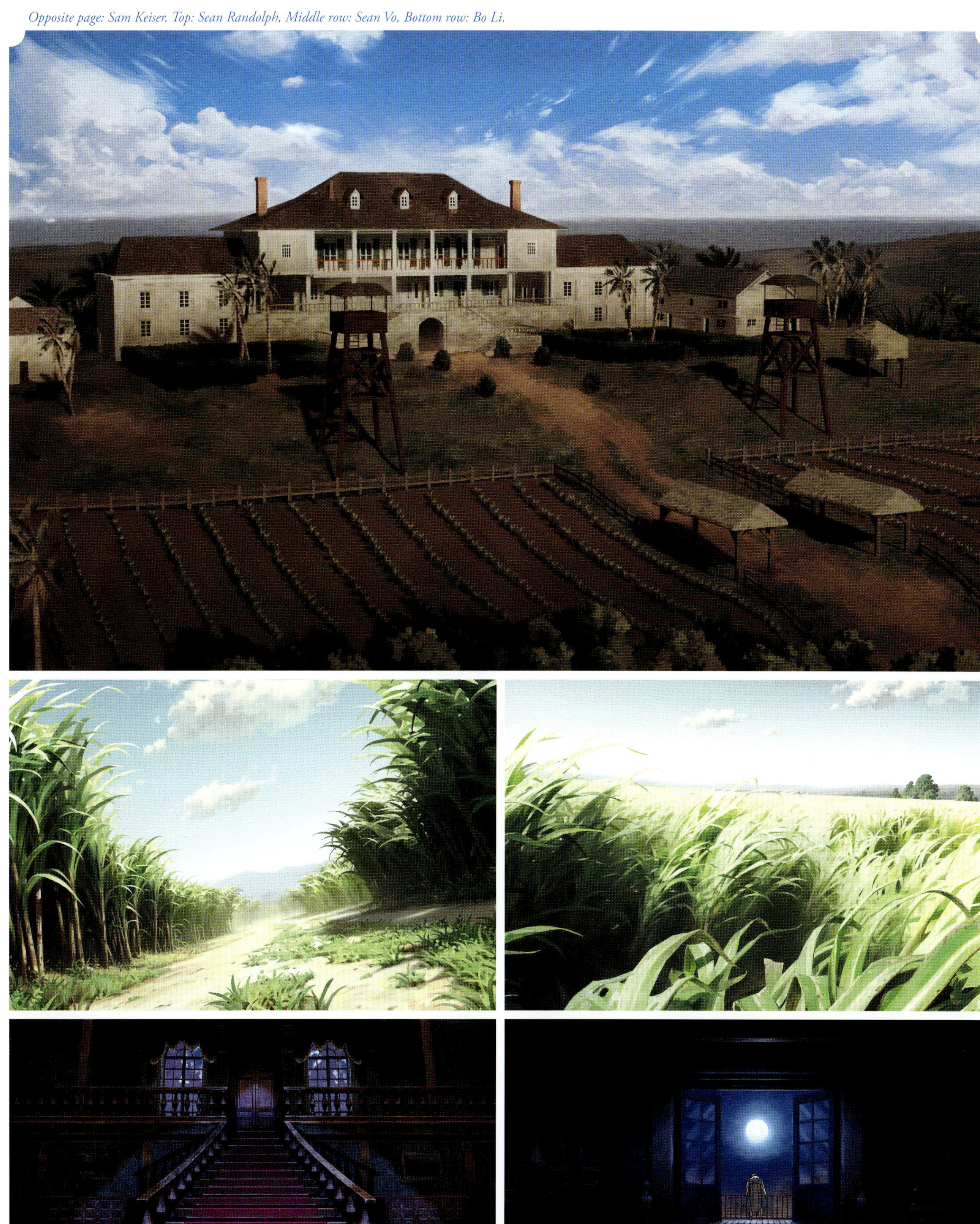

VAUBLANC PLANTATION

The Comte de Vaublanc is the wealthy owner of a sugar plantation that profits off of slave labor. Sean Randolph designed and modeled the entire plantation, but he joked he did too much because viewers only see the immediate area around the big house. He shared that the house leans into a "cheesy theme" he did with a couple of buildings, that places where the villains live should have bat ears in the design. So the two chimneys on either side of the house are meant to be like bat ears.

Top: Mark Adams, Insert: Stephen Stark, Bottom: Bo Li.

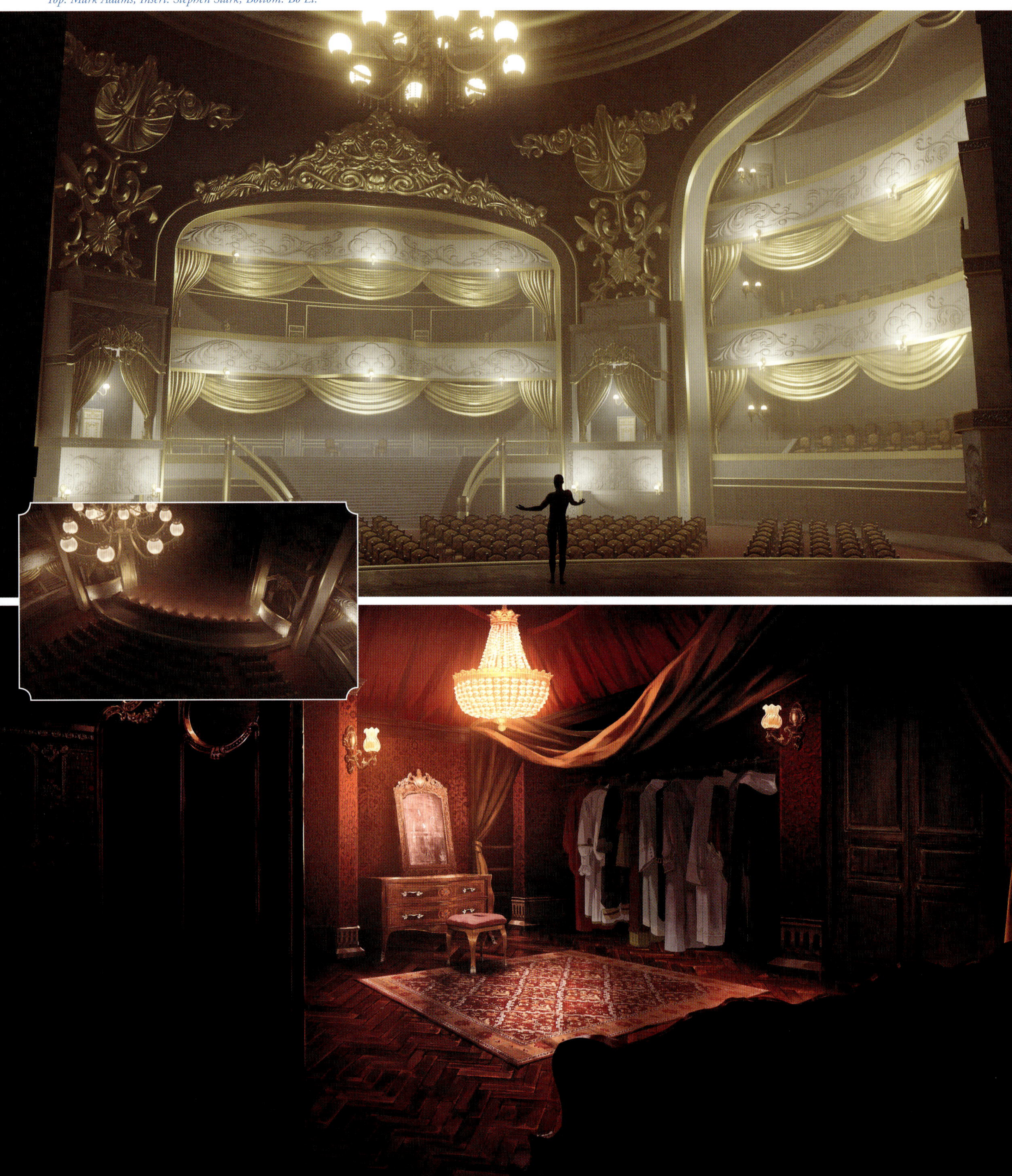

COMÉDIE DU CAP

With the real Comédie du Cap likely destroyed in a fire, the team didn't have a lot of historical images to draw from. But they did find a 3D construct of a theater in a different French colony and Frankensteined that with mainland French theaters from the time with the intent to make the theater look luxurious. Stark laid out the initial concept, and then Mark Adams completed the 3D model. If fans look closely at the clothes in the dressing room, they'll spot costumes for other *Castlevania* characters.

Art by Sam Keiser.

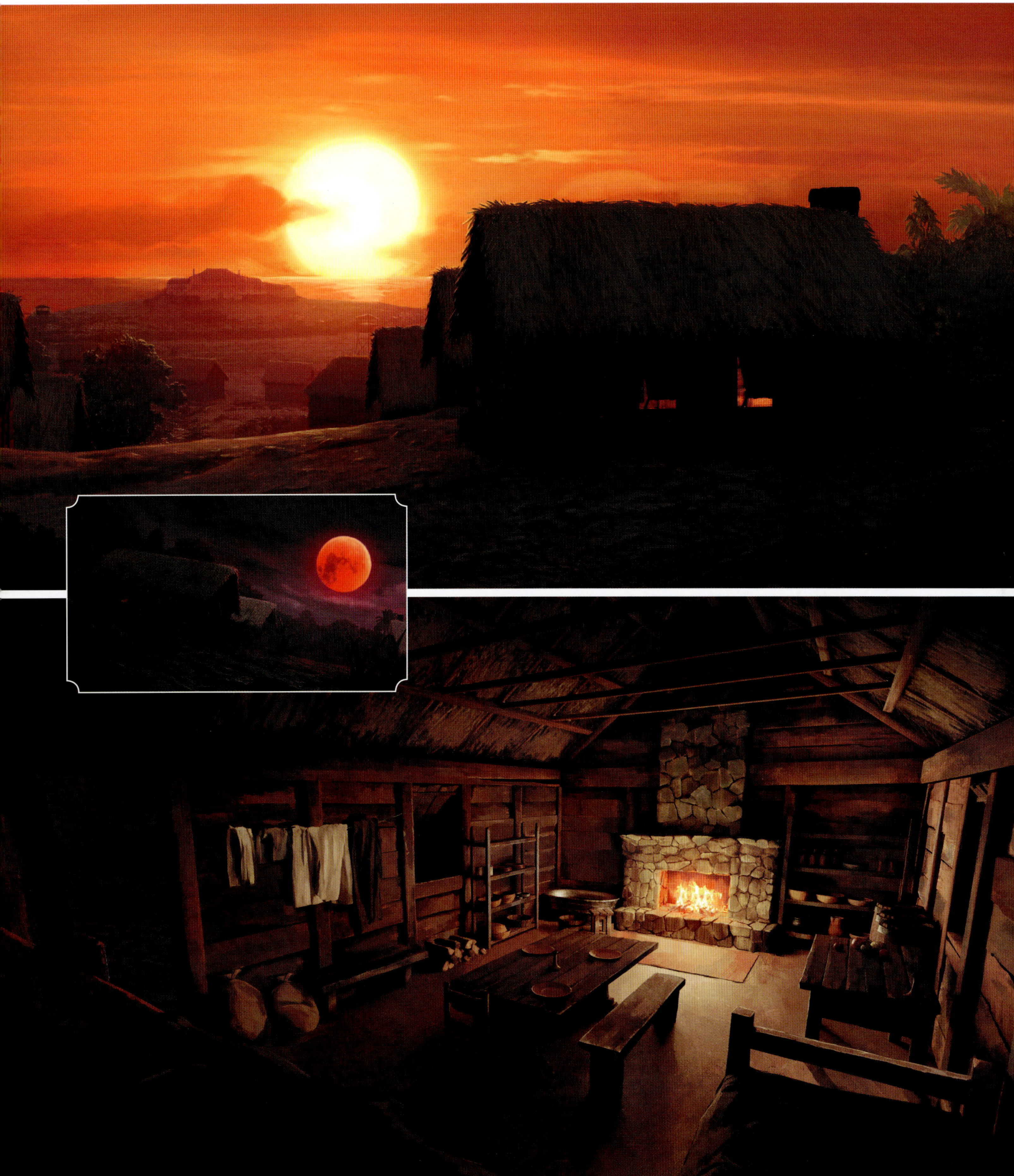

ESTHER'S CABIN

The prompt for Esther's Cabin, Keiser recalled, was to design slave quarters while still making it feel lived in and comfortable. Initially, Esther lived here alone, but that didn't make sense for the story. The background team filled in the space with a community area that's actually full of beds, a table, a bathtub in the corner, a place for laundry—they purposely wanted to make it feel overcrowded with stuff. They wanted it to look like Esther and her fellow slaves were trying to make the space feel cozy.

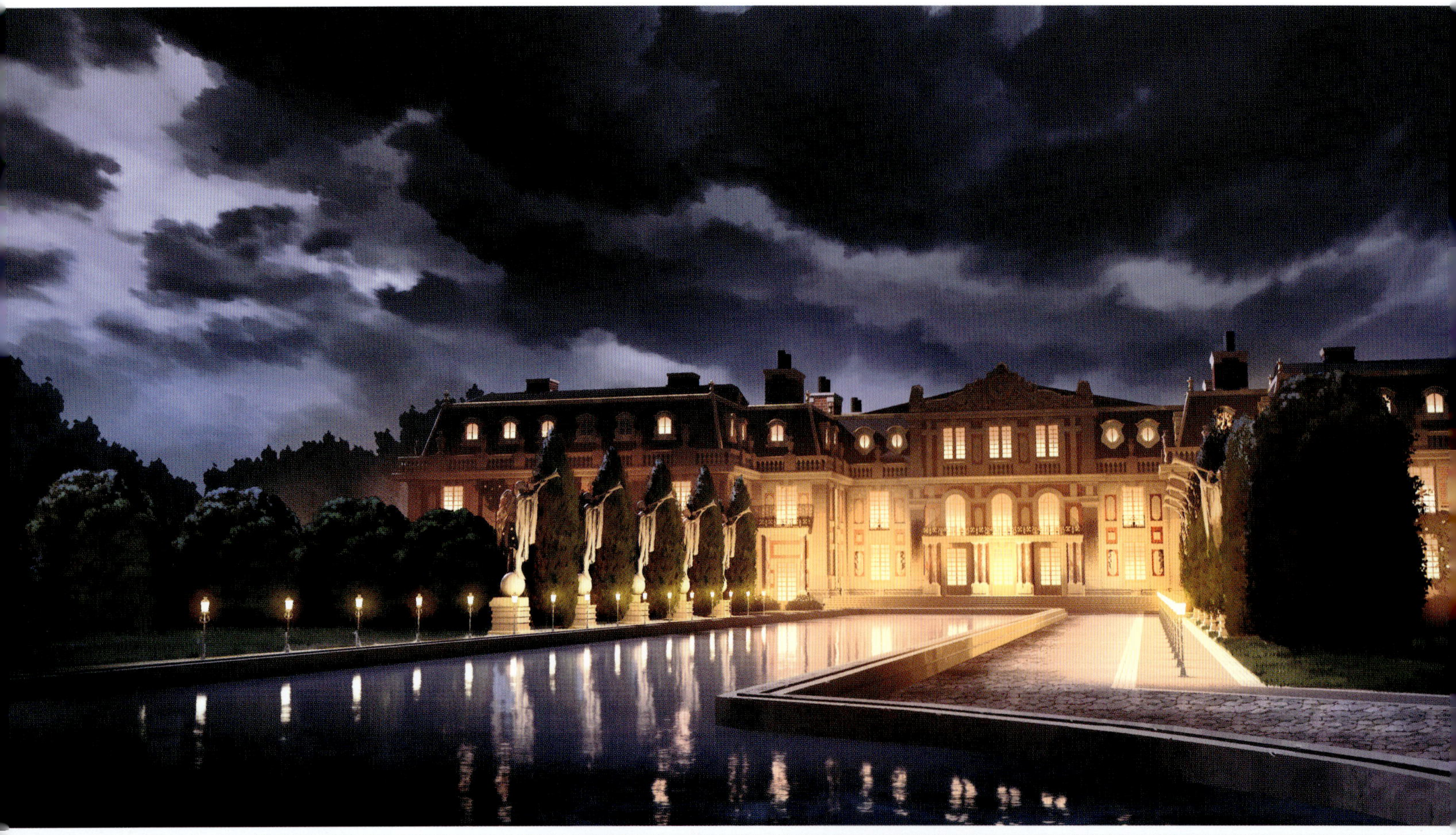

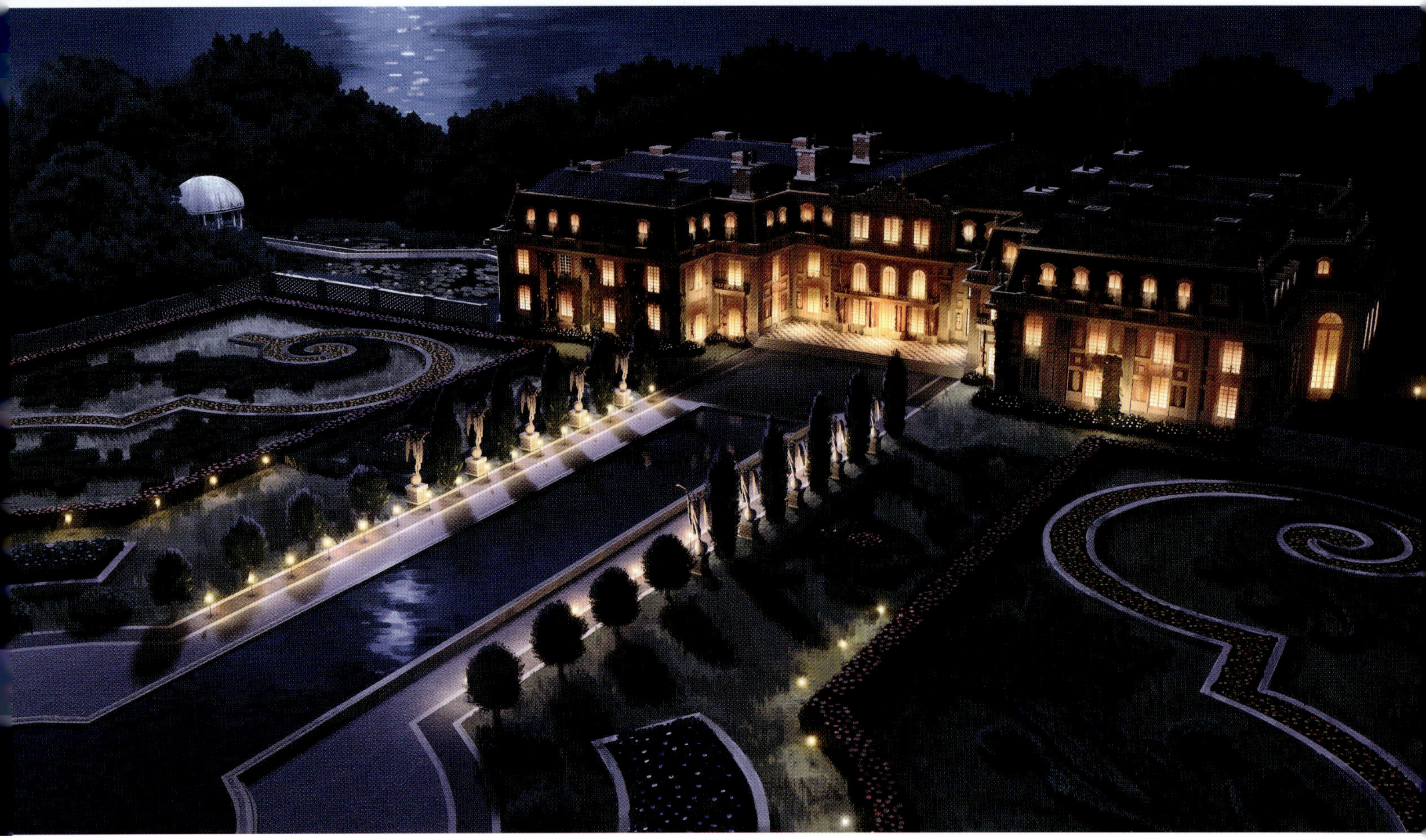

The Chateau

Grand scenes unfold at the Vendée, a decadent chateau owned by the Marquis, under the fist of vampire queen Erzsebet Báthory. Background designer and concept artist Bo Li took point on concepting the chateau's exterior and interior, with 3D generalist Mark Adams. King Louis XIV's Palace of Versailles is an obvious inspiration, but the idea was to make the Marquis's home more comfortable—less over the top. The idea was for it to appear like a pared-down version of Versailles with

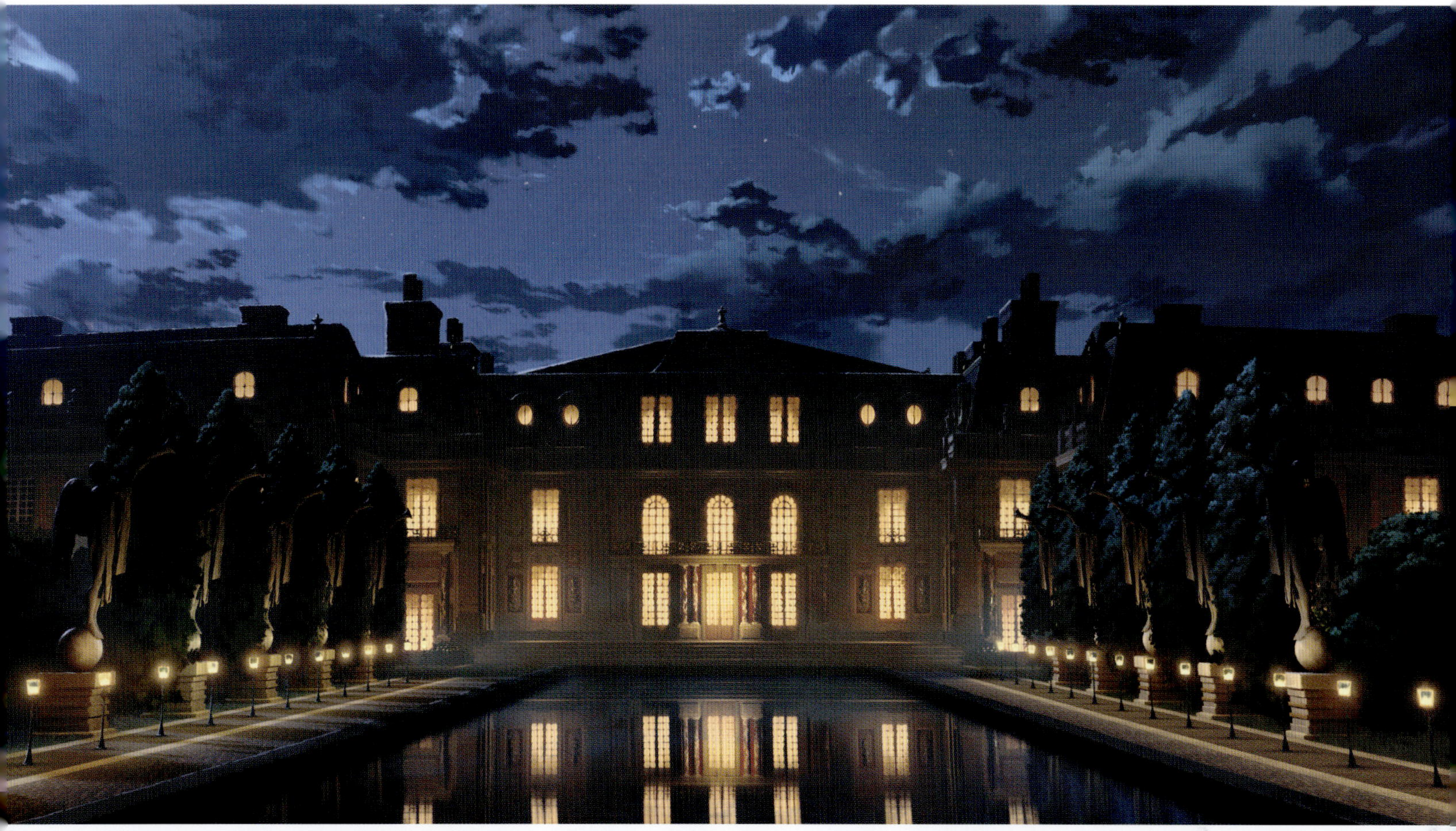

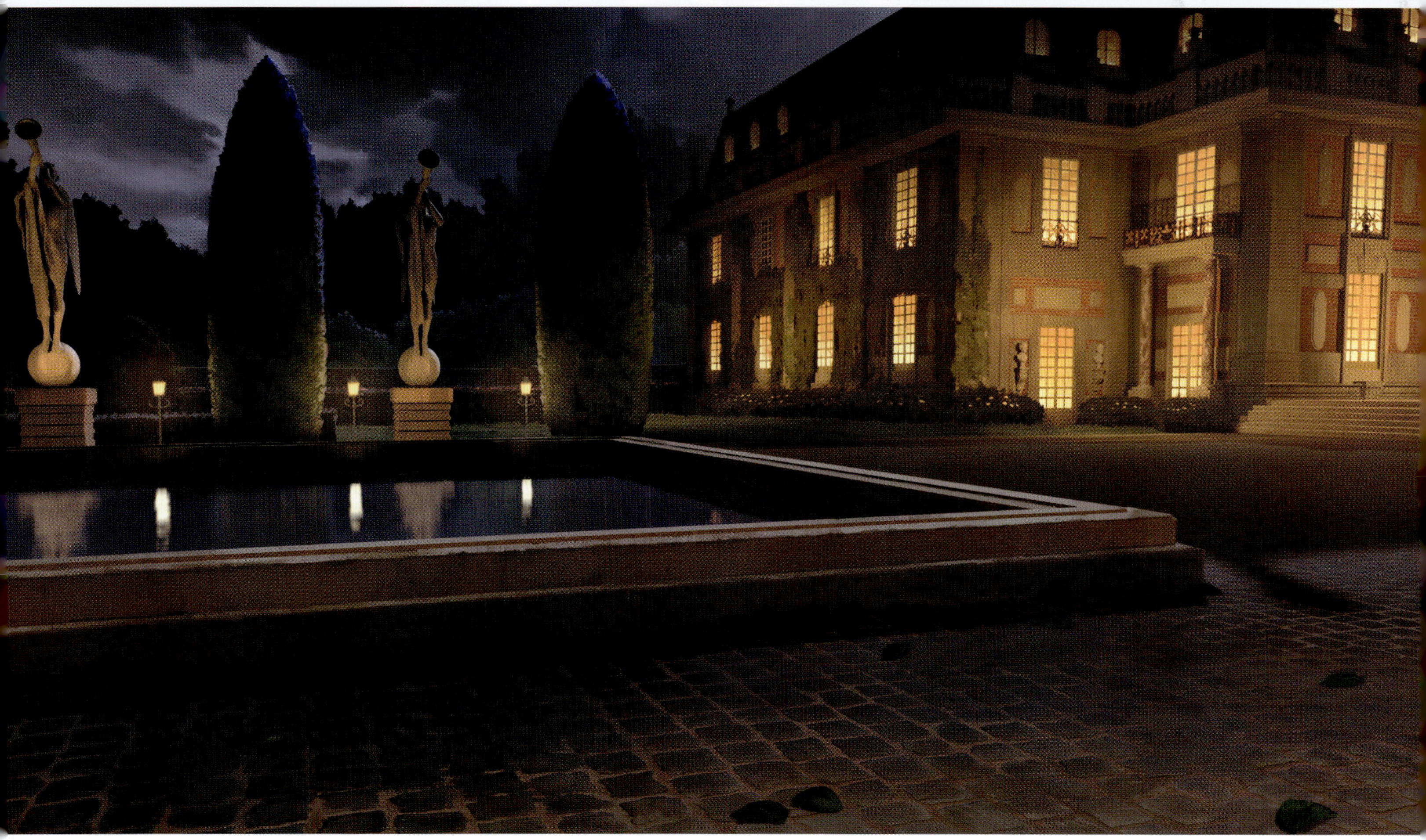

Opposite page: Bo Li. Top: Stephen Stark, Bottom: Bo Li.

similar opulence, but fewer rooms and less sprawl. It's scaled to match the Marquis's social status, too. Instead of functioning as a seat of court and government, it's more like a weekender home and a pseudo-escape from the city for the Marquis. The home is a place he can bring guests, including vampires, for elaborate parties and to show off his wealth.

Top and middle: Bo Li, Bottom left: Sean Randolph, Bottom right: Stephen Stark. Opposite top: Sabina Lewis, Opposite bottom: Sean Randolph.

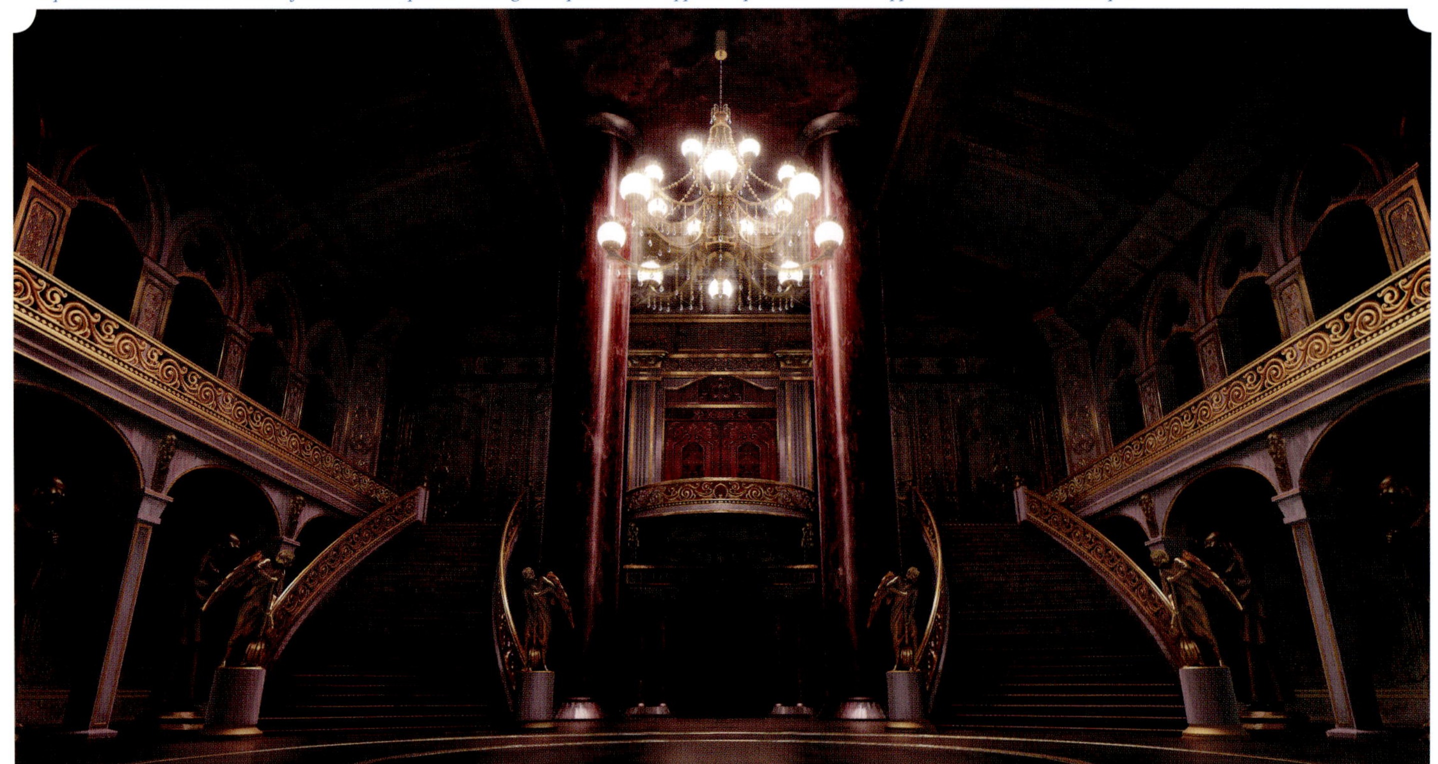

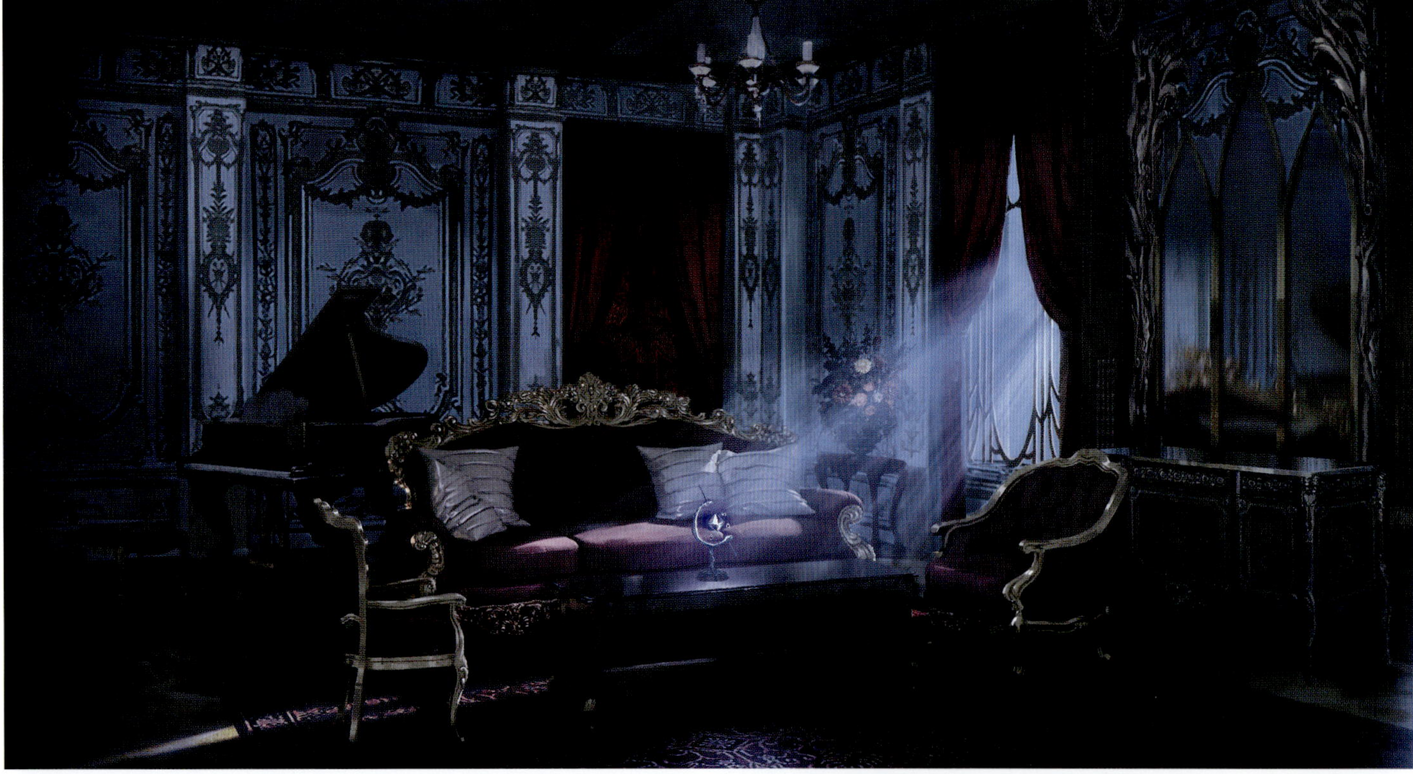

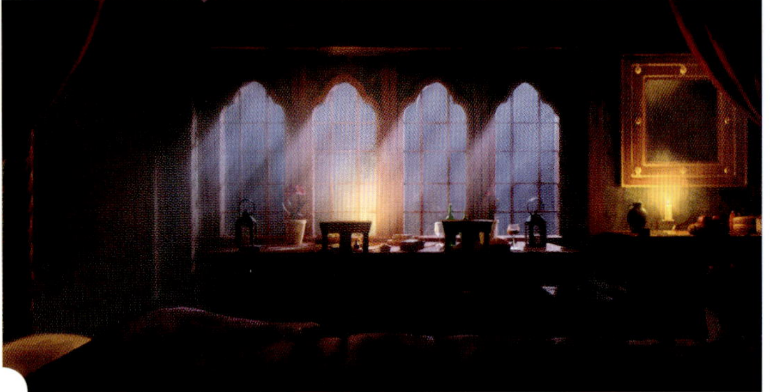

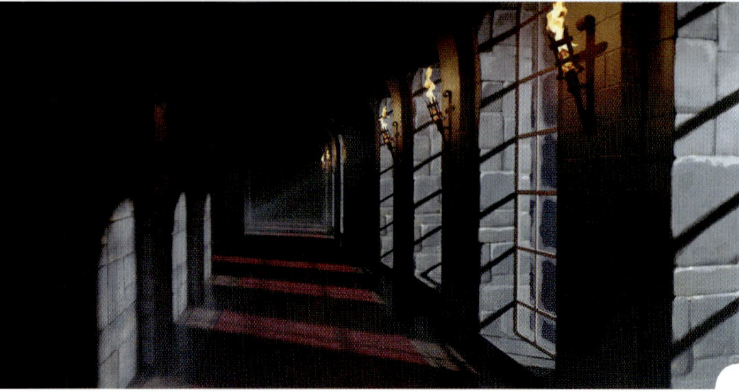

The Vendée's interior rooms, also by Bo Li, are moody with ornate decor and wall treatments. Stark remembers telling Li to look at *Vampire Hunter D* backgrounds for the top image, specifically to make it look like Carmilla's castle. That shot also shows off more of Adams's 3D sculpting. "We're capable of making cool backgrounds from scratch," Stark said, "but then you and a bunch of other artists have to do this same environment multiple times, and it's extremely tedious. Having Mark come out here to design the 3D models essentially saved us."

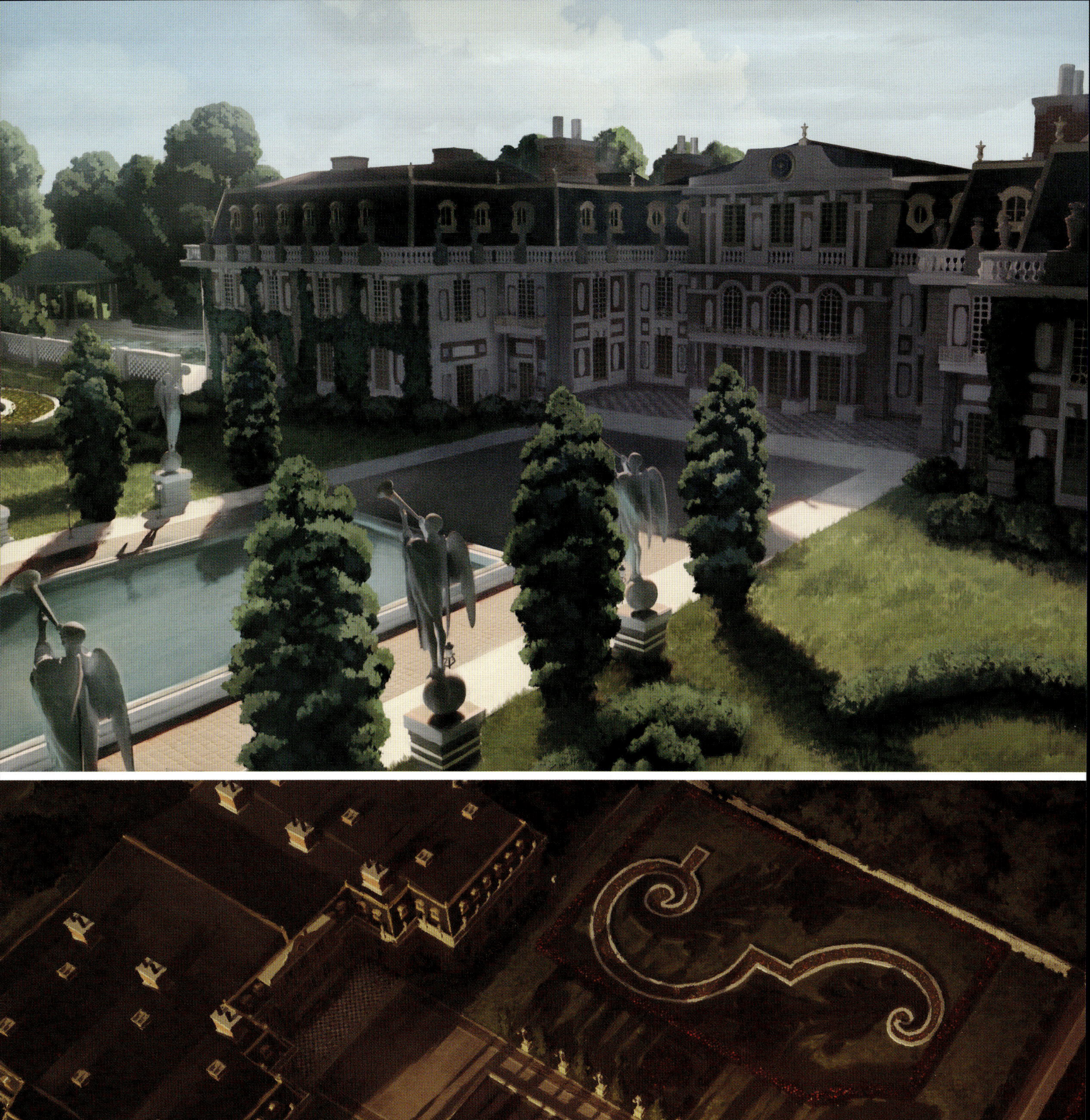

The Marquis and Marchioness do not do subtle. As vampire aristocrats, they have access to extreme wealth and eagerly offer it to Erzsebet by volunteering their chateau for her use and entertainment. The elaborate gardens around their weekend home are another example of their flamboyant extravagance.

Storyboards by Darius Rafil Vardiny.

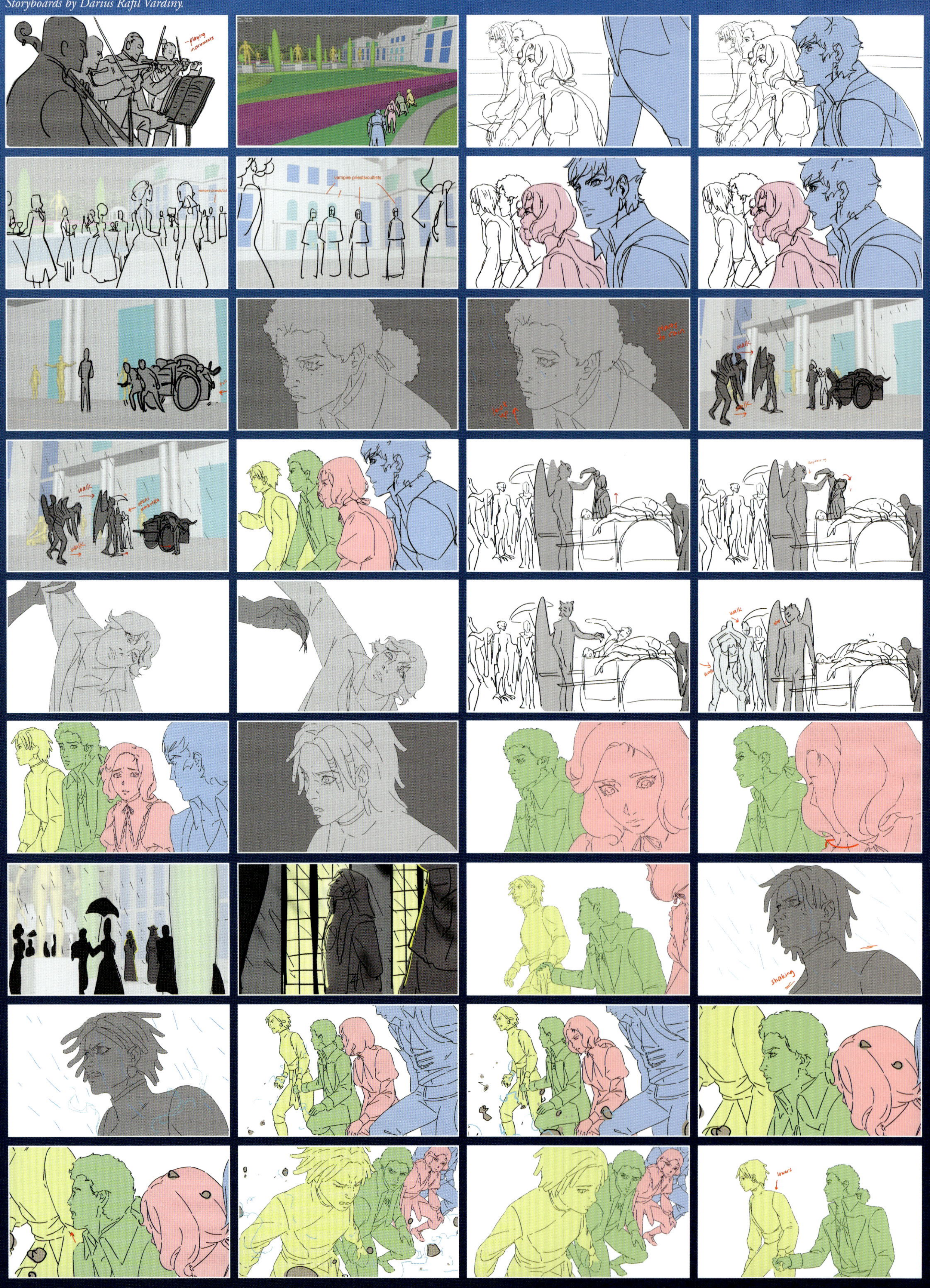

"Management of crowds is always the hardest, worst thing you can do in animation from every level on the boarding end, on the actual animation, and on the design end. It just hurts everything," Adam Deats noted. "And we unfortunately had too many crowds. The sequence in general was really tough."

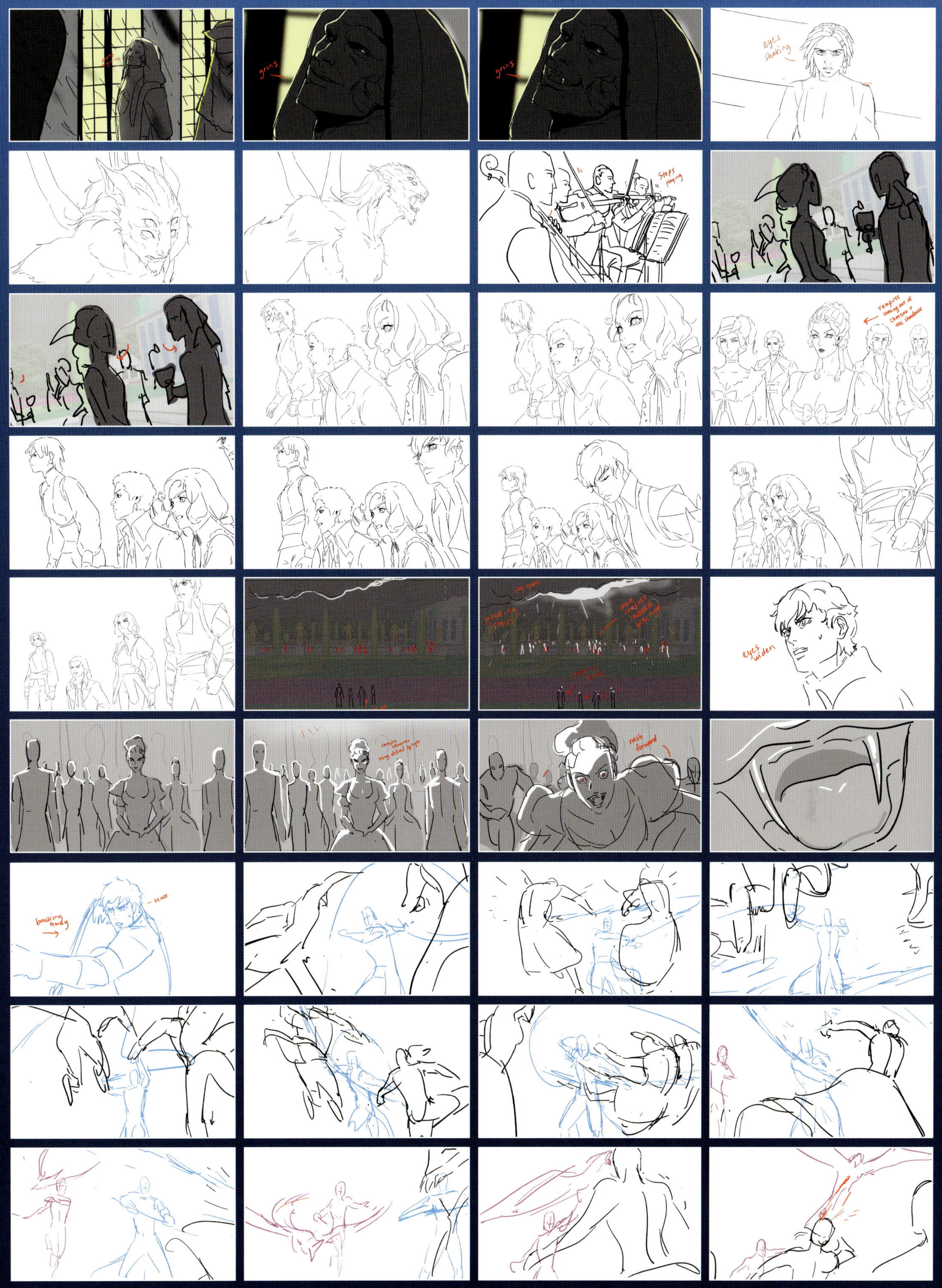

Sam noted Kamille Areopagita did the storyboards, and it was the first sequence he asked her to do. He said, in large part, it was about keeping logistics and staging in mind and then making sure that they weren't biting off more than they could chew. He joked, "We still ended up doing that, but we cut back on that as much as we could, too."

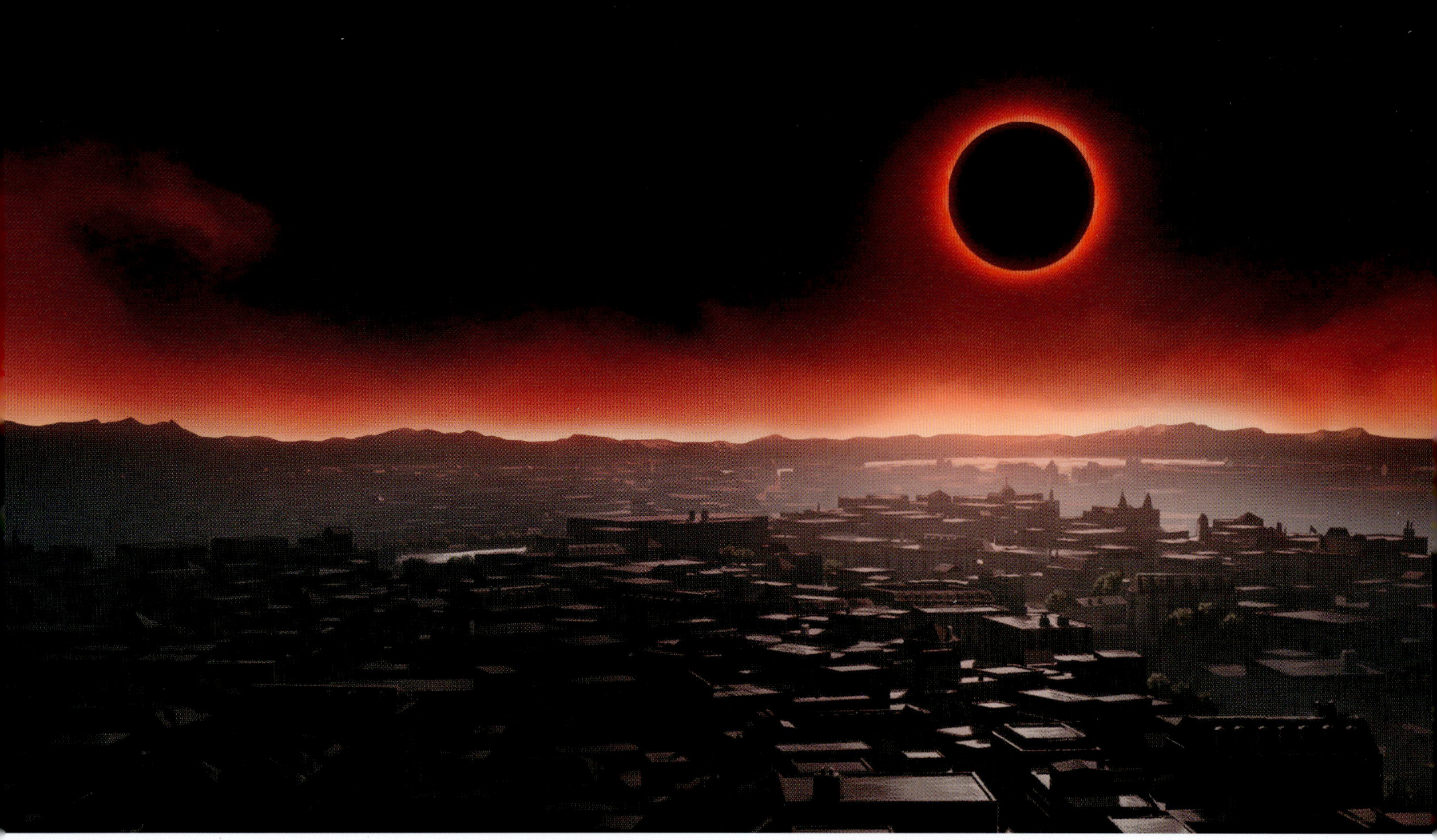

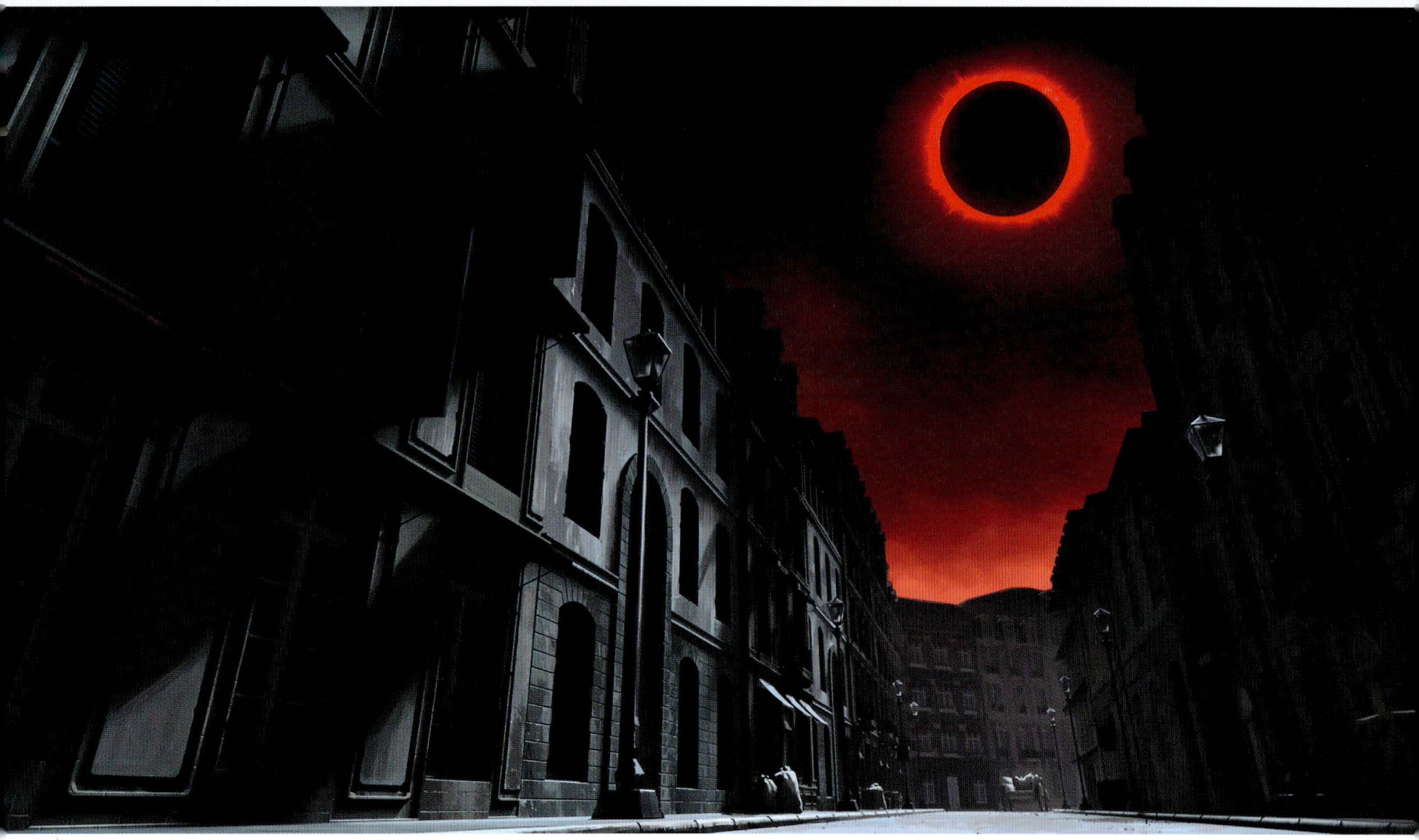

Paris

While the story of *Castlevania: Nocturne* is fantastical, with vampires and goddesses, the backdrop of Paris during the French Revolution is tangible and real. However, the creative team played a little fast and loose when it came to specifics in concept art and background designs. As executive producer Sam Deats noted, they didn't have a hundred-million-dollar budget to spend the time to figure out historically what buildings were where at the exact time period. The background team researched and referenced documentation they could find, but it wasn't, in some cases, clear. When it wasn't, the story provided the guidance for the overall direction and color palette.

Opposite top: Sean Randolph, Opposite bottom: Bo Li. Top: Sean Randolph, Middle: Sam Keiser, Bottom: Stephen Stark.

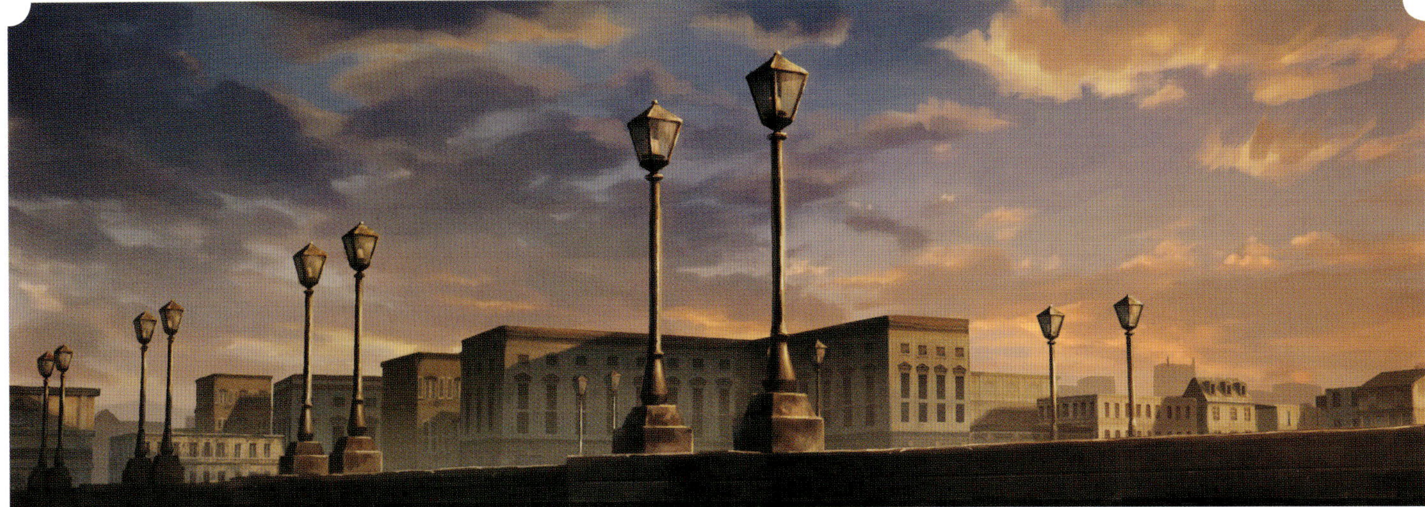

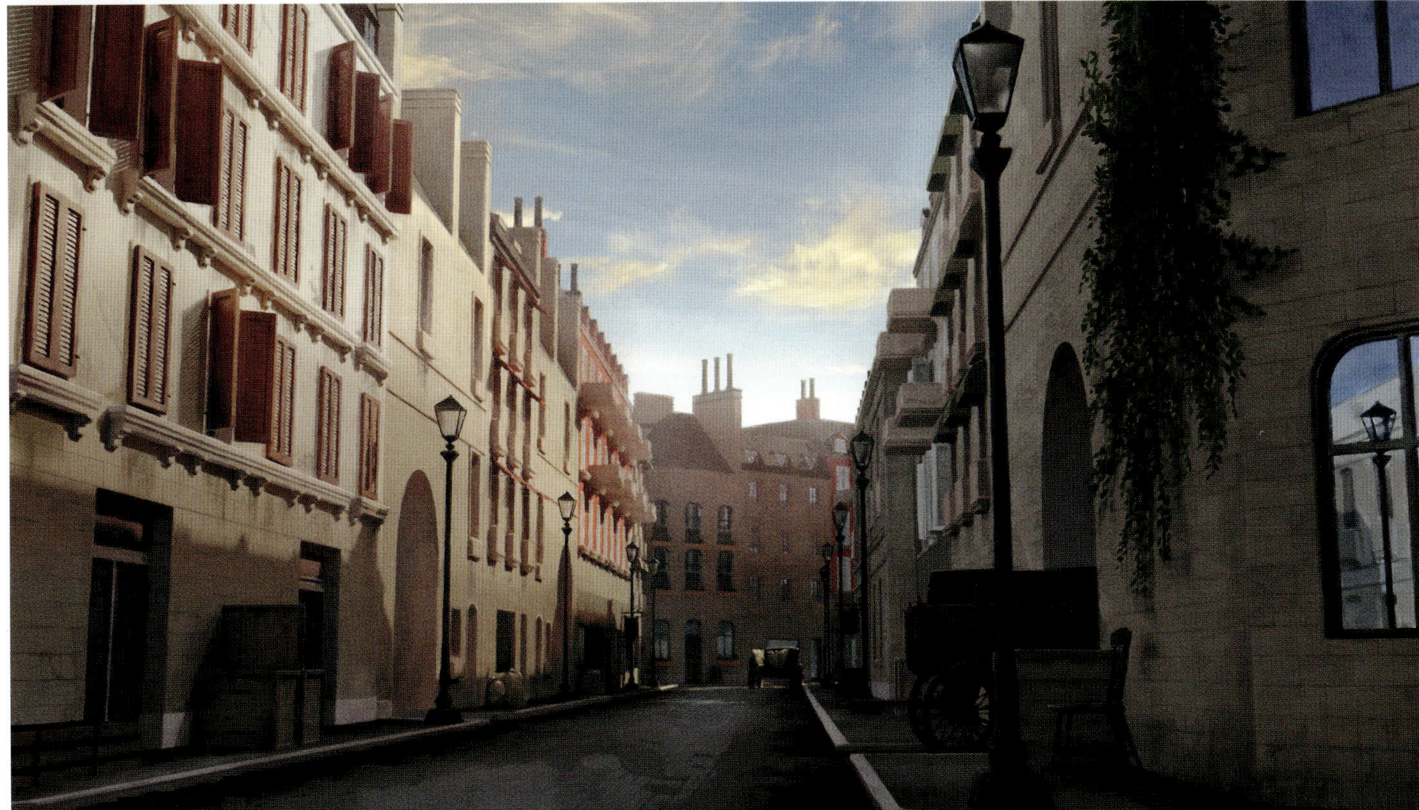

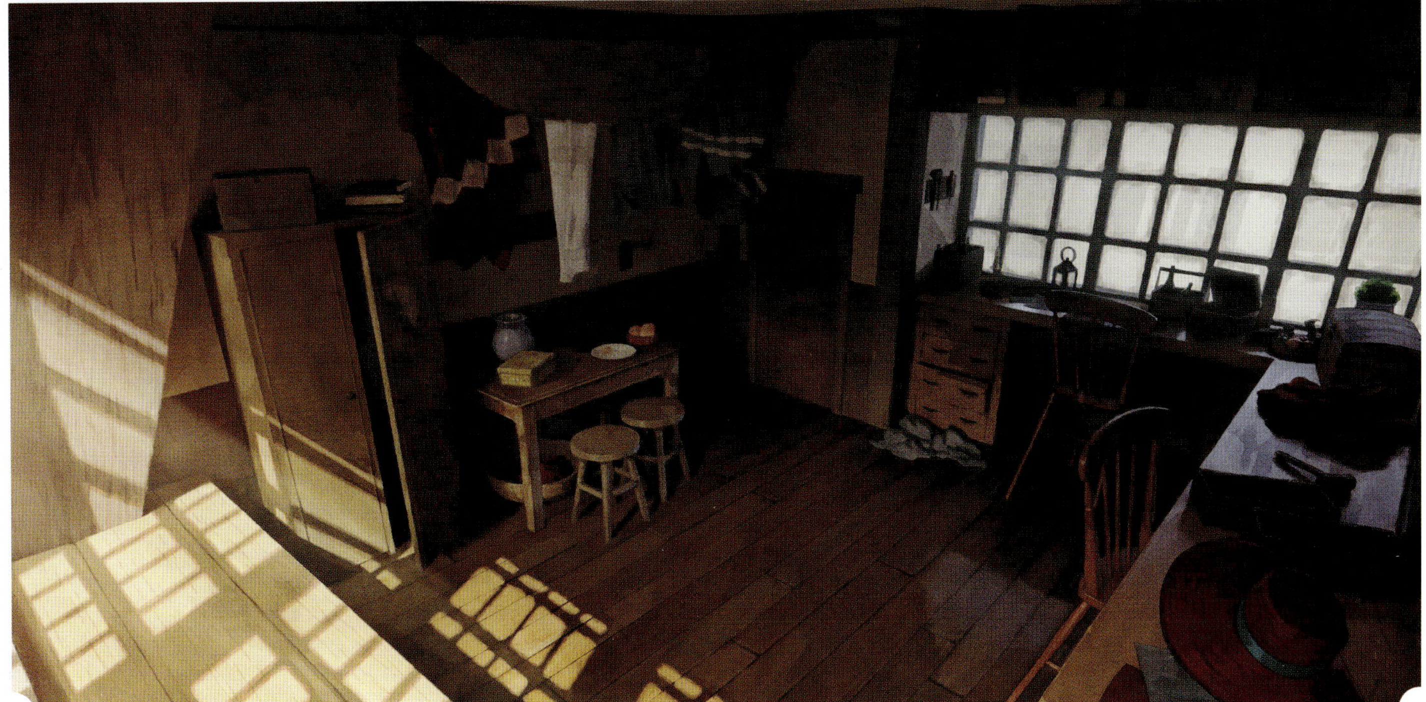

Top: Stephen Stark, Middle: Sam Keiser, Bottom row: Stephen Stark. Opposite top: Bo Li, Opposite bottom: Stephen Stark.

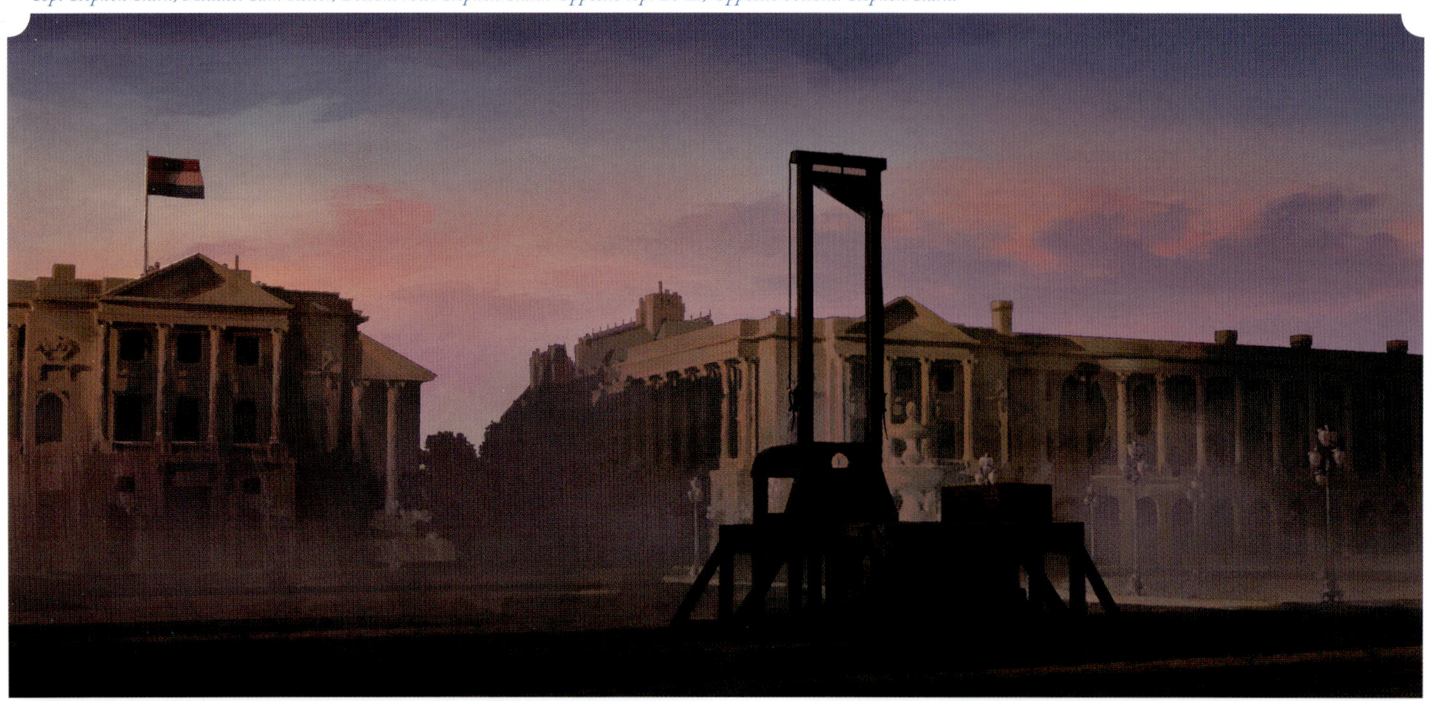

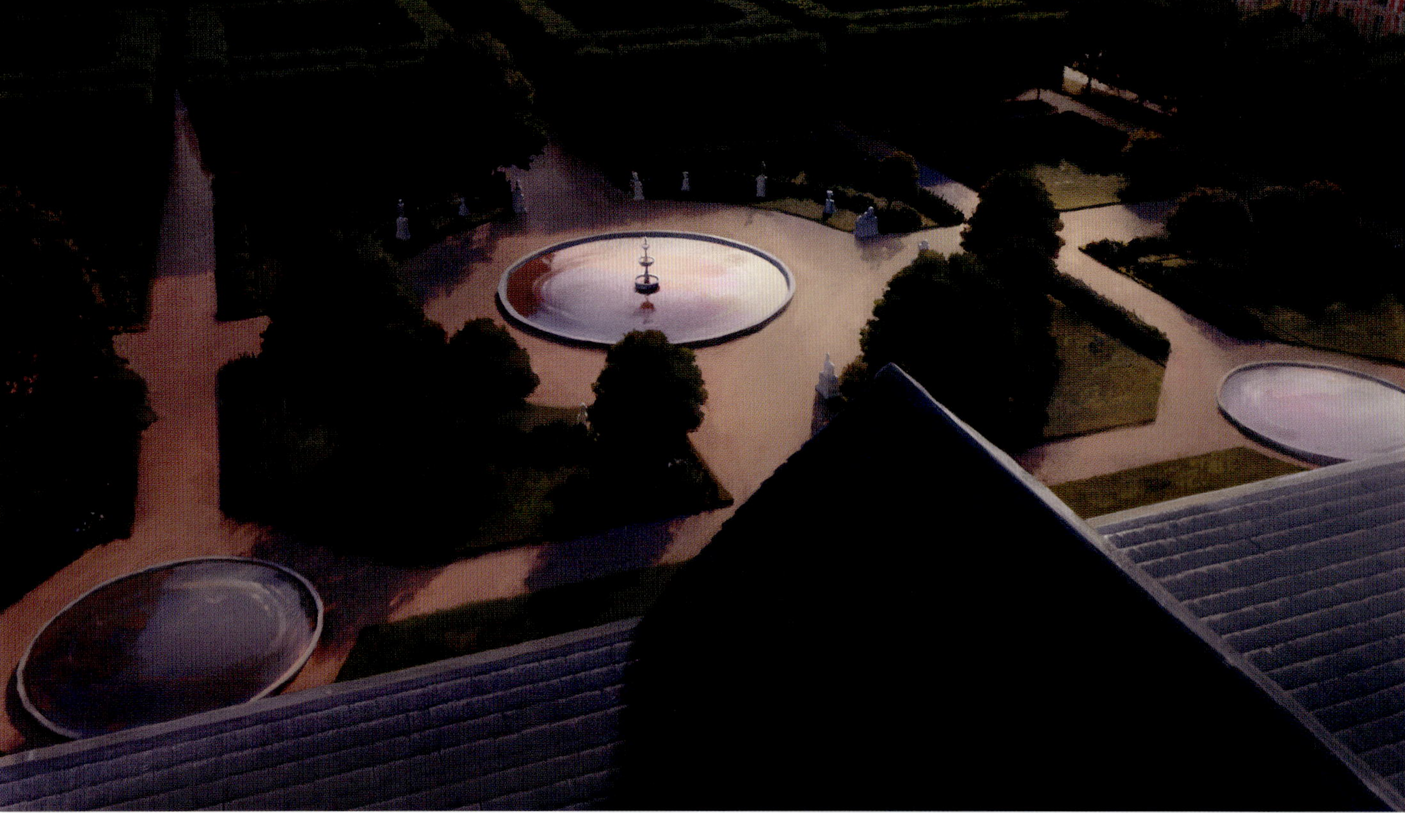

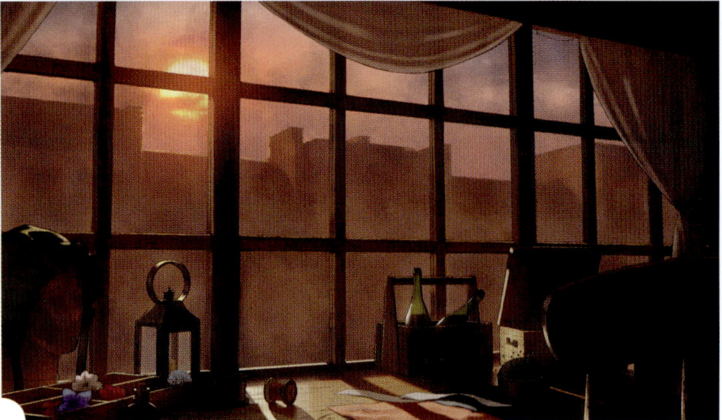

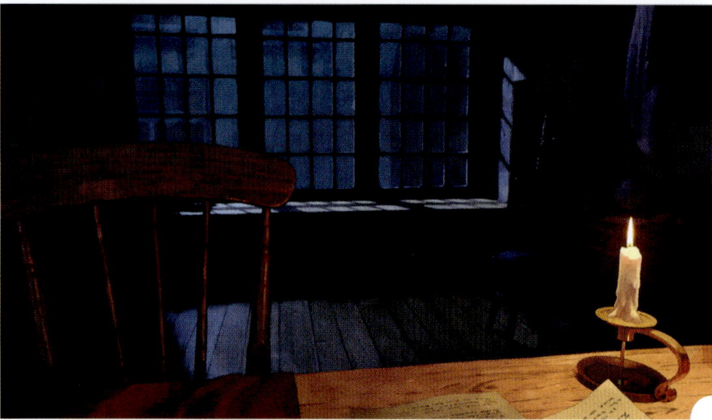

As they laid out Paris, they did their best to make sure there weren't obvious major landmarks that shouldn't be present during the era. They noted the city might be more built out in the series than it was in history, which is most visible in some of the aerial shots. Sam Deats said they did the best they could to find accurate maps.

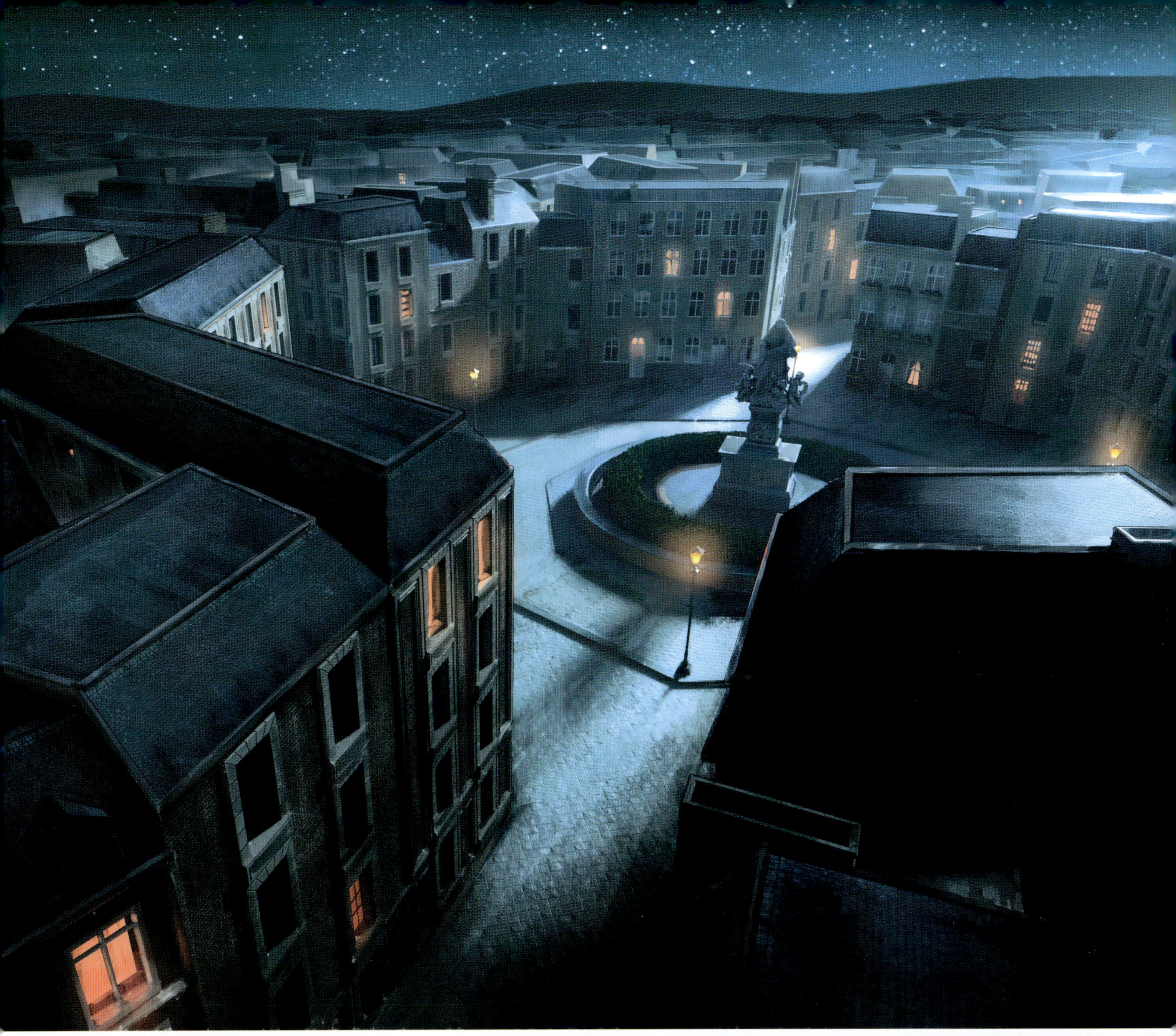

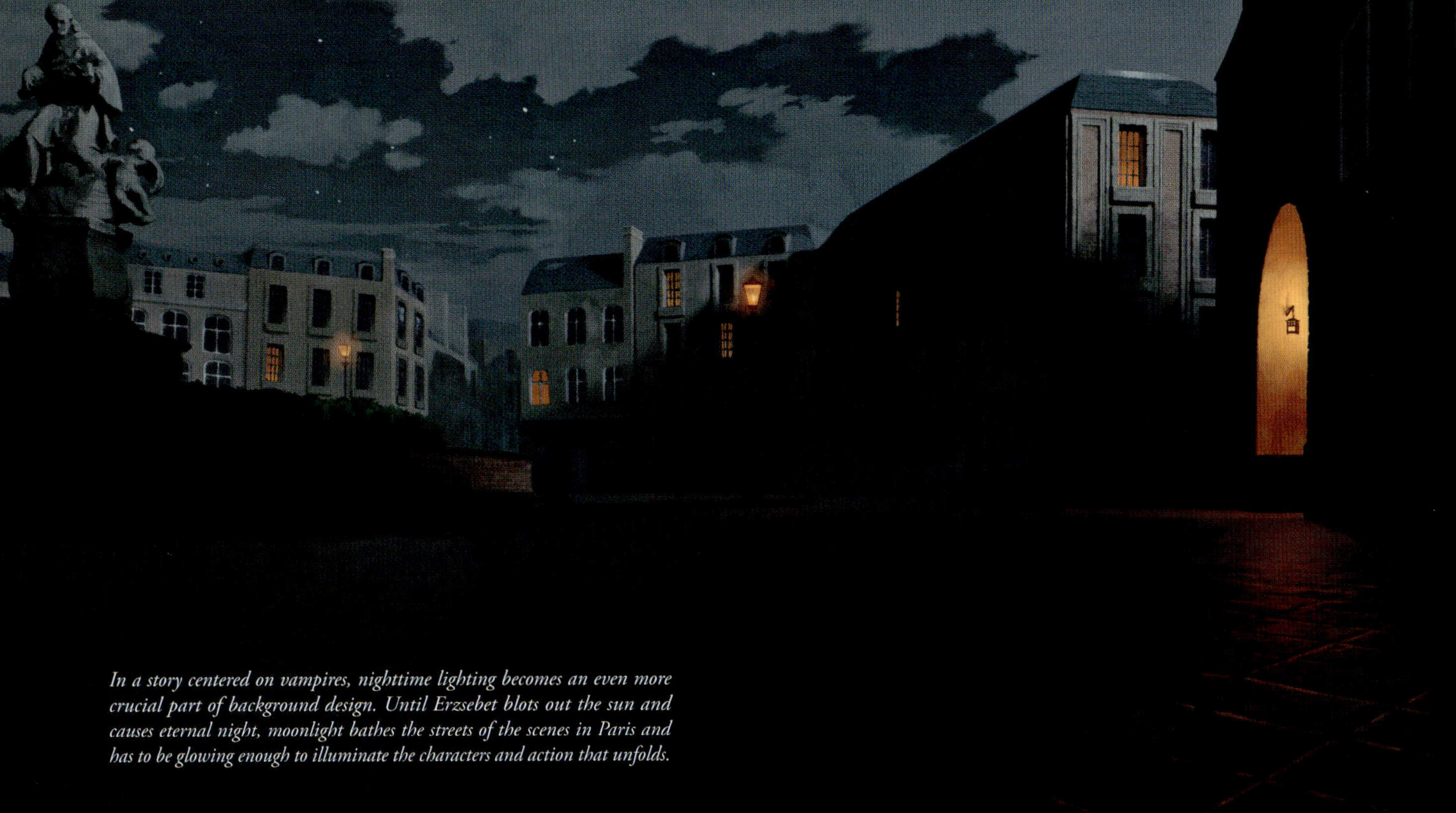

In a story centered on vampires, nighttime lighting becomes an even more crucial part of background design. Until Erzsebet blots out the sun and causes eternal night, moonlight bathes the streets of the scenes in Paris and has to be glowing enough to illuminate the characters and action that unfolds.

Top: Sean Randolph, Middle: Sean Randolph, Bottom left: Sabina Lewis, Bottom right: Bo Li. Opposite page: Stephen Stark.

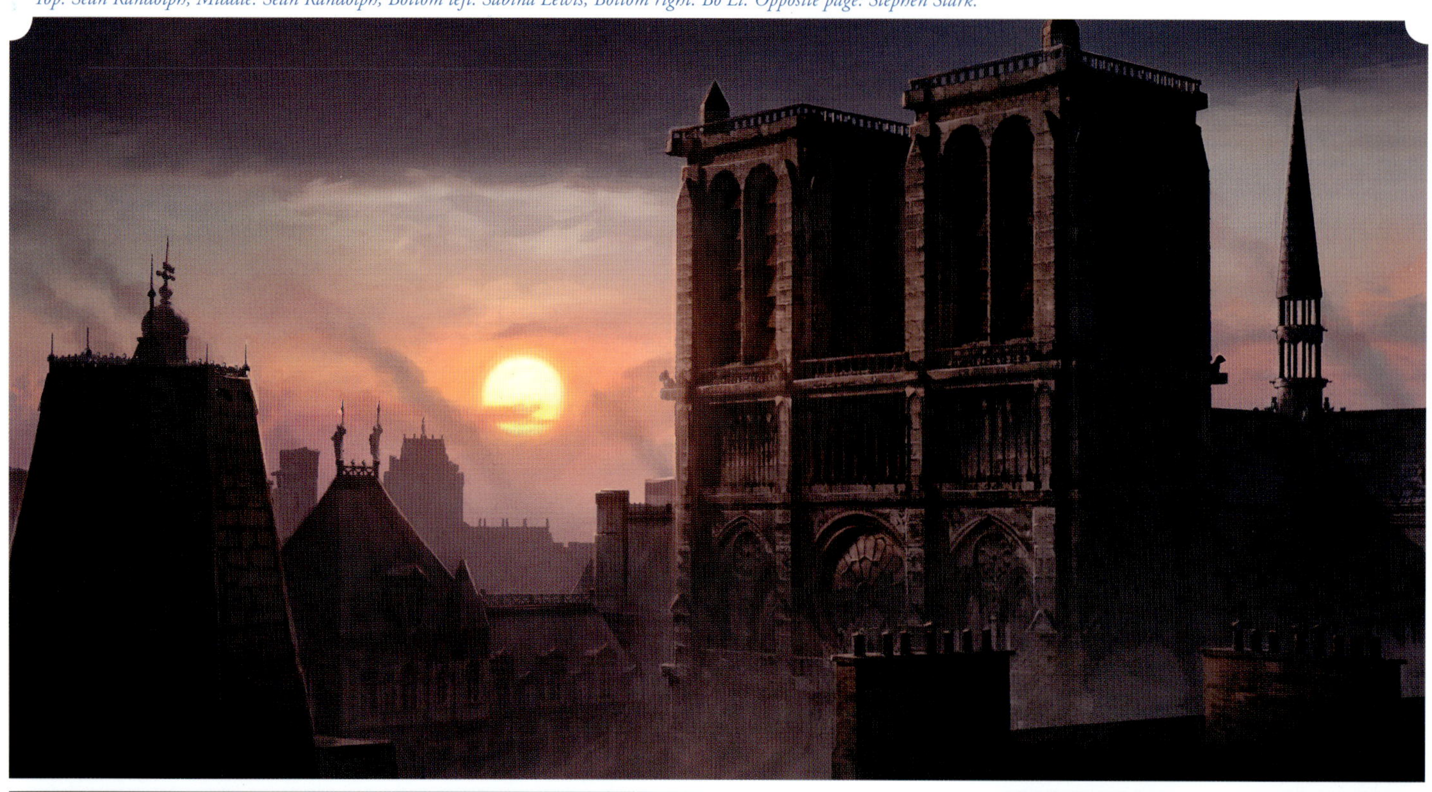

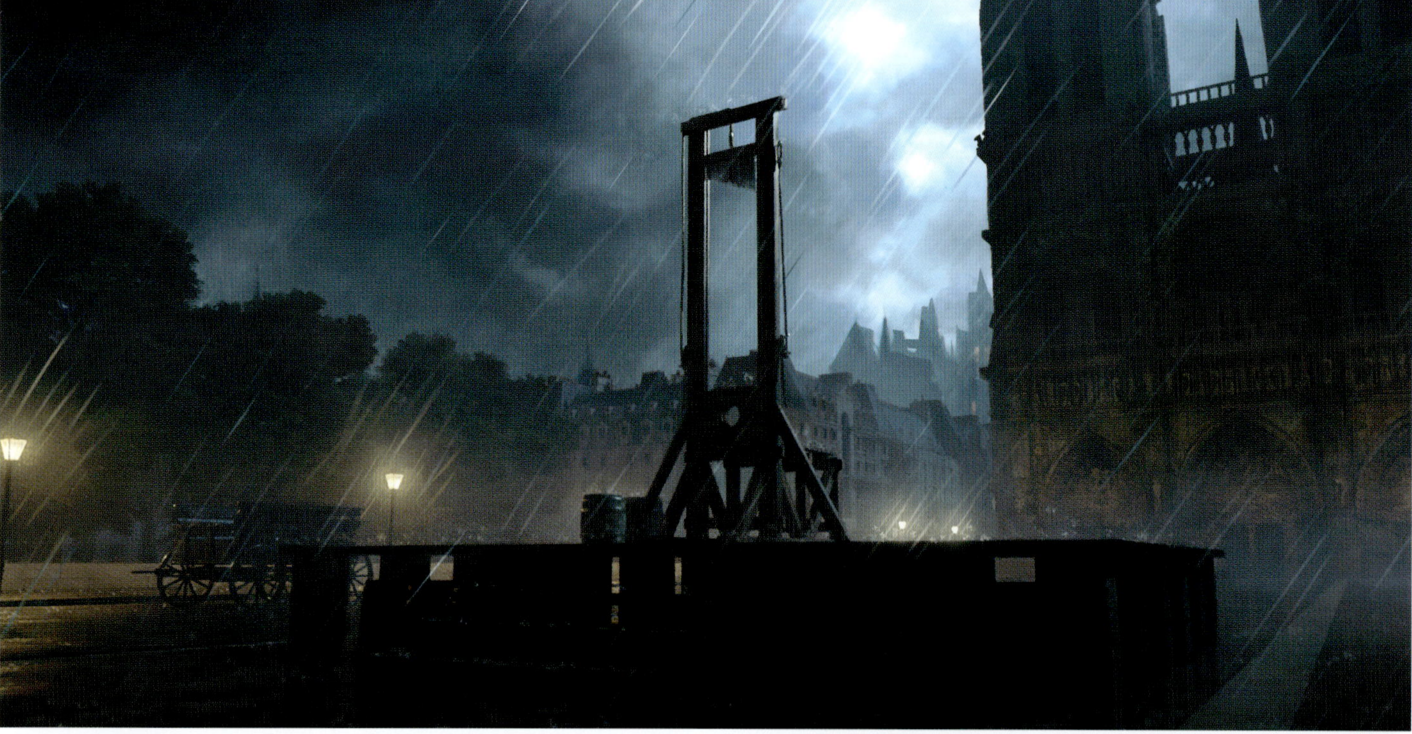

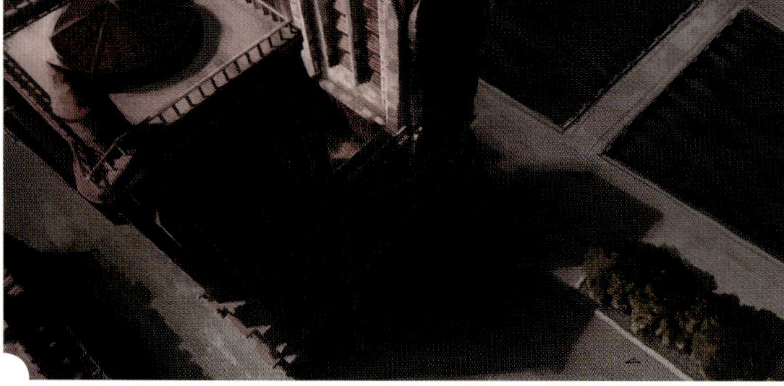

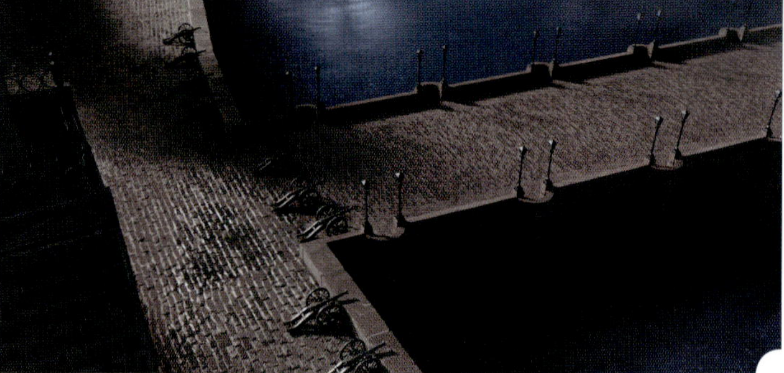

NOTRE DAME

One example of an aspect of Paris not being one hundred percent accurate is this bridge next to Notre Dame that goes towards the Place de Grève. The story was scripted assuming the bridge was present, but it turned out it wasn't built for another 15 years after the time period of *Nocturne*. With the series being about vampires, they decided not to adhere to the constraints of that particular real-world location.

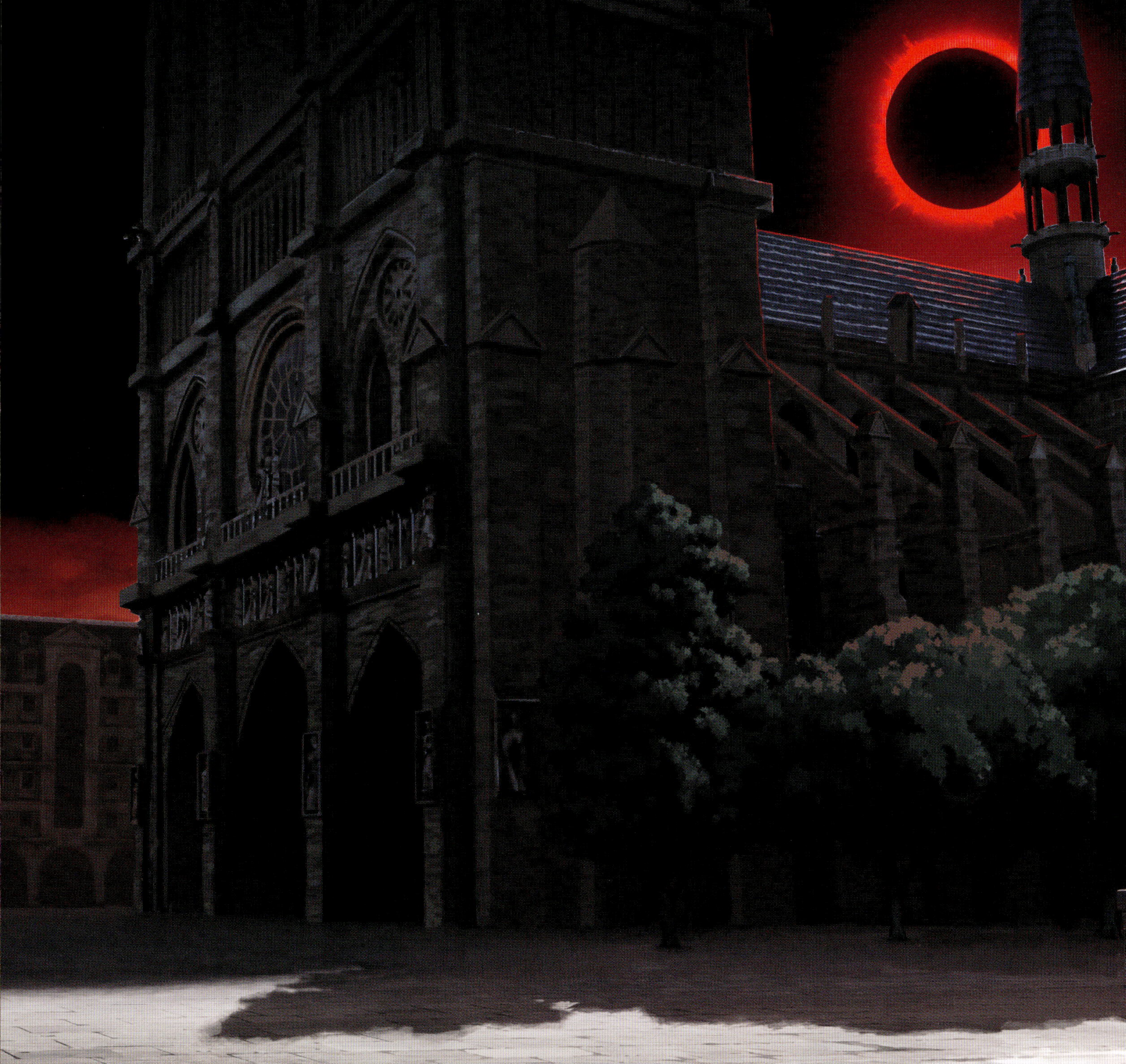

Top: Stephen Stark, Insert: Sean Randolph, Bottom: Sam Keiser. Opposite page: Mark Adams.

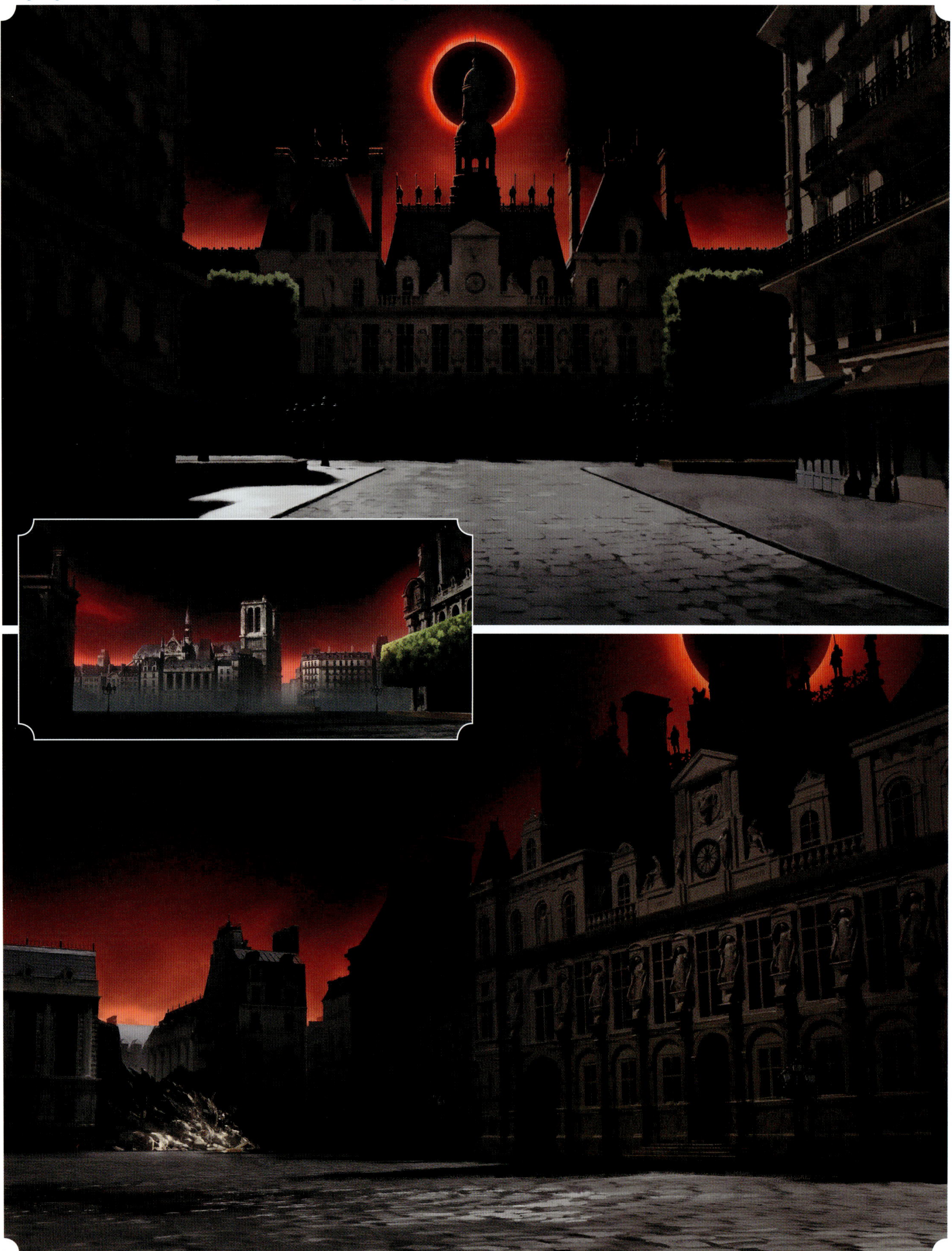

PLACE DE GRÈVE

When the eclipse comes at the end of the first season, Adam Deats said they purposefully sucked the color out of the scenes in contrast to what came before. Previously, the look was more romantic. He explained, "As the season goes on, things become a little bit less colorful, and by the end of the season it's back to being grim vampire territory. The tone shifts as we go. Our background manager did a really good job making sure that they're changing the way that they were painting backgrounds to match that look."

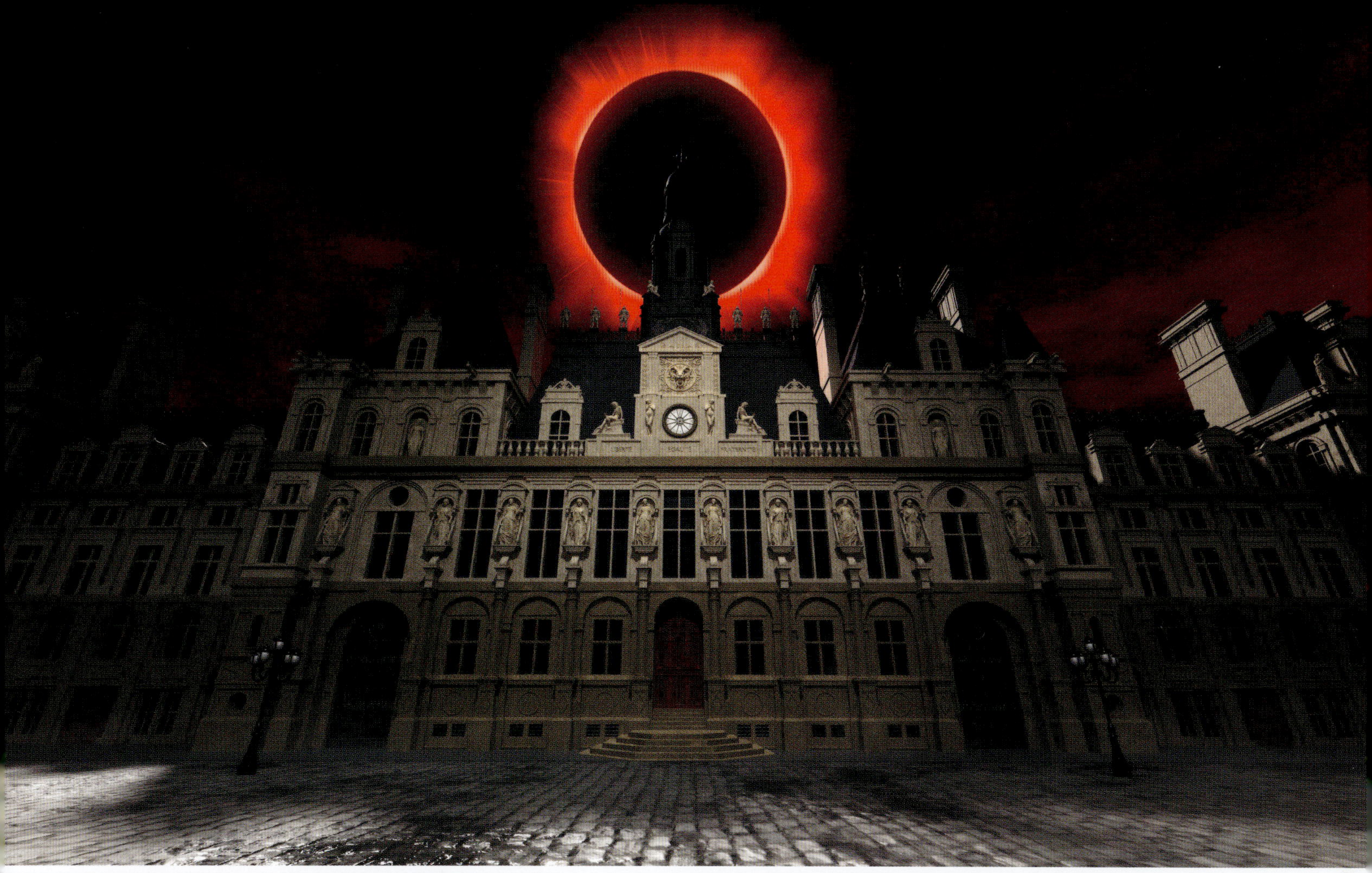

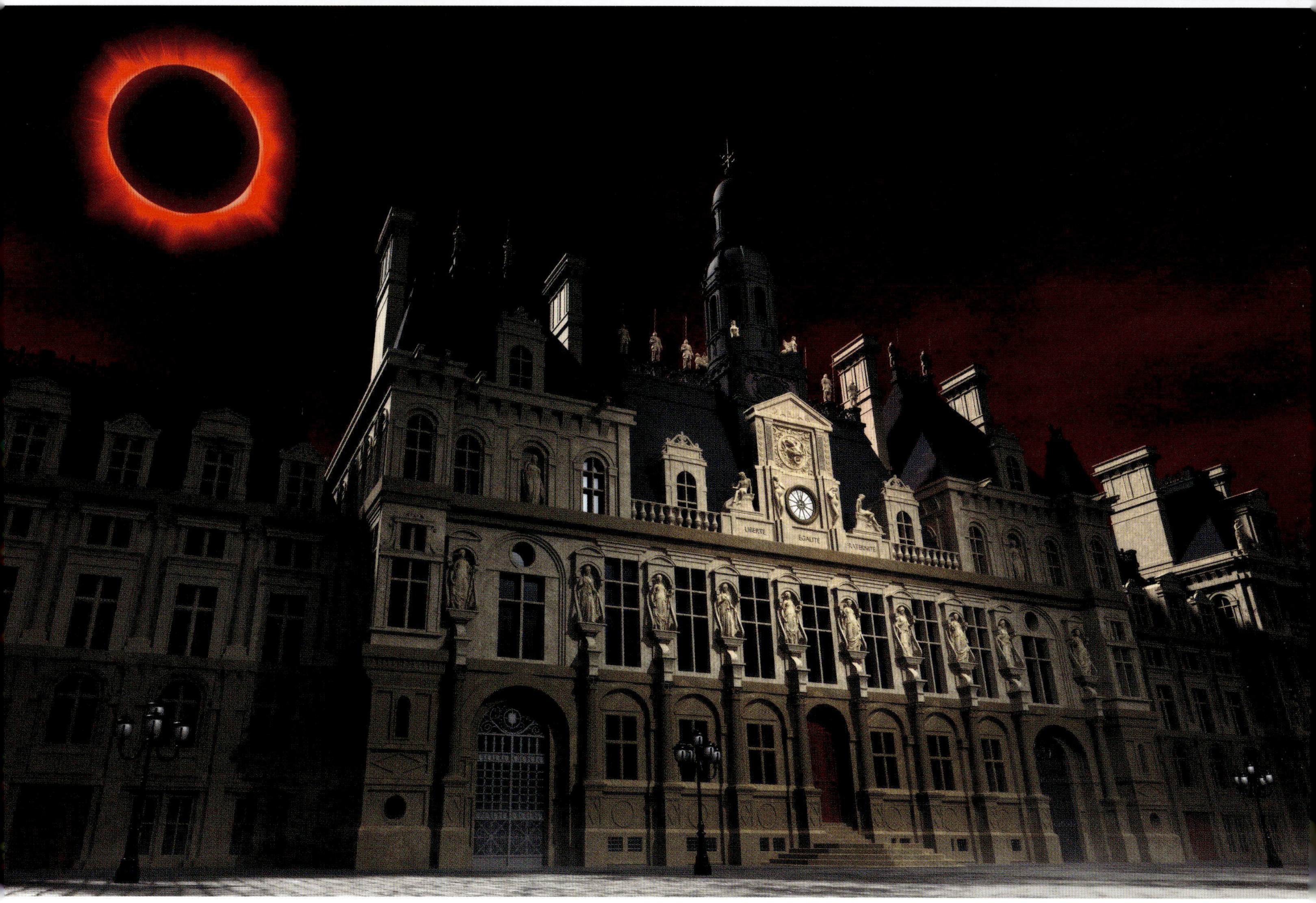

Art by Sam Keiser.

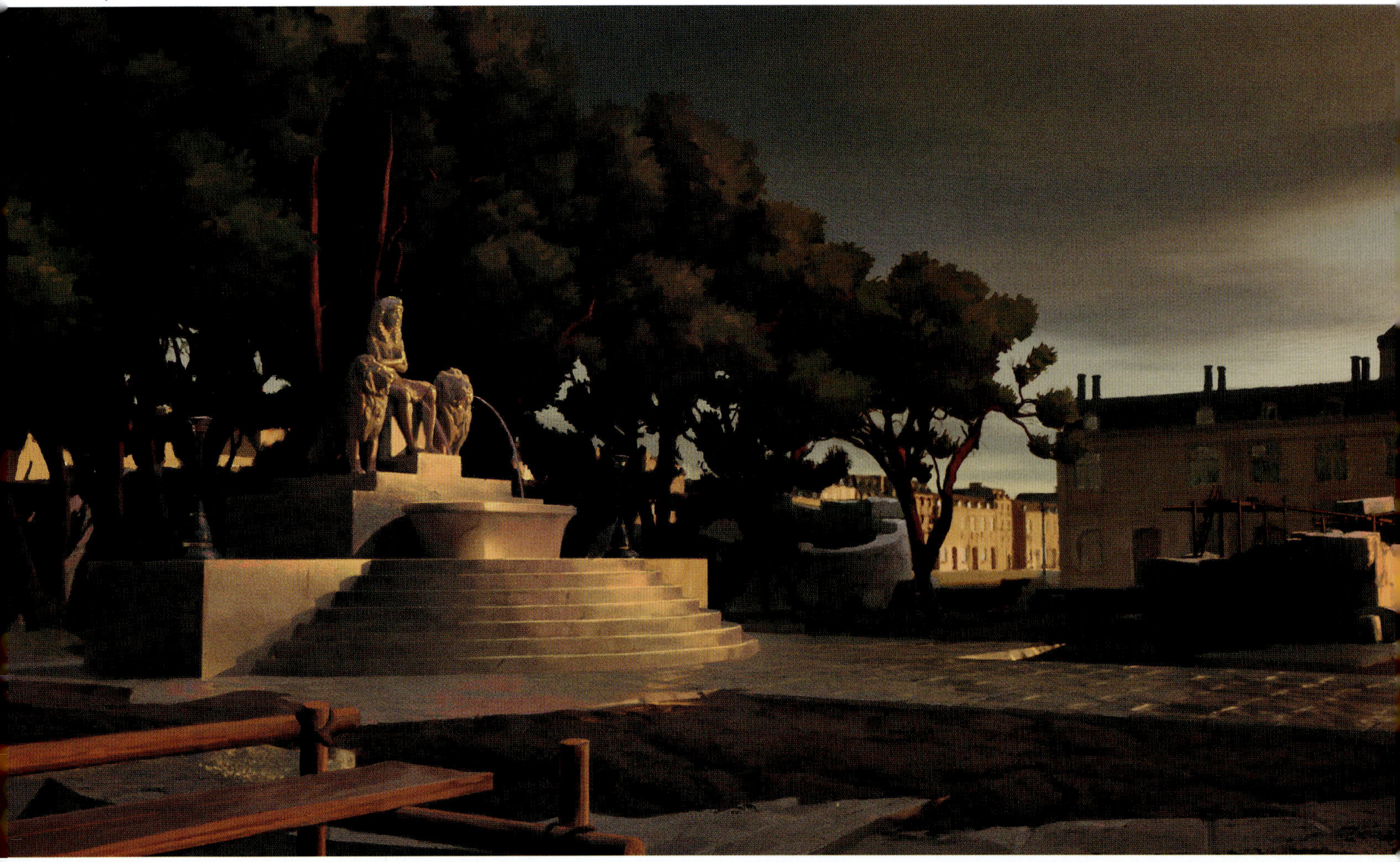

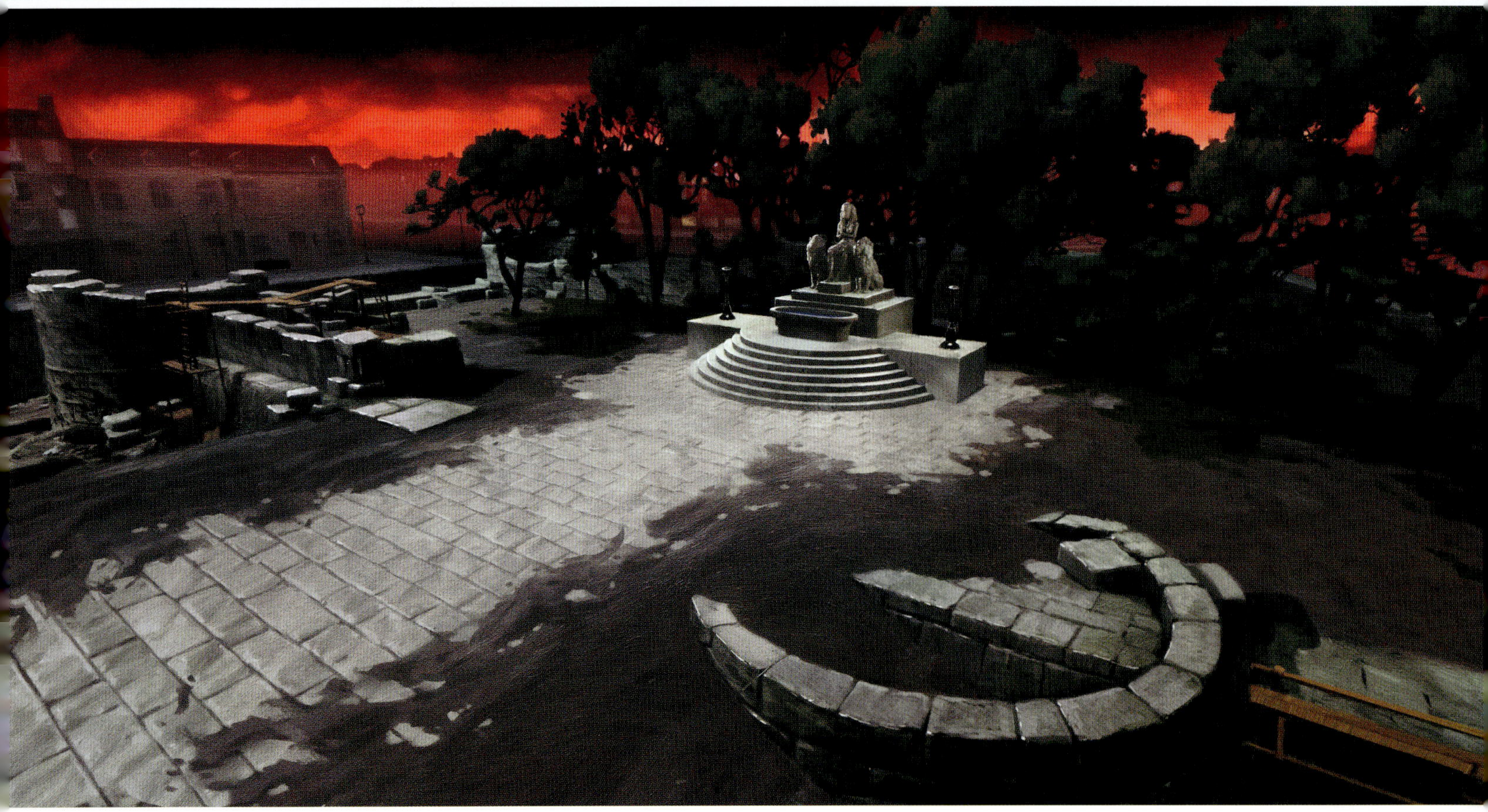

THE BASTILLE

Nocturne continually looked to history for background inspiration, even the ephemeral aspects. This temporary fountain, The Fountain of Regeneration, in the Bastille is an example. It featured Isis and sat atop the Bastille prison, where the French Revolution began. Keiser said, "It was weird to figure out this only existed for three years, and the timeline of when the show took place actually lined up for it. How do we play this up and actually do justice to this?"

Art by Sam Keiser.

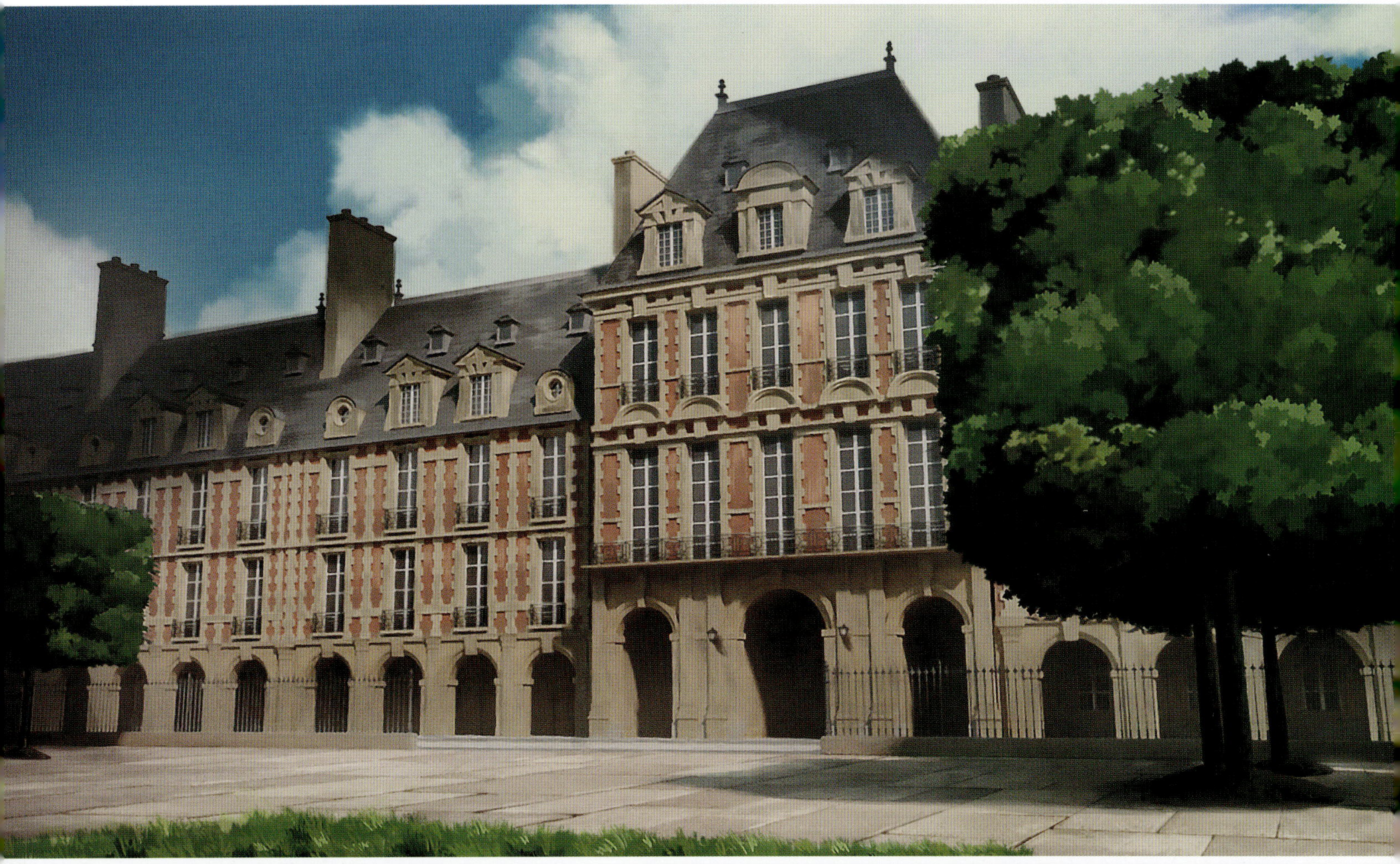

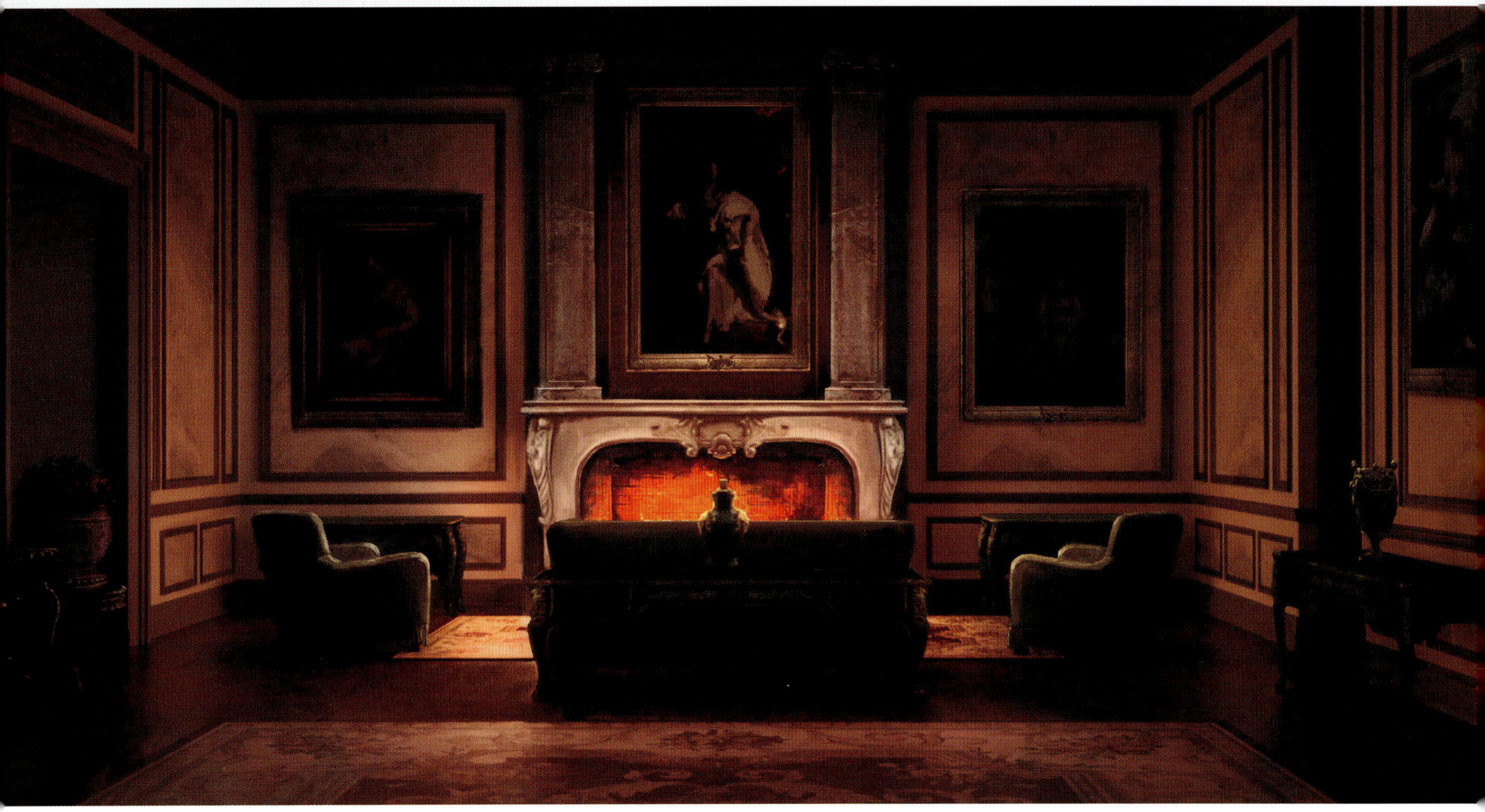

PLACE DES VOSGES

The Place des Voges, the oldest planned city square in Paris, is home to horrors in *Nocturne* (as are many of the locations in France). Drolta and her vampire cultists have human nobles under capture here, and it's where Drolta chooses a young woman to offer to Erzsebet as a sort of sacrifice. Sean Randolph tapped into the square's symmetry and brick arcades, using its structured elegance to contrast the chaos unfolding within.

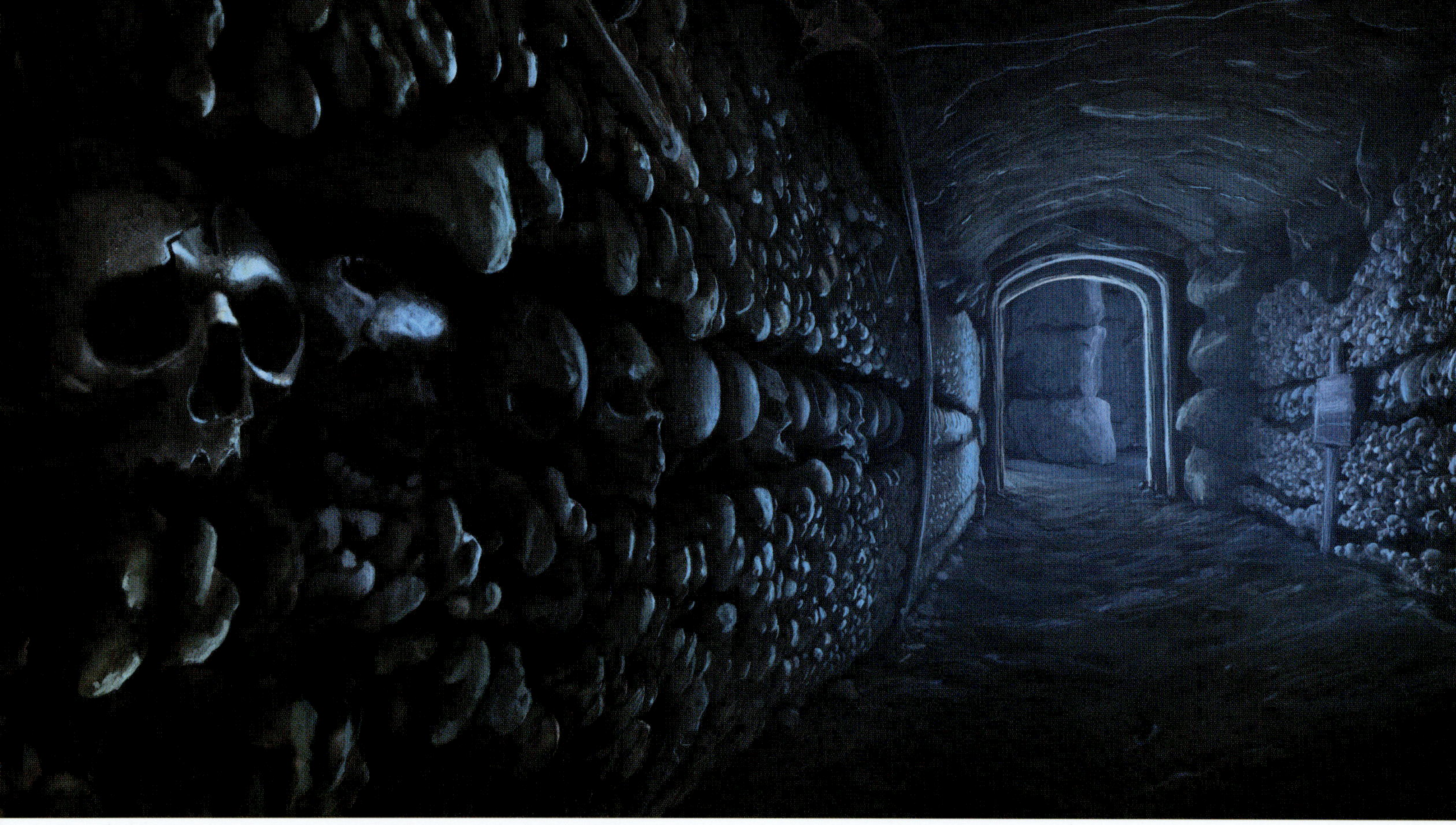

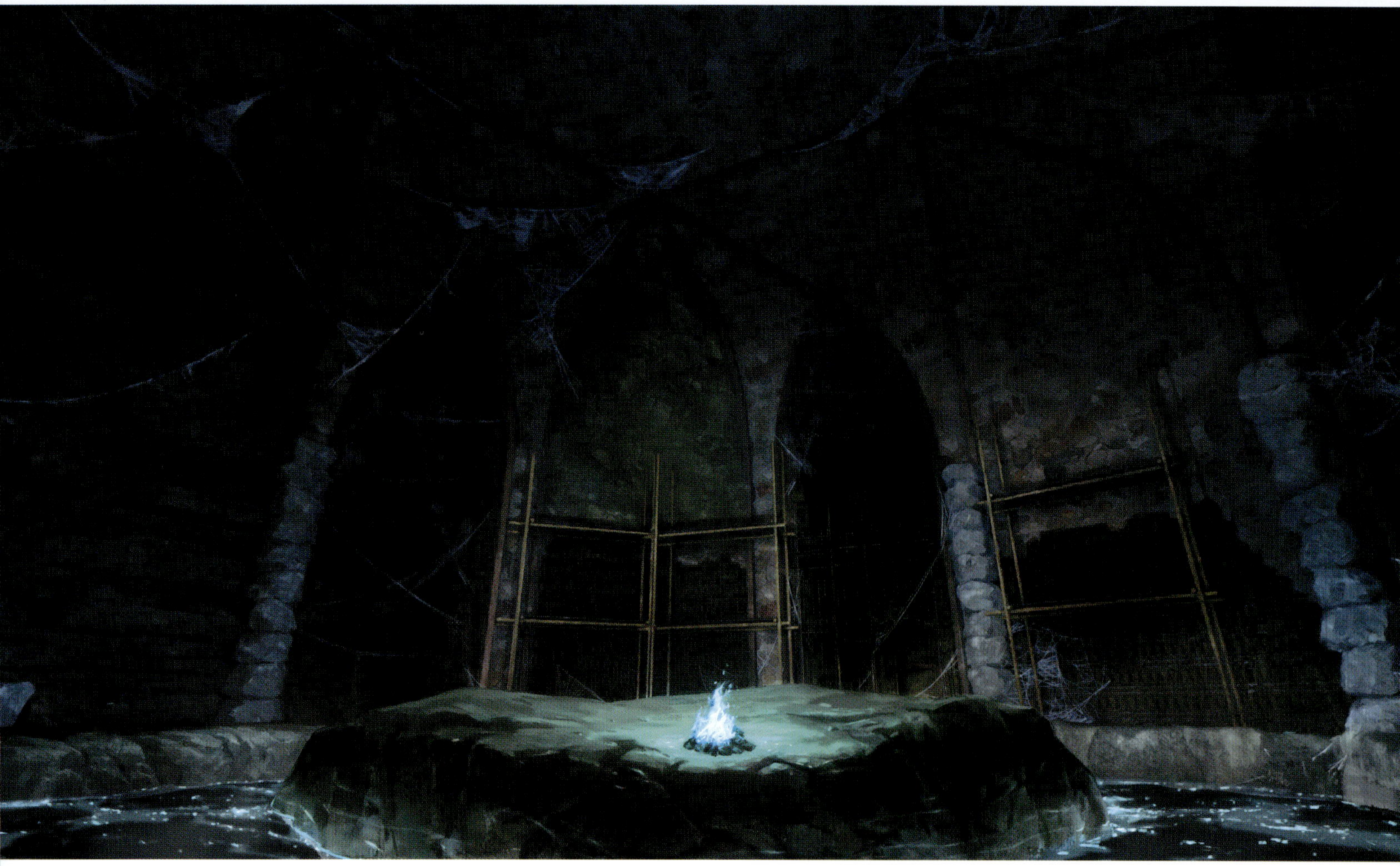

CATACOMBS

Catacombs under Paris hold the remains of millions of people. For the appearance of the ossuaries In *Nocturne*, Randolph turned to photos of those catacombs for real-life reference. He recalled he actually toned it down because these initial designs match how it is in the actual catacombs with sections where it's just walls of bones. In later iterations, he had skulls peeking out of the mortar here and there.

Opposite top: Sabina Lewis, Opposite bottom: Sam Keiser. Top: Sam Keiser, Insert: Sean Randolph, Middle: Bo Li, Bottom left: Sabina Lewis, Bottom left: Bo Li.

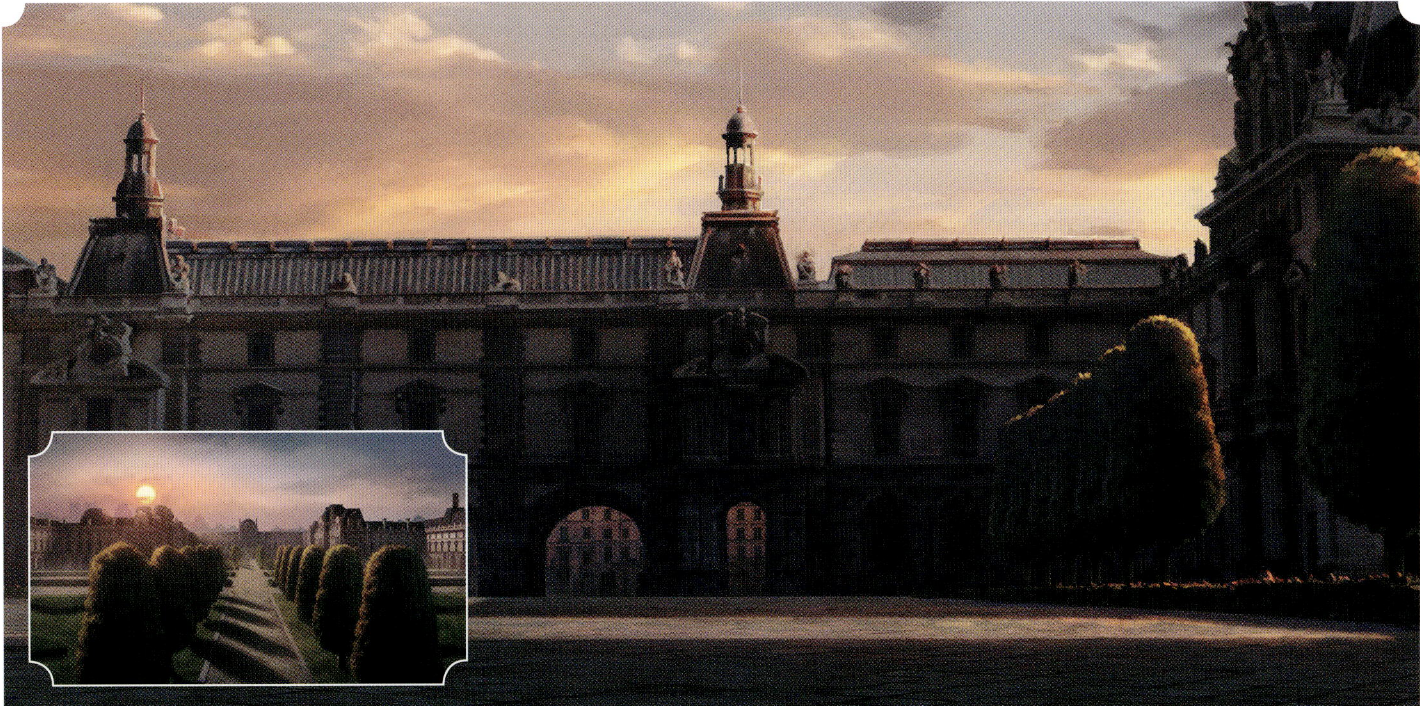

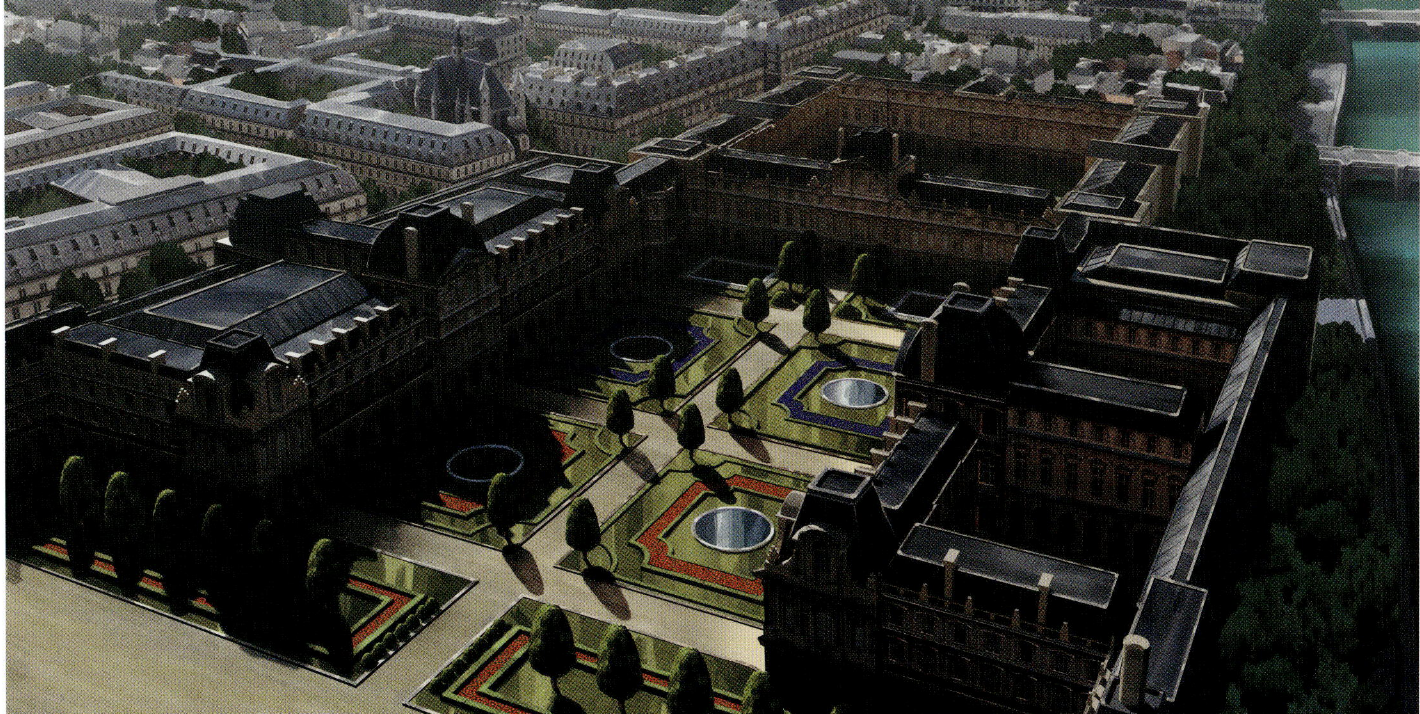

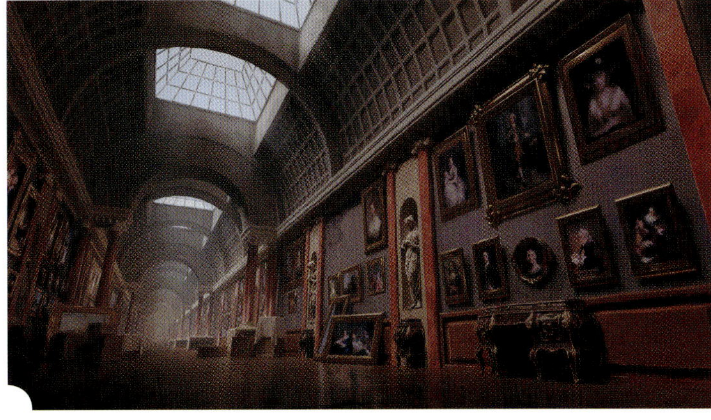

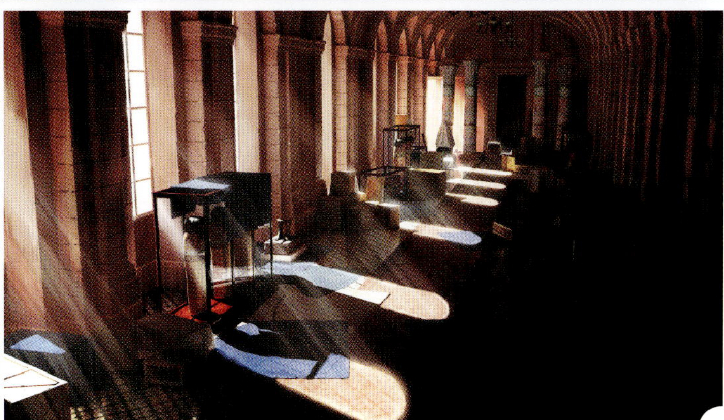

LOUVRE

To stop Erzsebet from consuming more of Sekhmet's soul and becoming unfathomably powerful, Richter, Annette, and Alucard must find Sekhmet's mummy in the Louvre. The iconic art museum in Paris houses a treasure trove of iconic artwork. The background design team got to create both the exterior and interior of the museum, re-creating some of the paintings (including the Mona Lisa) and studying the way natural light would filter through the spacious room.

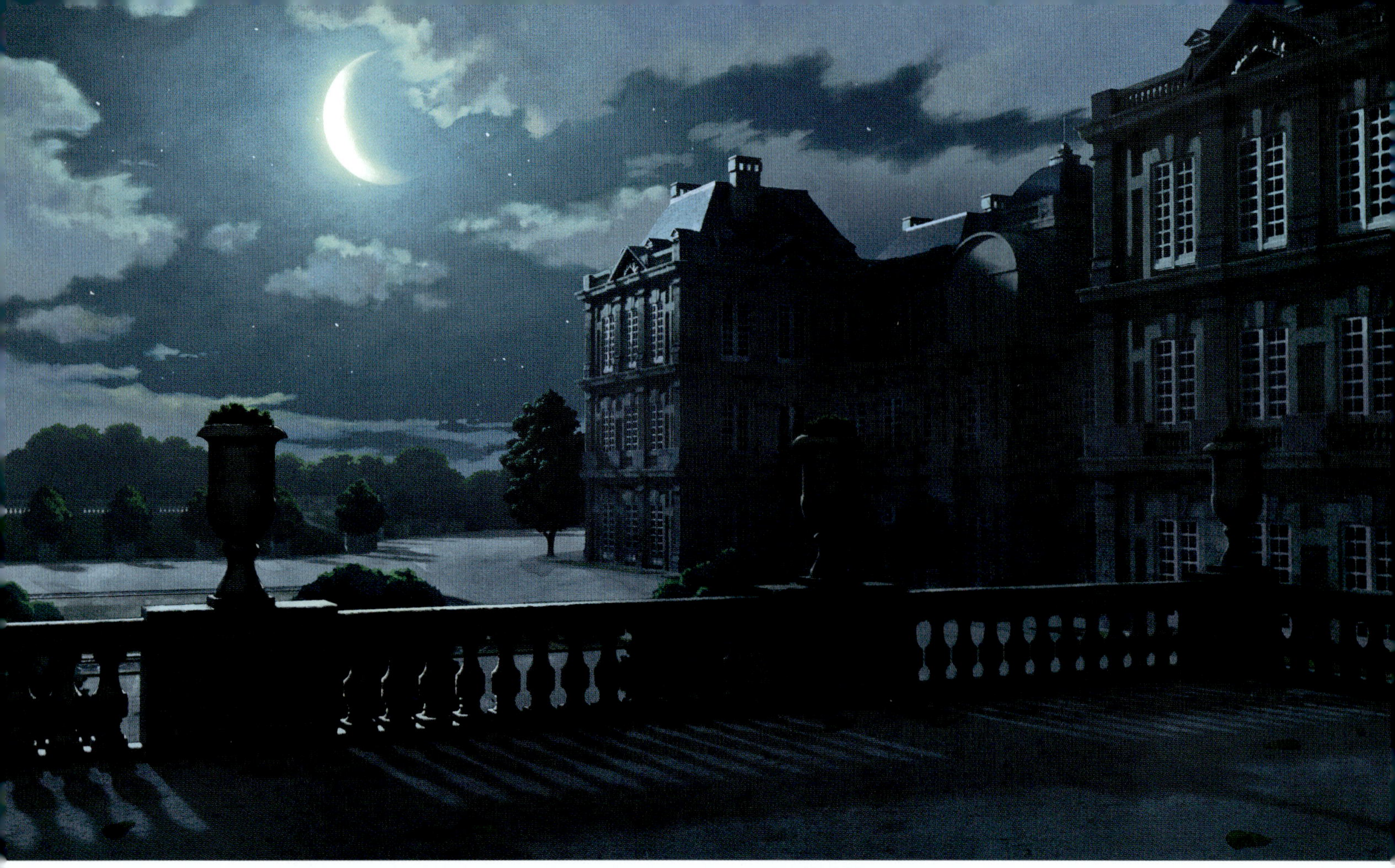

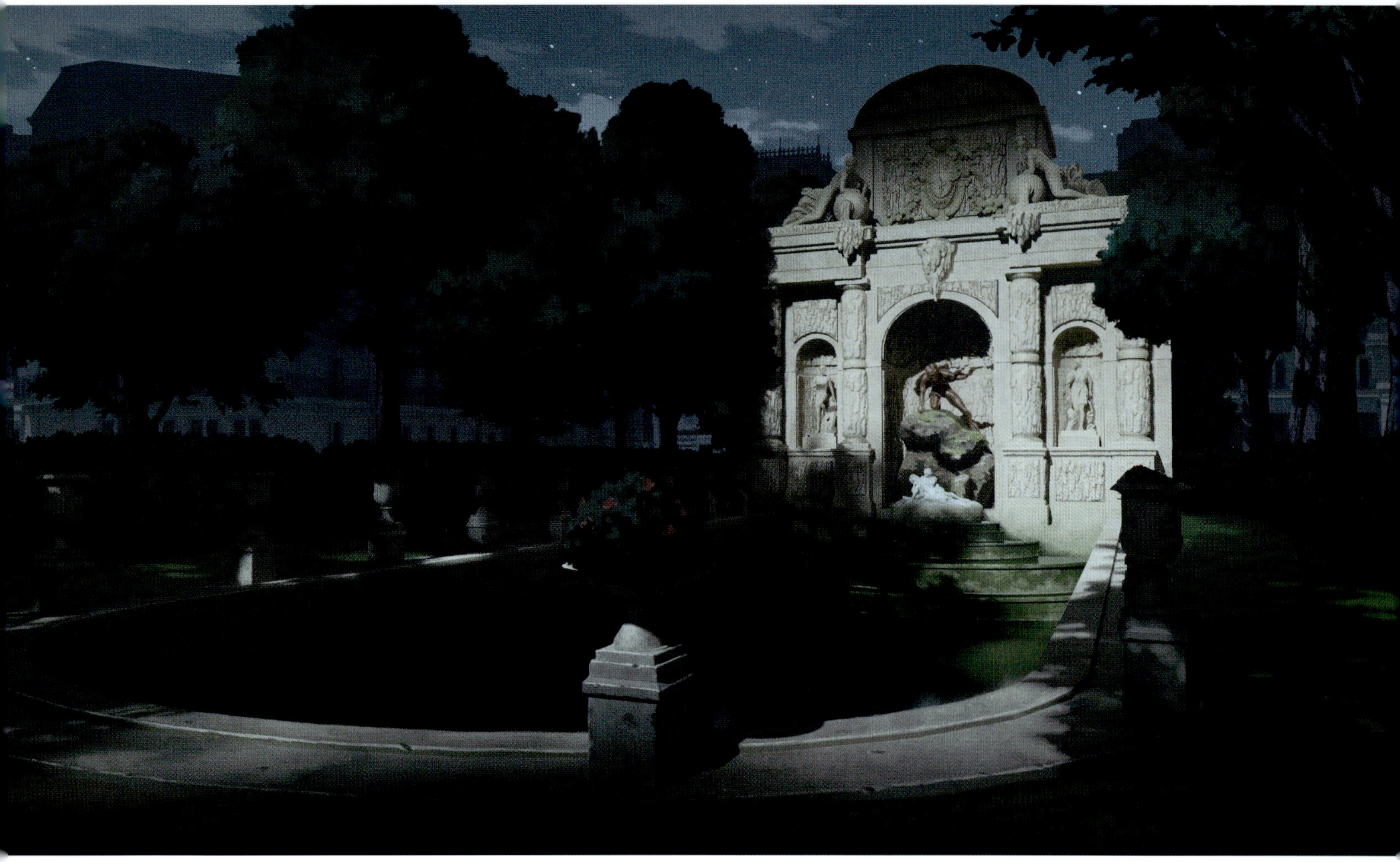

LUXEMBOURG

The Medici Fountain in the Jardin du Luxembourg was named in the script, though it only appears on screen briefly. Stark said if it's a real-life location, they strive to get it right regardless of the amount it's shown. "You have to model it out correctly," he said. "This is a good instance of that, of we barely ever see this, but I spent so long on it."

Opposite page: Stephen Stark. Top and middle: Sean Randolph, Bottom left: Stephen Stark, Bottom right: Bo Li.

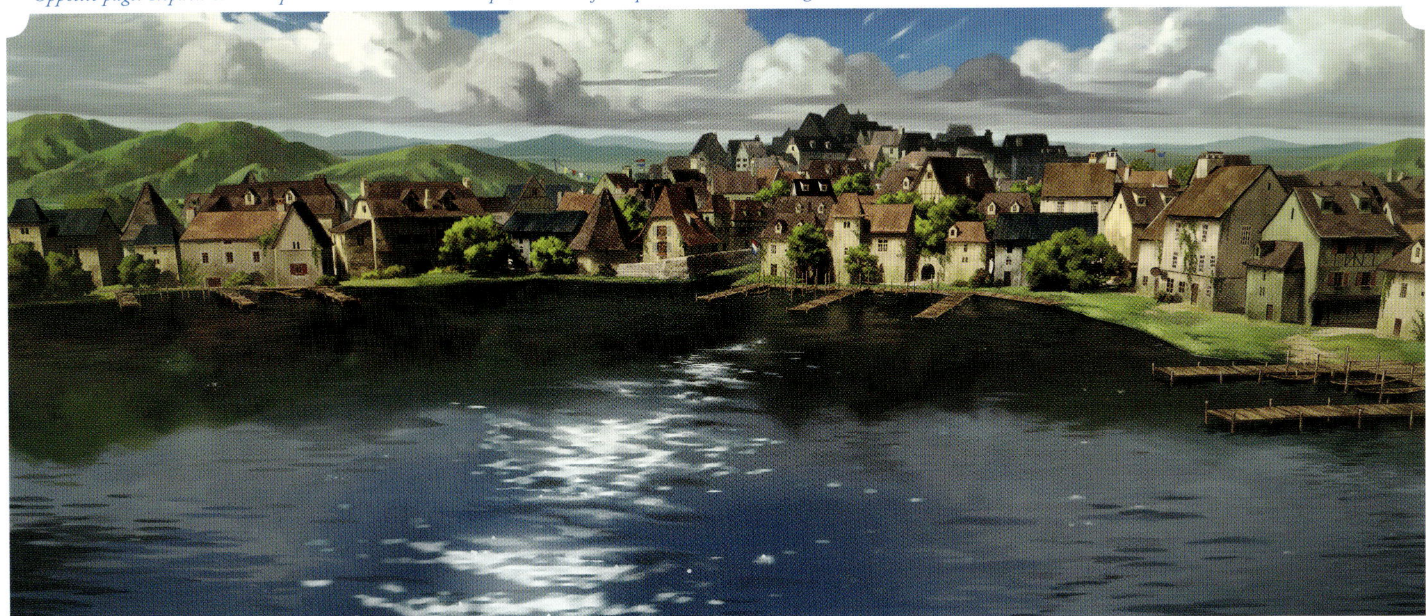

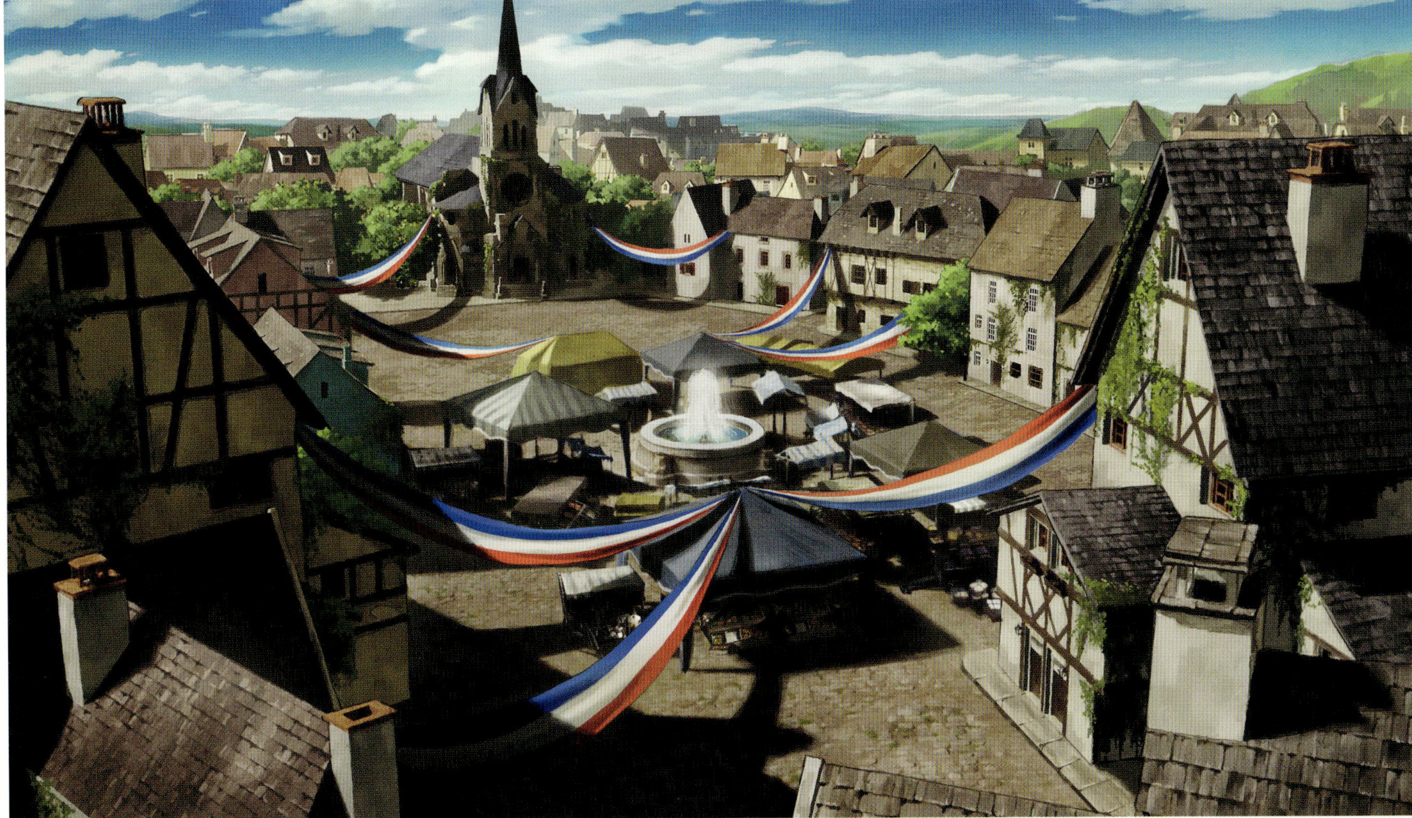

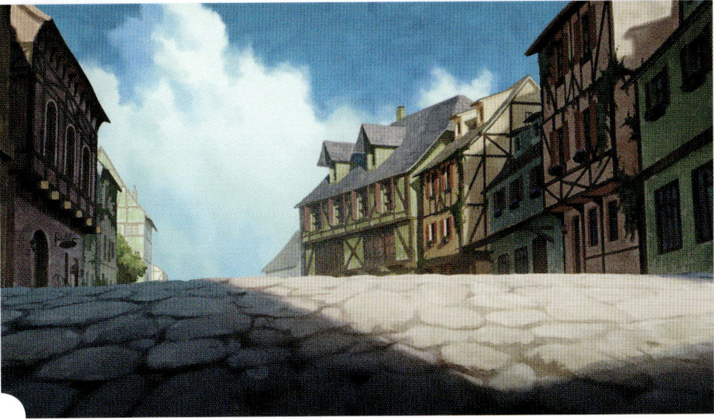

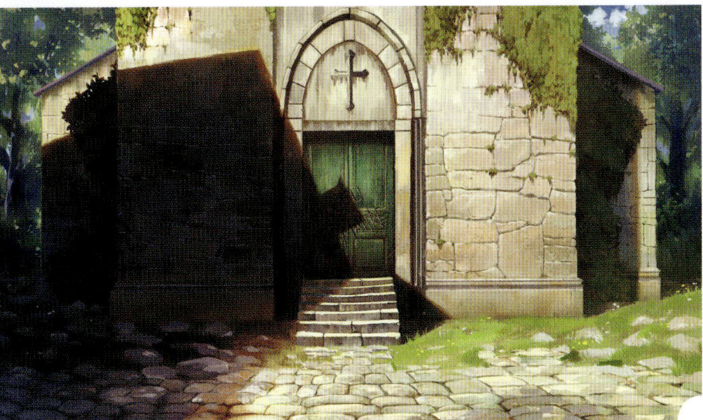

PICTURESQUE TOWN

This quaint town is an inviting respite from grander settings. It's here the team brought locations from other animation into their field of inspiration. The town in *Howl's Moving Castle* was a reference point for the designers. Stark said he intentionally didn't draw too much from the Studio Ghibli movie at other points in the series because he put the homage here. In addition to to the Studio Ghibli film, the setting also brings the provincial town from *Beauty and the Beast* to mind.

Art by Stephen Stark.

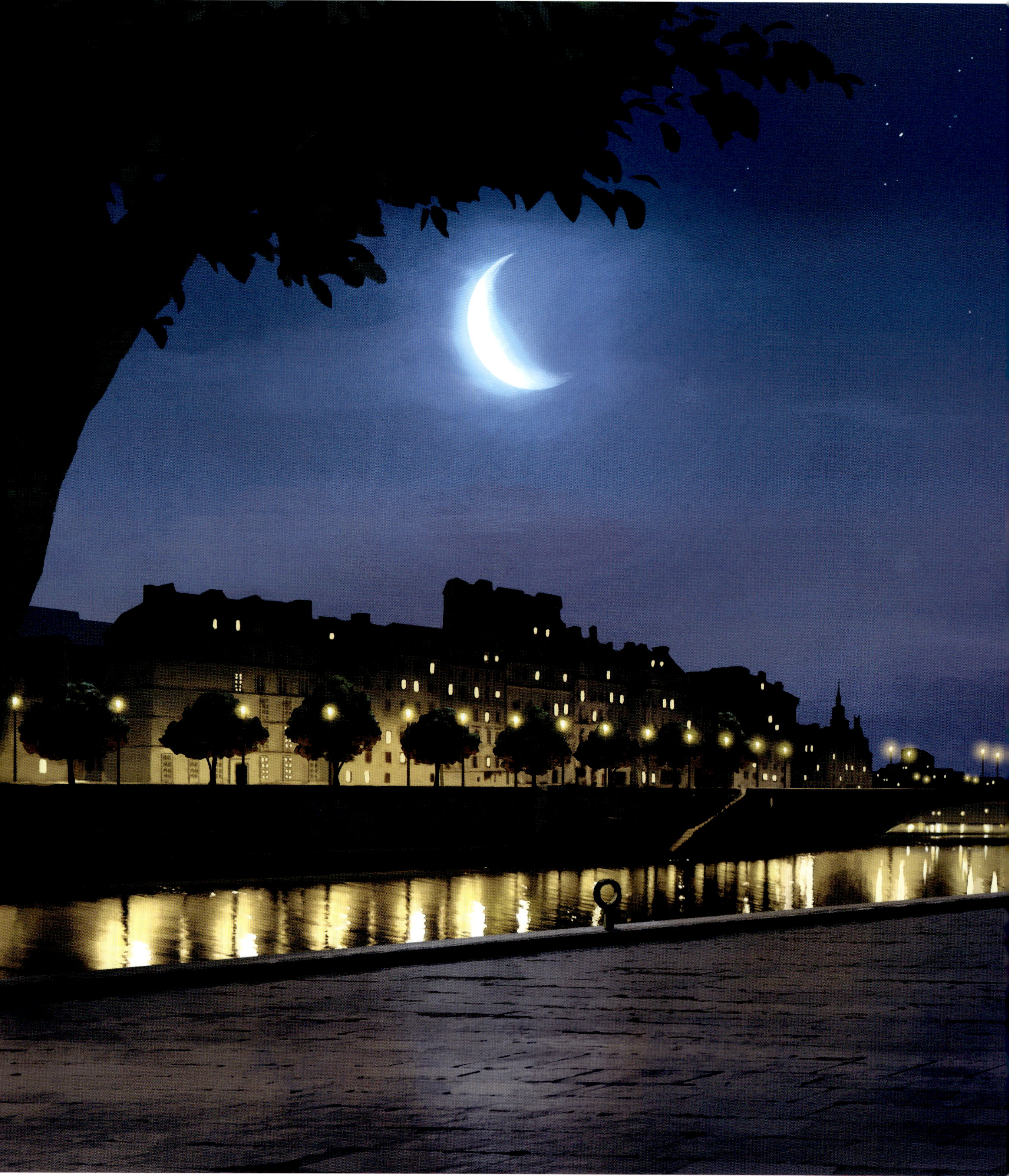

SEINE RIVER

The phases of the moon were key throughout the series, and the environment designers mentioned executive producer Sam Deats reminded them to pay attention to the phases of the moon—particularly since the story unfolds over a relatively short period of time. They showed a full moon in the night sky the majority of the time, but this concept for the Seine River shows a crescent moon. Regardless of the moon's phase, the artists often got to light scenes with moonlight. In this image, the moon's light casts stark shadows against the cobblestone.

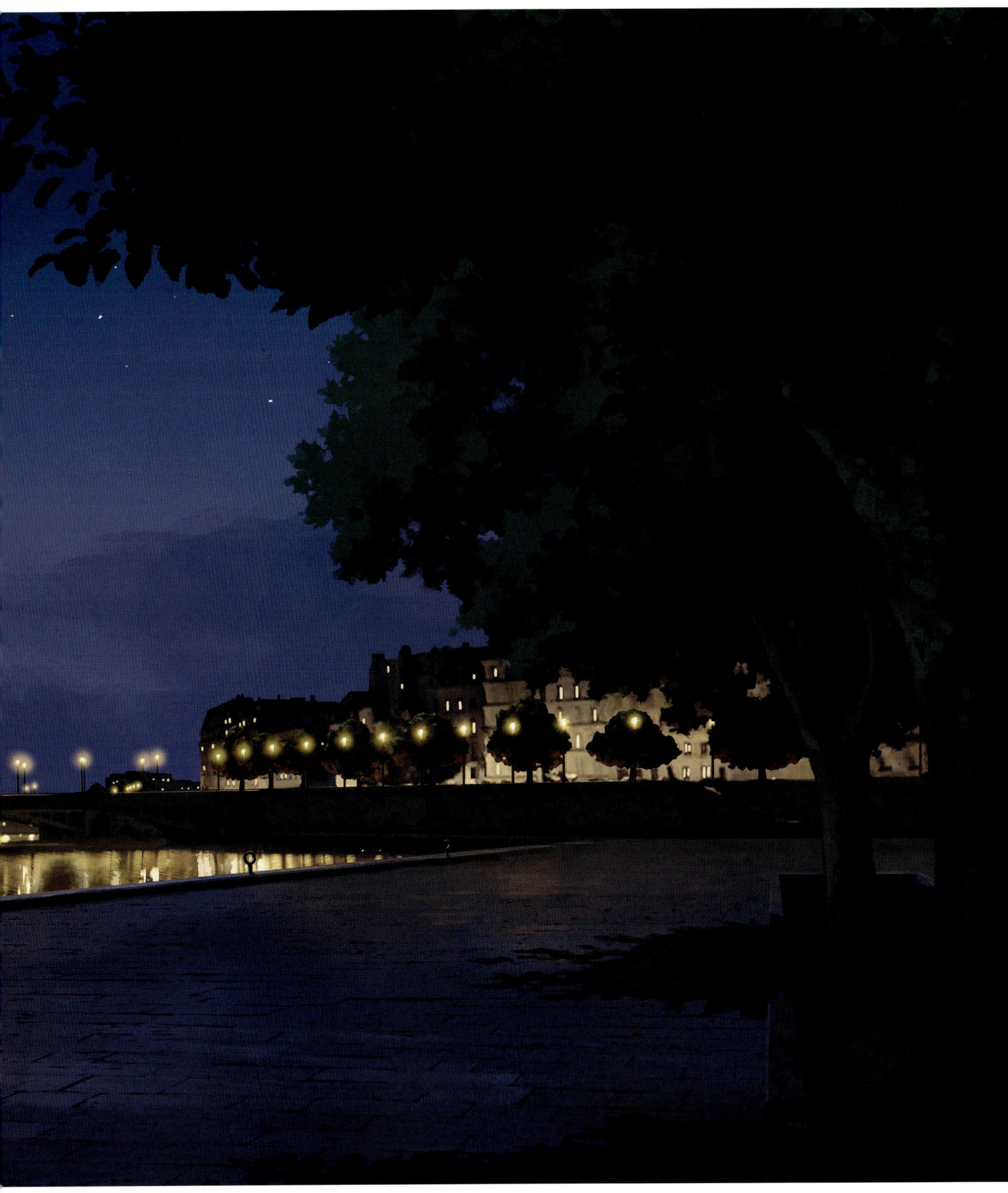

This scene also features soft lighting from glowing lamps. Sam Deats noted that they took some liberty with the lighting, because they're brighter than they actually would have been during that era. "We played with the modern lighting aesthetic for the romantic feeling that we wanted, which is classic filmmaking. If you want nice bright lights on things that maybe weren't realistic for the time, that's okay. It's better to hit the emotion than always adhere to perfect accuracy."

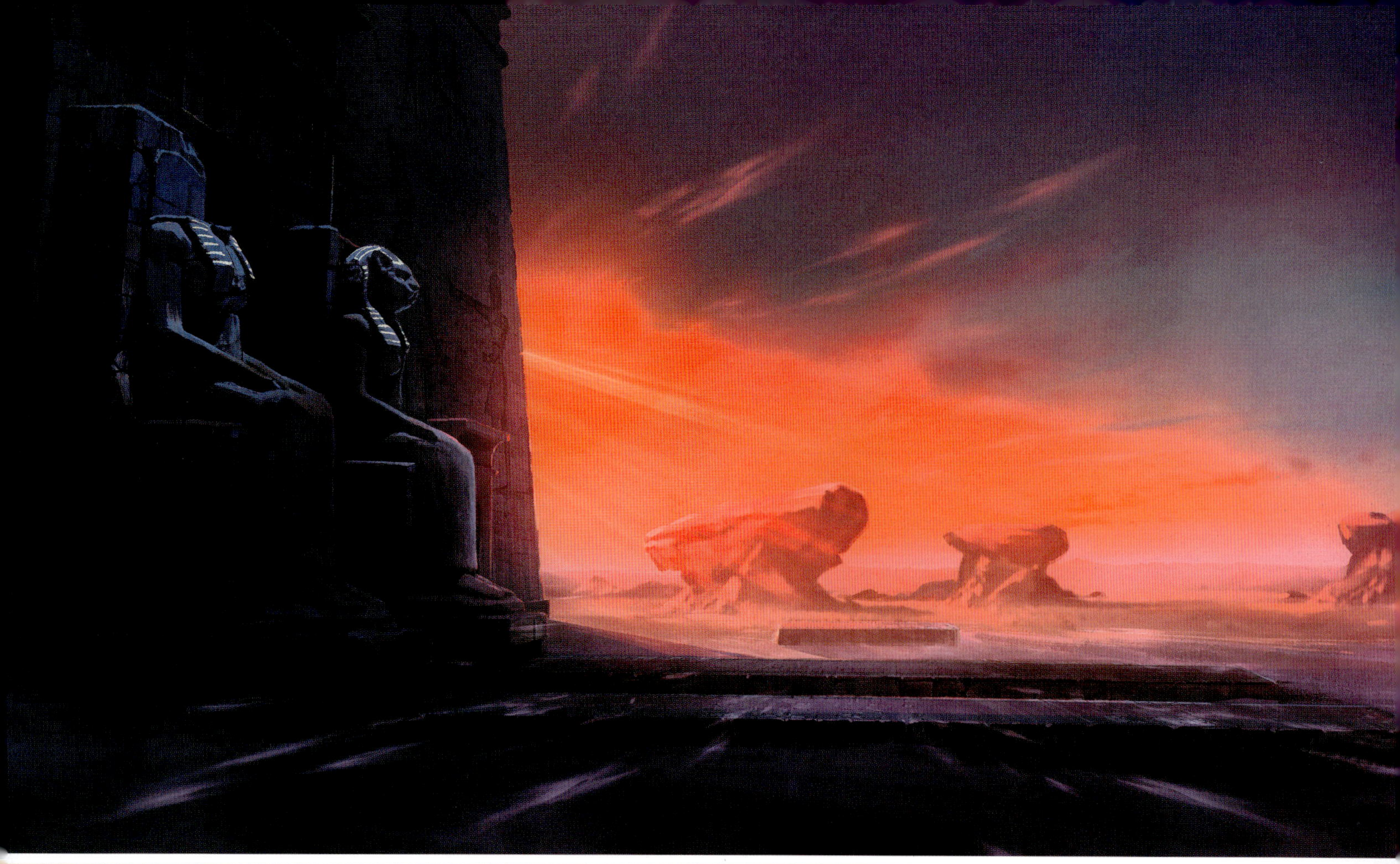

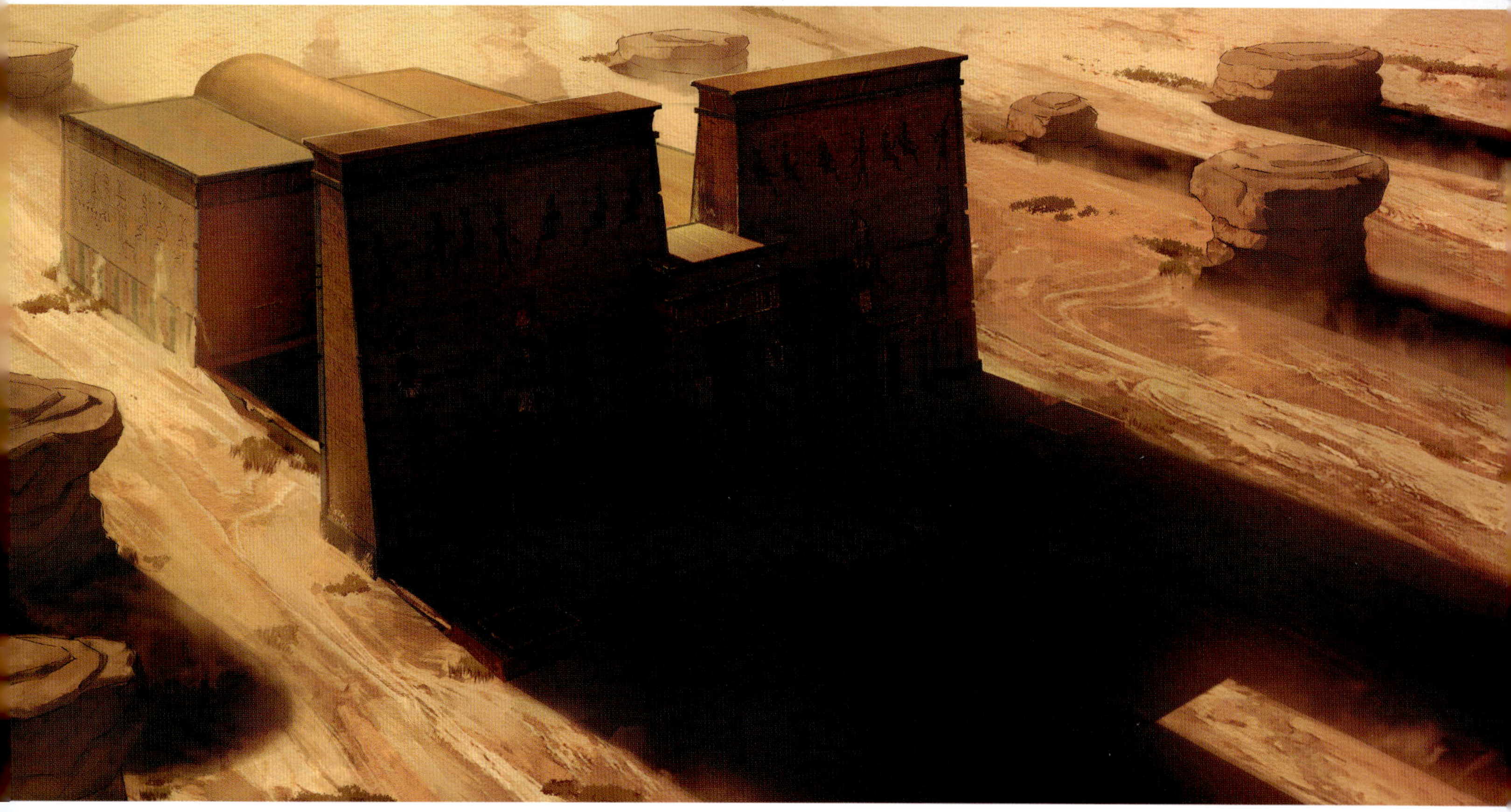

Sekhmet Temple

The place of worship for the warrior goddess Sekhmet appears in the story at different points of time. To showcase it in proper chronological context, background designer Sam Keiser created three versions: a super-ancient one with no paintings, another with super-polished paintings, and then a take that shows it's fallen on hard times again. Keiser based the look on the actual temple, as well as the Temple of Isis, and used textures to resemble the geographic area where it was built near Luxor, Egypt. In his words, he went "ham" building a super-robust model and going for as much historic accuracy as possible. Keiser called this set his baby. He designed and modeled it, handpainted the textures, and then lit the entire set for reference.

Opposite top: Sam Keiser, Opposite bottom: Bo Li. Storyboards by Victoria Li and Chance Kubesh.

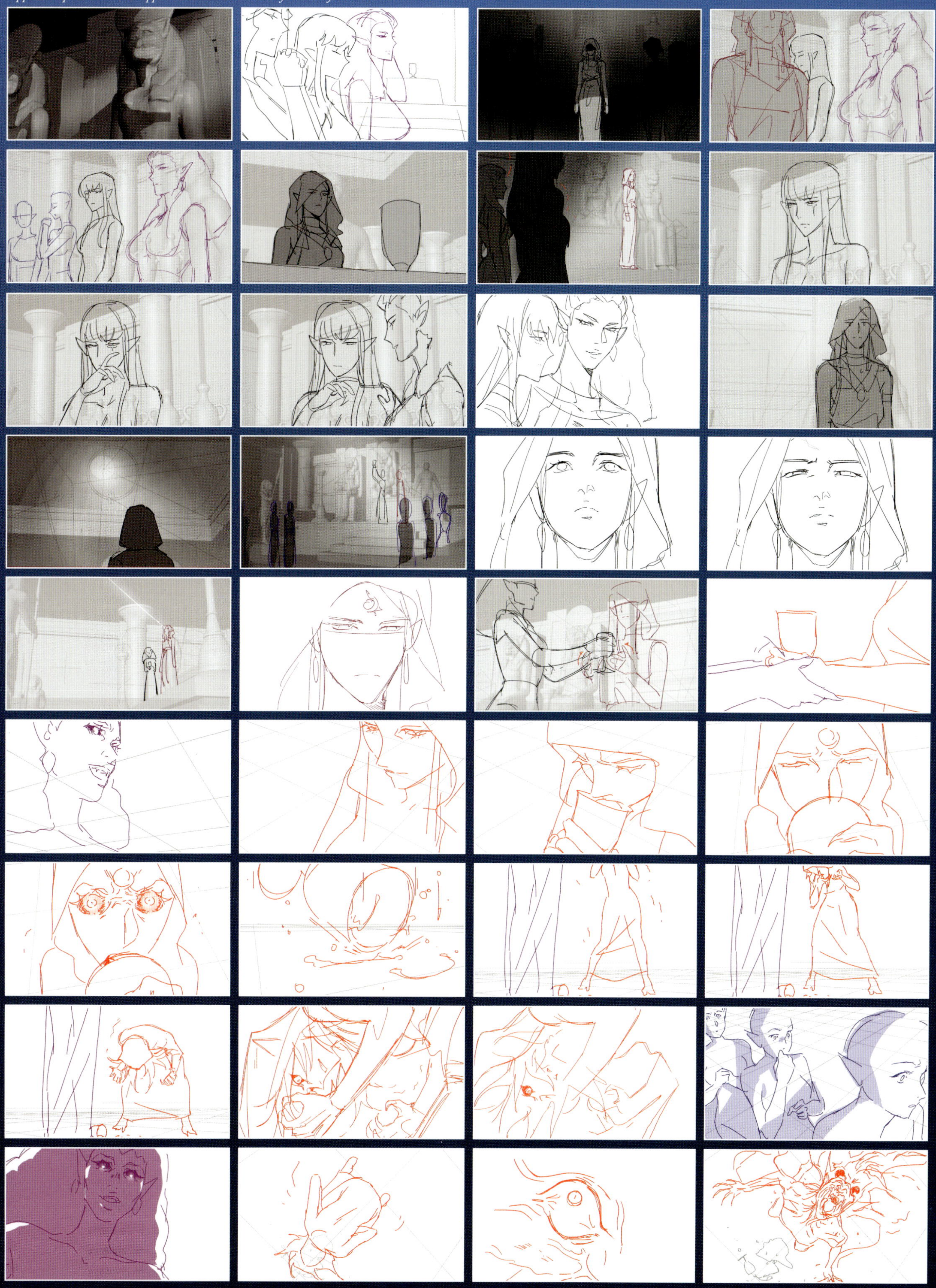

This early look at Drolta shows how different she once was. She was so sympathetic that watching people she loved and cared about die deeply affected her. That changed. Sam said, "We're seeing that obsessed religious side as she's distorted what her own gods actually want from her and showing that corruption."

Top: Sean Randolph, Middle row: Sabina Lewis, Bottom two rows: Sam Keiser.

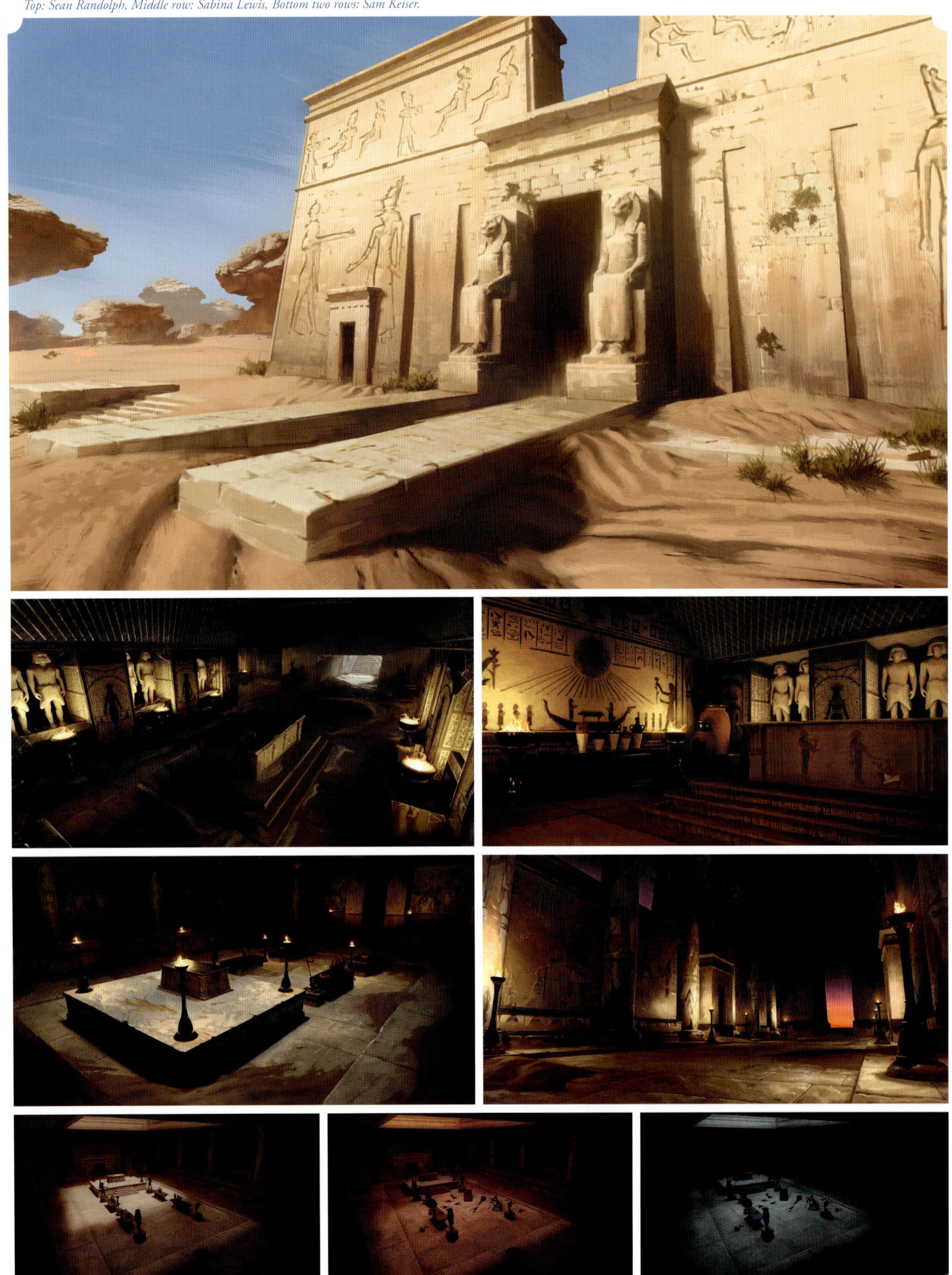

The inside of Sekhmet's temple brings atmosphere and intimacy while showing a stretching space worthy of a goddess. Massive columns, etched with hieroglyphs and gilded accents, rise toward vaulted ceilings, framed by dim, amber-lit sconces that cast shadows as though they were real flames. As the temple moves through time, it falls into disarray. Centuries of abandonment show chipped statues and damaged floor tiles. It's a visual representation of how time passes by us all and trying to stop it, though vampires may succeed for a period, is futile.

Storyboards by Lou O'Neil.

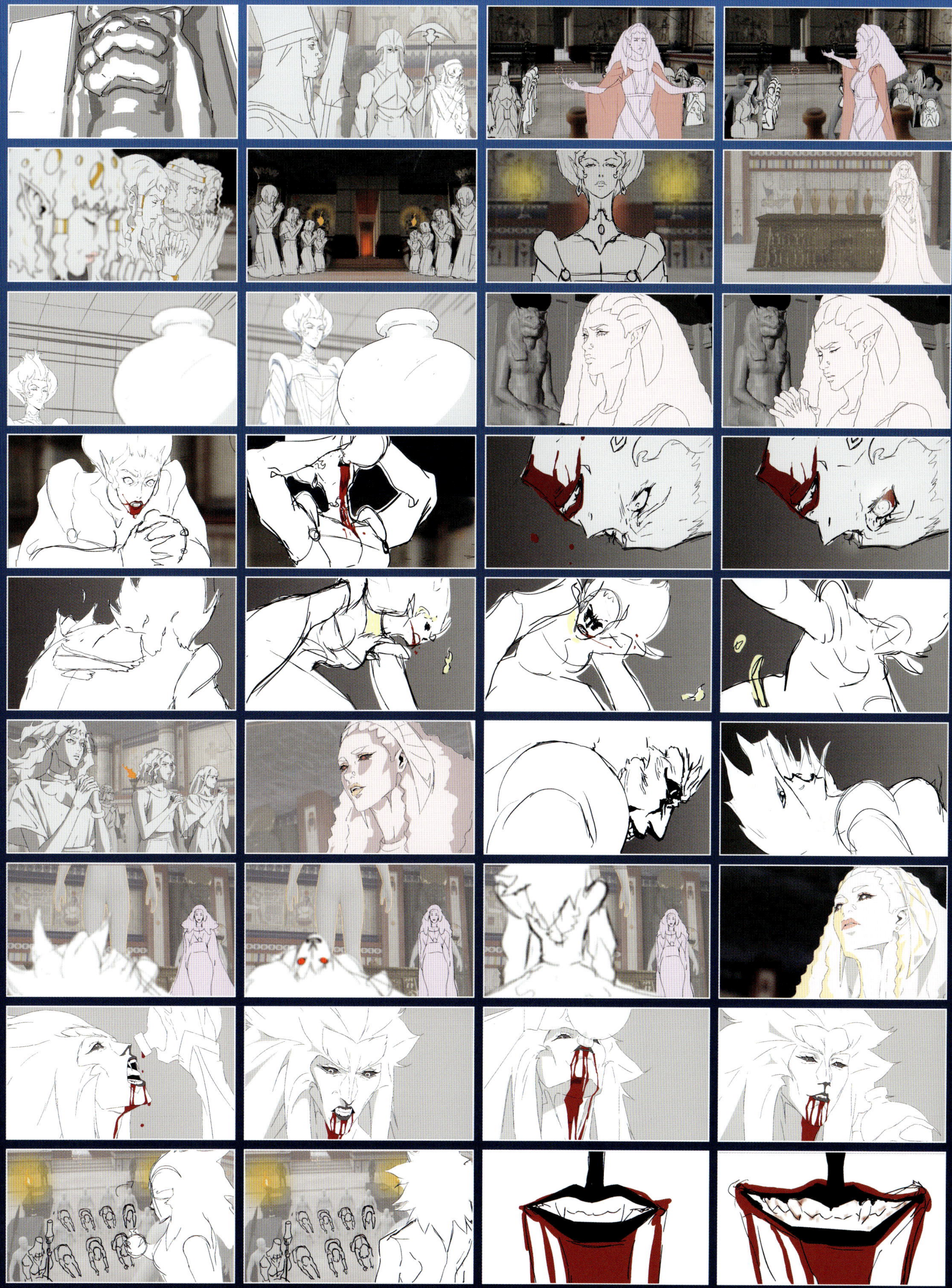

Chronologically this is the first time Erzsebet transforms, but it's the second transformation sequence in the series. Sam explained, "This sequence ended up getting cut down a bit from its original study for a variety of reasons. But we wanted to slip in the bit of lore that she had to build her body up to be ready for possession." These rough layouts plot the action that took place in the Sekhmet Temple.

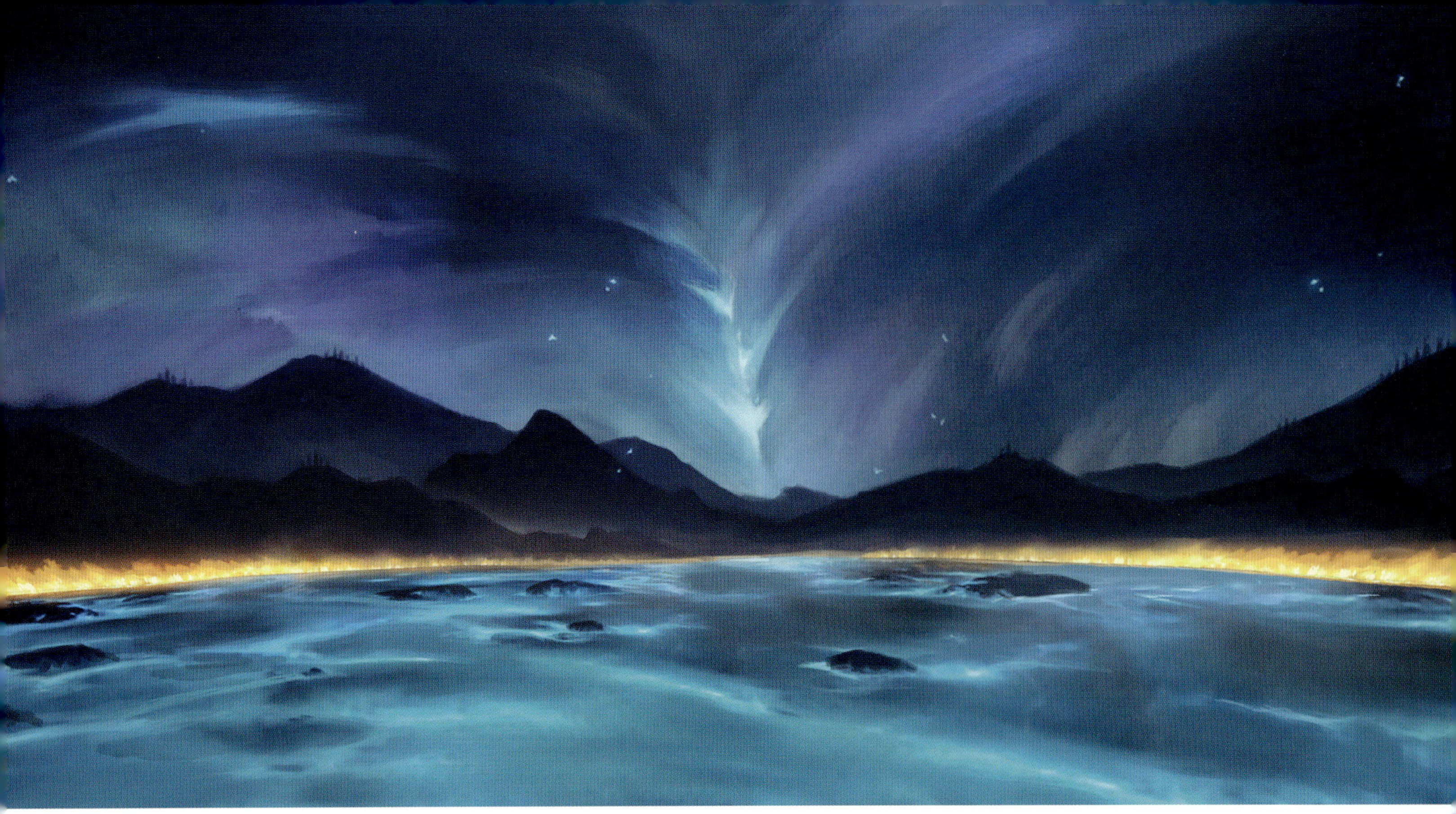

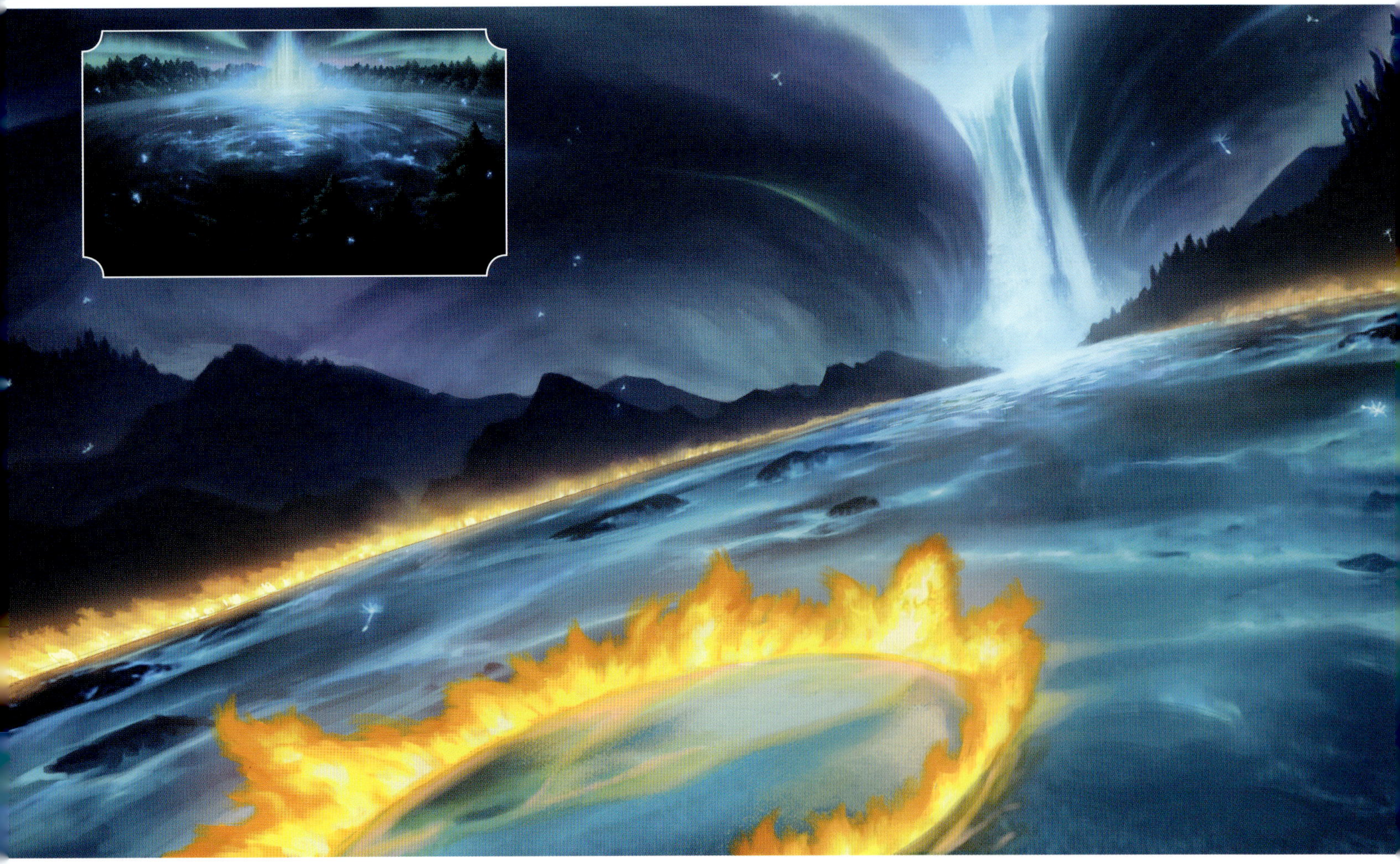

The Spirit World

An astral plane inhabited by the supernatural, ancestral, and divine, the Spirit World is a mystical place and the design reflects it. Background designer Sean Randolph said the initial idea he ran by Adam and Sam Deats was an image he found of the sky that almost looked like two tornadoes. "The sky on one side was twisting towards the other sky, so I took that image and then I just put a waterfall between the two twisting tornadoes. I ran with that [for Annette's first time in the Spirit World], but then when we returned to the Spirit World, I wanted it to feel somewhat similar to how we had seen it before, but to have more . . . The tinier image in the bottom image is when she full on ghosts in the Spirit World."

Opposite page: Sam Keiser. Top and middle row: Sean Randolph, Bottom: Stephen Stark and Mark Adams.

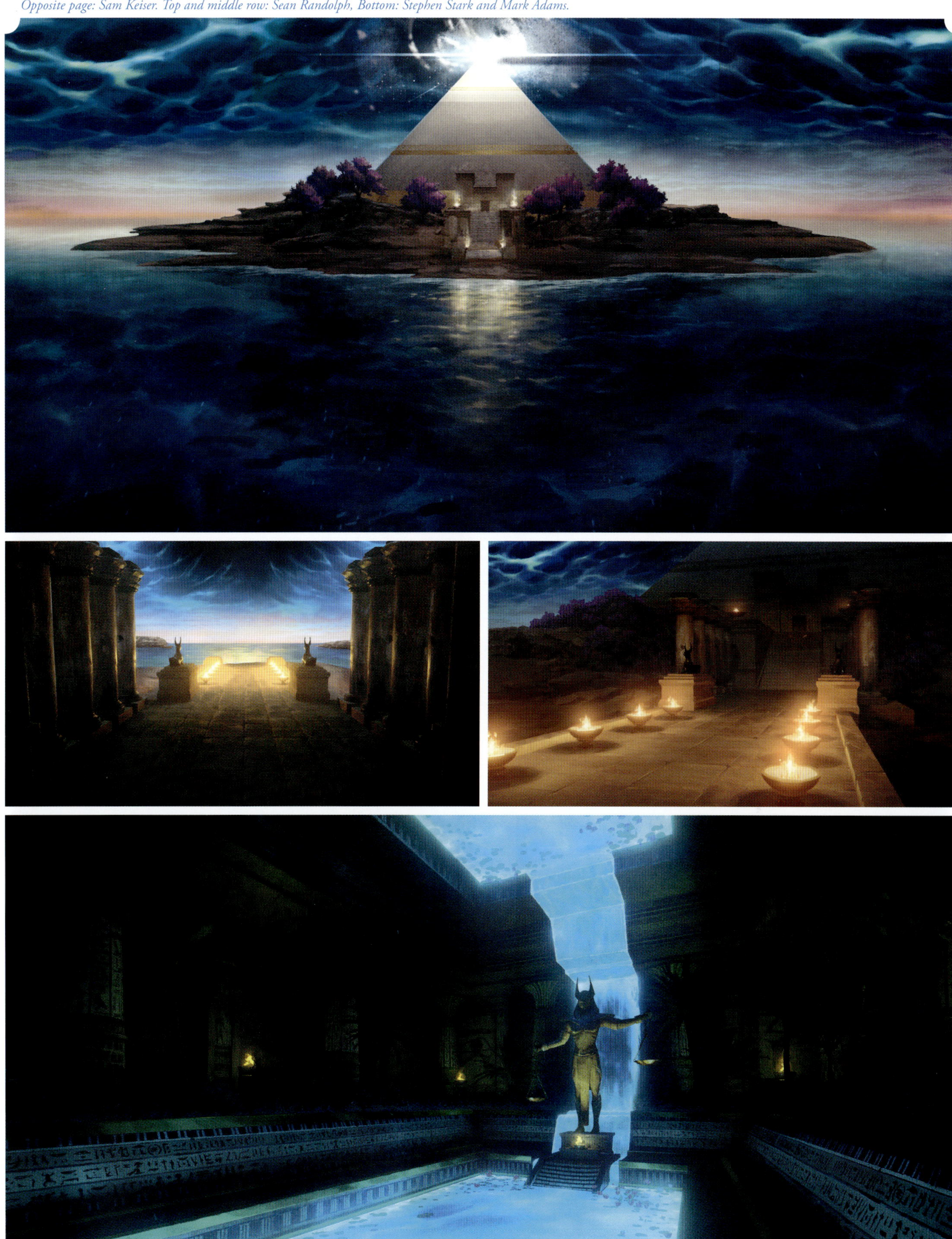

DUAT TEMPLE

The Spirit World connects an unspecified number of realms that seem to cross mythological boundaries. When Annette enters the supernatural plane, she speaks to her orisha ancestors, including Ogun. He sends her to the Duat temple to find Sekhmet, but he can't take her there himself because gods don't enter another god's realm. She arrives after crossing a river, and the designs from Stephen Stark and Sean Randolph evoke an ethereal place. Their designs paint a serene, sacred space for Sekhmet's rest.

Top: Sabina Lewis, Middle: Sean Randolph, Bottom: Bo Li.

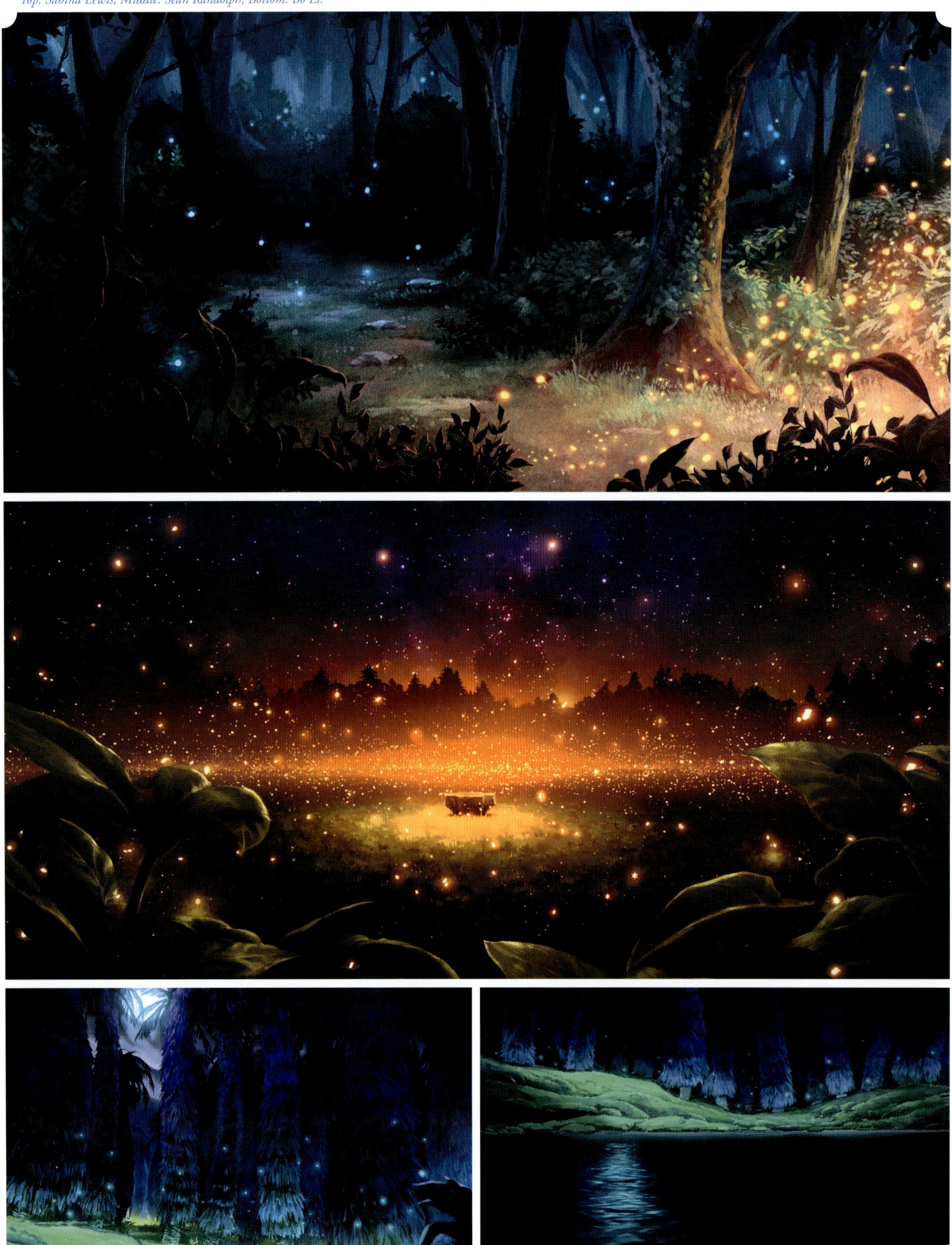

SPIRIT FOREST

As Annette traveled deeper into the Spirit World, Randolph wanted the foliage and locations to slowly start to become more African. He worked on the images with fellow background designer Bo Li, and they spun possibilities from plants and trees native to Africa. One type of palm tree that's covered in hair suited the magical and otherworldly look of the sparkling forests. The farther into the forest Annette goes, the closer she gets to the Duat Temple.

Storyboards by Armando Atencio.

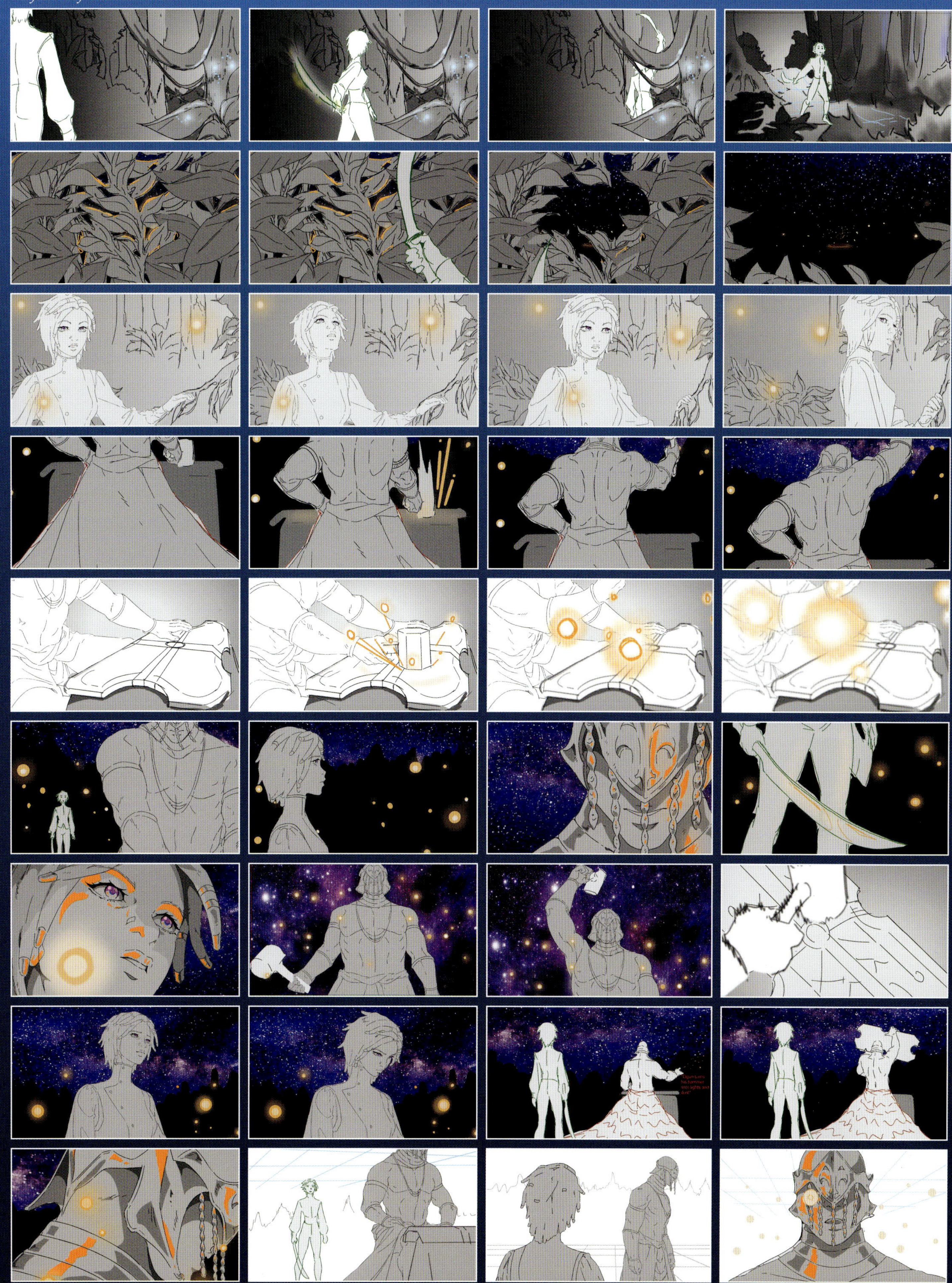

Storyboard artist Armando Atencio worked on this sequence between Annette and Ogun in the Spirit World. The story touched on the gods in season one, but they didn't know they'd actually get to show Ogun in season two. Sam said, "All of the embers are floating around like stars and it feels very celestial. With each hammer hit, each one becomes a part of the environment around them. That was just a really neat touch with the sequence that had a lot of fun depth." These rough layouts plot the scenes that took place in the spirit forest.

Art by Stephen Stark and Bo Li.

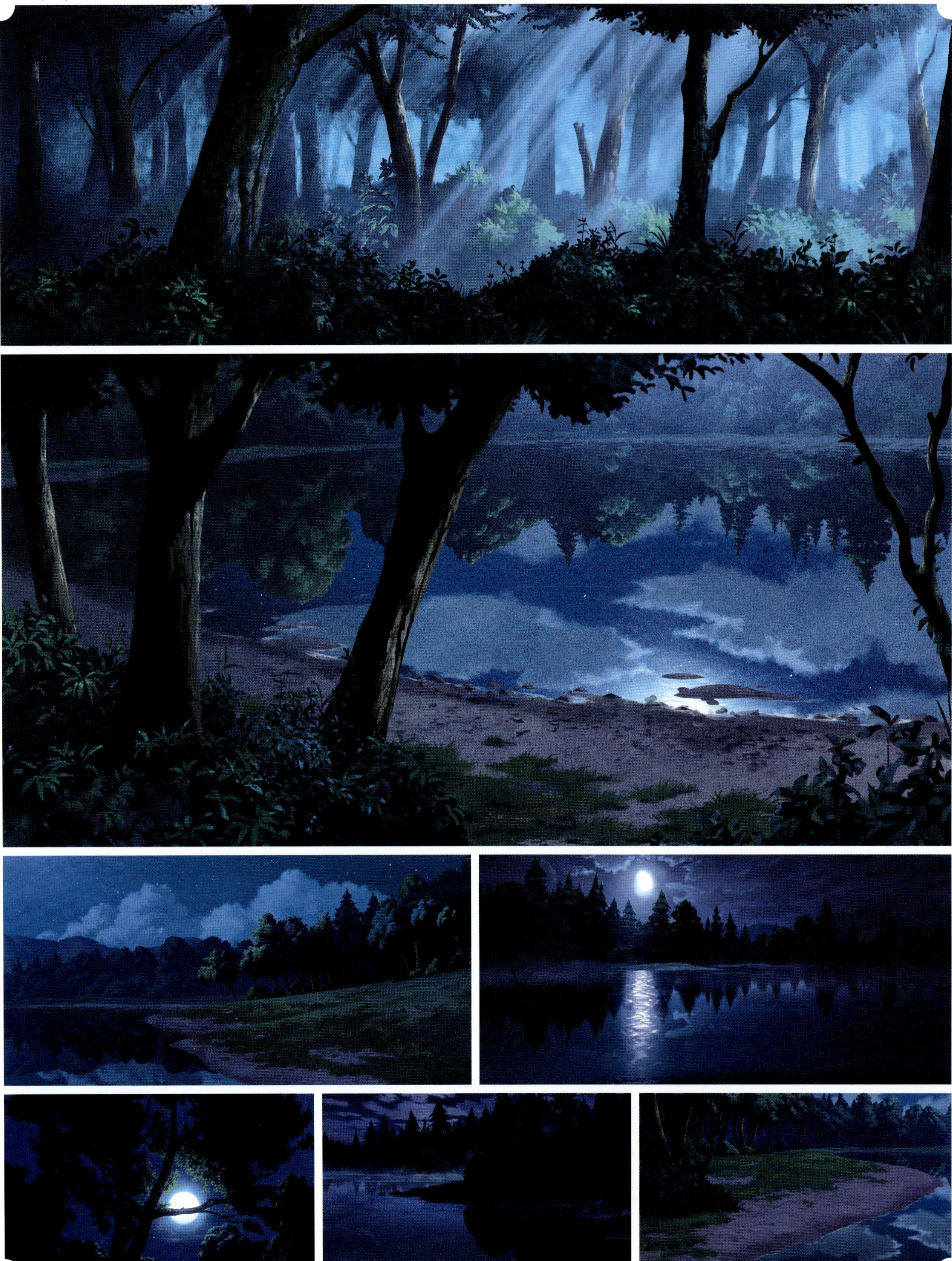

FRENCH FOREST

Supervising background designer Stephen Stark teased that he would grumble about all the forests and trees and then take them on anyway. Environments like these are in stark contrast to the orderly streets of Paris and allowed the background team to play with reflections, natural materials, and using the light of the full moon to bounce off leaves and water.

Top: Sam Keiser, Bottom: Sean Randolph.

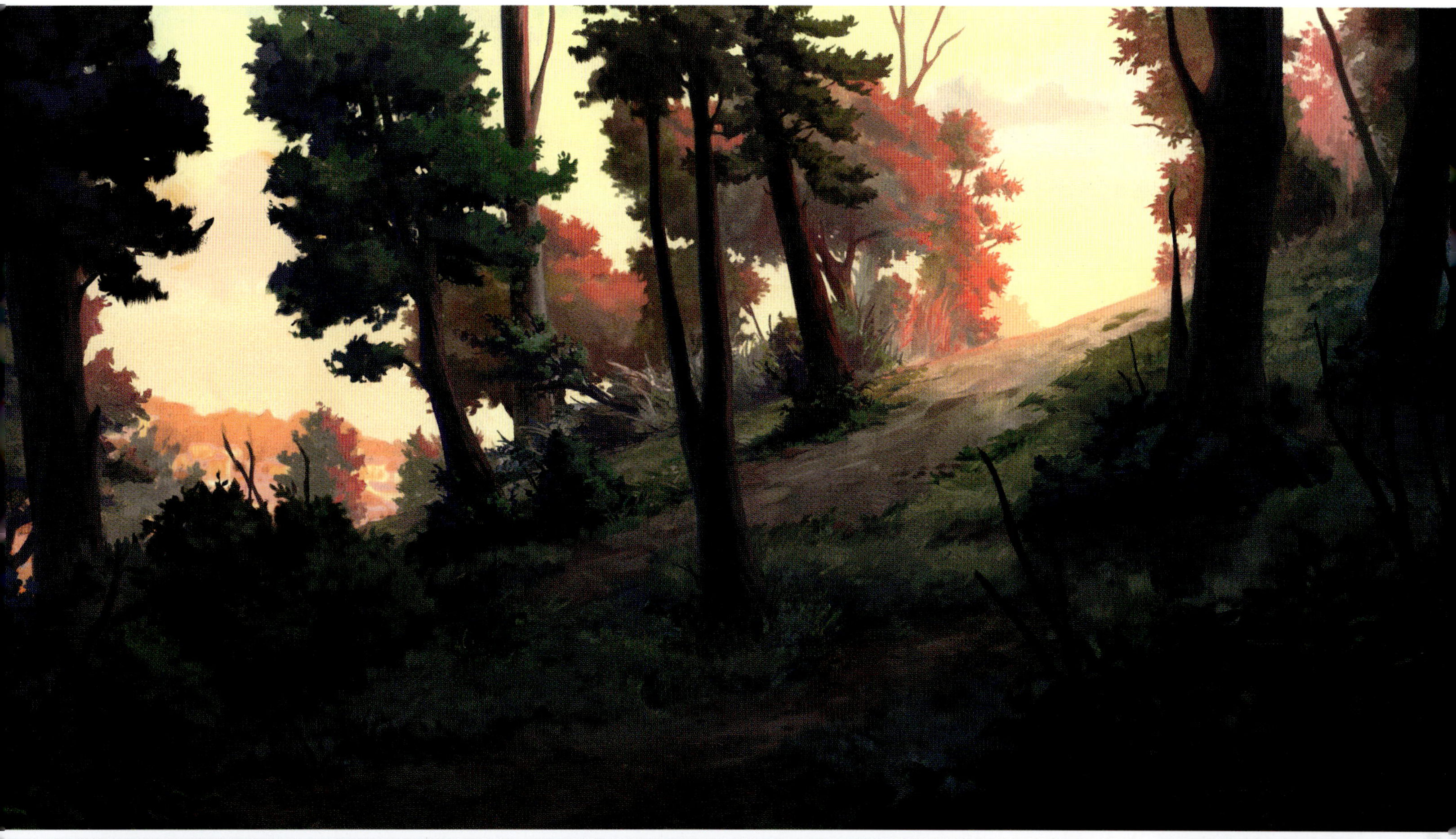

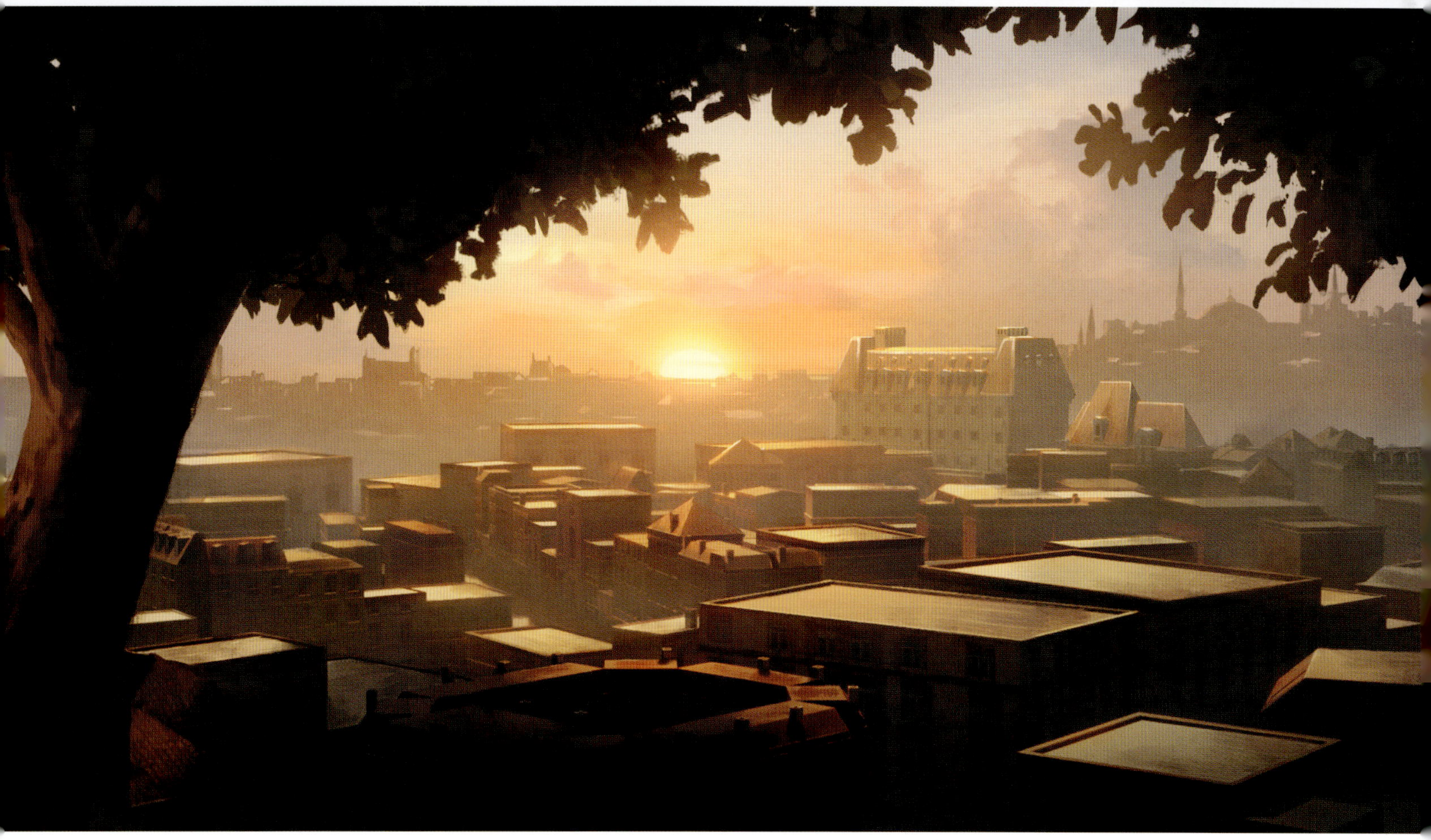

MONMARTRE

Montmartre is one of Paris's more romantic neighborhoods, known for its striking skyline along a large hill. The silhouettes of known buildings can be seen in the above concept. Every part of Paris looked more welcoming and lighter before Erzsebet's arrival in season one. The soft yellow of sunlight in these environment paintings emanates a warmth that becomes a distant memory after the solar eclipse.

Top: Sean Randolph, Middle: Blaise Rhein, Bottom: Stephen Stark.

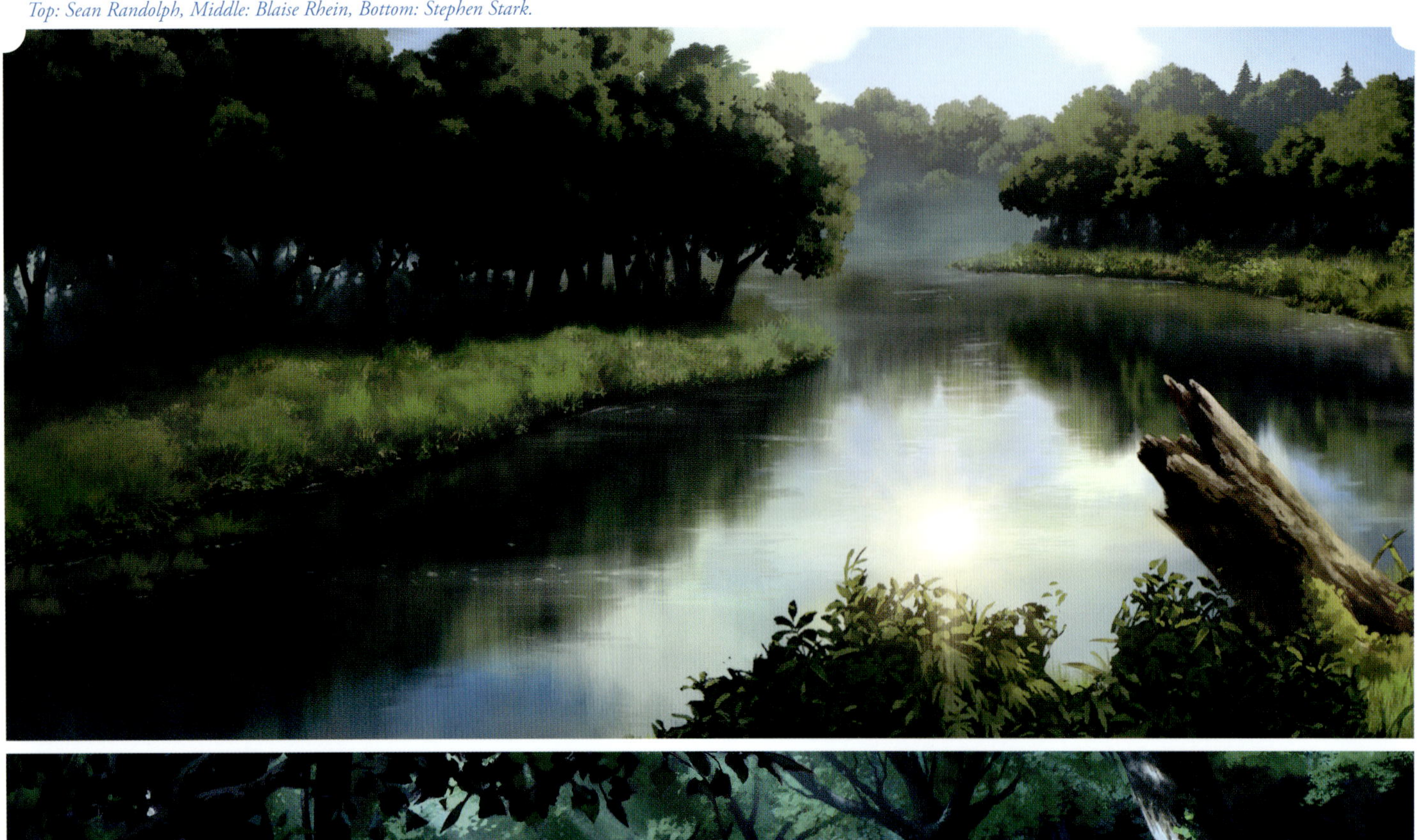

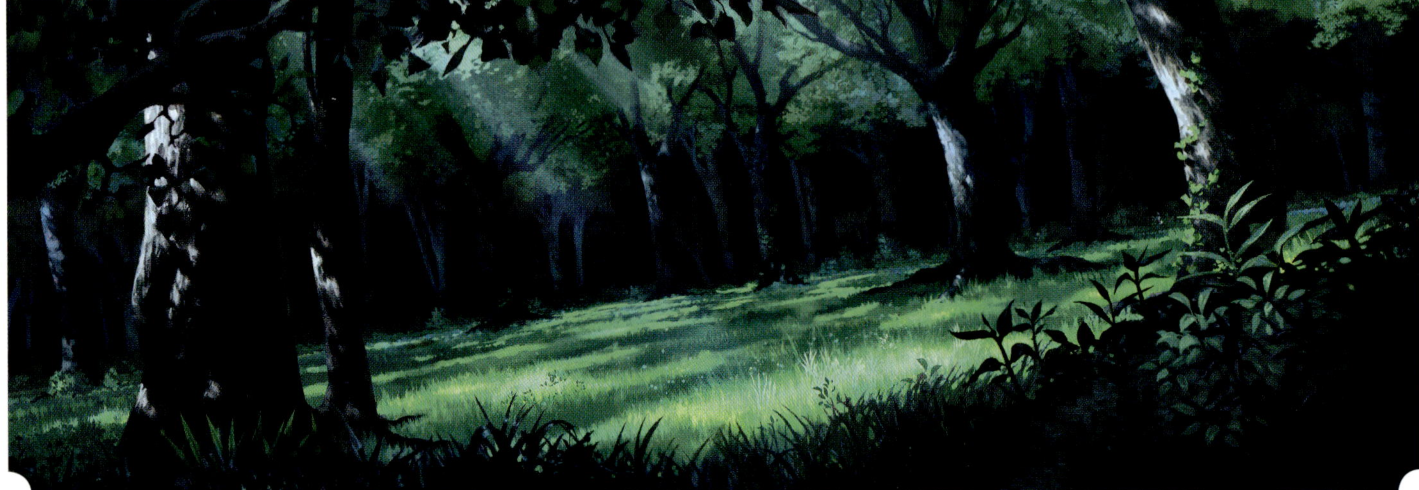

THE WOODLANDS

Tera's charming cottage is situated in an equally breathtaking setting. The woodland area outside of Machecoul looks like the type of place people flee to when they take vacations in the countryside. This is where Maria and Richter grow up together, and the whole location captures the mood of the carefree summers that often come with youth.

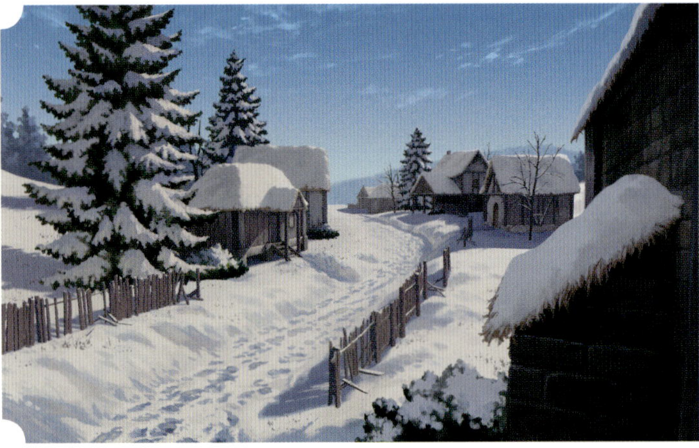

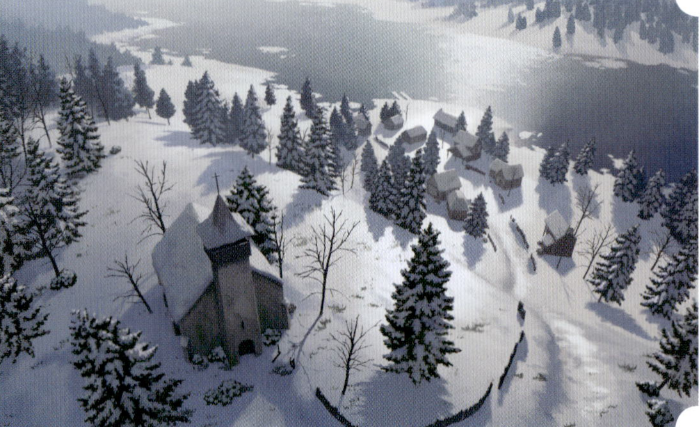

VOLGA VILLAGE

A flashback to Tera's childhood shows the Russian village she called home with her family and other Speakers. With its snow-covered homes and evergreen trees, it added another type of environment and lighting to the series. Though it was only on screen briefly, the background team needed to figure out how the snow would drape over buildings and what the sunlight would look like on snow versus forests or city streets.

Top: Bo Li, Middle and bottom rows: Sam Keiser.

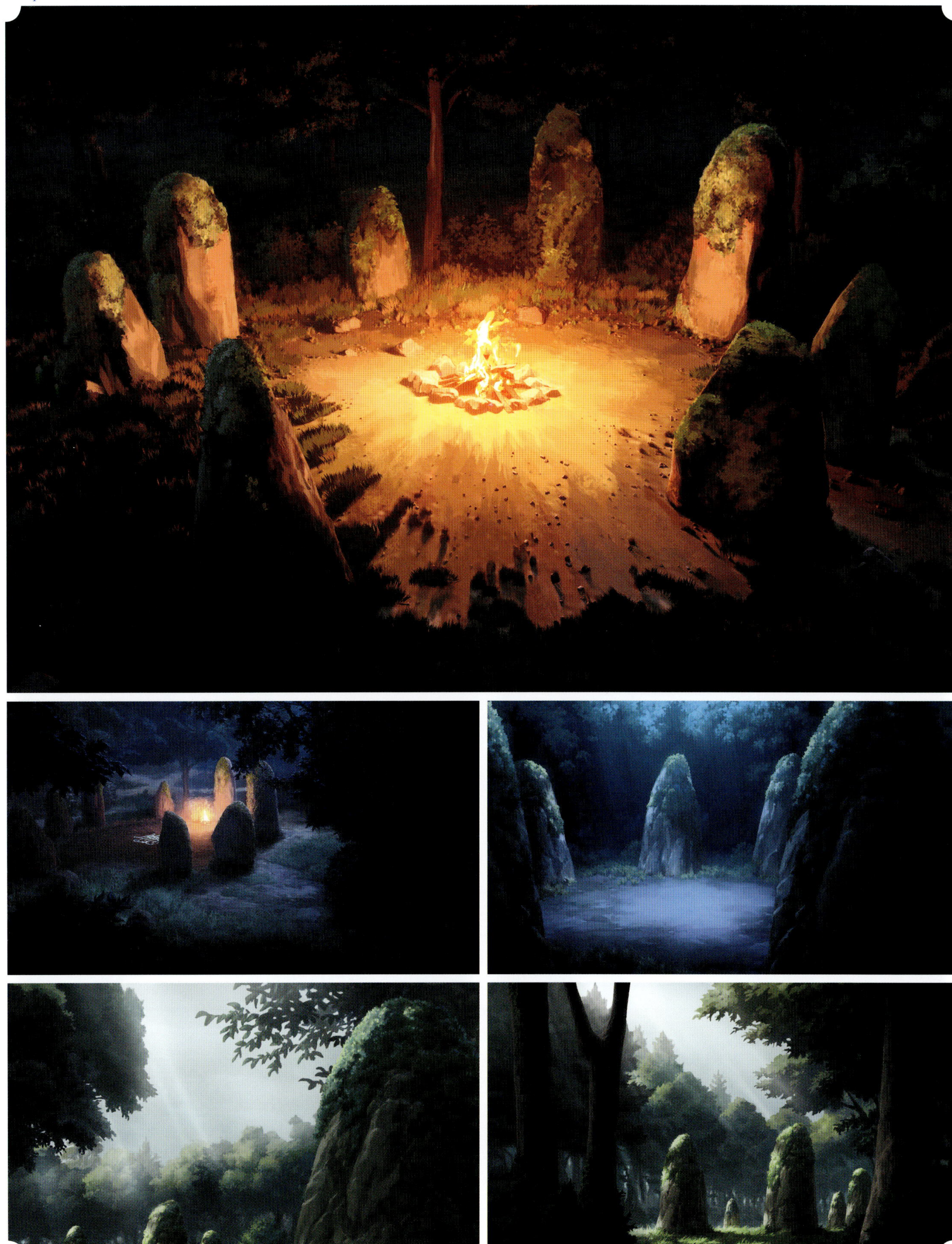

STONE CIRCLE

Like many places in Europe, the people of Machecoul in *Nocturne* connected religion and nature more strongly before the church gained strength. Maria explains to her friends that the stone circles in the woods around the town were built for communication with the Otherworld, not unlike the Spirit World Annette knows. The environment designers wanted the circle to look somewhat overgrown and like it's from another time—but in an enchanting way that suggests nature reclaiming what belongs to it.

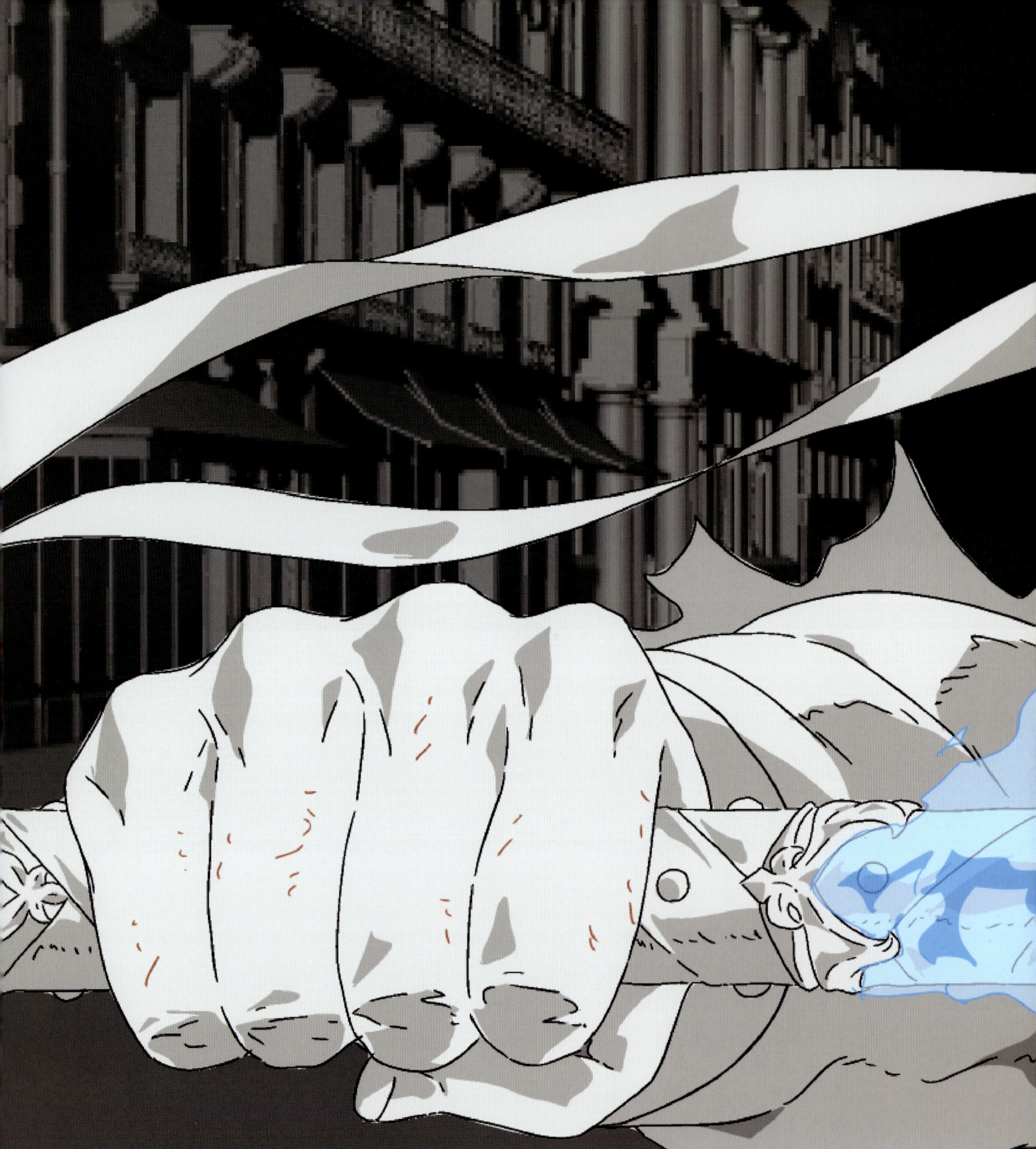

Art by Samuel Deats.

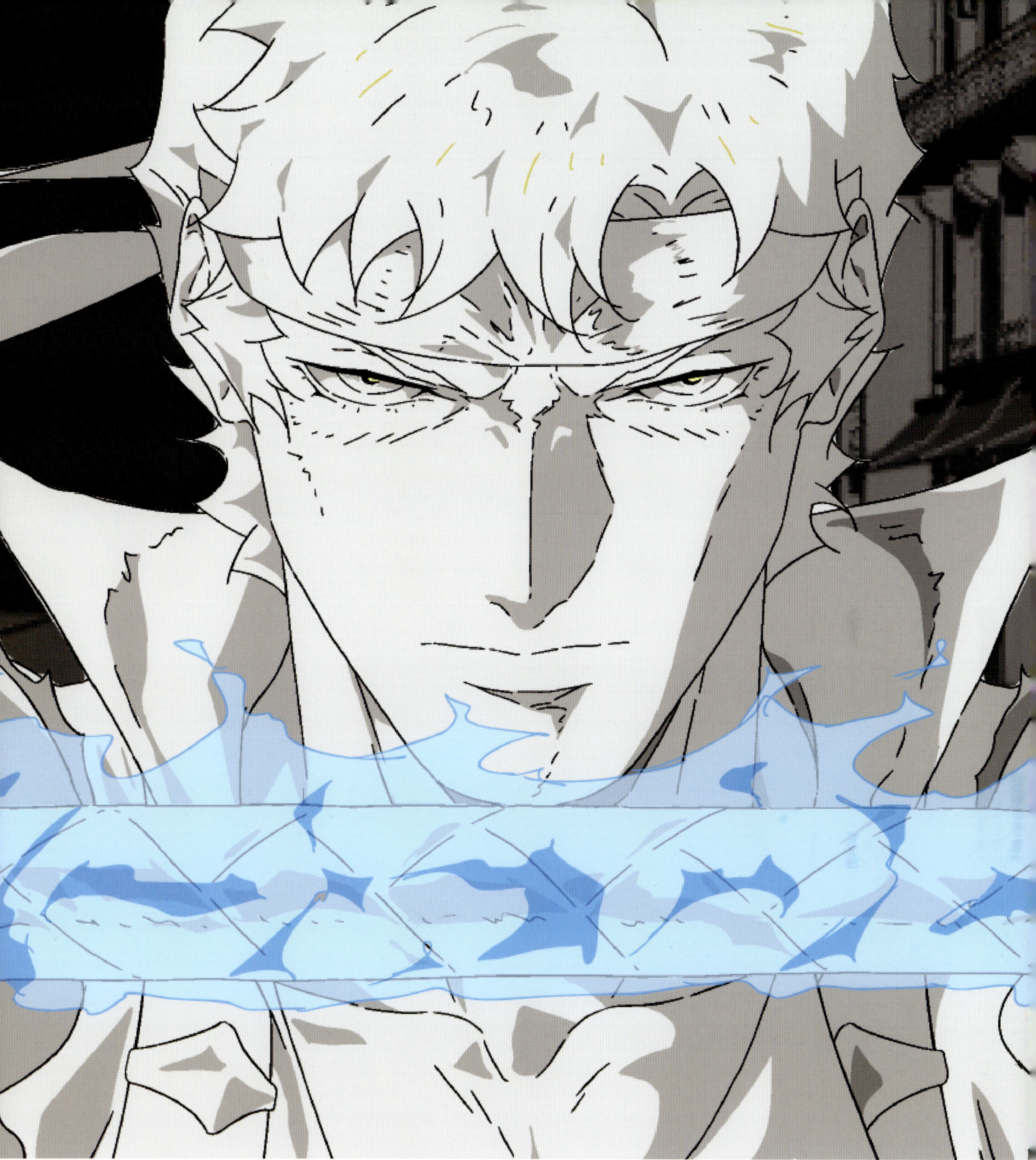

CHAPTER IV

Composing the Journey

PAIN AND LOSS

Richter carries heartache and trauma with him from an early age; he witnesses Olrox kill Julia, his mother, after an intense battle. Sam Deats noted this sequence was close to him so he wanted to be pretty hands-on with not only the storyboards, which are shown earlier in the book, but the drawings themselves. He got into the nitty-gritty for this scene with the layouts to set up the dynamic between these three characters.

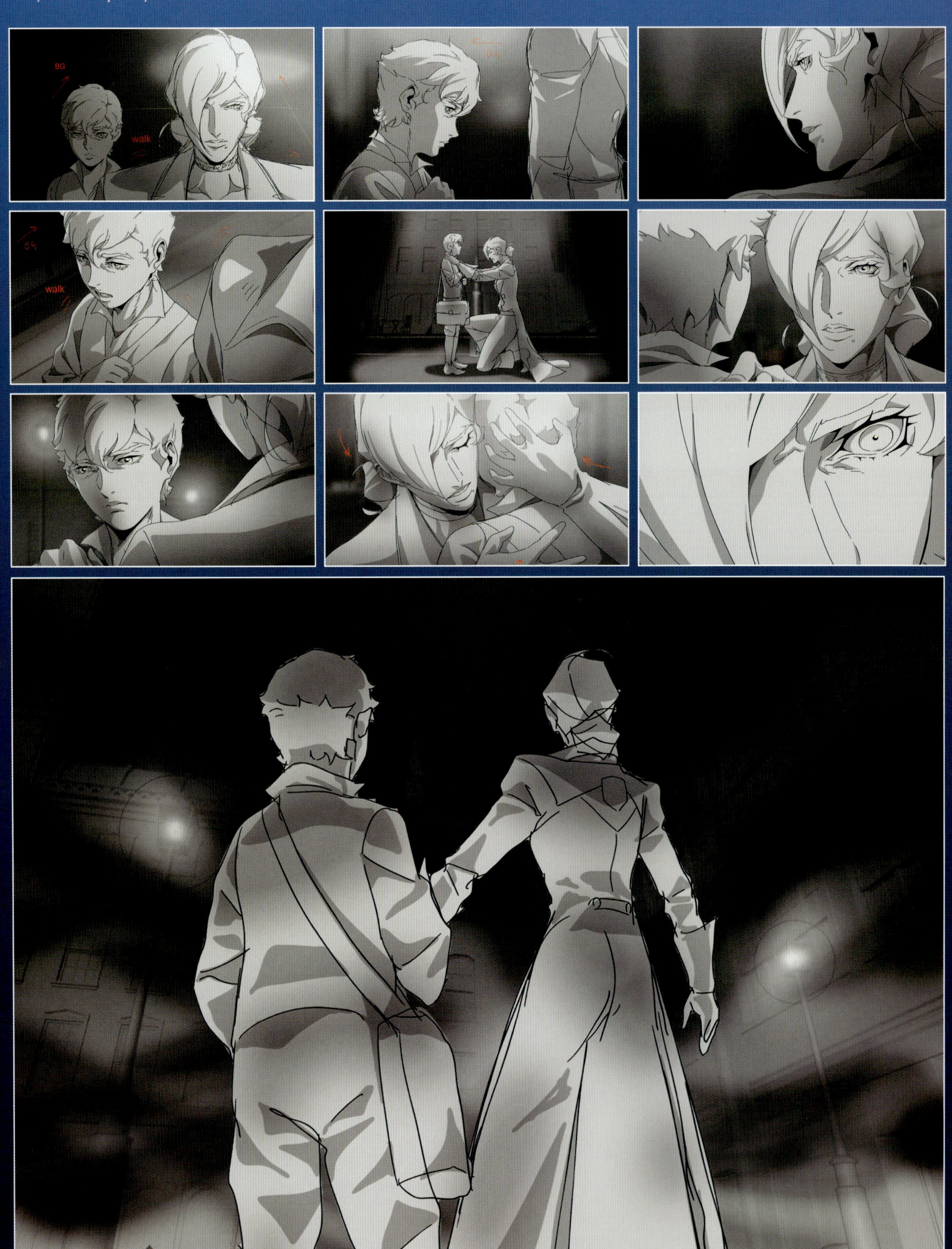

Storyboards by Samuel Deats.

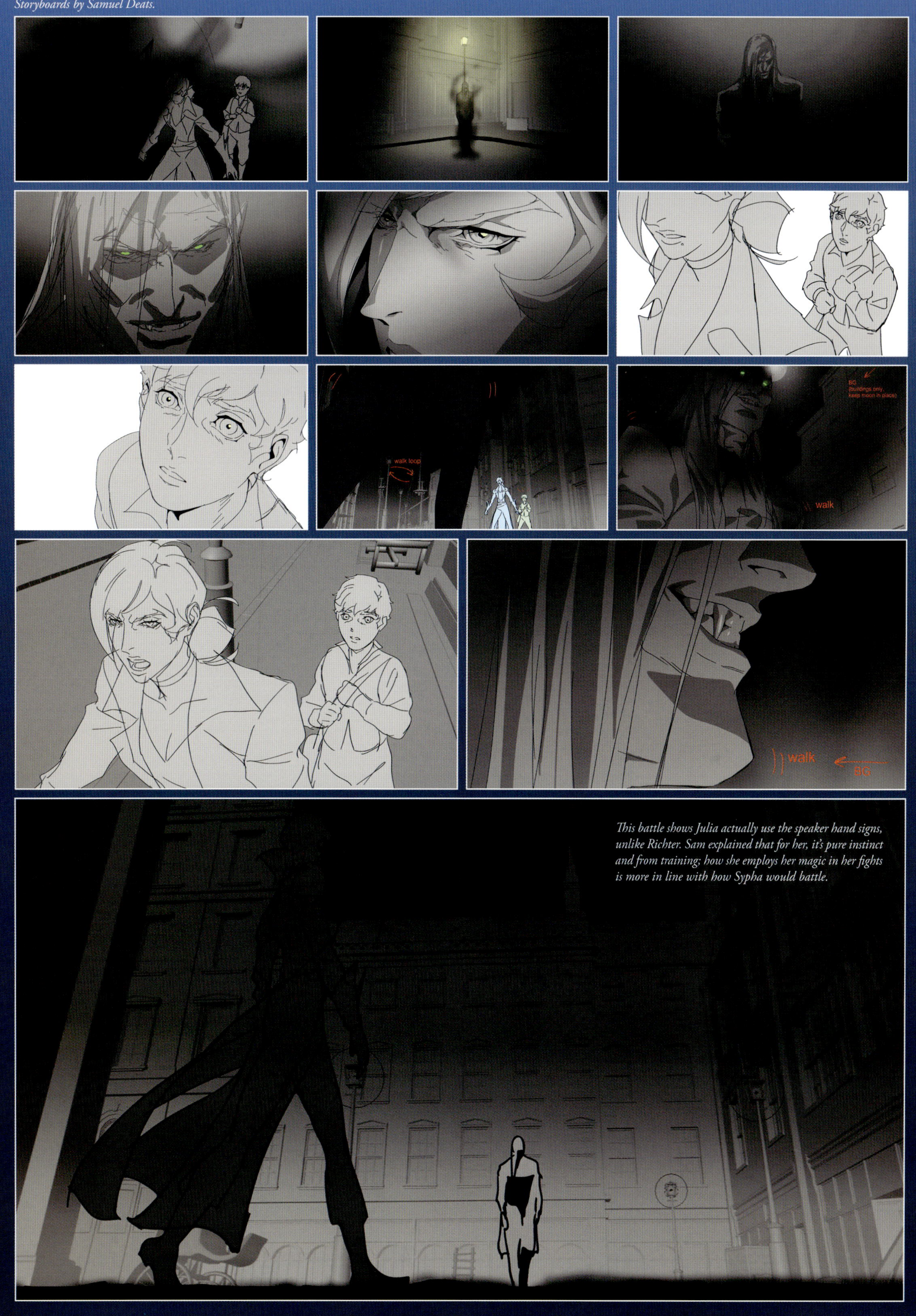

This battle shows Julia actually use the speaker hand signs, unlike Richter. Sam explained that for her, it's pure instinct and from training; how she employs her magic in her fights is more in line with how Sypha would battle.

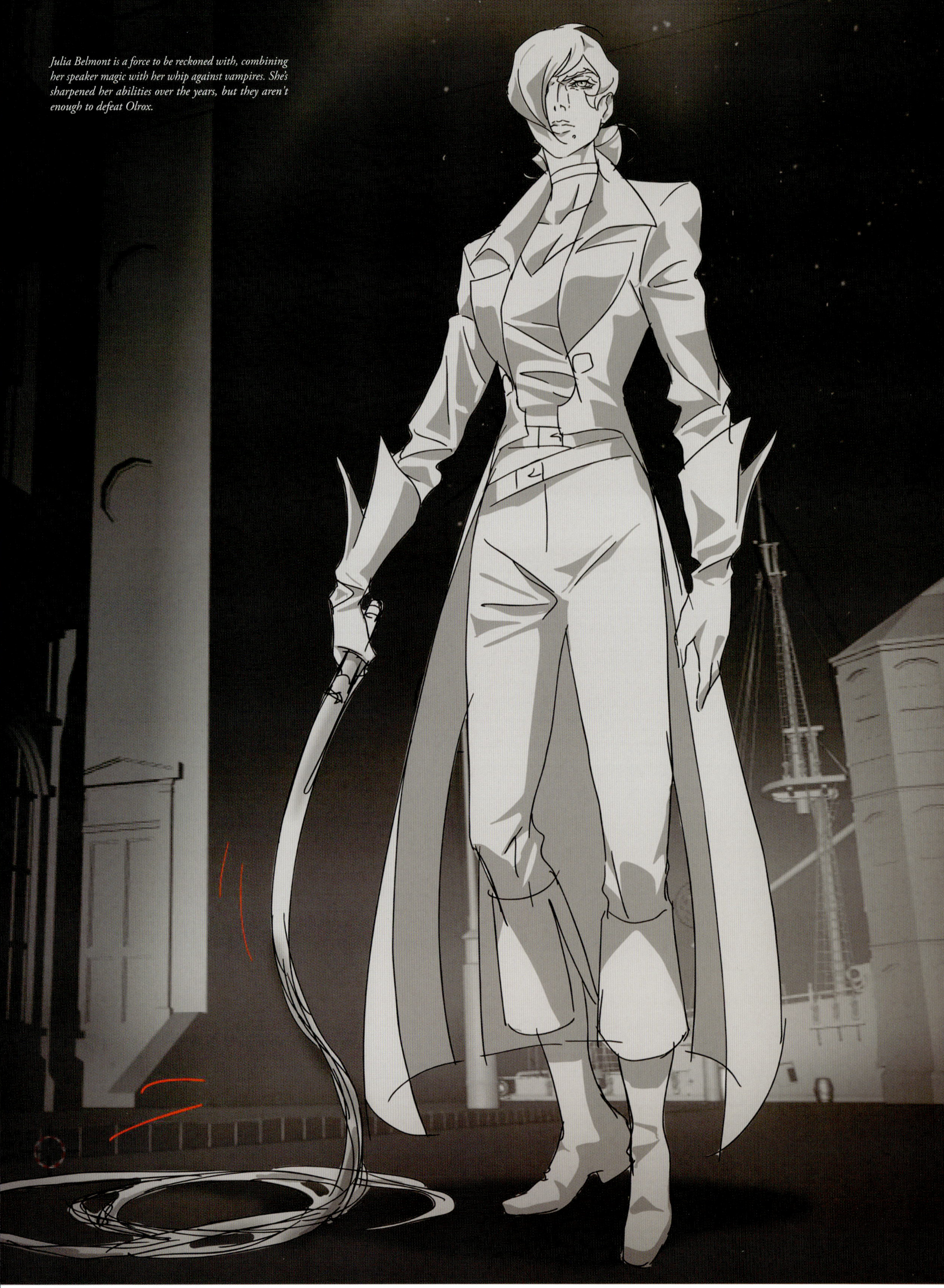

Julia Belmont is a force to be reckoned with, combining her speaker magic with her whip against vampires. She's sharpened her abilities over the years, but they aren't enough to defeat Olrox.

Storyboards by Samuel Deats.

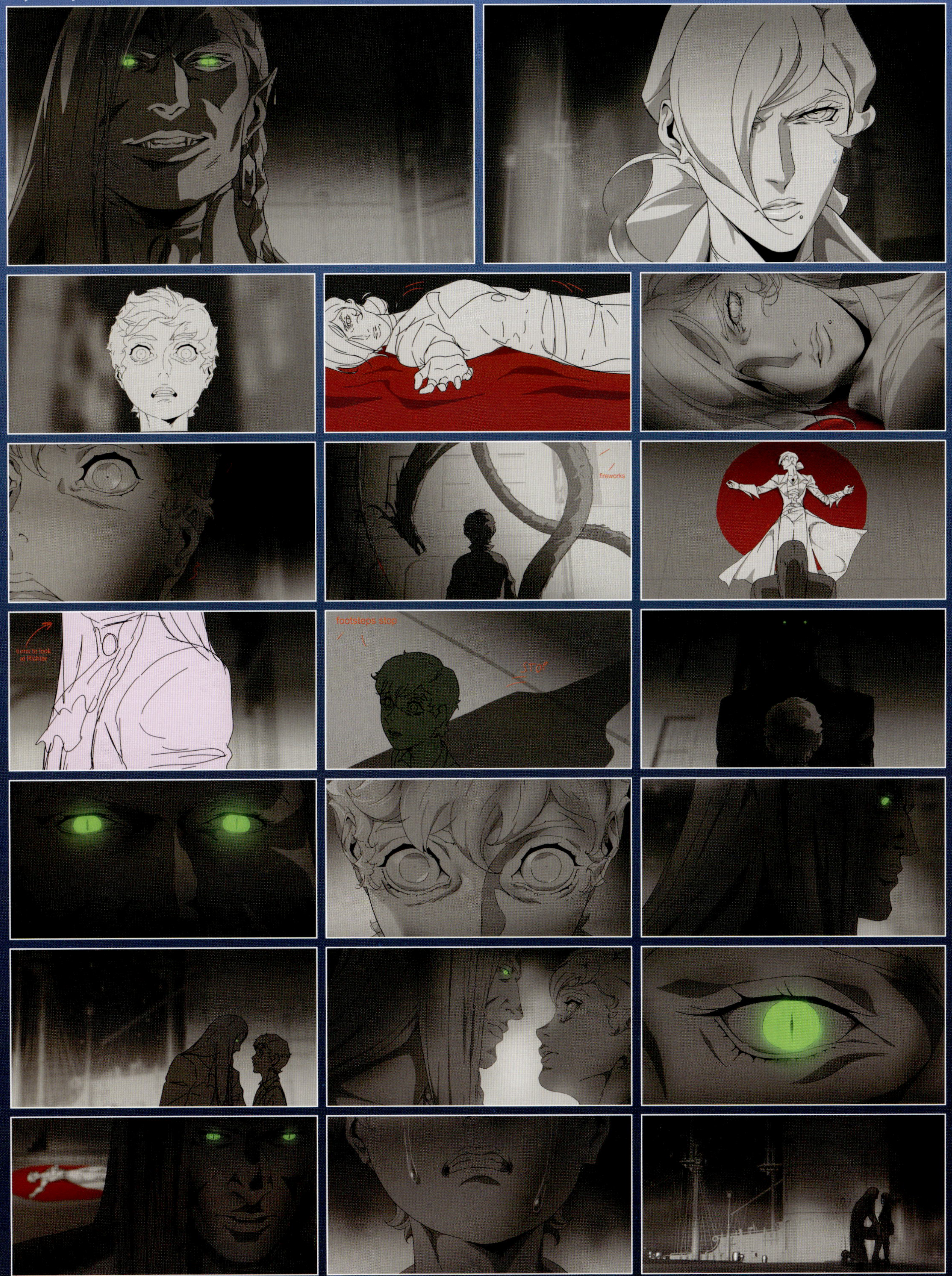

"Nailing the mood of this opening was really, really important, and I tried to put a lot of emphasis on showing the terror in young Richter's eyes and the shock of seeing someone so strong that he loves so much die in front of him," Sam said. The framing of many of the scenes with young Richter and Olrox intentionally mirror shots later when Richter gets his power back and fights vampires for the first time.

BELMONT TO BELMONT

Sam Deats brought the idea of including Juste Belmont to the table early in development. Juste shows Richter a version of himself he could end up becoming if things go wrong. "It was something I wanted to dig into," Sam said. "I always like to give things a breathing room and we don't always get the time or ability to let something sit and let your heart sink. This was a cool chance to do that and to really work out the feelings of these characters."

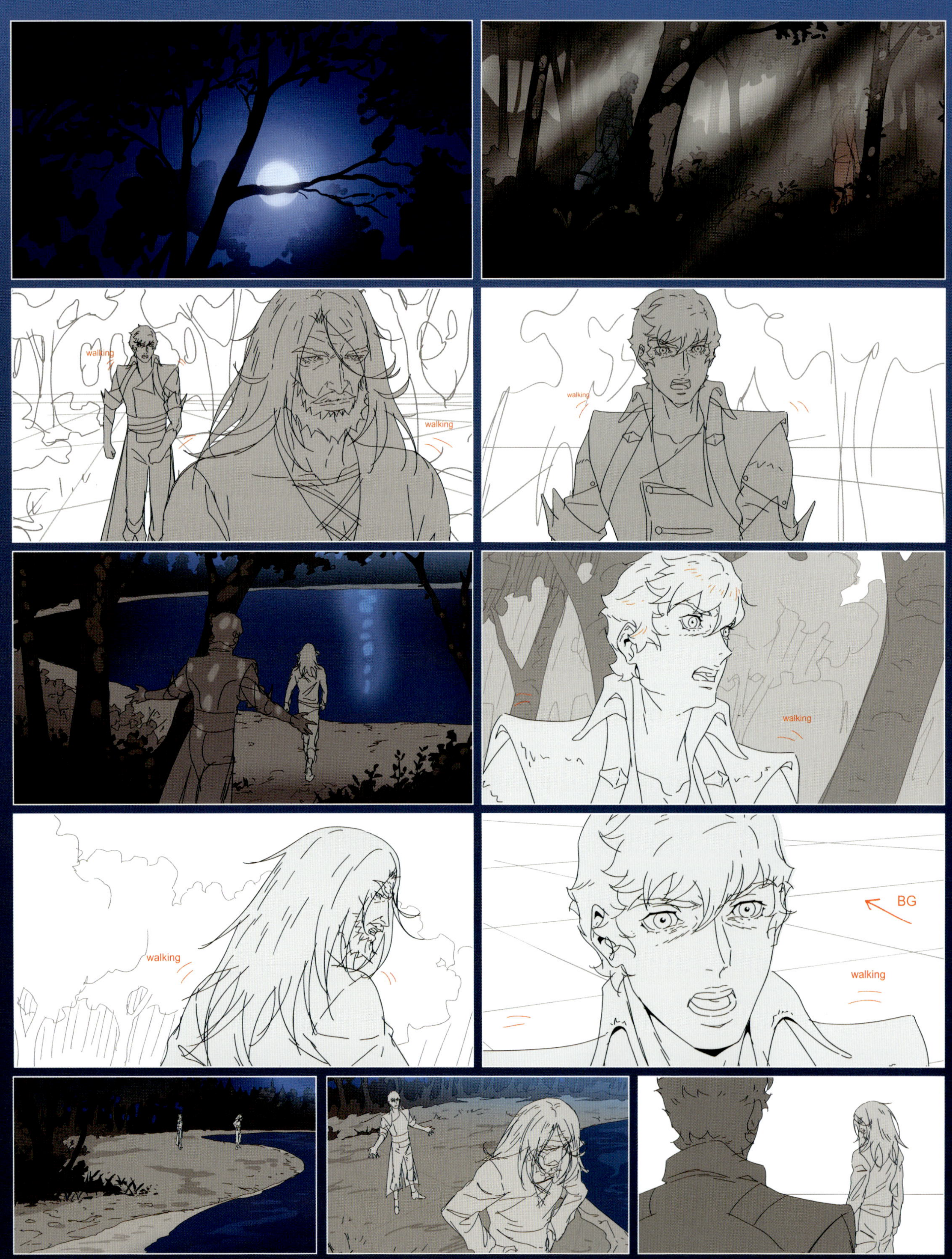

Storyboards by Samuel Deats.

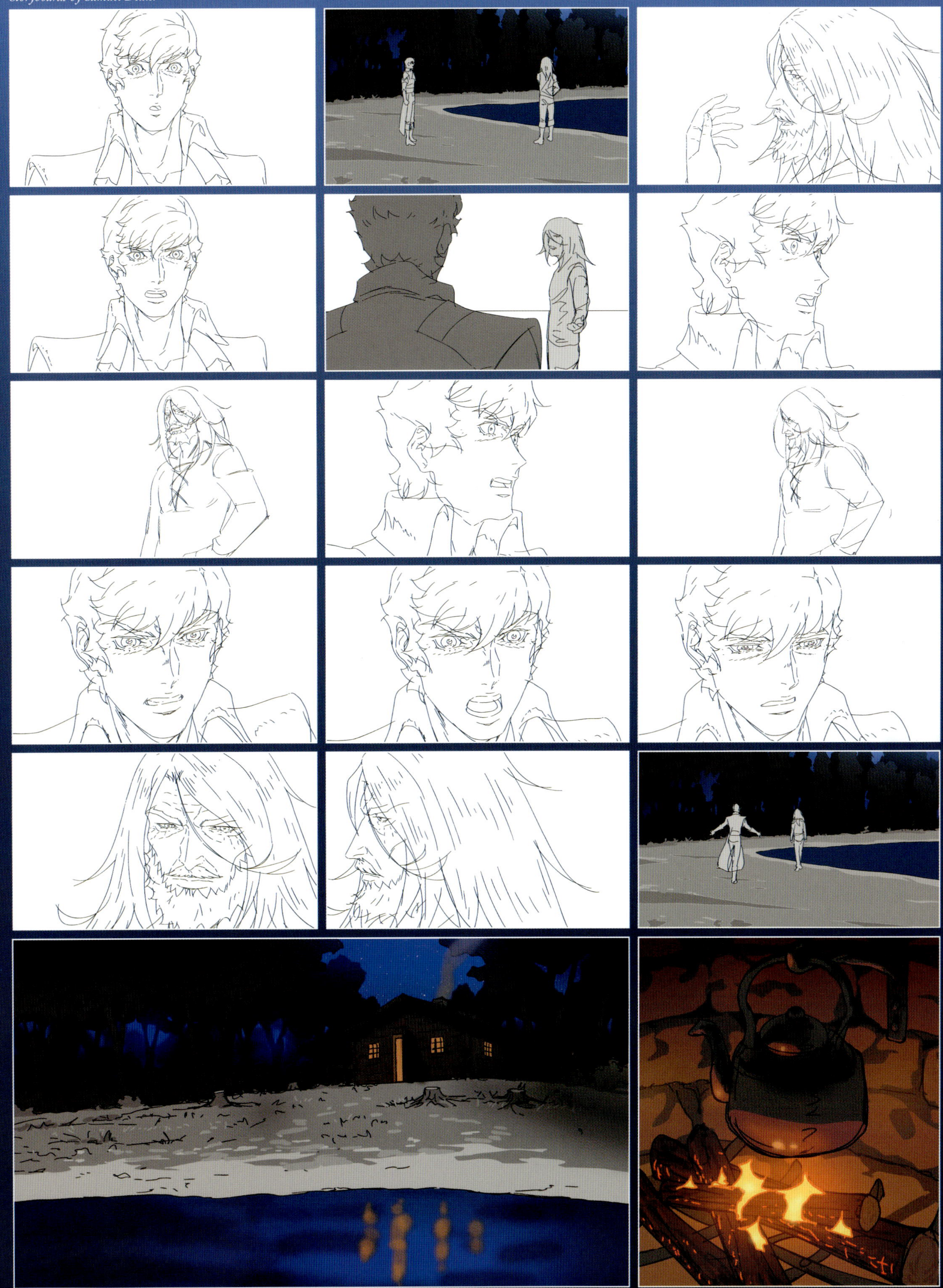

Juste ended up being more of a mentor-like figure to Maria rather than Richter, but given how Juste lost his daughter and the rest of his family, and his focus on magic as a Belmont, Sam said it made a beautiful sort of sense that he would be there for Maria instead.

Storyboards by Samuel Deats.

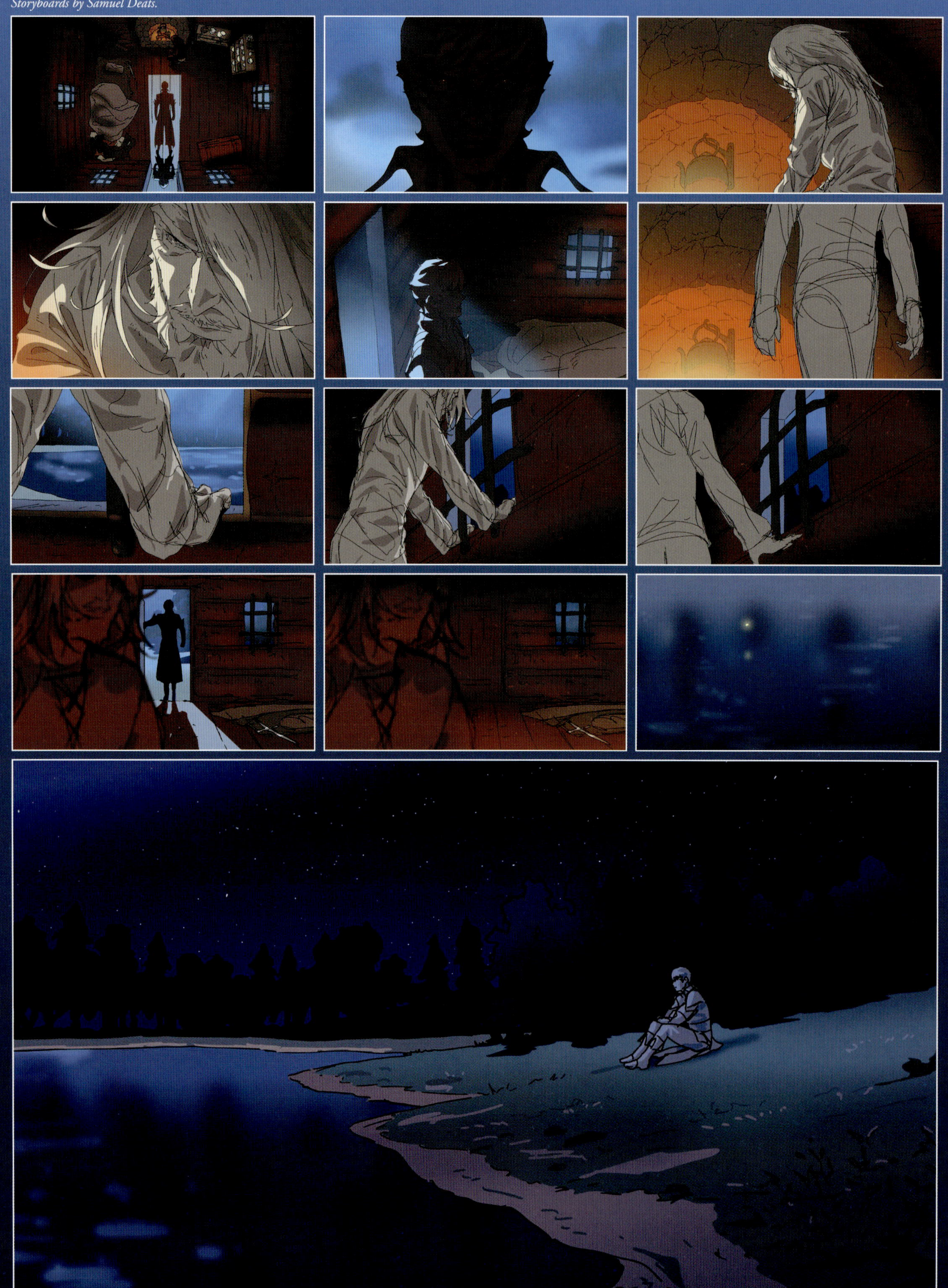

With Richter's silhouette in the doorway above, you get the blue light that's representative of him in the muddy reddish room closing in on him. Then the next shot is a closeup where he's lit with the red light. Sam explained, "This is him, like, peering at himself and his potential future."

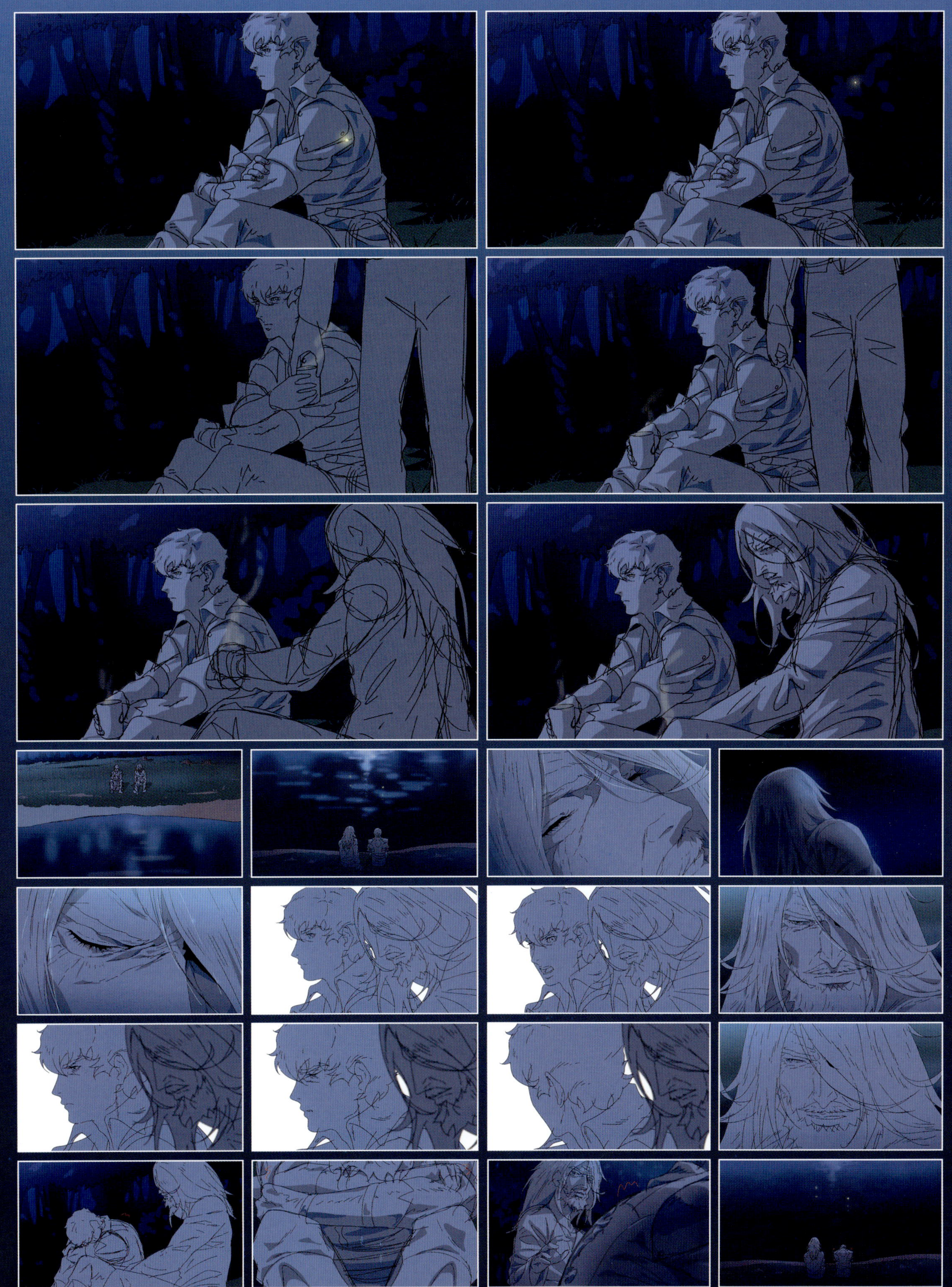

That moody blue is part of the scene by the lake, fireflies flickering. They also appear in subsequent scenes when Richter's about to get his power back. It's a small detail, but Sam noted three fireflies show up in that scene, representative of the three people he thinks of before his power returns.

RICHTER'S POWER-UP

The vampire attack triggers Richter to consider what he's recently seen of his grandfather and whether he wants that to be his future. He digs within himself and begins the sequence that leads to him discovering his strength. From the beginning, Adam recalled, Sam planned for it to have "Divine Bloodlines" from *Castlevania: Rondo of Blood* as part of the scene. Sam joked he didn't boot up *Dragon Ball* to make Richter's level-up a full Super Saiyan moment, but he did roll with that kind of vibe.

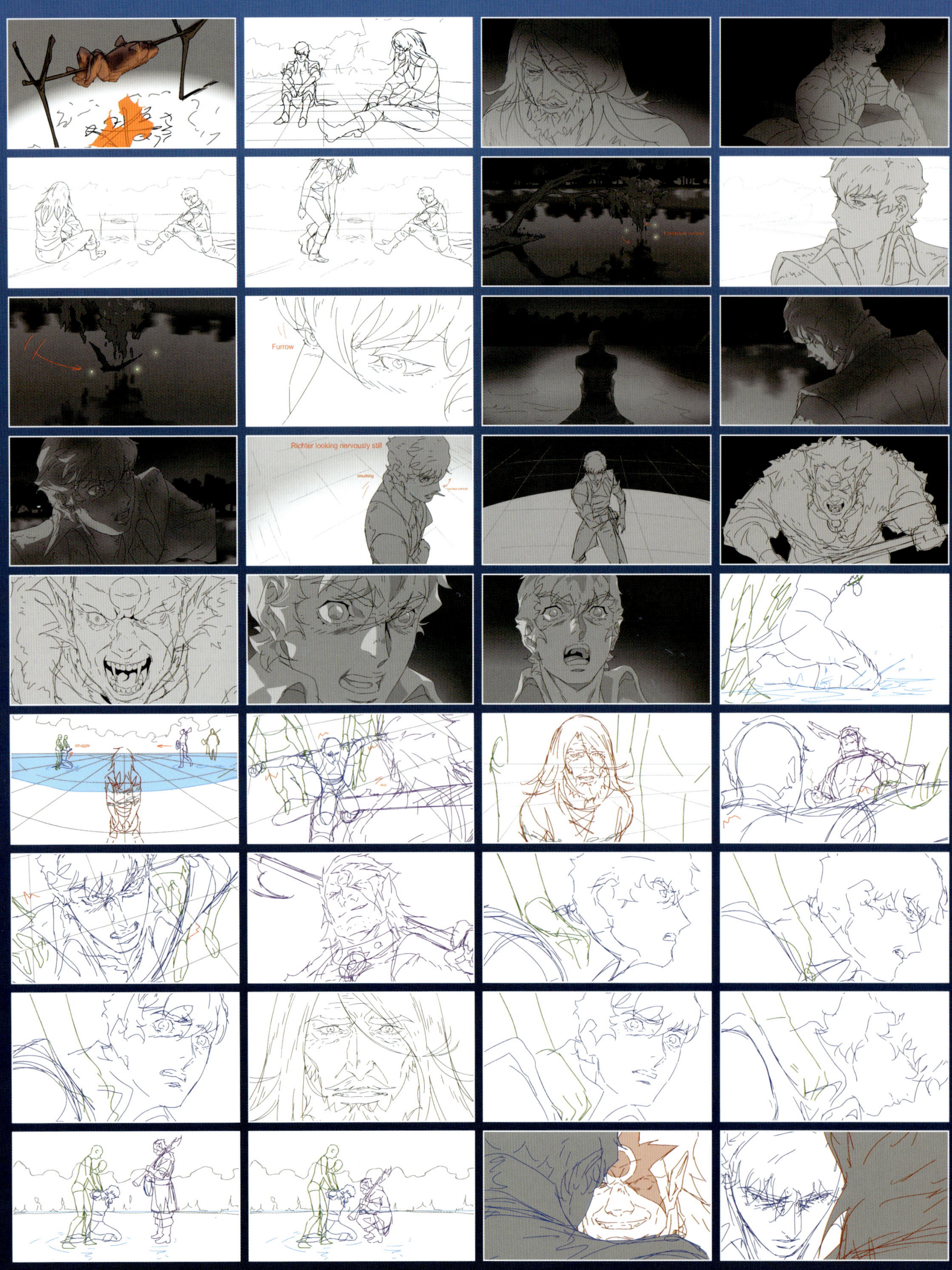

Storyboards by Samuel Deats.

The glowing blue cross is a nod to Richter's "Item Crash" attack from the Castlevania *video games, which Adam said was right for this power-up sequence. It also adds in some of the Belmont holy warrior imagery.*

Storyboards by Samuel Deats.

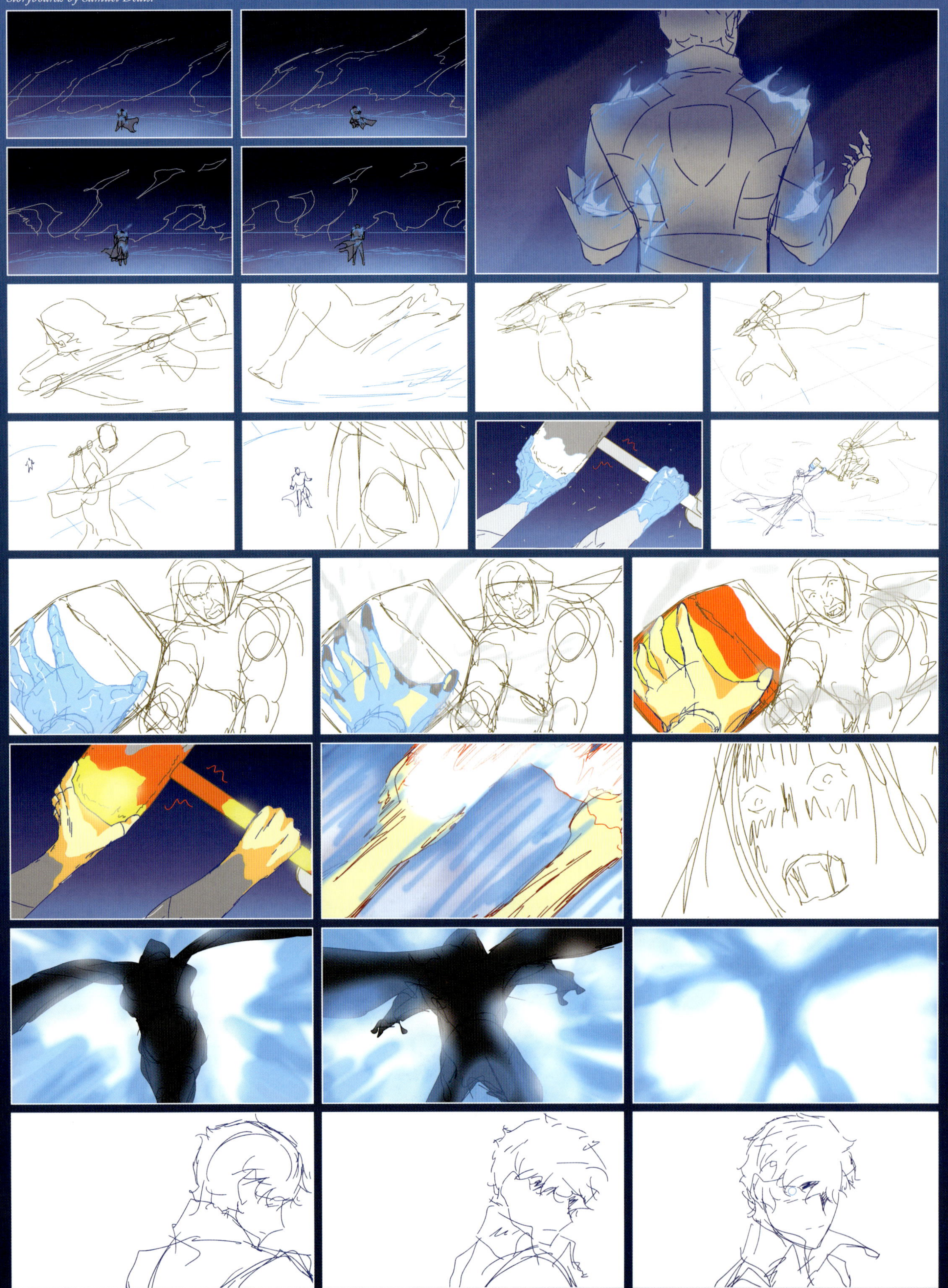

"When I thought about that sudden moment with that burst of power that he gets when he gets his magic back," Sam said, "it was the obvious choice to go with the Divine Cross. A big burst of blue flame and everything from the games was the perfect thing to go with there."

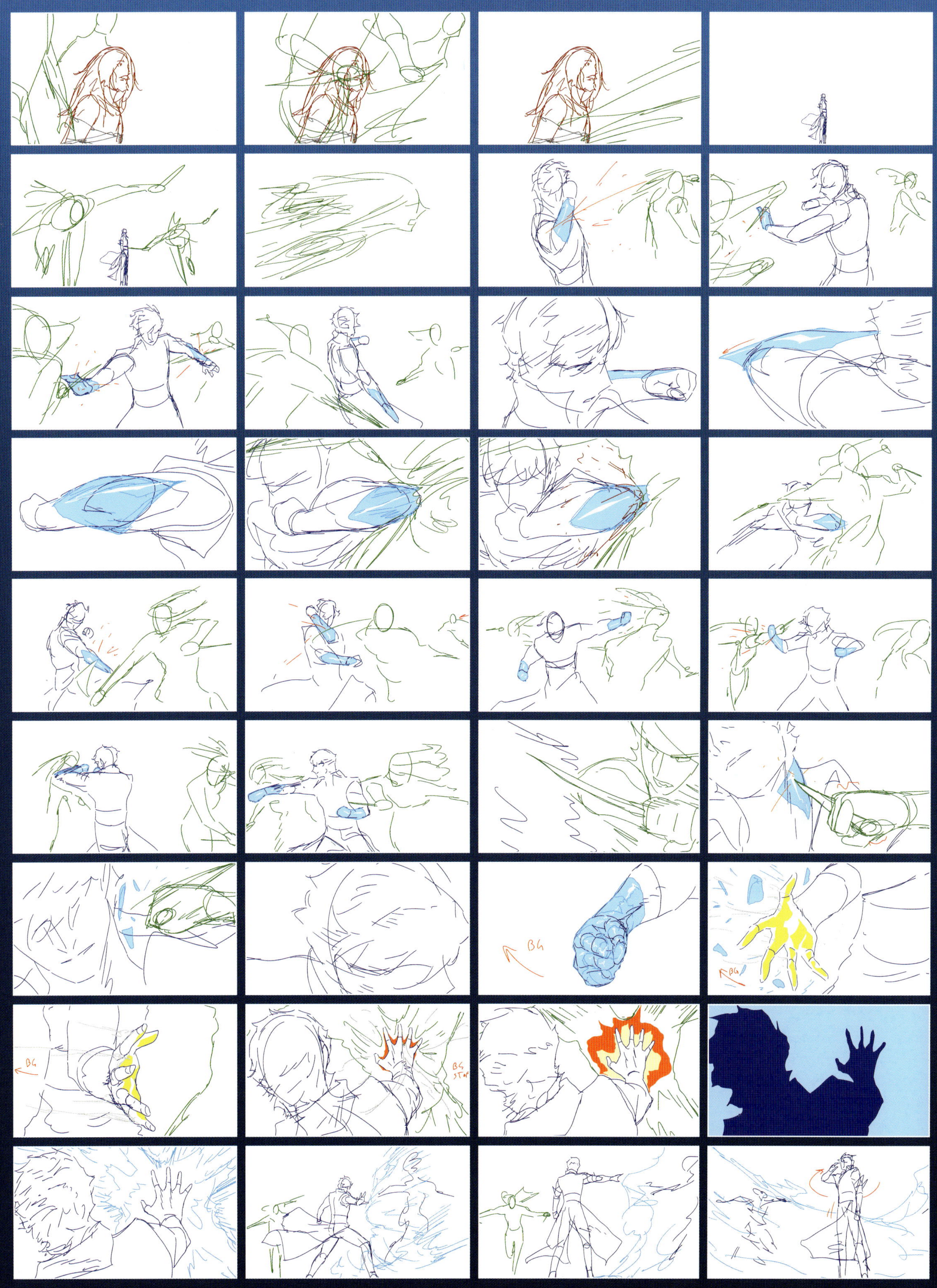

As this sequence progresses, they got to show, for the first time, how Richter would fight using his magic. Sam explained, “It was a really fun moment of getting to showcase that very specific fighting style that he’s putting into his ability set and his power, which is enhancing his attacks, his close-quarter combat, and his weapons.”

Storyboards by Samuel Deats.

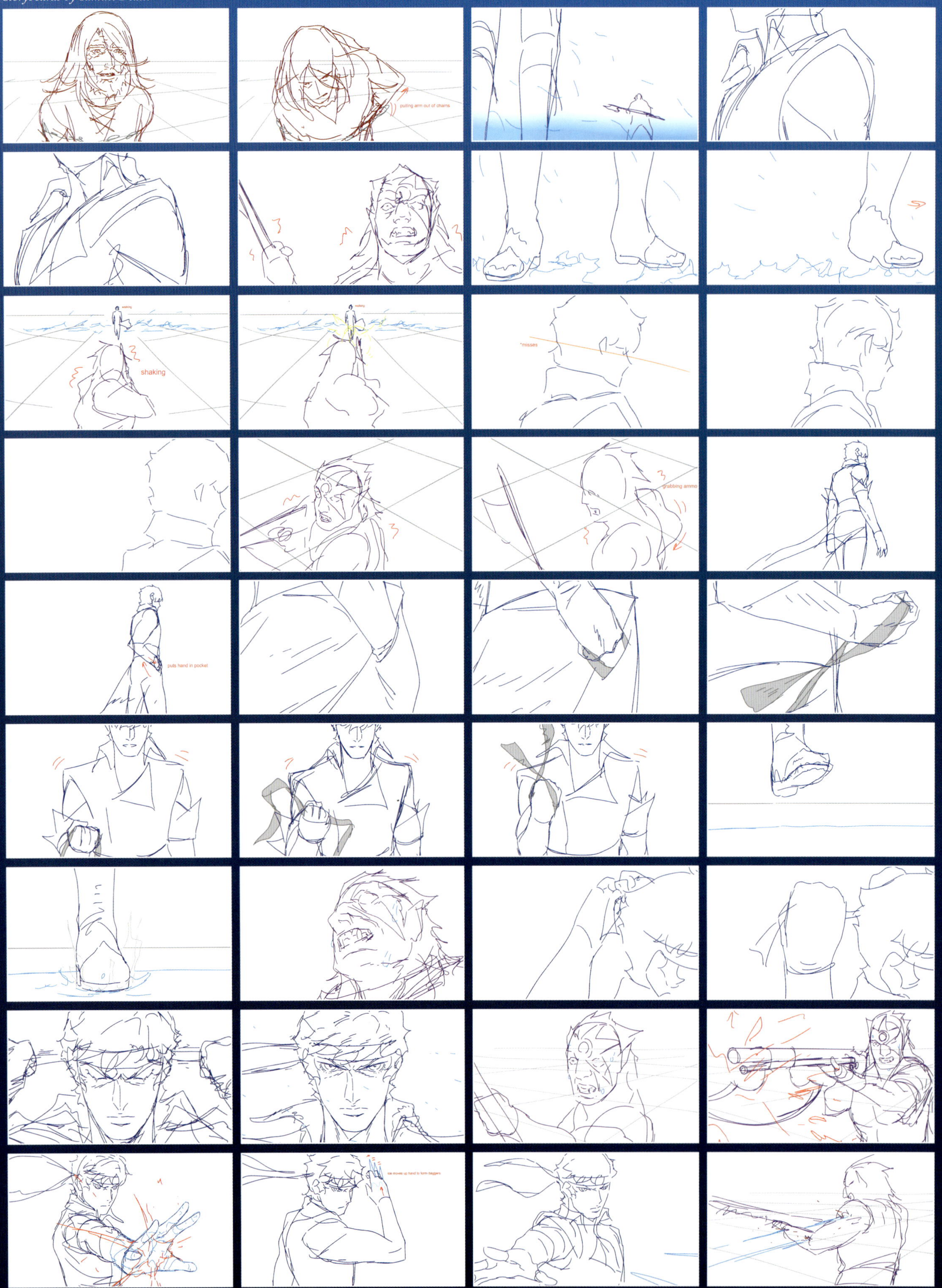

At first, Richter's power is raw and mixed with his preexisting skill set. Sam said, "I had this idea of wanting to have him form ice armor as his primary way of defending himself. It just appears where he needs it and in some ways it's automatic. He's instinctually using it."

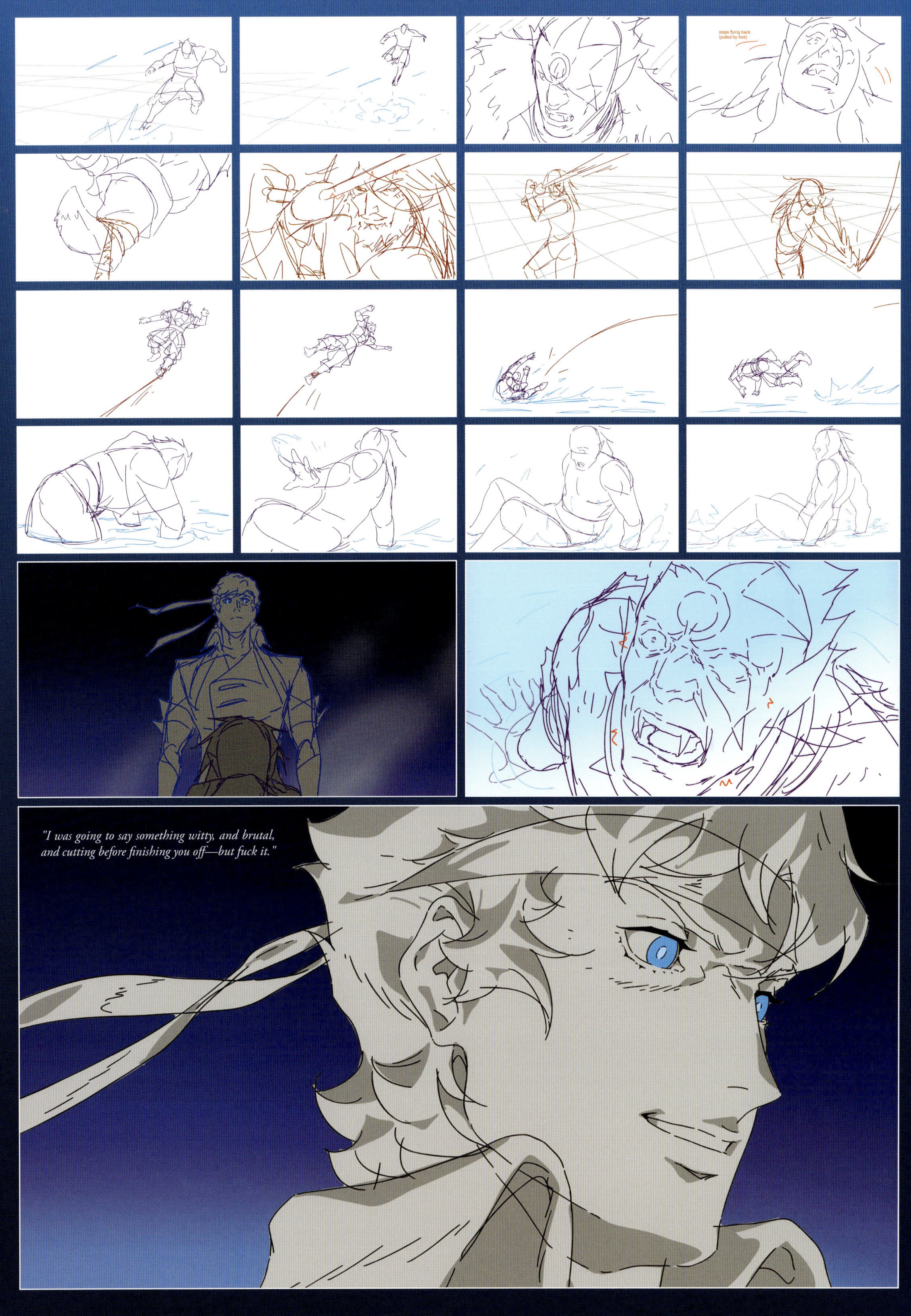
stops flying back
(pulled by foot)
"I was going to say something witty, and brutal,
and cutting before finishing you off—but fuck it."

Storyboards by Samuel Deats.

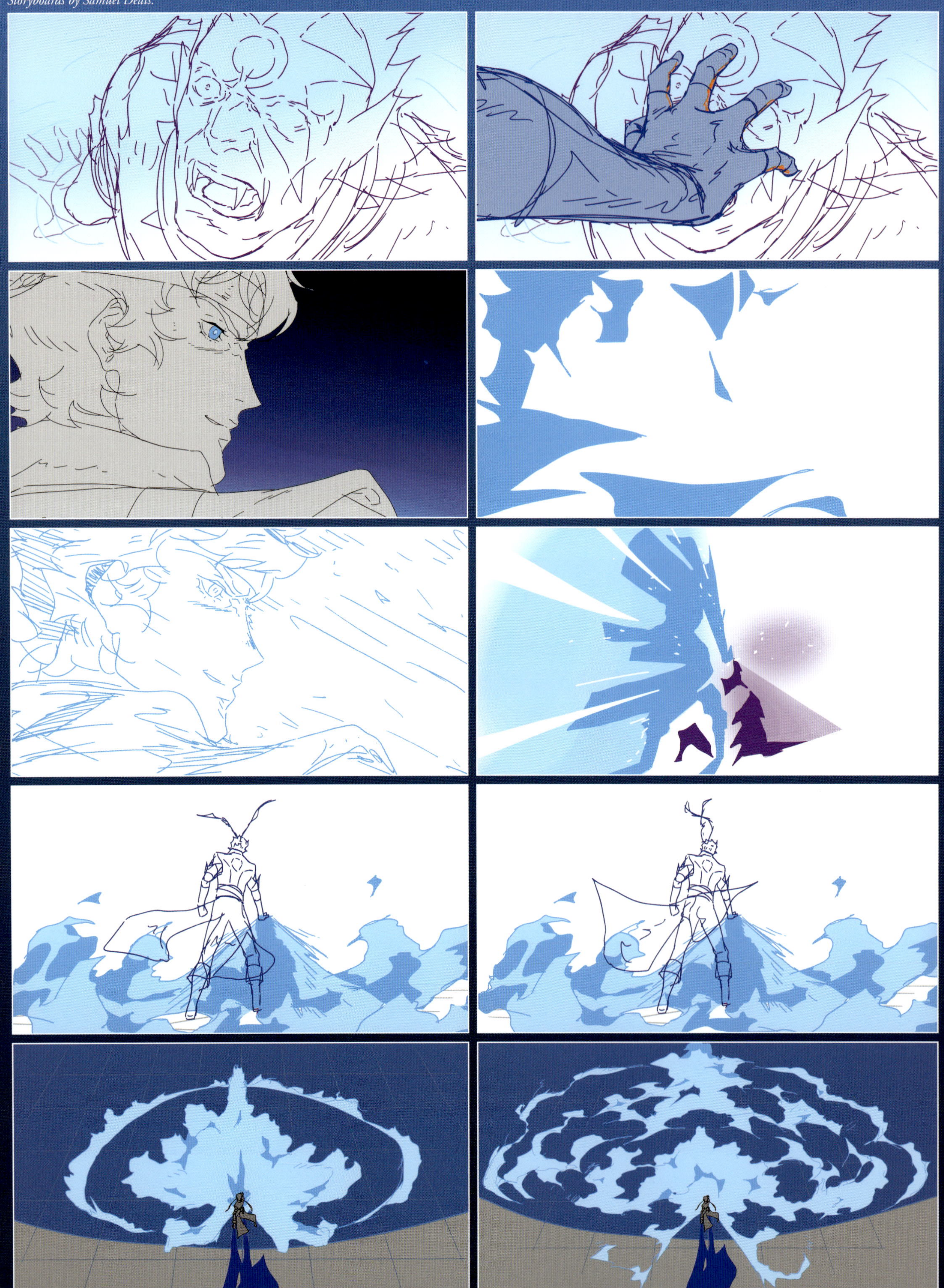

"This is that sequence where there's mirroring between the fight with Julia and Olrox," Adam pointed out. "When we get to the shot of Richter looming over Nikolai on the page on the right, it's pretty much a direct reference to the same shot of Olrox looming over kid Richter in the first episode."

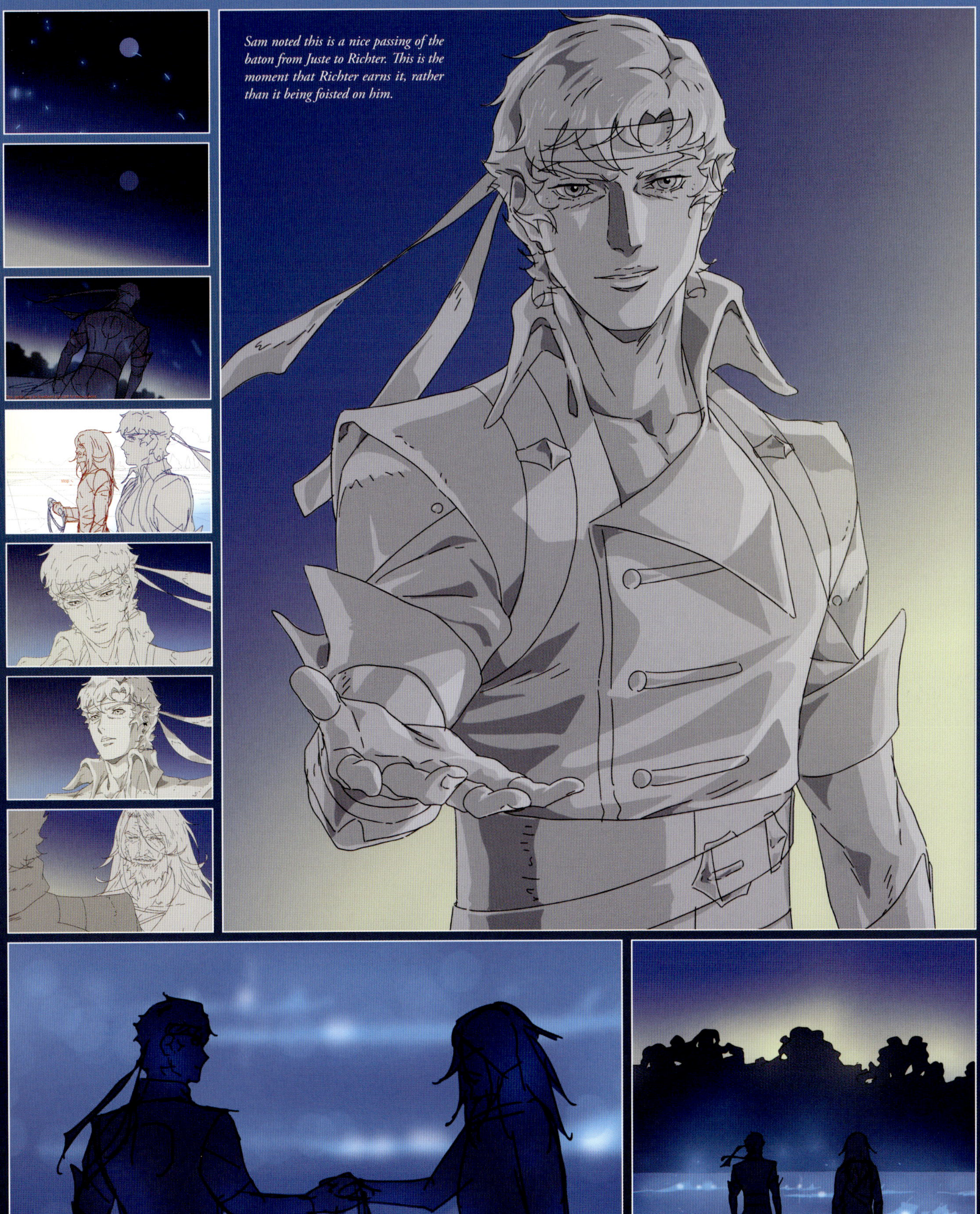

Sam noted this is a nice passing of the baton from Juste to Richter. This is the moment that Richter earns it, rather than it being foisted on him.

"I really liked this calm we got to work in at the end here, where suddenly there's this peace in the air and you have these blue flames, but they weirdly feel soothing rather than feeling like an inferno." —Sam Deats

POWER SHIFT

As characters, good and evil alike, embrace their identities, season two races towards a dramatic ending. This sequence in particular highlights some of Drolta's swagger and the general anxiety between characters. Sam called out the moment where Tera confronts the Abbot. He said, "I wanted to have everything go quiet there and soak in that moment and have the tears start streaming down his face. It was at that moment that that line from Tera finally cut through the noise and reached the Abbot."

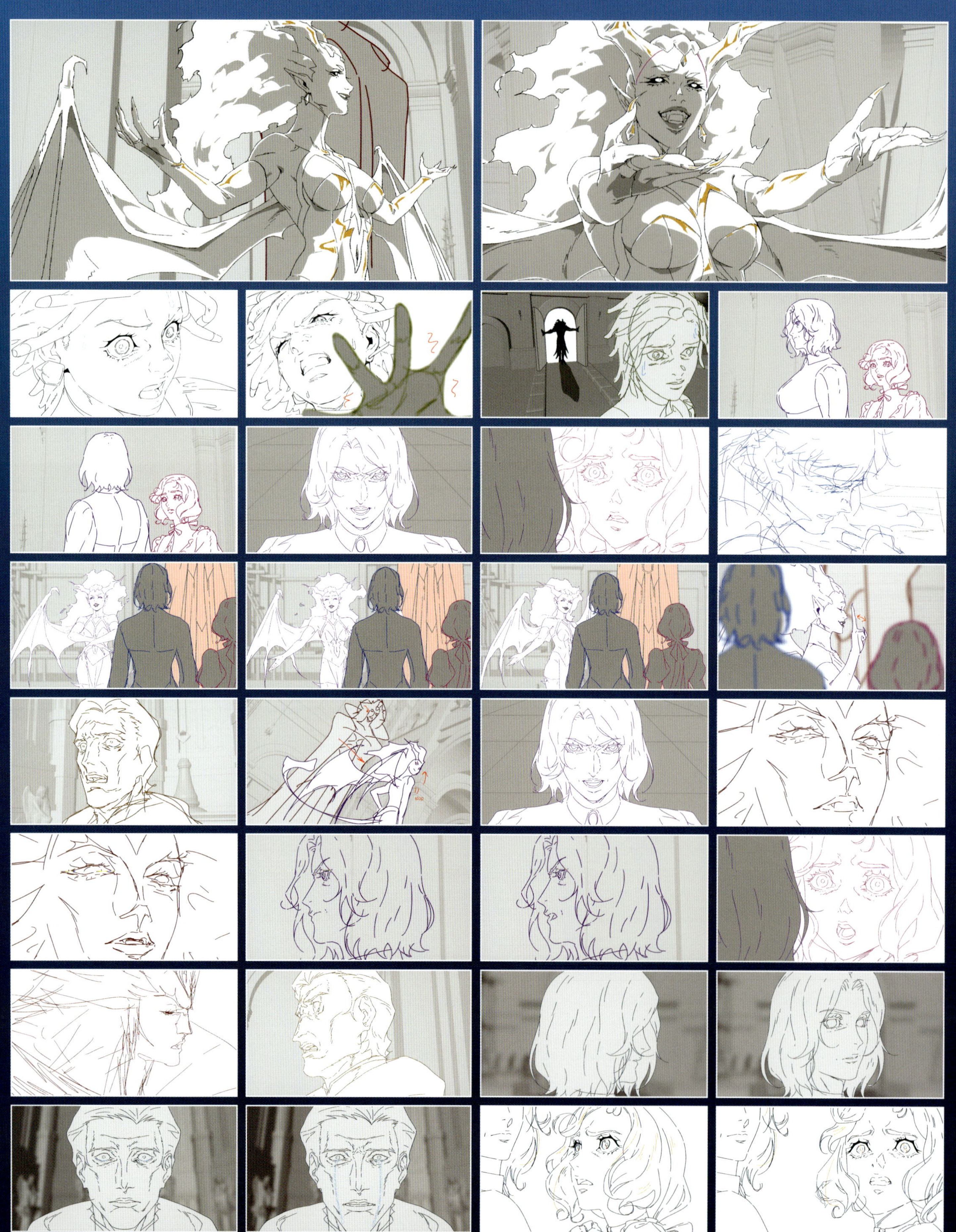

Storyboards by Samuel Deats, layouts by Katie Silva.

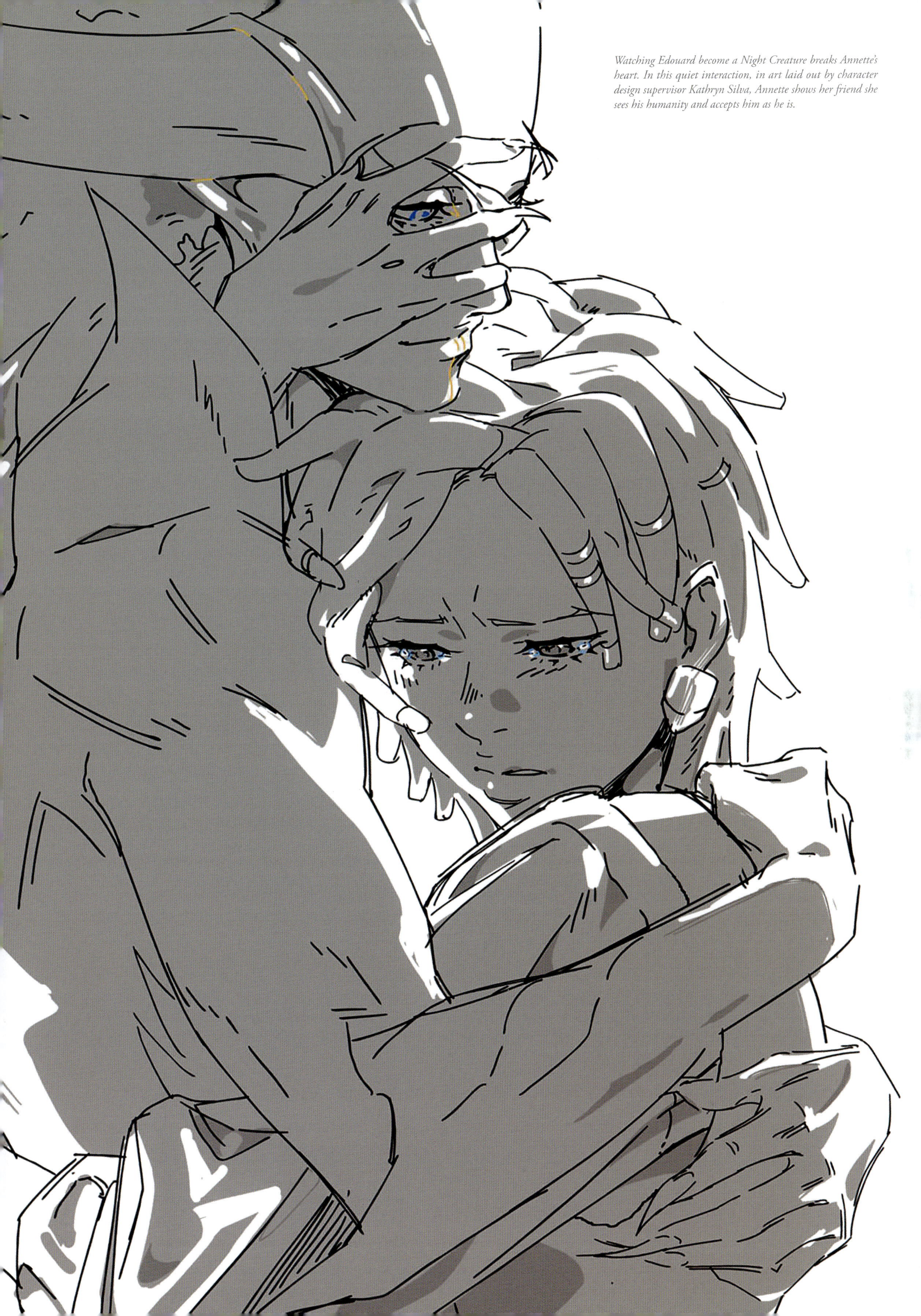

Watching Edouard become a Night Creature breaks Annette's heart. In this quiet interaction, in art laid out by character design supervisor Kathryn Silva, Annette shows her friend she sees his humanity and accepts him as he is.

ALUCARD AND RICHTER TEAM-UP

Drolta became so powerful over the course of the show that it took the joined forces of Alucard and Richter to take her on in an epic showdown. Adam Deats said if they'd had the time and resources, they could have easily spent triple the amount of time on the fight. One aspect Sam pitched was having Alucard go red-eyed and tapping into his father Dracula's powers, because it's something they hadn't shown Alucard doing before.

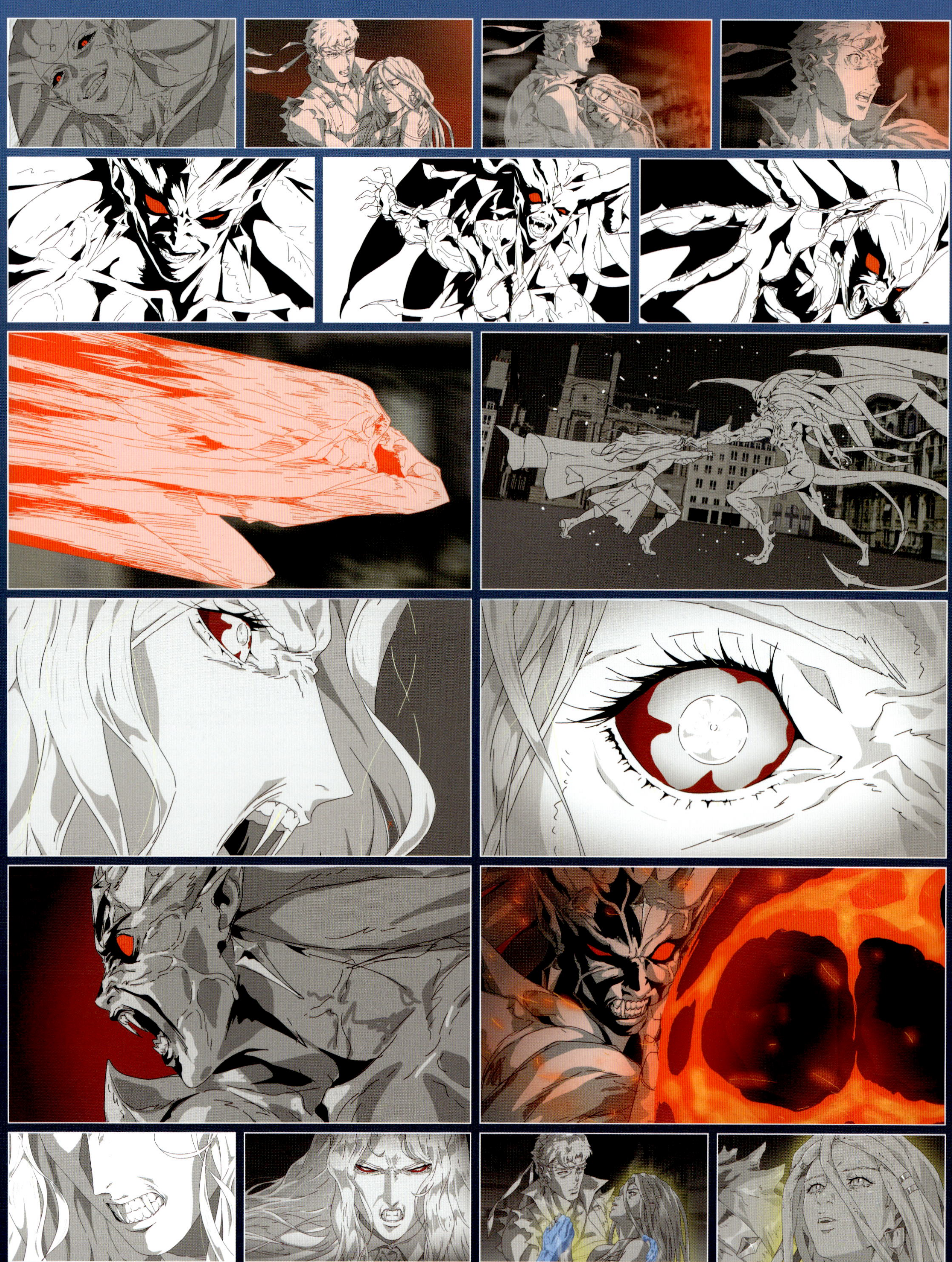

Storyboards by Samuel Deats.

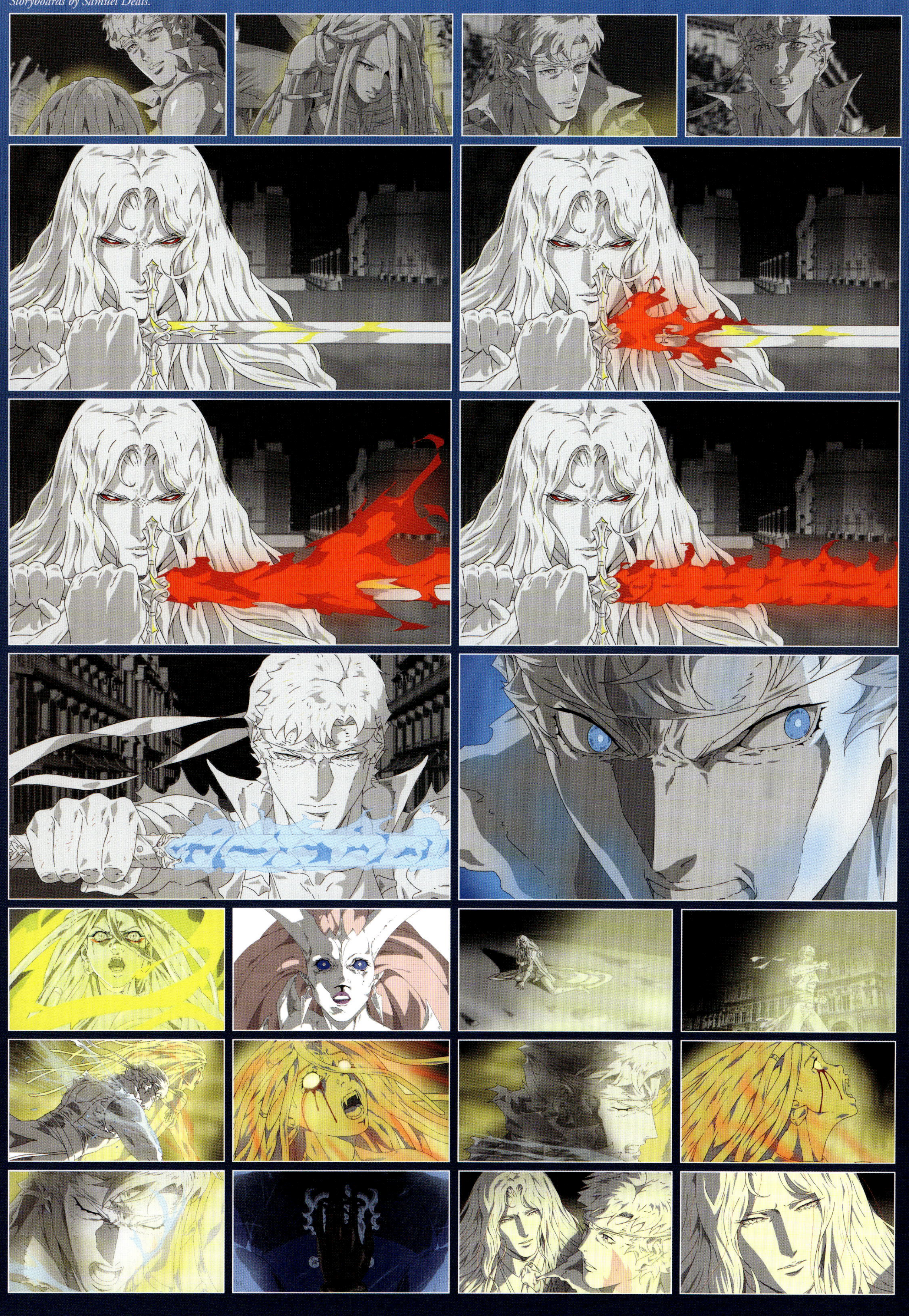

Storyboards by Samuel Deats.

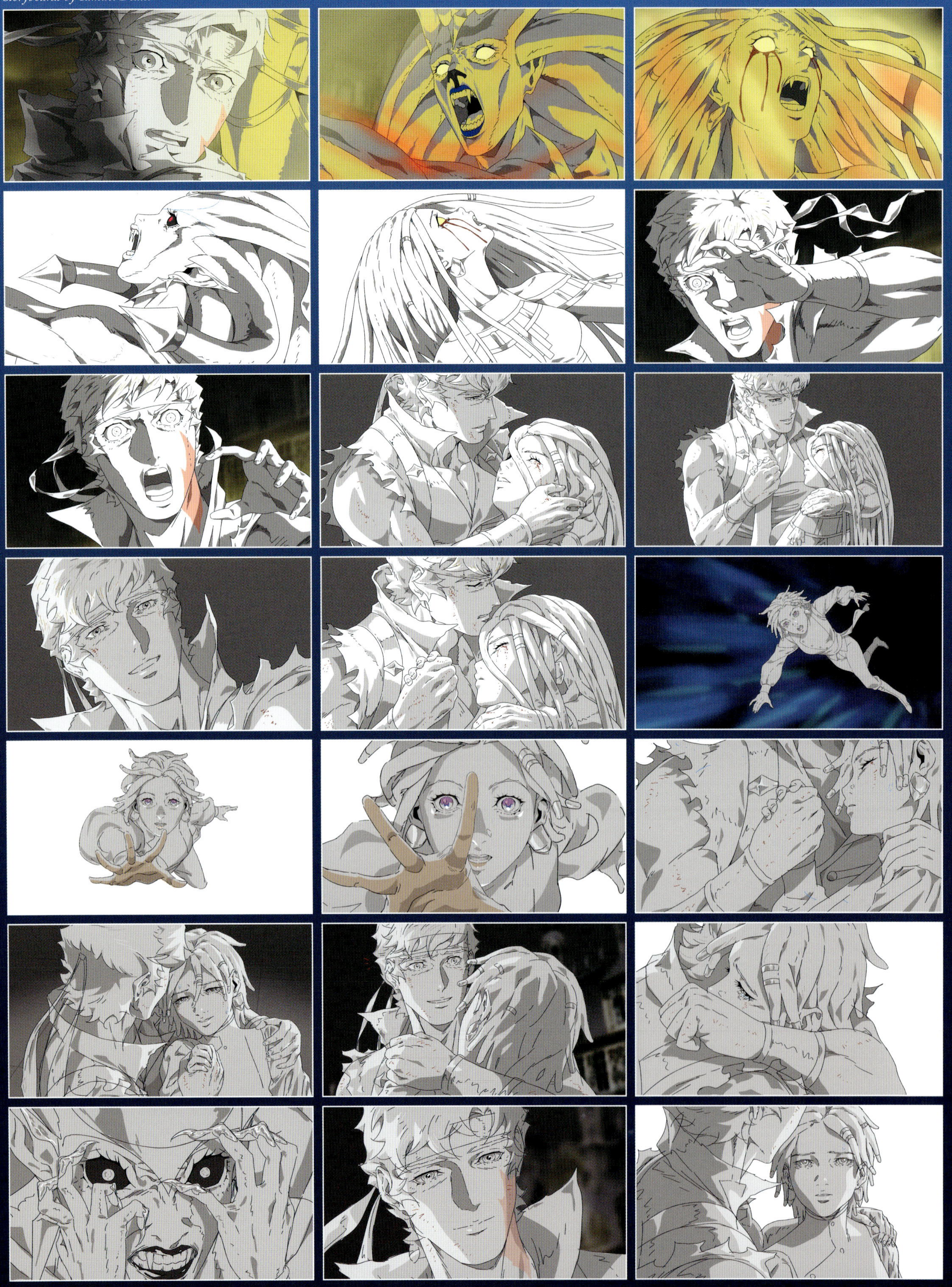

In the midst of the battle, we get a tender moment between Richter and Annette, who uses everything she has to fight both Sekhmet's possession and Drolta. Sam explained, "He's admitting that he's shown his weaknesses and his immaturity, but as he's doing that for the first time, he is probably looking his strongest, and so there was some intent about that. I wanted that to come through a bit in how he's drawn in these moments."

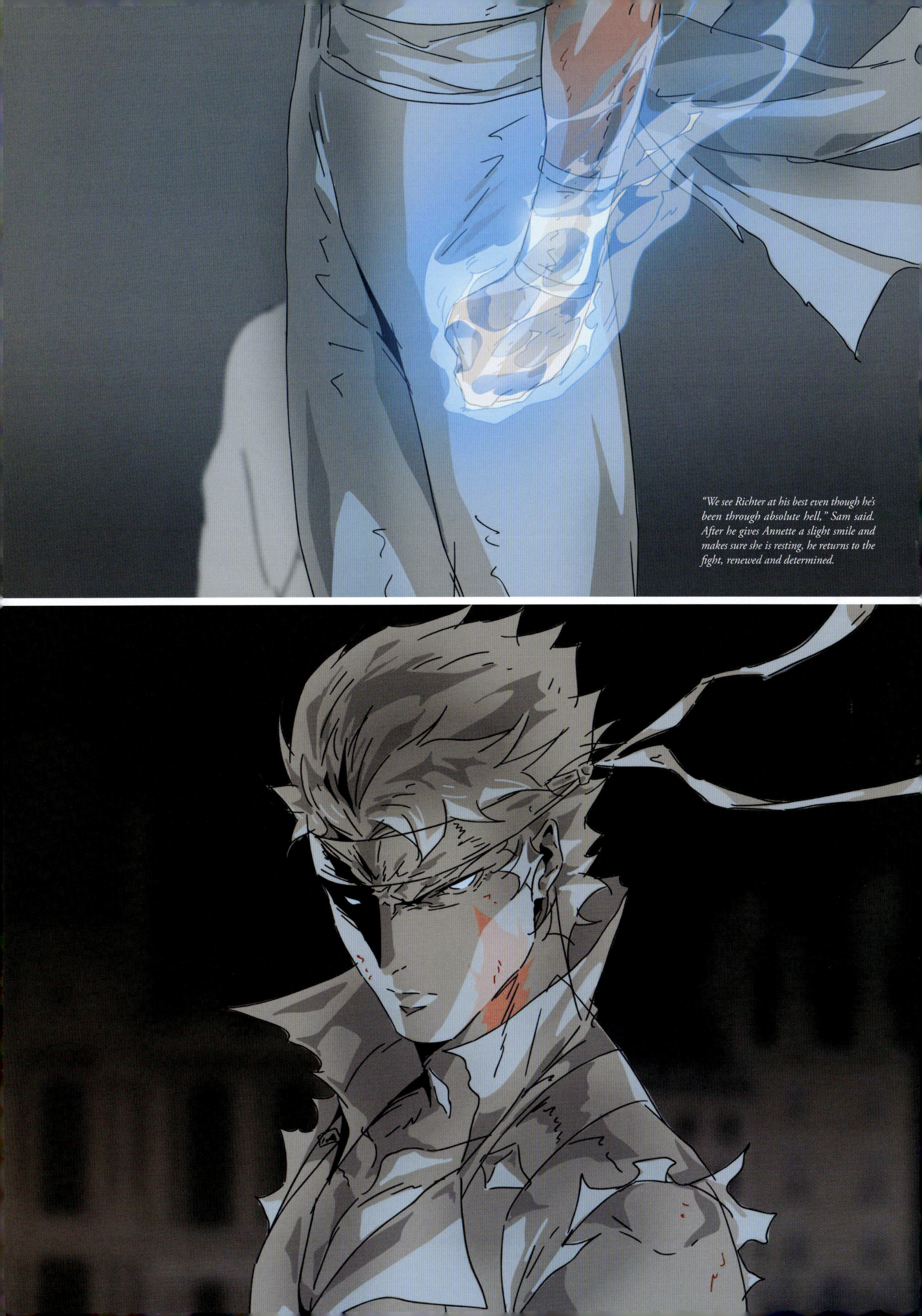

"We see Richter at his best even though he's been through absolute hell," Sam said. After he gives Annette a slight smile and makes sure she is resting, he returns to the fight, renewed and determined.

Storyboards by Samuel Deats.

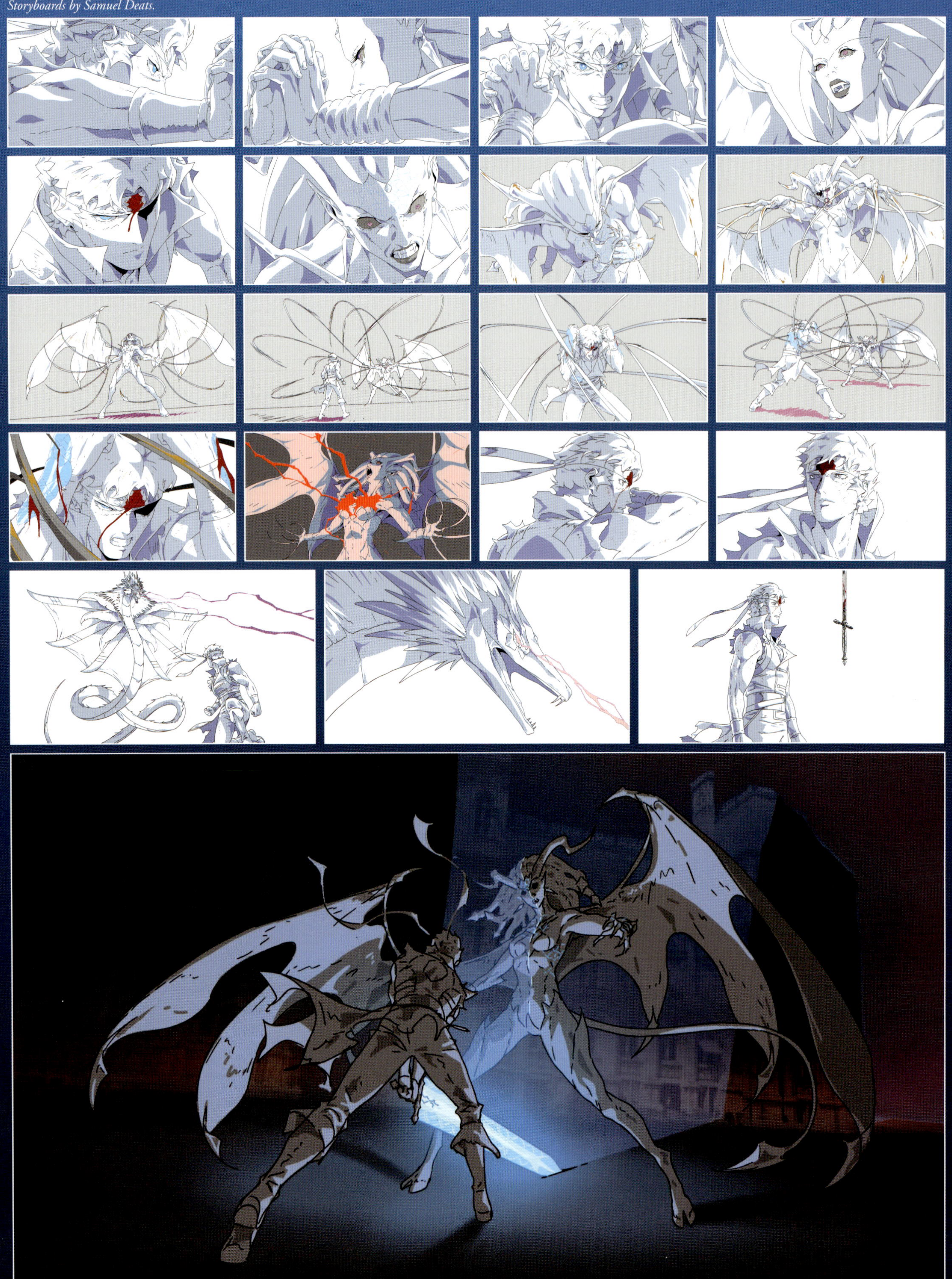

"I wanted to do a few things with Richter's character in this moment to really play out the drama for the final fight with Drolta and play out that moment with Alucard passing the sword to him. He's come to learn that this power he has gained and everything he's done is for that one final slash that will put an end to it. Olrox helps set him up at the end and then Richter finishes it off." —Sam Deats

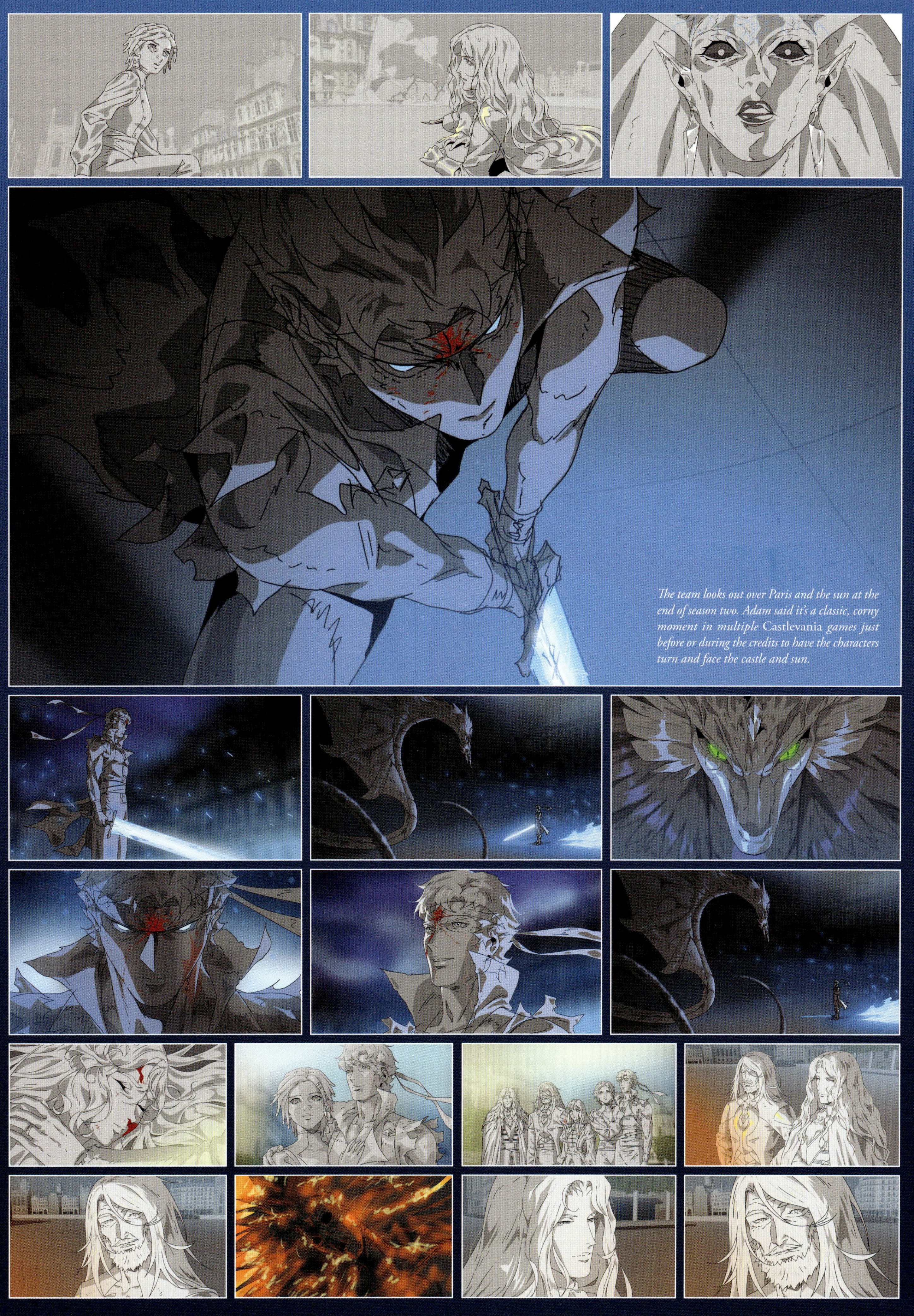

The team looks out over Paris and the sun at the end of season two. Adam said it's a classic, corny moment in multiple Castlevania *games just before or during the credits to have the characters turn and face the castle and sun.*

A TENDER MOMENT

Richter and Annette's blossoming romance becomes real at the end of the season. Sam said, "It's the first time we're, to an extent, getting to see these characters in their element when they're not having to fight for their lives, for freedom, against vampires or anything else. We're getting to see Annette, how she would normally be if she weren't having to fight, and we're getting to see Richter beyond his trauma and getting to be his normal self and at his best."

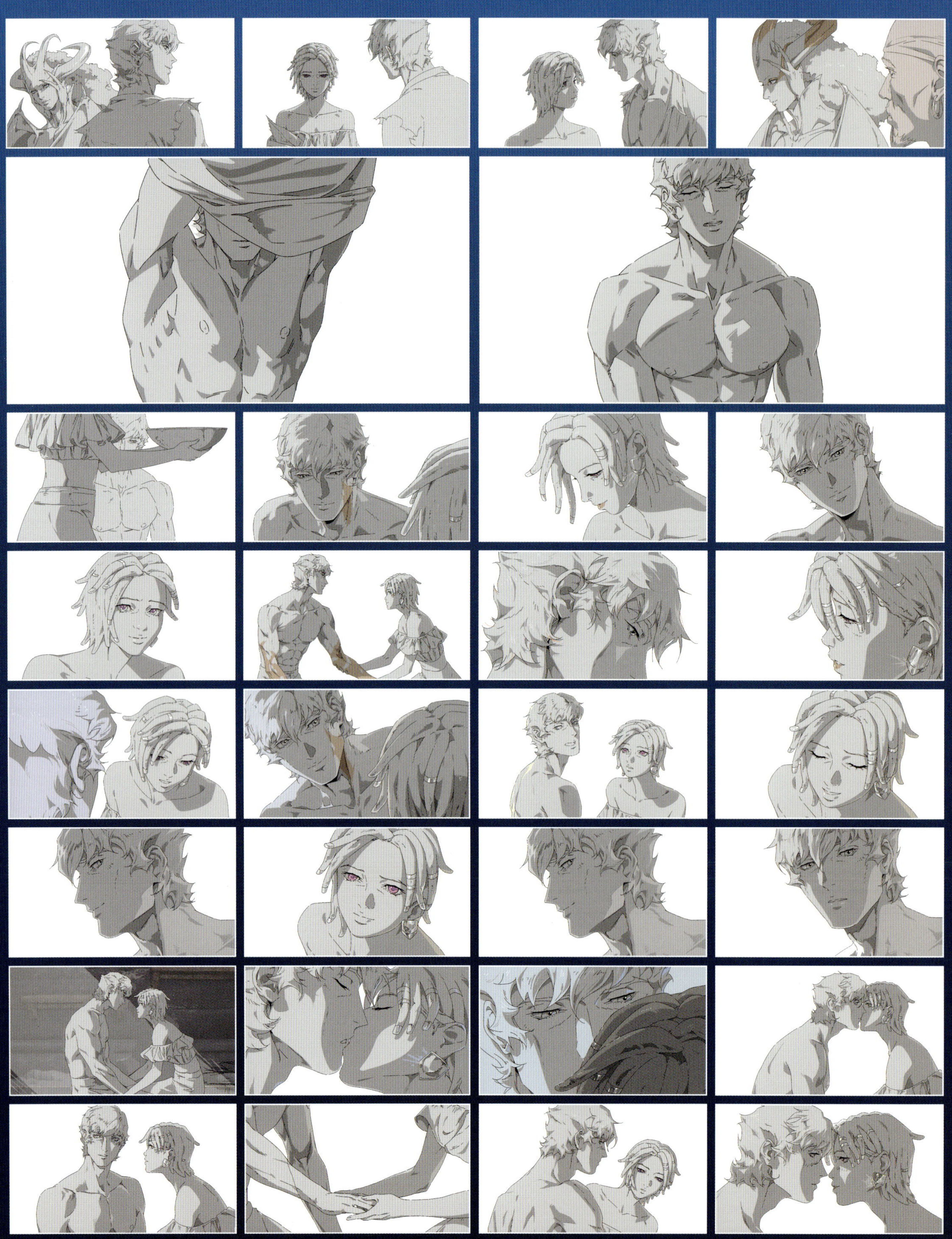

Storyboards by Amanda Sitareh B. and Jenn Doyle, layouts by Katie Silva.

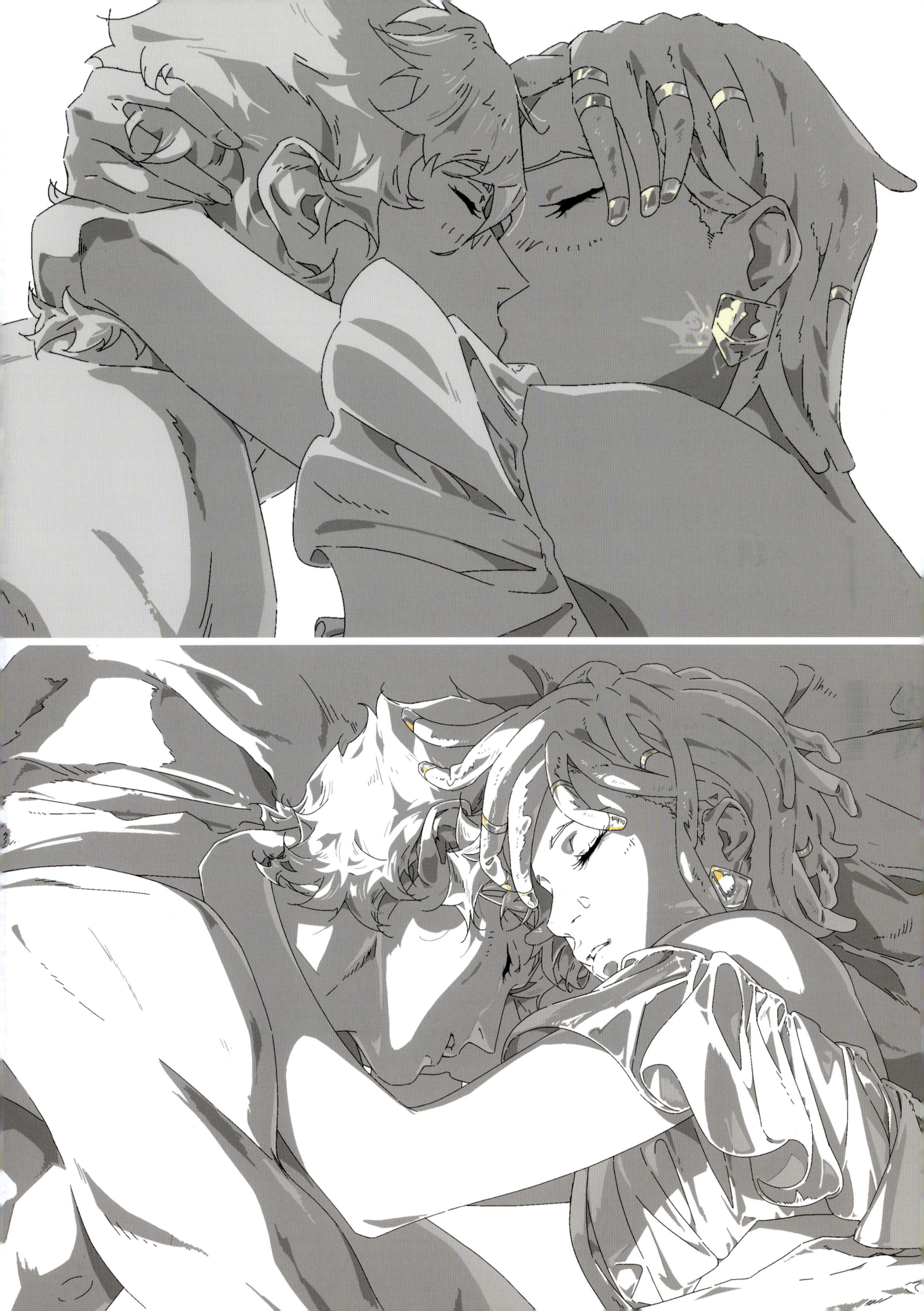

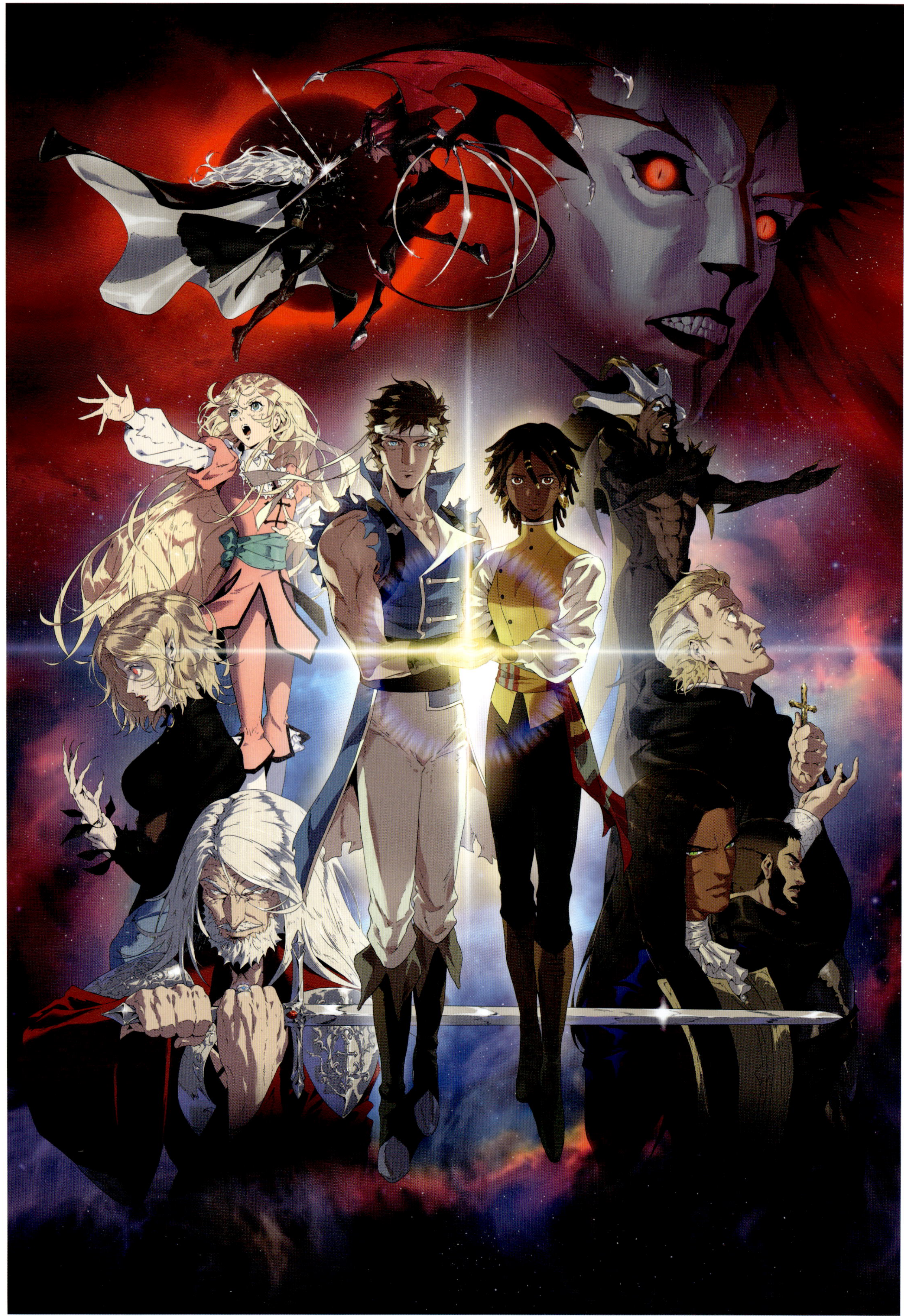

Art by Samuel Deats.

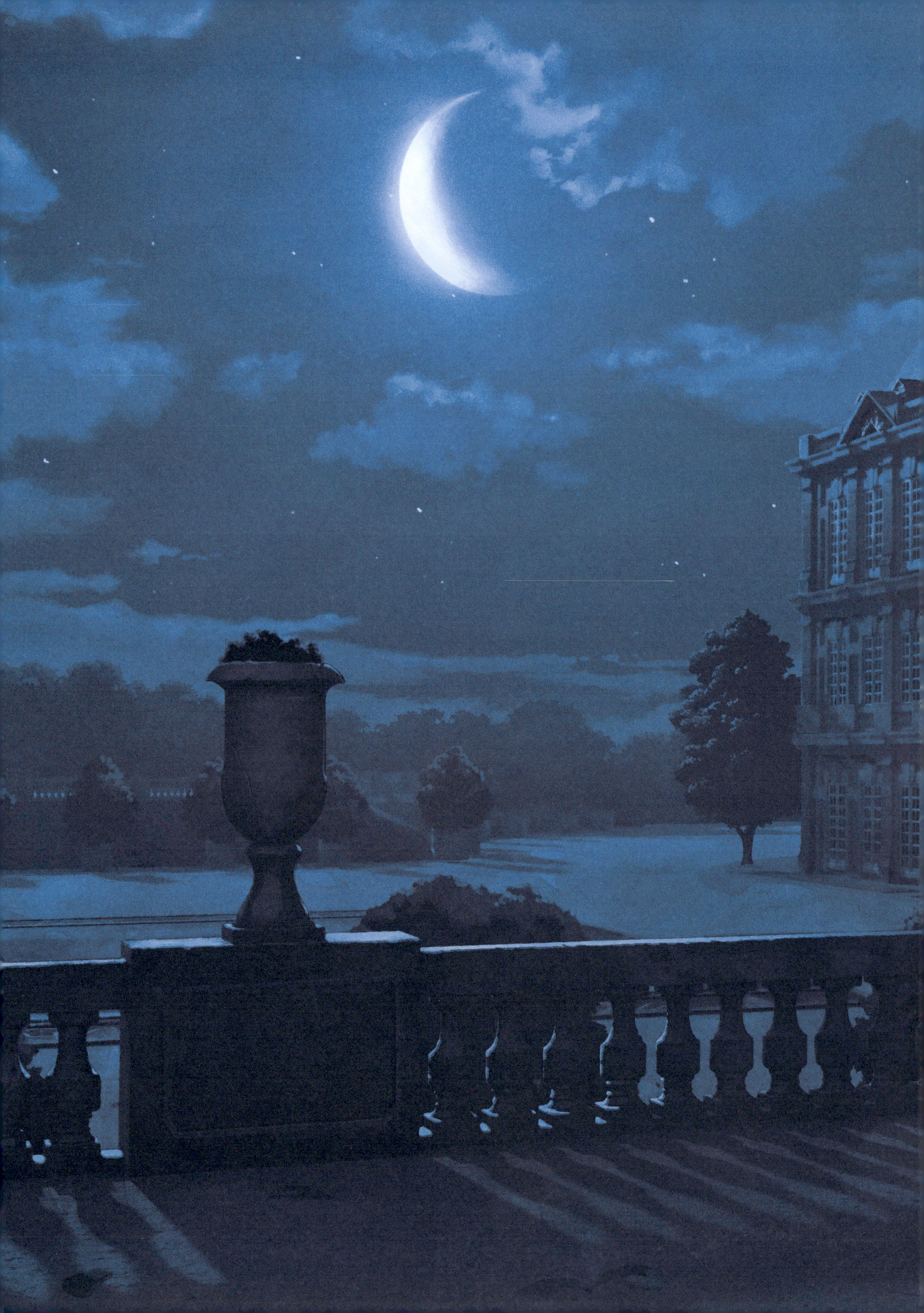